Corporate Finance

Version 2.1

Stan Eakins and William McNally

FlatWorld

978-1-4533-3746-2

Corporate Finance
Version 2.1

Stan Eakins and William McNally

Published by:

FlatWorld
292 Newbury Street
Suite #282
Boston, MA 02115-2832

Gen: 202201061603

Brief Contents

Contents

About the Authors

Stan Eakins, Ph.D.

Stan Eakins received his Ph.D. from Arizona State University in 1990. Prior to beginning his academic work, he gained practical experience serving as vice president and comptroller at the First National Bank of Fairbanks and as a commercial and real estate loan officer. A founder of Denali title and escrow agency, a title insurance company in Fairbanks, Alaska, he was also the chief finance officer for a multimillion-dollar construction and development company. After joining East Carolina University, Dr. Eakins served as the chair of the Department of Finance and as the Associate Dean of the College of Business prior to becoming the Dean. After eighteen years in administration he decided to return to teaching and writing. Dr. Eakins has had textbooks in continuous use since 1998. His research is focused primarily on the role of institutions in corporate control and how they influence investment practices. He is also interested in integrating multimedia tools into the learning environment and has received grants from ECU in support of this work.

William McNally, Ph.D.

William J. McNally is a Professor of finance at Wilfrid Laurier University. He earned a B.A. and M.A. in Economics from Queen's and Simon Fraser University, respectively. In 1993 he received his Ph.D. in finance from the University of Toronto. After Toronto, he taught at the University of Victoria until 1999. His primary research interests are in stock repurchases and insider trading. His research has been published in journals such as *Management Science* and *Financial Management*. He has received over $200,000 in research grants and has received two best paper awards. Professor McNally is a co-author (with Stanley Eakins) of *Corporate Finance* (FlatWorld), an online introductory finance textbook which is published in both the U.S. and Canada. Professor McNally has served as Finance Department chair and has supervised the Laurier Student Investment Fund since 2001 (AUM = ~$1M).

Dedication

Stan Eakins

I want to thank my wife, Laurie, for patiently reading draft after draft of this manuscript and for helping make this my best work. Through the years, her help and support have made this aspect of my career possible.

William McNally

To Catherine for her patience and support.

Preface

Welcome to *Corporate Finance*, v2.1! Whether it's your first time teaching or you are an experienced professor of finance, these course materials are probably unlike any that you have used in your career. Throughout the authors' combined 50+ years of teaching introductory finance, they noticed some dramatic changes in how students learn and how you teach their course. We created *Corporate Finance* to address these sweeping changes in the teaching and learning process.

Technology: Transforming Learning

The current generation of students (born after 1995) are the *iGeneration*.[1] So named because they were virtually born with a smartphone in hand. *iGeneration* students spend time outside of class on console gaming, watching YouTube videos, and on apps like SnapChat, Tik-Tok, Facebook, and Twitter. Today's students are intolerant of non-engaging teaching techniques. They expect their learning resources to be digital, graphic and wireless. We created *Corporate Finance* to meet the expectations of *iGeneration* students and so enhance their engagement in learning finance.

When creating this book, we weighed carefully which type of multimedia would best communicate and assess the information that students need to know and how you want to teach them. As a result, we leverage technology to make learning finance as easy and fun as possible.

Let *Corporate Finance* Teach the Mechanics Through Video Presentations

Education has two stages: 1) information transfer; and 2) assimilation. The assimilation stage is when students make their own mental model of the ideas. In traditional introductory finance courses, a lot of class time is spent teaching students the mathematical computations (information transfer) and not much time is left for teaching the application (assimilation).[1]

Corporate Finance is designed to shoulder the burden of teaching the formulas and computations. That way, you can use your class time to teach problem solving, analyze cases, or discuss current financial events. This design allows *Corporate Finance* to be used successfully in a traditional lecture-style course and equally well in online courses, hybrid courses, or flipped classrooms.

Corporate Finance key technological advantage lies in the wealth of author-recorded videos embedded in the digital text. The combination of text and video gives students multiple explanations for each idea so if they don't understand one, they have recourse to another. This teaching design greatly reduces learner frustration.

There are over 300 author-generated videos strategically placed throughout the text. Each video is between 1–5 minutes in length and can be used to introduce topics, explain operations, and provide 24/7 review so that students can learn anytime and anywhere they have live web connection. These embedded videos are divided into three categories:

- "Explain It" videos demonstrate key concepts and clarify topics that typically confuse learnings.
- "Explore It" videos provide richer context for an operation or calculation to illuminate the concept behind the mechanics.
- Solutions videos provide detailed explanations of solutions to examples in three ways: algebra, calculator, and downloadable Excel spreadsheet templates. The first shows the general approach to the solution, the algebra involved, and explains the intuition behind the solution. The other two solutions videos show the mechanics of the solution with either a financial calculator or Excel.

Finally, if you want your students to learn spreadsheet basics, *Corporate Finance* gives them the tools to learn them. Most examples have a downloadable spreadsheet template that is accompanied by a video explaining the layout and functions used in the spreadsheet.

Quizzes: Reading & Comprehension

A trend in university education is that students don't buy the textbook or, if they do, many don't read it. A significant proportion of those who read the text lack an effective reading strategy and therefore fail to absorb the main ideas. We have addressed both issues by embedding a large number of quiz questions, organized by section, throughout the online reader version of the book. This affords students the opportunity to self-test as they read. Reading comprehension is enhanced by the quizzes, because if students cannot answer the quiz question correctly, then they are immediately alerted that their grasp of the surrounding material is lacking. These online quizzes promote self-regulation: they empower students to take responsibility for their own learning.

Autograded Homework

Homework is where the bulk of learning happens, and *Corporate Finance* makes assigning homework easy. Each chapter in *Corporate Finance* has 50–70 corresponding questions in FlatWorld's online homework system that is available to adopters and their students at no additional charge. These problems have **multiple variations**, **detailed solutions**, and are **autograded**. With multiple variations of the same problem, students get different numbers. As a result, cheating isn't as simple as sharing the solution value. We have also found that students won't attempt problems without **detailed solutions** to help them better understand how the problem is correctly worked. Every problem has a detailed solution that students can view if they get the answer wrong. Finally, all homework problems are **autograded**, saving faculty the time-consuming process of hand grading, and student-performance data automatically flow to the associated gradebook. Thus, students receive immediate feedback on their progress and so do you. The gradebook is invaluable in helping to identify and remediate students who procrastinate or underinvest in homework or reading.

The problems are organized by major sub-section in FlatWorld Homework and, within each section, by degree of difficulty. The clear organization of problems makes customizing homework easy.

Rich Resources Support Effective Teaching

Corporate Finance comes with a suite of supplements (all written by the textbook authors) so it can be used in any course format.

Instructor's Manual with chapter overviews and summaries; classroom activities and discussion questions, a quick quiz, and a mini case ideal for flipped class implementation.

PowerPoint Slides include many original examples different from those in the text. These PPT slides have been extensively used by the authors over many years with their own students.

Test Item File contains over 2,000 items written by the authors and vetted with the authors own students over a period of two decades. The breadth of the test item file provides adopters with plentiful options for assessing student learning. Each question is classified by learning outcome and difficulty level. The test items are available as part of an online test generator powered by Cognero that enables printed tests. For faculty who are using a learning management system (LMS), the test items are also formatted and packaged for easy import into popular LMSs such as Canvas, Blackboard, Brightspace/D2L, Moodle, and Respondus.

Free Online Homework System—FlatWorld Homework Do you want to find out how your class is doing? Or know if your students comprehend the material being covered? Measuring class progress and comprehension is easy using FlatWorld's web-based homework system. And the best part: The system is free. Students get access to the homework system with their textbook at no extra cost. It's also easy to use—you can create an assignment in minutes by selecting questions from a pool of specifically designed, multi-format questions (plus some of your own if you want), and FlatWorld does the rest. The system provides feedback to each student and class statistics to you. It can be accessed through FlatWorld's stand-alone interface or through your learning management system (e.g., Canvas, Moodle, Brightspace/D2L, Blackboard). Students can complete their homework assignment from any device using a standard web browser. To learn more about the system and to watch a demo go to https://catalog.flatworldknowledge.com/homework.

Sample Syllabi provide useful templates to help new adopters easily transition their course to embrace *Corporate Finance* as the assigned text and lend insights to existing adopters on how to more effectively organize their classes.

Of course, *Corporate Finance*'s online delivery makes it ideal for online courses. But *Corporate Finance* can also be used in a variety of in-class formats. In a lecture format, faculty can use videos to supplement their own presentations. Those who want additional class activities can use those supplied in the Instructor's Manual. Adopting faculty implementing a flipped teaching model can use the online quiz questions embedded in the digital reader or create pre-lecture quizzes in FlatWorld Homework to motivate before-class reading, the mini cases for classroom activities, and FlatWorld Homework problems (and test bank problems) to generate after-class autograded assignments.

We are confident that *Corporate Finance* provides all the tools to transform your students to active, engaged learners, and motivates them to continue their studies in finance. We also hope that adopting *Corporate Finance* makes teaching finance more fun for you. It certainly has for us.

Thank you once again for choosing *Corporate Finance*.

Sincerely,

Stan Eakins

William McNally

Endnotes

1. While Millennials, who were born in the early 1980s, continue to mystify the world, there's an even more puzzling generation on the horizon—and they're going to change everything. Enter the iGeneration, also known as Generation Z, or those born in 1994 and later, who grew up with a smart-phone in hand. "How to Market to the iGeneration". *Harvard Business Review* hbr.org › 2015/05 › how-to-market-to-the-igeneration
1. https://harvardmagazine.com/2012/03/twilight-of-the-lecture

Acknowledgments

Grateful acknowledgment and thanks to FlatWorld sales representative Clarence Middlebrooks for bringing this book to the attention of Sean Wakely, Vice President, Product and Editorial, who became a champion to our cause. Thank you to Alastair Adam and John Eielson for their confidence in us and our book. We also want to thank KB Mello whose dedication and guidance were essential to the publication of this book. She burned the midnight oil to keep the book on schedule and applied her superior problem-solving skills to overcome obstacles posed by the publication effort. What she accomplished was truly unusual and remarkable.

We gratefully acknowledge our colleagues' time and insights in helping us create *Corporate Finance*:

Ahmed Al-Asfour, *Oglala Lakota*

Michael H. Anderson, *University of Massachusetts–Dartmouth*

Curt Bacon, *Southern Oregon University*

Karen Barr, *Penn State University–Beaver Campus*

Eric Blazer, *Millersville University*

Elizabeth Booth, *Michigan State University*

Mike Bowyer, *Montgomery Community College*

Carol Boyer, *Long Island University–CW Post*

Fritz Burkhardt, *Champlain College*

Deanne Butchey, *Florida International University*

Xiaowei Cai, *California Polytechnic State University*

Chuck Chahyadi, *Eastern Illinois University*

Meg Clark, *Cincinnati State Technical and Community College*

Thomas Coe, *Quinnipiac University*

Nandita Das, *Delaware State University*

Kate Demarest, *Carroll Community College*

Alexander Deshkovski, *North Carolina Central University*

Vern Disney, *University of South Carolina–Sumter*

Robert Donchez, *University of Colorado–Boulder*

Anne Drougas, *Dominican University*

Barbara Edington, *St. Francis College*

Susan Emens, *Kent State University–Trumbull*

Ted Eschenbach, *University of Alaska–Anchorage*

Jim Estes, *California State University–San Bernardino*

Dov Fobar, *Brooklyn College/CUNY*

Alex Gialanella, *Manhattanville College*

Scott Gibson, *Mason School of Business, College of William and Mary*

Ann Gillette, *Kennesaw State University*

Kimberly Goodwin, *University of Southern Mississippi*

Rachel Graefe-Anderson, *College of Charleston*

Michelle Hagadorn, *Roanoke College*

TeWhan Hahn, *Auburn University at Montgomery*
Mahfuzul Haque, *Scott College of Business, Indiana State University*
Wei He, *Mississippi State University*
Peter Holland, *Napa Valley College*
Susan Hume, *School of Business, The College of New Jersey*
Ed Hutton, *Niagara University*
Roger Ignatius, *Lane College*
Robert Irons, *Dominican University*
Thad Jackson, *University of Alabama*
Benjamas Jirasakuldech, *Slippery Rock University of Pennsylvania*
Raymond Johnson, *Auburn University–Montgomery*
Steve Johnson, *Sam Houston State University*
Travis Jones, *Florida Gulf Coast University*
Samuel Kohn, *Touro College*
Lynn Kugele, *University of Mississippi*
Manoj Kulchania, *Marquette University*
Adam Lei, *Midwestern State University*
Qian Li, *Midwestern State University*
John Masserwick, *Farmingdale State*
Denny McGarry, *Lake Erie College*
Jill Merle, *Anderson University*
Clay Moffett, *University of North Carolina–Wilmington*
Dianne Morrison, *University of Wisconsin–La Crosse*
Christian Ola, *Waynesburg University*
Ken O'Brien, *Farmingdale State*
Ohannes Paskelian, *University of Houston–Downtown*
Michael Phillips
Shoba Premkumar, *Iowa State University*
Charles Reback, *University of South Carolina–Upstate*
Jennifer Schneider, *Gainesville State College*
Adam Schwartz, *Washington and Lee University*
Sudhir Singh, *Frostburg State University*
Steven Slezak, *Cal Poly, San Luis Obispo*
Bradley Stevenson, *Bellarmine University*
Diana Tempski, *University of Wisconsin–La Crosse*
Rhonda J. Tenkku, *University of Missouri–St. Louis*
Gwendolyn Webb, *Baruch College/CUNY*
Shelton Weeks, *Florida Gulf Coast University*
Eric Wehrly, *Seattle University*
Michael Welker, *Franciscan University of Steubenville*
Jeff Whitworth, *University of Houston–Clear Lake*
Benjamin Woodruff, *Shelton State Community College*
Jie Yang, *Georgetown University*
Brian Young, *Mississippi State University*

CHAPTER 1

Introduction to Finance

Learning Objectives

By the end of this chapter you will be able to:

1. Understand the function of the financial system.
2. Distinguish between money and capital markets.
3. Tell the difference between primary and secondary markets.
4. Discuss the structure and governance of corporations.
5. List six important ideas in finance.

1.1 The Financial System

In this section, we provide an overview of the financial system, and in the two following sections we focus on financial markets. The **financial system**, as shown in Figure 1.1, transfers money from suppliers (such as individual households), to users, such as companies. Suppliers have savings that they want to invest to earn a return. Users need money to fund their activities. For example, individuals borrow to finance a home purchase, businesses expand their factories, and governments build roads. The financial markets are the places in which suppliers and users transact. They usually transact through intermediaries and seldom transact directly with each other. The intermediaries include (commercial) banks, investment banks, funds, and insurance companies.

financial system

The system that transfers money between suppliers and users. It comprises financial intermediaries, markets, and instruments (securities).

FIGURE 1.1 The Financial System

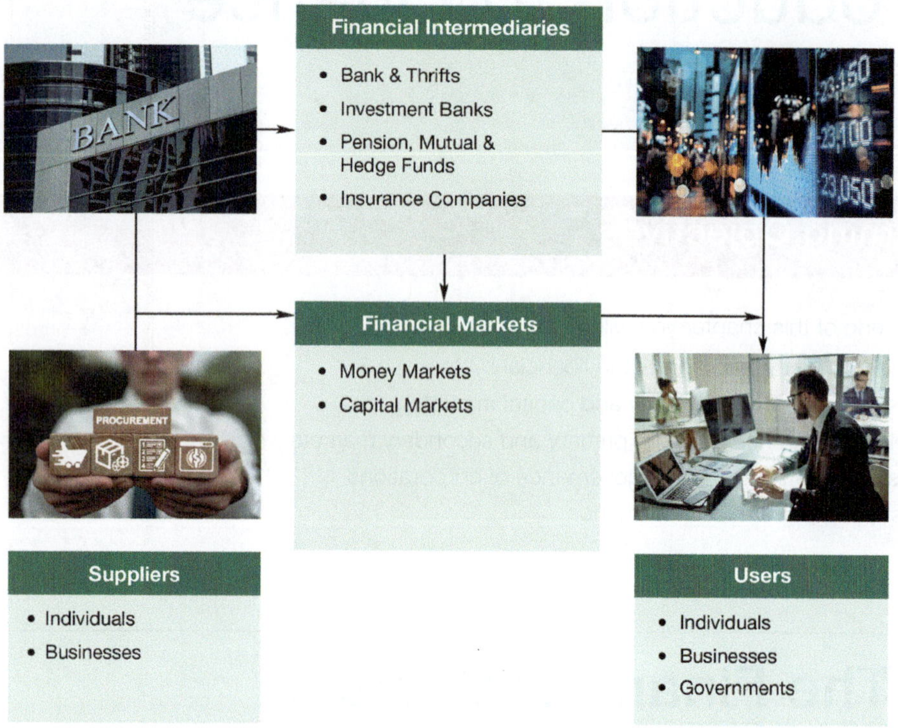

TABLE 1.1 Definitions of Terms in Figure 1.1

Individuals (Suppliers)	Individuals are the primary investors in the economy. Ultimately, they own every business asset. As individuals plan for retirement (or set aside money for other goals), they invest their savings in the financial system with the expectation of converting them into greater savings for the future.
Business (Suppliers)	Businesses supply funds in the form of retained earnings.
Individuals (Users)	Individuals borrow to finance homes, cars, and holidays.
Business (Users)	Businesses use money to start new projects. They borrow money and raise equity.
Government (Users)	Governments borrow to pay for operating deficits and to fund real capital—like new highways.
Banks & Thrifts (Financial Intermediaries)	Take deposits from savers and lend to individuals (i.e., mortgages) and businesses (i.e., lines of credit and commercial loans). Profit from spread between rate charged on loans and rate paid on deposits.
Investment Banks (Financial Intermediaries)	Help companies, municipalities and states raise capital by selling securities to public. Profit from spread between price paid to security issuer and price charged to investor. Provide financial consulting to companies.
Funds (Financial Intermediaries)	Invest in private businesses and financial securities on behalf of individual savers. Profit from management fees charged to savers.
Insurance Companies (Financial Intermediaries)	Collect premiums from individuals/businesses for life and property insurance. Invest premium income prior to paying out claims. Profit if premium plus investment income exceeds claims.

To give you a sense of who the suppliers and users are, let's look at two specific markets: the bond and equity markets. Figure 1.2 shows the users and suppliers of capital in the U.S. **bond market**.

bond market

The bond market is the market for coupon and zero-coupon bonds with maturities ranging from 1 to 30 years and includes bonds issued by governments and corporations.

FIGURE 1.2 U.S. Bond Market Suppliers and Users

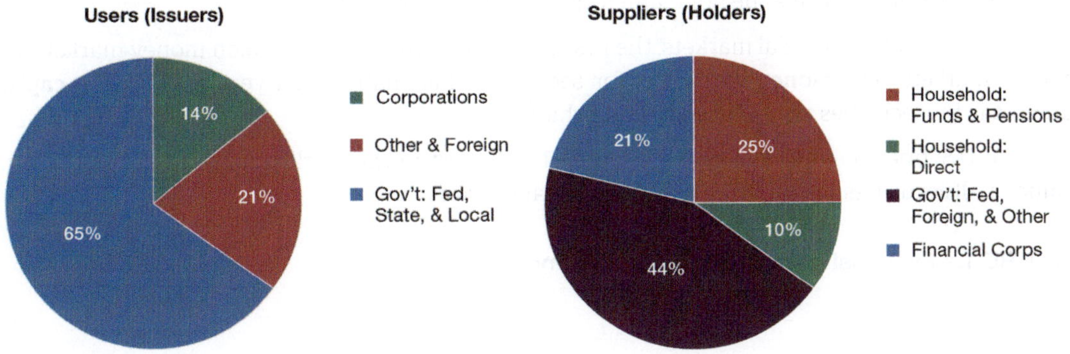

The largest user of capital in the bond market is the government. Federal, state, and local governments along with Agencies and Government Sponsored Enterprises (e.g., Freddie Mac) account for 65% of bond issuance. Corporations only account for 14% of bond market issuance. On the supply side, the largest supplier is domestic households who buy 35% of all bonds, but you should note that households don't generally buy bonds directly. Direct holdings account for only 10% of the market. It is more common for households to own bonds through mutual funds or through their retirement accounts. The bond markets are not retail markets in the sense that public investors buy the securities directly.

FIGURE 1.3 U.S. Equity Market Suppliers and Users

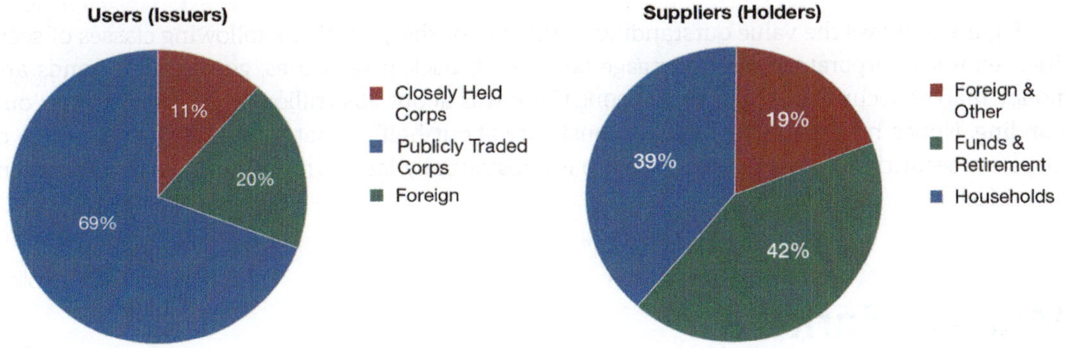

Not surprisingly, the largest issuer in the equity markets is publicly traded companies. The equity market is much more of a retail market as shown by the fact that households directly account for 39% of the supply capital. Of course, households also supply capital to equity markets indirectly through funds and retirement accounts.

1.2 Money and Capital Markets

stocks

A security that represents ownership in an incorporated company.

bonds

A debt instrument issued by governments and corporations with a maturity of more than 1 year. Coupon bonds pay periodic (annual or semi-annual) interest payments to the holder (called coupons) and pay a final lump-sum (called the face value) at maturity.

money market

The market for bonds with a maturity of less than 1 year. These bonds are all zero-coupon bonds and include bankers' acceptances, commercial paper, and government T-bills.

capital market

The market for long-term securities with original maturity greater than 1 year. The main securities are bonds and stocks issued by companies and governments.

As shown in Figure 1.1, the financial markets are the place in which suppliers and users of capital interact. They not only encompass a multitude of securities, including **stocks**, **bonds**, and other securities, but also span national borders. They exist physically (e.g., the New York Stock Exchange), and they exist virtually like the bond and foreign exchange markets.

To help classify financial markets, the first distinction we make is between money markets and capital markets. The **money market** is for securities that mature in 1 year or less. The **capital market** is for securities that mature in more than 1 year.

The U.S. financial markets are very large—the largest in the world. Figure 1.4 shows the total value of all securities outstanding in U.S. financial markets.

FIGURE 1.4 Financial Markets: Values Outstanding

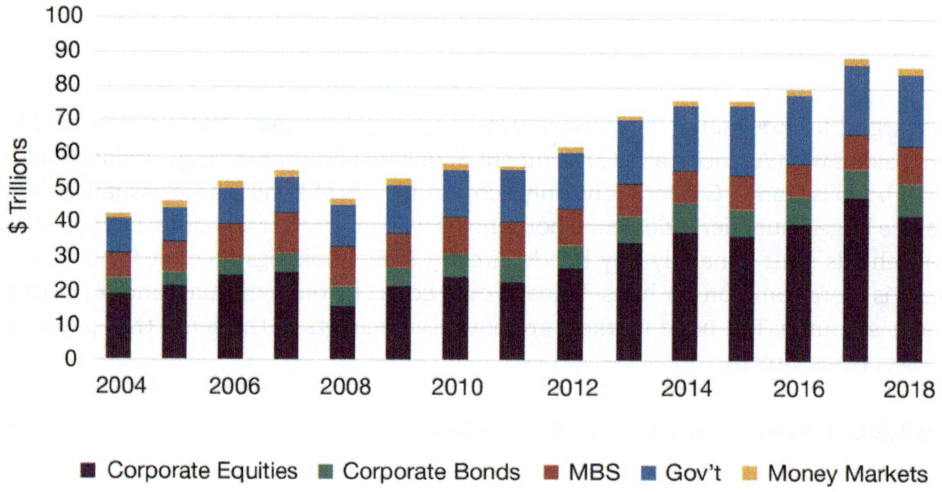

Figure 1.4 shows the value outstanding at the end of the year of the following classes of securities: equities, corporate bonds, mortgage (and asset) backed securities, government bonds and money market securities. At the end of 2018, there was about $85 trillion worth of securities outstanding. Notice how corporate equities constitute about half of that total and that the value of corporate securities (both equities and debt) is substantially larger than the value of government securities.

Money Markets

The term *money market* is a misnomer. Money is not traded in the money markets. However, in a money market, the securities

- are fixed income securities (i.e., bonds),
- are short term,
- are highly liquid (easy to sell), and
- mature in less than 1 year from their issue date.

Investors use the money market as an interim investment that provides a higher return than cash. Most investment funds and financial intermediaries (such as banks) hold money market securities to meet withdrawals. Money market securities have large face values (i.e., $1 million), which precludes most individual investors from buying them. As a result, individuals participate in the money market when they buy units in **money market mutual funds (MMMFs)**.

The sellers of money market securities find that the money market provides a low-cost source of temporary funds. Banks borrow in the money market to meet short-term reserve requirement shortages. The government funds a large portion of the national debt by issuing **Treasury bills (T-bills)**. Money markets permit finance companies, such as General Motors Acceptance Corporation (GMAC), to raise the funds it uses to make car loans. Figure 1.5 shows a diagram of the money market.

money market mutual funds (MMMFs)

A pooling of investor money that is professionally managed. The investors own shares (or units) in the pooled fund and are entitled to a proportionate share of earnings. Each fund has a specific investment objective that guides the types of securities that it owns. A money market fund owns money market securities.

Treasury bills (T-bills)

Bonds issued by the U.S. government that have maturities of 91 days, 182 days, or 52 weeks. T-bills are zero-coupon bonds.

FIGURE 1.5 The Money Market

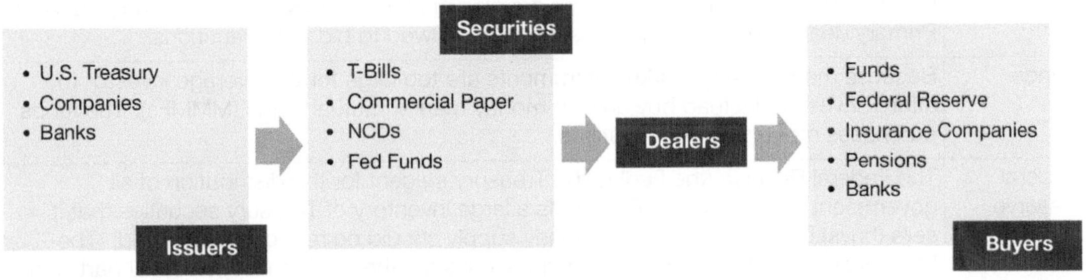

TABLE 1.2 Definitions of Terms in Figure 1.5

U.S. Treasury	The U.S. Treasury is the largest of all money market borrowers. It issues T-bills and other securities to finance the national debt. Short-term issues enable the government to raise funds until tax revenues are received.
Companies	Corporations use commercial paper to finance the loans they extend to their customers. For example, GMAC Financial Services borrows money by issuing commercial paper and uses the money to make loans, for example, to consumers buying General Motors cars, with repayment to come from customers making their monthly payments.
Banks (Issuers)	Banks are the major issuer of negotiable certificates of deposit (NCDs) and the only issuer of federal funds.
T-Bills	The most widely held money market security is the Treasury bill, or T-bill. Sold at a discount to par value. Lowest possibility of default of all money market securities. T-bills have 4-week, 13-week, 26-week, and 52-week maturities.
Commercial Paper	Commercial paper securities are unsecured promissory notes issued by corporations. Because these securities are unsecured, only the largest and most creditworthy corporations issue commercial paper. Commercial paper always has an original maturity less than 270 days, so as to avoid the need to register the security issue with the Securities and Exchange Commission (SEC). Most commercial paper actually matures in 20 to 45 days. Commercial paper is issued at a discount to its face value.
NCDs	A negotiable certificate of deposit (NCD) is a security issued by a bank that documents a deposit and specifies the interest rate and maturity date. Because a maturity date is specified, an NCD is a term security as opposed to a demand security. An NCD is also a bearer instrument, which means that whoever holds the instrument at maturity receives the principal and interest. The denominations of NCDs range from $100,000 to $10 million. Few NCDs are denominated less than $1 million. NCDs typically have a maturity of 1 to 4 months.

Fed Funds	Federal funds are funds that are used for borrowing or lending between financial institutions. The term of the loans is usually less than one day. The name "federal funds" ("fed funds") derives from the fact that the loan rates are close to the rate charged by the Federal Reserve. Fed funds are an alternative to borrowing from the Federal Reserve. Banks borrow from other banks so that they do not alert the Fed to liquidity problems. Banks lend in the fed funds market because money held at the Federal Reserve does not earn any interest. On a typical day, over $250 billion in fed funds are purchased. You are unlikely to ever buy or sell fed funds; however, their interest rates are the most closely watched and reported of all money market instruments. The Federal Reserve often announces its intention to raise or lower the fed fund rates. The Federal Reserve influences the fed funds market by buying (selling) government securities from (to) banks.
Dealers	The primary function of dealers is to make a market for money market securities by maintaining an inventory from which to buy or sell. These firms are very important to the liquidity of the market because they ensure that both buyers and sellers can readily market their securities. Money market dealers are commercial banks, investment banks and broker-dealers like Citibank, Bank of America, JP Morgan, GoldmanSachs, and Cantor Fitzgerald. These same firms are also primary dealers at U.S. Treasury auctions. Primary dealers are the institutions who are allowed to bid at the auctions.
Funds	Because many money market instruments are too large for the average investor to afford, investors instead buy units in money market mutual funds (MMMFs). The funds purchases money market securities.
Federal Reserve	The Federal Reserve (the Fed) is the Treasury's agent for the distribution of all government securities. The Fed holds a large inventory of Treasury securities that it sells (buys) if it believes that the money supply should be reduced (expanded). The Fed's responsibility for the money supply makes it the single most influential participant in the U.S. money market. By flooding the economy with money, the Fed can push down short-term borrowing rates.
Insurance Companies	Property and casualty insurance companies must maintain liquidity because of their unpredictable need for funds. For example, when Hurricane Katrina hit the Gulf Coast in 2005, insurance companies paid out billions of dollars in benefits to policy holders to help cover the $81 billion loss Katrina caused. To meet this demand for funds, the insurance companies had to sell a portion of their money market holdings.
Pensions	Pension funds maintain a portion of their funds in the money market so that they will be liquid enough to take advantage of investment opportunities. Additionally, pension funds must have sufficient liquidity to meet their obligations to beneficiaries.
Banks (Investors)	Commercial banks hold a larger percentage of U.S. government securities than any other group of financial institutions (approximately 12%). This is partly because of regulations that limit the investment opportunities available to banks.

Figure 1.6 compares the interest rates on selected money market instruments. On this graph, you will notice that all of the money market instruments appear to move together over time. This is because all are very low risk and have short-term maturities, so they are close substitutes Figure 1.6 also demonstrates the large drop in interest rates after the financial crises of 2008. Before 2008, rates ranged between 3% and 5%. Since the crises they have been below 1%. In 2015, the Federal Reserve began slowly raising rates, but Figure 1.6 doesn't tell the whole story because it ends at the end of 2019. In early 2020, the COVID-19 pandemic led to an economic lockdown of the economy. In response, the Federal Reserve lowered rates and the Federal Funds rate fell to about 0.10%.

FIGURE 1.6 Rates on Money Market Securities

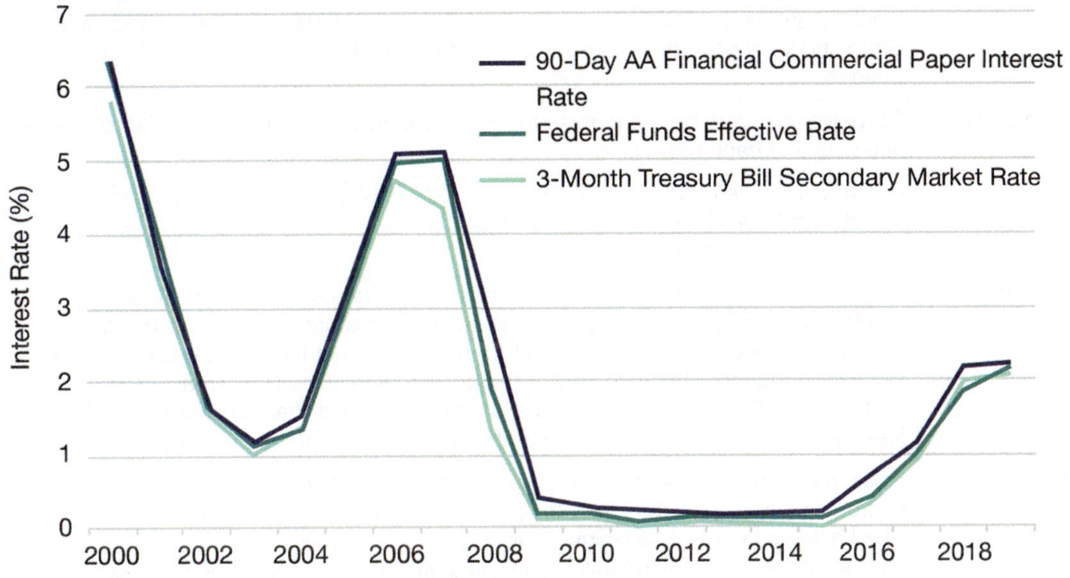

Capital Markets

Unlike money markets, capital markets are markets in which the securities have an original maturity greater than 1 year. The principal securities traded in the capital market are bonds and stocks.

Capital market participants have different motives from those of money market participants. The money markets are primarily for warehousing funds until a more important need arises. The securities traded on the capital markets fund long-term investments by companies and governments in projects like factories and highways.

FIGURE 1.7 The Capital Market

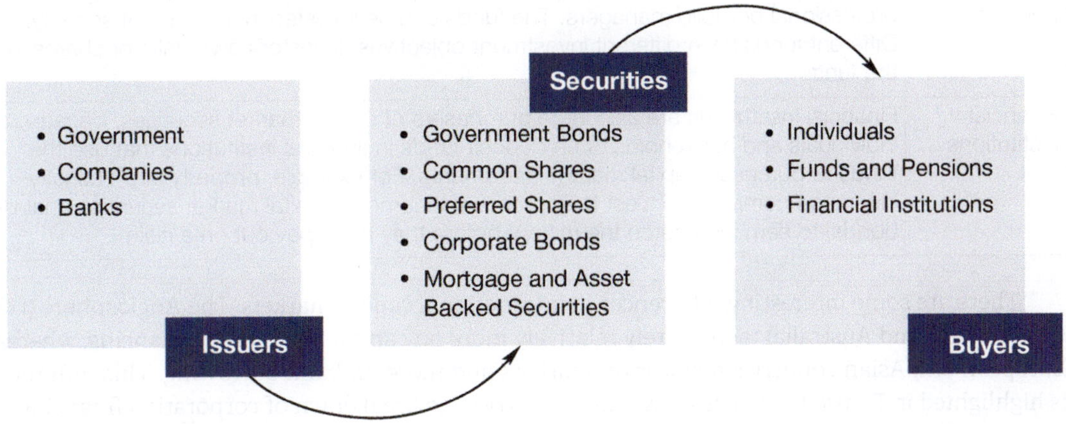

TABLE 1.3 Definitions of Terms in Figure 1.7

Government	The U.S. Treasury is the largest issuer of bonds and accounts for about 85% of the outstanding public debt. A number of federal agencies issue bonds, as do state and local governments. The federal government issues bonds to fund the national debt. State and local governments issue bonds to finance projects like schools and prisons.
Companies	Corporations issue bonds to raise funds for projects and acquisitions. Bonds are an alternative to bank borrowing.
Banks	Banks will initiate mortgages and then sell off bundles (say, 100 mortgages) to an investment bank. The investment bank sells the bundle to an investor. The bundles are called asset backed securities.
Government Bonds	A bond is a security that requires the issuer to make a series of annual (or semiannual) interest payments followed by a final maturity payment. A bond is like an i.o.u. Bondholders don't have to wait for maturity to get their money back, they can sell their bonds to other investors in the bond market. The U.S. Treasury issues T-Notes and T-Bonds (T-Bonds have a maturity greater than ten years). The Federal Reserve auctions new T-Notes and T-Bonds on behalf of the Treasury.
Common Shares	Stock represents ownership in a corporation. A stockholder owns a percentage interest in a firm consistent with the percentage of outstanding stock held. Stockholders are residual claimants in the sense that they get whatever is leftover after all of the company's liabilities are paid off. Common shareholders exercise their control of the corporation by voting for directors who sit on the board. (Typically one vote per share.) Common shareholders receive a dividend at the discretion of the board.
Preferred Shares	The preferred stockholder receives a fixed dividend that does not change. Preferred stockholders have a more senior claim against assets than common shareholders and are entitled to their dividends before common shareholders. Preferred stockholders usually do not vote.
Corporate Bonds	Corporate bonds are similar to government bonds, but corporate bonds can be more exotic in the sense of having more features. For example, some corporate bonds give the bondholder the option to convert into being a stockholder.
Mortgage- and Asset-Backed Securities	Mortgage-backed securities are bundles of mortgages. The owner of a mortgage-backed security receives the stream of interest and principal payments from the original borrowers. Asset-backed securities are similar to mortgage-backed, but they are bundles of car loans or credit card receivables instead of mortgages.
Individuals	The largest purchasers of capital market claims are households.Individuals, often through their employee-sponsored programs, invest in stocks and bonds as a means of preparing for retirement.
Funds and Pensions	Mutual funds, hedge funds and pensions are pools of money that are managed by professional portfolio managers. The funds can be invested in any type of security. Different funds have different investment objectives. Investors own units or shares in the fund.
Financial Institutions	Financial institutions are also large purchasers of capital market securities, because individuals and households often deposit funds in financial institutions that use the funds to purchase capital market instruments. For example, property and casualty insurance companies invest their premium income in capital market securities (mainly bonds) to earn income on the money before they must pay out on a claim.

There are some interesting differences in international capital markets. The Anglosphere (U.S., U.K., Canada, and Australia) tends to rely relatively more on capital markets for financing, whereas European and Asian countries rely less on markets and more on bank borrowing. This difference is highlighted in Figure 1.8, which shows the proportionate breakdown of corporation financing by source of financing.

FIGURE 1.8 Global Comparison of Corporate Financing by Source

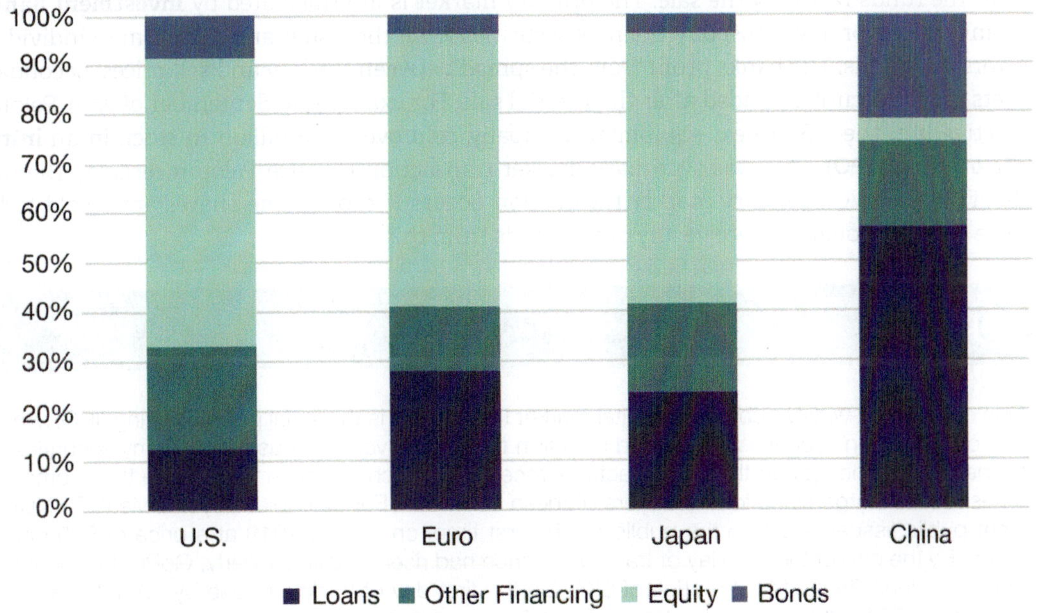

Note how the proportion of financing that U.S. corporations obtain from bank loans (the bottom part of the bar) is smaller than in Europe, Japan, and China. The other thing to notice is that the sum of financing from capital market sources (Equity plus Bonds) is larger in the U.S. (about 67%) than in Europe, Japan, and China.

1.3 Primary and Secondary Markets

Primary Markets

We divide the capital markets into two notional sub-markets: the primary and secondary markets. The **primary market** is the market for the first issuance of a security. The **secondary market** trades securities after their issuance. Secondary markets are much larger than primary markets.

primary market
The market where securities are traded for the first time and where initial offerings to the public are made.

secondary market
The market for trading securities after they have been issued.

investment bank

A financial intermediary that purchases securities from corporate and government issuers and resells them to the general public in the primary market.

initial public offering (IPO)

Where a firm first offers shares to the public and the firm becomes a public company.

Primary markets are for securities offered for sale for the first time. A primary market transaction is one in which there is an initial sale of a security by a firm or government and the issuer receives the funds raised by the sale. The primary market is intermediated by **investment banks**. The banks (alone or in groups) buy the new securities from the issuer and sell them to individual investors and funds. The banks profit from the spread between the buy and sell prices. Secondary markets are for securities traded after their initial sale. For example, in September of 2019, Peloton Interactive Inc., the U.S. fitness equipment company, sold over $1.16 billion in stock in an **initial public offering (IPO)**. This was a primary market transaction because Peloton received the proceeds of the sale. A secondary market transaction occurs if those same shares are resold today because Peloton would not receive any of the funds from this sale.

Explain It

One of the most widely publicized capital market transaction is the initial public offering (IPO). An IPO occurs when securities are offered by a firm that has never previously issued any securities to the public. The reason these transactions receive so much attention is because they sometimes result in large gains for the buyers of these securities. For example, Beyond Meat (BYND) went public (issued stock to the public for the first time) on May 1, 2019 at a price of $25 per share. By the end of the first day of trading, its price had risen 163%. Similarly, GoPro Inc., went public on June 26, 2014, at a price of $24. On the first day of trading it rose by 30%. By September 30, 2014, it had risen by 190%. There is no guarantee, however, that the price will rise after issue. Uber Inc. went public on May 9, 2019, at a price of $45. By the end of the trading day the price closed down 7.6%, and by the end of the year the stock was trading at $28 per share. Investors who participated in the new issue had lost close to half of their investment. Despite the hype surrounding IPOs, on average, an investment in an IPO underperforms investments in similar firms by 17%. This well-documented fact is exacerbated when the issuing firm is smaller. Another factor regarding IPOs is that your ability to buy shares depends on whether your broker chooses to sell shares to you. The better the prospects for the IPO, the less likely it is that a small investor will be able to buy any shares. Instead, these shares go to the broker's largest investors.

To understand the size of the primary markets, Figure 1.9 shows the dollar value of issuance of new securities in the U.S. capital markets.

FIGURE 1.9 Issuance of Securities

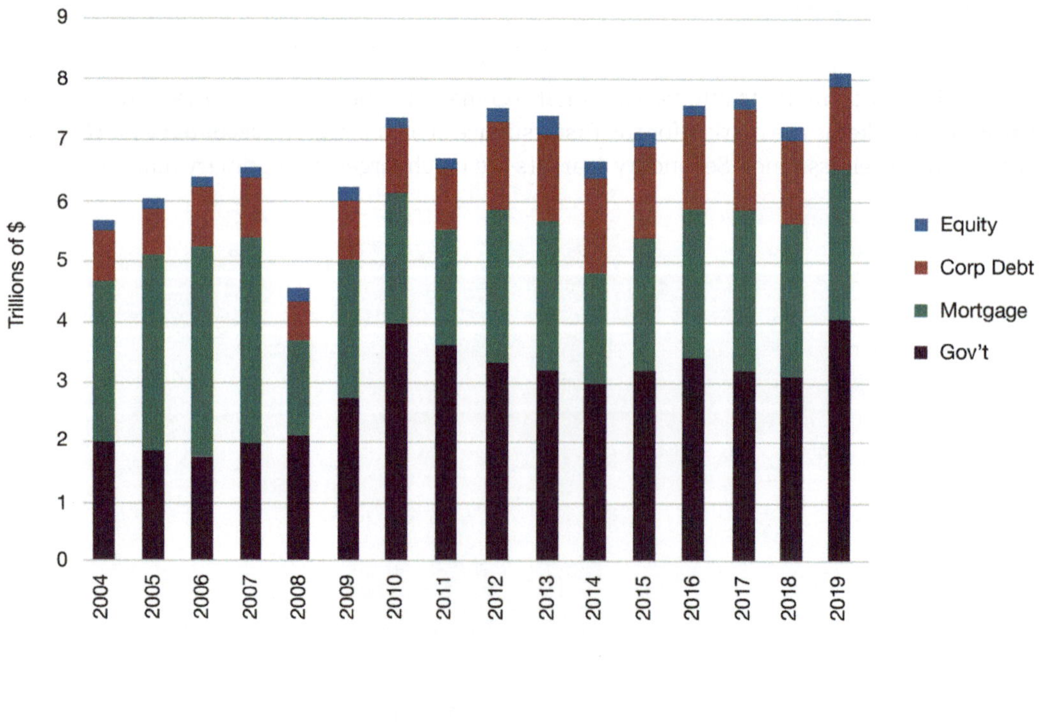

First note the scale on the y-axis. In 2019 (the bar on the far right), over $9 trillion of capital was raised in the U.S. capital markets. To benchmark that value, consider that the GDP of the U.S. in 2019 was about $21T. By far the largest issuer of securities was governments (Federal agencies, states, and municipalities). Note that corporations constitute about 20% of the capital markets and that equity is a smaller source of capital than debt.

Next, let's look at equity markets in more detail. Figure 1.10 shows common equity issuance by corporations.

FIGURE 1.10 Common Equity Issuance

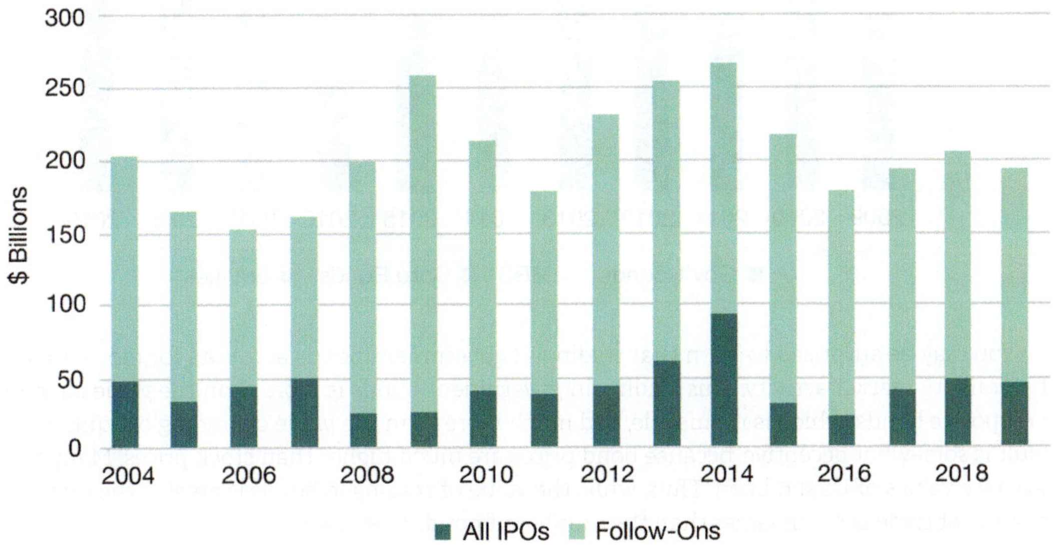

The first thing to notice is how small equity issuance is relative to total issuance in U.S. capital markets. In 2019, there was under $200 billion of common equity issued but total issuance was over U.S. $8T. Figure 1.10 divides common equity issuance into two parts: 1) IPOs and 2) follow-ons. Follow-ons are all subsequent issuances by companies after their IPO. Note how small IPOs are as a proportion of new equity issuances. To give you a sense of how infrequent they are, in 2018 there were only 197 IPOs in total.

Secondary Markets

Secondary markets are the markets for trading securities after they have been issued. The seller of the security in the secondary market is never the issuer, although many companies will buy back their own shares—share buybacks are an alternative to dividends and will be explained in more detail later in this book. To understand the scale of the secondary market and the relative sizes of the various sub-markets, Figure 1.11 shows average daily trading volume (in dollars) for government bonds, mortgage (and asset) backed securities, corporate bonds, and equities.

FIGURE 1.11 Average Daily Trading Volume (US)

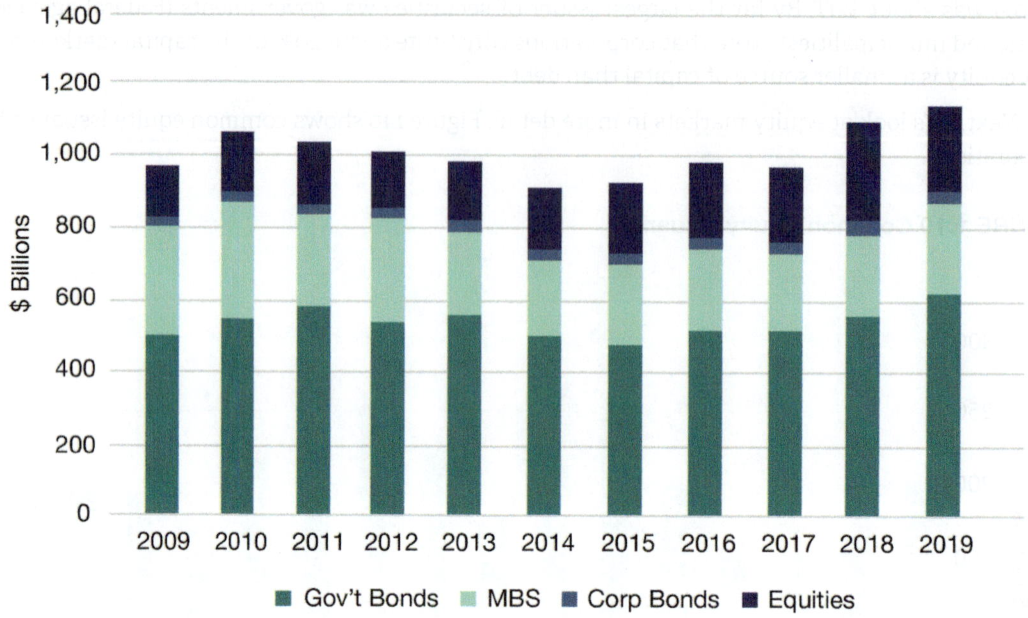

You may be surprised to learn that trading in government bonds accounts for more than half of secondary market activity. This trading in government bonds is more than the value of trading in corporate bonds, which is minuscule, and much more than the value of trading of equities. This result is somewhat deceptive, because bond prices are much higher than stock prices. Many bonds have face values of US$1 million. Thus, while the value of trading in bonds is greater, the number of shares that trade is much larger than the number of bonds that trade.

Another important fact to understand is that, in stocks, the U.S. markets represent a very large fraction of the global market for equities. Figure 1.12 shows the breakdown of global equity market capitalization by country. Equity market capitalization is simply the value of shares listed in the market (price times quantity). The total value of all shares listed globally at the end of 2018 was about US$75 trillion.

FIGURE 1.12 Global Equity Market Capitalization

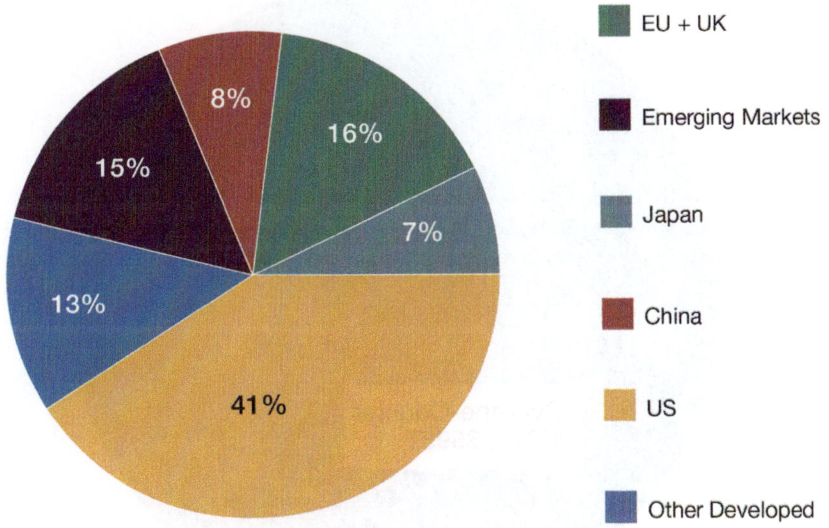

U.S. stock markets account for 41% of the value of all shares listed in all markets around the globe. The value is far greater than Europe and China, which both have economies about the same size as that of the U.S.

Another category of secondary markets is the derivative markets. Derivatives are securities like futures, options and swaps whose value is derived from the value of some other underlying security. Derivative markets are very large. Figure 1.13 shows the size of global derivatives markets. Size in Figure 1.13 is measured by something called the "notional principal value outstanding," which is similar to market capitalization. A more detailed explanation is beyond the scope of this introductory chapter.

FIGURE 1.13 Global Derivative Markets

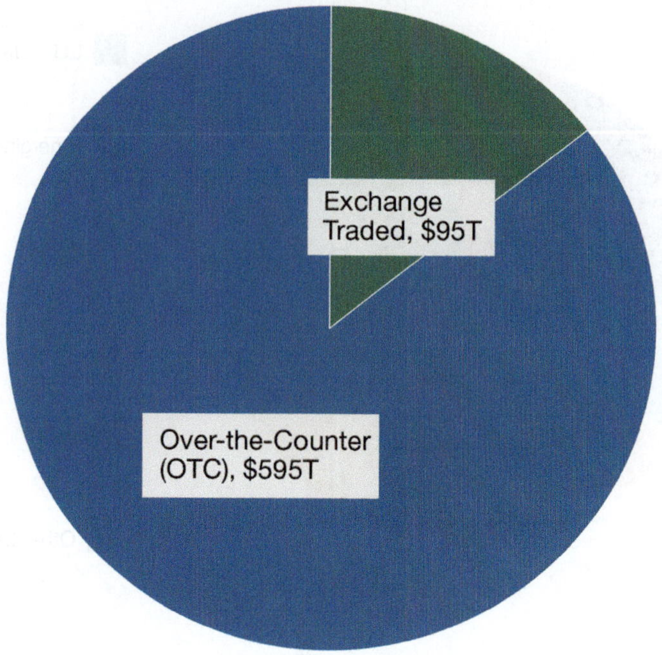

The total global notional principal value outstanding of derivative contracts at the end of 2018 was about US$690 trillion. This dwarfs the value of global equity markets, US$75T, and dwarfs the size of global bond markets which had about US$100T outstanding at the end of 2018. As Figure 1.13 shows, only about 14% of that trading happened on organized exchanges, whereas the other 86% occurred in the over-the-counter market. The difference between the exchanges and the over-the-counter market is the topic of the next section.

Types of Secondary Markets: Auction and Dealer

Secondary markets are further divided into two groups: (1) **auction** and (2) **dealer markets**. Auction markets trade in one physical or virtual location. A dealer market is characterized by multiple **dealers** who each hold an inventory of the security and who are each willing to buy or sell.

The **New York Stock Exchange (NYSE)** is an example of a physical auction market for stocks, because the NYSE still maintains a physical trading floor. (Only about 1% of NYSE volume is traded on its physical floor.) The Toronto Stock Exchange (TSX) is an online stock market with no physical trading floor. Both exchanges are auction markets. The key feature of an auction market is that all trading funnels through one location (real or virtual) and so there is only one best price at any given time. On the NYSE floor there are specific places (called trading posts) where particular stocks trade and the exchange assigns an auctioneer (specialist) to supervise the trading.

auction

A form of securities trading. It features many competitive buyers and sellers who simultaneously issue orders through brokers. The buyer's price is called the bid, and the seller's price is called the ask. A transaction occurs (and a price is set) when a buyer's bid price equals a seller's ask price. The New York Stock Exchange and Chicago Mercantile Exchange are examples of auction markets.

dealer markets

A form of securities market. An alternative to an auction market. Market participants trade over the phone or electronic network. Trading does not occur between buyers and sellers but, instead, through a network of middlemen called dealers. Dealers carry inventories of securities and stand ready to buy at their bid price and sell at their ask price. Some dealer markets, like NASDAQ, are centralized through a computer network; most are not (e.g., bond and foreign exchange markets). Also called an over-the-counter market.

dealers

An entity that stands ready to buy or sell a security to (from) its own inventory. Dealers post prices at which they will buy (bid price) or sell (ask price). Also known as a market-maker.

New York Stock Exchange (NYSE)

The largest stock exchange (by value) in the U.S. located in New York City. Owned by NYSE Euronext Inc.

electronic limit order books

A form of security market. The market is online and has no physical location. Trading is based around orders. Market orders are matched with the best available buy or sell order based on price and time priority. Limit orders are entered into the limit order book.

limit orders

A conditional order to buy or sell a security where it is only filled if the sell price is above a given level or the buy price is below a given level.

market orders

An order to buy or sell that is to be executed as soon as it is received by the broker.

Worldwide, auction markets are moving away from physical trading floors and are more commonly organized as **electronic limit order books**. In those markets, the order book is open to all traders. Traders either submit **limit orders** that offer to trade a specific quantity at a specific price or submit **market orders** that are matched with posted limit orders. Limit orders are recorded in the limit order book. Market orders are matched against the best buy or sell limit order based on priority rules (i.e., price and time).

Tip

In a limit order book market there are bid and ask prices, but they are set differently from those in dealer markets. The bid price is the price of the best offer to buy (the limit order to buy with the highest price), and the ask price is the price of the best offer to sell (the limit order to sell with the lowest price).

FIGURE 1.14 Dealer Markets

In dealer (**over-the-counter (OTC)**) markets, trading takes place in a variety of places. Figure 1.14 shows a dealer market. Trading usually occurs over the telephone or by computer. In a dealer market, multiple dealers simultaneously make a market in an individual security. Each dealer holds an **inventory** of the security, posts buy (**bid**) and sell (**ask**) prices, and stands ready to trade. Traders can transact with any dealer, and it is up to traders to compare prices before selecting their dealer to ensure the best price. The money market is a dealer market, as are the markets for foreign currencies and bonds. In the bond market, the buyers and sellers are mainly large institutions (i.e., mutual and pension funds) that trade through investment dealers. Dealers use a multitude of electronic trading platforms to trade with each other.

over-the-counter (OTC)

A form of securities market. An alternative to an auction market. Market participants trade over the phone or electronic network. Trading does not occur between buyers and sellers but, instead, through a network of middlemen called dealers. Dealers carry inventories of securities and stand ready to buy at their bid price and sell at their ask price. Some dealer markets, like NASDAQ, are centralized through a computer network; most are not (e.g., bond and foreign exchange markets). Also called an over-the-counter market.

inventory

To ensure an active market, dealers own an inventory of the security. The inventory is important because buy and sell orders do not arrive at the dealer at the same time. For example, it is unlikely that one customer will call the dealer wanting to buy a security just as another customer is selling it. The dealer adds and subtracts stock from this inventory as demand warrants. Dealers want to begin and end each day with approximately the same inventory level.

bid

In dealer markets, dealers buy at the bid price, so traders sell to the dealer and receive the bid. In auction markets, the bid price is the highest of the competitive offers to buy.

ask

In dealer markets, dealers sell at the ask price, so traders buy from the dealer and pay the ask price. In auction markets, the ask price is the lowest of the oompotitivo offers to sell.

Explain It: The Market Dealer, Part 1

View in the online reader

Explain It: The Market Dealer, Part 2

View in the online reader

The Role of Secondary Markets

The primary markets are the source of capital for businesses, so it is easy to understand their importance for a growing and vibrant economy. The role of secondary markets is harder to understand. Some criticize them as being glorified casinos. While prices certainly fluctuate in the secondary market, their primary role is to provide the means for investors to tailor their investment horizons (i.e., to sell their shares according to the personal financial needs). Without a secondary market investors would have to wait for a liquidation, takeover, dividend, or repurchase in order to get some or all of their money back. Those events don't often coincide with investors' need for cash, so an active secondary market is a critical feature of the stock markets.

Characteristics of Secondary Markets

Tip

Academic finance has an entire subdiscipline devoted to the study of how markets function. It is called market microstructure.

Given that secondary markets perform an important economic function, what are the characteristics of good markets? Among the most important are accurate pricing of stocks and **liquidity**.

liquidity

A securities market with a high volume of trading activity in which it is easy to buy and sell. Liquid markets also have depth, which means large quantities can be traded quickly without impacting the price adversely.

One of the most important roles of secondary markets is establishing security prices. Setting accurate prices is not trivial. Consider the case in which something is bought secondhand. Both buyer and seller want the exchange price to be fair. The problem is how to set a fair price when neither the buyer nor the seller knows the price other people have set for the item. Let us consider two secondhand items: a car and a desk.

Suppose you want to buy a 2014 BMW 328 from your neighbor. You would probably begin establishing the value of the car by consulting www.autotrader.com or www.kbb.com. The first is an online marketplace for used cars and the second estimates average prices by attending large car auctions. You and your neighbor then adjust the actual price up or down, depending on the condition of the car.

Now suppose that you want to buy your neighbor's antique Louis XV writing desk. The market for the desk is much thinner, meaning not many are bought or sold. Therefore, you will have a more difficult time establishing its true value. No central market exists in which similar desks are frequently traded and there is no value guide to consult. The result is that neither you nor your neighbor are sure what the true value of the desk should be. If you think it is worth less than what your neighbor thinks it is worth, then no transaction will occur.

What are the differences between the markets for used cars and custom furniture? First, there are many similar cars being bought and sold. In other words, there is standardization of the commodity, which allows **traders** to compare the price of one unit with another. Second, the market for cars is a much more liquid market because it is easy to convert the asset to cash. Figure 1.15 shows three important dimensions of liquidity.

traders

A large number of traders produces a competitive market in which no individual trader has monopoly power and there are many available traders.

FIGURE 1.15 Liquidity
Trades: A large number of trades means it is possible to buy or sell at any time. To give you a sense of how active the stock markets are, the NYSE Euronext market trades 3.5 billion shares per day in busy periods. **Traders:** A large number of traders produces a competitive market in which no individual trader has monopoly power and there are many available traders. **Depth** refers to the quantity of shares available to be traded. In a deep market, the quantities are large. When markets are deep, they can absorb large transactions while maintaining fair prices. When large pension funds or mutual funds sell hundreds of thousands of shares at a time, it is important that they not depress the market price of the securities.

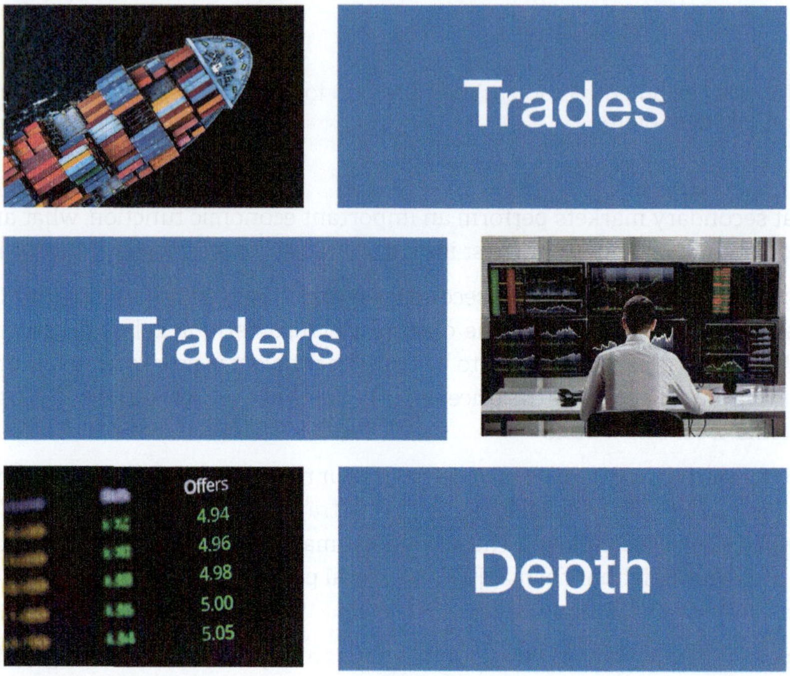

1.4 Corporate Governance

Governance refers to the way an organization is formed, structured, and controlled. It refers to the structure of authority within the organization. In this section, we first compare and contrast the three basic forms of business organization: **sole proprietorship**, **partnership**, and **corporations**. Then, we focus on corporations in more detail. We describe the legal structure of a corporation. We discuss the legal duty of the board of directors and the goals of management. We conclude with a discussion of governance problems, particularly the **principal–agent problem**.

governance

The way an organization is formed, structured, and controlled. It refers to the structure of authority within an organization.

sole proprietorship

A type of business entity owned and run by one person.

partnership

A type of business entity owned and run by two or more persons who have agreed to work together.

corporations

A type of business entity that is independent of its owners, the shareholders. Corporations may enter into contracts in their own name.

principal–agent problem

The problems and costs that occur when an agent does not maximize the utility of the principal.

Forms of Business Organizations

Table 1.4 lists the advantages and disadvantages of the three forms of business organizations: sole proprietorships, partnerships, and corporations.

TABLE 1.4 Forms of Business Organizations: Advantages and Disadvantages

Business Structure	Definition	Advantages	Disadvantages
Sole proprietorship	A type of business entity owned and run by one person.	1. Least regulated for a business; no license, charter, or agreement legally required 2. No conflict between owner and manager; manager acts in owner's best interests 3. Pay personal taxes on all business income	1. Unlimited liability; owner responsible for all business debts 2. No access to capital markets; just bank lending 3. Ownership difficult (impossible) to transfer
Partnership	A type of business entity owned and run by two or more persons who have agreed to work together.	1. No license, charter, or agreement legally required 2. Pay personal taxes on all business income	1. Partnership agreement recommended 2. Partners share joint liability for company's debts 3. No access to capital markets; just bank lending 4. Moral hazard; when profits are shared, each partner has an incentive to shirk on effort 5. Ownership difficult to transfer
Corporation	A type of business entity dependent of its owners, the shareholders; corporations may enter into contracts in their own name.	1. Ownership easy to transfer 2. Shareholders' liability limited to their investment; not liable for corporate debts beyond their investment 3. Corporation can outlive owners 4. Can raise money using capital markets (debt and equity)	1. Expensive to set up; must register with state government; need corporate charter 2. Pay corporate tax on business income and personal tax on distributions of profits 3. Agency problems due to separation of ownership and control

Figure 1.16 shows the breakdown of establishments and annual sales by organizational form in the United States. Although the majority of establishments are structured as sole proprietorships (61%), they only account for 2% of all sales. In contrast, corporations account for 91% of all sales. Given this statistic, you will not be surprised to know that we focus our attention on corporations (although many of the tools developed in this book are applicable to proprietorships and partnerships as well).

FIGURE 1.16 Number of Firms and Sales by Business Structure in the United States

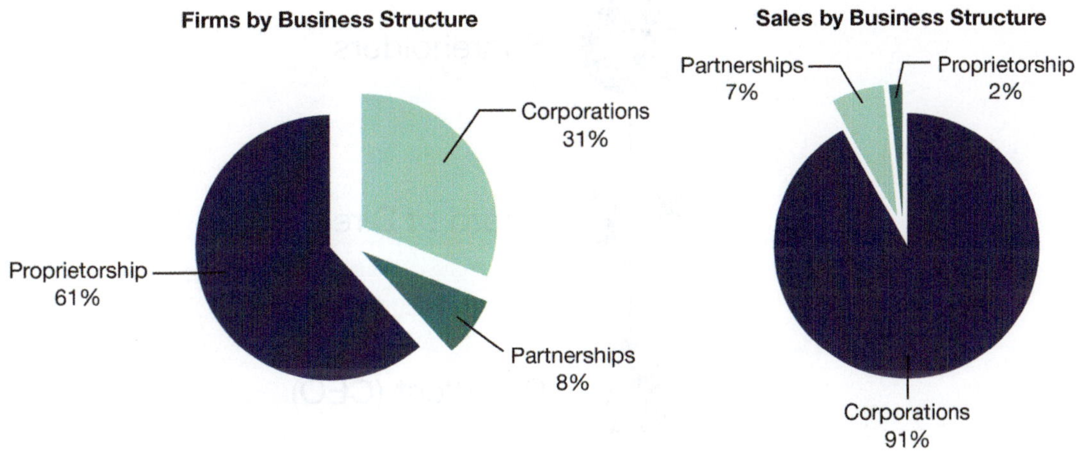

Source: Data from www.Bizstats.com

Corporations and Governance

In this section, we first review the legal structure of corporations. Then, we look at the legal duty of the board of directors and the goals of financial management. Finally, we look at the principal–agent problem, which is a breakdown in the relationship of shareholders and managers.

The Legal Structure of the Corporation

Figure 1.17 shows an organizational chart for a corporation. At the top are shareholders, who are the owners of the company. The owners' control of the corporation is exercised through their right to vote for members of the board of directors. The board of directors hires the senior management and sets their compensation. The board also reviews and votes on all major initiatives.

FIGURE 1.17 Organizational Structure as a Corporation

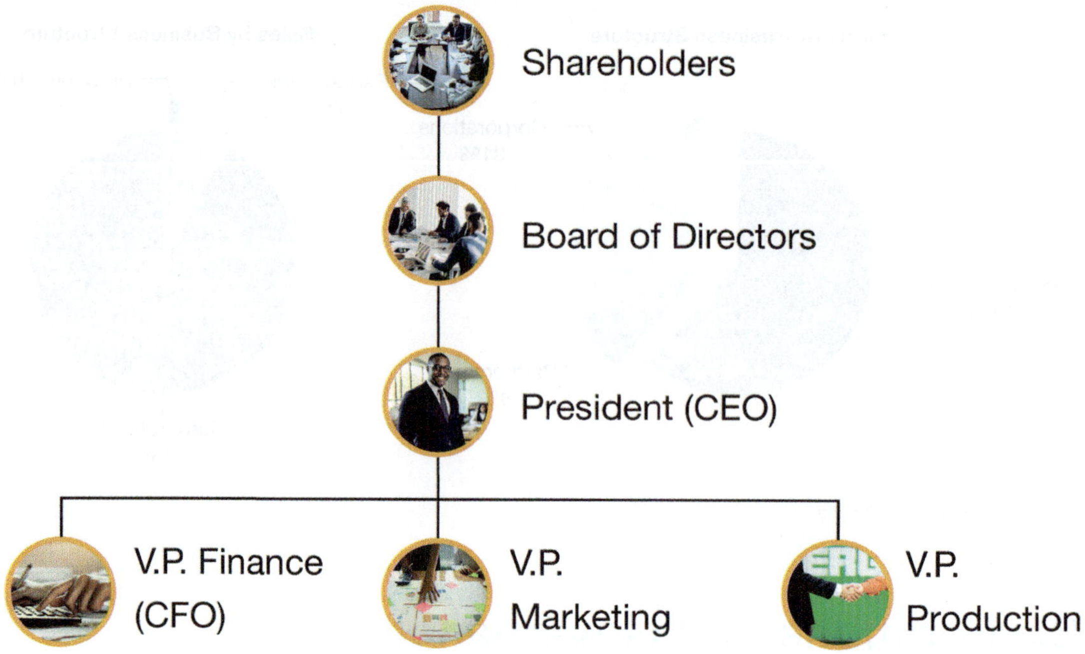

The Goals of Financial Management

In this textbook, we make recommendations about best financial practices. To recommend a best practice, we have to know the goal of the decision-maker (i.e., the board and the company's managers). What objective function should managers maximize? In a sole proprietorship, the manager maximizes the interests of the owner because the two individuals are one. In a corporation, ownership and control are separate, so the duty of the manager is less clear.

bondholders
The name of the owner of the bond.

The common law requires board members to have a fiduciary duty to the corporation. A fiduciary duty is a duty of care, loyalty, and good faith. But a corporation is just a nexus of contracts between stakeholders (i.e., shareholders, **bondholders**, employees, and suppliers). Recognizing this, the common law also stipulates that no one stakeholder group has legal primacy over any other (except in takeovers, in which the duty of the board is to shareholders). As you can imagine, this duty to the corporation is difficult to implement, since many decisions involve conflicts between stakeholder groups. The "Explain It" provides two examples of problems associated with the broad definition of the board's duty.

acquisition
An acquisition is when one company acquires control over another.

Explain It

Consider RJR Nabisco in the late 1980s. Its management wasted resources. For example, it abandoned a smokeless cigarette project costing over $400 million because the product smelled like horse manure. The stock price languished in the mid-$40s. Management needed to be removed. A management buyout offer led to a bidding war. The winning bidder offered over $110, which represented a gain of more than $15 billion to the shareholders. The winning bid depended on increasing the debt load of the company, which made the original bonds riskier and caused their price to fall. The bondholders sued, arguing that the board needed to weigh their loss against the shareholders' gain. The bondholders' suit did not derail the **acquisition**, but imagine if it did. Imagine if bondholders could have compelled the board to weigh their interests above those of the shareholders. The holders of $5 billion worth of bonds would have primacy over shareholders who stood to gain over $15 billion. That would have been a net loss to society. Alternatively, in late 2011, Chiquita Brands International Inc. (maker of the famous Chiquita banana) announced it was going to boycott oil from the Canadian oilsands because it felt the oilsands damaged the environment. The board made a decision in favor of one stakeholder, society, at the expense of another, the shareholders. This decision hurt shareholders because Chiquita Brands raised its energy costs by boycotting one of the cheapest supplies of fuel for its trucks. Motley Fool analysts awarded Chiquita Brands International Inc. a gold medal for being one of the worst food and beverage stocks of 2011.

Despite the confusion introduced by the common law, the legal structure of the corporation provides an answer to the question. Recall that shareholders elect board members. To be reelected, board members must act in the best interests of shareholders. The best interest of shareholders is that the stock price be as high as possible. Throughout this book, we assume that the goal of management is to maximize the share price—in other words, maximize shareholder wealth.

Principal–Agent Problem

All individuals act in their own interest. However, when managers put their interests before the interests of the stockholders, problems arise.

When principals (stockholders) cannot monitor agents (managers) easily, then managers have the opportunity to use corporate resources in ways that benefit themselves but may not benefit shareholders (e.g., empire building, perquisite consumption). This conflict of interest is called a *principal–agent problem*. To solve the principal–agent problem, shareholders need to spend resources to align managers' interests with their own. The loss of shareholder wealth associated with managerial waste and the cost of resources used to monitor agents' behavior and align incentives are called **agency costs**.

agency costs

The costs associated with principal–agent problems. The loss of the principal's wealth associated with the agent's waste and the cost of resources used to monitor agents' behavior and align incentives are called agency costs.

Principal–Agent Problem: Contractual Remedies

One possible remedy is an executive compensation plan that aligns the goals of managers more closely with those of shareholders. Giving executives stocks and stock options is considered one way of reducing agency costs. If executive compensation is tied to the stock price, then executives should make choices that maximize the stock price. Although this is true, it does not work perfectly. Executives who own stock can still make decisions in which they realize all of the benefits (e.g., executive jets) but incur only a fraction of the costs because the costs are spread across all the shareholders. When we study topics like **capital structure** and **distributions**, we discuss agency costs again because debt and **dividends** play a role in reducing agency costs.

capital structure

The mix of long-term debt and equity used by the firm to finance its assets.

distributions

A payment of cash to shareholders; either in the form of a dividend or share repurchase.

dividends

Periodic distributions of cash made by a firm to its stockholders, usually paid quarterly.

Principal–Agent Problem: Government Regulation

Explain It

Search the Internet for more information on any one of these three companies: Worldcom, Enron, or Tyco. Each case is a very interesting example of the principal–agent problem in practice.

The contractual remedies discussed have not completely solved the principal–agent problem. The Tech Bubble (1997–2000) produced three high profile cases of corporate fraud and abuse at Worldcom, Tyco, and Enron. In response, in the summer of 2002, the House of Representatives and Senate passed the Sarbanes-Oxley Act (SOX). SOX has five key provisions: (1) it mandates internal procedures to ensure accurate financial disclosure, and it requires that those procedures be audited; (2) it requires disclosure of all material off-balance sheet activities; (3) it requires a committee of outside directors to supervise and review the firm's audits; (4) it requires CEOs and CFOs to certify the financial statements; and (5) it has stiffened the criminal penalties for fraudulent disclosure.

The cost of compliance with SOX has been quite high. One study estimates about $1.7 million per company per annum.[1] The benefits are very difficult to quantify, so the net benefit of the law remains unknown.

1.5 Six Important Ideas in Finance

As you read, we would like you to keep in mind six key concepts. If you understand these six concepts thoroughly, it will greatly enhance your insight into financial issues.

Time Value of Money

Money has time value. A dollar today is worth more than the promise of a dollar next year. Human mortality makes us prefer current consumption over future consumption. When we evaluate securities or projects that generate cash over time, we have to be careful to discount the future.

Risk and Return

This is the finance equivalent of no pain, no gain. We should not expect to earn high returns without taking high risks. This derives from our natural aversion to uncertainty. Investors pay less for investments that have greater uncertainty, and so those investments generate higher returns (on average).

Explain It

Bernie Madoff conducted a Ponzi-scheme fraud for almost 20 years, until his arrest in December 2008. Over the period 1990–2008, Madoff's fund earned an average return of 10.45% per annum with a standard deviation of 2.45%. In contrast, over the same period, the annual return from investing in the S&P 500 was 9.64% with a standard deviation of 14.28%. Madoff's fund appeared to earn a higher return than the S&P 500 with less variability (risk). This is because Madoff fabricated his fund performance results to fool investors. Bernard and Boyle (2009) argue that regulators (and investors) should have been suspicious because it was too good to be true. There was too much gain and not enough pain![2]

Efficiency, Arbitrage, and Law of One Price

Explain It: Market Efficiency

View in the online reader

Investors are not stupid. The competition to find cheap securities and earn high returns is fierce. Thus, we should not expect to find mispriced securities. This idea is central to an understanding of the **efficient markets hypothesis**.

Like the efficient markets hypothesis, the **law of one price** is based on the idea that investors are not stupid. The law of one price states that, if two identical assets are traded in two different markets, then they must trade at the same price. For example, if the price of a six-pack of Coors is $4 at the Quick-E-Mart, but it is $5 at Safeway, then that is a violation of the law of one price.

The law of one price is enforced by **arbitrage**. Arbitrage is the practice of taking advantage of violations of the law of one price. In this situation, you should buy a six-pack for $4 at the Quick-E-Mart and then sell the beer for $5 outside of Safeway. If you repeat this transaction many times, then the excess demand will raise the price at the Quick-E-Mart and the excess supply will lower the price at Safeway. You will stop trading when the two prices are equal and the law of one price is restored.

efficient markets hypothesis

The hypothesis states that all relevant information is fully and immediately reflected in a security's market price.

law of one price

Law that says that two equivalent investments that trade in different markets must have the same price. If the prices aren't equal, then an arbitrage opportunity is created and the resulting trading pushes the prices back to equality. The equality implied by the law of one price only holds exactly if there are no trading frictions or barriers between the markets.

arbitrage

A trading strategy that involves the simultaneous purchase and sale of an identical security in two different markets at two different prices. Perfect arbitrage involves no investment and no risk.

Cash Is King

You cannot spend net income. It is an accounting number meant to represent the average profit available to shareholders. Net income is reduced by depreciation that is not an actual cash outlay, so net income is not equal to the amount of cash that owners actually have at the end of the year. In finance, we focus on actual cash receipts and disbursements. We use accounting numbers in our calculations, but we often have to make adjustments to get closer to an actual cash value.

Transaction Costs and Information Matter

In some financial models, we assume that markets are perfect, that contracts are costless to enforce, and that everyone has the same information. Reality is different. In reality, transaction costs make contracts work imperfectly and undermine the incentives of the transacting parties. One example is the agency problem previously described. When principals cannot monitor their agents, then the agents can take advantage of the principal.

Information asymmetry

When information is not spread evenly among all participants. When some know more than others.

Information asymmetry is another feature of reality. Information is not distributed evenly across economic agents (i.e., shareholders, bondholders, bankers, and managers). Information is the lifeblood of financial markets, so many institutions have arisen to signal information and to protect uninformed agents from exploitation. One example is the moral-hazard problem with insurance. Once you insure your car against damage, you have less interest in avoiding accidents. This affects the likelihood of a claim and the pricing and features of the insurance contract.

When we study financial institutions and contracts, we must realize that they occur in a world with transaction costs and information asymmetries. Sometimes, we observe arrangements that seem peculiar. That perception is usually the result of our failure to understand the particular costs and information problems encountered by the economic agents involved.

Rate of Return

profit

The profit from an investment comprises any change in value in the asset that was purchased plus interest, dividends, or other cash flows that the investor receives from owning the asset.

timeline

A horizontal line on which time 0 is the leftmost end and future periods are shown as you move from left to right; can be used to depict investment cash flows.

Throughout this book we calculate rates of return. We do it for loans, bonds, projects, and stocks. In finance, the return is the **profit** earned on an investment. The rate of return expresses the profit as a proportion of the original investment. The profit comprises any change in the value of the asset that was purchased plus interest, dividends, or other cash flows that the investor receives as a result of owning the asset. The investment is the amount of money paid by the investor to initiate the investment. Usually it is the cost of purchasing an asset, but in a loan it is the amount loaned (the principal). For example, say you give a friend \$100 today and he repays you \$200 in one year. First let's make a picture, called a **timeline**, that shows the information in the problem.

At the beginning of the year (time 0) you give your friend \$100. That is the investment. At the end of the year (time 1) you get \$200. Your profit is the difference between what you received and what you invested:

$$Profit = Cash\ Flows\ Received - Investment = \$200 - \$100 = \$100$$

Your rate of return is given by:

$$Return = Profit/Investment$$

or

$$Return = (Cash\ Flows\ Received - Investment)/Investment$$

The default unit of time is a year. If the time span is shorter or longer than a year, then we convert the return to an annual return using methods you will encounter later in the book.

Endnotes

1. Financial Executives International, "FEI 2007 Survey of SOX 404 Costs." Fei.mediaroom.com. April 30, 2008.
2. Bernard, Carole, and Phelim Boyle, "Mr. Madoff's Amazing Returns: An Analysis of the Split-Strike Conversion Strategy," *Journal of Derivatives* 17 (2009): 62–76.

CHAPTER 2

Financial Statements and Ratio Analysis

Learning Objectives

By the end of this chapter you will be able to:

1. Describe the three financial statements needed for financial analysis.
2. Explain the goals of financial statement analysis.
3. Perform financial statement analysis.
4. Prepare common-sized financial statements.
5. Evaluate company performance using the DuPont Ratios.
6. Integrate ratios together to perform company analysis.

Earlier, we learned that the goal of the financial manager is to maximize shareholder wealth, which occurs when the firm's stock price is maximized. In this chapter, we want to get more pragmatic. How does the financial manager know that he or she is moving the company in the right direction, and how do investors in the firm's stock evaluate the performance of the managers? The stakeholders look at the firm's financial statements for answers to these and other questions. Firm managers use accounting information to help them manage the firm. Investors and creditors use accounting information to evaluate the firm.

This chapter focuses on the interpretation and analysis of financial statements. To perform financial analysis, you will need to know how to use financial ratios, **common-sized financial statements**, and the DuPont ratio method. In addition, you will learn market-based ratios that provide insight about what the market for stocks and bonds believes about future prospects of the firm.

common-sized financial statements

Financial statements that have every line converted into a ratio by dividing income statement data by total sales and balance sheet data by total assets.

Financial analysis is the process of using financial information to assist in investment and financial decision-making. Financial analysis helps managers with efficiency analysis and identification of problem areas within the firm. Also, it helps managers identify strengths on which the firm should build. Externally, financial analysis is useful for credit managers evaluating loan requests and investors considering security purchases.

financial analysis

The process of using financial information to assist in investment and financial decision-making.

2.1 The Financial Statements

Three financial statements are critical to financial statement analysis: the balance sheet, the income statement, and the statement of cash flows. We provide a brief overview of each statement and describe what information it contains.

Balance Sheet

balance sheet

A snapshot of a firm at a particular point in time that shows its assets and liabilities.

The **balance sheet** provides the details of the accounting identity.

$$\textit{Assets} = \textit{Liabilities} + \textit{Owners}'\ \textit{equity}$$

or

$$\textit{Investments} = \textit{Investments paid for with debt} + \textit{Investments paid for with equity}$$

The balance sheet is a financial snapshot of the firm, usually prepared at the end of the fiscal year. That is, it provides information about the condition of the firm at one particular point in time. By reviewing a series of balance sheets from different years, the analyst can identify changes in the firm over time. Table 2.1 shows a sample balance sheet, and "Explain It: Balance Sheet Discussion" discusses its content.

Explain It: Balance Sheet Discussion

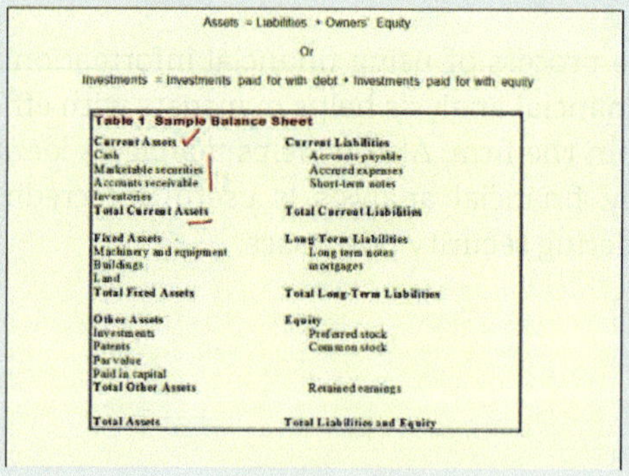

View in the online reader

TABLE 2.1 Sample Balance Sheet

ASSETS	LIABILITIES AND EQUITY
Current Assets	**Current Liabilities**
Cash	Accounts Payable
Marketable Securities	Accrued Expenses
Accounts Receivable	Short-Term Notes
Inventories	Total Current Liabilities
Total Current Assets	**Long-Term Liabilities**
Fixed Assets	Long-Term Notes
Machinery and Equipment	Mortgages
Buildings	**Total Liabilities**
Land	**Shareholders' Equity**
Other Assets	Preferred Stock
Investments	Common Stock
Patents	Paid in Capital
Intangible Assets	Retained Earnings
	Total Equity
Total Assets	**Total Liabilities & Equity**

It is important to note that assets are owned only for the income they can produce for the firm. Liabilities and owners' equity provide the funds for the purchase of these assets.

1. Assets generate income (the left-hand side)

   The left-hand side of the balance sheet lists the firm's assets. The only reason for a firm to hold an asset is if it produces income. There is no reason for a firm to hold an asset if it is not going to produce income.

2. Financing the assets (the right-hand side)

   For every dollar in assets the firm has, there will either be a dollar of liability or a dollar of equity on the right-hand side of the balance sheet. The right-hand side of the balance sheet shows how the firm is financing its assets. By adjusting the mix of debt and equity, the lowest cost of financing can be achieved.

In summary, the left-hand side of the balance sheet reports the assets that earn income and the right-hand side reports how these assets are financed.

Income Statement

Unlike the balance sheet, which tells us the state of the firm *at one point in time*, the **income statement** tells us how the firm has performed *over a period of time*.

Income statements usually have two sections. The first section reports the results of operating activities or operating income. This includes sales minus operating expenses. Financing activities are reported in the second section, where interest expense, taxes, and preferred dividends are subtracted to arrive at net income. Table 2.2 provides a sample income statement and "Explain It: Income Statement" discusses its content.

income statement

Provides a financial summary of the firm's operating results during a specified period.

Explain It: Income Statement

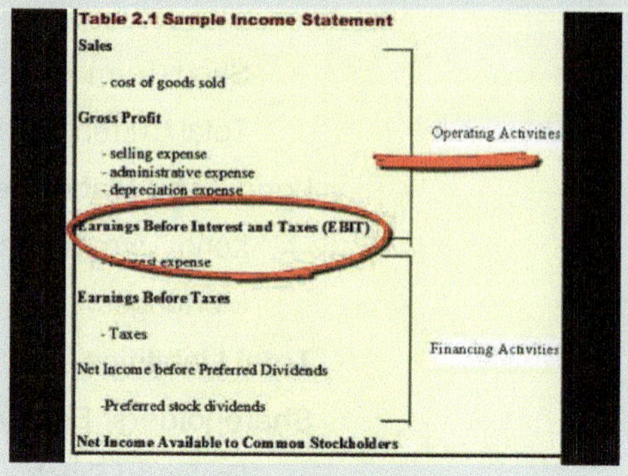

View in the online reader

TABLE 2.2 Sample Income Statement

Sales	
—Cost of Goods Sold	
Gross Profit	
—Selling Expense	Operating Activities
—Administrative Expense	
—Depreciation Expense	
Earnings Before Interest and Taxes (EBIT)	
—Interest Expense	
Earnings Before Taxes	
—Taxes	Financing Activities
Net Income Before Preferred Dividends	
—Preferred Stock Dividends	
Net Income Available to Common Stockholders	

Statement of Cash Flows

statement of cash flows

Provides a summary of the firm's operating, investment, and financing cash flows and reconciles them with changes in its cash and marketable securities during the period of concern.

Many students are not as comfortable with the **statement of cash flows** as they are with the income statement and balance sheet. It does, however, provide insight not readily available from the other statements. In finance, we are particularly concerned with cash flows rather than accounting earnings. Table 2.3 shows a sample statement of cash flows and "Explain It: Statement of Cash Flows" discusses its contents.

Explain It: Statement of Cash Flows

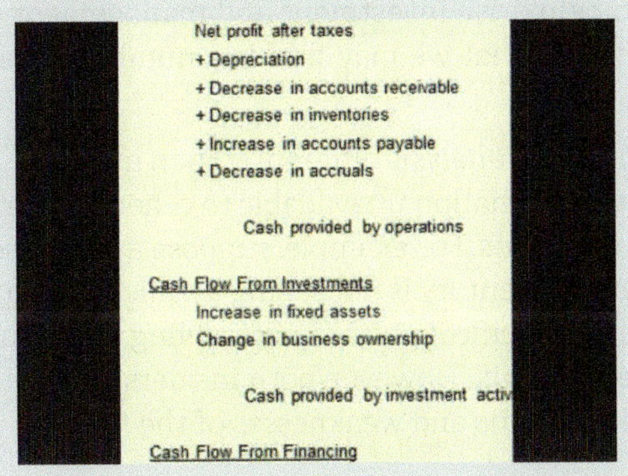

View in the online reader

TABLE 2.3 Sample Statement of Cash Flows

<u>Cash Flow from Operations</u>
Net Profit After Taxes
+ Depreciation
+ Decrease in Accounts Receivable
+ Decrease in Inventories
+ Increase in Accounts Payable
+ Decrease in Accruals
Cash Provided by Operations
<u>Cash Flow from Investments</u>
Increase in Fixed Assets
Change in Business Ownership
Cash Provided by Investment Activities
<u>Cash Flow from Financing</u>
+ Decrease in Notes Payable
+ Increase in Long-Term Debt
+ Changes in Stockholders' Equity
– Dividends Paid
Cash Provided by Financing Activities
Net Increase/Decrease in Cash and Marketable Securities

2.2 The Goals of Financial Analysis

Exactly what can we hope to accomplish by analyzing the financial aspects of a firm? Financial analysis is a powerful tool to help drive investment and management decisions. However, we will not find many absolute answers. What we may find is a number of red flags that help focus our attention.

Outsiders will conduct financial analysis differently than managers, also referred to as *insiders*. Clearly, insiders have access to information unavailable to others in the market. This gives them an advantage when ratios raise questions. For example, suppose a firm discovers it has a falling profit margin. It has also found that its inventory is not selling as quickly as in the past. Insiders can order an analysis to determine which specific items are not moving well. Outsiders may only speculate about the quality of the inventory mix. However, both insiders and outsiders have a common goal of attempting to identify the strengths and weaknesses of the firm.

Identify Company Weaknesses

One goal of financial analysis is to identify problems that affect the firm. By identifying problems early, managers can make corrections to improve firm performance. Some problems may be hard to identify. A firm that seems to be earning profits but is constantly short of cash may turn to financial analysis to identify why this is occurring.

Investors are also interested in identifying companies with problems as early as possible. No one wants to stay on a sinking ship any longer than necessary. Analysts hope they can identify firms with problems before other investors so they can sell their stock before the price drops.

Identify Company Strengths

Another equally important purpose of financial analysis is to identify company strengths so those strengths can be enhanced and used to their greatest potential. For example, in the early 1970s, falling inventory turnover ratios and return on equity ratios told JCPenney that it was not able to compete successfully with high-volume discount stores; however, it was able to sell good-quality clothing. This discovery led to a major refocusing of the firm that involved discontinuing its automotive, appliance, and furniture departments and upscaling its clothing lines. Because of these changes, it succeeded where many of its competitors failed.

2.3 Financial Statement and Ratio Analysis

In this section, we introduce and briefly discuss a number of the more common financial ratios. This is not an exhaustive list by any standard. There are many ratios that can be used. In fact, it is common for analysts to create specialized ratios to look at a factor peculiar to a firm or industry. For example, revenues and costs per mile flown are often computed for airlines.

The formulas presented here for each ratio may differ from those reported elsewhere. An effort has been made within this section to locate the most common definition for each formula, but for some there is simply no consensus among reporting agencies. This means that, when you compare ratios computed by different sources, you must be sure they are all computed in the same way.

Cross-Section Analysis

Most financial ratios mean little when viewed in isolation. For example, an inventory turnover ratio tells us how many times per year the company's inventory is sold (we discuss this ratio later in the chapter). A value of 20 is not interesting until we learn that other firms in the industry have an inventory turnover ratio of 3. Similarly, gross profit margins, liquidity ratios, and activity ratios all vary substantially depending on the industry. Clearly, a grocery store will turn over its inventory more frequently than an auto dealer will.

Cross-sectional analysis is the comparison of one firm to other similar firms. A cross section of an industry is utilized as a comparison for the firm's numbers. There are a variety of sources of cross sectional information. Value Line, Risk Management Association, and Dun & Bradstreet all publish industry average ratio statistics. One way to identify a firm's industry is by its Standard Industrial Classification (SIC) code. SIC codes are four-digit codes given to firms by the government for statistical reporting purposes.

cross-sectional analysis

The analysis of a firm's financial condition by comparing ratios of the firm to ratios of similar firms.

Explain It

The first digit of the four-digit SIC code puts the firm in a broad business type. Each succeeding digit breaks the industry type down into finer units. For example, all financial firms have an SIC code that begins with 6. This includes insurance firms, banks, and real estate firms. SIC codes starting with 60 are reserved for banks, 63 for insurance firms, and so on. Many firms are assigned multiple SIC codes. For example, Disclosure Inc. lists eight SIC codes for Xerox Corp. The first code listed is usually deemed the dominant industry for the firm.

Many firms do not have any clear industry to use for comparison, such as conglomerates that do business in dozens of different industries. There are no good guidelines for picking comparison numbers for these types of firms. In other cases, the firm under study so dominates the industry that the industry ratios are simply mirroring that firm. Consider General Motors (GM). With so few firms in the auto manufacturing business, what happens to GM happens to the industry.

Tip

Many times, firms may be included in an SIC category used for preparing industry ratios that are not appropriate comparisons. For example, SIC 2080 includes Coca-Cola and Pepsi. However, it also includes Molson Coors and Willamette Valley Vineyard Inc.

One solution to the problem of finding good comparison numbers is to create your own list of competitors. Compare the firm under analysis to the averages found from this list. Often, this approach yields far superior comparison numbers than can be found in the published reference materials.

Tip

If you are analyzing a firm, you will often know who the firm's main competitors are. These firms usually make the best comparisons for cross sectional analysis. Popular financial websites like Yahoo and Google provide a list of competitors for each company.

Time-Series Analysis

time-series analysis

Evaluation of the firm's financial performance over time utilizing financial ratio analysis.

Another equally important method of financial analysis is **time-series analysis**, which involves comparing the firm's current performance to prior periods. This method allows the analyst to identify trends, changes over time that are more or less consistent in one direction. Unless the firm has undergone some type of major restructuring, prior period numbers are a near perfect comparison against today's figures.

Both cross-sectional and time-series analysis are important. For this reason, analysts should use both.

Tip

Both cross-sectional analysis and time-series analysis raise red flags that inspire the analyst to investigate specific figures from the financial statements in greater detail. Ratios often raise more questions than they answer.

The Ratios

The ratios are presented in groups to facilitate understanding. We have grouped the ratios into five categories:

- Profitability ratios
- Liquidity ratios
- Activity ratios
- Financing ratios
- Market ratios

Different users put different levels of emphasis on the categories. For example, short-term lenders, like banks, focus on the liquidity ratios because they are concerned with evaluating how easily a company can pay its short-term liabilities. Managers focus on activity ratios as indicators of how well the company is running. Finally, stockholders focus on profitability and market ratios to select companies for their portfolio.

We use financial ratios because firms vary in scale and so we cannot compare the levels of various accounts. The ratios standardize the accounts to facilitate comparison over time and cross-sectionally. For example, if you want to compare the fuel efficiency of a sports utility vehicle (SUV) to a motorcycle, you wouldn't compare how far they each travel on a full tank of fuel. The comparison is unfair because the SUV probably has a larger fuel tank. Instead, we calculate a standardized measure of efficiency: the miles-per-gallon ratio. The ratio divides the number of miles travelled in a given journey by the amount of fuel consumed on the journey as follows:

$$\textit{Miles per gallon} = \frac{\textit{Number of miles traveled}}{\textit{Fuel consumed on the journey}}$$

The ratio is interpreted as the number miles the vehicle can travel for each gallon of gas consumed. The financial ratios are interpreted in exactly the same way: units of the numerator per unit of the denominator.

As you review this section, pay attention to what the ratio is intended to measure and whether it is generally better if the ratio is higher or lower. Also note the unit of measure and what change might improve the ratio.

After presenting the formula for each ratio, we will demonstrate how the formula is calculated using a simple balance sheet and income statement for a fictional company, Risky Ventures, Inc., presented in Table 2.4 and Table 2.5.

Digital Downloads

FS Financial _Statements_for_Risky_Ventures.xlsx
https://catalog.flatworldknowledge.com/a/34711/ FS_Financial__Statements_for_Risky_Ventures-7f8a.xlsx

TABLE 2.4 Sample Income Statement

Income Statement Risky Ventures Inc. Year Ending December 31	
Sales	$30,000,000
Cost of Goods Sold	21,000,000
Gross Profit	9,000,000
Selling Expense	2,500,000
General & Administrative Expense	1,500,000
Depreciation Expense	1,000,000
Operating Profit	4,000,000
Interest Expense	2,000,000
Net Profit Before Tax	2,000,000
Taxes (40%)	800,000
Net Profits After Tax	1,200,000
Preferred Dividends	200,000

TABLE 2.5 Sample Balance Sheet

Balance Sheet Risky Ventures Inc Year Ending December 31 ($000s)			
ASSETS		**LIABILITIES AND EQUITY**	
Current Assets		**Current Liabilities**	
Cash	$1,000	Accounts Payable	$8,000
Marketable Securities	3,000	Notes Payable	8,000
Accounts Receivable	12,000	Accruals	500
Inventories	7,500	Total Current Liabilities	16,500
Total Current Assets	23,500	**Long-Term Liabilities**	
Fixed Assets		Long-Term Debt	20,000
Land and Buildings	11,000	**Total Liabilities**	36,500
Machinery and Equipment	20,000	**Shareholders' Equity**	
Furniture and Fixtures	8,500	Preferred Stock	2,500
Total Gross Assets	39,500	Common Stock	5,000
Accumulated Depreciation	13,000	Paid in Capital	4,000
Net Fixed Assets	26,500	Retained Earnings	2,000
		Total Equity	13,500
Total Assets	$50,000	**Total Liabilities and Equity**	$50,000

Profitability Ratios

We begin our discussion of ratio analysis with the profitability ratios, reported in Table 2.6, because they are ultimately the most important. If a firm is generating acceptable profits, analysts tend to be more forgiving of deviations in other ratios. For example, low inventory turnover may be due to high prices. If this is a corporate strategy that produces high profits, investors are unlikely to complain. On the other hand, if the profits are not there, low inventory turnover will be viewed as a serious shortcoming.

Tip

One point made in this paragraph is so important that it bears repeating. Ratio analysis requires that you look for interactions. One ratio may give a clue that there is a problem, and that clue must be investigated by reviewing other ratios. Ratio analysis is a skill that can only be honed with practice.

Profitability ratios measure how effectively the firm uses its resources to generate income. The return on equity (ROE) and net profit margin are probably the best known and most widely used of all financial ratios. Investors are happier the greater the profitability ratios are.

The profitability ratios express various dollar measures of profit over a base—dividing the profitability measure by a base standardizes the ratio. In each case we interpret the ratio as dollars of profit per dollar of the denominator. The ratios in Table 2.6 have three different measures of profit and three different bases. The measures of profit range from a broad measure (gross profit) to an intermediate measure (operating profit) to a very precise measure (net profit). The bases are owners' equity, total assets, and sales.

Taken together, these profitability ratios give the analyst insight into the performance of the firm. For example, if the return on equity is not acceptable, you can review the various profit margin accounts to determine whether the problem lies with cost of goods sold, operating expenses, or financing cost.

TABLE 2.6 Profitability Ratios

Ratio Name	Equation Number	Equation
Return on Equity (ROE)	Equation 2.1	$\text{Return on equity} = \dfrac{\text{Net income}}{\text{Common stockholders' equity}}$
Return on Assets (ROA)	Equation 2.2	$\text{Return on assets} = \dfrac{\text{Net income}}{\text{Total assets}}$
Gross Profit Margin	Equation 2.3	$\text{Gross profit margin} = \dfrac{\text{Gross profit}}{\text{Sales}}$
Operating Profit Margin	Equation 2.4	$\text{Operating profit margin} = \dfrac{\text{Operating profit}}{\text{Sales}}$
Net Profit Margin	Equation 2.5	$\text{Net profit margin} = \dfrac{\text{Net income}}{\text{Sales}}$

Return on Equity (ROE)

The **return on equity ROE** tells us the amount of profit earned on every dollar of common equity. Many analysts consider ROE to be the most important of all ratios, which is why we present it first. The area of most concern to shareholders is the return they receive on their invested dollar. ROE is a measure of that return. (Note that the numbers used in all of the ratio examples are from the Risky Ventures financial statements shown above.)

return on equity ROE
Tells what the firm earns on every dollar of equity. Note that this return is based on the book value of equity, not current market value. Many analysts consider ROE the most important of all ratios. The area of most concern to shareholders is the return they receive on their invested dollar.

EQUATION 2.1

$$\text{Return on equity} = \frac{\text{Net income}}{\text{Common stockholder equity}}$$

$$\text{Return on equity} = \frac{\$1.2}{\$11.0} = 0.1091$$

Note that this return is based on the book value of equity. Because the market value of the stock may have changed substantially since it was booked, this is called an accounting rate of return rather than a market rate of return. The market return will usually be different than the accounting return, but the two should be highly correlated over time. To compute the common equity we subtracted the \$2.5 million in preferred from the \$13.5M in total equity. Some sources may use total equity in the denominator instead of common stock stockholder equity.

Return on Assets (ROA)

return on assets (ROA)

A measure of profit per dollar of assets, sometimes called a firm's return on investment. It measures the overall effectiveness of management in producing profits with available assets. It is computed as Net income/Total assets.

The **return on assets (ROA)** is a measure of profit per dollar of assets held in the firm:

EQUATION 2.2

$$\text{Return on assets} = \frac{\text{Net income}}{\text{Total assets}}$$

$$\text{Return on assets} = \frac{\$1.2}{\$50} = 0.02$$

This is sometimes also called the firm's return on investment. It measures the overall effectiveness of management in producing profits with available assets. For firms financed solely with equity, Total assets = Total equity, so ROA would equal ROE. However, because most companies have some debt, total assets for most firms exceed total equity and so the ROA is lower than ROE.

Gross Profit Margin

gross profit margin

The gross profit (before operating expenses, interest, taxes, and preferred dividends) earned on each dollar of sales.

The **gross profit margin** is the gross profit (sales minus cost of goods sold) earned on each dollar of sales:

EQUATION 2.3

$$\text{Gross profit margin} = \frac{\text{Gross profit}}{\text{Sales}}$$

$$\text{Gross profit margin} = \frac{\$9}{\$30} = 0.3$$

If we think of cost of goods sold as the marginal cost of making the firm's output, then we can think of the gross profit margin as the difference between price and marginal cost. Gross profit margins vary widely by industry depending on the industry structure. For example, grocery stores, which are in a very competitive industry, typically make very little on each sale so their gross profit margins are low, typically less than 4%. They make their profit by selling a high volume of low margin products. On the other hand, luxury car manufacturers have some price-setting power and so tend to have high gross profit margins but low volume.

Operating Profit Margin

operating profit margin

Goes one step further than the gross profit margin by subtracting operating expenses as well as the cost of goods sold from sales. The operating profit margin ignores any financial or tax charges and measures only the profits earned on operations.

The **operating profit margin** goes one step further than the gross profit margin by subtracting operating expenses as well as the cost of goods sold from sales, while holding the base (sales) constant. (Operating profits are also called "earnings before interest and taxes" or EBIT.)

EQUATION 2.4

$$\text{Operating profit margin} = \frac{\text{Operating profit}}{\text{Sales}}$$

$$\text{Operating profit margin} = \frac{\$4}{\$30} = 0.13$$

The operating profit margin ignores any financial or tax charges and measures only the profits earned on operations.

Net Profit Margin

The **net profit margin** is the profit that remains after all costs have been deducted, including taxes and preferred dividends, expressed per dollar of sales. The net profit margin is important since it tells us exactly how much income owners could take out of the company, while still meeting its obligations.

net profit margin

The percentage of each sales dollar that remains after all costs have been deducted, including taxes and preferred dividends. It is computed as Net income/Sales.

EQUATION 2.5

$$\text{Net profit margin} = \frac{\text{Net income}}{\text{Sales}}$$

$$\text{Net profit margin} = \frac{\$1.2}{\$30} = 0.04$$

Note that there are several different profit margins. Some reporting services are careless about disclosing which profit margin they are reporting. Generally, if a ratio is called the profit margin, the reference is usually to the net profit margin.

Taken together, these profitability ratios give the analyst insight into the performance of the firm. If the return on equity is not acceptable, the various profit margin ratios can be reviewed to determine whether the problem lies with cost of goods sold, operating expenses, or financing cost.

Explain It: Profitability Ratios

View in the online reader

Liquidity Ratios

A liquid firm is one that can meet its various short-term debt and credit obligations. Those who extend credit to a firm are particularly concerned with the firm's liquidity. It is not unusual for a firm to be making profits, but not have sufficient cash on hand to pay its creditors. The following liquidity ratios will help identify problems of this nature.

TABLE 2.7 Liquidity Ratios

Ratio Name	Equation Number	Equation
Current ratio	Equation 2.6	$\text{Current ratio} = \dfrac{\text{Current assets}}{\text{Current liabilities}}$
Quick ratio	Equation 2.7	$\text{Quick ratio} = \dfrac{\text{Current assets} - \text{Inventory}}{\text{Current liabilities}}$

The Current Ratio

current ratio

One measure of the firm's ability to meet its short-term obligations. In theory, current assets are converted into assets in 1 year, so they should be available to pay current liabilities. A current ratio of 1 would mean a firm has sufficient current assets to meet its current liabilities.

The **current ratio** is a widely reported ratio of particular interest to creditors. It is one measure of the firm's ability to meet its short-term obligations:

EQUATION 2.6

$$\text{Current ratio} = \frac{\text{Current assets}}{\text{Current liabilities}}$$

$$\text{Current ratio} = \frac{\$23.5}{\$16.5} = 1.42$$

In theory, current assets will be converted into cash within 1 year. The idea behind the current ratio is: if the firm converts its current assets to cash, then what proportion of current liabilities could be repaid? Of course, the exact timing of when assets are converted and when liabilities are due is not reflected by this ratio. A current ratio of 1 would mean that a firm has sufficient current assets to meet its current liabilities. Most firms prefer to have a safety margin to provide a cushion in case there are cash flow timing problems, unforeseen problems, or new opportunities.

The Quick Ratio

quick ratio

Similar to the current ratio, except that inventory is subtracted from current assets. Since inventory may not always be easily converted into cash, the quick ratio is a more conservative measure of liquidity than is the current ratio.

The **quick ratio** (or acid test) is very similar to the current ratio except that inventory is subtracted from current assets:

EQUATION 2.7

$$\text{Quick ratio} = \frac{\text{Current assets} - \text{Inventory}}{\text{Current liabilities}}$$

$$\text{Quick ratio} = \frac{\$23.5 - \$7.5}{\$16.5} = 0.97$$

Because inventory may not always be easily converted into cash (or may lose a lot of value when liquidated), the quick ratio is a more conservative measure of liquidity than is the current ratio.

There is a great deal of disagreement among analysts as to how liquid a firm should be. It is not necessarily bad for a firm to have low current and quick ratios if the firm can meet its obligations. Consider which firm you would rather own: one that could make $100 of sales with only $5 of inventory and $1 of cash or one that required $50 of inventory and $10 of cash to make that same $100 of sales. Many efficiently run companies get by with fewer current assets than poorly run firms.

Keep in mind that firms put a great deal of effort into strategies for minimizing inventory, such as just-in-time delivery. The more successful a firm is at this, the lower its current ratio. Don't penalize a firm by criticizing its liquidity when, in fact, it's well run.

Tip

Most students think that high current and quick ratios are good things, and they typically are for lenders, but consider that the field of inventory management, including just-in-time methods, is designed to reduce the need for current assets.

Explain It: Liquidity Ratios

View in the online reader

Activity Ratios

Activity ratios (also known as efficiency or asset management ratios) measure the efficiency with which assets are converted to sales. Generally, greater activity is good. Activity ratios go hand in hand with the liquidity ratios. For example, if inventory is not turning over, current assets are not being converted to cash and the firm will have trouble paying its bills. If problems are suggested by the liquidity ratios, the analyst can review the activity ratios to see whether they provide clues to the problem.

activity ratios

Used to measure the speed with which various assets are converted to sales or cash.

TABLE 2.8 Activity Ratios

Ratio Name	Equation Number	Equation
Inventory Turnover	Equation 2.8	$\text{Inventory turnover} = \dfrac{\text{Cost of goods sold}}{\text{Inventory}}$
Accounts Receivables Turnover	Equation 2.9	$\text{Accounts receivable turnover} = \dfrac{\text{Sales}}{\text{Accounts receivable}}$
Total Asset Turnover	Equation 2.10	$\text{Total asset turnover} = \dfrac{\text{Sales}}{\text{Total assets}}$
Average Collection Period	Equation 2.11	$\text{Average collection period} = \dfrac{\text{Acounts receivable}}{\text{Daily credit sales}}$

Inventory Turnover

inventory turnover

Measures how many times per year the inventory is completely sold and replaced.

The **inventory turnover** ratio measures how many times per year the inventory is completely sold and replaced:

EQUATION 2.8

$$\text{Inventory turnover} = \frac{\text{Cost of goods sold}}{\text{Inventory}}$$

$$\text{Inventory turnover} = \frac{\$21}{\$7.5} = 2.8$$

Tip

Some forms of this equation call for using average inventory in the denominator instead of end-of-period inventory. This is appropriate if beginning- and end-of-period inventory levels are very different. Average inventory is computed by summing the beginning and ending inventory levels and dividing by 2.

A high inventory turnover ratio is an indicator of efficient management, as long as the company isn't losing sales due to insufficient stock. A low inventory turnover ratio can be an indication of unsellable or obsolete inventory. On the other hand, if a company sells a small quantity of expensive items (i.e., luxury cars) then a low inventory turnover might be perfectly consistent with high profits. As always, a change in one ratio, say falling inventory turnover, must be viewed in context with other ratios, say increased gross profit margins.

Accounts Receivable Turnover

accounts receivable turnover

The accounts receivable turnover ratio is the number of times per year accounts receivable are paid and replaced.

The **accounts receivable turnover** ratio is the number of times per year accounts receivable are paid and replaced:

EQUATION 2.9

$$\text{Accounts receivable turnover} = \frac{\text{Sales}}{\text{Accounts receivable}}$$

$$\text{Accounts receivable turnover} = \frac{\$30}{\$12} = 2.5$$

As with all ratios, the analyst must be careful not to draw incorrect assumptions from changes in ratios. Slower accounts receivable turnover could be caused by collection problems, but it could also be caused by a new credit policy that gives customers more time to pay. If this new credit policy increases sales and net profits, it should not be criticized.

Total Asset Turnover

total asset turnover

An even broader measure of activity is the total asset turnover ratio. It is interpreted as the number of dollars of sales generated per dollar of assets.

An even broader measure of activity is the **total asset turnover** ratio. It is interpreted as the number of dollars of sales generated per dollar of assets.

EQUATION 2.10

$$\text{Total asset turnover} = \frac{\text{Sales}}{\text{Total assets}}$$

$$\text{Total asset turnover} = \frac{\$30}{\$50} = 0.6$$

Average Collection Period

The **average collection period** (also known as the days sales in receivables) is the average amount of time that it takes for the company to collect on its credit sales. Most firms do not publicly report their credit sales separately from their cash sales, so it is common to use total sales instead of credit sales. Internally, a firm that sells on credit pays close attention to how quickly (or slowly) its customers take to pay their invoices. An increasing average collection period may mean there are problems in the collection department or with the firm's customers.

average collection period

The average length of time it takes for the firm to collect on its credit sales. Collection periods = 365/ Receivable turnover or Average collection period = Accounts receivable/ Daily credit sales.

EQUATION 2.11

$$\text{Average collection period} = \frac{\text{Acounts receivable}}{\text{Daily credit sales}}$$

$$\text{Average collection period} = \frac{\$12}{\left(\frac{\$30}{365}\right)} = 146 \text{ days}$$

In the above example, we substituted total sales for daily credit sales. If all sales are not made on credit, this will underestimate the true average collection period.

An alternative method of computing the average collection period is to divide 365 by the account receivables turnover:

$$\text{Average collection period} = \frac{365 \text{ days}}{\text{Accounts receivable turnover}}$$

Explain It: Activity Ratios

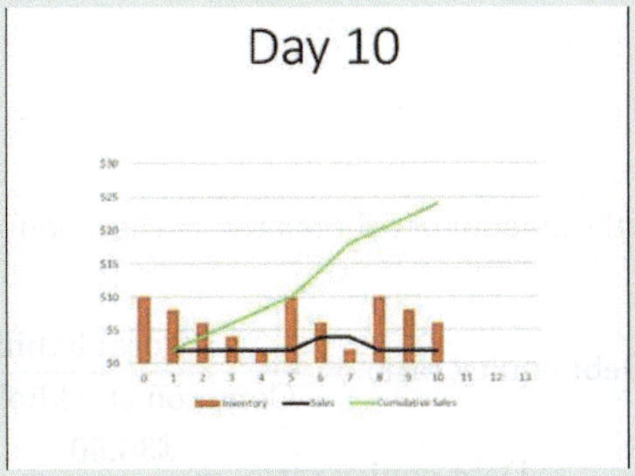

View in the online reader

Financing Ratios

Financing ratios measure how much money a firm has borrowed. In finance, borrowing is also called leverage, so the financing ratios measure how leveraged the firm is. For this reason, they are also called financial leverage ratios or simply leverage ratios. As we shall see when we cover capital structure, firm risk is closely tied to the firm's leverage.

TABLE 2.9 Financing Ratios

Ratio Name	Equation number	Equation
Debt Ratio	Equation 2.12	$\text{Debt ratio} = \dfrac{\text{Total liabilities}}{\text{Total assets}}$
Debt Equity Ratio	Equation 2.13	$\text{Debt equity ratio} = \dfrac{\text{Total liabilities}}{\text{Common stockholder equity}}$
Times Interest Earned Ratio	Equation 2.14	$\text{Times interest earned} = \dfrac{\text{Earnings before interest and taxes (EBIT)}}{\text{Interest}}$

Debt Ratio

debt ratio

A ratio that measures the proportion of assets financed by debt. The greater the debt ratio, the more leveraged and, hence, more risky the firm.

The **debt ratio** measures the proportion of assets financed by debt:

EQUATION 2.12

$$\text{Debt ratio} = \frac{\text{Total liabilities}}{\text{Total assets}}$$

$$\text{Debt ratio} = \frac{\$36.5}{\$50} = 0.73$$

We can interpret the debt ratio for Risky Ventures as saying that 73% of total assets are financed in some way through debt. The greater the debt ratio, the more leveraged, and hence, riskier is the firm. Note that the definition of debt here is liberal: all liabilities are considered debt. It is more common to reserve the term "debt" for money that is borrowed from a lender who expects interest.

Debt Equity Ratio

debt equity ratio

A ratio that shows the relationship between the suppliers of long-term debt and equity.

The **debt equity ratio** shows the amount of debt relative to the amount of equity:

EQUATION 2.13

$$\text{Debt equity ratio} = \frac{\text{Total liabilities}}{\text{Common stockholder equity}}$$

$$\text{Debt equity ratio} = \frac{\$36.50}{\$11} = 3.32$$

It is another measure of leverage that is used in conjunction with the debt ratio.

Times Interest Earned Ratio

The **times interest earned ratio**, often called the TIE ratio, measures the firm's ability to meet its interest payments:

times interest earned ratio

Often called the TIE ratio, measures the firm's ability to meet its interest payments. It does not actually measure leverage, rather it indicates the firm's ability to service the debt it already has incurred.

EQUATION 2.14

$$\text{Times interest earned} = \frac{\text{Earnings before interest and taxes (EBIT)}}{\text{Interest}}$$

$$\text{Times interest earned} = \frac{\$4}{\$2} = 2$$

For Risky Ventures, EBIT is twice as large as interest, so the company has more than enough money to pay its interest obligations. The TIE ratio does not actually measure leverage; rather, it indicates the firm's ability to service the debt it has already incurred. In finance, we use the term solvency to refer to a firm's ability to pay its debts and the interest on that debt. The TIE ratio measures one dimension of solvency: the ability to pay interest. The TIE ratio is primarily of interest to the firm's creditors, who want to be sure the firm can make its interest payments. Creditors like high TIE ratios and will be concerned about decreasing trends.

Explain It: Financing Ratios

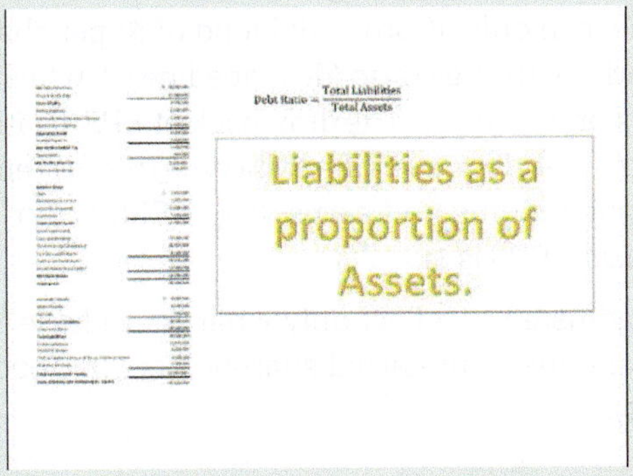

View in the online reader

Market Ratios

The market ratios are distinct from the other ratios in that they are based, at least in part, on information not contained in the firm's financial statements. The term "market" is used as a reference to the financial markets where security prices are established. Market ratios are closely watched by those considering security purchases.

TABLE 2.10 Market Ratios

Ratio Name	Equation Number	Equation
Earnings per Share (EPS)	Equation 2.15	$\text{EPS} = \frac{\text{Net income available to common shareholders}}{\text{Number of shares outstanding}}$
Price Earnings (P/E)	Equation 2.16	$\text{P/E} = \frac{\text{Market price of common stock}}{\text{Earning per share of stock}}$
Market to Book	Equation 2.17	$\text{Market to book} = \frac{\text{Market price of common stock}}{\text{Book value per share}}$

Earnings per Share (EPS)

earnings per share

Net income (less preferred share dividends) divided by the number of common shares outstanding.

The **earnings per share** ratio reports the net income per share of stock:

EQUATION 2.15

$$EPS = \frac{\text{Net income available to common shareholders}}{\text{Number of shares outstanding}}$$

$$EPS = \frac{\$1.2 - \$0.2}{1} = \$1$$

The EPS ratio is used by investors to predict a company's dividends per share, since dividends are paid out of net income. For example, Frisky Dentures Inc., a competitor to Risky Ventures, has EPS of $10. If both companies paid out all earnings as dividends, then Frisky could afford a dividend of $10 per share whereas Risky can only afford a dividend of $1 per share. The most important use of EPS is as an input to the price-earnings ratio (described next), which is used to gauge whether a company's stock price is cheap or expensive. The drawback of EPS, by itself, is that it will change if a company changes its shares outstanding, even if net income (profit) remains unchanged. For example, if a firm has 100 shares outstanding and earns $1,000, EPS is $10. If the firm has 1,000 shares outstanding and still earns $1,000, EPS is $1.

Note that net income is adjusted to reflect only what is available to shareholders by subtracting dividend payments that are due to preferred shareholders (100,000 preferred shares with a $2 per share dividend = $200,000).

Price/Earnings Ratio

price/earnings (P/E) ratio

The amount investors are willing to pay for $1 of income by the firm.

The **price/earnings (P/E) ratio** shows the relationship between the market price of its stock and the earnings per share. It is one of the most popular ratios and is widely reported and tracked.

EQUATION 2.16

$$P/E = \frac{\text{Market price of common stock}}{\text{Earning per share of stock}}$$

$$P/E = \frac{\$20}{\$1} = 20$$

The P/E ratio calculation requires that the analyst know the current market price of the firm's stock. At the time of writing, Risky Ventures was trading for $20.

The press uses various terminology when referring to a firm's P/E ratio. It may say the stock is selling for 20 times earnings or that the stock has a multiple of 20.

Another interpretation of the P/E is that it shows how much investors are willing to pay for each dollar of earnings. A firm with a P/E of 20 means investors are paying $20 for each dollar of earnings. Another way to interpret the P/E ratio is as the number of years it will take an investor to earn back their investment. If a company has earnings per share of $1 (and pays that out as a dividend) and if an investor pays $20 for a share, then it will take 20 years for the investor to earn back the money they paid for the share, if earnings remain constant.

If companies have different P/E ratios, then why would investors pay more per dollar of earnings for one stock than for another? Consider that when Facebook went public, its stock sold at 85 times earnings (P/E = 85), but, at the same time, Google Inc. (now Alphabet Inc.) had a P/E of about 19. One reason investors pay a premium for a stock is that they may think future earnings will be higher. Another reason is that investors may think the firm is less risky than another, so each dollar of earnings is more valuable.

Of course, as earnings fall, the P/E may rise and become very large. Most reporting services don't report the P/E when earnings are very small or negative.

Market-to-Book Ratio

The **market-to-book ratio** is the market price per share divided by the book value per share.

market-to-book ratio

Measures how the market values the firm. If the ratio is great than 1, the market is valuing the firm at a premium over the acquisition price of its assets.

EQUATION 2.17

$$\text{Market to book} = \frac{\text{Market price of common stock}}{\text{Book value per share}}$$

$$\text{Market to book ratio} = \frac{\$20}{\$13.5/1} = 1.48$$

The market value per share is simply the firm's stock price. The book value per share is computed by dividing total equity (not just common equity) by the number of shares outstanding. The book value per share is the liquidation value of a share. That is, it is approximately equal to the money a shareholder would receive if the company sold all of its assets at their book (depreciated) value and then repaid all of its liabilities.

The market-to-book ratio is another way of measuring how the market values the firm. If the ratio is less than one, it means the stock is very cheap: you can buy a share for less money than the liquidation value of the share. That situation is rare. It is more common for the market-to-book ratio to be above one.

Explain It: Market Ratios

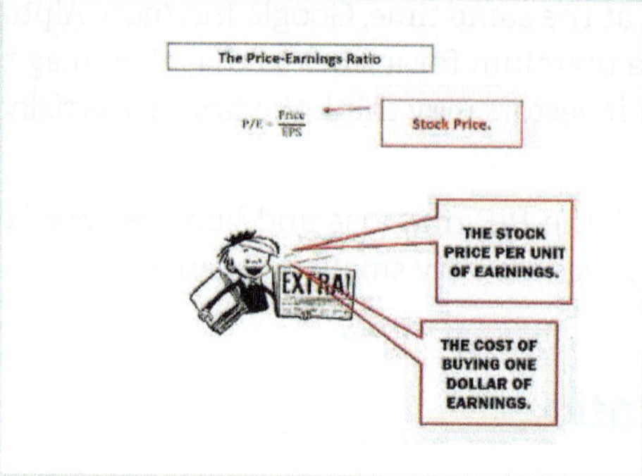

View in the online reader

2.4 Common-Sized Financial Statements

common-sized financial statements

Financial statements that have every line converted into a ratio by dividing income statement data by total sales and balance sheet data by total assets.

Financial statements themselves cannot be compared across an industry or across time because of scale differences. One way to standardize financial statements is to divide each line item by a constant. This standardized format is referred to as **common-sized financial statements**. In effect, this converts every entry into a ratio. Now, you can use them to make comparisons. Some of the ratios previously discussed are generated in this process, such as the debt ratio.

Explain It: Common-Sized Financial Statements

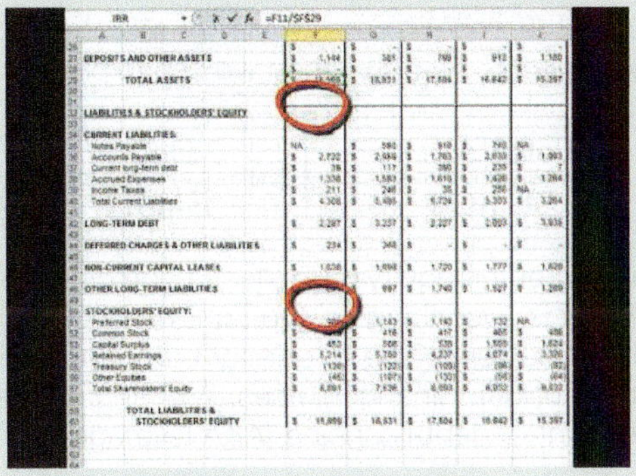

View in the online reader

To prepare a common-sized balance sheet, divide all balance sheet line items by total assets. Similarly, a common-sized income statement is prepared by dividing each line item by sales. Thus, common-sized statements are just a specialized type of ratio analysis in which the denominator of every ratio is either total assets or total sales.

2.5 DuPont Ratio Analysis

DuPont ratio analysis provides an effective method for identifying firm problems and for using ratios. This method of analysis was developed at the DuPont Corporation and is now frequently used by analysts.

DuPont ratio analysis

A method of financial analysis that provides a framework for dissecting a firm's financial statements and assessing its financial condition.

The DuPont system analyzes ratios from the point of view of the firm's shareholders. The focus of the DuPont system is on explaining differences in the ROE—differences across time or differences between the firm and a competitor. The DuPont system allows an analyst to explain why a firm's ROE changes in a particular way—to pinpoint the causal determinants.

The DuPont system begins by multiplying ROE by one, where one is judiciously defined as Total Assets divided by Total Assets (X/X = 1).

$$\text{ROE} = \frac{\text{Net Income}}{\text{Equity}} = \frac{\text{Net Income}}{\text{Equity}} \times \frac{\text{Total Assets}}{\text{Total Assets}}$$

We can rearrange the two ratios on the right-hand side to yield the following:

$$\text{ROE} = \frac{\text{Net Income}}{\text{Total Assets}} \times \frac{\text{Total Assets}}{\text{Equity}}$$

The first of these two ratios is just ROA and the second we call the equity multiplier.

EQUATION 2.18

$$\text{ROE} = \text{ROA} \times \text{Equity multiplier}$$

If ROE rises from one period to another, then the reason is either:

1. that the ROA is higher; or
2. that the amount of debt financing is higher.

Tip

If we define $\textbf{Debt} = \textbf{(Total Assets} - \textbf{Equity)}$ then we can express the equity multiplier as:

$$\frac{\textbf{Total Assets}}{\textbf{Equity}} = \left[1 + \frac{\textbf{Debt}}{\textbf{Equity}}\right]$$

This manipulation helps us interpret the equity multiplier as one plus the debt-to-equity ratio. Here debt is total liabilities and equity is everything on the right hand of the balance sheet that isn't a liability. The equity multiplier will be very close to one for companies with no debt (Debt = 0) and rises above one as the amount of debt financing rises. A change in the equity multiplier is interpreted as a change in the amount of debt financing (AKA leverage).

The DuPont system further breaks down this identity by multiplying ROA by 1, where 1 is judiciously defined as sales divided by sales:

EQUATION 2.19

$$\textbf{ROA} = \frac{\textbf{Net Income}}{\textbf{Total Assets}} = \frac{\textbf{Net Income}}{\textbf{Total Assets}} \times \frac{\textbf{Sales}}{\textbf{Sales}}$$
$$\textbf{ROA} = \frac{\textbf{Net Income}}{\textbf{Sales}} \times \frac{\textbf{Sales}}{\textbf{Total Assets}}$$

The first ratio on the right hand side of the equality is profit margin and the second is total asset turnover, thus ROA is the product of the profit margin and total asset turnover. The equality tells us that overall firm profitability derives from the ability to price above costs and the ability to use assets efficiently. Profitable firms either have some price-setting power or are very efficient in their use of assets.

If we substitute Equation 2.19 into Equation 2.18 we get the following:

EQUATION 2.20

$$\textbf{ROE} = \textbf{Net profit margin} \times \textbf{Total asset turnover} \times \textbf{Equity multiplier}$$

The final equation tells us that changes in ROE are due to changes in profitability, efficiency or leverage (as measured by the equity multiplier). If a change in ROE is due to changes in profitability or efficiency, then those dimensions can be further investigated with other ratios. So, a DuPont analysis isn't the end, it is the beginning and helps us decide where to dig deeper. You will get a better sense of this in the next section where we provide an example of a DuPont analysis for a company called Beamscope.

DuPont Analysis of Beamscope Inc.

Beamscope was a distributor of electronic products to over 7,000 retailers in the 1990s. It focused on consumer software and hardware, video entertainment, and digital technology. In March of 2001, Beamscope declared bankruptcy. Let's see if we can determine why by conducting a ratio analysis starting with a DuPont analysis.

Digital Downloads

FS Financial Statements for Beamscope.xls
https://catalog.flatworldknowledge.com/a/34711/ FS_Financial_Statements_for_Beamscope-5793.xls

TABLE 2.11 DuPont Ratios for Beamscope Inc.

	Beamscope Inc.		Industry Average	
	1999	**1998**	**1999**	**1998**
ROE	–29%	10%	5%	18%
TA/Equity	3.41	2.35	3.41	3.15
ROA	–8%	4%	1%	6%
Sales/Total Assets	2.5	2.4	2.8	3.2
Net Profit Margin	–3.4%	1.7%	0.5%	1.8%

Beamscope's ROE fell dramatically in 1999 to –29% from 10% in 1998. The fall in ROE is mirrored by a decrease in ROA, and net profit margin. The industry average profitability also fell in 1999 to 5%—well above Beamscope's performance. Some of Beamscope's poor performance can be attributed to industry-wide conditions, but clearly Beamscope underperformed the industry average and so there were also firm-specific factors at play.

Beamscope's leverage (as seen from its equity multiplier) actually increased in 1999, so the decrease in ROE is due to a decline in ROA from 4% to –8%. In turn, the decline in ROA can be explained by a decrease in the net profit margin. Asset efficiency—that is, sales per dollar of assets—stayed constant over the period. Net profit margin fell from 1.7% to –3.4%. The major source for the decline in ROE at Beamscope was a decline in its profit margin. However, in the next section we will examine the change in leverage, since the rising leverage offset the declining ROA and led to a smaller decline in ROE than would otherwise have occurred. In subsequent sections we will examine liquidity and activity ratios.

Leverage Changes at Beamscope Inc.

Table 2.12 shows that Beamscope's leverage (Debt Ratio) increased considerably in 1999 over 1998—from 57% to 71%. 1998, Beamscope's leverage was lower than the industry average; however it rose above average in 1999. The big change in leverage was short-term borrowing, which rose dramatically in 1999. Beamscope's interest coverage was above industry average in 1998 and fell well below in 1999. Clearly, Beamscope borrowed a great deal of money in 1999.

TABLE 2.12 Financial Ratios for Beamscope Inc.

	Beamscope Inc.		Industry Average	
	1999	**1998**	**1999**	**1998**
Total Debt Ratio	71%	57%	71%	68%
Short-Term Debt/Total Assets	31%	8%	14%	15%
Times Interest Earned	–5.24	8.50	4.80	4.70

Activity and Liquidity Rations at Beamscope Inc.

Table 2.13 shows selected activity and liquidity ratios. Although total asset turnover did not decline much from 1998 to 1999, this masks some significant changes. According to its quarterly update and its annual report, Beamscope wrote off large amounts of inventory and accounts receivable in 1999, thus improving the end-of-year figures. A closer inspection is therefore warranted.

TABLE 2.13 Activity and Liquidity Ratios for Beamscope Inc.

	Beamscope Inc.		Industry Average	
	1999	**1998**	**1999**	**1998**
Total Asset Turnover	2.5	2.4	2.8	3.2
Inventory Turnover	5.7	6.9	9.6	10.5
Average Collection Period	54.2	80.2	61.7	52.4
Current Ratio	1.4	1.7	1.4	1.4

Beamscope's current ratio fell in 1999 due to a decrease in current assets and an increase in current liabilities. The decline in current assets was largely due to the write-off of accounts receivable (more on this below) while the increase in current liabilities was due to increased short-term borrowing.

The average collection period falls in 1999 to 54 days from 80 days in 1998, which appears to be a huge improvement over time and relative to the industry average. The appearance of improvement is misleading, as we shall see below. Inventory turnover declined in 1998 well below the industry average indicating a rapidly expanding amount of inventory.

Beamscope's Quarterly Report for Q3 in 1999 explains the problem, which links all of the results discussed above. In 1999, Beamscope experienced a significant increase in unit volumes, which taxed the company's accounts receivable and inventory management processes. Beamscope lost control of its inventory, accounts receivable, and payables. It didn't know what it had, what it owed, or who owed it money! At year-end, it wrote off $16.0 million in respect of accounts receivable, recorded as a reduction of sales, and $19.8 million in respect of inventories and amounts charged to suppliers, recorded as an increase in cost of sales.

From this analysis you can see that the DuPont analysis, by itself, isn't sufficient to tell the whole story. It is a starting point that helps the analyst know where to dig deeper.

2.6 Putting the Ratios to Work

Now that we have a number of tools to use for analyzing firms, we need to decide how to proceed. The task can seem overwhelming until we decide on an organized approach.

The financial analysis of a firm should include the following steps:

1. Analyze the economy in which the firm operates.
2. Analyze the industry in which the firm operates.
3. Analyze the competitors that currently challenge the firm.
4. Analyze the strengths and weaknesses of the firm, using common-sized statements, ratios, and the DuPont analysis.

There are two primary methods to ascertain the strengths and weaknesses of a firm. The first and preferred approach uses the DuPont ratio analysis, which leads you through the ratios as described in the previous section. The second is to summarize the ratios by type. For example, summarize the profitability ratios, then the liquidity ratios, and so on. The problem with this approach is that it can hide causality in the sheer volume of ratios computed and does not help identify ratio interactions.

1. **Ratio Interaction** Ratio interaction refers to the effect one ratio has on another. For example, if sales fall, inventory turnover will also fall if inventory is held constant. The goal of ratio analysis is to locate the most fundamental cause of a firm's problem. We do not want to recommend that a firm adjust its inventory if the real problem is that its cost of goods sold is higher than that of its competitors. Because no two firms are likely to have the exact same problem, no two approaches to financial analysis are the same. The analyst must take on the role of a detective for whom ratios provide clues that must be tracked down and explained.
2. **Reading Between the Lines** Often, ratios simply will not tell the whole story. The analyst can only hope that the ratios will provide flags that prompt investigation and lead to the truth about the firm. For example, a banker will review the statements of a credit applicant, looking for items that stand out as unusual. These unusual items generate questions that can be posed to the borrower. The borrower's responses to these questions may lay the issue to rest or may generate new, more probing questions.

It is important to recognize that ratio analysis is not useful for all firms. Conglomerates are especially difficult to analyze because widely different divisions may be combined on the financial statements. Insiders to the firm usually have departmental or divisional statements to use for management purposes, but outsiders may not have sufficient details to draw meaningful conclusions.

CHAPTER 3

Introduction to the Time Value of Money

Learning Objectives

By the end of this chapter you will be able to:

1. Calculate simple interest and be able to to draw a timeline.
2. Calculate the future value of a sum.
3. Calculate and understand the effective interest rate.
4. Solve for the interest rate and number of time periods.
5. Calculate the present value of a sum.

In this chapter, you learn to compute how the value of money changes over time. In addition to corporate finance, this knowledge can come in handy for decision making on personal finance issues such as calculating car payments, mortgage payments, and retirement planning. In fact, understanding the Time Value of Money is one of the most important concepts you will learn in this book.

3.1 Interest and Timelines

Simple Interest

How do you calculate the future value of a sum—*one period*—in the future?

Suppose money is deposited in a bank account for 1 year. At the end of the year interest is computed and paid. The future value is simply the amount of money in the account at the end of the year.

Example 3.1 Simple Interest and One-Period Future Value

Compute simple interest earned on a 1-year \$100 deposit that earns 5% per year and compute the future value of the \$100 deposit.

SOLUTION:

Algebraic Solution

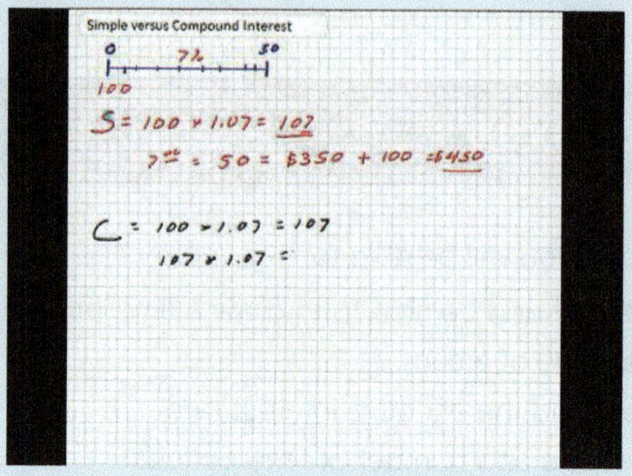

View in the online reader

The interest is computed as the deposit multiplied by the interest rate:

$$\text{Interest} = \text{principal} \times \text{interest rate}$$
$$\text{Interest} = \$100 \times 0.05 = \$5$$

The future value at the end of the year is the sum of the original deposit and the interest:

$$\text{Future value} = \$100 + \$5 = \$105$$

In the example, the \$5 of interest is simple because it is interest earned on the original principal. You can use the following formula to determine future value:

EQUATION 3.1

$$\text{FV} = \text{PV} + (\text{PV} \times \text{i}) = \text{PV} \times (1 + \text{i})$$

Synonyms and Notation

The original deposit is also called the principal or the **present value** and denoted *PV*. The interest rate, denoted *i*, is 5%. This rate is called the **quoted rate**, the **nominal rate**, or the **annual percentage rate (APR)**. Unless otherwise stated, you should assume that the interest rate is annual. The **future value** is denoted *FV*.

present value

The current dollar value of a future amount. The amount of money that would have to be invested today at a given interest rate over a specified period to equal the future amount.

quoted rate

The simple interest rate for a whole year, as opposed to the periodic rate, which is the rate for an individual compounding period. The quoted rate is equal to the periodic rate multiplied by the number of compounding periods in the year. A synonym for the nominal rate or APR.

nominal rate

The simple interest rate for a whole year, as opposed to the periodic rate, which is the rate for an individual compounding period. The nominal rate is equal to the periodic rate multiplied by the number of compounding periods in the year. A synonym for the quoted rate or APR.

annual percentage rate (APR)

The simple interest rate for a whole year, as opposed to the periodic rate, which is the rate for an individual compounding period. The APR is equal to the periodic rate multiplied by the number of compounding periods in the year. A synonym for the quoted rate or nominal rate.

future value

The value of a present amount at a future date, found by applying the compound interest rate over a specified period of time.

Simple versus Compound Interest

simple interest

Interest earned on the original principal only.

compound interest

Interest earned on the sum of the original principal plus reinvested interest from earlier periods.

When there is only one period the interest earned is called **simple interest** because no interest is earned on previously paid interest. In the next section, we calculate a *multiperiod* future value that will generate **compound interest**. Simple interest is interest earned on the original principal. Compound interest is interest earned on interest.

The Timeline

timeline

A horizontal line on which time 0 is the leftmost end and future periods are shown as you move from left to right; can be used to depict investment cash flows.

When you work on time value of money problems, a handy tool for organizing the data and visualizing the solution is a **timeline**. A timeline is a graphic representation of cash flows. For example, consider a question that says that you received $100 per year for 5 years. You need to know whether the money arrived at the beginning, the end, or in the middle of each year. A timeline helps clarify the exact timing of the cash flows. To understand the conventions of the timeline, review the following diagram and accompanying video:

FIGURE 3.1

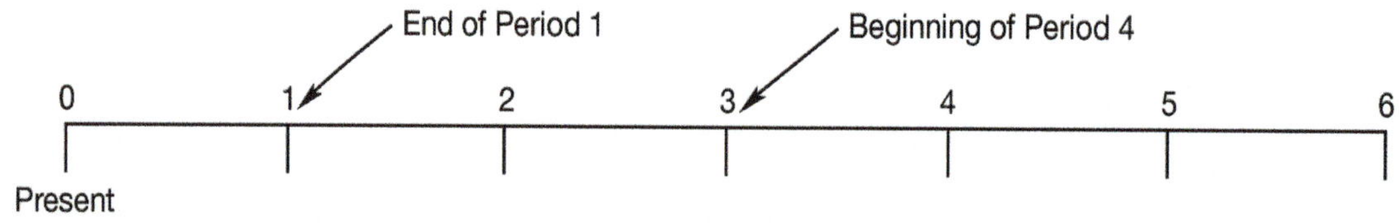

Explain It: The Timeline

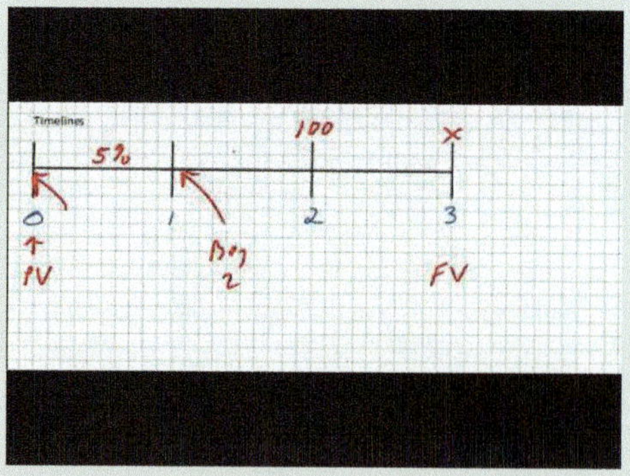

View in the online reader

Inflows and Outflows

Inflows, cash you receive, have a positive sign (typically, the + sign is dropped), as implied in the above examples. A cash outflow, cash you spend, has a negative sign, as shown in the following timeline:

FIGURE 3.2

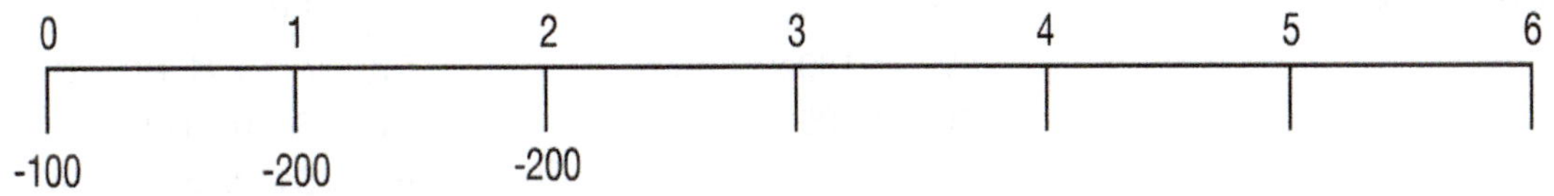

In Figure 3.2, a $100 investment is made at the beginning of the first period and $200 investments are made at the beginning of the second and third periods.

Financial calculators and some built-in spreadsheet functions require that you input cash flows with either a positive or negative sign to indicate inflows and outflows. However, when you solve time value of money problems algebraically, you do not make outflows negative. All cash flows are positive.

3.2 Future Value of a Sum

Compound Interest: Future Value over Multiple Periods

Simple interest is easy to compute, but most of the time, we want our interest payments to be reinvested. For example, if you put money into a savings account, the bank automatically deposits the monthly or quarterly interest payments back into the account. During subsequent periods, interest is earned on a higher balance. If the interest is reinvested, then, in later periods, interest is earned on earlier interest. This is compound interest. Virtually all of the calculations performed in finance assume that interest is compounded. We begin our study of compound interest by finding future balances over multiple periods with **annual compounding**.

annual compounding
Compound interest calculated with a compounding interval of 1 year.

Compound Interest: Future Value over One Year

As we saw in the introduction, if you make a $100 deposit into a bank that pays 5% interest once per year, you'll have $105 at the end of 1 year. The formula for computing the balance after one period is given in Equation 3.1.

EQUATION 3.2

$$FV_1 = PV_0 \times (1 + i)$$
$$FV_1 = \$100 \times (1 + 0.05) = \$105$$

This calculation is shown on the timeline in Figure 3.3. At time period 0, we see a present value of \$100. At time period 1, the future value is $FV_1 = \$105$. Notice the use of the subscripts in the above formula. The subscript denotes the point on the timeline when the cash flow occurs.

FIGURE 3.3

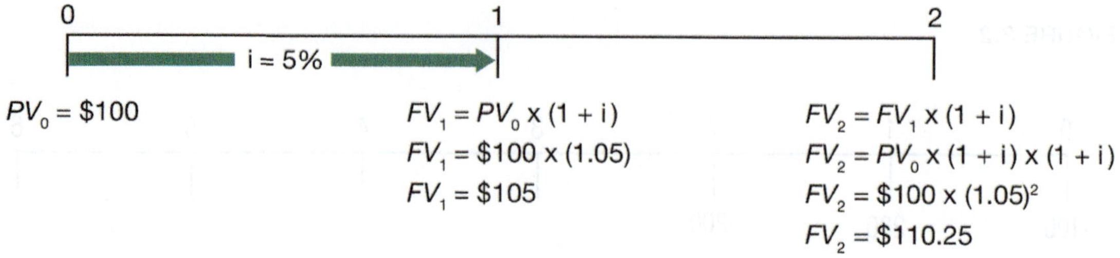

Compound Interest: Future Value over Two Years

Now suppose that you leave the deposit in the bank to compound for another year, without withdrawing any money. Using the above formula, the balance grows to \$110.25:

$$FV_2 = FV_1 \times (1 + i)$$
$$FV_2 = \$105 \times (1 + 0.05) = \$110.25$$

This calculation is shown under period 2 on the timeline in Figure 3.3.

Tip

You should have a calculator or spreadsheet available while reading this chapter. Work each example as each section builds on the previous example's concept.

During the first year, the account earned \$5, but during the second year, it earned \$5.25. The extra \$0.25 is interest earned on the first period's interest $(\$5.00 \times 0.05 = \$0.25)$—it is compound interest. We can simplify these calculations by noting that FV_1 is equal to $PV_0 \times (1 + i)$ and then by substituting $PV_0 \times (1 + i)$ for FV_1 into the equation:

$$FV_2 = PV_0 \times (1 + i)(1 + i)$$
$$FV_2 = PV_0 \times (1 + i)^2$$
$$FV_2 = \$100 \times (1 + 0.05)^2$$
$$FV_2 = \$100 \times 1.1025 = \$110.25$$

Explain It: Compound Interest

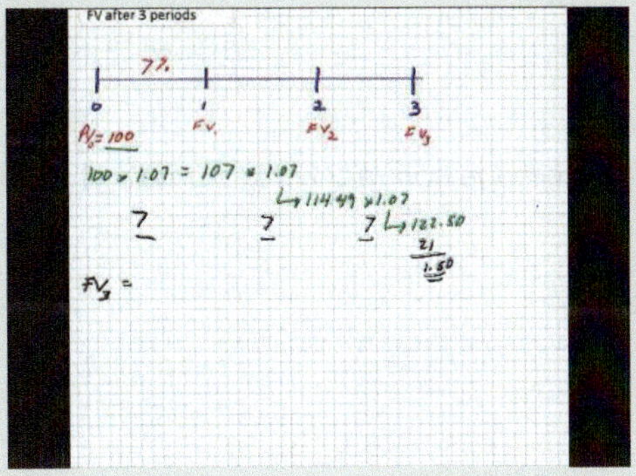

View in the online reader

The process of computing a future balance over multiple periods is called **compounding** because the investor is earning compound interest.

compounding

The process of computing future values where interest is earned on reinvested interest.

Tip

It may seem that this discussion is trivial and easy. We agree, but it is critical that you see exactly how compound interest is earned before we go on to tougher material.

Compound Interest: Future Value over Multiple Years

Similarly, each subsequent period of compounding increases the exponent by one. The generalized equation for finding the future value of a deposit is:

EQUATION 3.3

$$FV_n = PV_0 \times (1+i)^n$$

where

FV_n = the future value of a deposit at the end of the nth

PV_0 = the initial deposit

i = the interest rate earned during each period

n = the number of periods the deposit is allowed to compound

Tip

It's easy to compute y^x on your calculator using the **Y^x** key. For the example given, enter 1.05 and then press the **Yˣ** key. Next, enter the number of periods, 2, and press the = key. You should get 1.1025.

Let's illustrate with an example.

Example 3.2 Future Value over Multiple Years

Suppose your grandmother gave you $1,000 when you graduated from high school. Instead of using it to buy clothes, you decided to invest it and to not touch the balance for 40 years, until you retire. If you managed to earn 10% per year, what is the future value of your investment?

Digital Downloads

Example 3.2.xlsx
https://catalog.flatworldknowledge.com/a/34711/Example_3_2-f1ee.xlsx

SOLUTION:

Spreadsheet Solution

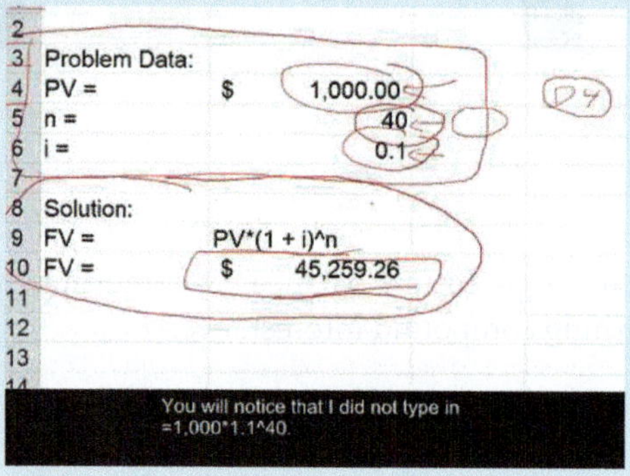

View in the online reader

Algebraic Solution

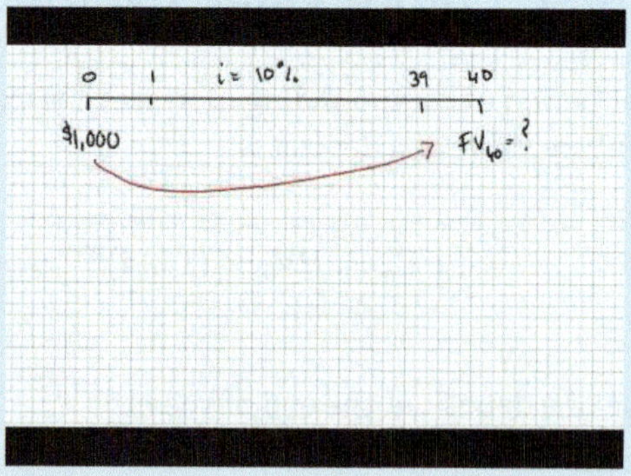

View in the online reader

Calculator Solution

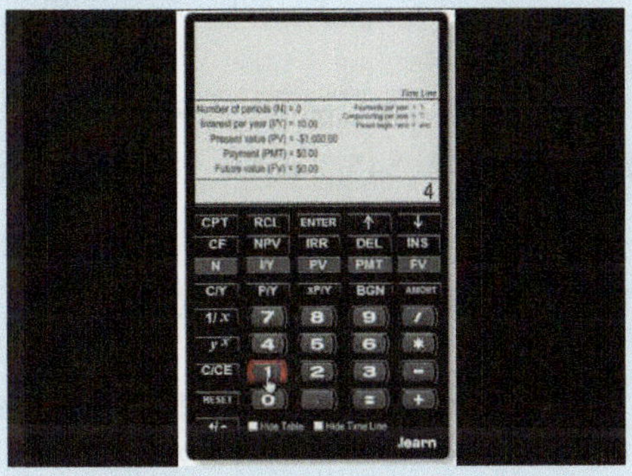

View in the online reader

To work out the future value of $1,000 invested for 40 years at 10%, let's first lay out the data that we have and draw a timeline to describe the problem. You should make a habit of doing this for each time value problem that you attempt.

The timeline for the problem is:

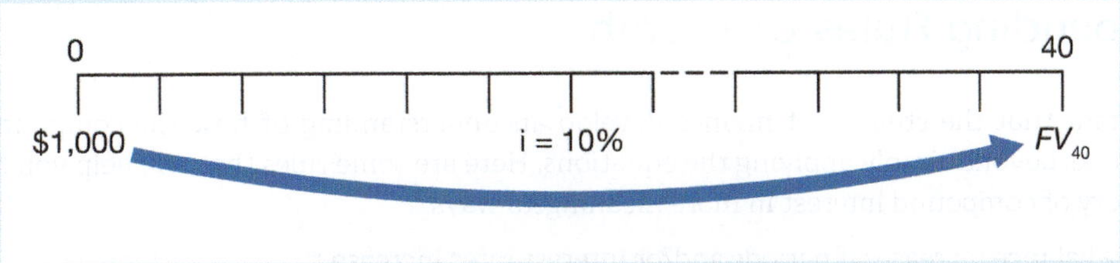

To find the future value of $1,000 over 40 years compounded at 10:

$$FV_n = PV_0 \times (1+i)^n$$

Tip

Rather than write down a number with only a couple of decimal places, use the calculator's memory if you are doing multistep problems. Accuracy is important since we are dealing with money. There is no hard rule of thumb for the number of significant figures. The goal in each problem is to produce an answer that is accurate to pennies.

$$FV_{40} = \$1,000 \times (1.10)^{40}$$
$$FV_{40} = \$1,000 \times 45.25926$$
$$FV_{40} = \$45,259.26$$

Tip

To see more decimal places on the TI calculator, press **2nd FORMAT**, enter the number of digits to the right of the decimal to show, and then press **ENTER**.

Calculating Interest Earned

To find the interest earned, we subtract the principal (the original amount) from the ending balance:

$$\text{Interest earned} = FV - PV$$
$$\text{Interest earned} = \$45,259.26 - \$1,000 = \$44,259.26$$

Simple and Compound Interest Compared

If simple interest, rather than compound interest, had been earned in "Example 3.2 Future Value over Multiple Years", then $100 per year would have been earned Over a period of 40 years, the total simple interest earned would have been 40 times $100 or $4,000. Since the total amount of interest earned was $44,259.26, the difference of $40,259.26 was earned because of compounding. Put another way, $40,259.26 in interest was earned on interest. In this example, more interest was earned on the interest than was earned on the original principal! *This is the magic of compound interest.*

Compounding Rules of Thumb

It's important that the student of finance develop an understanding of how the compounding process works beyond simply applying the equations. Here are some rules that will help you think of the theory of compound interest in more meaningful ways.

compounding period

The interval over which interest is accumulated before being paid. Typical compounding periods are annual, semi-annual, quarterly, monthly, semi-monthly (twice per month), biweekly (every 2 weeks), weekly, and daily. A synonym for conversion period or interest period.

conversion period

The interval over which interest is accumulated before being paid. Typical compounding periods are annual, semi-annual, quarterly, monthly, semi-monthly (twice per month), biweekly (every 2 weeks), weekly, and daily. A synonym for compounding period or interest period.

1. Future balance increases if periods and/or interest rates increase.

   First, as the *number of compounding periods increases*, the future balance increases. Second, as the *interest rate increases*, the future balance increases. The videos show how the future balance changes given different interest rates and numbers of compounding periods.

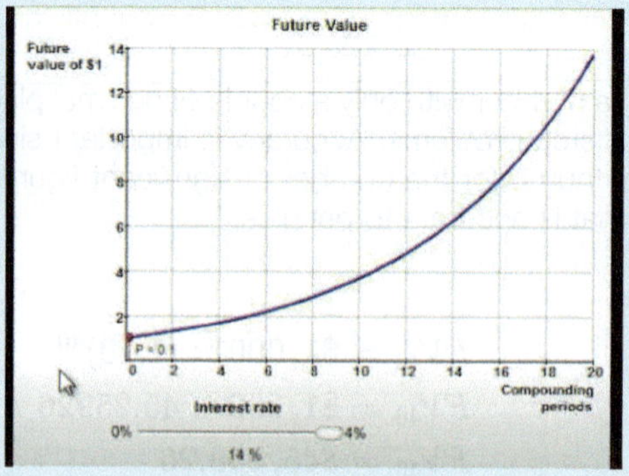

View in the online reader

2. Compound interest theory applies to any growth.

   One of the more important features of TVM calculations is that the methods can be applied to anything that grows. We can use the same equations to find future sales, if sales grow at a constant rate. The method can be applied to any constant growth situation, whether it be money, sales, profits, or dividends.

3. Any length of period can be used.

   Time does not have to be measured in years. The formula can be used with any length period: days, weeks, months, quarters, or years. This period is called the **compounding period** or the **conversion period**. This period is the basic unit of time in all time value of money problems. However, whatever compounding period is used, the interest rate must be defined over the same period. For example, if time is measured in months, then the interest rate must be expressed as a "per month" rate. If time is measured in weeks, then the interest rate must be expressed as a "per week" rate. When no compounding period is stated, then you should assume that interest is compounded annually.

Tip

Failing to adjust the interest rate to match the time period as described here is one of the most common mistakes students make early in their TVM careers. Don't get caught doing this.

Future Value of Mixed Streams of Cash Flows

Suppose you expect to receive a number of separate cash flows over time, which will be different from one another. Now, suppose you want to know what their combined future value will be. This might occur if you're interested in computing your retirement balance, but know you'll save a different amount each year as your salary increases. The solution is to compute the future value of each cash flow separately and add them together.

Example 3.3 Future Value of Mixed Streams

Digital Downloads

Example 3.3 Future Value of Mixed Streams.xls
https://catalog.flatworldknowledge.com/a/34711/Example_3_3_Future_Value_of_Mixed_Streams-6309.xls

You expect to receive $100 at the end of the first period, $200 at the end of the second period, and $300 at the end of the third period. If you will earn 10% by investing these cash flows, what will the future balance be at the end of the sixth period?

SOLUTION

Spreadsheet Solution

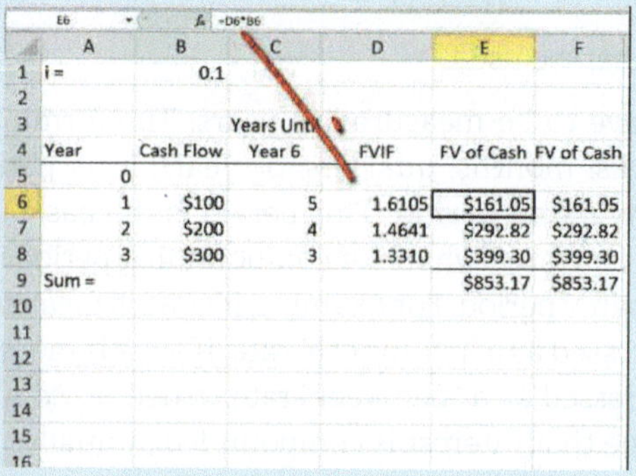

	A	B	C	D	E	F
1	i =	0.1				
2						
3			Years Until			
4	Year	Cash Flow	Year 6	FVIF	FV of Cash	FV of Cash
5	0					
6	1	$100	5	1.6105	$161.05	$161.05
7	2	$200	4	1.4641	$292.82	$292.82
8	3	$300	3	1.3310	$399.30	$399.30
9	Sum =				$853.17	$853.17

View in the online reader

Algebraic Solution

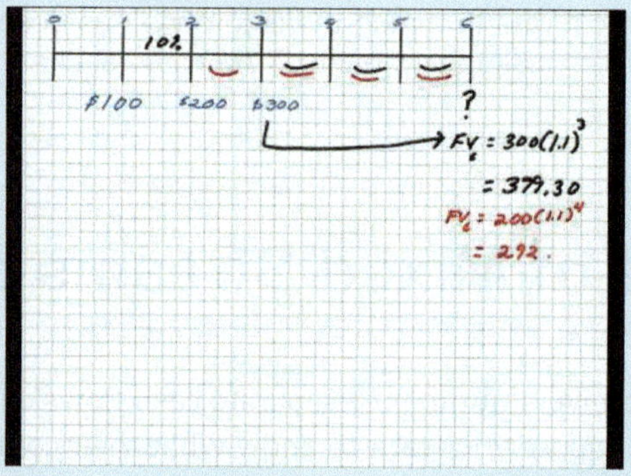

View in the online reader

Calculator Solution

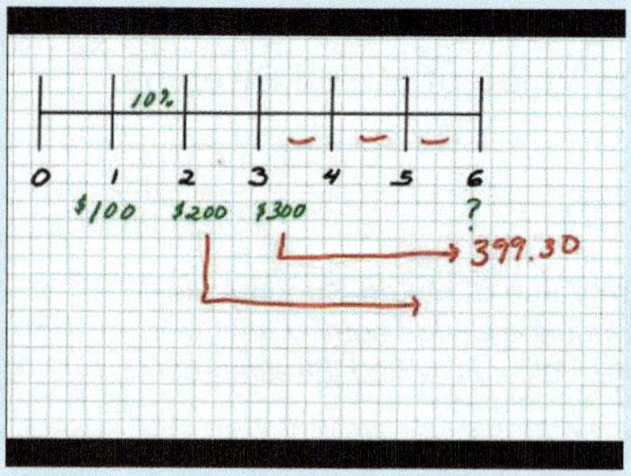

View in the online reader

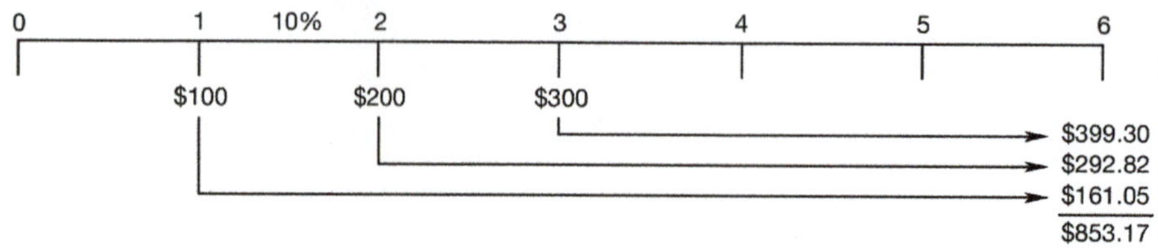

- The first cash flow ($100) goes forward 5 years (count the number of intervals in the time-line) so n=5. The future value at date 6 is: $\$100 \times (1.10)^5 = \$161.05$
- The date 2 cash flow ($200) compounds for four years (n=4) and the future value is $292.82.
- The date 3 cash flow ($300) compounds for 3 years (n=3) and the future value is $399.30.
- The sum of the three future values is $853.17.

Tip

If you have many cash flows to deal with, the computations can become tedious. Unfortunately, most financial calculators don't have the capability to compute the **FV** of mixed streams. The best alternative is to use a spreadsheet program, such as Excel, to perform the arithmetic.

Future Value with Non-Annual Compounding

Annual compounding refers to a situation in which interest is paid once per year. It is common for interest to be paid more frequently than once per year. Most bank accounts, for example, pay interest every month. We must adjust our formula to allow for any interest payment schedule that may arise. To calculate a future value with non-annual compounding:

1. Define m as the number of compounding periods in the year. For example, with semi-annual compounding, $m = 2$.
2. Always match the interest rate to the length of the compounding period. If there are m compounding periods, then the **periodic rate** for each period is i/m. For example, if the interest rate is 12% per year, then the semi-annual periodic rate is 6%, the quarterly rate is 3%, and the monthly rate is 1%.
3. Always adjust the number of periods by multiplying the number of years by the number of compounding periods per year. For example, 5 years $(n = 5)$ with semi-annual compounding $(m = 2)$ is 10 periods $(n \times m)$.

periodic rate

The rate of interest that prevails over a compounding period. The periodic rate is equal to the nominal rate (APR or quoted rate) divided by the number of compounding periods in the year.

The following formula adjusts the generalized equation for future value by inserting the periodic interest rate and the number of compounding periods.

EQUATION 3.4

$$FV_n = PV_0 \times \left(1 + \frac{i}{m}\right)^{n \times m}$$

Explain It: Future Value with Non-Annual Compounding

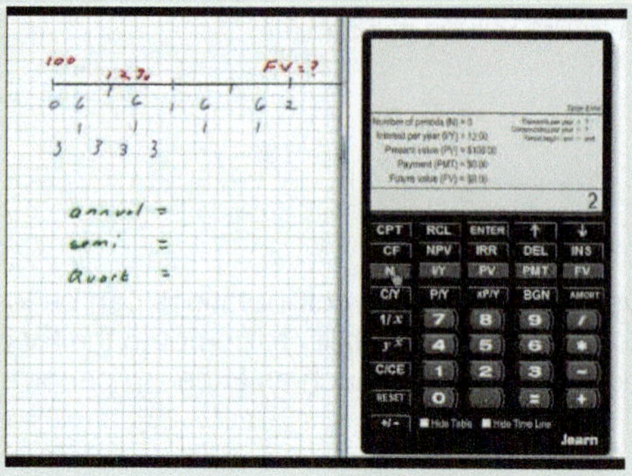

View in the online reader

Explore It: Future Value with Non-Annual Compounding

The Future Value with Non-Annual Compounding Explore It demonstrates the manipulation of the number of compounding periods, denoted *m* in Equation 3.3, to help you understand the difference between annual and non-annual compounding.

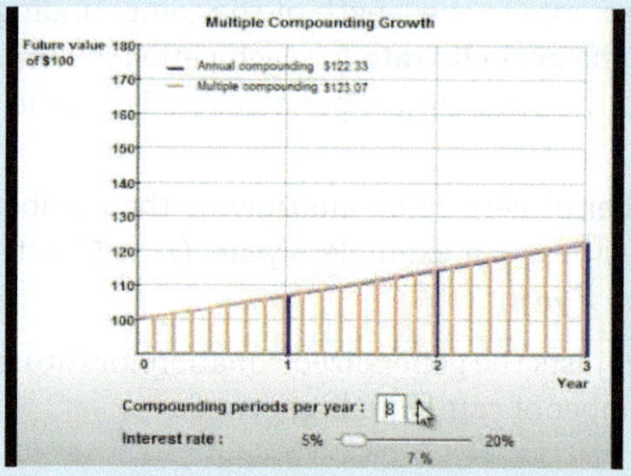

View in the online reader

Example 3.4 Multiple Compounding Periods per Year

Digital Downloads

Example 3.4 Multiple Compounding Periods per Year.xlsx
https://catalog.flatworldknowledge.com/a/34711/Example_3_4_Multiple_Compounding_Periods_per_Year-5fcd.xlsx

What is the future value of a $1,500 deposit after 20 years with an annual interest rate of 8% compounded quarterly?

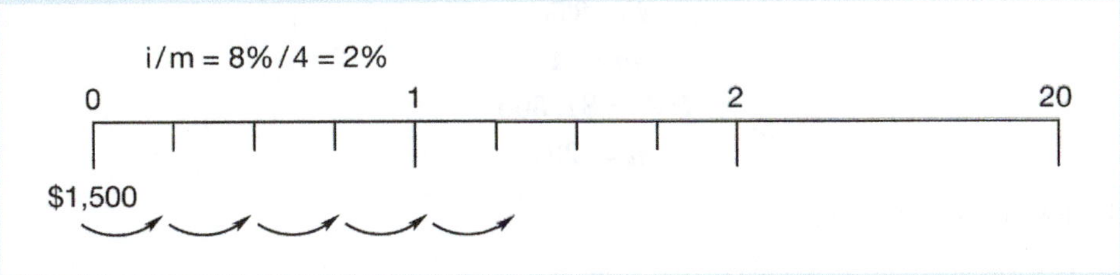

Spreadsheet Solution

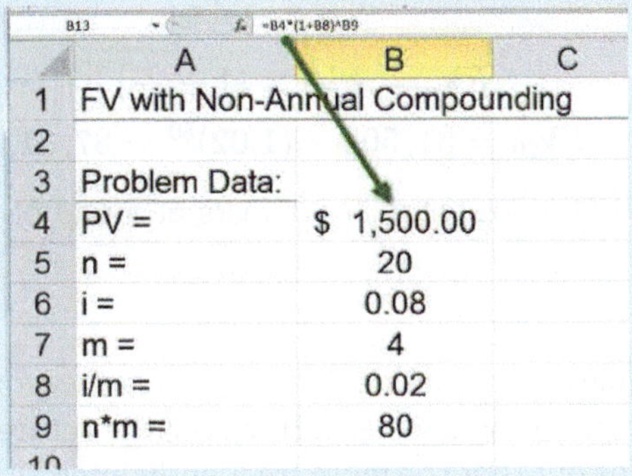

	A	B	C
1	FV with Non-Annual Compounding		
2			
3	Problem Data:		
4	PV =	$ 1,500.00	
5	n =	20	
6	i =	0.08	
7	m =	4	
8	i/m =	0.02	
9	n*m =	80	

View in the online reader

Algebraic Solution

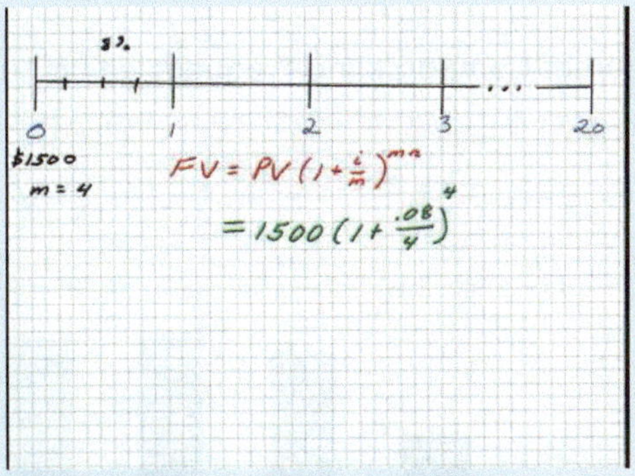

View in the online reader

Calculator Solution

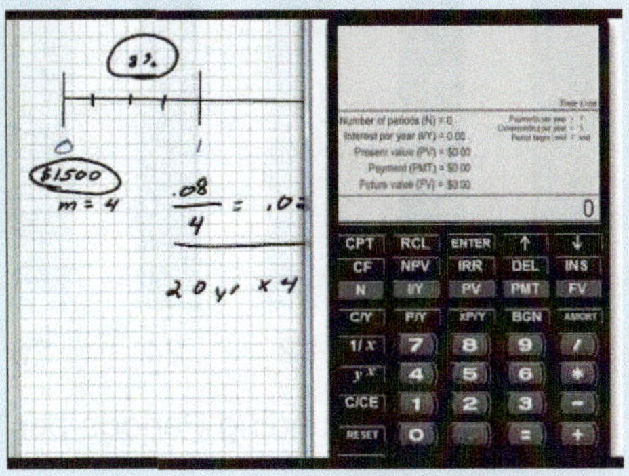

View in the online reader

In this example, we know that:

$$i = 8\%$$
$$m = 4$$
$$PV = \$1,500$$
$$n = 20$$

First, solve for the periodic rate:

$$i/m = 8\%/4 = 2\%$$

Second, substitute these numbers into Equation 3.4:

$$FV_n = PV_0 \times \left(1 + \frac{i}{m}\right)^{n \times m}$$
$$FV_{20} = \$1,500 \times (1.02)^{80} = \$7,313.16$$

The future value of a \$1,500 deposit after 20 years at a rate of 8% compounded quarterly is \$7,313.16.

In "Example 3.4 Multiple Compounding Periods per Year" we found that \$1,500 deposited for 20 years at 8% compounded quarterly is \$7,313.16. However, the future value with annual compounding is only \$6,991.44. It turns out that the more frequently interest is paid, the greater is the future value. Now, look at Figure 3.4. This figure shows the future value of \$100 at 12%, compounded at different frequencies. As the compounding periods get smaller the increase in future value from additional compounding periods increases at a decreasing rate.

FIGURE 3.4 Effect of Different Compounding Frequencies on Future Value (*i*=12%)

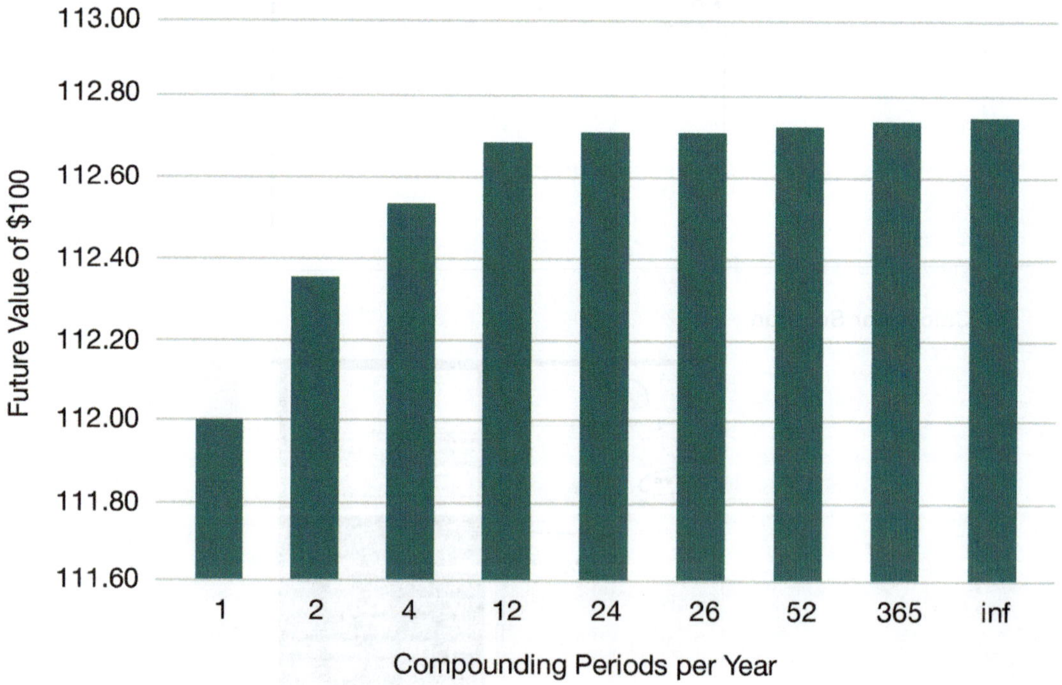

3.3 The Effective Interest Rate

The Effective Interest Rate

If you make a $100 deposit into an account that pays 12% compounded once per year, at the end of the year you will have $112. Would you be any better off if the bank compounded (made interest payments) any more frequently? To answer this let's compute what you would have if the deposit was compounded semi-annually. After 6 months, you would be paid half of the quoted rate, or $6. This $6 would then earn additional interest for you during the second half-year. The interest earned on this interest would be $0.36, or 6% of $6. Your total earnings would then be $6 each half year plus $0.36 or $12.36. So you are better off with compounding. The 12% in this example is the quoted interest rate and the 12.36% that is earned is the **effective interest rate (EIR)**. The EIR is the rate you actually earn on your investment after taking into account the compounding frequency.

effective interest rate (EIR)

A restatement of the annual quoted percentage rate, which adjusts earnings to reflect compounding. The EIR is the simple interest rate that is equivalent to a given quoted rate when compounded m times through a year.

Tip

Note that the effective interest rate is often referred to as the effective annual rate.

To determine the exact effective interest rate, given multiple compounding periods per year, we find the *FV* of $1 after 1 year and then subtract the initial dollar. What's left is the interest for the year, which is the effective interest rate. The FV of $1 is found by applying Equation 3.4 where PV = 1 and n=1. The effective interest rate is computed by subtracting 1.

EQUATION 3.5

$$\textbf{Effective interest rate} = \left[\mathbf{1} + \frac{i}{m}\right]^{m} - \mathbf{1}$$

where

$$i = \textbf{the quoted annual rate}$$
$$m = \textbf{the number of compounding intervals}$$

Example 3.5 Effective Interest Rate Calculation

What is the effective interest rate for a nominal rate of 12%, which is compounded monthly?

SOLUTION

Spreadsheet Solution

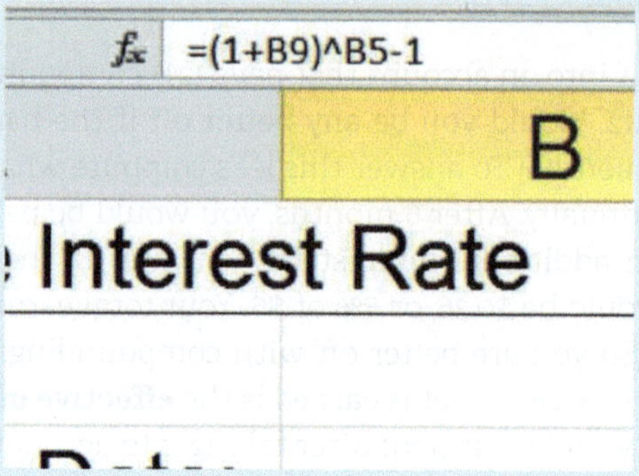

View in the online reader

Algebraic Solution

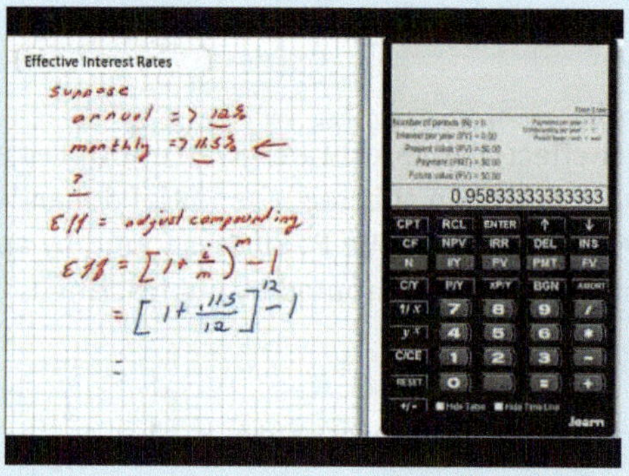

View in the online reader

In this example, we know that:

$$i = 12\%$$
$$m = 12$$

Substitute these numbers into Equation 3.5.

$$\text{Effective interest rate} = \left[1 + \frac{i}{m}\right]^m - 1$$

$$\text{Effective interest rate} = \left[1 + \frac{0.12}{12}\right]^{12} - 1$$

$$\text{Effective interest rate} = 0.1268 \text{ or } 12.68\%$$

An annually compounded interest rate of 12.68% is equivalent to earning a 12% annual rate compounded 12 times per year.

Table 3.1 shows the effective rate at different compounding intervals, when the annual rate is 12%. Suppose you are attempting to choose between two bank savings accounts. The first pays 5% compounded annually, and the second pays 4.9% compounded monthly. Which would you prefer? To answer this, you must compute the effective rate of each alternative and pick the largest one.

The effective rate of the first is unchanged, 5%. The effective rate of the second is 5.01%. So, you would choose the bank offering 4.9% compounded monthly.

Explain It: Effective Interest Rate

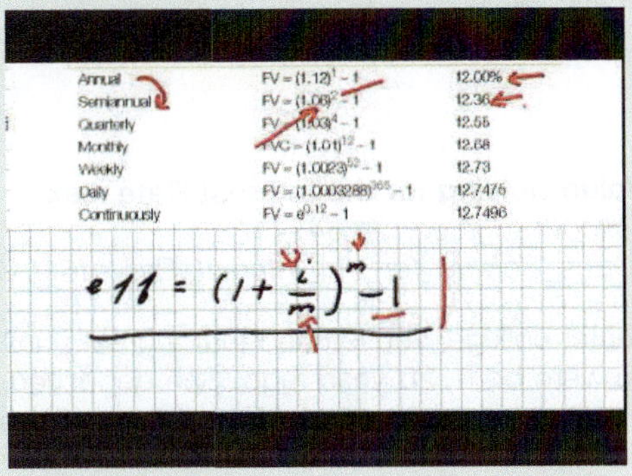

View in the online reader

TABLE 3.1 Effective Interest Rates with 12% Annual Rate

Compounding Interval	Equation 3.5	Effective Rate
Annual	$EIR=(1.12)^1-1$	12.00%
Semiannual	$EIR=(1.06)^2-1$	12.36
Quarterly	$EIR=(1.03)^4-1$	12.55
Monthly	$EIR=(1.01)^{12}-1$	12.68
Weekly	$EIR=(1.0023)^{52}-1$	12.73
Daily	$\text{EIR}=(1.0003288)^{365}-1$	12.7475

3.4 Solving for Rate and Time Periods

Solving for the Interest Rate

In all of the examples shown, we've used the basic future value equation to solve for how much a deposit today can grow to in the future. There are times, however, when we already know both the future and present values and want to know either the interest rate or the length of time it took to earn the future balance. Next, we learn how to find the interest rate, and then we learn how to solve for the length of time. We can use the future value of a lump sum from Equation 3.3 to solve for the interest rate (when it is the unknown):

$$FV_n = PV_0 \times (1 + i)^n$$
$$FV_n / PV_0 = (1 + i)^n$$
$$[FV_n / PV_0]^{1/n} = [(1 + i)^n]^{1/n} = (1 + i)$$

EQUATION 3.6

$$i = [FV_n / PV_0]^{1/n} - 1$$

Example 3.6 Future Value, Solving for the Interest Rate

Digital Downloads

Example 3.6 Future Value Solving for the Interest Rate.xlsx
https://catalog.flatworldknowledge.com/a/34711/ Example_3_6_Future_Value_Solving_for_the_Interest_Rate-d67f.xlsx

Just as you were about to enter college, you learned that a great aunt had established a college trust fund for you when you were born, 20 years ago. She deposited $5,000 initially. If the balance is now $19,348.42, what average compounded rate of return has been earned?

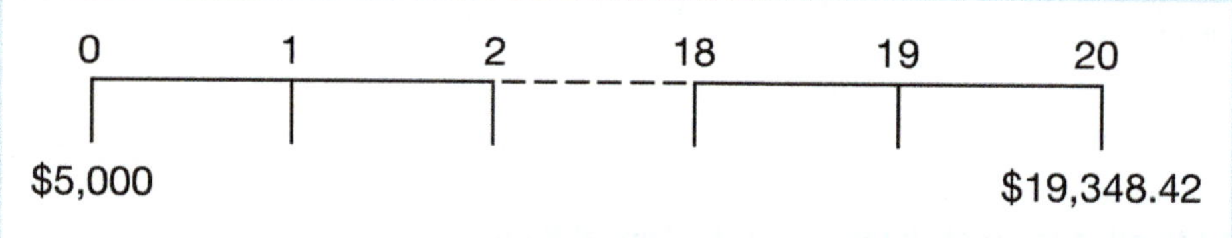

SOLUTION

Spreadsheet Solution

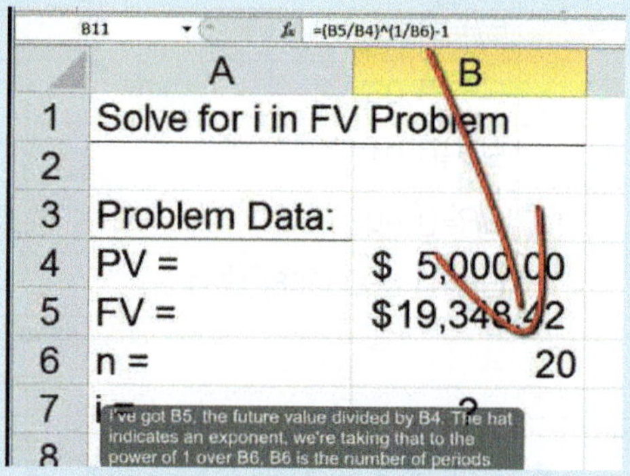

View in the online reader

Algebraic Solution

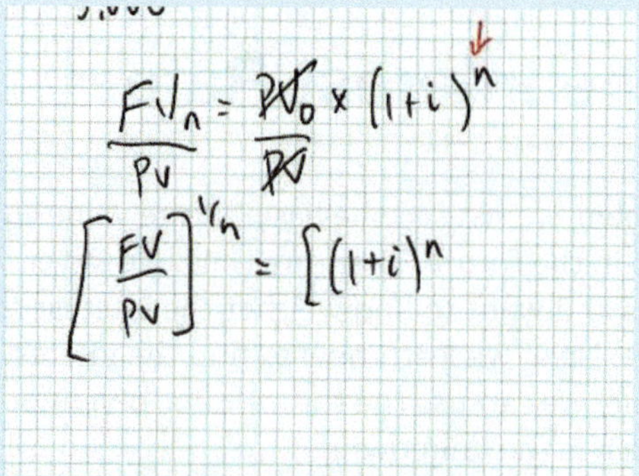

View in the online reader

Calculator Solution

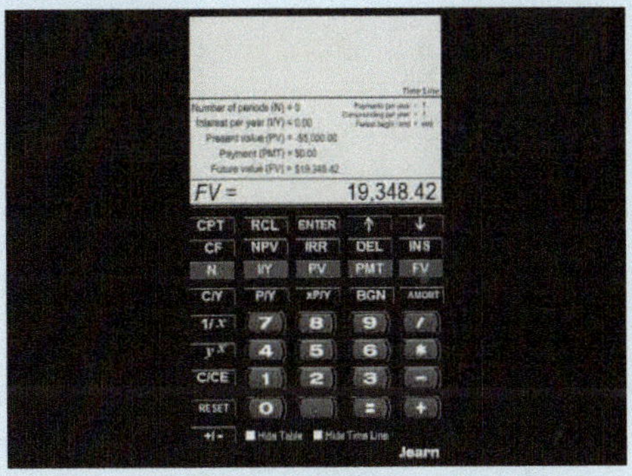

View in the online reader

We can use Equation 3.2 to solve for the unknown interest rate:

$$i = [19,348.42/5,000]^{1/20} - 1 = [3.8697]^{1/20} - 1$$
$$i = 1.0700 - 1 = 0.0700 \text{ or } 7\%$$

Tip

You can use the **Y^x** button on your calculator to compute the 20th root. *Y*=3.8697 and *x*=1/20=0.05.

Solving for the Number of Time Periods

If you know the *PV*, *FV*, and the interest rate you can compute the number of periods.

Example 3.7 Future Value, Solving for *n*

Digital Downloads

Example 3.7 Future Value Solving for n.xlsx
https://catalog.flatworldknowledge.com/a/34711/Example_3_7_Future_Value_Solving_for_n-bfb7.xlsx

How long does it take to double your money at 3%? For example, if inflation averages 3% per annum, then how many years will it take for the price of a pint of beer to double from $1.50 to $3.00?

SOLUTION

Spreadsheet Solution

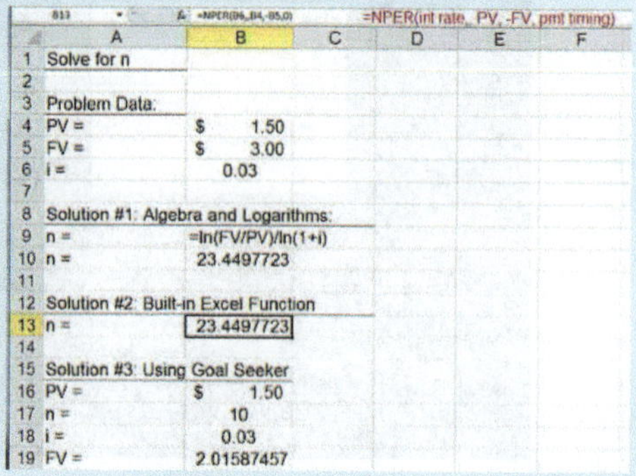

=NPER(int rate, PV, -FV, pmt timing)

	A	B	C	D	E	F
1	Solve for n					
2						
3	Problem Data:					
4	PV =	$ 1.50				
5	FV =	$ 3.00				
6	i =	0.03				
7						
8	Solution #1: Algebra and Logarithms:					
9	n =	=ln(FV/PV)/ln(1+i)				
10	n =	23.4497723				
11						
12	Solution #2: Built-in Excel Function					
13	n =	23.4497723				
14						
15	Solution #3: Using Goal Seeker					
16	PV =	$ 1.50				
17	n =	10				
18	i =	0.03				
19	FV =	2.01587457				

View in the online reader

Algebraic Solution

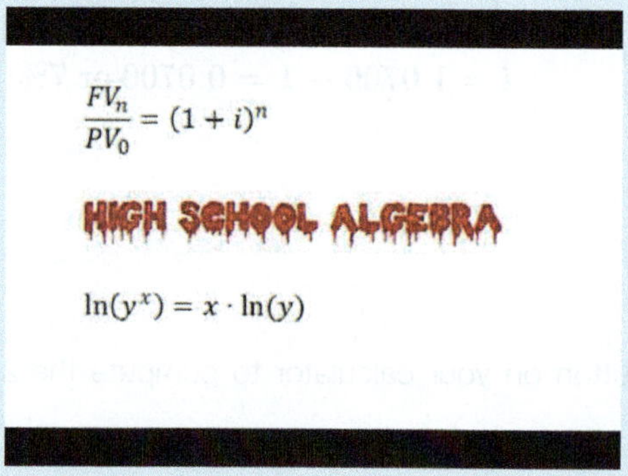

View in the online reader

Calculator Solution

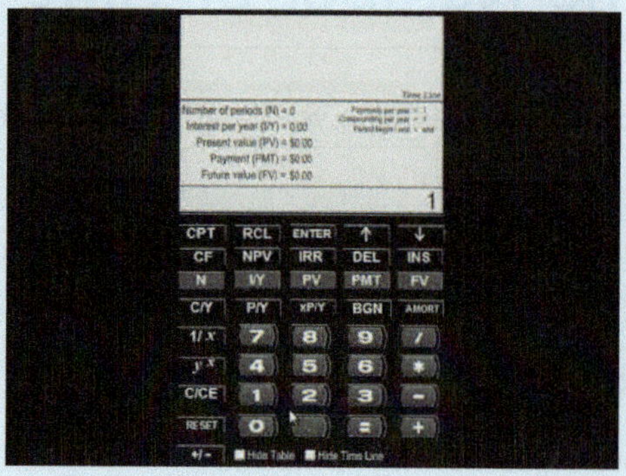

View in the online reader

$$PV_0 = \$1.50$$
$$FV_n = \$3$$
$$n = ?$$
$$i = 3\%$$

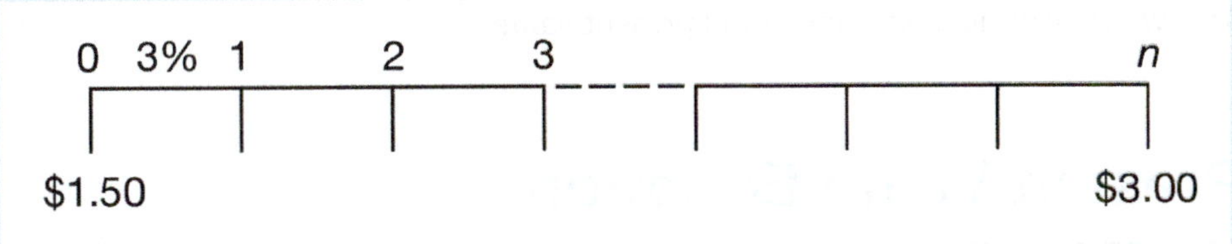

First, we set this up as a future value problem where the unknown is the number of compounding periods, *n*:

$$FV_n = PV_0 \times (1+i)^n$$
$$FV_n / PV_0 = (1+i)^n$$

The videos show how to solve for *n* with a financial calculator or spreadsheet. the following "Explain It: Solving for n" describes how to solve for *n* with algebra.

Explain It: Solving for *n*

Consider the following problem: How long does it take to double your money at some rate *i*%? We solve this by setting the problem up as a future value problem with an unknown number of compounding periods.

$$FV_n = PV_0 \times (1+i)^n$$
$$\frac{FV_n}{PV_0} = (1+i)^n$$

The trick to solving for periods is to remember the following rule of logarithms:

$$ln(y^n) = n \times ln(y)$$

We take the logarithm of both sides, apply the rule to the right-hand side, and simplify:

$$ln\left[\frac{FV_n}{PV_0}\right] = ln\left[(1+i)^n\right] = n \times \; ln(1+i)$$
$$n = \left[\frac{ln\left(\frac{FV_n}{PV_0}\right)}{ln(1+i)}\right]$$

If $PV = 1.5$, $FV = 3$, and $i = 3\%$, then:

$$n = \frac{ln\left(\frac{3}{1.5}\right)}{ln(1.03)} = \frac{ln(2)}{ln(1.03)} = 23.4498 \text{ year}$$

You can use any base logarithm to solve this problem.

3.5 Present Value of a Sum

Often, we need to determine what the value is today of sums that will be received in the future. For example, if a firm is evaluating an investment that will generate future income, it must compare today's expenditures with expected future revenues. To compare sums across time, future values must be adjusted to what they're worth today. Luckily, if the concepts discussed under future value make sense, it won't be difficult to understand present value.

The Present Value Equation

Explain It: Present Value

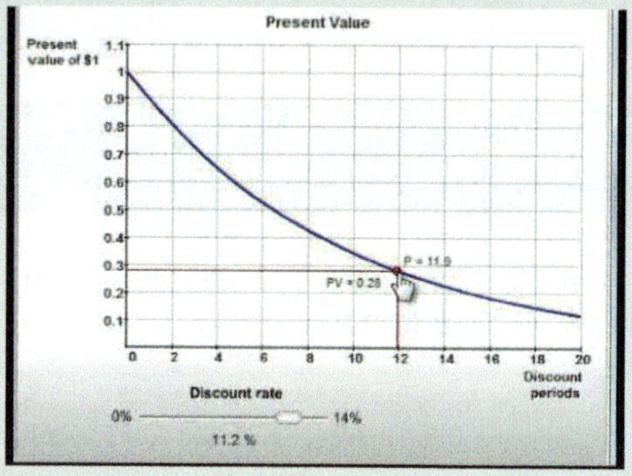

View in the online reader

Take another look at the future value equation (Equation 3.2):

$$FV_n = PV_0 \times (1 + i)^n$$

The future value is defined in terms of present value. To find the equation for computing present value, we need to rearrange Equation 3.2. If both sides are divided by $(1 + i)^n$, we get the equation for present value:

EQUATION 3.7

$$PV_0 = \frac{FV_n}{(1 + i)^n} = FV_n \times (1 + i)^{-n}$$

The term $1/(1 + i)^n$, or $(1 + i)^{-n}$ is called the present value interest factor.

Example 3.8 Solving for the Present Value

Digital Downloads

Example 3.8 Solving for the Present Value.xlsx
https://catalog.flatworldknowledge.com/a/34711/Example_3_8_Solving_for_the_Present_Value-5d10.xlsx

What is the present value of $100, which will be received in 10 years, if the interest rate is 5%?

SOLUTION

Spreadsheet Solution

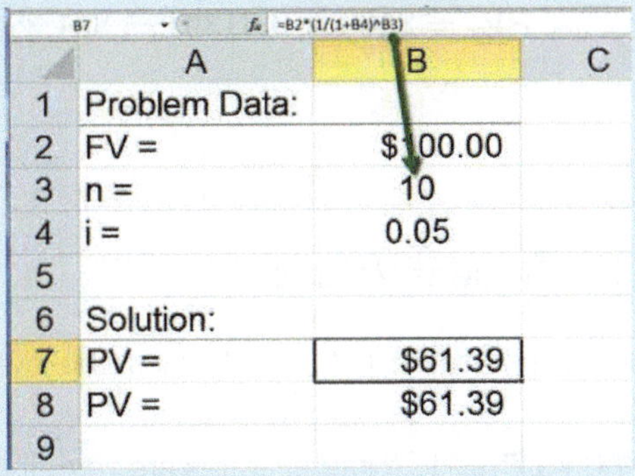

	A	B	C
1	Problem Data:		
2	FV =	$100.00	
3	n =	10	
4	i =	0.05	
5			
6	Solution:		
7	PV =	$61.39	
8	PV =	$61.39	
9			

View in the online reader

Algebraic Solution

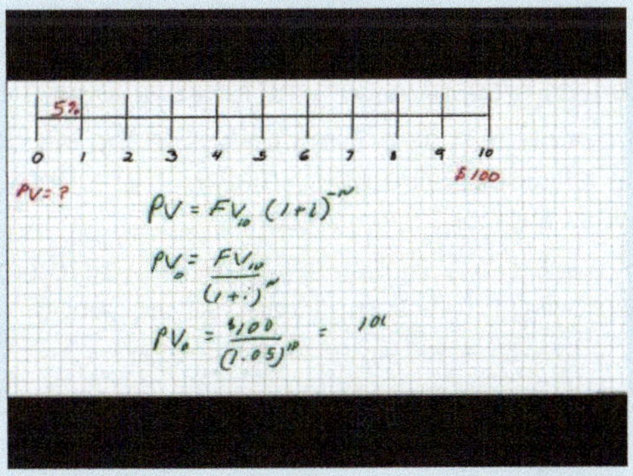

View in the online reader

Calculator Solution

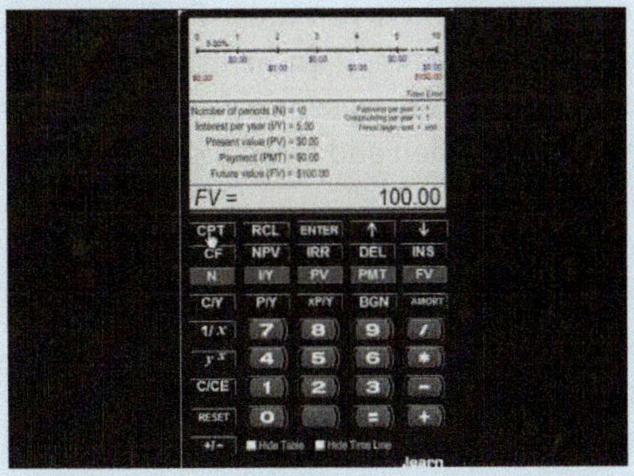

View in the online reader

$$FV = \$100$$
$$n = 10$$
$$i = 0.05$$

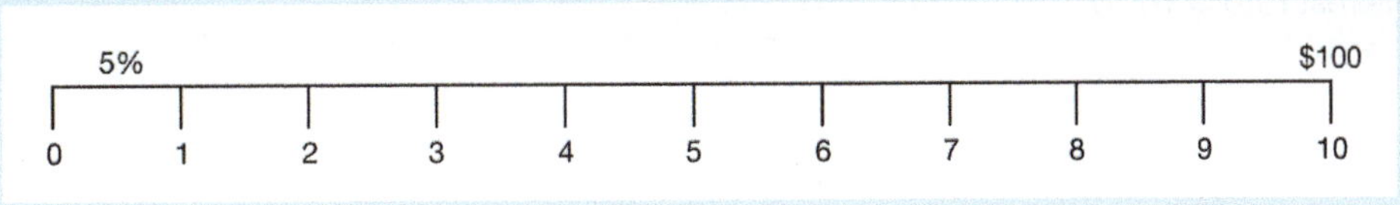

$$PV_0 = FV_n \times \frac{1}{(1+i)^n}$$
$$PV_0 = \$100 \times \frac{1}{1.05^{10}}$$
$$PV_0 = \$100 \times 0.61391 = \$61.39$$

discounting

The process of calculating the present value of a sum.

Some Insights about Present Values

1. The present value interest factor, $1/(1+i)^n$ is just the inverse of the future value factor, $(1+i)^n$.
2. if $i = 0$, then $1/(1+i)^n = 1$. If interest rates are zero, then future values are equivalent to present values.
3. Interest rates and the present value are inversely related. When the interest rate rises, the present value falls.
4. The process of computing the present value of a future sum is called **discounting**. Remember that a future sum isn't worth as much as a sum you have today. To convert future amounts to their present values, the future amount must be reduced, or discounted.
5. You can think of discounting as moving dollars to the left on a timeline. Whenever dollars are moved to the left, their value gets smaller. The further to the left and the higher the interest rate, the less the dollars are worth.
6. You don't always want to move cash flows all the way to time period 0. Present value calculations include moving future sums to any earlier period.

Present Value of Mixed Streams of Cash Flows

Thus far, we've focused on computing the present value of a single, lump-sum future cash flow. However, there are many occasions when you must find the present value of a series of unequal cash flows. For example, if you're evaluating an investment in a business, it's unlikely each year's cash flows will be the same. To find the present value of mixed streams, simply find the present value of each cash flow individually, then add them together.

Example 3.9 Present Value of Mixed Streams

Digital Downloads

Example 3.9 Present Value of Mixed Streams.xlsx
https://catalog.flatworldknowledge.com/a/34711/Example_3_9_Present_Value_of_Mixed_Streams-96f6.xlsx

You're contemplating introducing a new product line expected to generate cash flows of $100 at the end of the first year, $200 at the end of the second year, $300 at the end of the third year, and $400 at the end of the fourth year. What is the present value of the cash flows if the appropriate interest rate is 10%?

SOLUTION

Spreadsheet Solution

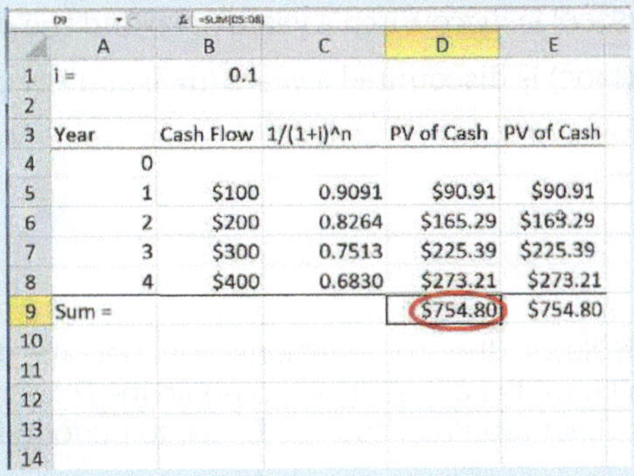

	A	B	C	D	E
1	i =	0.1			
2					
3	Year	Cash Flow	1/(1+i)^n	PV of Cash	PV of Cash
4	0				
5	1	$100	0.9091	$90.91	$90.91
6	2	$200	0.8264	$165.29	$165.29
7	3	$300	0.7513	$225.39	$225.39
8	4	$400	0.6830	$273.21	$273.21
9	Sum =			$754.80	$754.80
10					
11					
12					
13					
14					

View in the online reader

Algebraic Solution

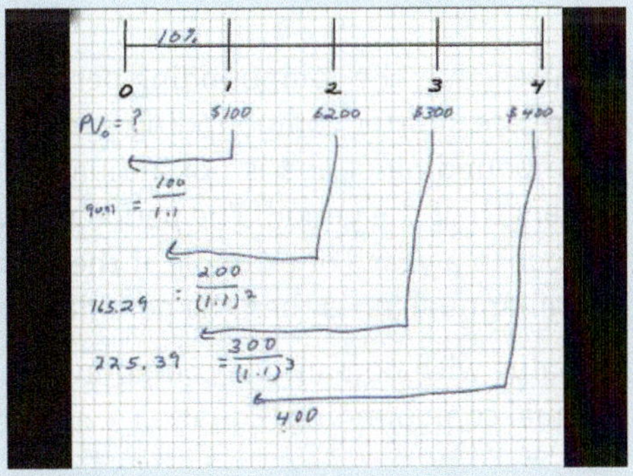

View in the online reader

Calculator Solution

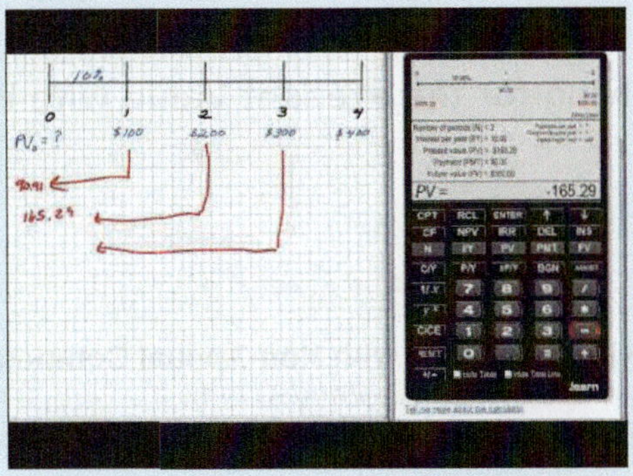

View in the online reader

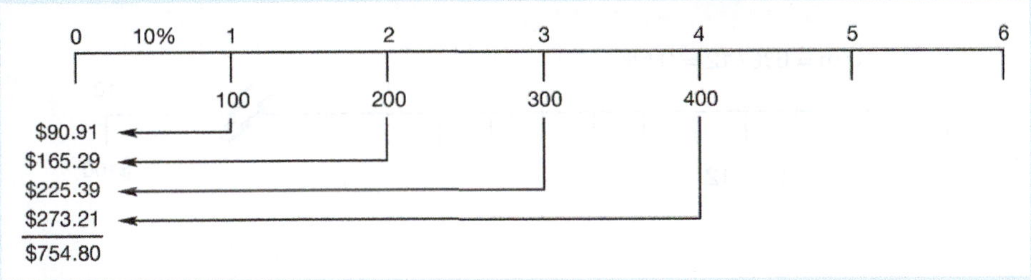

- The first cash flow ($100) is discounted 1 year (n=1) and the present value at date 0 is $\$100/(1.01) = \$90.91.$
- The date 2 cash flow ($200) is discounted 2 years (n=2) and the present value at date 0 is $\$100/(1.01)^2 = \$165.29.$
- The date 3 cash flow ($200) is discounted 3 years (n=3) and the present value at date 0 is $225.39.
- The date 4 cash flow ($400) is discounted 4 years (n=4) and the present value at date 0 is $273.21.
- The sum of the four present values is $754.80.

Tip

If you have many cash flows, the computations can become tedious. Unfortunately, many financial calculators don't have the capability to compute the *PV* of mixed streams. The best alternative is to use a spreadsheet program, such as Excel, to perform the arithmetic.

Present Value with Non-Annual Compounding

Just as we discussed with future value, the compounding period in Equation 3.7 does not have to be a full year. Frequently, there are shorter compounding periods such as semi-annual, monthly, weekly, or daily. When the compounding period is not annual we must be sure to use a periodic interest rate that reflects the length of the period. The periodic rate is simply i/m, where m is the number of compounding periods in a year. For example, if the nominal rate is 10% ($i = 10\%$) and the compounding period is semi-annual (m=2) then the periodic rate is $10\%/2$ or 5%.

The formula for present value with non-annual compounding is analogous to the formula for the future value with non-annual compounding (Equation 3.2):

EQUATION 3.8

$$PV_0 = FV_n \times \frac{1}{\left(1 + \frac{i}{m}\right)^{n \times m}}$$

Example 3.10: Solving for the Present Value with Non-Annual Compounding

Digital Downloads

Example 3.10 Solving for the PV with Non-Annual Compounding.xlsx
https://catalog.flatworldknowledge.com/a/34711/Example_3_10_Solving_for_the_PV_with_Non_Annual_Compounding-efb7.xlsx

What is the present value of $100, which will be received in 10 years, if the annual interest rate is 6% and there is monthly compounding of invested funds?

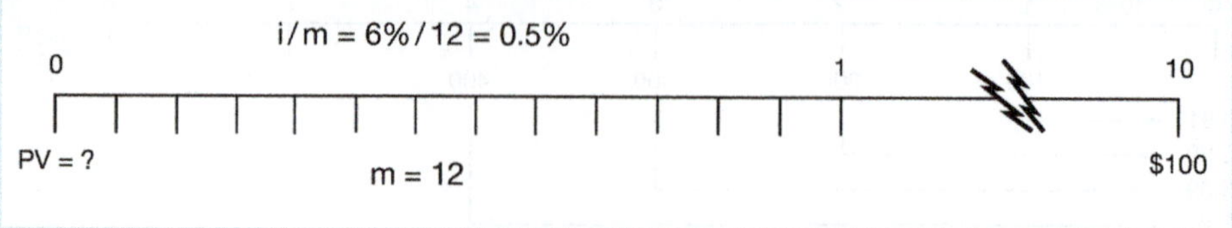

SOLUTION

Spreadsheet Solution

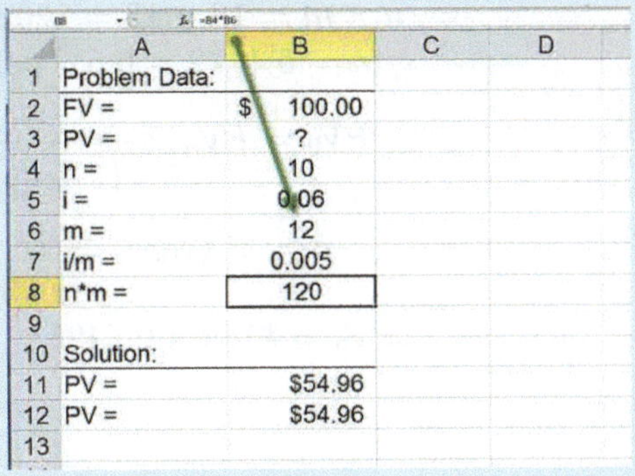

	A	B	C	D
1	Problem Data:			
2	FV =	$ 100.00		
3	PV =	?		
4	n =	10		
5	i =	0.06		
6	m =	12		
7	i/m =	0.005		
8	n*m =	120		
9				
10	Solution:			
11	PV =	$54.96		
12	PV =	$54.96		
13				

View in the online reader

Algebraic Solution

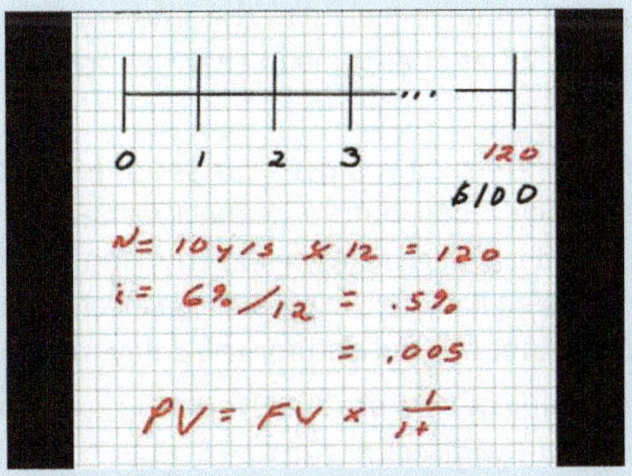

View in the online reader

Calculator Solution

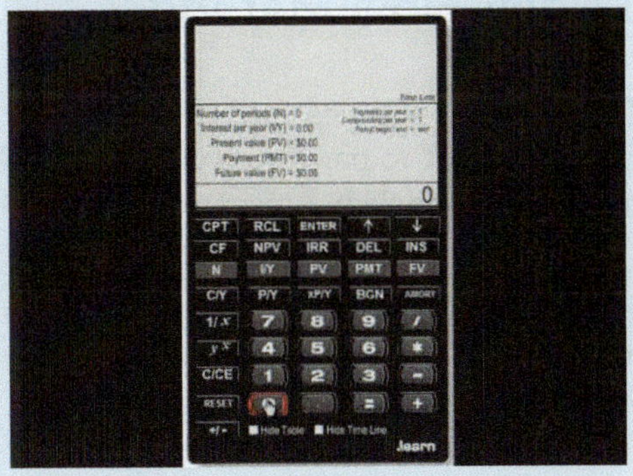

View in the online reader

$$FV = \$100$$
$$n = 10 \text{ years}$$
$$m = 12$$
$$n \times m = 10 \times 12 = 120 \text{ months}$$
$$i/m = 6\%/12 = 0.5\% \text{ per month}$$
$$PV_0 = FV_n \times \frac{1}{\left(1 + \frac{i}{m}\right)^{n \times m}}$$
$$PV_0 = \$100 \times \frac{1}{1.005^{120}}$$
$$PV_0 = \$100 \times 0.5496 = \$54.96$$

The Intuition behind Present Values

Because the concept of present value is central to the study of finance, you need to understand the intuition behind the numbers. What does it mean that the present value of $100 to be received in 1 year at 10% is $90.91?

1. *It means you're indifferent to which you get—the $90.91 today or the $100 in 1 year.* What if you don't really need the money today, but you expect to need it in 1 year? In that case, you can invest the $90.91 today and it will grow to be exactly $100 by the time you need it. The interest rate used to discount the $100 back to the present is selected so that you'll be properly compensated for the risk you may not be paid and for the delay in receiving the cash flow.
2. If you have the present value of a future sum, *you can exactly match that future sum by investing what you have today at the discount rate.*
3. It is the current value of a promised payment in the future.

The Discounted Cash Flow Method

discounted cash flow (DCF)

The valuation methodology whereby the value of an asset is equal to the present value of the asset's cash flows; the same as fundamental value.

There are a number of different methodologies used to find the fair value of assets. By fair value we mean the price that you would expect to pay (receive) if you buy (sell) the asset in a competitive market. The primary valuation methodology presented in this book is the **discounted cash flow (DCF)** method.

With the DCF methodology, the current value of an asset is the present value of all future cash flows. The current price must be such that the seller is indifferent between continuing to receive the cash flow stream provided by the asset and receiving the offer price. That is exactly what present values do.

Suppose you're interested in investing in a Van Gogh painting called *Sunflowers*. If you think you can hold the painting for 2 years and then resell it for $1,200,000, how much would you pay for the painting today? The only cash flow from this investment is the final sales price. No periodic payments will be received. To compute the current price of the painting, you will first need to determine an appropriate discount rate to use for computing the present value of the cash flows. Investments in art are high risk and therefore require a high discount rate. Let's assume you require a 16% return to compensate you for the risk of the investment.

Source: Vincent van Gogh / Public domain

To find the current price of the painting, discount the future cash flow back to the present at 16%. This provides a present value of $891,795.48. In fact, this painting actually sold for $883,123. The buyer must have expected a slightly lower future price or required a slightly higher return than assumed by our example.

A commercial building is valued using the same technique. The preferred way to value commercial real estate is the income approach, which involves computing the present value of the building's cash flows and using this to estimate the property's value.

Why did the Van Gogh painting not sell for the present value of its expected cash flows and why might a building not sell for its *PV* of projected income? It is because competition for valuable investments in the market causes prices to adjust so that they represent the best estimate of value by market participants. Not everyone agrees about what the future cash flows are going to be. Assets like these will sell to the investor who either expects the *largest cash flows* or sees the least risk in the investment.

Let's summarize how to find the DCF value of a business asset.

1. Identify the cash flows that result from owning the asset.
2. Determine what discount rate is required to compensate the investor for "the risk" of holding the asset.
3. Find the present value of the cash flows estimated in step 1 using the discount rate determined in step 2.

Castle in the Air (Bigger Fool) theory

An investment theory of valuation that posits that assets are worth the amount that the next bigger (greater) fool will pay for them; in contrast to the fundamental theory of valuation, which holds that assets are worth the present value of their future cash flows.

This discounted cash flow methodology is the process used to value all business assets and securities. We employ it repeatedly in the remainder of this book to value bonds, stocks, projects, and firms. The next video takes a brief look at an alternative valuation method called the **Castle in the Air (Bigger Fool) theory**.

Explain It: Castle in the Air Theory

View in the online reader

CHAPTER 4

Annuities and Loans

Learning Objectives

By the end of this chapter you will be able to:

1. Compute the future value of streams of payments.
2. Compute the present value of streams of payments.
3. Articulate strategies for solving advanced TVM problems.
4. Calculate a balloon loan payment.
5. Compute amortized loan payments and prepare amortization schedules.

This chapter extends the ideas presented in Chapter 3. The main extension is that this chapter presents tools for managing streams of cash flows. The first half of the chapter shows how to discount and accumulate level streams of cash flows known as annuities. The second half of the chapter explains loans and presents an in-depth analysis of amortized loans, which are a type of annuity.

4.1 Future Value of Streams of Payments

In the last chapter, we computed the future and present values of a *single deposit* or sum. Often, though, you want to know the future value of a series of *equal deposits* over a period of time. For example, you may make equal monthly deposits into a savings account. You could find the future value of these deposits by computing the future value of each one separately and then summing them. However, this method becomes tedious if there are many deposits. An easier way to find the future value of these deposits involves using annuities.

What is an Annuity?

An **annuity** is a series of equal payments made at equal intervals. Despite being called annuities, annuity payments don't have to be made annually. They can be made monthly, weekly, or even daily. The critical factors are that the payments equal each other and that the interval between them is the same.

An annuity in which payments are made at the *end* of each period is an **ordinary annuity**. An annuity in which payments are made at the beginning of each period is an **annuity due**. Ordinary annuities are more common than annuities due. In this text, the annuity may be assumed to be ordinary unless otherwise specified.

annuity

A stream of equal periodic cash flows. These cash flows can be inflows or outflows.

ordinary annuity

An annuity for which the payments occur at the end of each period.

annuity due

An annuity for which the payments occur at the beginning of each period.

Future Value of an Ordinary Annuity

Suppose you want to know the future balance in your interest-bearing bank account after 3 years if you make three annual $100 deposits. We will assume that your bank pays interest at the rate of 10% each year. The timeline of cash flows is shown in Figure 4.1.

FIGURE 4.1

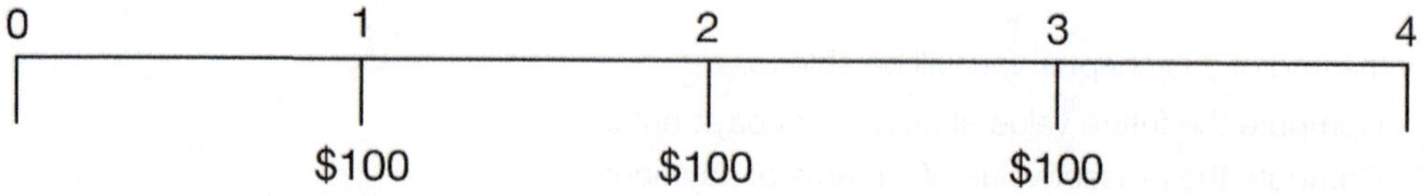

The "long" approach finds the future value of each cash flow and adds them up as shown in Figure 4.2. The values shown under date 3 on the timeline are just the future value of each corresponding cash flow.

FIGURE 4.2

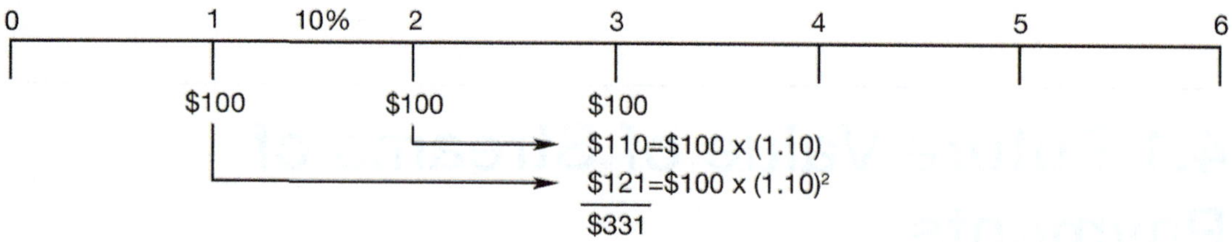

The total future value is the sum of the future values of the individual payments, so we can express the future value of the ordinary annuity as

$$FV_{anmiity} = PMT_1 \times (1+i)^{n-1} + PMT_2 \times (1+i)^{n-2} + \cdots$$
$$+ PMT_{n-1} \times (1+i)^1 + PMT_n \times (1+i)^0$$

Unfortunately, the equation above isn't much help in solving annuity problems. Students of algebra will recognize that the equation above is a geometric progression for which standardized solutions have been found.

After some algebra, the equation simplifies to:

EQUATION 4.1

$$FV_{\text{annuity}} = PMT \times \frac{(1+i)^n - 1}{i}$$

where

PMT = the periodic payment in the annuity
i = the interest rate
n = the number of payments

The term after the multiplication sign in Equation 4.1 is the **future value interest factor for an annuity (FVIFA)**. The acronym is useful because it is shorter than writing out the whole formula and here we use it interchangeably with the formula.

future value interest factor for an annuity (FVIFA)

FVIFA is the future value of an *n*-period ordinary annuity at rate *i* with payments of one dollar.

EQUATION 4.2

$$FVIFA_{i,n} = \frac{(1+i)^n - 1}{i}$$

Explain It: FVIFA

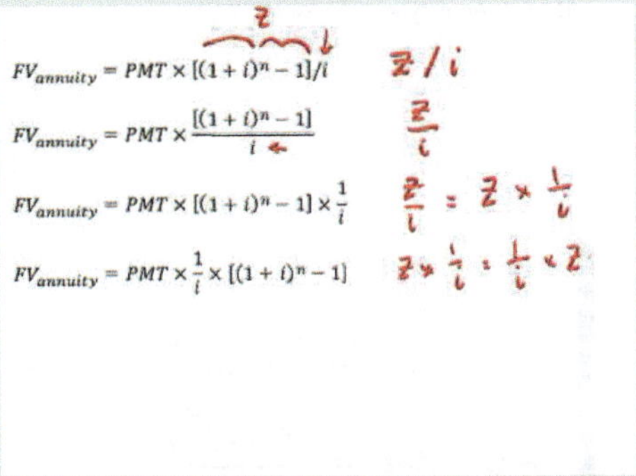

View in the online reader

Example 4.1 Future Value of an Ordinary Annuity: Accumulating a Nest Egg

Digital Downloads

Example 4.1 FV Value of an Ordinary Annuity.xlsx
https://catalog.flatworldknowledge.com/a/34711/Example_4_1_FV_Value_of_an_Ordinary_Annuity-988f.xlsx

Suppose you win the lottery. The winnings consist of 20 equal annual payments of $50,000. You decide to save all of this money for your retirement, and you deposit it into an account that earns 8% per year. What is the amount of your retirement nest egg?

SOLUTION

Spreadsheet Solution

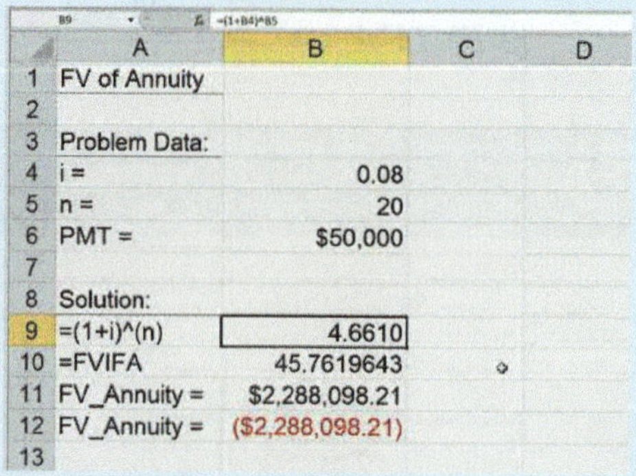

	A	B	C	D
1	FV of Annuity			
2				
3	Problem Data:			
4	i =	0.08		
5	n =	20		
6	PMT =	$50,000		
7				
8	Solution:			
9	=(1+i)^(n)	4.6610		
10	=FVIFA	45.7619643		
11	FV_Annuity =	$2,288,098.21		
12	FV_Annuity =	($2,288,098.21)		
13				

View in the online reader

Algebraic Solution

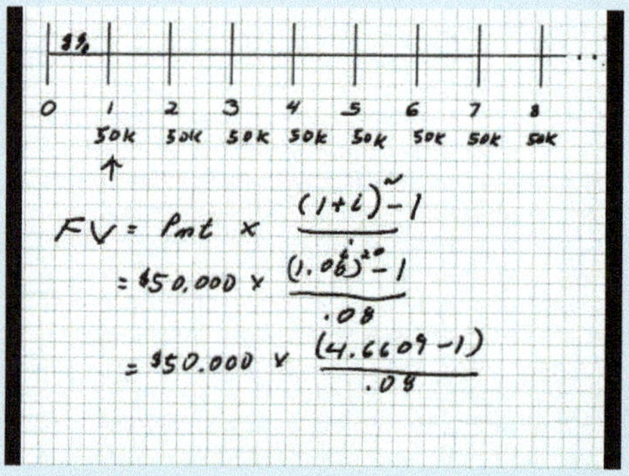

View in the online reader

Calculator Solution

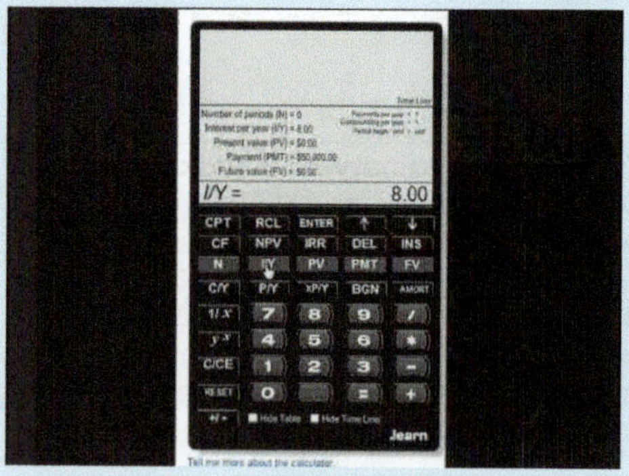

View in the online reader

In this example, find the future value of an ordinary annuity:

$$PMT = 50,000$$
$$i = 8\%$$
$$n = 20$$

This question asks for the future value of an ordinary annuity, so:

$$FV_{\text{annuity}} = PMT \times FVIFA_{i,n}$$

$$FVIFA_{8\%,20} = \frac{(1+0.08)^{20}-1}{0.08} = 45.76196$$

$$FV_{\text{annuity}} = 50,000 \times 45.76196 = \$2,288,098.21$$

Tip

Incorrect rounding can cause wrong answers when doing problems and often leads to frustration. Always carry as many digits as you can forward in each step.

A Note about Rounding

A good rule of thumb is to carry enough significant digits so that you can round your solution to the nearest penny. The future value of an annuity is very sensitive to changes in the interest rate.

Solving for Payments in a Future Value Annuity Problem

At times you will know how much you want to accumulate. The question will be how much you need to *save* each period to reach the goal. We can solve for the payments by substituting the definition of the annuity factor, FVIFA, into Equation 4.1, which yields:

$$FV_{\text{annuity}} = PMT \times FVIFA_{i,n}$$

We can easily rearrange terms to solve for the payments.

$$PMT = \frac{FV_{\text{annuity}}}{FVIFA_{i,n}}$$

Example 4.2 Solving for Payments

You hope to retire in 35 years and you need $1,000,000 in the bank to live the life you want after retirement. You can earn 7% per year on your investments. How much must you save every year to reach your goal?

Digital Downloads

Example 4.2 Solving for Payments.xlsx
https://catalog.flatworldknowledge.com/a/34711/Example_4_2_Solving_for_Payments-9a87.xlsx

SOLUTION

Spreadsheet Solution

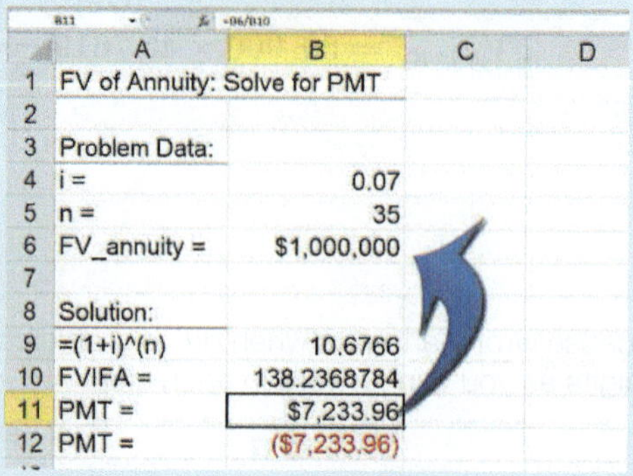

	A	B	C	D
1	FV of Annuity: Solve for PMT			
2				
3	Problem Data:			
4	i =	0.07		
5	n =	35		
6	FV_annuity =	$1,000,000		
7				
8	Solution:			
9	=(1+i)^(n)	10.6766		
10	FVIFA =	138.2368784		
11	PMT =	$7,233.96		
12	PMT =	($7,233.96)		

View in the online reader

Algebraic Solution

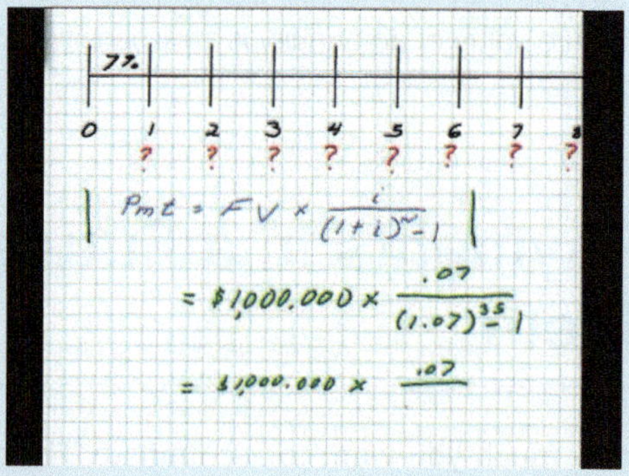

View in the online reader

Calculator Solution

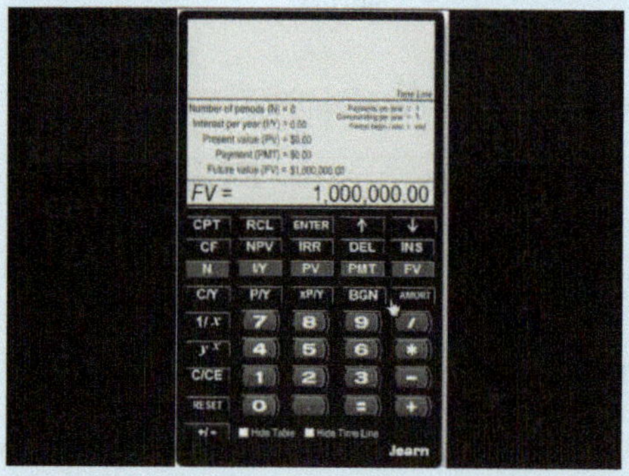

View in the online reader

Find the payment needed to accumulate $1 million.

$$FV_{\text{annuity}} = 1 \text{ million}$$
$$i = 7\%$$
$$n = 35 \text{ years}$$
$$PMT = \frac{FV_{\text{annuity}}}{FVIFA_{i,n}}$$
$$FVIFA_{7\%,35} = \frac{(1+0.07)^{35} - 1}{0.07} = 138.23688$$
$$PMT = \frac{\$1,000,000}{138.23688} = \$7,233.96$$

You will have to save $7,233.96 per year to have $1 million in your retirement fund after 35 years.

Future Value of Annuity Due

As we noted earlier, when an annuity's payments occur at the beginning of each period, we call the cash flows an annuity due. Figure 4.3 shows two variations of the 3-year bank deposit example (with annual deposits of $100). The example on the top line has end-of-period timing and is an ordinary annuity. The example on the bottom line has beginning-of-year payments and is an annuity due.

FIGURE 4.3

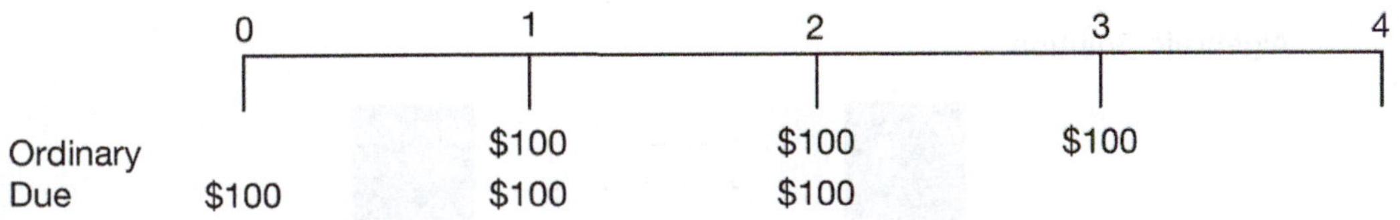

The equation for the FV of an annuity, (Equation 4.1) introduced earlier, provides the FV at the point in time when the last payment is made. When we apply our equation to the annuity due in Figure 4.3, we get a FV at the end of period 2, not 3. To get the FV at the end of period 3, we need to move the balance forward one period. This is done by multiplying the accumulated total at period 2 by $(1+i)$.

More generally, for any size of payment and number of time periods, the future value of an annuity due is equal to:

EQUATION 4.3

$$FV_{\text{annuity due}} = PMT \times \frac{(1+i)^n - 1}{i} \times (1+i)$$

We can simplify this by using the future value interest factor (Equation 4.2) for an (ordinary) annuity:

$$FV_{\text{annuity duc}} = PMT \times FVIFA_{i,n} \times (1+i)$$

The only difference between Equation 4.1 and Equation 4.3 is the last term $(1+i)$. Because of their similarity, we won't introduce a separate annuity due interest factor. Instead, we simply multiply the ordinary annuity factor by $(1+i)$.

Tip

Remember when using your financial calculator or a spreadsheet the number of actual payments in your annuity has to match number of periods you input. You can't find the FV of an annuity due simply by adding a period because this would assume too many payments have been made.

Example 4.3 FV of an Ordinary Annuity and an Annuity Due

You have been offered an investment opportunity that will pay you $5,000 per year for 6 years. What is the value of this stream of cash flows at the end of year 6 if you receive payments at the end of each year and you require a return of 7%? What if you receive payments at the beginning of each year?

SOLUTION

Spreadsheet Solution

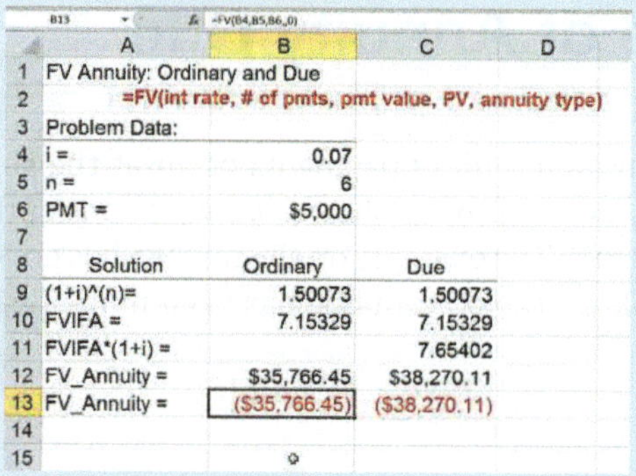

	A	B	C	D
1	FV Annuity: Ordinary and Due			
2	=FV(int rate, # of pmts, pmt value, PV, annuity type)			
3	Problem Data:			
4	i =	0.07		
5	n =	6		
6	PMT =	$5,000		
7				
8	Solution	Ordinary	Due	
9	(1+i)^(n)=	1.50073	1.50073	
10	FVIFA =	7.15329	7.15329	
11	FVIFA*(1+i) =		7.65402	
12	FV_Annuity =	$35,766.45	$38,270.11	
13	FV_Annuity =	($35,766.45)	($38,270.11)	
14				
15				

View in the online reader

Algebraic Solution

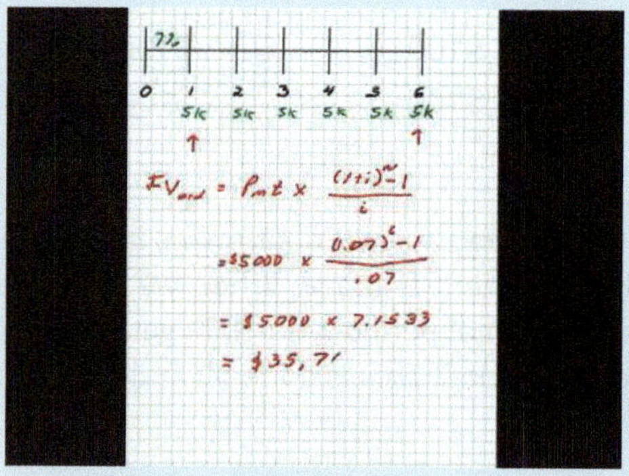

View in the online reader

Calculator Solution

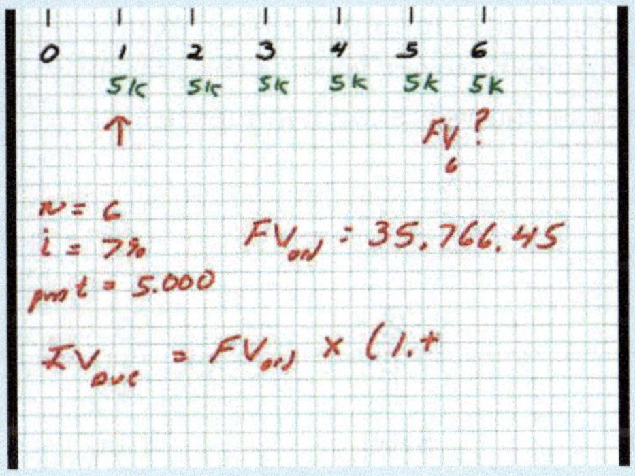

View in the online reader

In this example,

$$PMT = 5,000$$
$$i = 7\%$$
$$n = 6$$

for the ordinary annuity timing, the solution is:

$$FV_{\text{ord annuity}} = PMT \times \frac{(1+i)^n - 1}{i}$$

$$FV_{\text{ord annuity}} = \$5,000 \times \frac{(1.07)^6 - 1}{0.07} = \$35,766.45$$

For the annuity due timing, the solution is:

$$FV_{\text{annuity due}} = PMT \times \frac{(1+i)^n - 1}{i} \times (1+i)$$

$$FV_{\text{annuity due}} = \$5,000 \times \frac{(1.07)^6 - 1}{0.07} \times (1.07) = \$38,270.11$$

4.2 Present Value of Streams of Payments

Just as we sometimes need to find the future value of a stream of equal cash flows, we also may need to find the *present value* of a stream of equal cash flows. In this section, we find the present value of an ordinary annuity, an annuity due, and a perpetuity. Note that if the cash flows are different from each other, there's no equation-based shortcut. You have to compute the present value of each cash flow separately and add them together using a calculator or a spreadsheet.

Present Value of an Ordinary Annuity

Consider the following present value annuity problem. You won the lottery and the prize is $100 per year at the end of each of the next 4 years. What is the present value of the prize if the interest rate is 10%? The timeline of the cash flows is shown in Figure 4.4.

FIGURE 4.4

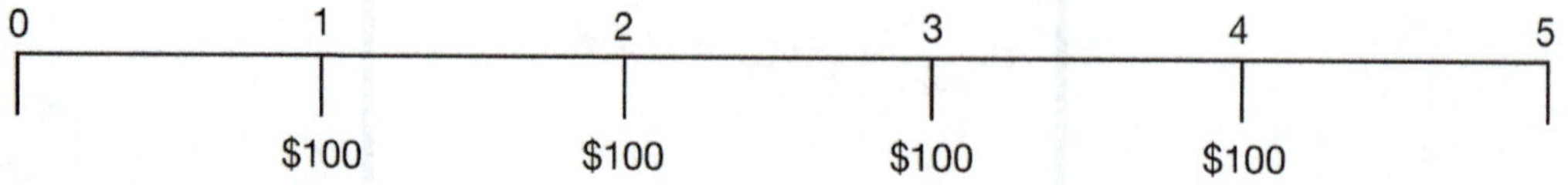

One way to find the present value of the prize annuity is to find the present value of each cash flow separately and add them together. This "longhand" approach is shown in Figure 4.5.

FIGURE 4.5

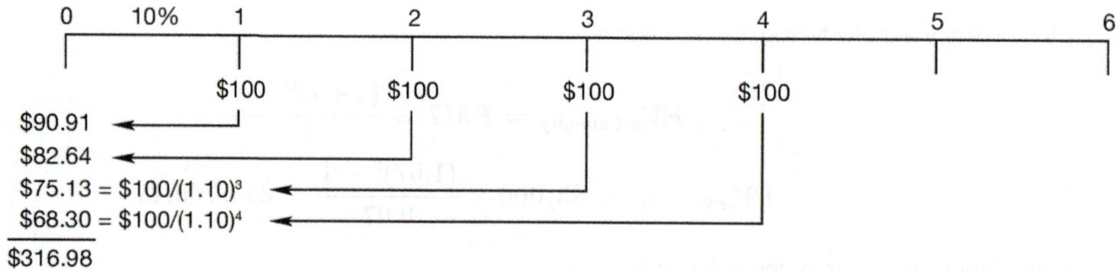

Following this method, the general expression for the present value of an annuity is:

$$PV_{\text{annuity}} = PMT \times \left[\frac{1}{(1+i)^1} + \frac{1}{(1+i)^2} + \cdots + \frac{1}{(1+i)^n} \right]$$

This is another example of a geometric progression that has a standardized solution. This solution to the equation can be written as:

EQUATION 4.4

$$PV_{\text{annuity}} = PMT \times \frac{1 - \frac{1}{(1+i)^n}}{i}$$

where

$$PMT = \text{the periodic payment in the annuity}$$
$$i = \text{the interest rate}$$
$$n = \text{the number of payments}$$

Explain It: PVIFA

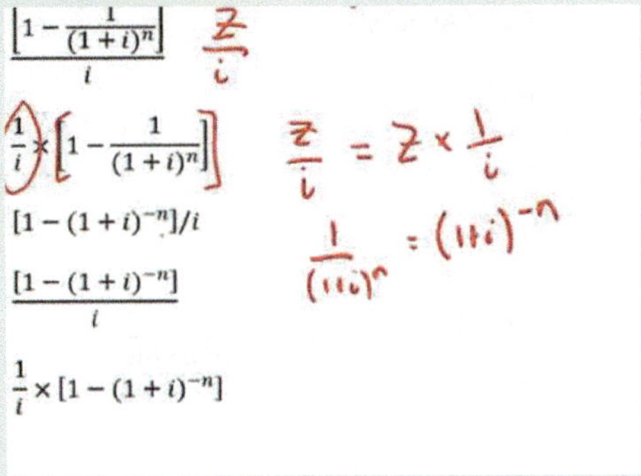

View in the online reader

The term after the multiplication sign in Equation 4.4 is the **present value interest factor for an annuity (PVIFA)**. The acronym is useful because it is shorter than writing out the whole formula and here we use it interchangeably with the formula.

present value interest factor for an annuity (PVIFA)

PVIFA is the present value of an n-period ordinary annuity at rate i with payments of one dollar.

EQUATION 4.5

$$PVIFA_{i,n} = \frac{1 - \frac{1}{(1+i)^n}}{i}$$

Example 4.4 PV of Ordinary Annuity

Digital Downloads

Example 4.4 PV of Ordinary Annuity.xls
https://catalog.flatworldknowledge.com/a/34711/Example_4_4_PV_of_Ordinary_Annuity-7a61.xls

You won the lottery! The prize is $100 paid at the end of each of the next 4 years. What is the present value of the lottery annuity if the interest rate is 10%?

SOLUTION

Spreadsheet Solution

B10 f_x =(1-B9)/B4

	A	B	C
1	PV of Annuity		
2			
3	Problem Data:		
4	i =	0.1	
5	n =	4	
6	PMT =	$100	
7			
8	Solution:		
9	1/(1+i)^(n) =	0.6830	
10	PVIFA =	3.169865446	
11	PV =	$316.99	

View in the online reader

Algebraic Solution

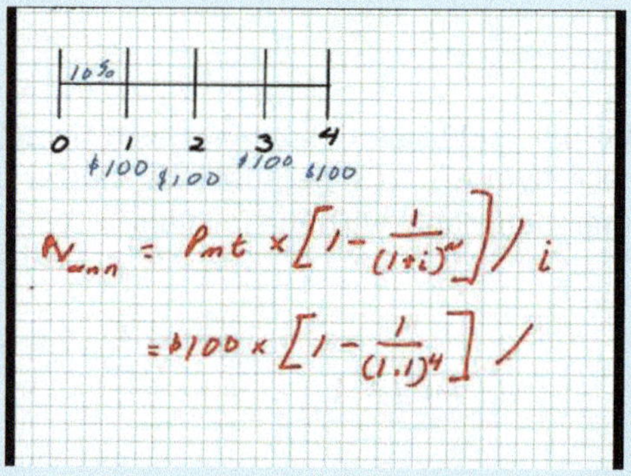

View in the online reader

Calculator Solution

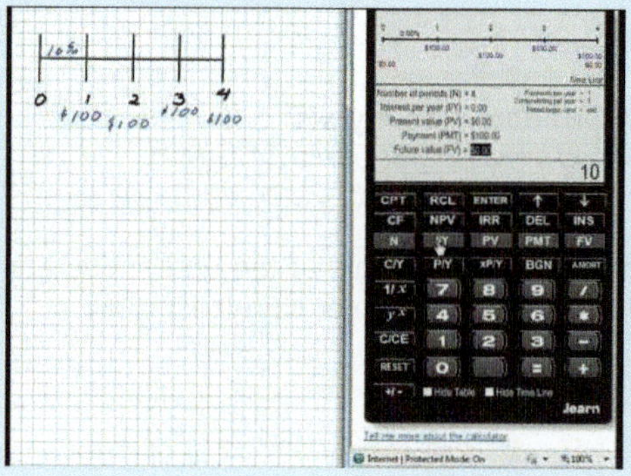

View in the online reader

In this example,

$$PMT = 100$$
$$i = 10\%$$
$$n = 4$$

this question asks for the present value of an ordinary annuity, so:

$$PV_{\text{annuity}} = PMT \times PVIFA_{i,n}$$

$$PVIFA_{10\%,4} = \frac{1 - \frac{1}{(1+0.10)^4}}{0.10} = 3.16987$$

$$PV_{\text{annuity}} = \$100 \times 3.16987 = \$316.99$$

We've just discovered that the present value of a four-period stream of \$100 cash flows is \$316.99. This is the present value of the lottery prize. You would be indifferent between the four payments of \$100 or a \$316.99 lump sum today.

It is also illuminating to think about the present value of the annuity from the point of view of the government (which runs the lottery). If the government has \$316.99 to invest today, then it has just enough money to fund each of the \$100 payouts. The government treasurer could invest the \$316.99 at 10% and have \$348.69 1 year later. The first \$100 prize is then subtracted from the balance, which is reinvested. One year later, the balance is \$273.56 and an additional \$100 is subtracted. This process continues as shown in Figure 4.6 until the final \$100 is subtracted and the remaining balance is zero.

FIGURE 4.6

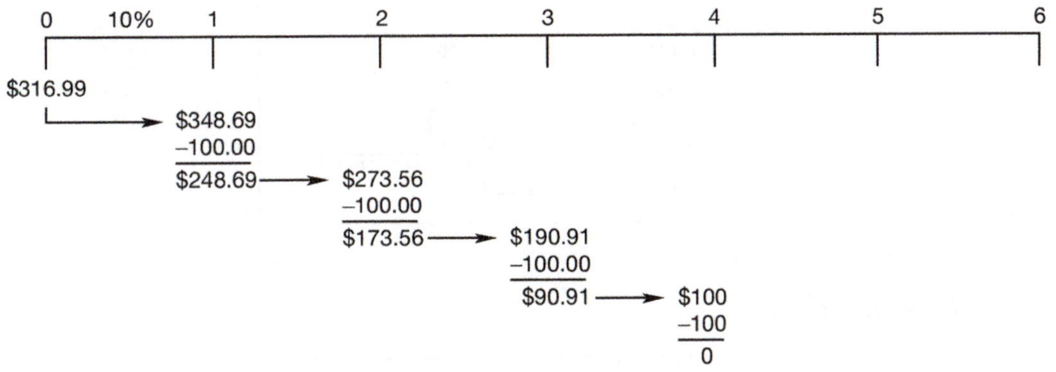

This example provides an important clue as to when you'll want to use present value equations. Anytime you want to know how much you need today to create a future cash flow stream, find the present value of the cash flows. For example, if you plan to retire at age 65 and will need \$50,000 per year for the next 30 years, you compute the PV of a 30-year \$50,000 annuity. (If we assume an 8% return, then you would need \$562,889 in your retirement account to meet this cash requirement.)

Finding the Interest Rate in a PV Annuity Problem

Example 4.5 Finding the Interest Rate

Digital Downloads

Example 4.5 Finding the Interest Rate.xlsx
https://catalog.flatworldknowledge.com/a/34711/Example_4_5_Finding_the_Interest_Rate-e365.xlsx

Let's look at the retirement question from another viewpoint. Suppose you have saved $562,889 and want to withdraw $50,000 per year for 30 years. What rate of return would you need to earn?

SOLUTION

Spreadsheet Solution

	A	B	C	D
1	PV of Annuity--Solve for i			
2				
3	Problem Data:			
4	i =	0.1		
5	n =	30		
6	PMT =	$50,000		
7				
8	Solution:			
9	1/(1+i)^(n) =	0.0573		
10	PVIFA =	9.426914467		
11	PV_Annuity =	$471,345.72	($471,345.72)	
12	Goal =	$562,889.00		
13				

View in the online reader

Algebraic Solution

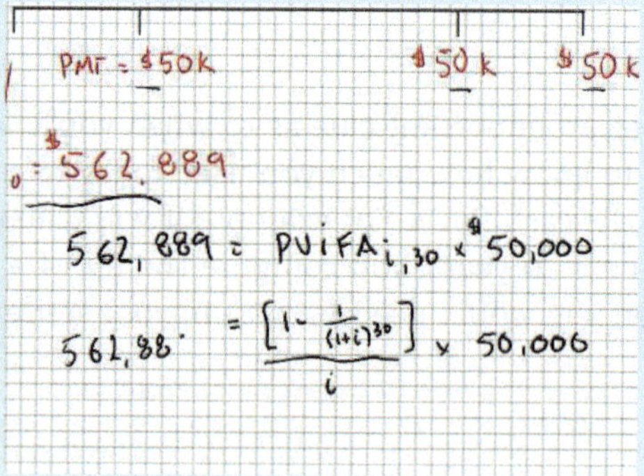

View in the online reader

The question can be answered using the present value annuity formula (Equation 4.4). In this example, we know the present value, the annuity payments, and the term. The unknown is the interest rate. Since this is a problem with one equation and one unknown, we can insert the variables that we know into Equation 4.4 and solve for *i*.

$$\$562,889 = \$50,000 \times \frac{1 - \frac{1}{(1+i)^{30}}}{i}$$

The rate, *i*, appears in two places, so simplifying for the rate is not going to be easy.

To avoid the algebra, let's get the computer to solve for the rate using trial and error. Excel has a tool called Goal Seeker that is perfect for this job. You can also use your calculator to compute the answer.

The solution value is $i = 8.00\%$ If you start with $562,889 and invest the remaining balance each year at 8%, then you will be able to withdraw $50,000 per year for 30 years.

Tip

If $n \geq 5$, then there is no solution for the roots of the polynomial, so don't try solving this algebraically!

Present Value of an Annuity Due

The retirement annuity problem just presented assumes end-of-period payments. The first payment occurs 1 year from today. The alternative timing assumption is beginning of period payments as shown in Figure 4.7. The PV of an annuity equation presented earlier provides the PV on period before the first payment is due. Just as we did for future value, we adjust our equation to multiply by $1+i$ to find the PV of an annuity due at time 0.

FIGURE 4.7

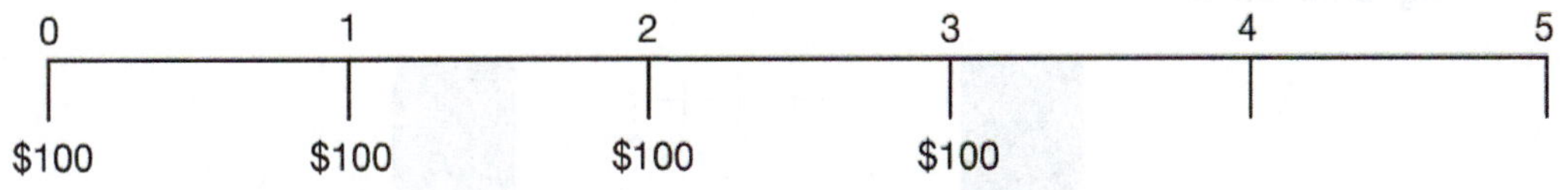

The equation for finding the present value of an annuity due is:

EQUATION 4.6

$$PV_{\text{annuity due}} = PMT \times \frac{1-\frac{1}{(1+i)^n}}{i} \times (1+i)$$

We can simplify this by using the present value interest factor for an (ordinary) annuity:

$$PV_{\text{annuity due}} = PMT \times PVIFA_{i,n} \times (1+i)$$

The only difference between Equation 4.6 and Equation 4.4 is the last term, $(1+i)$. Because of their similarity, we won't introduce a separate annuity due interest factor. Instead, we simply multiply the ordinary annuity factor by $(1+i)$.

Example 4.6 Present Value of an Annuity Due

Digital Downloads

Example 4.6 PV of an Annuity Due.xlsx
https://catalog.flatworldknowledge.com/a/34711/Example_4_6_PV_of_an_Annuity_Due-a6ee.xlsx

You won the lottery! The prize is $100 paid at the beginning of each of the next 4 years (starting today). What is the present value of the lottery annuity if the interest rate is 10%?

SOLUTION

Spreadsheet Solution

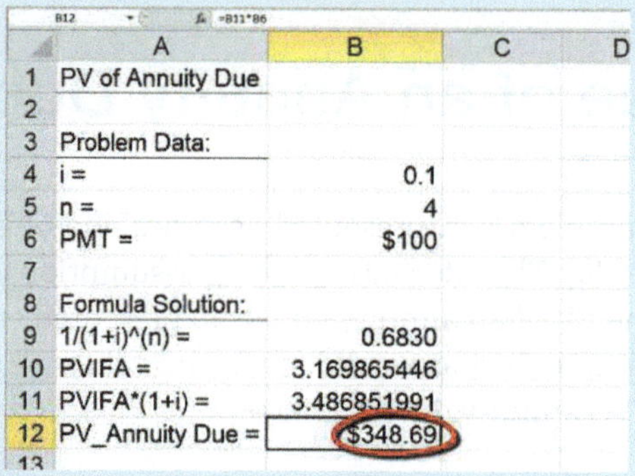

	A	B	C	D
1	PV of Annuity Due			
2				
3	Problem Data:			
4	i =	0.1		
5	n =	4		
6	PMT =	$100		
7				
8	Formula Solution:			
9	1/(1+i)^(n) =	0.6830		
10	PVIFA =	3.169865446		
11	PVIFA*(1+i) =	3.486851991		
12	PV_Annuity Due =	$348.69		
13				

View in the online reader

Algebraic Solution

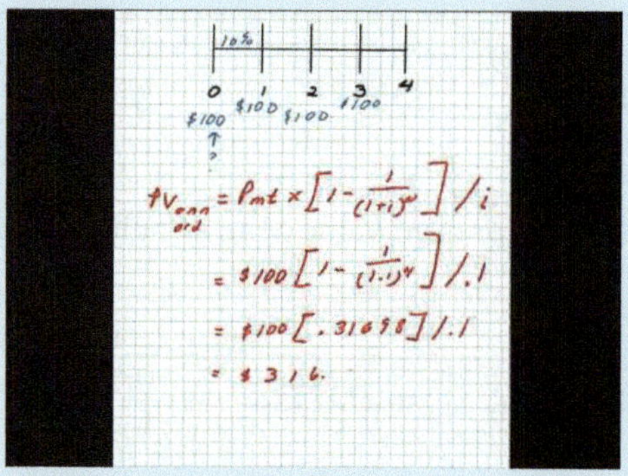

View in the online reader

Calculator Solution

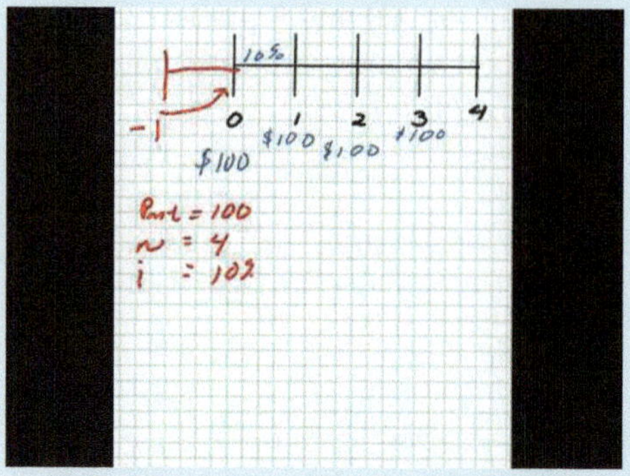

View in the online reader

In this example,

$$PMT = 100$$
$$i = 10\%$$
$$n = 4$$

the question asks for the present value of an annuity due, so:

$$PV_{\text{annuity due}} = PMT \times PVIFA_{i,n} \times (1+i)$$

$$PVIFA_{10\%,4} = \frac{1-\frac{1}{(1+0.10)^4}}{0.10} = 3.16987$$

$$PV_{\text{annuity due}} = \$100 \times 3.16987 \times (1.10) = \$348.69$$

Present Value of a Level Perpetuity

Annuities are streams of equal payments that go on for a fixed number of periods. If the annuity continues forever, it's called a **perpetuity**. The term *perpetuity* comes from the word *perpetual*, which means "continual or everlasting."

perpetuity

A stream of fixed payments paid at regular time intervals that goes on forever.

There are a few real examples of perpetuities. One example is a Consol bond (short for *consolidated annuity*) issued by the Bank of England. Consol bonds were perpetual and paid a fixed rate of interest. The first consol was issued in 1752 with an annual interest rate of 3.5%.

The cash flows from a level perpetuity (with a $100 payment) are illustrated by the following timeline. Note that the timeline incorporates an end-of-period timing assumption: the first cash flow on the timeline is at date 1.

FIGURE 4.8

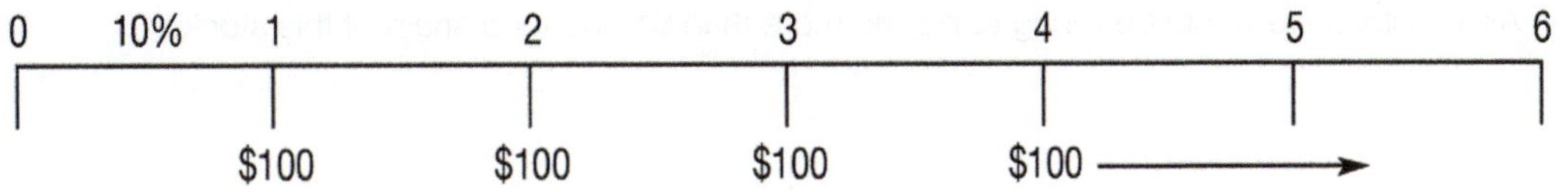

Tip

A level perpetuity has a series of equal payments that continue forever. In another chapter we introduce growing perpetuities that have payments that grow at a constant rate forever.

To derive the equation for the present value of a perpetuity, consider the following. Think of the cash flows in Figure 4.8 as a series of withdrawals from a bank account that pays 10% interest. At the start of each year, starting at time 0, you will invest an amount in the account. At the end of the year you will withdraw interest and reinvest the principal. How much do you have to invest at time 0 to be able to withdraw $100 at the end of year 1? The first interest payment at the end of 1 year is: $Interest = Principal \times i$. You want interest of $100 and the interest rate is 10%, so the principal is $1,000. Dividing both sides of the equation by the interest rate yields a formula for the principal that you must invest. Since this investment strategy (invest $1,000, withdraw $100 interest, and reinvest $1,000) yields a perpetuity of $100, then the equation for the principal is also the equation for the *PV* of a perpetuity (where the annual cash flow is denoted *PMT*).

EQUATION 4.7

$$PV = \frac{PMT}{i}$$

Example 4.7 Preferred Share Valuation Using the Present Value of a Perpetuity

Suppose we want to determine the present value of the dividends paid by a share of preferred stock. We know that the stock promises to pay the holder an annual $100 dividend forever, and we assume a 10% interest rate. We also assume that the first dividend will be paid in 1 year.

SOLUTION

Algebraic Solution

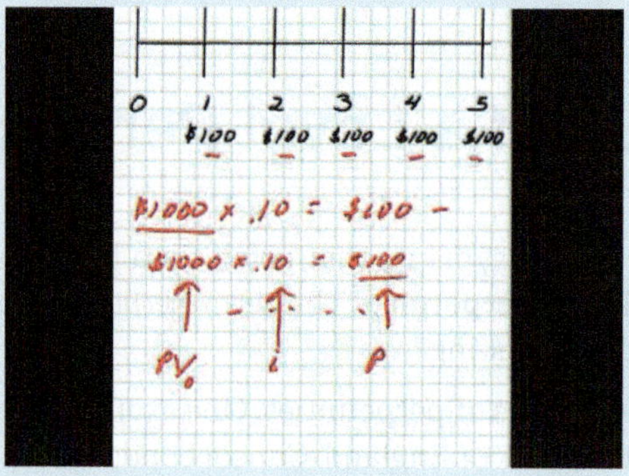

View in the online reader

$$PMT = 100$$
$$i = 10\%$$

This question asks for the present value of a level perpetuity, so:

$$PV_{\text{perpetuity}} = PMT/i = \$100/0.10 = \$1,000.00$$

As investors, we would be willing to pay no more than $1,000 for a share of this stock.

4.3 Help with Advanced Time Value Problems

The equations presented in this chapter are not difficult to calculate and do not, of themselves, present an obstacle to solving time value of money problems. The main obstacle that students face in solving advanced time value of money problems is choosing the correct equation to apply to a given scenario. This section provides some general ideas to aid in solving time value problems and presents a class of problems, imbedded annuities, that many students find difficult.

Tips for Solving Time Value of Money Problems

Explain It: Solving TVM Problems

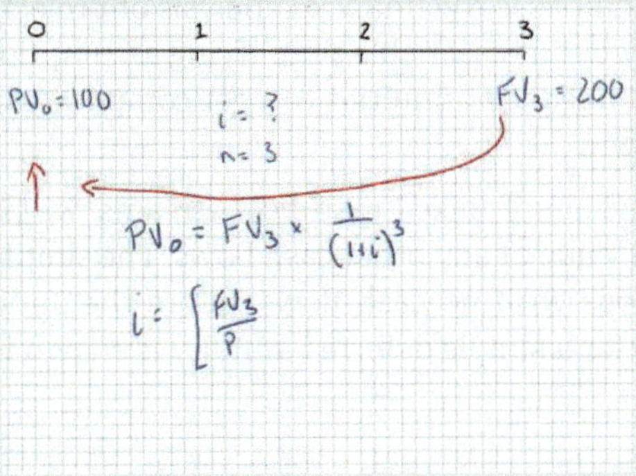

View in the online reader

Almost all time value of money problems are word problems, but to solve them they must be expressed in the form of an equation with one unknown. Luckily, almost every problem that we confront (in this text) involves only one unknown and one equation. In time value of money mathematics, the equation is known as an **equation of value**. An equation of value is an equality between cash inflows and outflows after they have all been accumulated or discounted to a common point in time. This common point in time is called the **focal date**. The focal date is central to solving time value of money problems. Because money is more valuable the sooner it is received, we can't equate a dollar today with a dollar next year. Either we accumulate today's dollar to next year or discount next year's dollar to today. In many examples, the focal date is arbitrary; it simply acts as a common point to which we can bring all payments so that an equation of value can be obtained.

equation of value

An equality between cash inflows and outflows after they have all been accumulated or discounted to a common point in time.

focal date

A common point in time to which we bring all payments so that an equation of value can be obtained.

To determine how to solve TVM problems, and to pick which equation of value to use, follow these steps:

1. Review the information given in the problem and jot down what is known.
2. Draw a timeline.
3. Select a focal date. There are only two directions that you can move money: forward or backward. If you pick a focal date at the end of the timeline, then you are moving cash forward (a future value). If you pick a focal date at the beginning of the timeline, then you are moving cash backward (discounting).
4. Determine whether the cash flows are lump sums or annuities. If you have a single cash flow or if there are multiple cash flows of varying amounts, then you are dealing with lump sums. If there are multiple cash flows with the same value, then you have an annuity. (If the annuity goes on forever, then you have a perpetuity.)
5. Determine the compounding frequency of the problem (e.g., annual, monthly, or weekly) and decide whether the cash flows are beginning-of-period or end-of-period.

Here's one last suggestion. Not every problem can be solved immediately with one of the basic equations of value presented in this chapter. If you're attempting to solve a problem and find you can't determine what to plug into the equation for each of the variables, it may be because you're using the wrong equation of value. Try another.

Imbedded Annuities

imbedded annuity

An annuity within a cash flow stream that includes payments other than the series of fixed payments.

deferred annuity

A series of equal payments that does not begin immediately, but rather at some future date.

It's not unusual that cash flows have some payments that differ, as well as some that are the same. When an annuity is mixed with other irregular payments, we have an **imbedded annuity**. The most common use of imbedded annuities is the financial analysis of projects. We can often estimate the first few cash flows accurately, but a reasonable simplifying assumption is that later cash flows are all the same. Problems with imbedded annuities can get complicated, so we want to take time to walk through an example slowly.

To solve for the present value of mixed cash flow streams, we find the present value of the annuity, then add the present value of any other cash flows. The simplest mixed cash flow is one in which there are several periods with no cash flows before the annuity begins. This is called a **deferred annuity**. A timeline for a simple deferred annuity is shown in Figure 4.9. We will assume an interest rate of 10%.

FIGURE 4.9

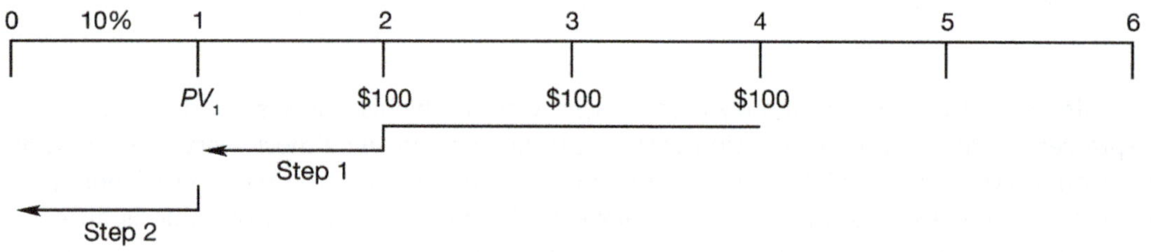

We solve this problem in two steps. First, we apply the present value method to the annuity. When we do this using Equation 4.4, we find the value of the annuity one period before the first payment. (We label this point as PV_1 on the timeline.)

STEP 1:

$$PV_1 = \$100 \times \left[1 - \frac{1}{(1.1)^3}\right] / 0.1$$

$$PV_1 = \$100 \times 2.4869 = \$248.69$$

We're not finished yet because we need the value at time 0, not at time 1 (the end of the first period). To move the value of the annuity back in time one more period, we treat the solution to Step 1 as a lump sum on date 1 and find its present value:

STEP 2:

$$PV_0 = PV_1 \times \frac{1}{(1+i)^1}$$

$$PV_0 = \$248.69 \times 0.909 = \$226.07$$

Let's review carefully what we've done. Step 1 discounts the value of the three-period annuity to the end of period 1.

Tip

The number of periods in the annuity is always equal to the number of payments, even when the annuity is deferred. One way to view ordinary annuities is to recognize that the annuity begins one period before the first payment is made and ends when the last payment is made.

Step 2 discounts the present value of the annuity back to time 0.

A slightly more complex example has two annuities. In the following example, find the present value of each annuity separately and add them together.

Tip

The most common mistake students make when solving these problems is not recognizing that the *PV* of an ordinary annuity calculation provides a result one period *before* the first cash flow.

Example 4.8 Present Value of Two Annuities

Digital Downloads

Example 4.8 PV of Two Annuities.xlsx
https://catalog.flatworldknowledge.com/a/34711/Example_4_8_PV_of_Two_Annuities-57c1.xlsx

Suppose you have two 3-year annuities, one beginning one period from now (with $200 payments) and another beginning four periods from now (with $100 payments). What are the present values of each of the annuities, and what is their combined PV? Assume an interest rate of 10%.

SOLUTION

Spreadsheet Solution

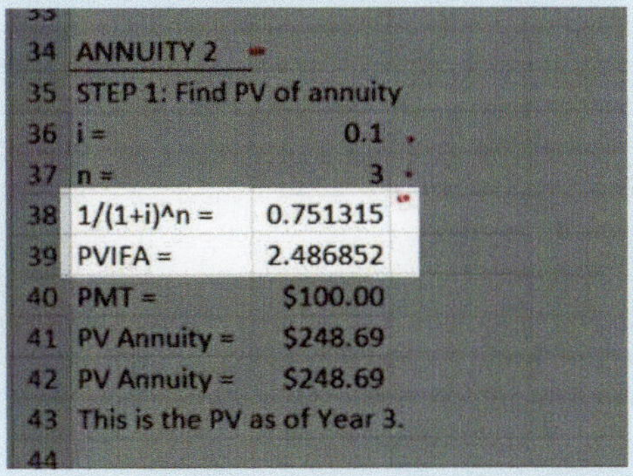

34	ANNUITY 2	
35	STEP 1: Find PV of annuity	
36	i =	0.1
37	n =	3
38	1/(1+i)^n =	0.751315
39	PVIFA =	2.486852
40	PMT =	$100.00
41	PV Annuity =	$248.69
42	PV Annuity =	$248.69
43	This is the PV as of Year 3.	
44		

View in the online reader

Algebraic Solution

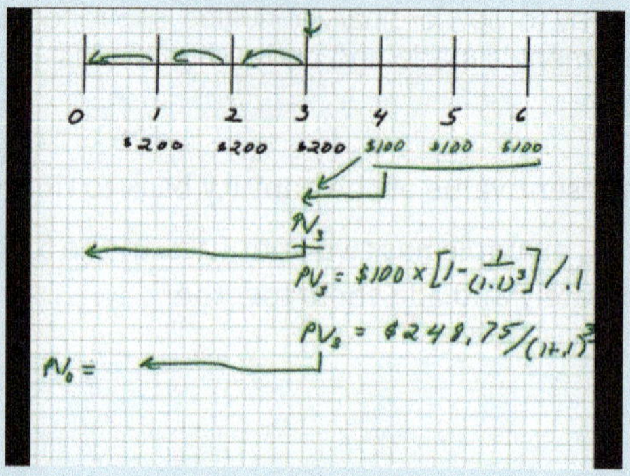

View in the online reader

Calculator Solution

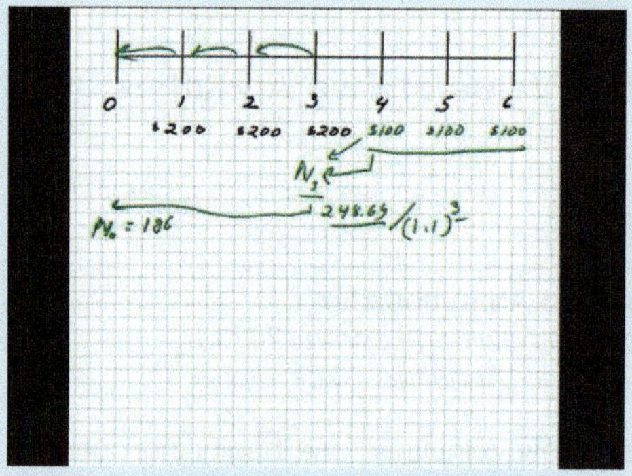

View in the online reader

We begin by drawing a timeline. These are especially important with complicated problems like this one.

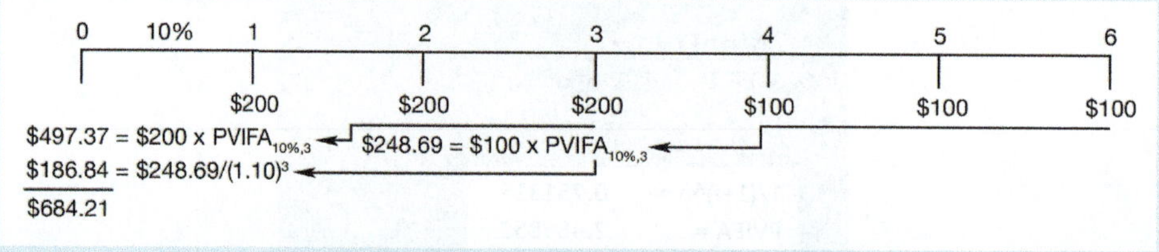

The focal date of this problem is time 0. To solve this problem, find the present value of each annuity separately (at time 0) and then sum the two present values. The combined present value is $\$497.37 + \$186.84 = \$684.21$.

4.4 Balloon Loans

The next two sections present an overview of two types of loans: (1) **balloon loan** and (2) **amortized loan**. We start with balloon loans to establish a basic understanding of how interest is calculated for a loan. Second, we present amortized loans. Car loans and mortgages are examples of amortized loans. First, we show how to calculate the payments for an amortized loan. Then we show how to separate the loan payments into their principal and interest components and how to calculate the principal outstanding using an **amortization schedule**.

A balloon loan is a loan where the principal and interest (sometimes just the principal) are paid at the end of the loan term. The end-of-term payment is referred to as the balloon payment.

Balloon loans are very common in business. For example, short-term construction loans are often structured with a balloon loan during the construction phase followed by a long-term amortized loan.

Here, we only analyze balloon loans where the balloon payment includes both the principal and interest. In that case, the balloon payment is just the future value of the principal when compounded at the loan rate (*i*) over the loan term (*n*). The equation of value for balloon loans is just the basic future value equation.

EQUATION 4.8

$$Balloon_n = FV_n = Principal_0 \times (1 + i)^n$$

Example 4.9 Balloon Loan: Solve for the Balloon Payment

Your friend, Ernest Defraud, wants to borrow $1,000 for 3 years. Let's assume that you want to earn interest at 5% compounded annually. What is the balloon payment? How much interest do you earn on the loan?

SOLUTION

Algebraic Solution

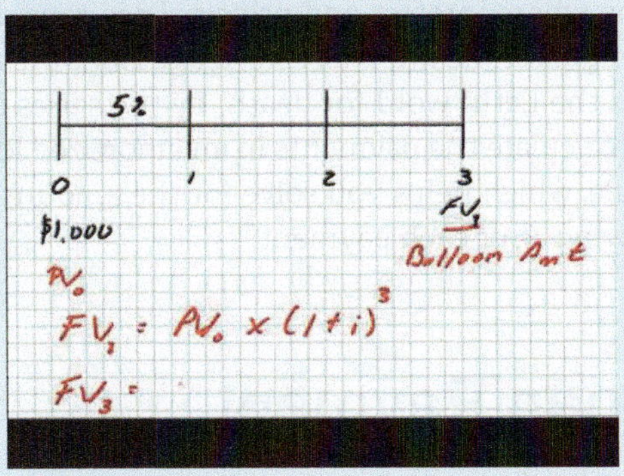

View in the online reader

balloon loan

A loan where zero or low payments are due while the loan is outstanding and the balance is due at maturity.

amortized loan

A loan where the borrower repays the loan with level and regular periodic payments. Each payment incorporates a blend of interest and principal. The payments are applied first to interest and the remainder is applied to principal.

amortization schedule

A complete table of periodic loan payments, showing the amount of principal and the amount of interest that compromise each payment until the loan is paid off at the end of its term.

Calculator Solution

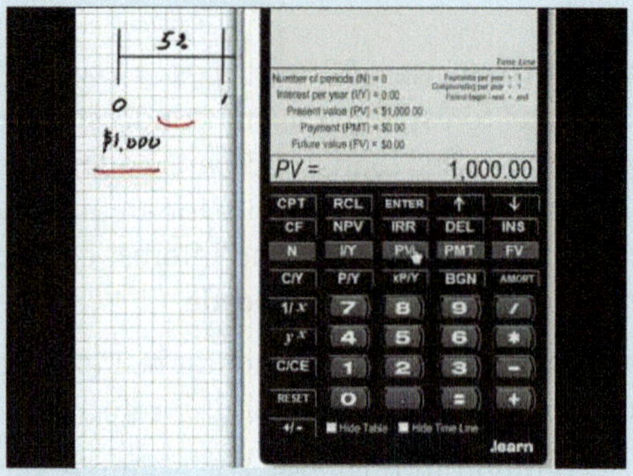

View in the online reader

$$Principal = \$1,000$$
$$i = 5\%$$
$$Balloon_3 = \$1,000 \times (1+i)^n$$
$$Balloon_3 = \$1,000 \times (1.05)^3 = \$1,157.63$$

Since the principal of the loan is $1,000, the amount of interest earned by the lender is:

$$Interest\ earned = \$1,157.63 - \$1,000 = \$157.63$$

4.5 Amortized Loans

Amortized loans are loans where interest and principal are repaid with a constant series of payments, which are paid at regular time intervals. Mortgage loans are an example. The loan obligation is literally killed (*mortis* is the Latin word for death) by the series of constant payments. The first subsection shows how to calculate the payments in an amortized loan and the second presents the loan amortization schedule, which helps you solve for the amount of interest paid with each payment and the principal owing after each payment.

Amortized Loan Payment

Let's reconsider the $1,000 loan to Ernest Defraud. Instead of a balloon loan, assume that the loan is structured as an amortized loan with three annual, end-of-year payments as shown in the following timeline.

FIGURE 4.10

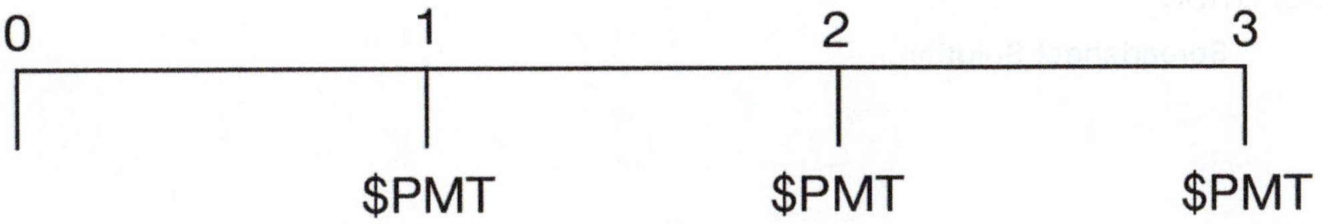

What set of end-of-year payments does the lender require? Here is a hint: Wouldn't the lender be happy to exchange the principal for the payments if the present value of the payments is the same as the principal? The hint suggests that the focal point is time 0. Notice that the payments look like an ordinary annuity. We know how to find the present value of annuity payments (recall Equation 4.4 and Equation 4.5). The equation of value for an amortized loan is the equality between the principal and the present value of ordinary annuity payments.

EQUATION 4.9

$$Principal = PMT \times PVIFA_{i,n}$$

We call Equation 4.9 the amortized loan equation. The equation involves four variables: the principal, the payments, the interest rate, and the number of payments. We can use it to solve for any one variable if the other three are given. In the Ernest Defraud example, the unknown is the annuity payment (*PMT*). We can rearrange Eq. 4.9 to solve for payments as follows.

EQUATION 4.10

$$PMT = \frac{\text{Principal}}{PVIFA_{i,n}}$$

For the loan to Ernest, the interest rate is 5% $(i = 5)$ and there are three payments $(n = 3)$. So, $PVIFA_{5\%,3} = 2.723248$. The amortized loan payments are:

$$PMT = \$1,000/2.723248 = \$367.21$$

reinvestment rate assumption

The assumption that as funds are received they will be reinvested at the interest rate required by the investor.

Example 4.10 Amortized Loans, Interest, and the Reinvestment Rate

Digital Downloads

Example 4.10 Amortized Loans Interest and the Reinvestment Rate.xlsx
https://catalog.flatworldknowledge.com/a/34711/Example_4_10_Amortized_Loans_Interest_and_the_Reinvestment_Rate-dfd7.xlsx

Your friend, Ernest Defraud, wants to borrow $1,000 for 3 years. He has proposed an amortized loan with payments of $367.21. What is the future value of the payments if you can reinvest the first and second payments at 5%? How much interest do you earn from reinvestment and how much interest is included in the payments themselves?

SOLUTION

Spreadsheet Solution

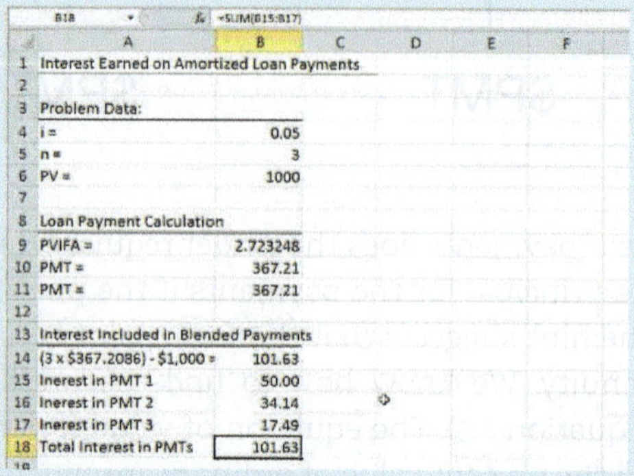

B18 =SUM(B15:B17)

	A	B
1	Interest Earned on Amortized Loan Payments	
2		
3	Problem Data:	
4	i =	0.05
5	n =	3
6	PV =	1000
7		
8	Loan Payment Calculation	
9	PVIFA =	2.723248
10	PMT =	367.21
11	PMT =	367.21
12		
13	Interest Included in Blended Payments	
14	(3 x $367.2086) - $1,000 =	101.63
15	Inerest in PMT 1	50.00
16	Inerest in PMT 2	34.14
17	Inerest in PMT 3	17.49
18	Total Interest in PMTs	101.63

View in the online reader

Algebraic Solution

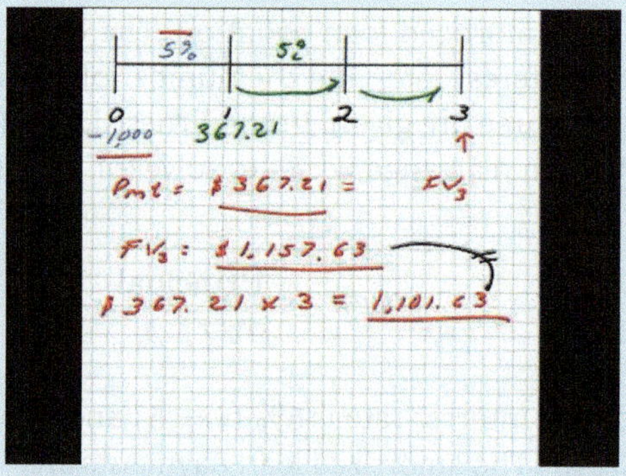

View in the online reader

At year 3, the future value of the payments can be calculated by finding the future value of a three-period ordinary annuity at a rate of 5%. The future value of the annuity is:

$$FV_{\text{annuity}} = PMT \times \frac{(1+i)^n - 1}{i}$$

$$FV_{\text{annuity}} = 367.21 \times \frac{(1.05)^3 - 1}{0.05} = \$1,157.63$$

The amount of interest earned due to reinvestment is just the difference between the future value of the three payments and the sum of the three payments. The sum is what you would have at year 3 if you didn't earn any interest by reinvesting (for example, if you put the payments in your mattress)!

$$\textit{Reinvestment interest} = \$1,157.63 - (3 \times \$367.21) = \$56$$

The amount of interest that is included in the three payments is the difference between the sum of the three payments and the principal of the loan.

$$\textit{Interest in payments} = (3 \times \$367.21) - \$1,000 = \$101.63$$

This example highlights two important points about amortized loans:

1. Interest on amortized loan payments comes in two forms: (1) each payment contains interest and (2) the lender receives the payments before the end of the term and so can earn interest by investing them.
2. The future value of the amortized loan payments is only equal to the balloon payment if the lender can reinvest intermediate payments at the loan rate (try it with a different rate to see). Thus, lenders only earn *i*% on amortized loans if they can reinvest at *i*%. This is called the **reinvestment rate assumption**.

Example 4.11 Solving for Amortized Loan Payments: the Car Loan

Digital Downloads

Example 4.11 Solving for Amortized Loan Payments.xlsx
https://catalog.flatworldknowledge.com/a/34710/Example_4_11_Solving_for_Amortized_Loan_Payments-eb24.xlsx

Source: Pavlo Baliukh / Shutterstock.com

Car loans are amortized loans. Consider the Ferrari California, shown here. The California has a V8 engine that generates 450 hp. Its top speed is 193 mph, and it can reach 60 mph in less than 4 seconds. The price of a Ferrari California is $190,000. Let's say that your bank will lend you the money to buy the car at a rate of 6% for a 6-year term with monthly payments. What are the monthly payments on the car loan?

SOLUTION

Spreadsheet Solution

B9 fx =1/(1+B6)^(B8)

	A	B	C
1	Monthly Car Loan Payments:		
2	Solving For PMT with Non-Annual Compo		
3			
4	i =	0.06	
5	m =	12	
6	i/m =	0.005	
7	n =	6	
8	n*m =	72	
9	PVIF =	0.69830243	
10	PVIFA =	60.3395139	

View in the online reader

Algebraic Solution

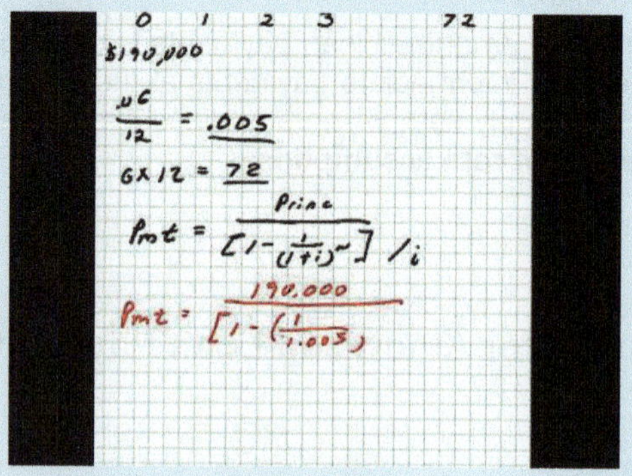

View in the online reader

Calculator Solution

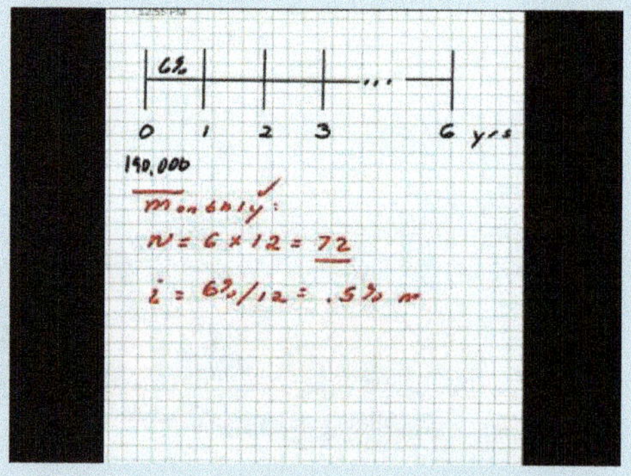

View in the online reader

In this example, $i = 6\%$, $n = 6$ and $m = 12$. The monthly interest rate is the periodic rate $i/m = 0.06/12 = 0.005$. The number of monthly payments is $n \times m = 6 \times 12 = 72$. The monthly payments on the loan can be solved using a monthly variation of the amortized loan identity (Equation 4.9).

$$PMT = \frac{\text{Principal}}{PVIFA_{i/m,n\times m}}$$

$$PVIFA_{0.5\%,72} = \frac{1 - \frac{1}{(1.005)^{72}}}{0.005} = 60.3395$$

$$PMT = \frac{\$190,000}{60.3395} = \$3,148.85$$

For only $3,148.85 (per month) you could reach 60 mph in under 4 seconds and drive the hottest car in your neighborhood.

Explain It: The Car Loan Calculator

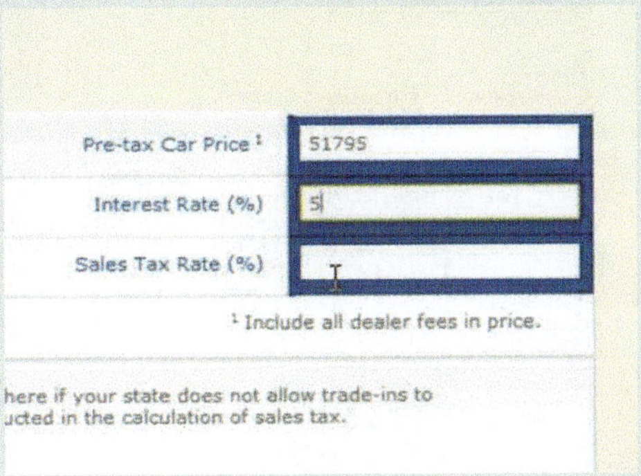

View in the online reader

Loan Amortization Schedule

Amortized loan payments are a blend of interest and principal. However, the portion of each payment that is interest and principal changes. Each payment reduces the principal owing and so reduces the amount of interest owing in the next period. We can calculate the amount of interest and principal in each payment using a loan amortization schedule. The schedule is very useful in business because interest payments are tax deductible. We will demonstrate the loan amortization schedule for you by means of an example.

Example 4.12 Principal Outstanding on an Amortized Loan

Digital Downloads

Example 4.12 Principal Outstanding on an Amortized Loan.xlsx
https://catalog.flatworldknowledge.com/a/34711/Example_4_12_Principal_Outstanding_on_an_Amortized_Loan-41f0.xlsx

Consider an amortized loan with principal of $10,000, a 5-year term, and an interest rate of 10%. Calculate the following: 1) the annual payments; 2) interest owing at the end of the first year; 3) principal repaid in the first payment; 4) the principal owing at the end of the first year; and 5) complete the rest of the amortization schedule.

SOLUTION

Spreadsheet Solution

	A	B	C	D	E
1	Amortization Table				
2					
3	i =	0.1			
4	n =	5			
5	Principal =	$10,000.00			
6	PMT =	$2,637.97			
7					
8		Interest		Principal	Principal
9	Year	Owing (EOY)	Payment	Repaid	Owing
10	1	$1,000.00	$2,637.97	$1,637.97	$8,362.03
11	2	836.20	2,637.97	1,801.77	6,560.25
12	3	656.03	2,637.97	1,981.95	4,578.30
13	4	457.83	2,637.97	2,180.14	2,398.16
14	5	239.82	2,637.97	2,398.16	0.00
15					
16					
17					

View in the online reader

The annual payments are:

$$PMT = \frac{Principal}{PVIFA_{i,n}} = \$10,000/3.790787 = \$2,637.97$$

At the end of the first year the interest owing is:

$$Interest\ owing = 0.10 \times \$10,000 = \$1,000$$

The payment at the end of the first year is $2,637.97, thus the principal repaid at the end of the year is the amount left over after interest is paid:

$$Principal\ repaid = \$2,637.97 - \$1,000 = \$1,637.97$$

The repayment of principal lowers the balance owing (at the end of the first year) to:

$$Principal\ owing = (\$10,000 - \$1,637.97) = \$8,362.03$$

The full schedule of payments, interest, and principal payments is as follows.

	A	B	C	D	E
1	Year	Interest Owing at End of Year	Payment	Principal Repayment	Principal Owing at End of Year
2	1	1,000.00	2,637.97	1,637.97	8,362.03
3	2	836.20	2,637.97	1,801.77	6,560.26
4	3	656.03	2,637.97	1,981.94	4,578.32
5	4	457.83	2,637.97	2,180.14	2,398.18
6	5	239.82	2,637.97	2,398.15	0.00

Look at the row labeled "Year 2," which shows values for the second year of the loan. Notice how interest owing at the end of the second year is $836.20, which is simply 10% of the principal owing at the end of the first year. Look at the final row of the table. Notice how the last payment covers the last amount of interest owing and repays the remaining principal. Very tidy!

Principal Outstanding

Look at the solution to "Example 4.12 Principal Outstanding on an Amortized Loan". In particular, notice that there is a balance of $8,362.03 still owing at the end of the first year. This is amount is also called the principal outstanding. It is the amount that is owed to the lender after the first payment. If you want to calculate the principal outstanding, there is a quicker method than building a loan amortization schedule. The short-cut involves using the amortized loan equation Equation 4.9. However, we change the focal date to the date of an intermediate payment *t* (where *t* is between 0 and *n*, and *n* is the maturity date).

EQUATION 4.11

$$Principal_t = PMT \times PVIFA_{i\%,\ n-t}$$

This equation expresses the fact that the principal outstanding on the loan is the present value of the remaining payments. In actuarial mathematics, this is called the prospective method for solving for the loan balance.

Example 4.13 Principal Outstanding on an Amortized Loan

Consider an amortized loan with principal of $10,000, a 5-year term ($n = 5$), and an interest rate of 10%. ($i = 0.10$). The annual payments are $2,637.9748. How much principal is owed after the first payment is made?

SOLUTION

We can solve for the principal outstanding using Equation 4.11 where *t*=1.

$$\text{Principal}_t = PMT \times PVIFA_{i\%,n-t}$$

$$PVIFA_{10\%,4} = \frac{1-\frac{1}{(1.10)^4}}{0.10} = 3.169865$$

$$\text{Principal}_1 = \$2,637.9748 \times 3.169865$$

$$\text{Principal}_1 = \$8,362.03$$

There is $8,362.03 owing after the first loan payment is made.

CHAPTER 5

Introduction to Risk and Return

Learning Objectives

By the end of this chapter you will be able to:

1. Describe the risk-return relationship.
2. Calculate the expected return on a single asset.
3. Compute the risk of holding a single asset.
4. Calculate the expected return for a portfolio of assets.
5. Explain diversification and portfolio risk.

There are many financial securities available to investors. Each has different levels of **expected return** and different **risks**, that is, ranges of returns that could be realized. This chapter investigates the relationship between risk and return. It will come as no surprise that increasing risk is sometimes accompanied by an increasing return. What may surprise you is that there is more than one type of risk. For some types of risks, the return is not necessarily increased *despite* the increased risk of the investment.

expected return

The return that is expected to be earned each period on a given asset in the future. A probability weighted average of the returns in each state of nature.

risks

The variability in outcomes coupled with the possibility of harm.

5.1 The Risk–Return Relationship

Investors study an asset's characteristics and develop expectations regarding the likelihood of the actual cash flows matching the projections. The less certain the investor is about the projected cash flows, the riskier the investment becomes. This risk and return relationship is explored in "Explain It: The Risk–Return Relationship".

Explain It: The Risk–Return Relationship

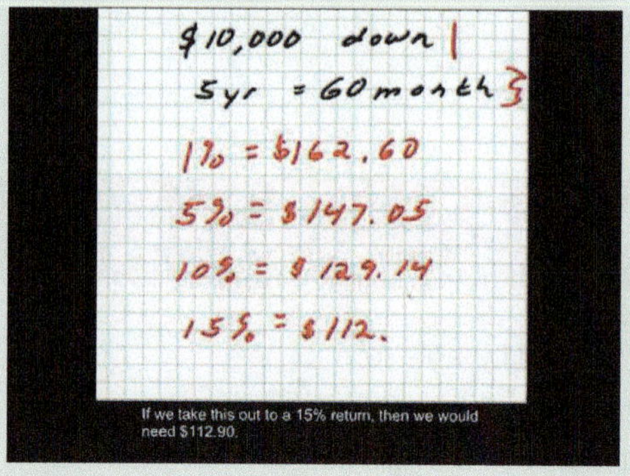

View in the online reader

What makes the investor uncertain about the projections? Often, uncertainty arises from factors that are difficult to predict and will influence the firm's future. For example, it is challenging to predict the probability and length of a foreign country's recession. Let's suppose Sunbeam sells toasters in the Asian markets. If this region suffers a recession, Sunbeam will also suffer, but it's very hard to predict exactly how large the effect will be. The point is that risk (1) is determined by the uncertainty of future cash flows, and (2) this uncertainty is the result of factors peculiar to each asset.

Once investors establish the riskiness of the asset, the market allows the price of the asset to adjust so the expected return on the asset fairly compensates investors for their perceived risk. The perceived risk of the asset is determined first and then the market establishes the price that will provide an expected return sufficient to induce investors to buy the asset. We expect return to increase as risk increases, as seen in "Explain It: Risk–Return Trade-off".

FIGURE 5.1 Risk–Return Trade-off

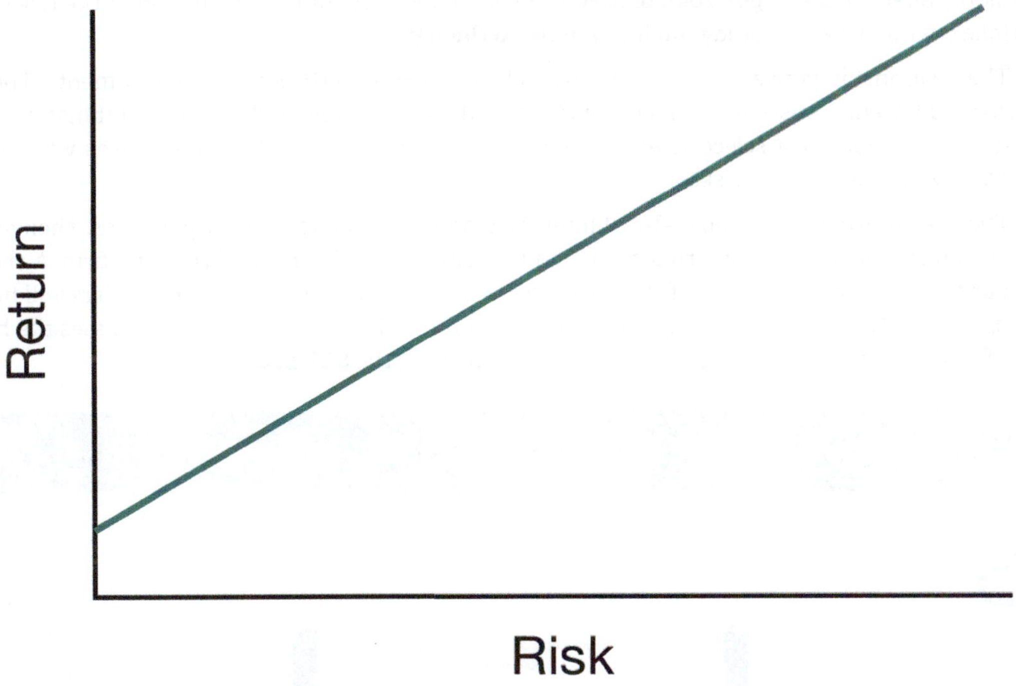

Explain It: Risk–Return Trade-off

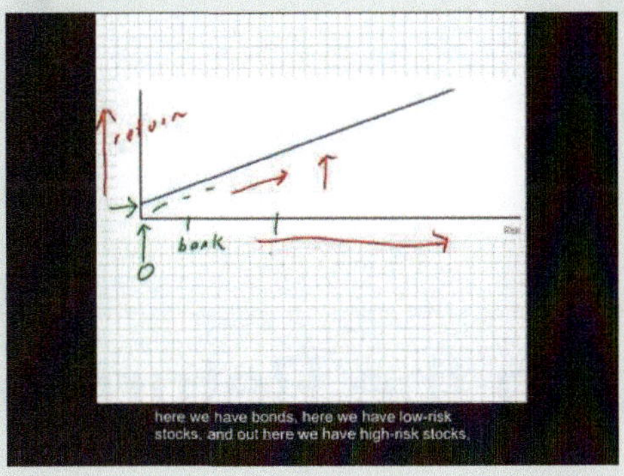

View in the online reader

In this chapter, we focus on how to measure return and risk. We learn:

- how to compute the return on a single asset.
- how to compute the risk of a single asset.
- how to compute the expected return on a portfolio of assets.
- how to compute the risk of a portfolio of assets.

portfolio of assets

A collection or group of assets.

modern portfolio theory

The theory that all investors hold a portfolio of assets called the market portfolio and that risk is measured by the correlation of an asset to this portfolio. The relationship between risk and return is captured by the CAPM equation.

S&P 500

An index formed by tracking the performance of 500 of the largest U.S. companies. The index was originally formed by Standard and Poor's.

Computing the returns on investments is straightforward. It's also not too difficult to compute the risk of a single asset. The challenging part is to determine the risk of a group of assets, more commonly referred to as a **portfolio of assets**. We learn more about the calculation of the risk of a portfolio later on when we study **modern portfolio theory**.

The relationship between risk and return is fundamental to the study of investments. There are many different investment vehicles and each offers a different risk–return combination. To invest properly, you must select investments that best suit your need for high returns while not exceeding your tolerance for risk.

The risk–return relationship is also of interest to financial managers of corporations. Their goal is to maximize the price of the firm's stock and this price depends on the risk of the firm. A thorough understanding of the types of risk that affect the return demanded by shareholders will help managers keep their firms on the right course. "Explain It: A History of Returns" discusses the history of returns earned on the popular stock indexes, such as the **S&P 500**.

Explain It: A History of Returns

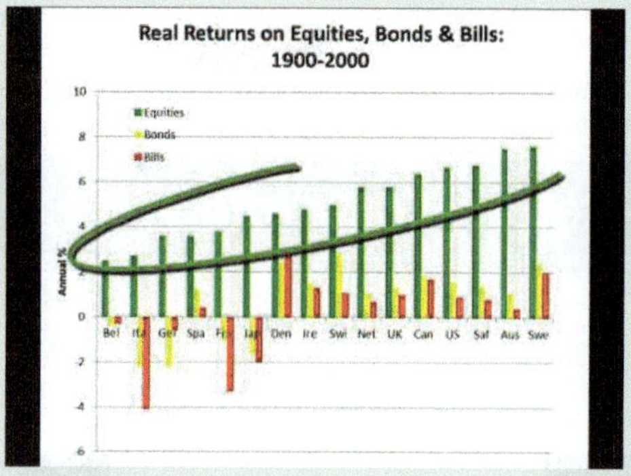

View in the online reader

5.2 Computing the Return on a Single Asset

In this section, we compute the return on an asset held in isolation. Later, we show that the wise investor won't willingly invest in single assets by themselves. This section provides a foundation for computing the return on a portfolio of assets.

Computing Simple Returns

Suppose you bought a share of Walmart stock at a price of $50.50 per share. A year later, you sell your share for $61.00. Additionally, Walmart sent you a dividend of $0.20 at the end of the year. The timeline of cash flows is shown in Figure 5.2.

FIGURE 5.2 Timeline of Walmart Trades

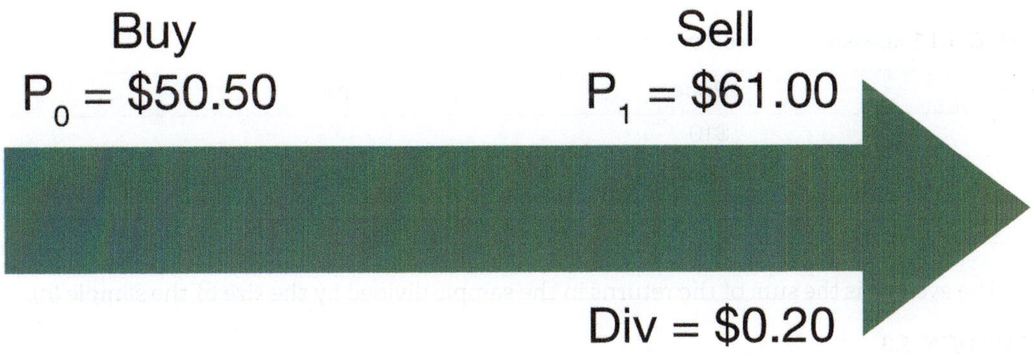

The **holding period return (HPR)** consists of the earnings from dividends paid, plus the return from appreciation (**capital gain**) in the stock's price. The HPR is simply the percent your investment earned during the time you held it. The formula for calculating holding period return is shown in Equation 5.1.

holding period return (HPR)
The return earned on an investment since its inception, not annualized.

capital gain
Earnings that are due to an increase in the price of security.

EQUATION 5.1

$$HPR_i = \frac{\text{Ending price} - \text{Beginning price} + \text{Dividends}}{\text{Beginning price}}$$

For your investment in Walmart, the return is:

$$HPR_i = \frac{\$61.00 - \$50.50 + \$0.20}{\$50.50} = 0.2119 = 21.19\%$$

We can separate Equation 5.1 into two parts:

EQUATION 5.2

$$HPR_i = \frac{\text{Ending price} - \text{Beginning price}}{\text{Beginning price}} + \frac{\text{Dividends}}{\text{Beginning price}}$$

The first part is the price of appreciation, which is called the *capital gain*, and the second part is the **dividend yield**. The HPR is equal to the sum of the capital gain and the dividend yield.

dividend yield
The ratio of the dividends paid in a year divided by the current price.

Average versus Compound Average

arithmetic average return

The simple average of a time series of returns. The sum of the returns in each period divided by the number of periods.

geometric (compound) average return

The return computed that recognizes that interest or earnings are paid on accumulated interest or earnings. It is also called a compound return.

If you have a sample of returns (say a mutual fund's past 10 years of returns), then there are two alternatives for summarizing the fund's past performance: **arithmetic average return** and **geometric (compound) average return**.

The arithmetic average return is simply the garden-variety sample average (also known as the *mean*). For a simple example, consider the data below for the Explosive Mutual Fund Inc. The first return is 100% and the second is –50%.

TABLE 5.1 Explosive Mutual Fund Inc's Annual Returns

Year	Price	Return
0	$10	
1	$20	100%
2	$10	-50%

The average is the sum of the returns in the sample divided by the size of the sample (n).

EQUATION 5.3

$$\textit{Average return} = \frac{1}{n}\sum_{i=1}^{n} k_i$$

In the case of Explosive, the average return is 25%.

$$\left(\textit{Average return} = \frac{(100\% + -50\%)}{2} = 0.25\right)$$

The compound average return is:

EQUATION 5.4

$$\textit{Compound average return} = \left(\frac{\text{ending value}}{\text{beginning value}}\right)^{\frac{1}{\#\text{ of years}}} - 1$$

In the case of Explosive, the compound average return is 0%.

$$\textit{Compound return} = \left[\frac{\$10}{\$10}\right]^{\frac{1}{2}} - 1 = 0$$

Tip

You may remember seeing this equation before. It was introduced in Chapter 3 as the compound average interest rate.

The example of Explosive shows clearly why the compound average is better than the garden-variety average for summarizing investment returns. If you look at the price of the fund, you see that it started at $10 and ended at $10. An investor who bought at Year 0 and sold at Year 2 would have earned nothing! Yet, the average return is 25%! The compound average is the annual return that would have made $10 grow into $10 over 2 years with compounding. The only return that can do that is 0%, so 0% is the compound average return for Explosive. Mutual fund companies are required by law to report the compound average, not the arithmetic average.

Computing Expected Returns

Risk derives from the uncertainty of future events. Objects that have more than one possible outcome and for which the magnitude of the outcomes is uncertain beforehand are called **random variables**. The possible outcomes of random variables are called *states of nature*. States of nature are just future scenarios. For example, the states of nature for tomorrow's weather are rain, sun, clouds, and so on. Stock returns are random variables and the states of nature are economic scenarios.

random variables

Variables with no identifiable relationship between each other.

States of nature are possibilities. They don't occur with certainty. Thus, there are probabilities associated with them. Probabilities quantify the likelihood or chance of these events occurring.

With many states of nature, we need a summary measure of the possible rates of returns. The expected return reflects the investor's evaluation of the probable yield of an investment. This evaluation is neither the same as the historic return computed above, nor the required return that we'll compute later in this chapter. The expected return is the weighted average of all the possible future returns, wherein the weights reflect the probabilities of each possible return.

The expected return is computed using information available at the time the projection is made. The expected return and the actual return can differ and they often do. Apple Computers' low stock price of $3.28 in December 1997 reflected the low probability that management could pull the firm out of its problems quickly and effectively. What was the expected return for Apple in 2021, by which time its price was $136 (even after four stock splits)? With Apple stock at an all-time high, investors clearly expect high returns in the future.

Explain It: Expected Returns

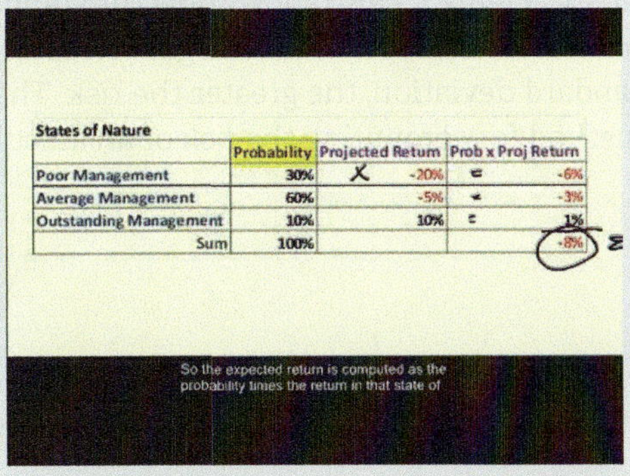

View in the online reader

In the video example, only three possible outcomes were listed—poor, average, and outstanding. Of course, there is an infinite number of possible states of the world to be considered and investors can't evaluate all of them. The expectations concept is still valid, however. Expected returns reflect investors' best projection of a firm's future, in which the projection is based on the weighted average of the possible outcomes. Equation 5.5 shows the generalized equation for computing the expected return.

EQUATION 5.5

$$Expected\ return = E(k) = Pr_1 k_1 + Pr_2 k_2 + \ldots + Pr_n k_n$$

where

$$k_i = \text{return in } i \text{ th state of nature}$$
$$Pr_i = \text{probability of occurrence of the } i \text{ th outcome}$$
$$n = \text{number of possible outcomes}$$

5.3 Evaluating the Risk of Holding a Single Asset

standard deviation

A popular statistical measure that quantifies the dispersion around the expected value.

Risk entails two essential components: harm and uncertainty. In finance, *harm* means small or negative returns. The other component of risk is *uncertainty*, which is the variability in outcomes (i.e., returns or cash flows). Consider the case of a man who jumps from an airplane with no parachute. He faces harm but no uncertainty. The harm is his impending death, but because his death will occur with certainty, there is no risk. Risk requires both harm and uncertainty. To define risk, we need a statistic that captures both the likelihood of small and negative returns and also the variability of returns. The **standard deviation** does this.

Computing the Risk of a Single Asset

The standard deviation is a measure of the risk of a single asset. Figure 5.3 shows the steps in the process of computing this statistic. Figure 5.3 also shows how the standard deviation measures risk. Greater deviations from the mean, whether positive or negative, result in a greater standard deviation. Thus, the greater the standard deviation, the greater the risk. These characteristics make the standard deviation a viable method for computing the risk of an asset held by itself.

FIGURE 5.3

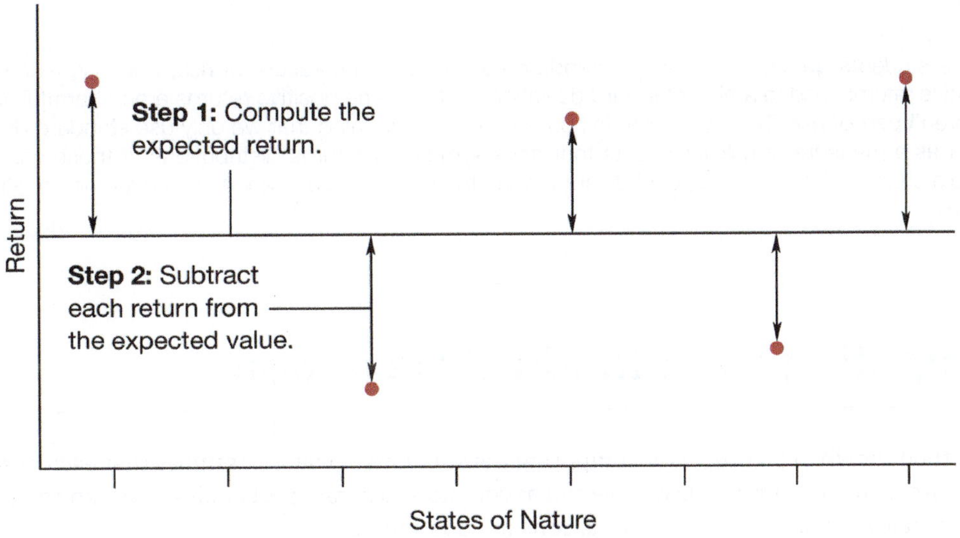

Step 3: Square each deviation to remove negative signs.

Step 4: Multiply each squared deviation by 0.25 (assuming each of the four states of nature is equally probable) and sum.

Step 5: Take the square root.

Explain It: Standard Deviation

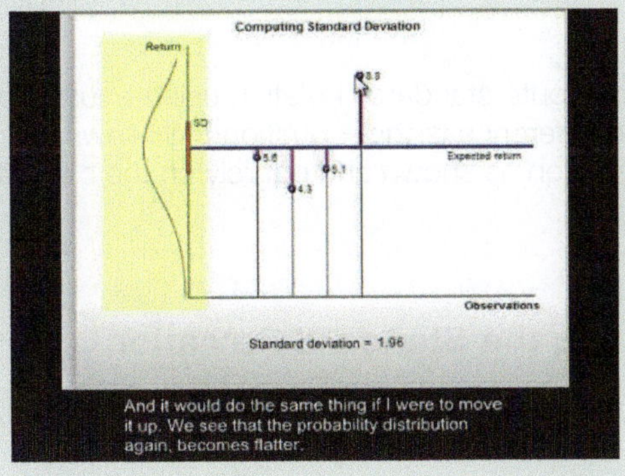

View in the online reader

Tip

Some students get confused about standard deviation as a measure of risk, because extreme positive returns lead to a high standard deviation. But extreme positive returns aren't harmful and so aren't part of risk. That reasoning is correct, but keep in mind that we only use standard deviation as a measure of risk for assets that have symmetric returns distributions. If those assets have a chance of an extreme positive return, then they also have a chance of an extreme negative return.

Computing the Standard Deviation

The method shown in Figure 5.3 for computing the standard deviation assumes that each observation occurs with equal probability. If we can assign more accurate probabilities, we can compute a more accurate standard deviation. This is done in Equation 5.6.

EQUATION 5.6

$$\text{Standard deviation} = \sqrt{\sum_{i=1}^{n} (k_i - E(k))^2 \times Pr_i}$$

where

$$E(k) = \text{expected return}$$
$$k_i = \text{return for } i \text{ th outcome}$$
$$Pr_i = \text{probability of occurrence of the } i\text{th outcome}$$
$$n = \text{number of outcomes evaluated}$$

Tip

Your calculator and Excel compute standard deviation using equal probabilities, not the method shown in Equation 5.6. The difference is that Equation 5.6 allows for unequal probabilities. You must compute standard deviation as shown and not rely on the calculator's functions.

Example 5.1 Computing the Standard Deviation

Digital Downloads

Example 5.1_computing_standard_deviation.xls
https://catalog.flatworldknowledge.com/a/34711/Example_5_1_computing_standard_deviation-eb0b.xls

Use the data provided in the table to calculate the standard deviation of returns for More Dollars Inc. The three states of nature correspond to the three possible performance levels of the management team. The expected return for MD is 8%.

Management Quality	Probability (*Pr*)	Projected Return (*k*)
Poor	0.30	−0.20
Average	0.60	−0.05
Outstanding	0.10	0.10

SOLUTION

Spreadsheet Solution

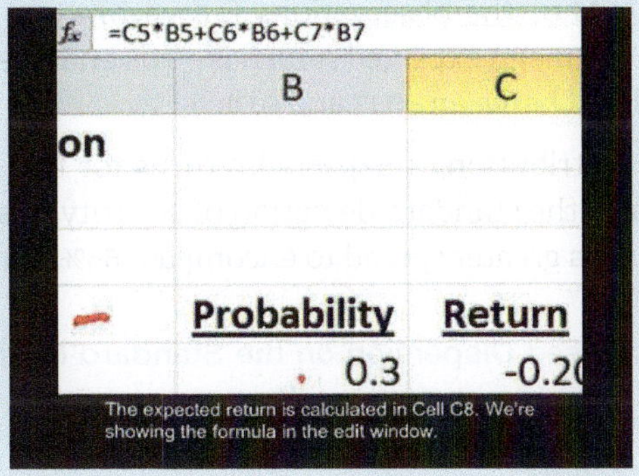

View in the online reader

Algebraic Solution

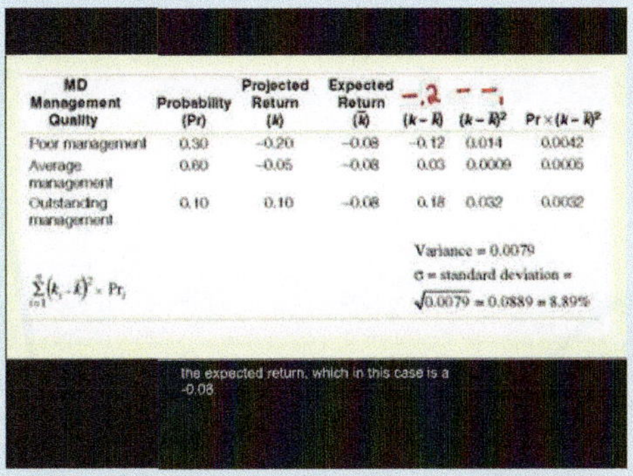

View in the online reader

MD Management Quality	Probability (*Pr*)	Projected Return (*k*)	(*k*–*E*(*k*))	$(k–E(k))^2$	*PR* × $(k–E(k))^2$
Poor	0.30	−0.20	−0.12	0.0144	0.00432
Average	0.60	−0.05	0.03	0.0009	0.00054
Outstanding	0.10	0.10	0.18	0.0324	0.00324

Use Equation 5.6.

$$\sigma = \sqrt{\sum_{i=1}^{n} (k_i - E(k))^2 \times Pr_i} = \sqrt{0.0081} = 0.0900 = 9.00\%$$

Standard deviation makes a lot of sense as a measure of risk. It starts with the expected return, which we can think of as our best guess forecast. The squared deviations are the (squared) forecast errors in each state of nature. That is, the (squared) difference between the actual return in the state of nature and the forecast. A forecast is only wrong when we are surprised, so these are squared surprises. The variance is the probability weighted average of the squared surprises. This is an excellent measure of risk. To be risky, an investment should generate some nasty surprises, but they also have to be reasonably likely. So, it makes sense to measure risk with the both the size of the surprise and likelihood of it happening, and that is what standard deviation (variance) does.

$$-0.08 + 0.09 = 0.01$$
$$\textbf{and}$$
$$-0.08 - 0.09 = -0.17$$

If we assume that the returns to More Dollars follow a normal probability distribution, we can use the standard deviation to establish confidence intervals for the expected returns. For a normal probability distribution, 68% of the observations fall within one standard deviation above and below the mean. Because the mean expected return is –0.08 and one standard deviation is 0.09, 68% of the time the return will fall between –0.17 and 0.01:

Figure 5.4 shows the distribution of expected returns for two securities. The standard deviation of security A is 10% and the standard deviation of security B is 5%. Security A, with the larger standard deviation, requires a greater spread to encompass 68% of the observations.

FIGURE 5.4 Effect of Increased Dispersion on the Standard Deviation

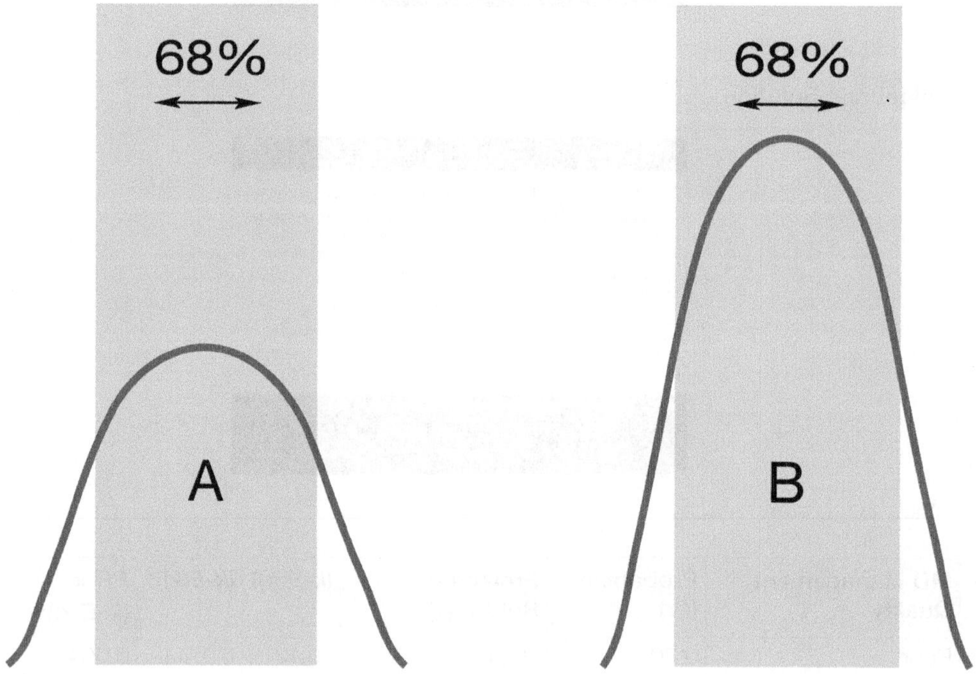

Explain It: Graphing Standard Deviation

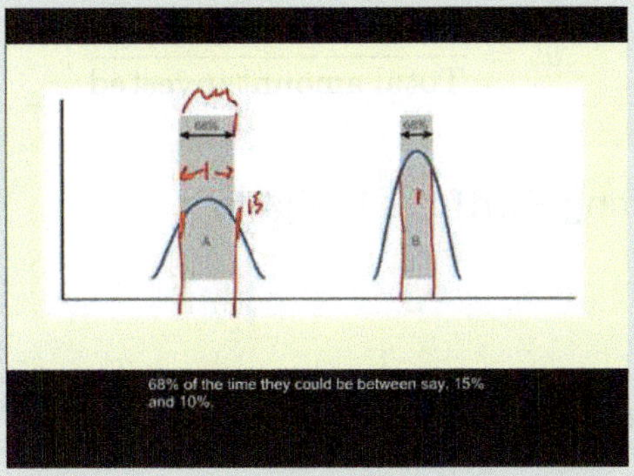

View in the online reader

5.4 Computing the Expected Return for a Portfolio of Assets

The preceding discussion was about the expected return of a single asset. Occasionally, an investor holds only one asset. For example, some firms invest employee retirement money in the firm's stock. If this is the employee's only investment, the appropriate measure of risk is the standard deviation. Most of the time, however, investors hold more than one asset. This section shows how to compute the expected return on a group of assets.

Tip

Another example where you might hold only one asset is if you own a business. So much of your wealth could be required to fund its growth that you cannot afford to invest in anything else.

A portfolio is a collection, or group, of assets held as an investment. An investment portfolio may contain a group of stocks, a group of bonds, or a combination of stocks and bonds. A portfolio also may include real estate, gold, options, and other income-producing assets.

How to Compute the Expected Return on a Portfolio

The expected return for a portfolio is the weighted average of the expected returns for each individual security, where the weights are the percentage of wealth invested in each security.

Portfolio Weights

The portfolio weights in the calculation of expected return (denoted w_i) are simply the amount invested in asset i divided by the total amount invested in the portfolio.

EQUATION 5.7

$$w_i = \frac{\text{Amount invested in } i}{\text{Total amount invested}}$$

Example 5.2 Computing Portfolio Weights

Digital Downloads

Example 5.2_Portfolio_Weights.xls
https://catalog.flatworldknowledge.com/a/34711/Example_5_2_Portfolio_Weights-0079.xls

You have $7,925 to invest. You create a two-asset portfolio consisting of 100 shares of Caltron at $24.50 and 100 shares of Bisbee at $54.75. What are the portfolio weights?

SOLUTION

Spreadsheet Solution

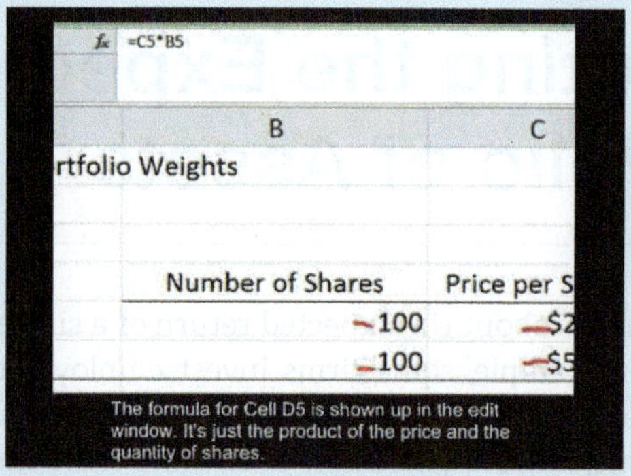

View in the online reader

Algebraic Solution

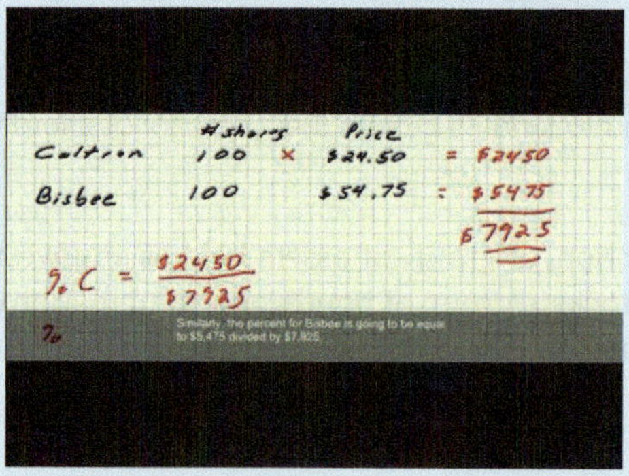

View in the online reader

	Number of Shares	Price per Share	Amount Invested	Portfolio Weight
Caltron	100	$24.50	$2,450.00	0.309
Bisbee	100	$54.75	$5,475.00	0.691
Total			$7,925.00	1.000

Two caveats about portfolio weights: First, in Equation 5.7 we labeled the numerator of a portfolio weight as the amount invested in asset *i*. You can also think of this as the amount spent on the purchase of the asset. The purchase is shown as a positive value. In contrast, if you were to short sell the asset, then you would receive the proceeds from the sale. The amount received would be in the numerator and would have a negative sign. Receipts from short sales are shown as negative purchases. Thus, short positions have negative portfolio weights.

The second caveat involves the denominator. In Equation 5.7 we labeled the denominator as the total amount invested. Think of this as the total amount that you invest. It is your equity in the portfolio—the total amount that you contributed. Later, we will consider portfolios where we borrow money and the total amount invested in the portfolio will be the sum of our equity and the amount borrowed. However, even then, the denominator of the portfolio weight will be our equity—the total amount we invested.

Expected Return

Equation 5.8 shows how the expected return for a portfolio is computed.

EQUATION 5.8

$$Expected\ return\ on\ portfolio = E(k_p) = w_1 E(k_1) + w_2 E(k_2) + \cdots + w_n E(k_n)$$

where

$$w_1 = \text{portfolio weight of asset } i$$
$$E(k_1) = \text{expected return on asset } i$$

In the simplest case, you could have half your money in one stock and half in another; thus, you could just compute a simple average. (Add the two returns together and divide by 2.) Equation 5.8 provides for the more common situation, where you have unequal amounts invested in multiple securities.

Tip

We've already computed a number of weighted averages and you will need to compute them throughout this course. If you are not comfortable with the process, review the examples again carefully.

Example 5.3 Expected Return on a Portfolio, Table Approach

Digital Downloads

Example 5.3_Expected_Return_Portfolio.xls
https://catalog.flatworldknowledge.com/a/34711/Example_5_3_Expected_Return_Portfolio-19ca.xls

Suppose you hold a two-asset portfolio consisting of 100 shares of Caltron at $24.50 and 100 shares of Bisbee at $54.75. Assume you've computed the expected return on Caltron and Bisbee at 22.17% and 21.81%, respectively. What is the expected return from the portfolio?

SOLUTION

Spreadsheet Solution

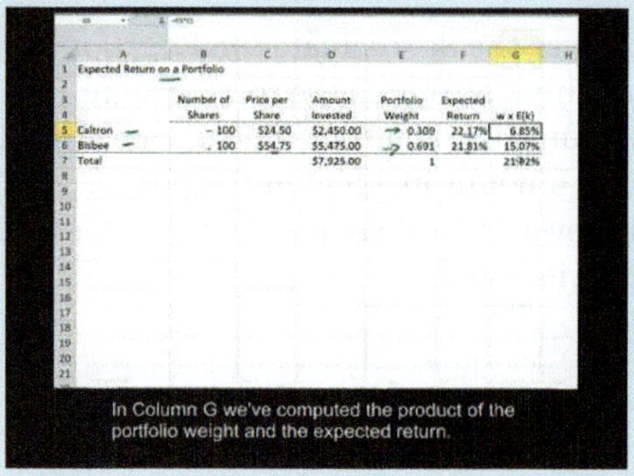

View in the online reader

Algebraic Solution

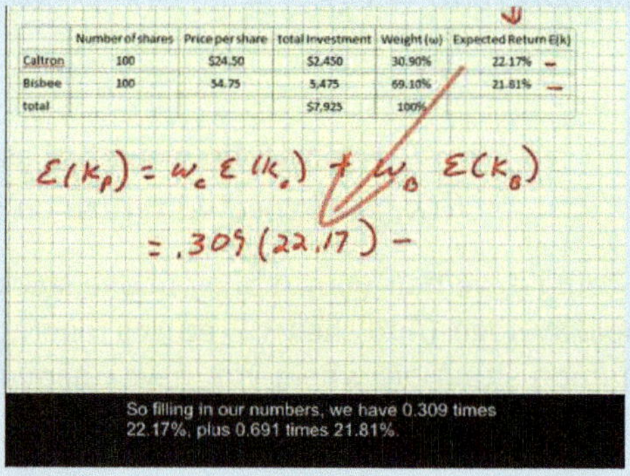

View in the online reader

	Number of Shares	Price per Share	Total Investment	Weight (*w*)
Caltron	100	$24.50	$2,450	30.90%
Bisbee	100	$54.75	$5,475	69.10%
Total			$7,925	100%

The expected return for this portfolio is 21.92%.

5.5 Evaluating the Risk of a Portfolio of Assets

Before attempting to compute the risk of a portfolio, let's conduct a brief review of what we have determined so far about the risk–return relationship.

- To compute the expected return on a single asset, we take the weighted average of the possible outcomes, where the weights reflect the probability of each outcome.
- To compute the risk of a single asset, we compute the standard deviation of the returns in each state of nature.
- To compute the expected return on a portfolio of assets, we find the weighted average of the expected returns of the assets in the portfolio.

We now need to find the risk of a portfolio of assets. Can you guess how we would do this?

Many students logically suggest that the risk of a portfolio can be determined by simply computing the weighted average standard deviation. Let's look at that method. In Figure 5.5, asset A and asset B both have a standard deviation of 1. If you invest 50% of your wealth in A and 50% of your wealth in B, the weighted average of the standard deviations is $1\ (0.5 \times 1) + (0.5 \times 1) = 1$. In fact, any combination of A and B will produce a weighted average standard deviation of 1. Now, look at the variation in the return to the holder of this portfolio. When A is high, B is low. When B is high, A is low. *The variation in one asset exactly offsets the variation in the other*. The resulting return is represented by the horizontal line. This portfolio actually has zero variation in returns over time, so it has no risk. The standard deviation of the portfolio is 0, not 1. What went wrong? Why didn't the weighted average method work?

FIGURE 5.5 Diversification Lowers Return Variability

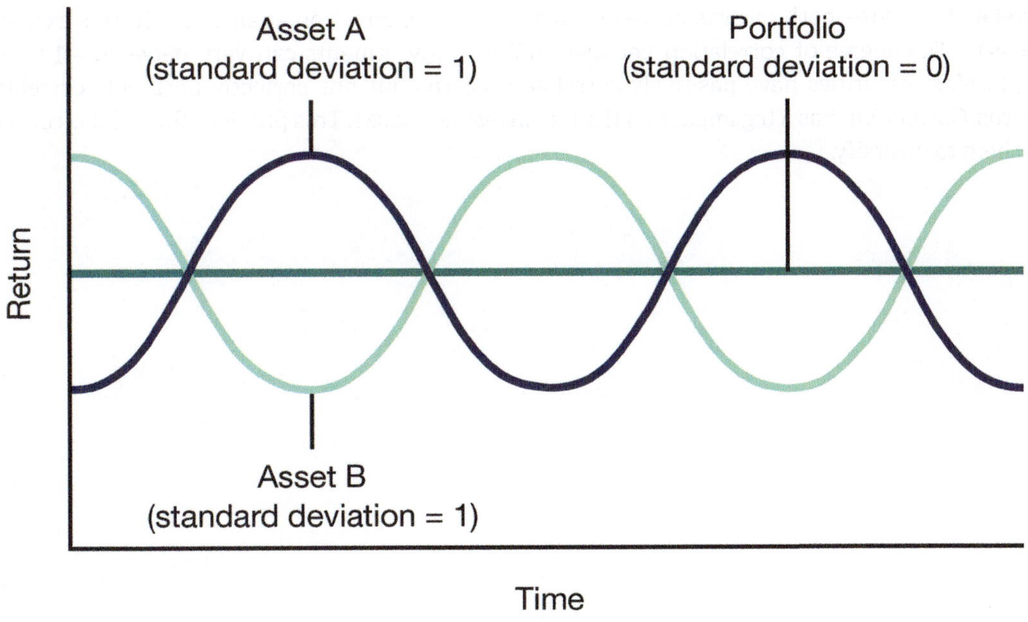

Explain It: Risk of a Portfolio of Assets

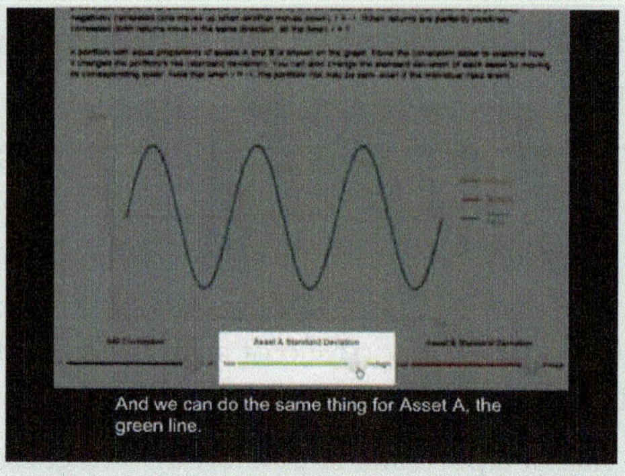

View in the online reader

Correlation

correlation

A relationship between observations, in which the movement over time of one item is related to the movement of another.

The problem is that the returns to assets A and B, in Figure 5.5, are correlated. **Correlation** means there's a predictable relationship between two series of numbers. This relationship is measured by the correlation coefficient, r. In Figure 5.5 the returns are perfectly negatively correlated—when one moves up, the other moves down. When returns are perfectly negatively correlated, they have a correlation coefficient equal to -1.0 . Figure 5.6 shows the relationship between perfectly positively correlated returns—both returns move in exactly the same direction at all times. In this example, $r = +1$. The degree of correlation between different investments can vary between -1.0 and $+1.0$. Most securities have positively correlated returns but not perfectly positively correlated returns. Correlation has a big impact on the risk investors realize. This provides financial incentives for them to diversify.

FIGURE 5.6 Perfectly Positive Correlation Does Not Lower Risk

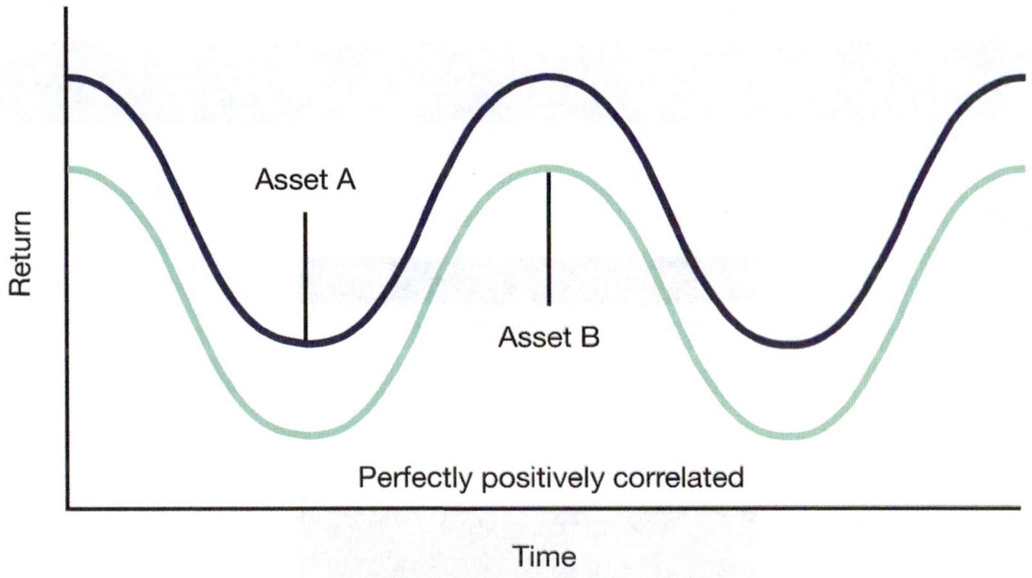

Explain It: Positive Correlation

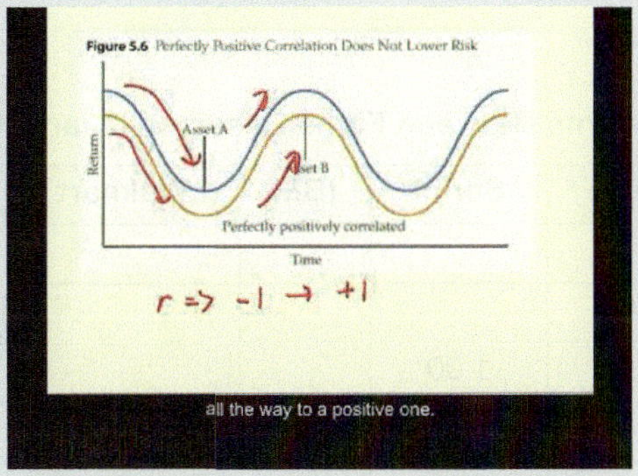

View in the online reader

Diversification

Explain It: Diversification

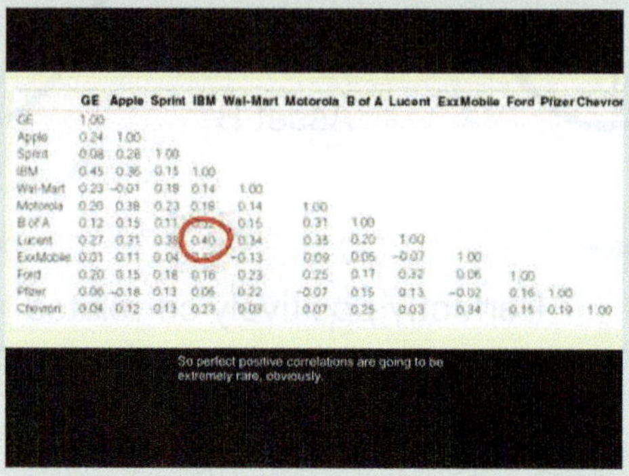

View in the online reader

Table 5.2 shows the correlation matrix for a sample of familiar companies. The table was prepared by computing the correlation between 10 years of quarterly returns. Most pairs of stocks have correlation coefficients between 0.2 and 0.5. For example, the correlation between IBM and Apple was 0.36.

TABLE 5.2 Correlation of Returns Between Firms Based on Quarterly Returns for 10 Years

	GE	Apple	Sprint	IBM	Walmart	Motorola	B of A
GE	1.00						
Apple	0.24	1.00					
Sprint	0.08	0.28	1.00				
IBM	0.45	0.36	0.15	1.00			
Walmart	0.23	–0.01	0.18	0.14	1.00		
Motorola	0.20	0.38	0.23	0.18	0.14	1.00	
B of A	0.12	0.15	0.11	0.32	0.15	0.31	1.00

Because the stocks of different companies aren't perfectly correlated, you can reduce risk but never completely eliminate it by holding more than one stock. "Explain It: Portfolio Risk" shows how two imperfectly correlated stocks combine to produce a portfolio with less risk than if either security were held by itself.

Explain It: Portfolio Risk

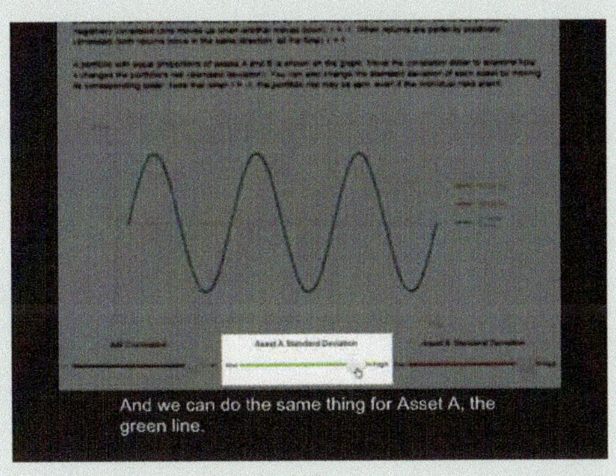

View in the online reader

Earlier, we tried to compute the risk of a portfolio as the average of the individual standard deviations and found that it did not work. Instead, we found that through holding multiple securities (diversification), some risk is eliminated. This leads to an amazing conclusion: *You can hold risky investments and, by combining them, end up with a portfolio less risky than if any of the investments were held by themselves.* Since you can eliminate some risk for free through the simple act of diversification, it is natural to ask two questions: (1) What is the risk that remains after diversification and (2) how is that risk related to expected returns?

It turns out that these questions have intrigued researchers for decades. The answers became the foundation of modern portfolio theory and resulted in multiple Nobel Prizes. Modern portfolio theory is such an important topic in finance that we devote an entire chapter to it.

CHAPTER 6
Portfolio Theory

Learning Objectives

By the end of this chapter you will be able to:

1. Understand the mathematics of portfolio risk and diversification.
2. Explain the importance of the market portfolio, construct a value-weighted portfolio, and be familiar with stock market Indexes.
3. Define and calculate systematic risk.
4. Graph portfolio possibility lines with lending and borrowing and calculate the Treynor Index.
5. Learn about the security market line, which is the equilibrium relationship between risk and return.

This chapter builds on the tools and insights presented in Chapter 5. In that chapter we did the following:

1. We looked at the historic returns on three asset classes (T-bills, bonds, and stocks) and saw that the safest asset, T-bills, had the lowest average return and the most worrisome asset, stocks, had the highest average return.
2. We showed how to measure expected returns on single assets and portfolios.
3. We showed that risk can be measured by the standard deviation of returns across potential states of nature. Since stocks have the highest standard deviation of returns, they aren't just worrisome, they are risky!
4. Finally, we looked at correlation.

In this chapter we are going to derive a new measure of risk and show how it ought to be related to expected returns, culminating in the security market line (SML), which is a line that maps risk to return. The SML is the conclusion of the Capital Asset Pricing Model. This chapter presents the derivation of the model. In the remainder of this introduction we give you an overview. You should reread it once you have finished the chapter and it will help fit the pieces together.

The standard deviation of a portfolio is critically dependent on the correlations of the assets in the portfolio. Our examples all focus on two asset portfolios, but when you analyze the return and risk of larger portfolios, as Professor Harry Markowitz did, you reach some surprising conclusions. First, Markowitz discovered that there are some portfolios that are better diversified than others. He called these the "efficient set of portfolios." Economist William Sharpe extended Markowitz's analysis by introducing a risk-free asset. When you add that, the efficient set changes a bit, so he called it the "new efficient set." The implication of the new efficient set is that when people invest in risky assets they all pick a common portfolio. Since everyone holds the same portfolio of risky assets, that portfolio must include every risky asset that is observed in the capital markets. Sharpe called this the "market portfolio."

If everyone holds the market portfolio, then we are all very well diversified and so our view of risk changes. We don't care about the standard deviation of returns on individual assets because a lot of that risk is diversified away in the portfolio. We call that "diversifiable risk," since it is eliminated by diversification. The remaining risk (nondiversifiable or systematic risk) is related to how sensitive the market portfolio is to the particular asset. We call that measure of risk "beta." Beta is the relevant risk for estimating asset returns because beta is all that is relevant to well-diversified investors. In the final part of the chapter we show that if capital markets obey the law of one price, then there is an equilibrium relationship between beta and expected returns. That relationship is the security market line.

6.1 Diversification

diversification

The act of giving something variety. In the context of investing, diversification manages the risk of a portfolio by including a variety of assets.

Diversification is the act of giving something variety. In the context of investing, diversification manages the risk of a portfolio by including a variety of assets.

How does diversification work? What does diversification teach us about the nature of risk? This section addresses these questions.

Portfolio Standard Deviation

True or false? A low-risk portfolio is constructed by selecting low-risk stocks. [*Hint*: Watch the following video.]

Explain It: Diversification

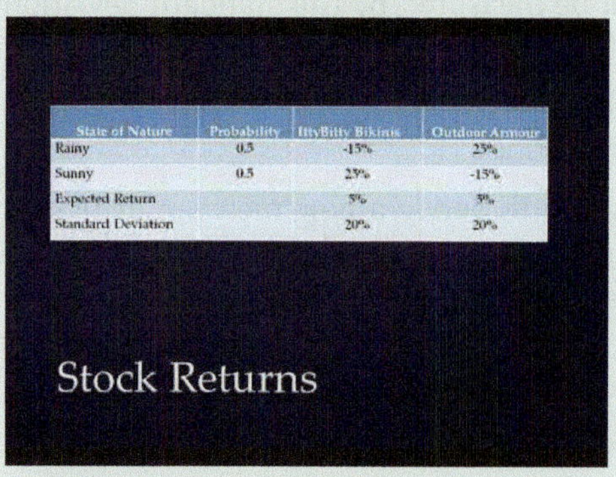

View in the online reader

"Explain It: Diversification" suggests that the answer is false. To build a low-risk portfolio, we should collect stocks that are negatively correlated. In this section, we look at the mathematics of portfolio risk and show you the precise role of correlation.

Standard Deviation of a Two-Asset Portfolio

From "Explain It: Diversification", we know that diversification reduces risk and that the reduction in risk depends on the correlation between the assets. Equation 6.1 formalizes this by showing the formula for the standard deviation of a two-asset portfolio:

EQUATION 6.1

$$\sigma_p = \sqrt{w^2\sigma_1^2 + (1-w)^2\sigma_2^2 + 2w(1-w)\rho_{1,2}\sigma_1\sigma_2}$$

where

$$\sigma_p = \text{the standard deviation of the returns on the portfolio}$$
$$w = \text{the portfolio weight of asset 1}$$
$$\sigma_1(\sigma_2) = \text{the standard deviation of the returns on asset 1 (or 2)}$$
$$\rho_{1,2} = \text{the correlation between the returns on assets 1 and 2}$$

Tip

When there are only two assets in a portfolio we don't need two portfolio weights. If we invest the fraction w in one asset, then we must be investing the fraction $(1-w)$ in the other.

Recall that the definition of correlation is:

$$\rho_{1,2} = \frac{COV(k_1, k_2)}{\sigma_1\sigma_2}$$

We can rearrange this to solve for *COV* as follows:

$$COV(k_1, k_2) = \rho_{1,2}\sigma_1\sigma_2$$

Thus, the covariance is equal to the product of the correlation and the two standard deviations. Notice that the right-hand side of this equality is the last part of Equation 6.1. So, the last part of Equation 6.1 is really just the covariance between the returns on the two assets. We use the product instead of the covariance because we have a better intuitive understanding of correlation. We can investigate the effect of correlation on portfolio risk by using Equation 6.1 to compute the risk of a portfolio for two correlation scenarios: when the assets have perfect positive correlation and when the assets have less than perfect correlation.

Example 6.1 Portfolio Standard Deviation

Digital Downloads

Example 6.1_Two_Asset_Portfolio_Standard_Deviation.xls
https://catalog.flatworldknowledge.com/a/34711/Example_6_1_Two_Asset_Portfolio_Standard_Deviation-fc41.xls

Compute the portfolio standard deviation for a portfolio with 45% of Delta Air Lines stock and 55% of AT&T stock, assuming:

a. the correlation between the two securities is equal to 1, and then
b. the correlation is 0.2.

Assume the standard deviation of returns for Delta is 17.1% and for AT&T is 20.8%.

SOLUTION

Spreadsheet Solution

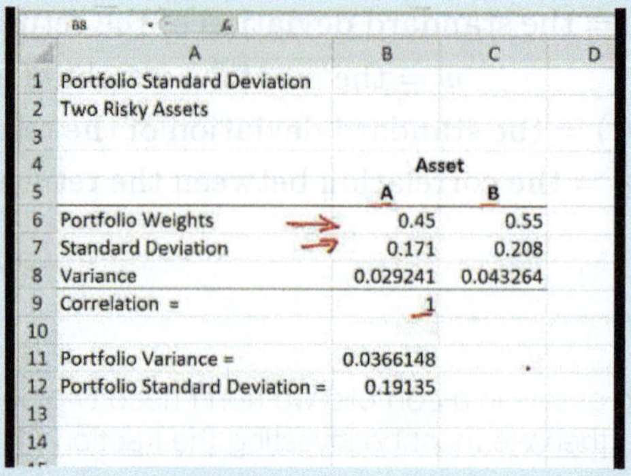

	A	B	C	D
1	Portfolio Standard Deviation			
2	Two Risky Assets			
3				
4		Asset		
5		A	B	
6	Portfolio Weights	0.45	0.55	
7	Standard Deviation	0.171	0.208	
8	Variance	0.029241	0.043264	
9	Correlation =	1		
10				
11	Portfolio Variance =	0.0366148		
12	Portfolio Standard Deviation =	0.19135		
13				
14				

View in the online reader

Algebraic Solution

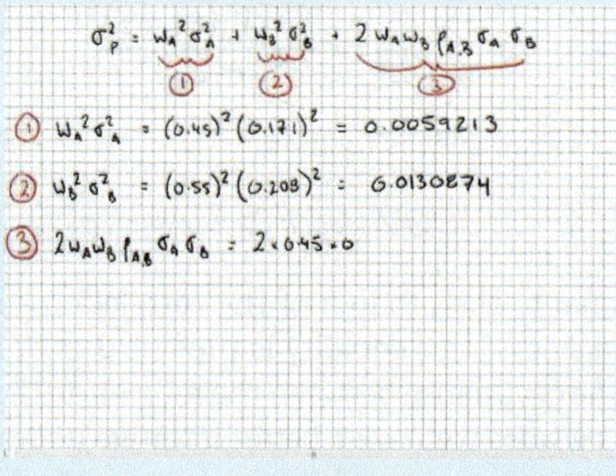

View in the online reader

a. Use Equation 6.1 to compute the portfolio standard deviation.

$$\sigma_p = \sqrt{(0.45)^2(0.171)^2 + (1-0.45)^2(0.208)^2 + 2(0.45)(1-0.45)(1)(0.171)(0.208)}$$

$$\sigma_p = 0.19135$$

Note this is simply the weighted average of the two individual standard deviations.

$$Average = 0.45 \times 0.171 + 0.55 \times 0.208 = 0.19135$$

When the correlation coefficient is equal to 1, there's no bonus from diversification. The portfolio standard deviation falls between the standard deviations of the individual securities.

b. Again, use Equation 6.1 to compute the standard deviation of the portfolio. This time the correlation coefficient is equal to 0.2.

$$\sigma_p = \sqrt{(0.45)^2(0.171)^2 + (1-0.45)^2(0.208)^2 + 2(0.45)(1-0.45)(0.2)(0.171)(0.208)}$$

$$\sigma_p = 0.1501$$

The portfolio standard deviation falls from 19.135% to 15.01% as the correlation falls from +1 to 0.2.

Tip

With perfect positive correlation, diversification can reduce risk, but the risk of the portfolio cannot fall below the level of the least risky asset. With less than perfect positive correlation, portfolio risk can be less than the least risky asset. That is the "bonus" of diversification.

In "Example 6.1 Portfolio Standard Deviation", we see that the portfolio standard deviation falls about 22% when the correlation coefficient falls from +1 to +0.2. If the correlation coefficient is –0.2 the portfolio standard deviation falls to about 12.4%. With a –1 correlation coefficient, the portfolio standard deviation is 3.74%.

Also notice that, in "Example 6.1 Portfolio Standard Deviation", the portfolio standard deviation computed in part (b) is actually less than the standard deviation of either security held independently (15.01% versus 17.1% and 20.8%). This is an important finding. We can combine two risky securities and end up with a portfolio less risky than either security held outside of a portfolio.

Tip

A spreadsheet is the best tool for calculating the portfolio return and standard deviation because you can repeat the calculation for many different input values without a lot of tedium.

We have learned that the effectiveness of diversification depends on the correlation of the returns. When the returns are perfectly positively correlated, then forming a portfolio does not reduce risk very much. However, when returns are less than perfectly correlated, a portfolio can substantially reduce risk.

Standard Deviation of a Portfolio with Many Assets

Equation 6.1 shows the standard deviation for a two-asset portfolio. What if you have more than two assets? If there are three assets in the portfolio, then Equation 6.1 expands to include nine terms: three variance terms and six correlation terms. With a 20-stock portfolio, the equation has 400 terms of which 380 correlate. As the number of stocks gets very large (assuming equal weighting across stocks), the risk of each stock matters less and less and the variance of the portfolio converges toward the average of the pairwise covariances. In other words, the risk is driven by the average degree of covariance.

Explain It: The Risk of a Large Portfolio

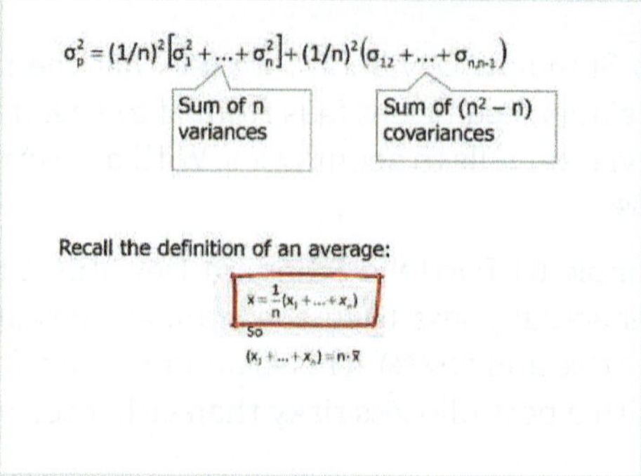

View in the online reader

This result turns our intuition about portfolio risk upside down! At the beginning of this section, we asked you this true-or-false question: Is a low-risk portfolio constructed by selecting low-risk stocks? You may have thought it was true. Now you know it to be false. It doesn't matter how risky each of the stocks is. If you want to build a low-risk portfolio, then you pick stocks with low covariances (correlations).

Types of Risk

In reality, it is hard to find two stocks that are perfectly negatively correlated. But the good news is that diversification works as long as stocks are less than perfectly positively correlated. In the process of looking at "Explain It: Types of Risk", we see that risk can be divided into two parts: diversifiable and nondiversifiable risk.

EQUATION 6.2

$$Total\ risk = Nondiversifiable\ risk + Diversifiable\ risk$$

Nondiversifiable risk is also called **market risk** or **systematic risk**. Henceforth, we mainly use the term systematic risk. Systematic risks include events such as wars, oil price shocks, surprise changes in monetary policy, and sovereign defaults. They are events that affect all assets to some extent.

Diversifiable risk is also called **firm-specific risk** or **unsystematic risk**. Unsystematic risks include events such as strikes, input price shocks, loss of a major customer, or technological obsolescence. These events affect one firm or a few firms.

nondiversifiable risk

Risk that cannot be eliminated through diversification. Also called systematic risk and market risk. Measured by beta.

market risk

The risk of holding the market portfolio. Market risk cannot be eliminated through diversification. Also called nondiversifiable risk or systematic risk.

systematic risk

Risk that is systemwide. Systematic risk cannot be eliminated through diversification. Also called nondiversifiable risk and market risk. Measured by beta.

diversifiable risk

Risk that can be eliminated through diversification. Also called unsystematic risk or firm-specific risk.

firm-specific risk

The risk of holding one (or a few) firms in a portfolio. This is risk that can be eliminated through diversification. Also called diversifiable risk or unsystematic risk.

unsystematic risk

Risk that is not systemwide. This is risk that can be eliminated through diversification. Also called diversifiable risk or firm-specific risk.

Explain It: Types of Risk

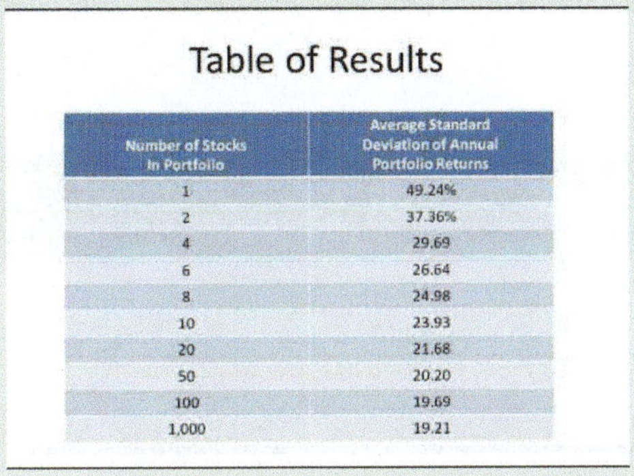

Table of Results

Number of Stocks in Portfolio	Average Standard Deviation of Annual Portfolio Returns
1	49.24%
2	37.36%
4	29.69
6	26.64
8	24.98
10	23.93
20	21.68
50	20.20
100	19.69
1,000	19.21

View in the online reader

6.2 The Market Portfolio

The Efficient Set

Naive diversification, which we described in "Explain It: Types of Risk", is not the most effective approach to portfolio creation. In this section, we summarize a better approach to portfolio selection devised by Harry Markowitz[1] and William Sharpe.

naive diversification

The strategy of investing equal amounts of money in a portfolio of randomly selected stocks.

efficient set

The set of all efficient portfolios across all levels of standard deviation. Harry Markowitz derived a formula for solving for the portfolio weights for each of the portfolios in the efficient set.

risk-free asset

An asset with no variation in its return and no risk of default. The best example is a U.S. government T-bill.

Explain It

Markowitz approached portfolio construction as an optimization problem: maximize return and minimize risk. Markowitz's optimization routine produces the portfolio weights for the best portfolio (highest expected return) at each level of standard deviation. He called those portfolios the **efficient set**.

William Sharpe added a **risk-free asset** to Markowitz's efficient set.[2] What is a risk-free asset? The only truly risk-free asset is a U.S. government zero coupon bond, since the return is known with certainty once the price is established.

Tip

The security is only risk free if there is no possibility of default. This is almost true for U.S. government bonds.

Explain It: Risk-Free Asset

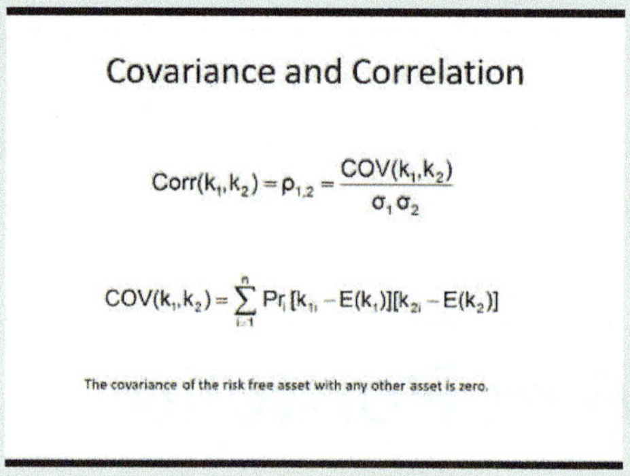

View in the online reader

Consider a T-bill with a face value of $1,000 that matures in 1 year and that costs $952.38. The return on the T-bill denoted k_F is 5%. Because it is guaranteed by the U.S. government, the T-bill return does not vary across states of nature (you always get 5%). The invariance of the return drives the following two facts about the risk-free asset:

1. The standard deviation of returns is zero.

   The formula for the standard deviation of returns for the risk-free asset is:

   $$\sigma_F = \sqrt{\sum_{i=1}^{n} \text{Pr}_i \times (k_{F,i} - E(k_F))^2}$$

   Because the return on the risk free asset is the same in every state of nature, the return is always equal to its average (expected value) so the difference in the parentheses is always zero.

2. The correlation of risk-free returns with the returns of any other asset is zero.

The formula for correlation between the return on any risky asset and the risk free asset is: $\rho_{A,F} = \dfrac{\text{COV}(k_A, k_F)}{\sigma_A \times \sigma_F}$

Since σ_F (the standard deviation of returns for the risk-free asset) is zero, the correlation is also zero. The covariance in the numerator is also zero, again because the return on the risk-free asset is always equal to its expected value in every state of nature.

Explain It

Sharpe's analysis showed that all investors hold two assets: (1) a common risky portfolio from Markowitz's efficient set and (2) the risk-free asset. The only difference between investors are their portfolio weights for the two assets. Sharpe called the set of all combinations of the two assets the **new efficient set**. If everyone holds a common portfolio of risky assets, then that portfolio must contain every risky asset in the capital market. The common portfolio is called the **market portfolio**.

The market portfolio is very large and well diversified. Since it is in Markowitz's efficient set, it has no unsystematic (firm-specific) risk. Thus, investors in Sharpe's model care only about systematic risk.

new efficient set

The set of portfolios formed by combining the risk-free asset and the market portfolio.

market portfolio

The portfolio that includes every capital asset held in proportion to its market value relative to the market value of all assets in total.

Value-Weighted Portfolios

The market portfolio is a value-weighted portfolio. To understand a value-weighted portfolio, consider a market with two assets: the shares of Big Corp. and Small Inc. Table 6.1 shows market data at two points in time: year 0 and year 1.

TABLE 6.1 Price, Shares Outstanding, and Value for Big and Small

	Year 0			Year 1		
	# of Shares	Stock Price	Value	# of Shares	Stock Price	Value
Big	4	$50	$200	4	$60	$240
Small	2	$25	$50	2	$35	$70

The market portfolio includes all of the shares of Big plus all of the shares of Small. The total value of the market portfolio in Year 0 is $250.

The portfolio weights for the market portfolio are the relative values of the two stocks. In year 0, Big is 80% of the total value of the stocks in the portfolio and Small is 20% Because the weights of the market portfolio are the proportionate values, the market portfolio is a **value-weighted portfolio**.

value-weighted portfolio

In a value weighted portfolio, the portfolio weights are equal to the value of each asset relative to the total value of the assets in the portfolio.

Sharpe's model predicts that every investor in this capital market (who invests in risky assets) has a portfolio with 80% of Big and 20% of Small. The aggregate of all of the individual investor portfolios is the market portfolio.

Each investor's portfolio return is equal to the return on the market portfolio. From Table 6.1, the return on Big, k_B , is 20% and the return on Small, k_S , is 40% The total value of shares in Year 1 is $310, so the market is up by 24%.

The return on an individual investor's portfolio is equal to:

$$k_p = w_B k_B + w_S k_S$$
$$kp = 0.8 \times 20\% + 0.2 \times 40\% = 24\%$$

We have learned the following:

1. The market portfolio is value-weighted: the weights are the relative values of each asset in the portfolio.
2. According to Sharpe's model, all investors should optimally hold a portfolio with the same assets in the same proportions (and will earn the same return).
3. The market portfolio is the aggregation of the individual investor portfolios.

Stock Market Indexes

stock market index

A statistical indicator showing the relative value of a basket of stocks compared to their value in a base year. Indexes are created by a variety of entities (i.e., Standard and Poor's) using different baskets of stocks and different weighting schemes (i.e., value or price weighting). Indexes measure the ups and downs of the stock market.

exchange traded fund (ETF)

Investment companies, like mutual funds, that are legally classified as open-end companies or trusts. Most ETFs seek to achieve the same return as a particular market index, and so hold a basket of stocks that mimics the composition of the target index. There are a number of important differences between ETFs and indexed mutual funds. The ETF can be traded within the day, can be shorted, and can be purchased on margin.

Sharpe's market portfolio includes all risky assets—not just stocks. It includes assets such as private corporations, real estate, precious metals, jewelry, and art. Many of those assets are difficult to trade, and so, in practice, we use a proxy for the market portfolio. The most common proxy is a value-weighted **stock market index**; view the Explain It video for a description of value-weighted indexes. The most popular market proxy is the S&P 500 index because it includes many of the largest companies in the country, so it is highly correlated with the market portfolio. The "Explain It" below describes a product called an **exchange traded fund (ETF)**, which makes it easy for investors to trade market proxies like the S&P 500 index.

Explain It

An ETF is simply a company (or trust) that holds a portfolio of assets. The company's shares (or the trust's units) are listed on an exchange. When you buy a share (unit) you are entitled to a proportion of the portfolio and the return on your share (unit) matches the portfolio's return. There are hundreds of ETFs listed on NYSE-Euronext exchange. Three examples are SPDRs, Diamonds, and iShares. SPDRs (Standard and Poor's Depositary Receipts) mimic the S&P 500 and are traded on the NYSE ARCA exchange with ticker symbol SPY. The manager (and trustee) is State Street Global Advisors who set up a trust that owns a basket of stocks exactly mimicking the S&P 500 (see www.spdrs.com). Diamonds are similar but mimic the Dow Jones Industrial average. iShares are managed by Black Rock. Black Rock manages more ETFs than any other company (see us.ishares.com). You can easily buy and sell ETFs using an online brokerage account. Unlike mutual funds, ETFs can be traded all through the day.

6.3 Systematic Risk

William Sharpe derived an equilibrium risk–return relationship for individual assets, which is now famous and is called the **capital asset pricing model (CAPM)**. The CAPM showed that investors who hold the market portfolio do not care about unsystematic risk. The CAPM yields a measure of systematic risk called **beta** and an equilibrium relationship between beta and expected returns. In this section, we discuss beta. We show you how to measure beta and present some properties of beta.

capital asset pricing model (CAPM)

Describes the relationship between the required return, or cost of common stock equity capital, and the nondiversifiable risk of the firm as measured by the beta coefficient.

beta

The measure of systematic risk. Equal to the covariance of returns between the asset and the market portfolio divided by the variance of returns of the market. Measures the marginal change to the risk of the market portfolio from the changing quantity of a given asset. Also measures the amount of systematic risk in a given asset.

marginal risk

The increase in a portfolio's risk resulting from the addition of one more unit of a particular asset to the portfolio. With the market portfolio, marginal risk is measured by the beta of the asset.

Explain It

In 1965, the CAPM was also derived simultaneously and independently by John Lintner (Harvard), Jan Mossin (Bergen), and Jack Treynor (MIT). In 1990, Sharpe and Markowitz were awarded the Nobel Prize in Economics for their contribution to the theory of finance.

Systematic Risk and Beta

William Sharpe showed that all investors hold the market portfolio. Suppose you are one such investor and are offered one more share in Company A. How do you evaluate its risk? As you hold the market portfolio, you aren't concerned with the total risk of the stock because you can diversify away much of that risk in the portfolio. The relevant risk is the marginal risk. That is, how will the risk of the market portfolio change if you add one more share of this particular stock? Sharpe shows that the **marginal risk** is equal to the covariance between the returns on the asset and the market portfolio. We standardize the covariance by dividing it by the variance of returns on the market portfolio, and call the resulting measure beta.

EQUATION 6.3

$$\beta_i = \frac{\mathrm{COV}(k_i, k_M)}{\sigma_M^2}$$

where

$$COV(k_i, k_M) = \text{the covariance of the return on stock } i \text{ with the return on the market portfolio}$$

$$\sigma_M^2 = \text{the variance of returns on the market portfolio}$$

Beta is the key measure of risk for large portfolio holders. It shows the marginal contribution of an individual asset to the overall risk of the market portfolio. Beta also measures the amount of market (systematic) risk possessed by an individual asset. In Equation 6.3 we argued that total risk is the sum of two pieces: systematic and unsystematic risk. The systematic portion is proportionate to beta. Stocks (and portfolios) with a large beta have a large amount of systematic risk.

Next, you learn how to calculate beta and the properties of beta.

Estimating Beta

To estimate beta, we start by graphing the returns on the asset against the returns on the market portfolio (S&P 500 index is a good proxy). The slope of the line of best fit (the ordinary least-squares regression line) is the beta for that asset.

characteristic line

The line of best fit (regression line) when the return of an asset is plotted against the return on the market portfolio.

Figure 6.1 graphs the monthly returns for ABC Company and the market portfolio over a 5-year period. Each monthly return for the company is graphed against the return earned during that same month by the market. A line is drawn on the chart that best fits the data. This line relates the return on ABC to the return on the market, and it's called the **characteristic line**. The slope of the characteristic line is the beta of the security. Note that there are many points that don't fall on the line. These variations result from firm-specific (unsystematic) risk factors.

FIGURE 6.1 Characteristic Line for ABC Company

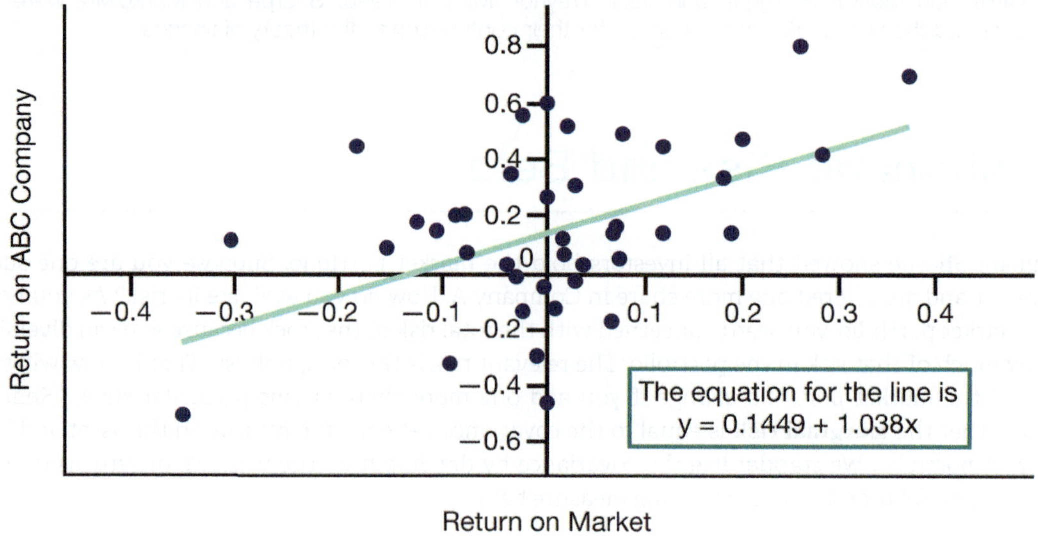

Explain It: Intuition Behind Beta

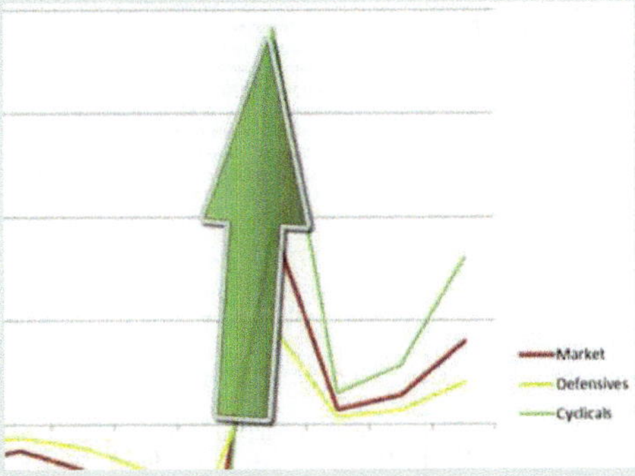

View in the online reader

The equation for the line is reported on the graph as $y = 0.1449 + 1.083x$. This equation means that the slope of the line is 1.083 and the y-intercept is 0.1449. Over this period of time, using this data, the beta of ABC is 1.083. As the beta of ABC is approximately equal to 1, we can say the systematic risk for ABC is about average for the whole market.

Example 6.2 Estimating Beta

Digital Downloads

Example 6.2 Estimating Beta.xls
https://catalog.flatworldknowledge.com/a/34711/ Example_6_2_Estimating_Beta-7a1a.xls

Given the following table of returns, plot the characteristic line and estimate beta.

Date	Return on Zoro Inc.	Return on the Market Portfolio
January	10%	5%
February	7	3.5
March	0	0
April	5	2.5
May	−15	7.5%

SOLUTION

Spreadsheet Solution

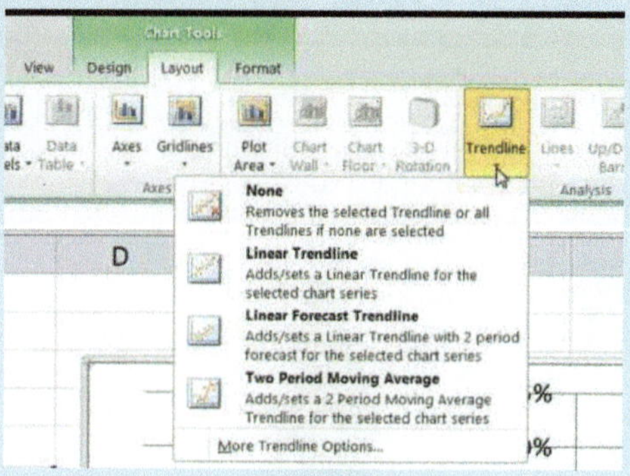

View in the online reader

Algebraic Solution

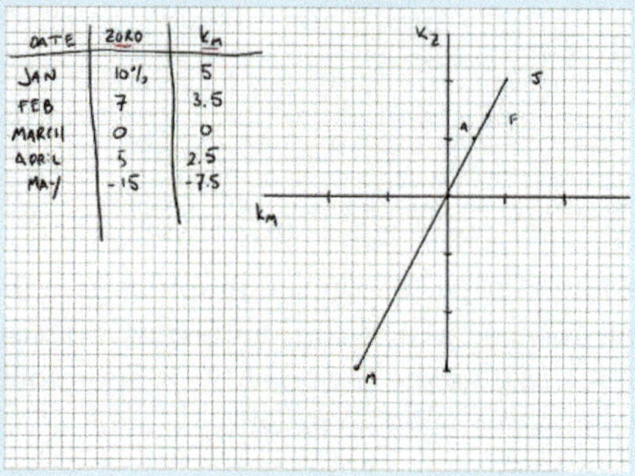

View in the online reader

Put the market returns on the *x*-axis and those of Zoro Inc. on the *y*-axis, as plotted below.

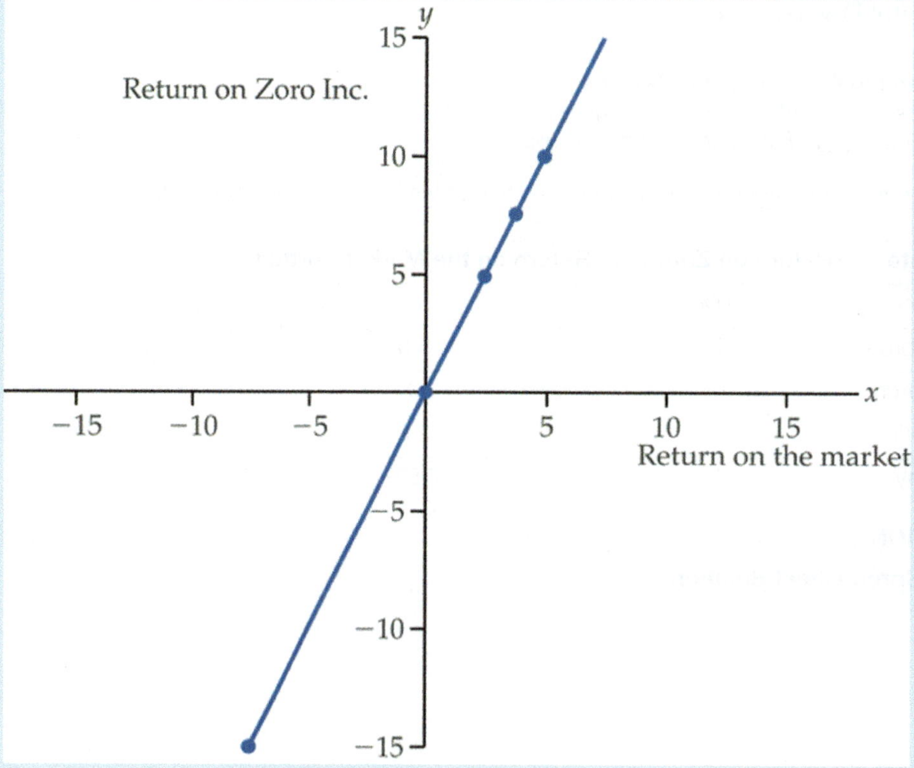

The slope is equal to the rise over the run (e.g., $10\%/5\% = 2$). In practice, betas can be computed as shown in this example or they can be obtained from third-party sources like Bloomberg, Yahoo! Finance, or Google Finance.

Explore It: Characteristic Line

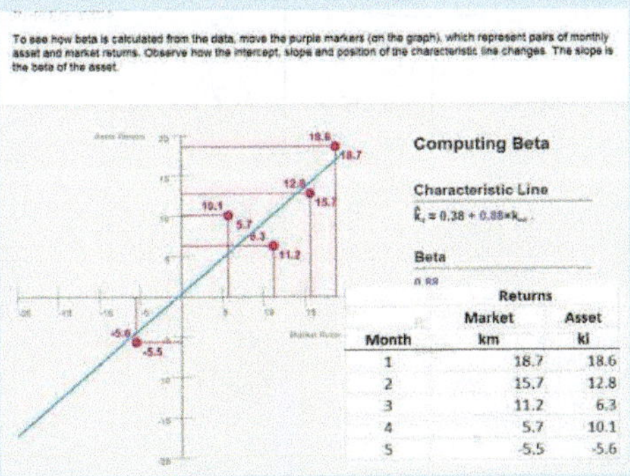

View in the online reader

Properties of Beta

The Market's Beta is Equal to 1

Notice that beta is defined with respect to the market portfolio. If we replaced ABC with the market portfolio in Figure 6.1, then the line would be a perfect diagonal with a slope of 1. While this seems obvious, we use this fact later and so you shouldn't forget it.

The Risk-Free Asset's Beta is Equal to 0

Earlier, we argued that the correlation (covariance) of the returns on the risk-free asset with the returns on any other asset is zero. In Equation 6.3 the numerator is the covariance. If the covariance is zero, then so is the beta. We could also think about replacing ABC with the risk-free asset in Figure 6.1; then the line would be flat (slope of zero), since the risk-free return doesn't change as the return on the market changes.

Portfolio Beta

The beta of a portfolio is the weighted average of the individual betas. The formula for calculating the portfolio beta is:

EQUATION 6.4

$$\beta_p = w_1\beta_1 + \ldots + w_n\beta_n$$

where w_1 is the portfolio weight for asset 1.

Example 6.3 Portfolio Betas

Suppose you held a portfolio with 60% of your funds in Intel $(beta = 1.7)$ and 40% of your funds in Progress Energy $(beta = 0.5)$. Compute the portfolio beta.

SOLUTION

Algebraic Solution

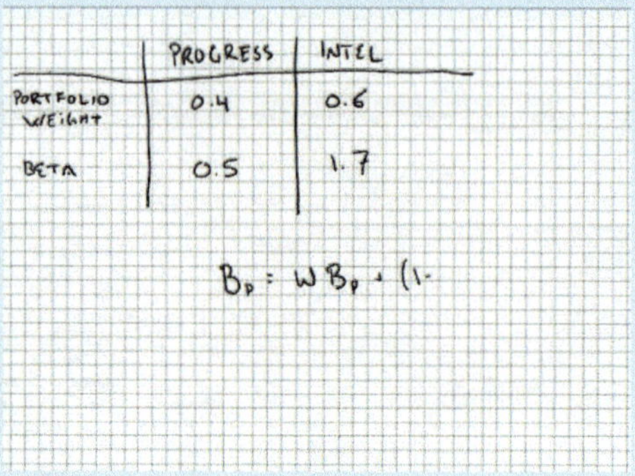

View in the online reader

Using Equation 6.4, the portfolio beta is:

$$\beta_p = (0.60 \times 1.7) + (0.04 \times 0.5) = 1.22$$

6.4 Portfolios with the Risk-Free Asset

The CAPM shows that asset returns are related to systematic risk (as opposed to unsystematic risk). The intuition for the theory is as follows. Unsystematic risk can be eliminated at no cost by holding a large portfolio (by diversifying). Since it can be eliminated at no cost, investors don't need to be compensated (with a higher return) for bearing it. Investors only need to be compensated for the risk that they can't diversify, which is systematic risk. The implication is that a security's expected return should be related to the portion of its risk that cannot be eliminated through diversification (the systematic risk).

In this section we cover the following three topics: First, we calculate the return and beta of portfolios that combine the risk-free asset and a risky asset. The graph of the set of risks and returns produced by those portfolios are called the **portfolio-possibility lines**. Second, we calculate the slope of those lines, which is known as the **Treynor Index**. Finally, we use the Treynor Index to derive an equilibrium relationship between return and risk.

portfolio-possibility line

A line in expected return-risk space. The line shows all of the risk and return combinations that can be achieved by forming two-asset portfolios with the risk-free asset and a risky asset. Each risky asset has its own portfolio possibility line.

Treynor Index

The ratio of the return premium for an asset to its systematic risk (beta). The return premium is the difference between the expected return on an asset and the return on the risk-free asset. Named after Jack Treynor.

Explain It: Systematic Risk Principle

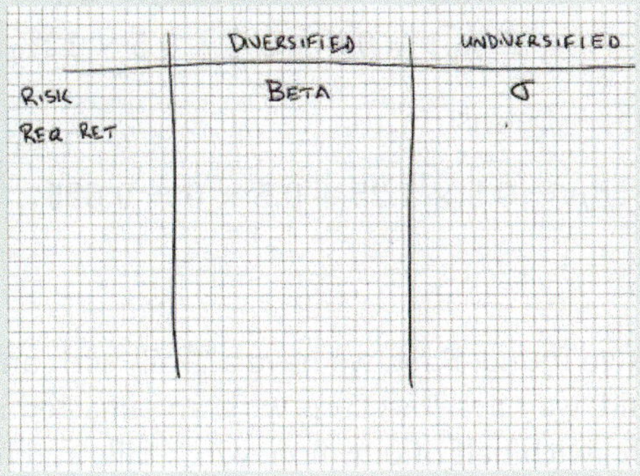

View in the online reader

Portfolios with Lending

Example 6.4 Risk and Return for a Two-Asset Portfolio Including the Risk-Free Asset

Consider a portfolio where half of the money is invested in T-bills and half is invested in shares of RiskCorp Inc. The expected returns and betas of the two assets are shown in this table. What is the expected return and beta of the portfolio?

	E(*k*)	Beta
RiskCorp	12%	1.25
Risk-free Asset	5%	0

SOLUTION

Algebraic Solution

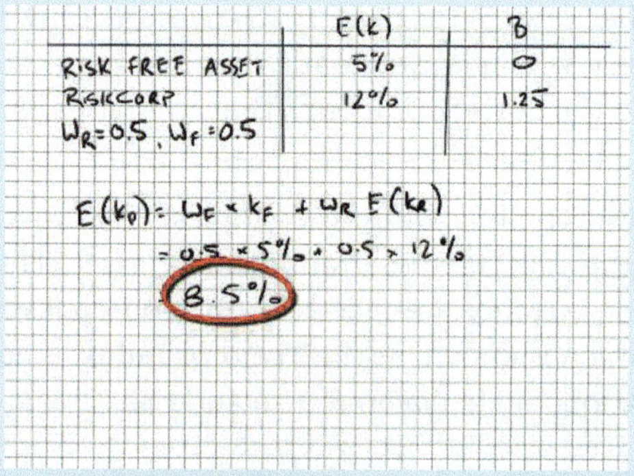

View in the online reader

The portfolio weights are $w_F = 0.5$ and $w_R = 0.5$. A positive portfolio weight for the risk-free asset means that we are long the risk-free asset. When you buy a risk-free asset (i.e., T-bill) you are lending money to the government. The expected return is:

$$E(k_p) = w_F \times E(k_F) + w_R \times E(k_R)$$
$$E(k_p) = 0.5 \times 5\% + 0.5 \times 12\% = 8.5\%$$

Using Equation 6.4, the portfolio beta is:

$$\beta_P = 0.5 \times 1.25 + 0.5 \times 0 = 0.625$$

Let's summarize what we've found. First, we have a T-bill with an expected return of 5% and a beta of zero (no risk). Second, we have RiskCorp with an expected return of 12% and a beta of 1.25. Finally, we built a portfolio with half of our money in T-bills and half in RiskCorp that has an expected return of 8.5% and a beta of 0.625. In Figure 6.2 we graph these three possible risk–return combinations. Below the figure is an Explain It video that works through the construction of the line in Figure 6.2.

FIGURE 6.2 Portfolio Possibility Line with RiskCorp

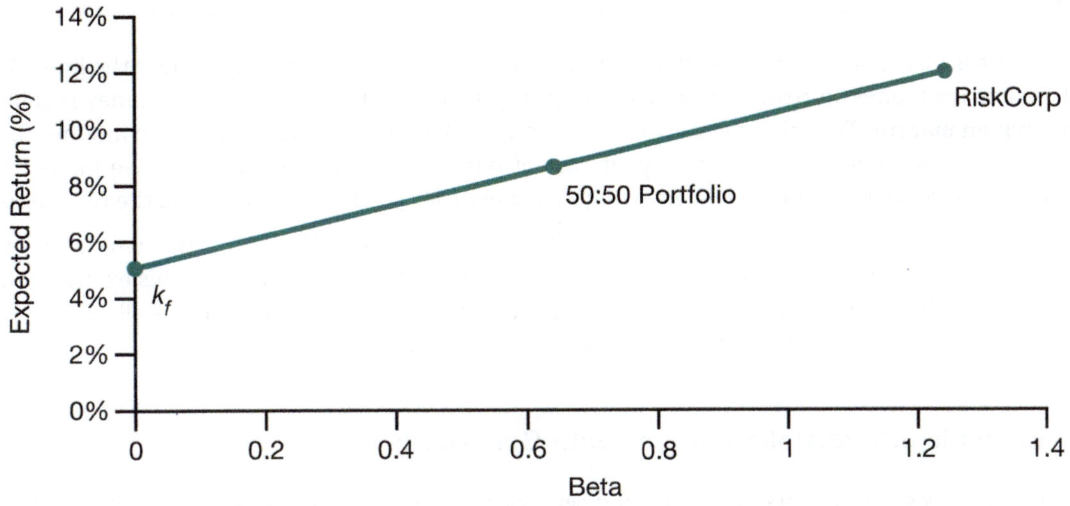

This line is called a *portfolio possibility line*.[3] The point where the line hits the *y*-axis is the risk–return combination for the T-bill. The right-hand end of the line is the risk–return combination for RiskCorp. The point in the middle of the line marked (50:50) is the half-and-half portfolio from "Example 6.4 Risk and Return for a Two-Asset Portfolio Including the Risk-Free Asset".

Explain It: Portfolio Possibility Line

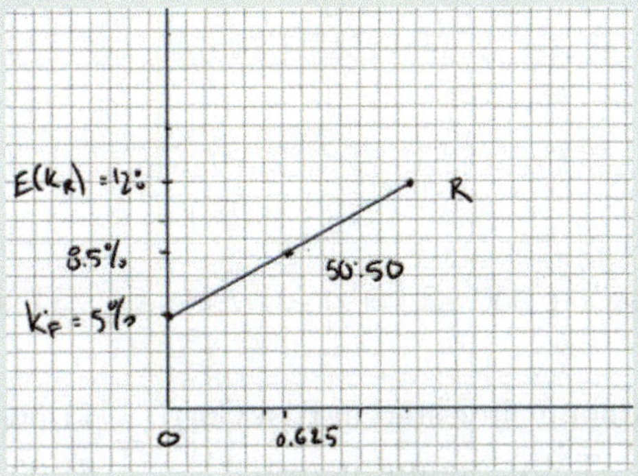

View in the online reader

Portfolios with Borrowing

buying on margin

The process of buying an asset where part of the purchase is financed with borrowed funds. The amount of money provided by the investor is called the margin.

long

A trading position in which an asset is bought and owned with the expectation that it can be sold at a higher price. The opposite of a short position.

short

A trading position in which an asset is sold with the expectation that it can be bought back at a lower price. The asset must be borrowed so that it can be delivered to the buyer. The opposite of a long position.

In Figure 6.2, the portfolio possibility line stops at RiskCorp. Is there a way to extend the line? Yes, if we borrow money. Borrowing to buy more than you can afford with your own money is called **buying on margin**. Typically, you borrow from your broker. Instead, we are going to assume that you borrow by issuing T-bills and so your cost of borrowing is the risk-free rate. We make this assumption so that we can model borrowing as just another portfolio of T-bills and the risky asset.

How is borrowing just another portfolio with T-bills? If we buy T-bills, then we own them—we are **long** T-bills. When we are long T-bills, we lend money to the government. In this example, the government borrows money, so it has the opposite position from us: it is **short** T-bills. When we borrow by issuing T-bills we are taking a short position in T-bills.

Example 6.5 Portfolio Weights with Borrowing

Imagine investing \$1 of our own equity and also borrowing \$0.50. We use the total (\$1.50) to buy shares of RiskCorp. We borrow the \$0.50 by issuing a T-bill with a face value of \$0.525. Let's assume that the yield on T-bills is 5%, so we receive \$0.50 $(= \$0.525/(1.05))$ when it is sold at auction. What are the weights for the portfolio?

SOLUTION

Algebraic Solution

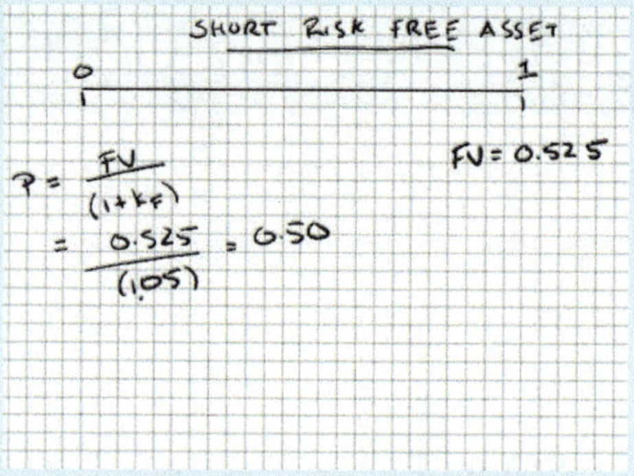

View in the online reader

We purchased \$1.50 of RiskCorp and our personal investment is \$1, so the weight on RiskCorp is:

$$w_R = \frac{\text{Amount invested in RiskCorp}}{\text{Total amount invested}} = \frac{\$1.50}{\$1.00} = 1.50$$

We issued \$0.5 of T-bills, so we are short T-bills. Short positions are represented by negative portfolio weights, so the weight on the risk-free asset is:

$$w_F = \frac{\text{Amount invested in RiskFree}}{\text{Total amount invested}} = \frac{-\$0.50}{\$1.00} = -0.50$$

This makes sense for two reasons: a positive weight means buying, so a negative weight means selling. Also, the weights have to sum to one.

Tip

Recall that the denominator of a portfolio weight, which we label as the "Total amount invested," is the equity provided by the investor—it doesn't include borrowed funds.

Example 6.6 Risk and Return of a Portfolio with Borrowing

Consider a portfolio where we buy $1.50 of RiskCorp and borrow $0.5 (by issuing T-bills). What is the expected return and beta of the portfolio? The expected returns on RiskCorp and the risk-free asset are 12% and 5%, respectively. The beta of RiskCorp is 1.25.

SOLUTION

Algebraic Solution

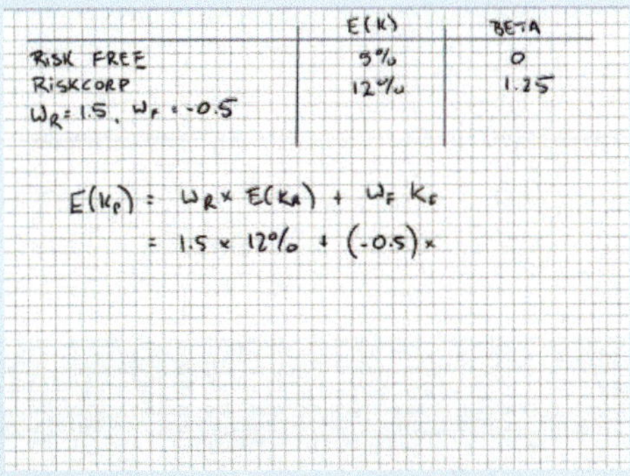

View in the online reader

As we discovered in "Example 6.5 Portfolio Weights with Borrowing", the portfolio weights are $w_F = -0.5$ and $w_R = 1.5$. Thus, the expected return is:

$$E(k_p) = w_F \times k_F + w_R \times E(k_R)$$
$$E(k_p) = -0.5 \times 5\% + 1.5 \times 12\% = 15.5\%$$

The portfolio beta is:

$$\beta_p = 1.5 \times 1.25 - 0.5 \times 0 = 1.875$$

We have added this risk and return combination to those calculated above and shown them all in a new portfolio possibility line in Figure 6.3. The portfolio with borrowing (labeled the margin portfolio) offers a higher expected return, but more risk. Notice that the risk–return point associated with buying on margin (borrowing $0.50) is just an extension of the original line.

FIGURE 6.3 Portfolio Possibility Line with Borrowing

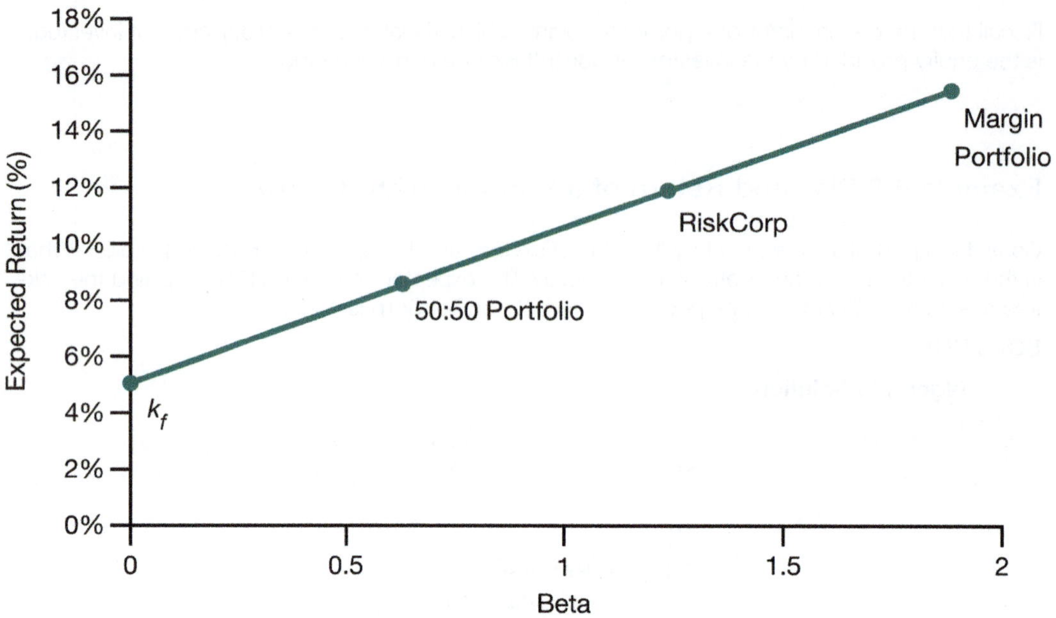

Explain It: Portfolio Possibility Line with Borrowing

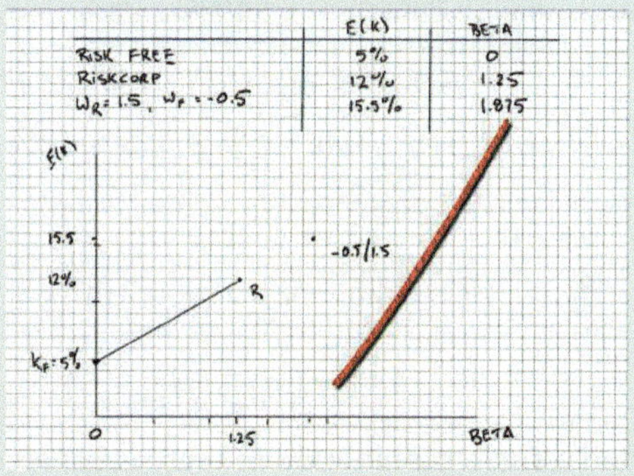

View in the online reader

The Treynor Index

In *Harvard Business Review*, Jack Treynor proposed that the slope of the portfolio-possibility line be used as a performance metric for evaluating risky investments.[4] Figure 6.4 shows the portfolio possibility line for RiskCorp. We can measure the slope using rise-over-run. The rise (the green arrow) is from the risk-free rate, 5%, to RiskCorp's expected return of 12%. The run (the blue arrow) is from the beta of the risk-free asset (0) to the RiskCorp's beta (1.25). The slope is 7%/1.25 or 5.6%. The slope of the portfolio possibility line is called the Treynor Index.

FIGURE 6.4 Portfolio Possibility Line for RiskCorp

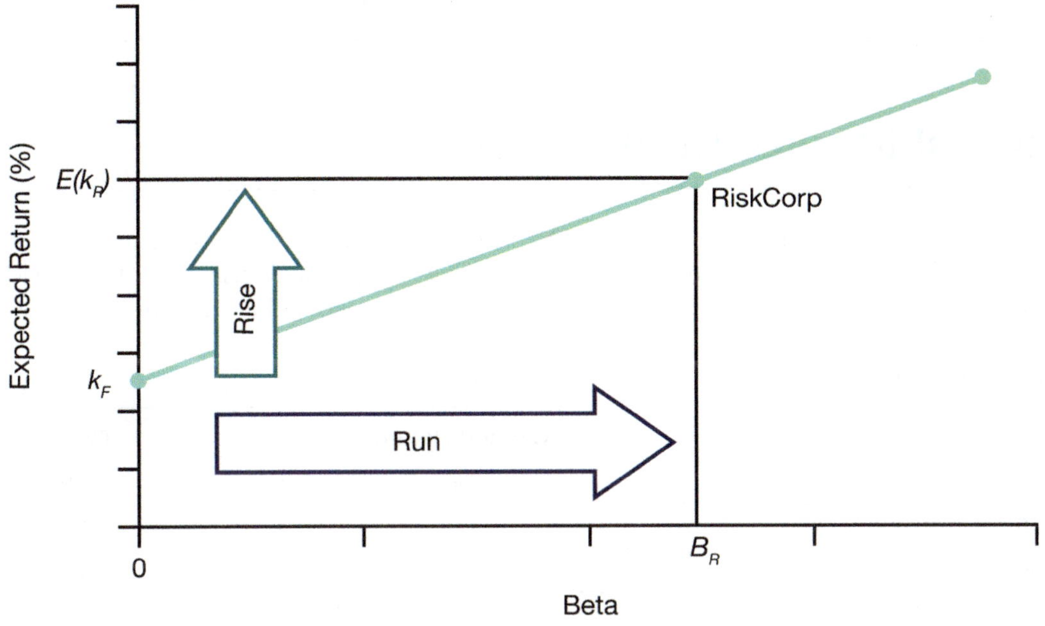

Explain It: The Treynor Index

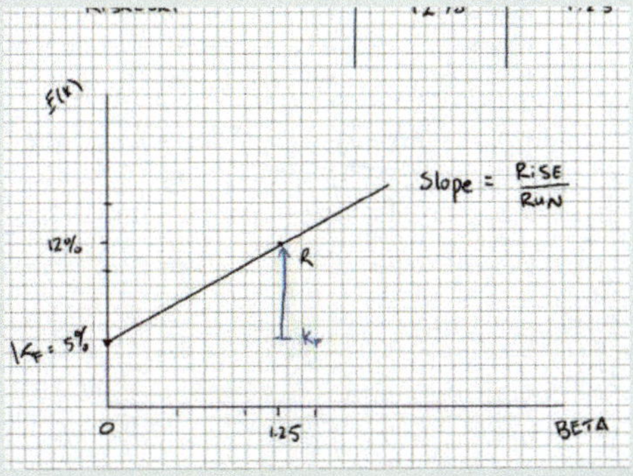

View in the online reader

The formula for the Treynor Index is:

EQUATION 6.5

$$Treynor\ Index = \frac{E(k_i) - k_F}{\beta_i}$$

The Treynor Index measures the excess of the asset's return over the risk-free return per unit of its systematic risk. The excess return is also called the risk premium. For RiskCorp, we interpret its Treynor Index value as telling us that the stock generates 5.6% of risk premium per unit of its beta risk.

6.5 Risk and Return in Equilibrium

Capital Market Equilibrium

Consider the two stocks outlined in Table 6.2. Which stock will be the better investment this coming year? Atlas has a higher expected return, but it also has higher systematic risk. Thus, it is not clear which is better. We can make a distinction between them by comparing their Treynor Indexes.

TABLE 6.2 Returns and Betas for RiskCorp, Atlas, and T-Bills

	Expected Return	Beta
RiskCorp	12%	1.25
Atlas	15%	2.25
T-Bills	5%	0

Example 6.7 Treynor Index

Calculate the Treynor Index for RiskCorp and Atlas using the data provided in Table 6.2.

SOLUTION

Algebraic Solution

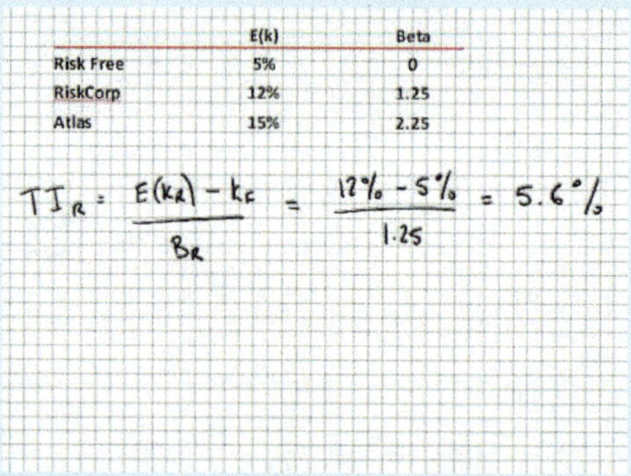

View in the online reader

The Treynor Index for RiskCorp is:

$$\textit{Treynor Index} = (12\% - 5\%)/1.25 = 5.6\%$$

The Treynor Index for Atlas is:

$$\textit{Treynor Index} = (15\% - 5\%)/2.25 = 4.44\%$$

The Treynor Index for RiskCorp is substantially greater than the Treynor Index for Atlas. RiskCorp generates more risk premium per unit of systematic risk than Atlas, so it is the better of the two stocks.

In Figure 6.5, we graph the portfolio-possibility lines for RiskCorp and Atlas.

FIGURE 6.5 Portfolio Possibility Lines for RiskCorp and Atlas

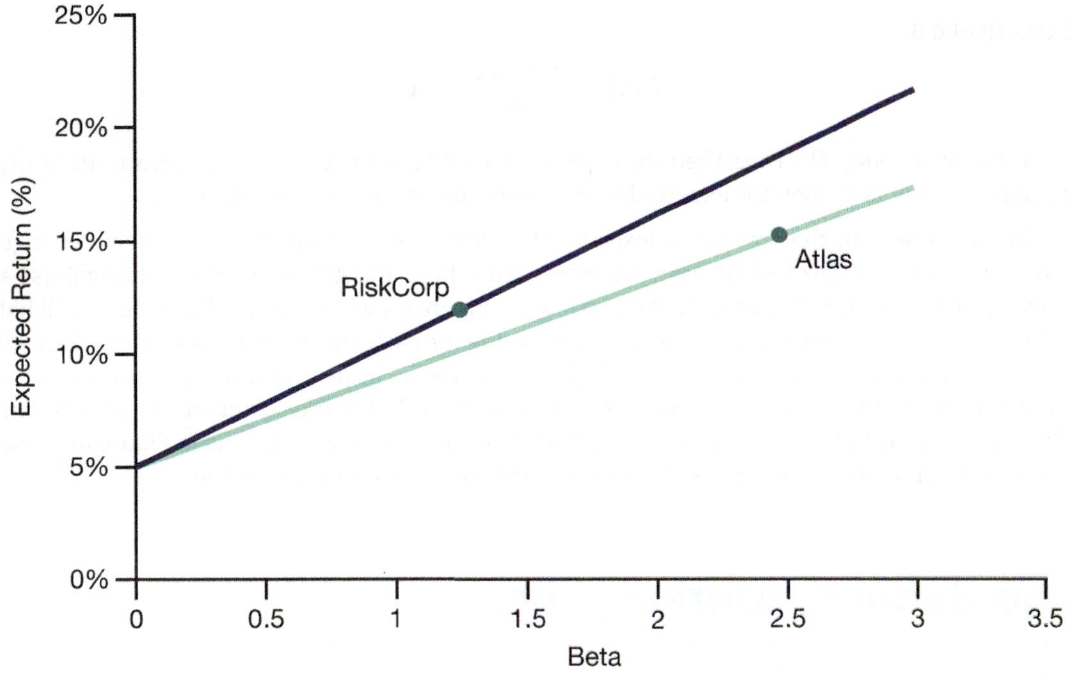

Explain It: Portfolio Possibility Line for Two Stocks

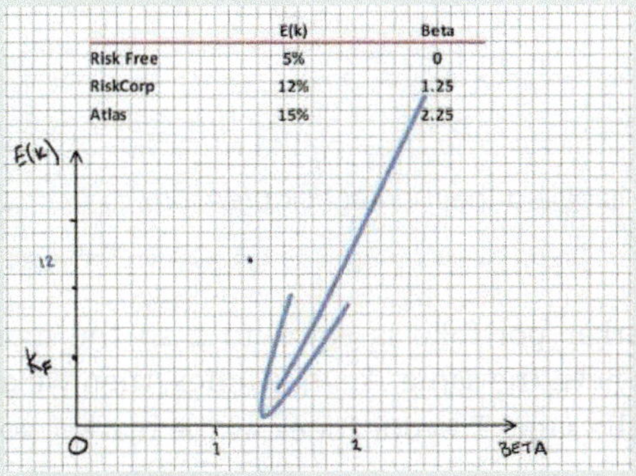

View in the online reader

The Treynor Index for each stock is just the slope of the line. The line for RiskCorp is steeper and so it generates a higher rate of return at every level of systematic risk. (The CAPM assumes that markets are efficient. It assumes that investors buy stocks with high Treynor Indexes and sell stocks with low indexes.)

How would you trade if you were presented with the information about RiskCorp and Atlas? Because RiskCorp generates more return per unit risk, you would want to buy RiskCorp and sell Atlas. The buying pressure for RiskCorp creates excess demand, which pushes its price up. The selling pressure for Atlas creates excess supply, which pushes its price down. The changes in today's prices will change the stocks' expected returns.

If we ignore dividends and assume that the future is fixed, then we can express the expected return as:

EQUATION 6.6

$$E(k) = \frac{E(P_{t+1})}{P_t} - 1$$

If the price today, P_t , rises, then the expected return falls. That is what happens to RiskCorp. If the price today falls, then the expected return rises. That is what happens to Atlas.

What happens to the Treynor Indexes for the two stocks as their expected returns change? RiskCorp's Treynor Index will fall as its expected return falls, and Atlas's Treynor Index will rise as its expected return rises. Graphically, the two lines in Figure 6.5 will converge. The process will halt when the two lines meet and the Treynor Index value for each stock is the same. Only then will there be no incentive to buy one stock or sell the other. That is the definition of equilibrium—when there is no force for change. Thus, we can characterize capital market equilibrium as occurring when the Treynor Indexes of all assets are equal—they all lie on the same line in Figure 6.5. What is that line? What are its coordinates? In the next subsection, we derive that line.

The Security Market Line

In the last section, we discovered that in equilibrium all securities have the same Treynor Index. That is, all securities plot on the same line. If all securities plot on the line, then the market portfolio must also, and that allows us to pin down the precise coordinates of the line. The market portfolio's Treynor Index is:

EQUATION 6.7

$$Treynor\ Index\ for\ market = \frac{E(k_M) - k_F}{\beta_M}$$

Tip

The difference $E(k_M) - k_F$ is called the *market risk premium*.

But the beta of the market portfolio is equal to 1, so the market's Trynor Index is just $E(k_M) - k_F$. If all securities have the same Treynor Index, then we can pick any security "*i*" and, in equilibrium, it must have the same Treynor Index as the market portfolio. Thus, we can equate their Treynor Indexes:

EQUATION 6.8

$$\frac{E(k_i) - k_F}{\beta_i} = E(k_M) - k_F$$

With a little algebra, we can rearrange that equality to derive an expression for the expected rate of return on any security "*i*" in equilibrium:

EQUATION 6.9

$$E(k_i) = k_F + \beta i \times [E(k_M) - k_F]$$

Look at Equation 6.9 carefully. It says that the expected return on a risky asset is equal to the return you would earn by investing in a riskless asset plus an additional return to compensate you for the risk of the investment. This additional return is the market risk premium multiplied by beta. "Explain It: Market Risk Premium" provides some evidence as to the size of the market risk premium.

Explain It: Market Risk Premium

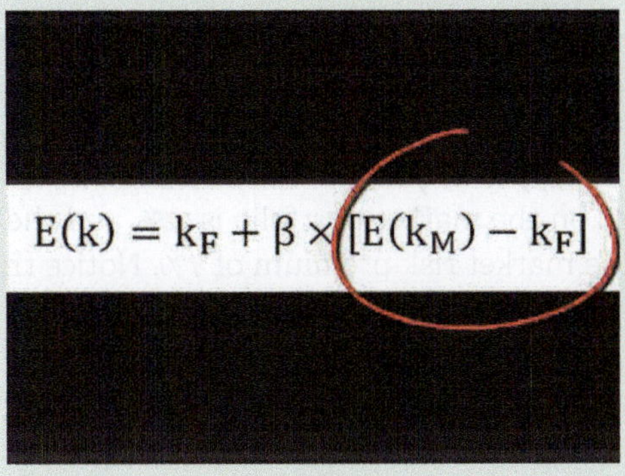

View in the online reader

Another thing to notice about Equation 6.9 is that the only type of risk that contributes to the required return is the kind that's measured by beta. We know that beta only measures systematic risk. Firm-specific risk never enters into the calculation of the required return.

Example 6.8 The Equilibrium Expected Return

If the beta for Intel is 1.7, the risk-free rate of interest is 5%, and the expected return on the market portfolio is 12%, what return must Intel provide investors to compensate them for the risk of the security?

SOLUTION

Algebraic Solution

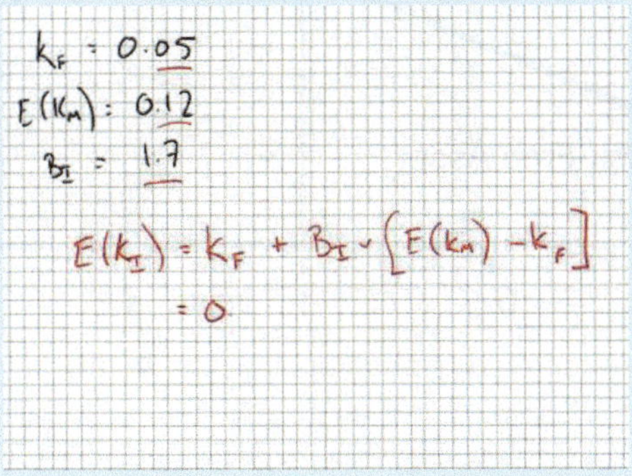

View in the online reader

Substituting these figures into Equation 6.9:

$$E(k_i) = k_F + \beta_i \times [E(k_M) - k_F]$$
$$E(k_i) = 5\% + 1.7 \times [12\% - 5\%]$$
$$E(k_i) = 16.9\%$$

security market line (SML)

The linear (straight-line) relationship between expected return and systematic risk (beta). The SML is the conclusion of the capital asset pricing model.

The graph of the CAPM equation (Equation 6.9) is called the **security market line (SML)**. Remember that the function for a straight line is $y = b + mx$ where *b* is the *y*-intercept and *m* is the slope of the line. The *y*-intercept of the CAPM is the risk-free rate of interest (k_F) and the slope is the market risk premium $(E(k_M) - k_F)$. Figure 6.6 shows the security market line. The risk-free rate is 5%, the expected return on the market portfolio is 12%, and the market portfolio has a beta of 1. The slope of the line is the market risk premium of 7%. Notice that, even when $beta = 0$ (i.e., zero risk), you still require a return.

Tip

It is tempting to think of beta as the slope of the security market line. This is incorrect. The *x*-axis is beta, and the slope is the market risk premium.

Security Market Line

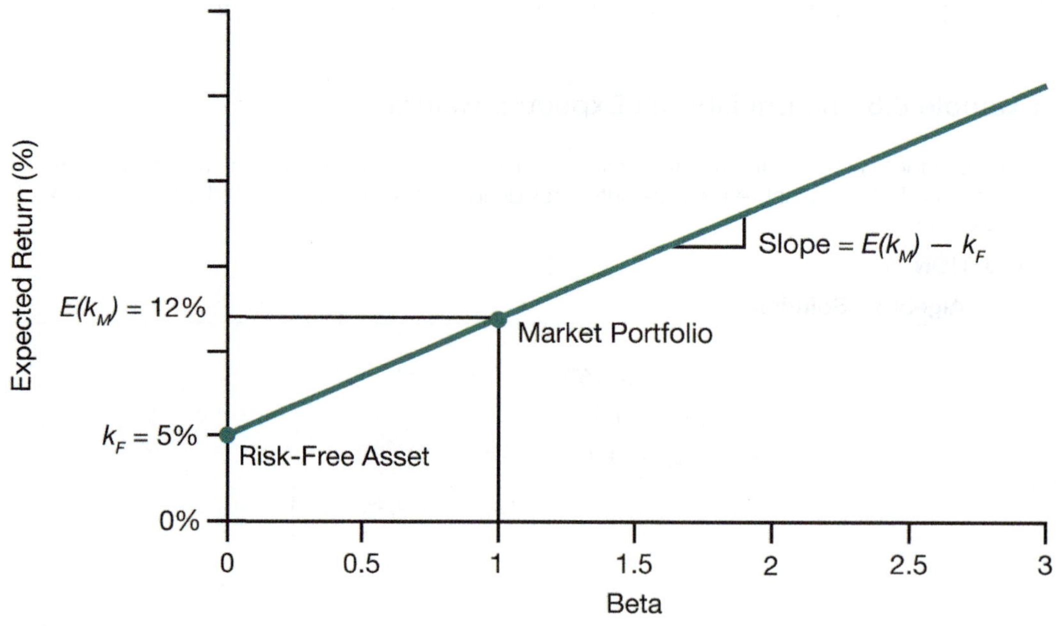

Example 6.9 Using the CAPM

Suppose you are considering the purchase of shares in Gap Inc., a chain of retail clothing stores. After studying the financials, you project the future return on investment to be 13.5%. The risk-free rate is 5%, the expected return on the market is 12%, and Gap's beta is 1.3. Should you buy the stock?

SOLUTION

Algebraic Solution

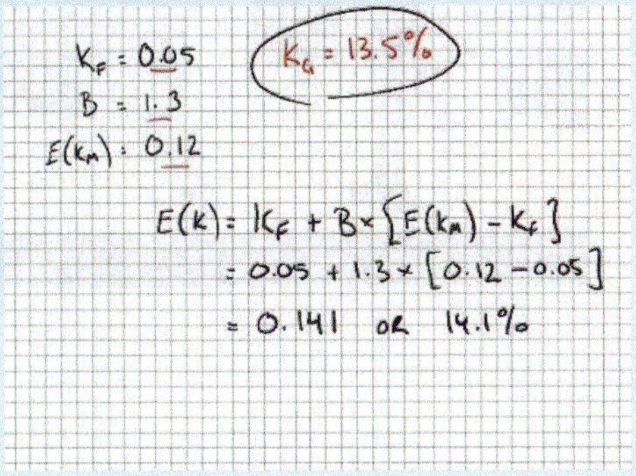

View in the online reader

To answer this question, you must first compute the expected return using the SML (Equation 6.9):

$$E(k_i) = 5\% + 1.3 \times [12\% - 5\%] = 14.1\%$$

According to the CAPM, in equilibrium you should earn an average return of 14.1% to compensate you for a beta of 1.3. Since you expect this stock to generate a return of only 13.5%, you should not invest. The CAPM return is the fair return in equilibrium, and we will sometimes refer to it as the "required" return. You require the CAPM return in order to be fairly compensated for the risk that you take.

Let's summarize the CAPM. The theory assumes that the market is filled with many well-diversified portfolio holders who measure systematic risk with beta. Those investors are rational and constantly search for mispriced securities. Mispriced securities are those whose Treynor Index does not equal the market risk premium. When a mispriced security is located, investors trade the security until the price adjusts and the mispricing disappears. The result is that all securities are on (or moving towards) the security market line and the expected return equals the required return.

Conclusions

A fair question to pose at this juncture is whether the CAPM actually reflects what happens in the markets. One problem with the CAPM is that the market portfolio is unobservable.[5] It is difficult (impossible) to estimate returns on many assets such as real estate, jewelry, and private companies. Another problem is that the CAPM beta does not appear to be the only measure of systematic risk.[6]

Explain It: Mutual Fund Performance

View in the online reader

"Explain It: Mutual Fund Performance" summarizes research conducted by Burton Malkiel on mutual fund performance.[7] Malkiel collected return data on U.S. equity mutual funds and plotted their returns and betas against the security market line. He found that funds plotted below the SML. This result is important because it indicates that the market is quite efficient (as the CAPM assumes). It appears that mutual fund companies, with all of their resources, cannot find lots of mispriced securities and so boost their returns above what the CAPM predicts.

Malkiel's result has powerful implications for individual investors. We can achieve risk-and-return points along a homemade SML by investing in money market mutual funds (which mostly hold T-bills) and stock market index ETFs. Since we can achieve the SML, Malkiel's result suggests that we can outperform most mutual funds with simple homemade portfolios.

Endnotes

1. Harry Markowitz is the father of portfolio theory. His Ph.D. dissertation at the University of Chicago led to his famous 1952 article titled "Portfolio Selection," published in the *Journal of Finance* (March 1952): 77–91.
2. Sharpe, William F. "Capital Asset Prices: A Theory of Market Equilibrium under Conditions of Risk," *Journal of Finance 19*, no. 3 (1964): 425–42.
3. Treynor, Jack, "How to Rate Management of Investment Funds," *Harvard Business Review 43* (1965): 63–75.
4. Treynor, Jack, "How to Rate Management of Investment Funds," *Harvard Business Review 43* (1965): 63–75.
5. Roll, Richard, "A Critique of the Asset Pricing Theory's Tests, Part I: On Past and Potential Testability of the Theory," *Journal of Financial Economics 4*, no. 2 (1977): 129–76.
6. Fama, Eugene F., and Kenneth R. French, "The Cross-Section of Expected Stock Returns," *Journal of Finance 47*, no. 2 (1992): 427–65.
7. Malkiel, Burton G., "Returns from Investing in Equity Mutual Funds 1971–1991," *Journal of Finance 50, no. 2* (1995): 549–72.

CHAPTER 7

Interest Rates and Bonds

Learning Objectives

By the end of this chapter you will be able to:

1. Discuss the features of zero coupon bonds and the markets they trade in.
2. Calculate zero coupon bond yields and prices.
3. Understand the factors that determine the shape of the spot rate yield curve.
4. Understand the features of coupon bonds and the markets they trade in.
5. Calculate coupon bond yields and prices.
6. Understand the properties of coupon bond prices.

Fixed income securities are a class of securities that pay a fixed income to the holder. The class includes bonds, which are the focus of this chapter. **Bonds** represent loans from the holder to the issuer. For example, when the U.S. government borrows money, it issues bonds, which are purchased by individual investors. The purchase of the bond represents a loan to the U.S. government. The bond stipulates how and when the money will be paid back as well as how much interest will be paid. The biggest difference between a loan and a bond is that the lender can get his money back early by selling the bond to another investor. With a loan, the lender has to wait until maturity to get his money back.

This chapter focuses on the two main types of bonds: zero coupon bonds and coupon bonds. We present most of the basic ideas about bonds in the context of zero coupon bonds because they are simple and easy to understand.

fixed income securities

A class of securities that is not equity and that makes payments to the holder on a fixed schedule (e.g., bonds).

bond

A debt instrument issued by governments and corporations with a maturity of more than 1 year. Coupon bonds pay periodic (annual or semi-annual) interest payments to the holder (called coupons) and pay a final lump-sum (called the face value) at maturity.

7.1 Zero Coupon Bond Features and Markets

An example of a zero coupon bond is shown in Figure 7.1.

FIGURE 7.1 Zero Coupon Bond
1. Face value = $100,000. The face value is the amount the issuer pays the holder at maturity. 2. Issuer: The name of the company (government or agency) that issued the bond. 3. The date that the face value is payable to the bond holder (April 6, 1970). 4. The date that the bond was issued to the (original) bond holder (October 9, 1969).

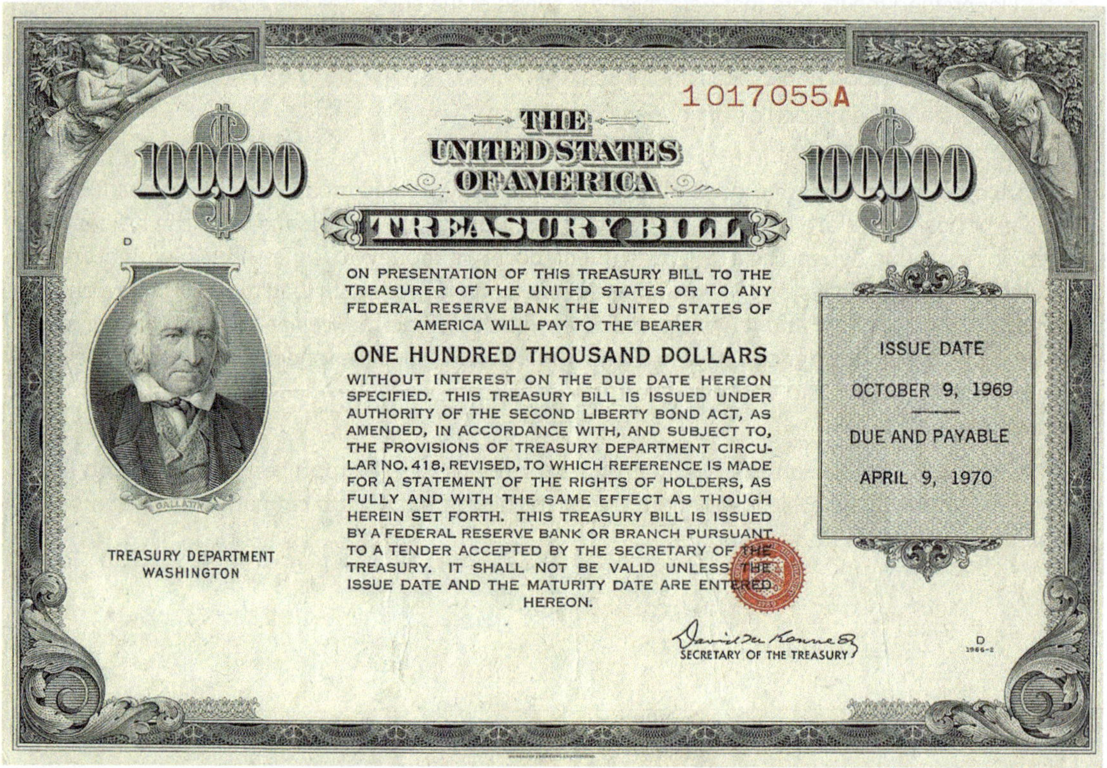

By JHerbstman - Own work, The Joe I. Herbstman Memorial Collection of American Finance, Public Domain, https://commons.wikimedia.org/w/index.php?curid=55835862

zero coupon bond
A bond that does not pay coupons.

This bond is called a **zero coupon bond** because it does not offer any coupons. (This will be clearer after we describe a coupon bond.) With a zero coupon bond, the holder (or lender) pays a price that is less than the face value, and then receives the face value at maturity. The difference between the price and the face value is the interest earned by the holder.

Zero Coupon Bond Markets

Short-maturity zero coupon bonds (with less than or equal to 1 year) are traded on the **money market**. These bonds include **commercial paper** and government **T-bills**. At the end of 2019, there was almost $3.5 trillion worth of money market securities outstanding (see Table 7.1). To put this in perspective, there was $45T worth of securities outstanding in the U.S. fixed income market at the end of 2019, so the money market constitutes less than 8% of the fixed income market. Buyers of money market securities include pension funds and **mutual funds**. Money market mutual funds are simply a portfolio of these securities.

TABLE 7.1 U.S. Money Markets—Face Value Outstanding at Year End (USD Billions)

	Paper	T-Bills	Total
2006	1,974.0	912.0	2,886.0
2010	1,051.0	1,789.0	2,839.0
2014	930.0	1,457.0	2,387.0
2018	996.0	2,340.0	3,336.0
2019	1,045.2	2,416.9	3,462.1

Data from Securities Industry and Financial Markets Association (SIFMA), www.sifma.org; Department of the Treasury.

The U.S. government does not issue zero coupon bonds with maturities greater than 1 year. However, many financial intermediaries strip T-bonds (and, to a lesser extent, T-notes) and sell the stripped coupons at face value as zero coupon bonds. At the end of 2019, there was $2.4 trillion of U.S. government T-bonds outstanding and about 14% of that total had been stripped (over $323 billion).[1]

Explain It: Strip Bonds

View in the online reader

money market

The market for bonds with a maturity of less than (or equal to) 1 year. These bonds are all zero-coupon bonds and include bankers' acceptances, commercial paper, and government T-bills.

commercial paper

A short-term, unsecured promissory note issued by a corporation that has a very high credit standing, having a yield above that paid on U.S. Treasury issues and comparable to that available on negotiable CDs with similar maturities.

T-bills

Bonds issued by the U.S. government that have maturities of 91 days, 182 days, or 52 weeks. T-bills are zero-coupon bonds also known as treasury bills.

mutual funds

A professionally managed pool of money. The money comes from a disparate group of investors who exchange their money for units (if the fund is organized as a trust) or shares in the fund. The money can be invested in any type of security depending on the goals of the fund.

7.2 Zero Coupon Bond Yields and Pricing

Zero Coupon Bond Yields

A zero coupon bond promises the holder a fixed sum of money (the face value of $*FV*) at a fixed date in the future (date *T*). The timeline of cash flows from a zero coupon bond is shown below.

FIGURE 7.2 Timeline of Cash Flows for Zero Coupon Bond

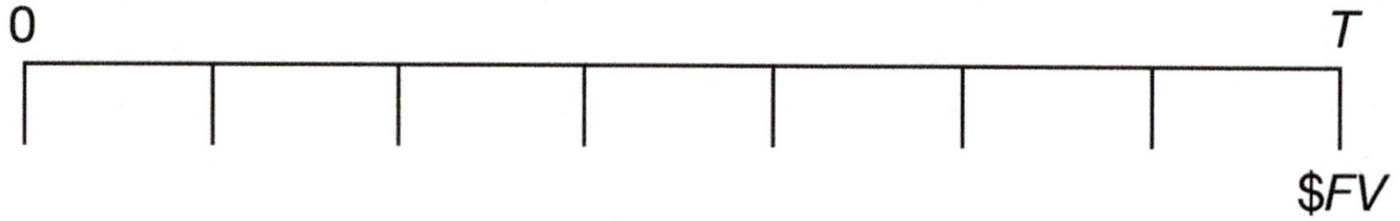

If interest rates are positive (which they usually are), then the price of the bond is less than the face value. The dollar amount of interest earned on the bond is the difference between the face value and the price.

Explain It

Interest rates aren't always positive. In mid-2011, prices of Swiss 3-month treasury bills rose above face value and yields became negative. With the high risk of default on bonds issued by the PIGS (Portugal, Italy, Greece, and Spain), investors were willing to pay for the security offered by Swiss government bonds. In October of 2015, U.S. Treasury Bills with a 3-month maturity were auctioned with a 0% yield. That was the lowest yield on record. German 2-year government bonds (Bunds) have had negative yields since late 2014 until the time of writing—October 2020.

The return on the bond is the rate that the price grows to equal the face value at maturity. If we think of the price as a present value and the face value as a future value, then we can use the future value formula to solve for the return.

EQUATION 7.1

$$FV = Price \times (1 + k)^n$$

where

$$FV = \text{the face value of the bond}$$
$$Price = \text{the price of the bond at the time } 0$$
$$k = \text{the return on the bond (yield to maturity)}$$
$$n = \text{the number of years until maturity}$$

Tip

Bond yields are quoted in nominal terms (not effective) and are expressed per annum. In this chapter, all long-term zero coupon bonds will have maturities that are an integer value, so the nominal yield equals the effective yield.

We can solve for the return on the bond by simplifying Equation 7.1.

EQUATION 7.2

$$k = \left[\frac{FV}{\text{Price}}\right]^{1/n} - 1$$

The return is also called a **yield to maturity (or yield)** of the bond. The returns on U.S. government zero coupon bonds are also called **Treasury spot rates**. Treasury yields are the building block for all yields because they are essentially default free; there is almost no risk that the U.S. government will fail to pay its obligations.

yield to maturity (or yield)

An estimate of the annual return an investor will earn if they buy a bond and hold it to maturity.

Treasury spot rates

The yield on a default-free zero-coupon treasury where the yield is quoted for immediate settlement.

Example 7.1 The Yield on a Zero Coupon Bond

Digital Downloads

Example 7.1 The Yield on a Zero Coupon Bond.xls
https://catalog.flatworldknowledge.com/a/34711/Example_7_1_The_Yield_on_a_Zero_Coupon_Bond-067f.xls

Consider a zero coupon bond with a maturity in 2 years and a face value of $1,000. Assume that the price of the bond is $907.03. If you buy the bond at that price and hold it until maturity, then what is the yield on the bond?

SOLUTION

Spreadsheet Solution

	A	B
1		
2		
3	Problem Data:	
4	Price =	$ 907.03
5	FV =	$ 1,000.00
6	n =	2
7	k =	?
8		

View in the online reader

Algebraic Solution

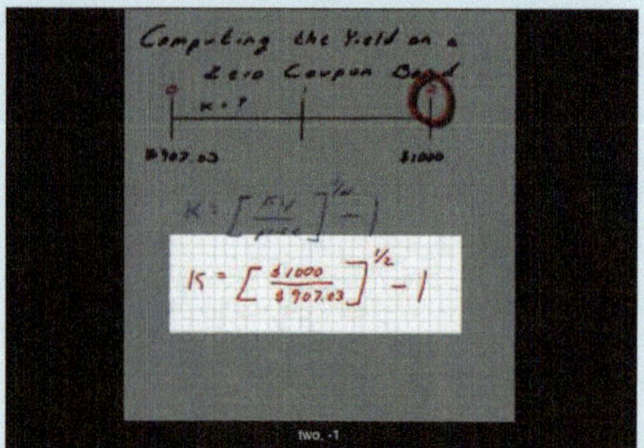

View in the online reader

Calculator Solution

View in the online reader

$$FV = \$1,000$$
$$\text{Price} = \$907.03$$
$$n = 2$$
$$k = \left[\frac{FV}{\text{Price}}\right]^{1/n} - 1$$
$$k = \left[\frac{\$1,000}{\$907.03}\right]^{1/2} - 1 = 0.05 \text{ or } 5\%$$

The yield on the bond is 5% per annum.

The Term Structure of Rates and the Yield Curve

Assume that you are an investor who is interested in buying U.S. government zero coupon bonds, but you are uncertain about what maturity you want. You call your broker for prices on five bonds with terms of 1, 2, 3, 4, and 5 years, and she replies with the information in Table 7.2.

TABLE 7.2 Zero Coupon Bond Prices and Yields for Different Maturities

Maturity Date	Price ($100 face value)	Yield to Maturity
1	$99.009	1%
2	$96.117	2%
3	$91.514	3%
4	$85.480	4%
5	$78.353	5%

The yields across the different maturities are called the **term structure of interest rates** because they are the interest rates for different maturities (terms).

term structure of interest rates

The relationship between term (maturity date) and interest rates.

The Yield Curve

If the term structure of rates is graphed against the respective maturities, then the resulting curve is called the yield curve. The **yield curve** of the Treasury spot rates is known as the Treasury spot rate yield curve. If we use the spot rates from Table 7.2, then the Treasury spot rate yield curve is shown in Figure 7.3.

yield curve

A graphical representation of the term structure. A graph of yields on the y-axis against time to maturity (term) on the x-axis.

FIGURE 7.3 Treasury Spot Rate Yield Curve

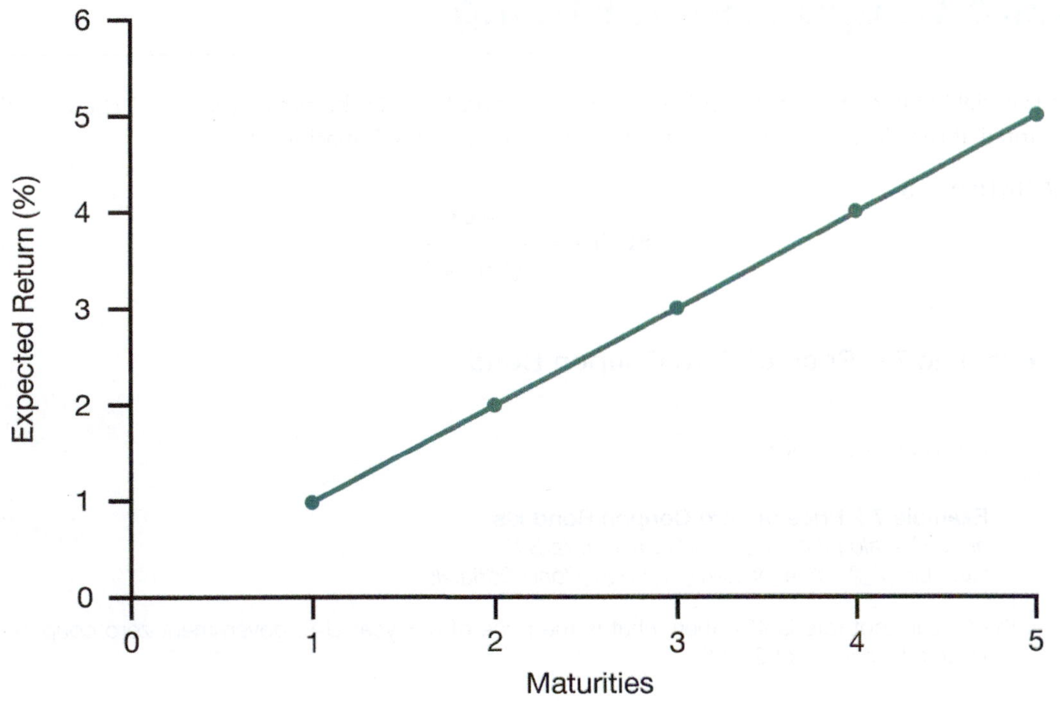

Each point on the yield curve represents the return earned on a U.S. government zero coupon bond with the indicated maturity.

Explain It: Treasury Spot Rate Yield Curve Over Time

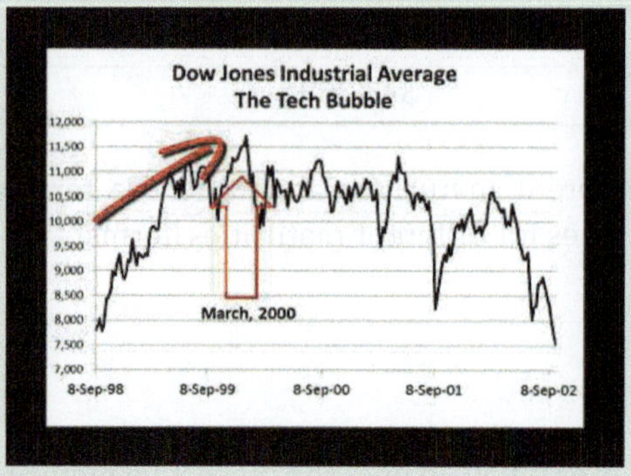

View in the online reader

Zero Coupon Bond Pricing

If the yield is known then the price of a zero coupon bond is the present value of the face discounted at the yield. We can solve for the price by rearranging Equation 7.1.

EQUATION 7.3

$$\$\text{Price} = \frac{\$FV}{(1 + k_n)^n}$$

Example 7.2 Price of Zero Coupon Bond

Digital Downloads

Example 7.2 Price of Zero Coupon Bond.xls
https://catalog.flatworldknowledge.com/a/34711/
Example_7_2_Price_of_Zero_Coupon_Bond-9d5a.xls

If the 3-year spot rate is 4%, then what is the price of a 3-year U.S. government zero coupon bond with a face value of $100?

SOLUTION

Spreadsheet Solution

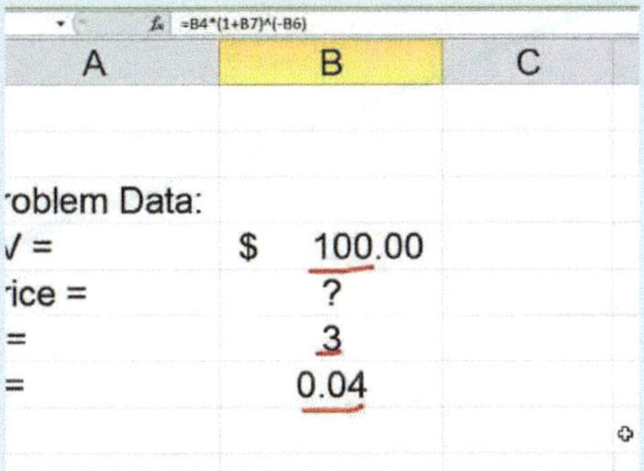

View in the online reader

Algebraic Solution

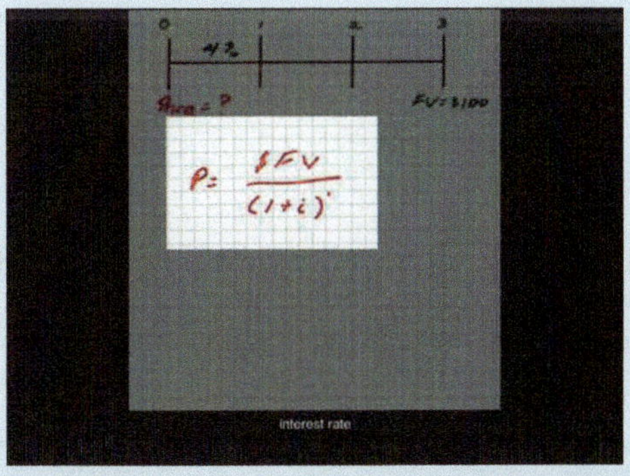

View in the online reader

$$\$FV = 100$$
$$n = 3\text{-year}$$
$$k_3 = 4\%$$

The price of the bond is:

$$\begin{aligned}\$\text{Price} &= \frac{\$FV}{(1+k_3)^3}\\ &= \frac{\$100}{(1.04)^3}\\ &= \$88.90\end{aligned}$$

The Inverse Relationship Between Bond Prices and Yields

Bond prices and interest rates move inversely: If yields rise, then bond prices fall. To see this relationship, look at Equation 7.3: The yield is in the denominator of the right-hand side of the equation—when the yield increases the ratio declines. You can also see this by increasing the yield in the spreadsheet that accompanies Figure 7.4. The graph in Figure 7.4 shows the prices of a 2-year bond at different yields.

FIGURE 7.4 Prices versus Yields for a 2-Year Zero Coupon Bond

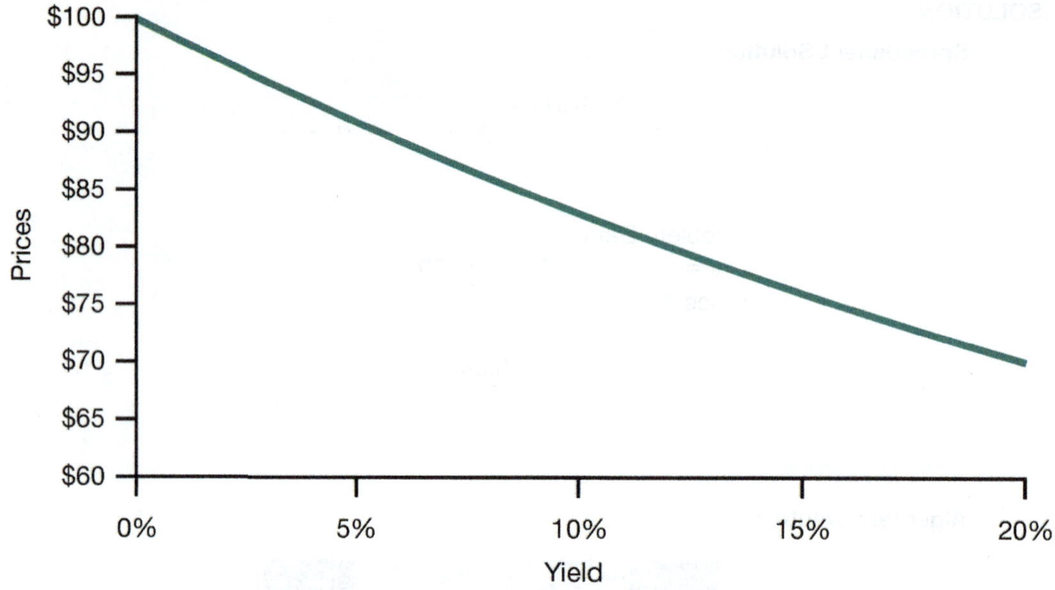

Digital Downloads

Spreadsheet Graph of Prices and Yields of Zero Coupon Bond.xls
https://catalog.flatworldknowledge.com/a/34711/
Spreadsheet_Graph_of_Prices_and_Yields_of_Zero_Coupon_Bond-e8d5.xls

Explain It: Zero Coupon Bond Prices and Yields

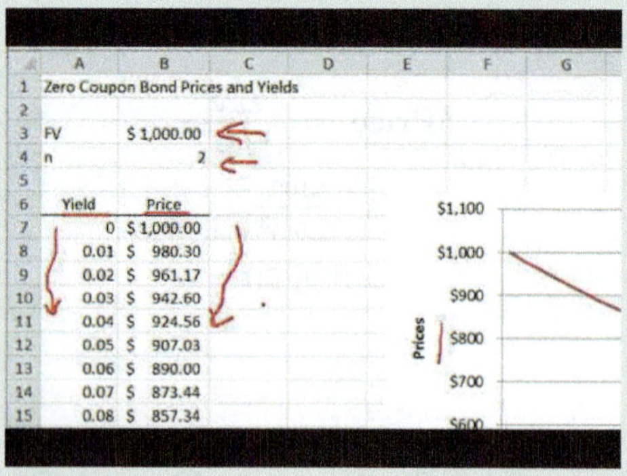

View in the online reader

Explore It: Zero Coupon Bond Price

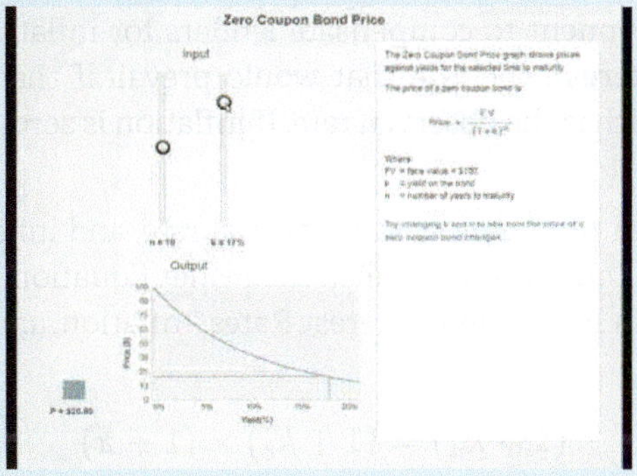

View in the online reader

7.3 Determinants of the Shape of the Yield Curve

The yield curve is not constant over time. In the early 1980s, short-term rates were very high. However, investors expected them to fall in the future, so long-term rates were lower and, as a result, the yield was downward sloping. Downward-sloping yield curves are unusual. For this reason, an upward-sloping yield curve is called a normal yield curve and a downward-sloping yield curve is called an **inverted yield curve**.

inverted yield curve

A yield curve that is downward-sloping.

There are five factors that determine the position and shape of the spot rate yield curve: (1) real interest rates; (2) inflation; (3) maturity preference; (4) default risk; and (5) liquidity. We will discuss each in turn.

Tip

This list of factors is general. Different bonds are affected by these factors by different amounts. For example, U.S. government bonds have very little default risk.

Interest Rates and Inflation

real rate of interest

The rate of interest that would prevail if there was no inflation.

nominal rate of interest

The rate of interest that incorporates compensation for inflation.

Interest rates include a component to compensate lenders for inflation. Inflation drives a wedge between the **real rate of interest**, the rate that would prevail if there was no inflation, and the **nominal rate of interest**, which is the observed rate. If inflation is zero, then the real rate equals the nominal rate.

The relationship between the nominal rate, the real rate, and inflation was derived by American economist Irving Fisher. Equation 7.4 is called the Fisher Equation. The derivation of the Fisher Equation is shown in "Explain It: Nominal Interest Rates, Inflation, and Real Rates".

EQUATION 7.4

$$(1 + k_n) = (1 + k_r) \times (1 + \pi)$$

where

$$\begin{aligned} k_n &= \textbf{the nominal interest rate} \\ k_r &= \textbf{the real interest rate} \\ \pi &= \textbf{the expected rate of inflation} \end{aligned}$$

We can simplify the Fisher Equation to obtain an expression for the nominal interest rate:

EQUATION 7.5

$$k_n = k_r + \pi + (k_r \times \pi)$$

Tip

The third term is called the product term. The product term is quite small and so some people, mistakenly, think that the nominal return is the sum of the real return plus inflation. You know better!

Explain It: Nominal Interest Rates, Inflation, and Real Rates

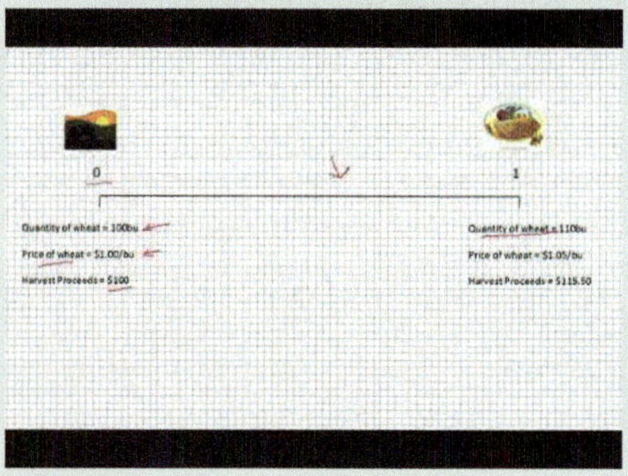

View in the online reader

Example 7.3 Nominal Rates, Real Rates, and Inflation

If the real rate is 10% and inflation is 5%, then what is the nominal rate?

SOLUTION

Algebraic Solution

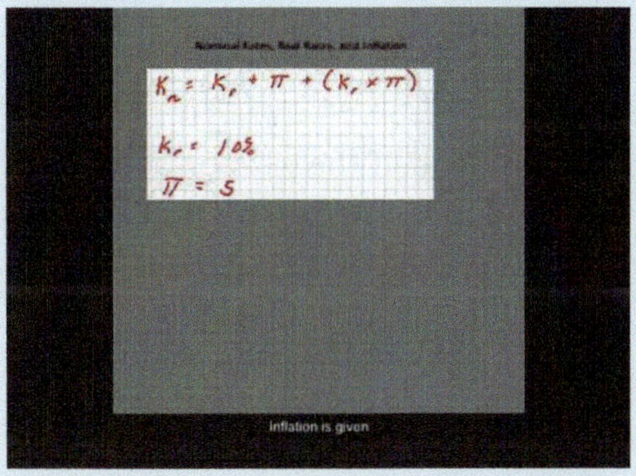

View in the online reader

Notice that π is defined as the *expected* rate of inflation. Lenders set interest rates before lending funds. Lenders set interest rates to compensate them for giving up the use of the money during the loan period. Of course, the actual inflation rate for the *next* year is not known when the lender establishes the interest rate. The lender must guess. When inflation rates are stable, as they have been since 1991, this is much easier to do. However, when they are volatile, as they were between 1970 and 1985, this is much more difficult. Inflation rates can be estimated using the rate of change of the **Consumer Price Index (CPI)**.

Consumer Price Index (CPI)

The Consumer Price Index (CPI) is an indicator of the relative level of consumer prices. It is obtained by comparing the cost of a fixed basket of goods and services to the cost of that basket in the base year.

Because we don't know what the market expects inflation to be (how do you accurately measure expectations?), we cannot directly compute the real rate. Rather, we observe the real rate retrospectively once we observe the nominal rate and inflation.

Expectations Theory

Consider an investor with a two-year investment horizon. The investor has two investment strategies (shown in Figure 7.5): 1) buy a 2-year bond with a yield of k_2 per annum; or 2) buy a 1-year bond with a yield of k_1 and roll over the investment into another one-year bond at Date 1. We refer to the first strategy as the "lock in" and the second as the "roll-over."

FIGURE 7.5 Timelines for Lock-In and Roll-Over

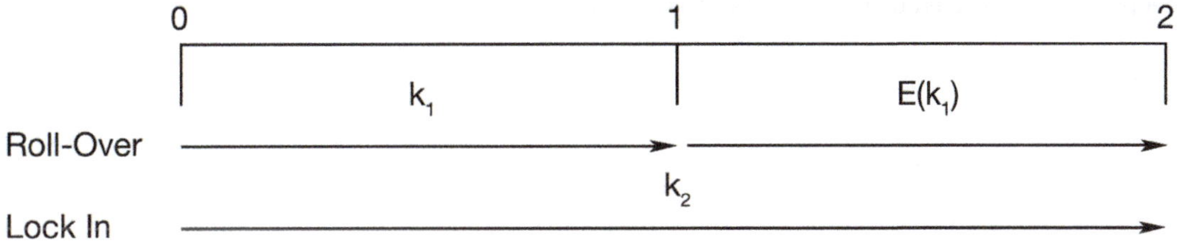

We know the spot rates for the one- and two-year maturities (k_1 and k_2), since those bonds are traded today. The market's consensus forecast of next year's spot rate is called the "expected future spot rate." It is denoted $E(k_1)$.

expectations theory

Long-term bond yields are the geometric average of the expected intermediate bond yields.

The **expectations theory** holds that the yield on a long-term bond (i.e., the 2-year bond) is a (geometric) average of the 1-year spot rate and the expected future spot rate. In particular, the rates are connected through the following equality:[2]

EQUATION 7.6

$$(1+k_2)^2 = (1+k_1)(1+E(k_1))$$

Consider the yield on a 2-year bond. If the yield on a 1-year zero coupon bond (which is issued today) is 10% and the expected spot rate next year is 12%, then the 2-year rate would be 10.99%.

$$(1+k_2)^2 = (1+k_1)(1+E(k_1))$$
$$k_2 = [(1+k_1)(1+E(k_1))]^{0.5} - 1$$
$$k_2 = [(1.10)(1.12)]^{0.5} - 1 = 0.109955$$

In the previous example, spot rates were expected to rise (from 10% to 12%) and so the yield curve was upward sloping (the two year rate was higher than the one year rate). We learn from the Expectations Theory that the shape of the yield curve is determined by expectations about future interest rates; the yield curve is upward sloping when rates are expected to rise and downward sloping when they are expected to fall.

Expectations about future interest rates are largely based on expectations of inflation and monetary policy. As we saw from the Fisher Equation (Equation 7.4), nominal interest rates are a function of real interest rates and expected inflation. Expectations of inflation are strongly influenced by monetary policy. As Milton Friedman, the Nobel Laureate in Economics, famously put it: "Inflation is always and everywhere a monetary phenomenon."[3] The Federal Reserve has a number of policy levers that it uses to affect the level of short-term interest rates. Those policies affect the real rate of interest by changing supply and demand conditions in the money and bond markets, and they also affect the market's expectations of inflation.

The Maturity Preference Theory

maturity preference theory

Bond investors prefer short maturities, so long-term bond yields incorporate a premium to compensate investors for the disutility of holding them.

maturity risk premium (MRP)

The premium incorporated in long-term bond yields to compensate investors who prefer shorter maturities. See maturity preference theory.

The **maturity preference theory** assumes that investors prefer short maturities and so like to roll-over rather than lock-in. To compensate for this preference, borrowers (bond issuers) must provide investors with higher yields to induce them to buy longer-term bonds. Under the maturity preference theory, the 2-year rate would be a little larger than predicted by Equation 7.6. Continuing the example from the last section, if the one year spot rate is 10% and the expected future spot rate is 12%, then the two year rate might be 11.10% (rather than 10.99%). The difference in rates ($11.10\% - 10.99\% = 0.11\%$) is called the **maturity risk premium (MRP)**. As a result of the premiums in longer term yields, the maturity preference theory implies that the yield curve is a little steeper than predicted by the expectations hypothesis.

The maturity preference theory assumes that investors prefer shorter maturities. That assumption derives from a more basic assumption about investor attitudes to two types of risk: **interest rate risk** and **reinvestment rate risk**. The lock-in strategy (discussed in the previous section) is exposed to interest rate risk. That is the risk associated with fluctuations in the price of the long-term bond before it matures (in this example, the risk that the rate in year 2 fluctuates). Recall that bond prices move inversely with rates. If the spot rate rises, then the bond price will fall and a bond holder who sells before maturity (at date 1) will experience a loss. The roll-over strategy isn't exposed to interest-rate risk, because it matures at date 1 before the interest rate for period 2 changes. But the roll-over is exposed to re-investment rate risk, which is the risk that the interest rate in period 2 falls (relative to the expectation of it at date 0).

interest rate risk

The risk of a capital loss on a bond investment. If interest rates rise, then bond prices fall. For an investor who has to sell a bond before maturity, an interest rate increase will cause a capital loss.

reinvestment rate risk

The risk that rates in the future will fall and thus reduce the future value of a bond investment. Bond strategies that involve a sequence of short-term investments or coupon bonds that pay large coupons are both subject to reinvestment rate risk.

The maturity preference theory assumes that investors are more concerned with the interest rate risk than they are with the reinvestment rate risk and so have a preference for shorter maturity bonds. "Explain It: Interest Rate Risk, Reinvestment Risk, and the Maturity Preference Theory" works through an example of interest rate risk and reinvestment rate risk.

Explain It: Interest Rate Risk, Reinvestment Risk, and the Maturity Preference Theory

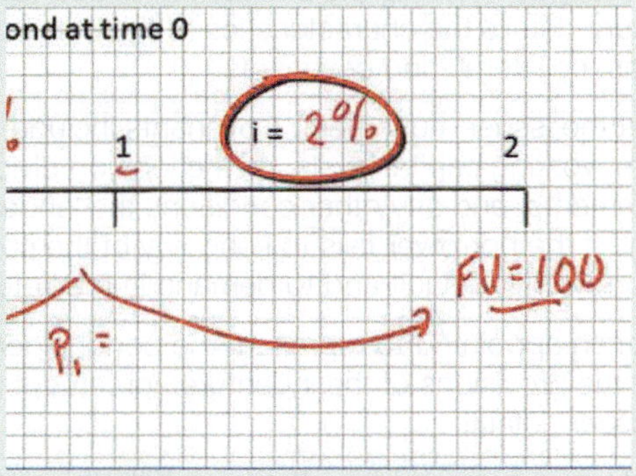

View in the online reader

Default Risk

Default means the failure to fulfill an obligation. In the context of loans and bonds, default can occur in a number of ways, such as failure of the borrower to make interest or principal payments or to follow the terms of the loan. Default is the major risk associated with corporate and foreign government bonds, and so a number of conventions have arisen in the bond markets to deal with it. These conventions are described in Figure 7.6 and the accompanying video.

default

The failure to fulfill an obligation. For example, the failure of the borrower to make interest or principal payments or to adhere to covenants.

FIGURE 7.6 Default

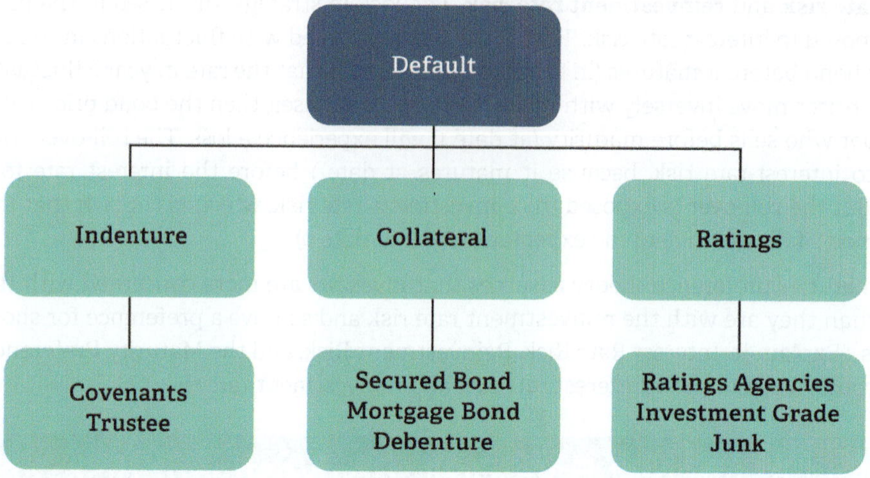

TABLE 7.3 Definitions for Terms in Figure 7.6

Default: The failure to fulfill an obligation. For example, the failure of the borrower to make interest or principal payments or to adhere to covenants.
The **indenture** is the loan agreement. All corporate bonds with a face value exceeding $10M must have an indenture. The indenture details the characteristics of the bonds such as face value, coupon rate, maturity, repayment terms, collateral, and covenants.
Covenants are conditions that the issuer must meet. Covenants include such things as maximum debt-to-equity ratios, minimum working capital levels, restrictions on dividend policy and capital expenditures, reporting requirements, and any other conditions the lender feels will increase the probability of timely repayment. If the borrower fails to keep *any* of the covenants, then the lender has the right to declare the borrower in default and to demand immediate repayment.
Trustee: A trust company is often appointed to represent the bondholders. The trustee's responsibility is to ensure that the provisions of the indenture agreement are followed and to defend the bondholders should the issuer default.
Collateral is assets that are pledges as security for the loan. If the borrower defaults, then the collateral is sold and the proceeds are used to satisfy any remaining obligations of the borrowers.
If a bond has collateral, then it is called a **secured bond**.
A bond secured with land is called a **mortgage bond**.
Unsecured bonds are called **debentures**.
Bond ratings help investors predict the probability of default. Higher ratings (i.e., AAA) correspond with a low probability of default, and lower ratings, (i.e., CCC) indicate a higher probability of default.
Debt **ratings agencies**, such as Standard & Poor's and Moody's rate bonds.
The term **investment grade** is used to refer to bonds from issuers with a rating of BBB (Baa) or higher.
The term **junk** is used to refer to bonds with a grade of BB (Ba) or lower.

Explain It: Default Risk

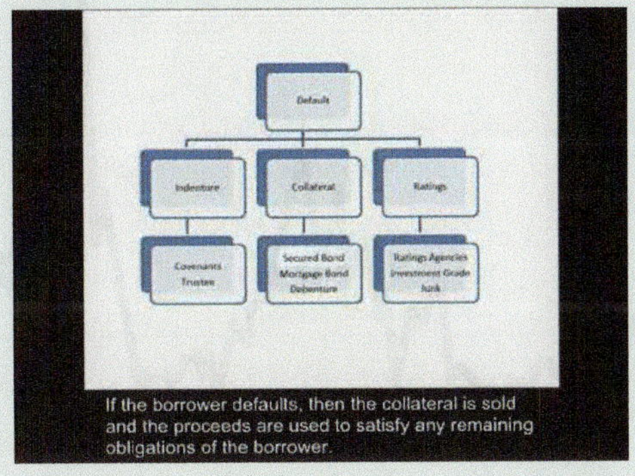

View in the online reader

The only way that bond investors can be compensated for higher levels of default risk is by paying a lower price for the bonds and so earning a higher return. As a result, bonds from issuers with higher default probabilities (lower ratings) have higher yields than bonds from issuers with a lower likelihood of default (higher ratings). This difference in yields is called the **default risk premium (DRP)**.

Figure 7.7 shows the **yield spread** between corporate bonds with a rating of Baa and U.S. 10-year T-bonds. A yield spread is just a difference in yields. This yield spread is the default risk premium associated with a Baa rating. The compensation for default risk varies with the probability of default. In turn, the probability of default varies with the business cycle. Figure 7.7 shows how the default risk premium rises with recessions (e.g., the 2008 financial crisis and the 2020 pandemic lockdown).

default risk premium (DRP)

A component of a bond yield that compensates the bondholder for the possibility that the issuer might default.

yield spread

A difference in yields.

FIGURE 7.7 Yield Spread Between Baa and U.S. T-Bond

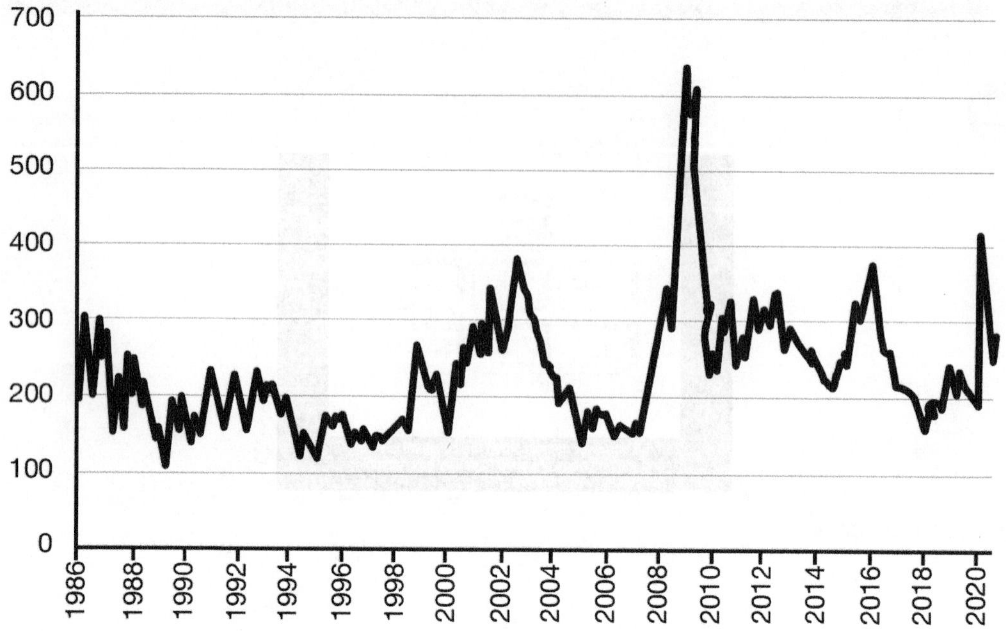

Data from Federal Reserve, www.federalreserve.gov.

Both sets of bonds have a maturity of 10 years. The bond yields shown in the graph are for coupon bonds, but the same point applies for zero coupon yields. U.S. T-notes have no default risk since the promise to repay is backed by the Federal government's ability to tax. The Baa rating is Moody's lowest investment grade rating. The y-axis reports basis points. A basis point is 1/100 of 1% or 0.01%.

Liquidity

Liquidity is defined as the ease with which an asset can be converted to cash. NYSE listed stocks are liquid assets because it is easy and cheap to sell a share on the NYSE. Real estate is illiquid because it is time-consuming and expensive to sell a house or property. Bonds vary in their degree of liquidity. Recently issued T-notes and T-bonds are very liquid. Older corporate bonds issued by small companies can be difficult and expensive to sell—difficult in the sense that you may have trouble finding a dealer who will buy them from you and expensive in the sense that you will receive less than fair value when you sell them. Liquidity is obviously not a problem for investors who plan to hold to maturity. Investors who buy illiquid bonds anticipate the costs of selling the illiquid assets and thus pay less for those bonds. As a result, illiquid bonds have a higher yield than equivalent liquid bonds. This difference in yields is called the **liquidity risk premium (LRP)**.

liquidity

Liquidity is the ease with which an asset can be converted to cash. Liquid markets are those in which it is easy to buy and sell. Liquid markets have depth, which means that large quantities can be traded quickly without adversely impacting the price. A liquid corporation is one that can meet its short-term obligations. Corporate liquidity is measured with ratios like the current and quick ratios.

liquidity risk premium (LRP)

A component of a bond yield that compensates the bondholder for the potential costs in selling the bond.

Reconciling Theories

In this section, we have identified five factors that affect bond yields. Which of these factors influence the yield to maturity? They all do. First of all, yields depend on expectations of future interest rates, which in turn are based on expectations about monetary policy and inflation. Following the maturity preference theory, longer maturity bonds will have higher yields than predicted by the expectations theory. Illiquid bonds have higher yields to compensate buyers for the cost, time, and inconvenience associated with bonds that may be hard to sell. Finally, bond investors are compensated for the risk of default through higher yields—a default risk premium. As a simple generalization (and a first approximation), we can say that the yield on any bond with maturity in year *t* is equal to the following:

EQUATION 7.7

$$YTM_t = k_{rt} + INF_t + MRP_t + LRP_t + DRP_t$$

where

$$YTM_t = \text{the yield to maturity of a bond with maturity in year t}$$
$$k_{rt} = \text{the real rate of return on a government bond with maturity in year t}$$
$$INF = \text{the inflation premium} = \pi_t + (k_{rt} \times \pi_t)$$
$$MRP_t = \text{the maturity risk premium for maturity t}$$
$$LRP_t = \text{the liquidity risk premium for maturity t}$$
$$DRP_t = \text{the default risk premium for maturity t}$$

7.4 Coupon Bond Features and Markets

Features of a Coupon Bond

coupon bond

A debt instrument that pays periodic (annual or semi-annual) interest payments to the holder (called coupons) and pays a final lump sum (called the face value) at maturity. Coupon bonds are issued by governments and corporations.

A **coupon bond** is one that makes periodic interest payments in addition to paying a lump sum at maturity. A coupon bond is shown in Figure 7.8. The holder of the bond is promised to receive $5 on July 1, 1866. (History pop quiz: Why did the State of Arkansas need money in 1861? Did the holder receive the $5 at maturity?)

Explain It

The State of Arkansas needed money to finance the Civil War. That is why the bond is labeled "War Bond." The State of Arkansas sided with the Confederacy. The Confederacy surrendered in April 1865, so the holder of the bond did not receive a payment of $5 at maturity in 1866.

FIGURE 7.8 Coupon Bond

1. Coupon amount: $0.20 is paid to the holder on the coupon date. 2. Coupon date: The date that this coupon is paid to the holder. 3. Issuer: Government or corporation that issued the bond. 4. Maturity date: When the issuer must pay the holder the face value of the bond. 5. Face value: The amount that the issuer must pay the holder at maturity. 6. Issue date: The date that the bond was first sold.

Arkansas War Bond, ASA currency collection, Arkansas State Archives, Little Rock, Arkansas.

Coupon bonds can also have several other features.

1. A **convertible bond** allows the holder of the bond to convert the face amount into a fixed number of common shares at any time before the maturity of the bond if they so choose.
2. A **callable bond** is one where the issuer has the right to force early redemption of the bond (before the maturity date). When a bond is called, the holder must return the bond to the issuer. In exchange, the issuer pays the holder the face value of the bond. In some cases, the holder may receive a call premium, which is a small payment (over and above the face value) to compensate for the inconvenience of the call.
3. A **foreign bond** is a bond that is issued in a particular country and is denominated in that country's currency (but issued by a foreigner). It is generally kept distinct from domestically issued bonds for tax and disclosure purposes.
4. Finally, a bond may have a variable coupon. These bonds are called **floating rate bonds**. In this case, rather than having a fixed **coupon rate**, the coupon rate fluctuates with some benchmark rate, such as the LIBOR (London InterBank Offer rate). For example, if the coupon rate is stated as LIBOR plus 100 **basis points (bps)**, and LIBOR is 3%, then the coupon rate for the current period is 4%.

convertible bond

A corporate bond, which gives the bondholder the right to convert the bond into a fixed number of shares.

callable bond

A call feature allows the issuer to require the bondholders to redeem their bonds. Bondholders must return their bonds to the issuer in exchange for a payment of the face value.

foreign bond

A bond that is issued in a particular country and is denominated in the country's currency (but is issued by a foreigner).

floating rate bonds

A bond where the coupon is tied to a variable interest rate (i.e., LIBOR) and is recalculated each time the variable interest rate changes.

coupon rate

The annual dollar value of the coupons divided by the face value of the bond.

basis points (bps)

A basis point is 1/100 of 1% or 0.01%.

Coupon Bond Issuers

Bonds may be issued by federal, state, and municipal governments, government-sponsored enterprises (e.g., Fannie Mae and Freddie Mac), federal government–owned corporations (e.g., Amtrak, Tennessee Valley Authority, PBS), and private-sector corporations. Table 7.4 shows the value of bonds issued by issuer type and by year.

TABLE 7.4 Issuance in the U.S. Bond Markets (USD Billions)

Year	Corporate[4]	Mortgage-Backed[5]	Federal Agency	Treasury[6]	Municipal	Total
1999	629	1,318	548	416	225	3,136
2004	812	2,759	878	853	358	5,661
2009	979	2,350	1,244	2,197	410	7,180
2014	1,477	1,833	559	2,215	339	6,423
2019	1,417	2,418	989	2,935	426	8,186

Data from Securities Industry and Financial Markets Association (SIFMA), www.sifma.org.

In 2019, new bond issues totaled $8.2 trillion. To put this in perspective, the gross domestic product of the United States in 2019 was about $22T. Corporate issues accounted for only 17% of all new issues in the debt markets in 2019. The federal government (and agencies) was the largest issuer of bonds in that year, accounting for nearly half of all issuance.

Coupon Bond Markets

Coupon bonds trade in what is aptly called the bond market. The bond market is the market for both coupon and zero coupon bonds with maturities ranging from 1 to 30 years and includes bonds issued by governments and corporations. The value of daily trading in the bond market is shown in Table 7.5. Treasury securities constitute about 67% of bond market trading. In contrast, corporate bonds constitutes less than 4% of the market. The final column shows average daily trading volume of NYSE and NASDAQ listed stocks. Notice how the dollar volume of trading in stocks is less than half of the value of trading in Treasury securities. This is a bit deceptive, because the volume of shares traded is far larger than the volume of bonds traded. The reason for the big difference between dollar volume and quantity of paper traded is that bonds have face values in hundreds of thousands or millions of dollars whereas stocks are usually priced at less than one hundred dollars.

TABLE 7.5 U.S. Bond & Stock Markets—Average Daily Trading Volume (USD Billions)

	Municipal	Treasury	Mortgage Related	Corporate Bonds	NYSE & NASDAQ Shares
2011	11.3	567.8	249.2	20.6	176.4
2015	8.6	490.0	197.6	27.9	206.6
2019	11.5	593.6	251.9	33.9	246.6

Data from Securities Industry and Financial Markets Association (SIFMA), www.sifma.org.

Both the money market and the bond market are **over-the-counter** or **dealer markets**. This means that there are no centralized physical or computerized exchanges for bonds. Transactions for bonds are privately negotiated through multiple **dealers** (or **market-makers**), such as banks and large brokerages, which post prices and stand ready to buy and sell bonds at those prices. The prices are posted on proprietary computer systems, such as Reuters, and buyers and sellers trade on electronic platforms and via telephone. The market-maker's clients tend to be large institutions such as pensions and mutual funds.

over-the-counter

A form of securities market. An alternative to an auction market. Market participants trade over the telephone or electronic network. There is no central exchange or meeting place. Trading does not occur between buyers and seller, but, instead, through a network of middlemen called dealers. Dealers carry inventories of securities and stand ready to buy and sell at posted prices.

dealer markets

A form of securities market. An alternative to an auction market. Market participants trade over the phone or electronic network. Trading does not occur between buyers and sellers but, instead, through a network of middlemen called dealers. Dealers carry inventories of securities and stand ready to buy at their bid price and sell at their ask price. Some dealer markets, like NASDAQ, are centralized through a computer network; most are not (e.g., bond and foreign exchange markets). Also called an over-the-counter market.

dealer

An entity that stands ready to buy or sell a security to (from) its own inventory. Dealers post prices at which they will buy (bid price) or sell (ask price). Also known as a market-maker.

market-makers

An entity that stands ready to buy or sell a security to (from) its own inventory. Market-makers post prices at which they will buy (bid price) or sell (ask price). Also known as a dealer.

Bond Price Reporting

A selection of bond prices is printed in the financial daily press and shown on financial websites. The prices are quotes from a particular market-maker with which the media company has a contract. An example of selected Treasury bond quotes from Bloomberg is show in Figure 7.9. The price is expressed as a percentage of the face value. For example, if a coupon bond is quoted as 101.59, then the price of that bond is 101.59% or 1.0159 times the face value.

FIGURE 7.9 United States Government Bonds

Treasury Yields

NAME	COUPON	PRICE	YIELD
GB3:GOV **3 Month**	0.00	0.06	0.06%
GB6:GOV **6 Month**	0.00	0.08	0.08%
GB12:GOV **12 Month**	0.00	0.10	0.10%
GT2:GOV **2 Year**	0.13	100.01	0.12%
GT5:GOV **5 Year**	0.38	100.07	0.36%
GT10:GOV **10 Year**	0.88	99.64	0.91%
GT30:GOV **30 Year**	1.63	99.53	1.64%

Source: Bloomberg Business, https://www.bloomberg.com/markets/rates-bonds/government-bonds/us

7.5 Coupon Bond Yields and Pricing

This section starts by showing the cash flows of a coupon bond. A coupon bond can be thought of as a collection (or portfolio) of zero coupon bonds. This intuition leads to a basic relationship between zero coupon bond prices and coupon bond prices. If a coupon bond's price is known, then we can calculate the yield to maturity, which is (approximately) the return an investor would earn if they bought the bond and held it to maturity. Conversely, if the yield to maturity for a bond is known, then we can calculate the bond's price. Finally, we show how to calculate the yield on a semi-annual coupon bond.

All of the yield and pricing formulas presented in this chapter are for the issue date or the point in time just after a coupon is paid. We leave pricing between coupon dates to a more advanced text.

Coupon Bond Cash Flows

Coupon bonds pay the holder annual (or semi-annual) coupons (*C*), as well as the face value (*FV*), at maturity. The coupons are usually expressed as a percentage of the face value and this percentage is known as the coupon rate.

Consider a U.S. government bond with 2 years to maturity, a face value of $*FV*, and annual coupons of $*C*. The timeline for this bond's cash flows is shown in Figure 7.10.

FIGURE 7.10 Timeline of 2-Year Coupon Bond

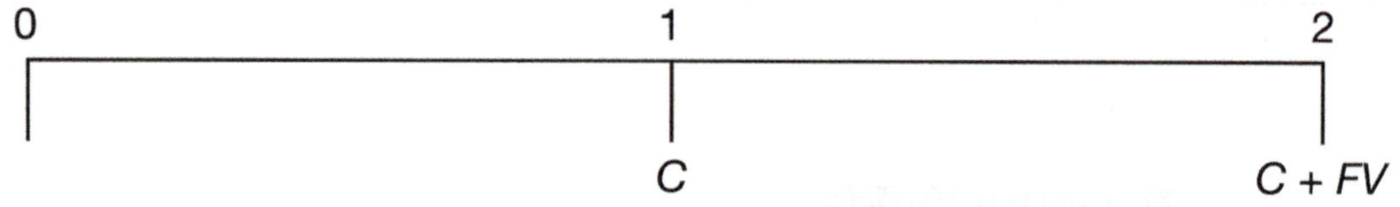

The Relationship Between Coupon and Zero Coupon Bond Prices

Pricing a coupon bond is straightforward if we think of the coupon bond as a portfolio of zero coupon bonds because we already know how to price zero coupon bonds.

Example 7.4 The Prices of Two Zero Coupon Bonds

Digital Downloads

Example 7.4 The Prices of Two Zero Coupon Bonds.xls
https://catalog.flatworldknowledge.com/a/34711/Example_7_4_The_Prices_of_Two_Zero_Coupon_Bonds-30f2.xls

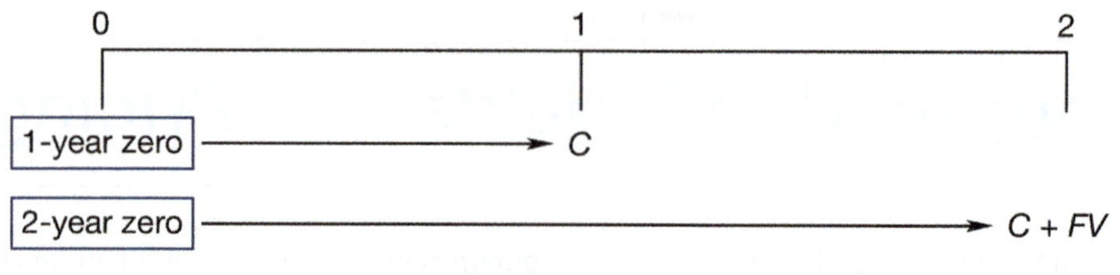

The timeline shows the face values for zero coupon bonds. A 1-year zero coupon bond has a face value of \$*C*, where \$*C* = \$10. A 2-year zero coupon bond has a face value of $(\$C + \$FV)$, where \$*C* = \$10 and *FV* = \$100. What are the prices of the bonds if the 1-year spot rate is 1% and the 2-year spot rate is 2% $(k_2 = 2\%)$? The cash flows of the two bonds are shown in the figure.

SOLUTION

Spreadsheet Solution

Price =	?	?
n =	1	
k =	0.01	0.0
Solution:		
Price =	FV * (1+ k)^(-n)	
Price =	\$ 9.90	\$105.7

View in the online reader

Algebraic Solution

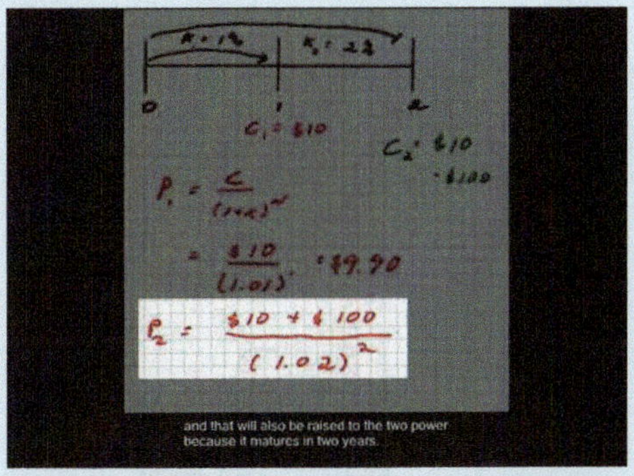

View in the online reader

Calculator Solution

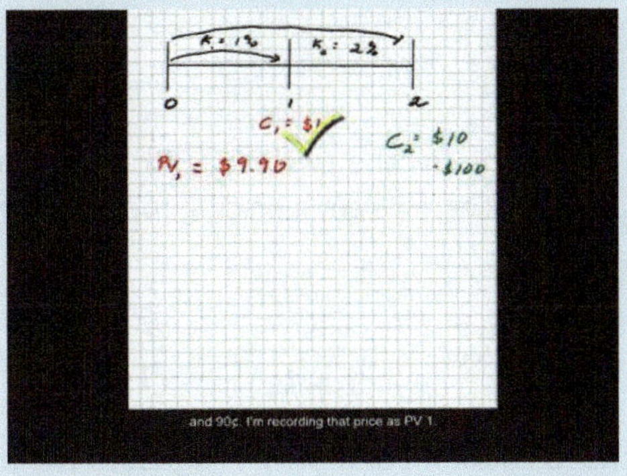

View in the online reader

The 1-year zero price, P_1, is (from Equation 7.3):

$$P_1 = \frac{C}{(1 + k_1)^1} = \frac{\$10}{(1.01)^1} = \$9.901$$

The 2-year zero price, P_2 , is:

$$P_2 = \frac{C + FV}{(1 + k_2)^2} = \frac{\$10 + \$100}{(1.02)^2} = \$105.729$$

law of one price

Law that says that two equivalent investments that trade in different markets must have the same price. If the prices aren't equal, then an arbitrage opportunity is created and the resulting trading pushes the prices back to equality. The equality implied by the law of one price only holds exactly if there are no trading frictions or barriers between the markets.

The cash flows from a portfolio comprising the two zero coupon bonds are equivalent to the cash flows from the 2-year coupon bond shown in Figure 7.10. Because the coupon bond and the package of zeros are equivalent (in cash flows, default risk, etc.), the price of the 2-year coupon bond, P_{bond} , must equal the sum of the prices of the two zero coupon bonds. This is an application of the **law of one price**. The law of one price asserts that two identical securities that are sold in two different markets must sell at the same price.

EQUATION 7.8

$$P_{bond} = P_1 + P_2$$

Explain It: The Relationship Between Zero Coupon Bond Prices and Coupon Bond Prices

View in the online reader

If we substitute the equations for the two zeros from "Example 7.4 The Prices of Two Zero Coupon Bonds" into Equation 7.8, then we get a pricing formula for a 2-period coupon bond.

EQUATION 7.9

$$P_{bond} = \frac{C}{(1 + k_1)^1} + \frac{C + FV}{(1 + k_2)^2}$$

Equation 7.9 shows that a coupon bond price is equal to the present value of the bond's cash flows when each cash flow is discounted at the appropriate spot rate from the yield curve. Following Equation 7.9 and Example 7.4, we now know that the price of a 2-year coupon bond with a face value of \$100 and a 10% coupon rate is \$115.63 $(P_{bond} = \$9.901 + \$105.729 = \$115.63)$.

More generally, for any number of coupons, *n*, we can express the price of a coupon bond as follows:

EQUATION 7.10

$$P_{bond} = \sum_{t=1}^{n} \frac{C_t}{(1+k_t)^t} + \frac{FV}{(1+k_n)^n}$$

Tip

The k_t in Equation 7.10 are the spot rate yields for term *t* from the Treasury spot rate yield curve. k_n is the spot rate corresponding to the maturity date of the coupon bond.

Yield-to-Maturity

Given a bond price, one obvious question is: "What return will the bond holder earn if he buys the bond and holds it to maturity?" The actual return is not known until the last coupon is received (and the interest from reinvested coupons is calculated), but a good estimate of the return is called the yield-to-maturity.

The yield to maturity is calculated by finding the single rate, which discounts the bond's cash flows so that the present value equals the bond's price. In other words, the yield-to-maturity is the solution to the following problem:

EQUATION 7.11

$$P_{bond} = \sum_{t=1}^{n} \frac{C_t}{(1+k_d)^t} + \frac{FV}{(1+k_d)^n}$$

Where the bond price P_{bond} is known, *n* is the number of coupon periods to maturity, and k_d is the yield to maturity that must be solved.

Note that the discount rate in Equation 7.11, k_d , is different than the rates used in Equation 7.10. In Equation 7.10, each coupon is discounted at a different rate k_t , which is the spot rate (from the spot rate yield curve) for that maturity. In Equation 7.11, we are looking for a common rate for all maturities.

Tip

We can interpret the yield-to-maturity of a coupon bond as a (complicated) average of the underlying spot rates from the spot rate yield curve. Thus, the yield-to-maturity for coupon bonds will change as the spot rate yield curve changes.

Equation 7.11 is tedious to use if there are many coupons. Since each of the coupon payments is the same, and we are discounting them with a common rate, k_d , we can use the equation for an annuity. Using present value interest factor notation, Equation 7.10 is rewritten as:

EQUATION 7.12

$$P_{bond} = C \times PVIFA_{n,k_d} + \frac{FV}{(1+k_d)^n}$$

$$PVIFA_{n,k_d} = \frac{1 - \frac{1}{(1+k_d)^n}}{k_d}$$

The yield is best solved using trial and error, as the following example shows. The procedure for finding the yield is the same as we used to find the interest rate in a present value annuity problem in "Example 4.5 Finding the Interest Rate".

Tip

Do not use the coupon rate in the denominator instead of the yield to maturity. The coupon rate is only used to compute the coupon payment.

Example 7.5 Calculate the Yield-to-Maturity

Digital Downloads

Example 7.5 Calculate the Yield to Maturity.xls
https://catalog.flatworldknowledge.com/a/34711/Example_7_5_Calculate_the_Yield_to_Maturity-5c91.xls

A 2-year coupon bond has a coupon rate of 5% and a face value of $1,000. The price of the bond us $1,038.75. What is the yield-to-maturity of the bond?

SOLUTION

Spreadsheet Solution

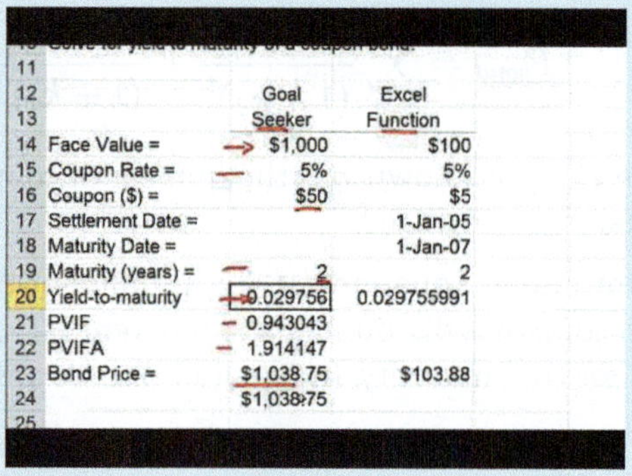

11			
12		Goal	Excel
13		Seeker	Function
14	Face Value =	$1,000	$100
15	Coupon Rate =	5%	5%
16	Coupon ($) =	$50	$5
17	Settlement Date =		1-Jan-05
18	Maturity Date =		1-Jan-07
19	Maturity (years) =	2	2
20	Yield-to-maturity	0.029756	0.029755991
21	PVIF	0.943043	
22	PVIFA	1.914147	
23	Bond Price =	$1,038.75	$103.88
24		$1,038.75	
25			

View in the online reader

Algebraic Solution

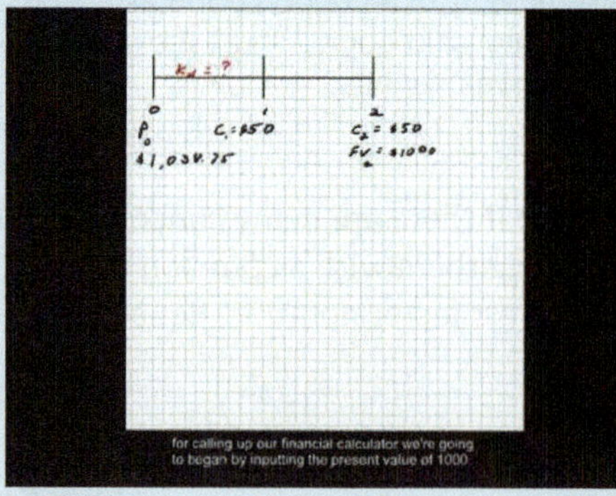

View in the online reader

Calculator Solution

View in the online reader

The yield-to-maturity is the value for the variable, k_d , in the following equation:

$$\$1,038.75 = \$50 \times PVIFA_{2,k_d} + \frac{\$1,000}{(1+k_d)^2}$$

$$\$1,038.75 = \$50 \times \left(\frac{1}{k_d}\right) \times \left(1 - \frac{\$1}{(1+k_d)^2}\right) + \frac{\$1,000}{(1+k_d)^2}$$

The solution value is $k_d = 2.976\%$.

Some Insights about Yield-to-Maturity

Here are three insights about yield-to-maturity:

1. The yield-to-maturity is approximately equal to the return that the bond holder will earn if she pays the price (P_{bond}) and holds the bond to maturity.
2. The yield-to-maturity calculation implicitly assumes that intermediate coupons can be reinvested at the solution rate, or 2.976%. If the bond holder's reinvestment rate differs, then her actual return will not equal the yield-to-maturity. (And that is why we used the word "approximately" in the last point.)
3. The yield to maturity can only be calculated if the bond price is known. The yield is thus interchangeable with the price. In other words, if we are given the price, then we can solve for the yield-to-maturity. Or, if we are given the yield-to-maturity, then we can solve for the price.

Pricing a Coupon Bond Given the Yield-to-Maturity

If the yield-to-maturity is given, then we can solve for the price of a coupon bond using Equation 7.12 as in the following example.

Example 7.6 Bond Valuation with Annual Coupons

Digital Downloads

Example 7.6 Bond Valuation with Annual Coupons.xls
https://catalog.flatworldknowledge.com/a/34711/Example_7_6_Bond_Valuation_with_Annual_Coupons-5b1a.xls

Suppose you found a bond in your great, great aunt's attic. It has 2 years before it matures (it has been in that shoe box for 28 years now), a 10% coupon rate, and a $1,000 face value. If interest is paid annually and the yield to maturity of the bond is 9%, then what is the current price of this bond?

$$n = 2$$
$$k_d = 9\%$$
$$C = \$100$$
$$FV = \$1,000$$

SOLUTION

Spreadsheet Solution

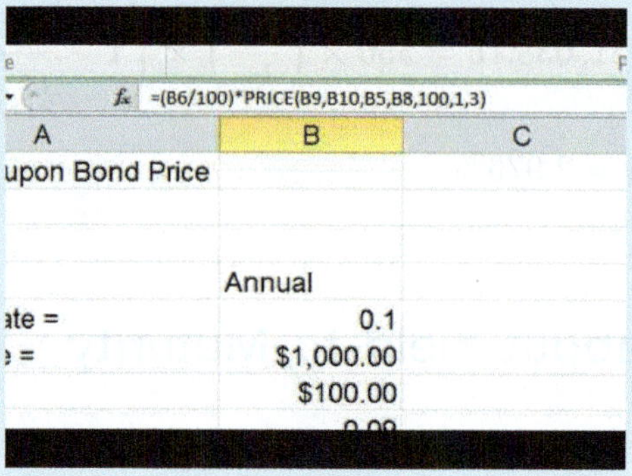

View in the online reader

Algebraic Solution

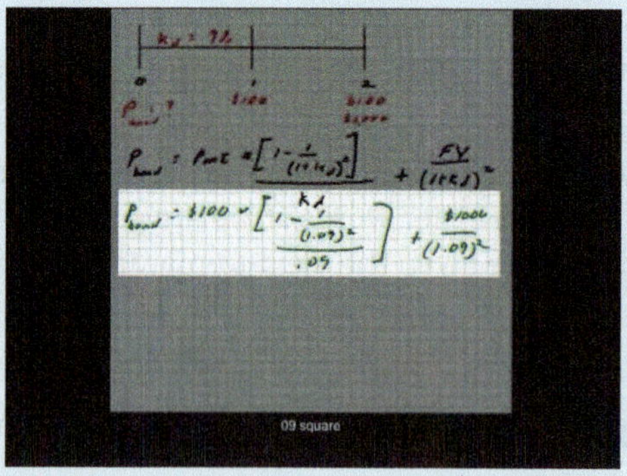

View in the online reader

Calculator Solution

View in the online reader

$$P_{bond} = C \times PVIFA_{n,k_d} + \frac{FV}{(1+k_d)^n}$$

$$P_{bond} = \$100 \times \frac{\left[1 - \frac{1}{(1.09)^2}\right]}{0.09} + \$1,000 \times \frac{1}{(1.09)^2}$$

$$P_{bond} = \$100 \times 1.75911 + \$1,000 \times 0.84168$$

$$P_{bond} = \$175.91 + \$841.68 = \$1,017.59$$

Semi-Annual Coupon Bonds

Most bonds pay interest semi-annually. To find the yield for a semi-annual coupon bond, we can use a variation of Equation 7.12, but we have to make three adjustments:

1. To find the semi-annual coupon, divide the annual coupon payment by two since only half of the annual payment is paid each 6 months. If the annual coupon is C, then the semi-annual coupon $= C/2$.
2. Discount the semi-annual coupons with the semi-annual yield. To find the yield for one-half of the year, we divide the annual yield by two. The semi-annual yield is $k_d/2$.
3. Finally, double the number of periods since there will be two coupon payments per year. The number of periods $= 2n$.

   With semi-annual compounding, Equation 7.12 becomes the following:

EQUATION 7.13

$$P_{bond} = \frac{C}{2} \times PVIFA_{2n,k_d/2} + \frac{FV}{(1+k_d/2)^{2n}}$$

bond equivalent yield

A calculation for restating semi-annual, quarterly, or monthly discount-bond or note yields into an annual yield. Multiply the periodic yield by the number of terms in 1 year (e.g., for semi-annual bonds, m=2).

The effective annual rate on a semi-annual bond is bigger than k_d , since we are compounding the periodic rate $k_d/2$ twice (semi-annually). Nonetheless, it is the market convention to solve for the yield, as shown in Equation 7.13, and then report the nominal annual rate (k_d) rather than the effective annual rate. The nominal rate is know as the **bond equivalent yield.**

If we are given the yield to maturity, then we can use Equation 7.13 to solve for the bond's price, as is shown in the following example.

Example 7.7 Bond Valuation with Semi-Annual Coupons

Digital Downloads

Example 7.7 Bond Valuation with Semi Annual Coupons.xls
https://catalog.flatworldknowledge.com/a/34711/ Example_7_7_Bond_Valuation_with_Semi_Annual_Coupons-dffe.xls

Let us compute the price of a Chrysler bond. The bonds have a 10.95% coupon rate that is paid semi-annually, a $1,000 face value, and mature in 20 years $(n = 20)$. Assume semi-annual compounding and that the yield to maturity is 12%.

SOLUTION

Spreadsheet Solution

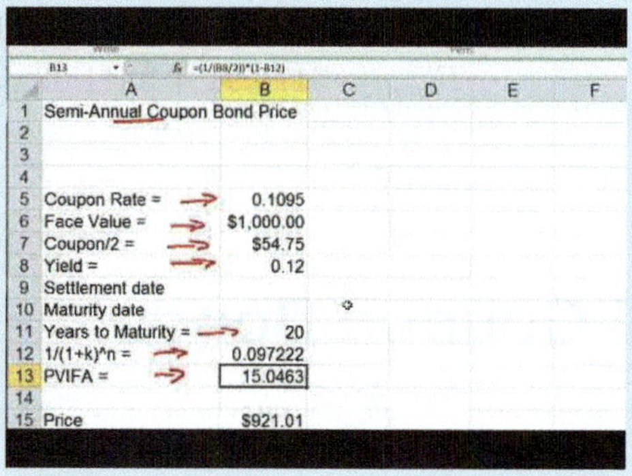

View in the online reader

Algebraic Solution

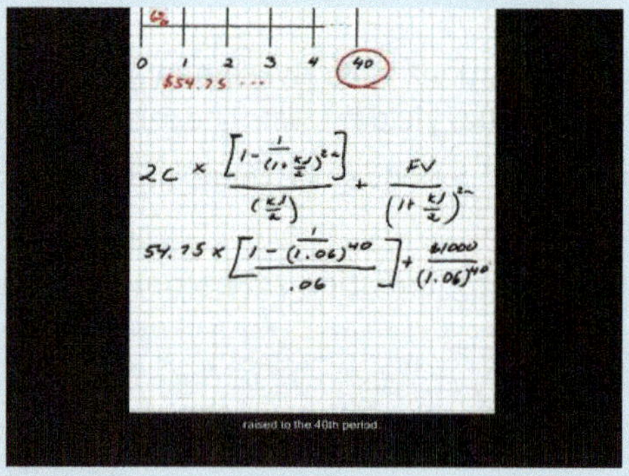

View in the online reader

Calculator Solution

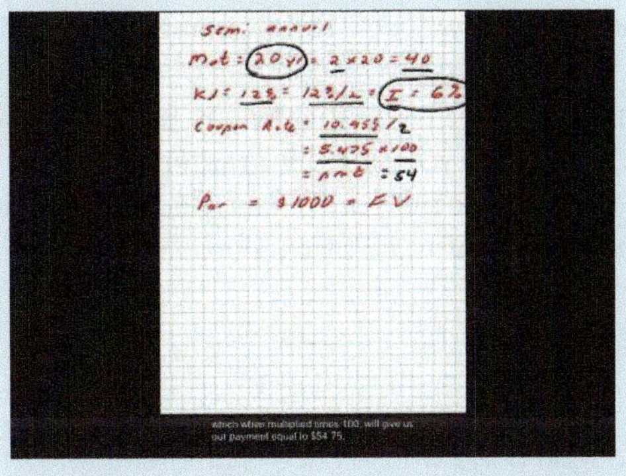

View in the online reader

Step 1: Calculate semi-annual coupon amount:

$$\textit{Annual coupon} = C = 0.1095 \times \$1,000 = \$109.50$$
$$\textit{Semi} - \textit{annual coupon} = \textit{Annual coupon}/2 = C/2 = \$109.50/2 = \$54.75$$

Step 2: Calculate semi-annual yield to maturity:

$$\textit{Yield to maturity} = k_d = 12\%$$
$$\textit{Semi} - \textit{annual yield to maturity} = k_d/2 = 12\%/2 = 6\%$$

Step 3: Note that with semi-annual compounding the number of periods must be doubled. This means that there are 40 coupon payments and 40 periods $(2n)$.

$$P_{bond} = \frac{C}{2} \times PVIFA_{2n, k_d/2} + \frac{FV}{\left(1 + k_{d/2}\right)^{2n}}$$

$$P_{bond} = \$54.75 \times \frac{\left[\left(1 - \frac{1}{(1.06)^{40}}\right)\right]}{0.06} + \$1,000 \times \frac{1}{(1.06)^{40}}$$
$$P_{bond} = \$54.75 \times 15.0463 + \$1,000 \times 0.09722$$
$$P_{bond} = \$823.785 + \$97.22 = \$921.01$$

7.6 Coupon Bond Price Properties

In this section, we present the properties of bond prices. We explain why some bonds are priced less than their face value and some bonds are priced higher. We show that bond prices and interest rates move inversely. We explain interest rate risk and show that longer maturity bonds and bonds with low coupon rates have more interest rate risk. Finally, we separate bond yields into their capital gain yield and coupon yield components and show how bond prices change as time passes to maturity.

Premiums and Discounts

premium

A premium bond is one that trades for a price that is above its face value. In the context of options, the premium is the price that the owner of an option pays to the seller when the contract is initiated.

discount

An expression used to refer to a coupon bond that trades for a price that is less than its face value.

par

Synonym for face value. A bond that trades at "par" has a price equal to its face value.

What determines whether a bond will sell for a **premium** or a **discount**? Suppose that you are asked to purchase an old bond that has a coupon rate of 10% and $1,000 face value. New bonds with similar risk yield 12%. You would not be willing to pay $1,000 for the old bond. Instead, you would want to pay less than $1,000 so that your yield is greater than 10%. In fact, the price would have to be low enough that your yield on the old bond exactly equals the yield on new bonds. Thus, the old bond would have to sell at a discount to its face value.

Tip

A premium bond is a coupon bond whose price is greater than its face value. A discount bond is one whose price is less than its face value.

Example 7.8 Discount and Premium Coupon Bonds

Digital Downloads

Example 7.8 Discount and Premium Coupon Bonds.xls
https://catalog.flatworldknowledge.com/a/34711/Example_7_8_Discount_and_Premium_Coupon_Bonds-2f8f.xls

Consider three annual coupon bonds each with a face value of $1,000 and 10 years remaining to maturity. The first bond has a coupon rate of 8%, the second has a coupon rate of 10%, and the third has a coupon rate of 12%. Assume that the yield to maturity of the bonds is 10%. Which bond trades at a premium, which trades at a discount, and which is at **par**?

SOLUTION

Spreadsheet Solution

	A	B	C	D	E
3					
4		Discount	Par	Premium	
5	Coupon Rate =	0.08	0.1	0.12	
6	Face Value =	$1,000.00	$1,000.00	$1,000.00	
7	Coupon =	$80.00	$100.00	$120.00	
8	Yield =	0.1	0.1	0.1	
9	Settlement date	15-Oct-62	15-Oct-62	15-Oct-62	
10	Maturity date	15-Oct-72	15-Oct-72	15-Oct-72	
11	Years to Maturity =	10	10	10	
12					
13					
14					
15	Price	$877.11	$1,000.00	$1,122.89	
16					
17					

View in the online reader

Algebraic Solution

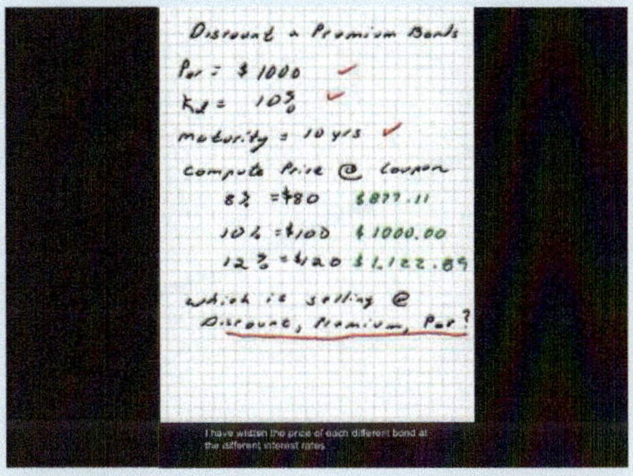

View in the online reader

Calculator Solution

View in the online reader

$$P_{8\%\text{ Coupon}} = \$80 \times PVIFA_{10,10\%} + \$1,000 \times \frac{1}{(1.10)^{10}} = \$877.11$$

$$P_{10\%\text{ Coupon}} = \$100 \times PVIFA_{10,10\%} + \$1,000 \times \frac{1}{(1.10)^{10}} = \$1,000.00$$

$$P_{12\%\text{ Coupon}} = \$120 \times PVIFA_{10,10\%} + \$1,000 \times \frac{1}{(1.10)^{10}} = \$1,122.89$$

The 8% coupon bond trades at a discount, the 10% coupon bond trades at par, and the 12% coupon rate bond trades at a premium.

Bond Prices and Interest Rates Move Inversely

Bond prices and interest rates move inversely. We saw this for zero coupon bonds (Figure 7.4), and it is also true for coupon bonds. Figure 7.11 shows the prices of a 10-year, 6% coupon bond at different yields. The spreadsheet download provides the data underlying Figure 7.11. Beneath Figure 7.11 is "Explain it: Coupon Bond Price", which explores the price-yield relationship and see how that relationship changes as the bond's time to maturity changes.

FIGURE 7.11 Prices versus Yields for a 10-Year, 6% Coupon Bond

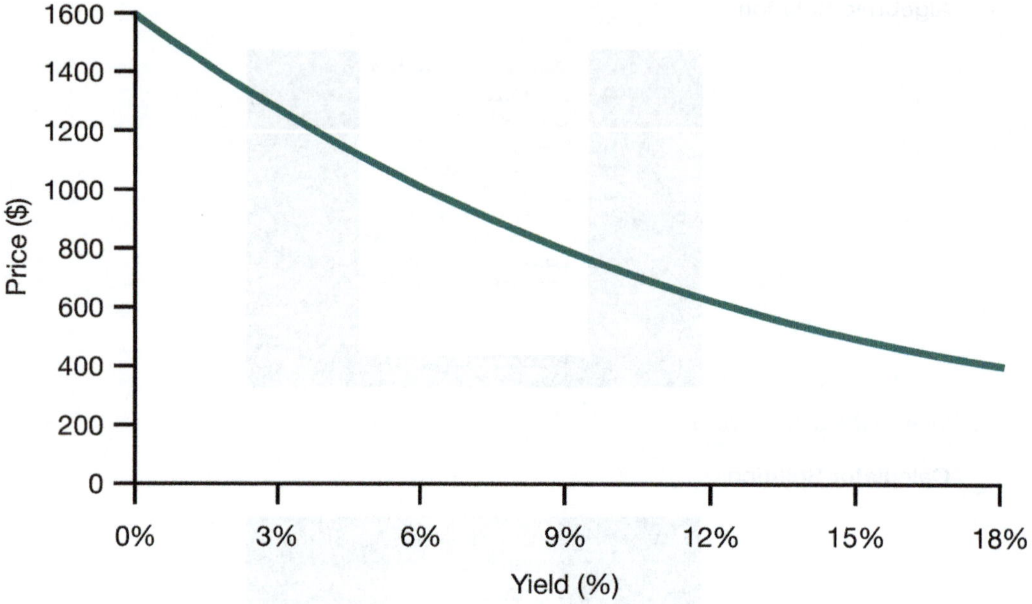

Digital Downloads

30yr Bond w:Different Coupon Rates and a 1% Change in Yields.xls
https://catalog.flatworldknowledge.com/a/34711/30yr_Bond_w_Different_Coupon_Rates_and_a_1_Change_in_Yields-72f9.xls

Explain it: Coupon Bond Price

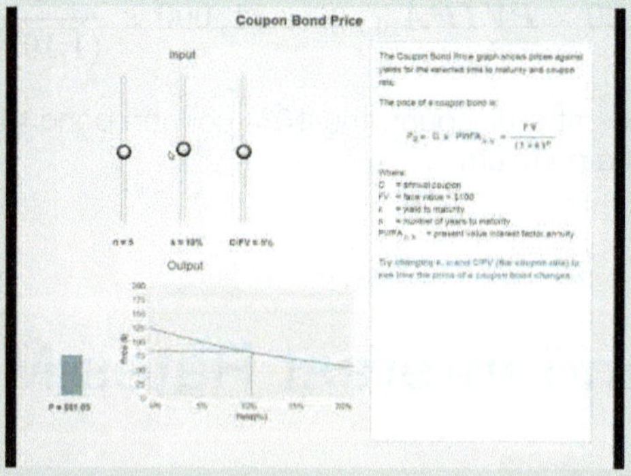

View in the online reader

Longer Maturity Bonds Have More Interest Rate Risk

When interest rates change, long-term bond prices change more than short-term bond prices. In other words, long-term bonds have more interest rate risk.

This principle follows from the time value of money mathematics. The present value of a near-term cash flow doesn't change much when rates change because it isn't discounted much. However, more distant cash flows are discounted many periods and the change in rates has a compound effect.

Table 7.6 shows the market price of 10% coupon bonds with 1, 10, and 30 years to maturity at three different yields. Notice that the change in the value of the bonds is much greater for bonds with longer maturities. A 1% drop in yield (moving from the middle column to the left-hand column) results in a $9.17 increase in price if the bond has 1 year to maturity. That same 1% drop in yield results in a $102.74 increase in price if there are 30 years to maturity. We can conclude that interest rate risk increases with increasing maturity. Beneath Table 7.5 is a spreadsheet download containing the same data as the Table and, below the spreadsheet, is a video which describes that spreadsheet.

TABLE 7.6 Price of a 10% Coupon Bond with Different Maturities and Yields

	Yield		
Years to Maturity	**9%**	**10%**	**11%**
1	$1,009.17	$1,000.00	$990.99
10	1,064.18	1,000.00	941.11
30	1,102.74	1,000.00	913.06

Digital Downloads

10% Coupon Bond with Different Maturieis and Yields (w Table 7.5).xls
https://catalog.flatworldknowledge.com/a/34711/10_Coupon_Bond_with_Different_Maturieis_and_Yields_w_Table_7_5_-6e64.xls

Explain It: Price of a 10% Coupon Bond with Different Maturities and Yields

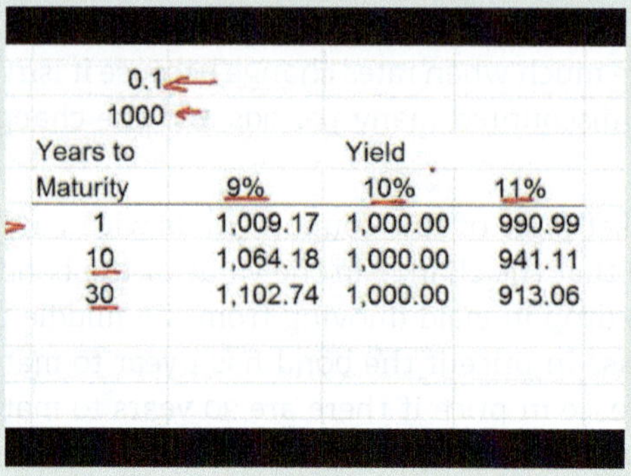

0.1
1000

Years to Maturity	Yield 9%	Yield 10%	Yield 11%
1	1,009.17	1,000.00	990.99
10	1,064.18	1,000.00	941.11
30	1,102.74	1,000.00	913.06

View in the online reader

interest rate expectation

A bond portfolio management strategy predicted on the successful prediction of future interest rates. It involves increasing a portfolio's average maturity if interest rates are expected to fall and reducing it if interest rates are expected to rise.

Bond portfolio managers take advantage of this bond pricing property by using a strategy called **interest rate expectation**. Interest rate expectation involves speculating on unanticipated interest rate changes. In effect, bond portfolio managers are using interest rate risk for profit. For example, consider a bond portfolio manager with a mix of short- and long-term bonds. If the manager thought that interest rates were going to fall (more than anticipated), then she would sell some or all of her short-term bonds and buy longer-term bonds. If rates did fall, then the prices of all of her bonds would rise, but the long-term bond prices would rise more than the original mix of short- and long-term bonds. She would subsequently sell the long-term bonds and buy short-term bonds, thus returning her portfolio to its original maturity structure. By buying long-term bonds, she would have increased the value of the portfolio by more than if she had held the original mix of short- and long-term bonds.

Bonds with Low Coupon Rates Have More Interest Rate Risk

One last factor that affects the level of interest rate risk is the coupon rate. As we know, the cash flows from a coupon bond consist of a series of coupon payments followed by the final face value. Consider summing those cash flows and calculating the proportion attributable to coupons and the proportion attributable to the face value. For example, a 10-year 1% coupon bond with a face value of $100 will pay $10 of coupons ($1 × 10) and $100 of face value. Total cash flows from the bond are $110 and the face value accounts for 90.91% of the total cash flows. Alternatively, a 10-year 10% coupon bond (with a $100 face value) pays the holder a total of $200 of which 50% is attributable to the face value. The low coupon rate bond pays proportionately more of its cash flow at maturity. The higher coupon rate bond spreads its cash flows out more smoothly over the life of the bond.

We know from the last section that the present values of longer maturity cash flows change more (following a change in interest rates) than the present values of shorter maturity cash flows.

Since low coupon rate bonds have more of their cash flows arriving at longer maturities, the present value of their cash flows (the bond price) changes more for a given change in yield compared to an otherwise equivalent high coupon rate bond. We can see this numerically in Table 7.7.

Digital Downloads

30 year Bonds with Different Coupon Rates and a 1% Change in Yields.xls
https://catalog.flatworldknowledge.com/a/34711/30_year_Bonds_with_Different_Coupon_Rates_and_a_1_Change_in_Yields-86f9.xls

TABLE 7.7 Prices of 30-Year Bonds with Different Coupon Rates and a 1% Change in Yields

	Yield=Coupon Rate		Yield>Coupon Rate		
Coupon Rate	Yield	Bond Price	Yield	Bond Price	Change in Price
0%	0%	$1,000	1%	$741.92	–25.8%
5%	5%	$1,000	6%	$862.35	–13.8%
12%	12%	$1,000	13%	$925.04	-7.5%

In Table 7.7, the market price of 30-year bonds is computed assuming yields increase by 1% above the bond's coupon rate. You can see the bond prices when the yield is equal to the coupon rate in the columns labelled "Yield = Coupon Rate" and you can see the prices after the 1% increase in yields in the columns labelled "Yield > Coupon Rate." When rates go up, the price of the zero coupon bond decreases by 25.8%, compared to 13.8% for the 5% bond and only 7.5% for the 12% bond. We can conclude from this that the lower the coupon rate, the greater the interest rate risk.

Bond Price Changes Over Time

First, we calculate the **capital gain yield**, which is just the percentage change in a bond price. We show you how the capital gain yield is related to the yield to maturity. Then, in the second subsection, we explore how bond prices change as the maturity date approaches even when interest rates (and yields) do not change.

capital gain yield
The percentage change in an asset's price.

Capital Gains, Coupon Yields, and the Yield to Maturity

Consider an annual coupon bond issued by Chrysler Corp. The bond has a 10.95% coupon rate, a $1,000 face value, and matures in 20 years. The yield to maturity is 12%. The bond is priced at $921.57. Assume that you buy it today, hold it for 1 year, and sell it after the next coupon. Assume that interest rates do not change during the year and so the yield is constant. What is the price change over the year, and what return do you earn on the bond? The data for the Chrysler Corp. Bond is shown in Figure 7.12.

FIGURE 7.12 Timeline of Chrysler Bond Cash Flows

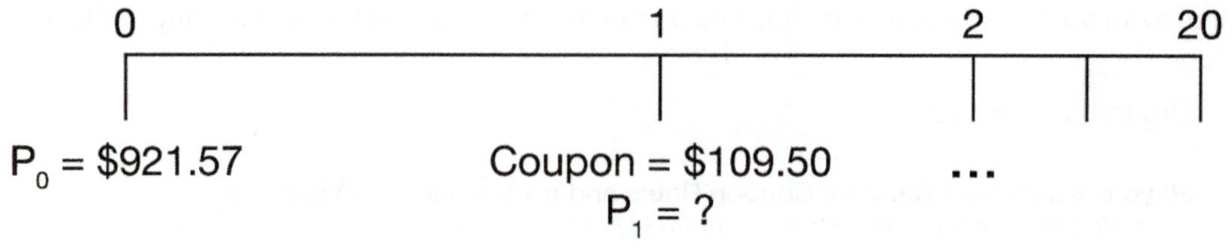

To calculate the change in price over the year we first need to calculate the price after the first coupon. Using Equation 7.12, the data given above, and $n = 19$, we find that the Chrysler bond price is $922.66 after the first coupon is paid.

The price of the bond rises over the year even though interest rates and the yield don't change.

An investor who buys the bond at the beginning of the year and sells it after the first coupon earns the following return:

EQUATION 7.14

$$HPR = \frac{\text{Price}_1 - \text{Price}_0 + C}{\text{Price}_0}$$

$$HPR = \frac{\$922.66 - \$921.57 + \$109.50}{\$921.57} = 0.12 \textit{ or } 12\%$$

The holding period return (HPR) on the bond is equal to the yield to maturity of the bond.

The holding period return can be divided into two components.

EQUATION 7.15

$$HPR = \frac{\text{Price}_1 - \text{Price}_0 + C}{\text{Price}_0}$$

$$HPR = \frac{C}{\text{Price}_0} + \frac{\text{Price}_1 - \text{Price}_0}{\text{Price}_0}$$

coupon yield

The annual coupon expressed as a percentage of the bond's price.

The first part is the **coupon yield**. It is the coupon interest payment divided by the current market price of the bond. In this example, the coupon yield is $\$109.50/921.57 = 0.1188$ or 11.88%.

Tip

Given Equation 7.15, a short-cut method for estimating the price change is to subtract the coupon yield away from the yield to maturity. Of course, this assumes no changes in the level of interest rates during the year.

The second part is the capital gain yield, which is just the percentage change in the price of the bond. In this example, the capital gain yield is $\$1.0885/921.57 = 0.00118$, or 0.118% . "Explain It: Capital Gains, Coupon Yield, and the Yield to Maturity" reviews these calculations by calculating the holding period return for the next year in the Chrysler Corp. bond example.

Explain It: Capital Gains, Coupon Yield, and the Yield to Maturity

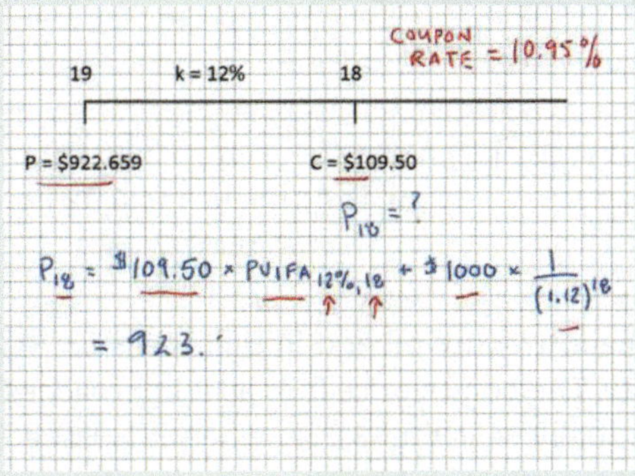

View in the online reader

Again, you can see why bonds with coupon rates lower than their yields trade at a discount. The yield to maturity in this example is 12%, but the coupon rate is only 10.95%. The coupons alone aren't enough to generate a sufficient return to satisfy investors. The low coupon rate has to be supplemented with a capital gain yield, so the bond trades at a discount to face value and slowly rises in price as the maturity date approaches (assuming no changes in the overall level of interest rates). When you buy a bond at a discount, you will receive the benefit of price appreciation as the maturity date approaches. This is in addition to the coupon payments. If you buy a premium bond, you will suffer a price decline as the maturity date approaches.

Bond Prices and Time to Maturity

The relationship between the time to maturity and the price of a discount bond, a premium bond, and a par value bond is graphed in Figure 7.13. The lines in Figure 7.13 show bond prices over 30 years (on coupon dates) between issue and maturity. In each case, the bond has the same features: a $1,000 face value and a 10% coupon rate. The three lines correspond to three different yields. The top line shows the price path of the bond if the yield is 8%, the middle line shows the price path if the yield is 10%, and the bottom line shows the price path if the yield is 12%.

FIGURE 7.13 Prices Over Time for a 10% Coupon Bond at 8%, 10%, and 12% Yields

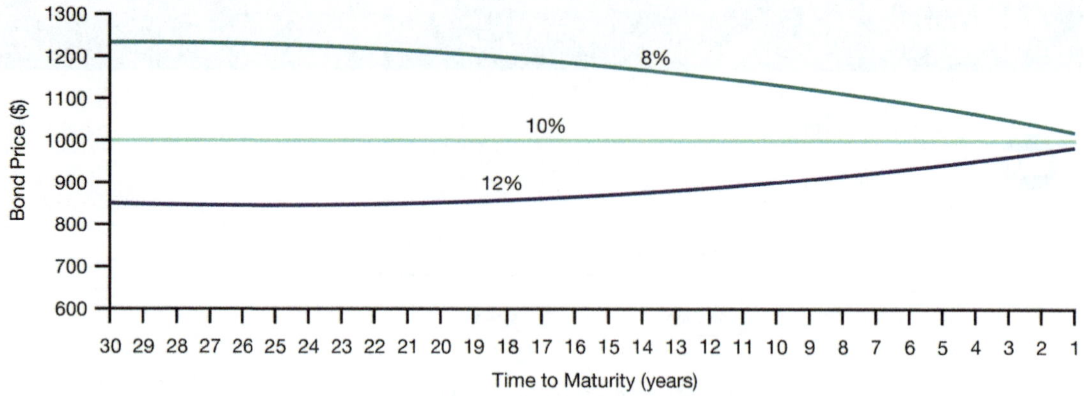

If the yield is 8%, then the 10% coupon bond initially sells for $1,225.16 when it is issued with 30 years remaining to maturity. The bond's price falls as it approaches maturity. If the yield is 12%, then the 10% coupon bond initially sells for $838.90 when it is issued. The bond's price rises as it approaches maturity. The 10% coupon bond has a constant value of $1,000 when the yield is also 10%. The spreadsheet below contains the data used in Figure 7.13. The Explain It video describes the contents of the spreadsheet and the calculations underlying the figure.

Digital Downloads

Spreadsheet Bond Prices and Time to Maturity (w Explain It Video).xls
https://catalog.flatworldknowledge.com/a/34711/Spreadsheet_Bond_Prices_and_Time_to_Maturity_w_Explain_It_Video_-31b3.xls

Explain It: Bond Price Changes Over Time

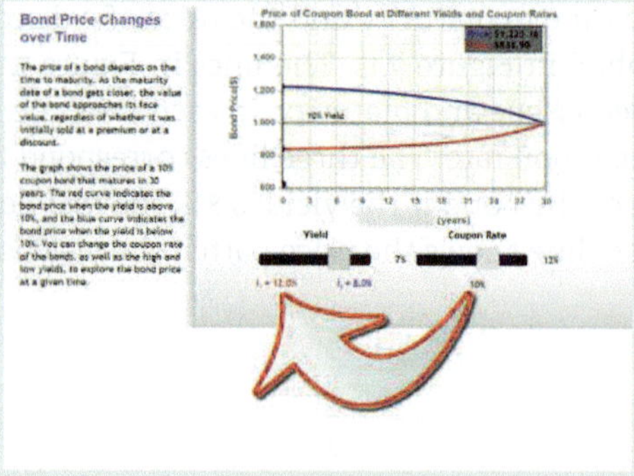

View in the online reader

7.7 Appendix: Forward Rates, Expectations, and Maturity Preference

In this appendix, we explain the Expectations Theory in more detail, describe and forward rates and revisit the maturity preference theory.

The Expectations Theory

The Expectations Theory assumes that investors are indifferent between the roll-over and lock-in strategies show in Figure 7.5. That is, if the two strategies yield the same return, then investors are indifferent between them. If the assumption is true, then the expectations theory predicts that Equation 7.6 will hold in equilibrium.

To understand why, we first need to broaden Equation 7.1 to allow for fractional bond purchases. Say you are interested in the two year zero-coupon bond shown in "Example 7.1 The Yield on a Zero Coupon Bond". The bond has a face value of $1,000, yields 5% and is priced at $907.03. Let's say that you only have $453.515 to invest. If we assume that bonds can be divided into fractions, then you can buy half of one bond and you will receive half of the face value at maturity. We can still use Equation 7.1 to characterize your investment, but with one adjustment:

$$f \times FV = f \times Price \times (1+k)^n$$

where *f* is the fraction of the bond that was purchased. In our example, $f = 0.5$ and the amount invested was half of the price or $453.515. The amount invested in the bond is f x Price and the future value of that investment is $f \times FV$. So, Equation 7.1 can be generalized to:

EQUATION 7.16

$$FV = \$Inv \times (1+k_n)^n$$

where $\$Inv$ is the dollar amount invested in the zero coupon bond, *FV* is the future value of that investment, and k_n is the spot rate for the maturity in *n* years.

With this equation in mind, let's compare the roll-over to the lock-in strategy.

Example 7.9 Comparing Roll-Over and Lock-In

The following table shows yields and prices for three zero coupon bonds (with face values of $100).

Term	Yield	Price
1 year (starting today)	$k_1 = 1\%$	$99.010
2 years (starting today)	$k_2 = 2\%$	$96.117
1 year (starting next year)	$E(k_1) = 3.01\%$	$97.078

Consider investing one dollar in each of the two investment strategies (roll-over and lock-in). What is the (expected) future value of the dollar under each strategy? (Assume that you can buy fractions of a bond so you can use Equation 7.16.)

SOLUTION

Under the lock-in strategy, you buy 2-year bonds and hold to maturity. The 2-year bond yields 2%. With $1 to invest, the future value (using Equation 7.16) of the investment is:

$$FV_2 = \$1 \times (1.02)^2 = \$1.0404$$

Under the roll-over strategy, you buy the 1-year bond and, when it matures, use the face value to buy a 1-year bond again (next year). At Date 0, the 1-year bond yields 1%. With $1 to invest, the future value of the investment after one year is:

$$FV_1 = \$1 \times (1.01) = \$1.01$$

At Date 1, you invest this money in another 1-year bond (with a yield of 3.01%). The future value of this at Date 2 is:

$$FV_2 = \$1.01 \times (1.0301) = \$1.0404$$

Algebraic Solution

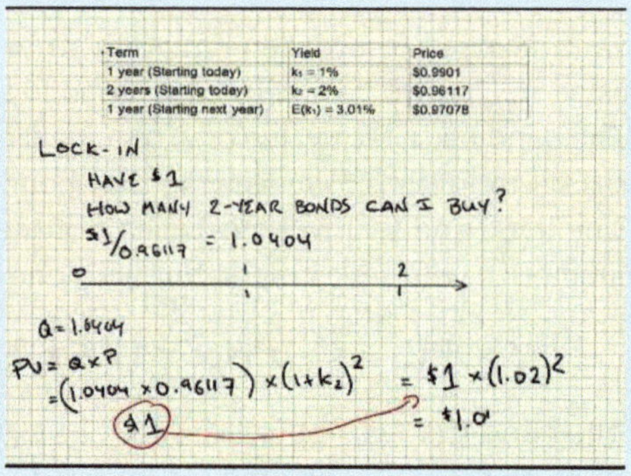

View in the online reader

The interest rates used in "Example 7.9 Comparing Roll-Over and Lock-In" conform to the relationship shown in Equation 7.6. With those rates, Example 7.9 shows that the lock-in and the roll-over strategies yield the same investment outcomes at Date 2. This is an equilibrium under the expectations theory. With these rates (and the assumption that investors are indifferent between the two strategies) there is no force to change the bond prices (and yields). "Explain It: EH and and the Law of One Price" uses a law of one price argument to show why Equation 7.6 must hold in equilibrium.

Explain It: EH and and the Law of One Price

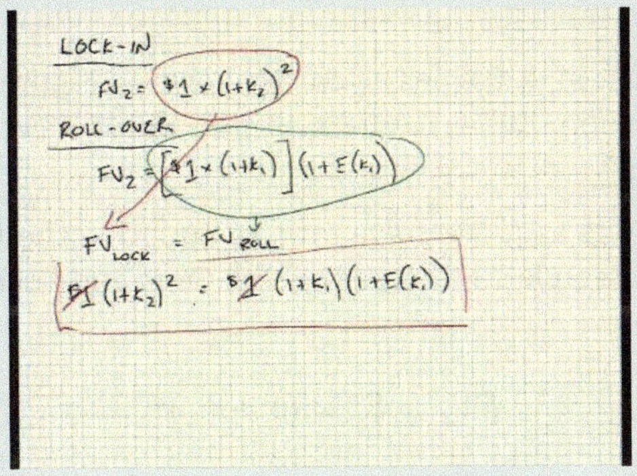

View in the online reader

The Expectations Theory and the Shape of the Yield Curve

Next we will use the expectations theory and Equation 7.6 to show that the main determinant of the shape of the yield curve is expected future interest (spot) rates. Consider the following example.

Example 7.10 The 2-year Spot Rate when Spot Rates are Expected to Fall

Assume that the one year spot rate is 1% $(k_1 = 1\%)$ and the expected future spot rate is lower, say $E(k_1) = 0.5\%$. What 2-year spot rate is consistent with these values under the expectations theory?

SOLUTION

We can use Equation 7.6 to solve for the 2-year spot rate.

$$k_2 = \sqrt{(1 + k_1) \times (1 + E(k_1))} - 1$$
$$k_2 = \sqrt{(1.01) \times (1.005)} - 1 = 0.0075$$

If $k_1 = 1\%$ and $E(k_1) = 0.5\%$, then $k_2 = 0.75\%$.

If we were to graph the spot rate yield curve using the two spot rates from "Example 7.10 The 2-year Spot Rate when Spot Rates are Expected to Fall", it would be downward sloping. We have learned that if interest rates are expected to fall (from 1% this year to 0.5% next year), then the yield curve is downward sloping.

Under the expectations theory, the shape of the yield curve is determined by expectations of future interest rates, which are, in turn, largely determined by expectations of future inflation rates. If inflation is expected to rise, then spot rates in the future will be higher than current rates, and long-term spot rates will be higher than short-term spot rates—the yield curve will be upward sloping.

Forward Rates

Consider the roll-over and lock-in strategies again, as shown in Figure 7.5. The forward rate is the answer to the following question: "What future spot rate would have to prevail to make the roll-over equivalent to the lock-in?"

We denote the forward rate as f. We solve for f by equating the future values of $1 invested in each strategy similar to "Example 7.9 Comparing Roll-Over and Lock-In". The future value of $1 invested in the lock-in is:

$$FV_2 = \$1 \times (1 + k_2)^2$$

The future value of $1 invested in the roll-over is:

$$FV_2 = \$1 \times (1 + k_1) \times (1 + f)$$

The roll-over strategy is reinvested at the forward rate, f, in the second year and then we solve for the forward rate, which equates the two future values (set the two future values, above, equal to one another):

EQUATION 7.17

$$(1 + k_2)^2 = (1 + k_1) \times (1 + f)$$

The solution for f is:

EQUATION 7.18

$$f = \frac{(1 + k_2)^2}{(1 + k_1)} - 1$$

As Equation 7.18 shows, the forward rate is derived from the spot rates. Equation 1.18 seems to suggest that there is only one forward rate from year 1 to year 2. Actually, there are many forward rates: one for each year in the future. Once we know the term structure of interest rates, then we can use the logic underlying Equation 7.18 to calculate one year forward rates between each of the maturity dates. The following example shows how to calculate the forward rate for year 3.

Tip

Don't try to memorize the Equation 7.18 as "the" forward rate formula. Instead, remember the process for solving for the rate: we equate the future value of the lock-in and the roll-over.

Example 7.11 The Forward Rate for Year 3

Consider the spot rates given in the table below. What is the forward rate between year 2 and year 3?

Maturity	Yield (Spot Rate)
1	1%
2	2%
3	3%

SOLUTION

The future value of $1 invested in the year 3 lock-in is:

$$FV_3 = \$1 \times (1 + k_3)^3 = (1.03)^3 = 1.0927$$

The future value of $1 invested in the roll-over is equal to the $1 compounded for two years at the two year spot rate and then the resulting future value compounded for one year at rate f:

$$FV_3 = \$1 \times (1 + k_2)^2 \times (1 + f) = (1.02)^2 \times (1 + f)$$

The forward rate is the rate that equates the two future values:

$$(1.02)^2 \times (1 + f) = (1.03)^3$$
$$f = [1.0927/1.0404] - 1 = 0.0503 \text{ or } 5.03\%$$

Algebraic Solution

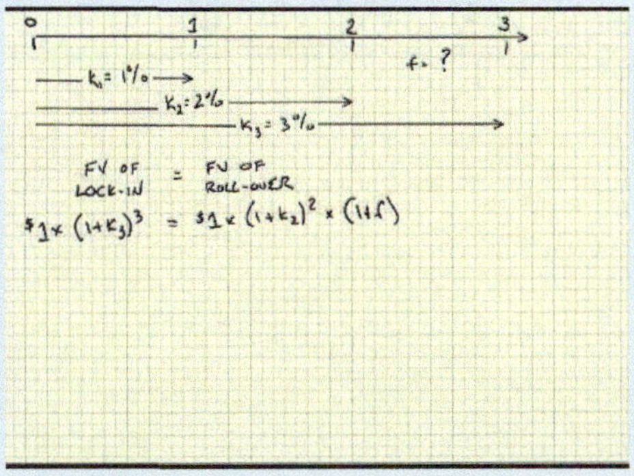

View in the online reader

How do we interpret the forward rate?

The expectations theory assumes that investors are indifferent between the lock-in and the roll-over strategies. That assumption yields the equilibrium relationship between spot rates given in Equation 7.6. But take a look at Equation 7.17, which is the set-up for solving for the forward rate. It looks almost identical to Equation 7.6. The only difference is that Equation 1.17 has the forward rate, *f*, and Equation 7.6 has the expected future spot rate, $E(k_1)$. If both equalities hold, then the forward rate must be equal to the expected future spot rate. In other words, under the expectations theory, the forward rate can be interpreted as the market's expectation of the future spot rate.

This is very useful! If you are ever asked to forecast future interest rates, then you don't need a complicated macroeconomic model. Instead, just download the term structure of interest rates from the Federal Reserve website and solve for the forward rate.

The Maturity Preference Theory and Forward Rates

As Figure 7.5 shows, there are two strategies for achieving any given long-term maturity: the roll-over and the lock-in. The lock-in strategy is exposed to interest rate risk. That is the risk associated with fluctuations in future spot rates and the associated (inverse) fluctuations in bond prices. If spot rates rise higher than expected, then the mid-term price of a long-term bond will be lower than expected. A lock-in investor who needs to sell their bond before it matures is exposed to interest rate risk.

The roll-over strategy faces re-investment rate risk. With the roll-over strategy, the investor doesn't know future spot rates with certainty. If future rates fall below what is expected, then she will earn less than if she had adopted the lock-in strategy. "Explain It: Interest Rate Risk and Reinvestment Rate Risk" describes an example with interest rate risk and re-investment rate risk.

Explain It: Interest Rate Risk and Reinvestment Rate Risk

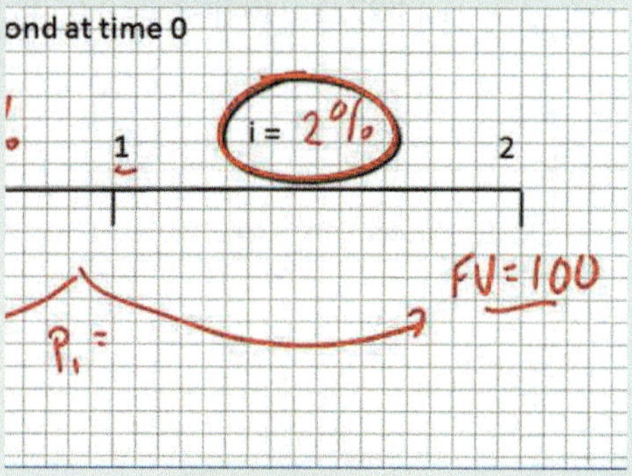

View in the online reader

The maturity preference theory assumes that investors are more concerned with the interest rate risk than they are with the re-investment rate risk. In that case, investors prefer to roll-over if the two strategies are otherwise equivalent. With this preference, we would not expect the future value of the roll-over to equal the future value of the lock-in as we showed in Equation 7.17. If they were equal, then maturity preference investors would always choose the roll-over. This argument implies that the lock-in must have a greater future value than the roll-over.

$$(1 + k_2)^2 > (1 + k_1) \times (1 + E(k_1))$$

To make this inequality hold, long-term rates (in this case the two-year spot rate) have to include a premium (over and above the level predicted by the expectations theory) to attract investors. We refer to the premium as the maturity risk premium (MRP).

Consider the following example. Let's assume that the one year spot rate is 1% and that the market expects the spot rate to be 1% next year. Under the expectations theory, the equilibrium 2-year spot rate is 1% and the yield curve should be flat. Under the maturity preference theory, the

2-year spot rate will include a maturity risk premium, even if future spot rates are expected to be unchanged, and so the yield curve will have a slight upward slope. In general, the maturity preference theory implies that the yield curve will be slightly steeper than the expectations theory predicts.

Another implication of the maturity preference theory is that forward rate is not exactly equal to the expected future spot rate. When we solve for the forward rate as we did with Equation 7.18, the result will be slightly larger than the expected future spot rate. Note that this difference isn't very large and is smaller the shorter is the maturity of the bond. The size of the maturity risk premium will vary over time as investor preferences vary.

Let's summarize what we have learned from the last four sections:

1. The expectations theory assumes that investors are indifferent between the lock-in and the roll-over strategies.
2. Under the expectations theory, the shape of the yield curve is determined by expectations about future interest rates.
3. If interest rates are expected to be higher (lower), then the yield curve is upward (downward) sloping.
4. Under the expectations theory, the forward rate can be interpreted as the market consensus expectation of the future spot rate.
5. The maturity preference theory assumes that investors prefer to roll over.
6. Under the maturity preference theory, the yield curve is a little steeper than predicted by the expectations theory and the forward rate is a little larger than the expected future spot rate.

Estimating Future Bond Prices with Forward Rates

At any point in a bond's life, its price is equal to the present value of the remaining cash flows. This calculation is easy to conduct today, because we know all of the spot rates from the spot-rate yield curve. Estimating a bond's price at a future intermediate date is more difficult, because we need all of the spot rates from that date until the dates of each of the remaining cash flows. However, as we observed above, the forward rate gives us an estimate of the expected future spot rates (assuming the expectations theory holds), which we can use to estimate a bond's price in the future. We show this in the next example.

Example 7.12 Estimating a Future Bond Price

Today's spot rates are given in the table, below. There is a T-Note with a face value of $100, 2 years to maturity, and an annual coupon rate of 4%. What is the bond's price today, and what is its expected price next year after the first coupon?

Maturity	Yield (Spot Rate)
1	1%
2	2%

SOLUTION

The price of the bond today is determined using Equation 7.9:

$$P_0 = \frac{\$4}{(1+0.01)} + \frac{\$4+\$100}{(1+0.02)^2} = \$103.92$$

To find the price at Date 1, we must discount the face value and second coupon at the spot rate that is expected to prevail between Date 1 and Date 2. If the expectations theory holds, then a good estimate of that expected future spot rate is given by the forward rate in Equation 7.18.

$$f = \frac{(1+k_2)^2}{(1+k_1)} - 1 = \frac{(1.02)^2}{(1.01)} - 1 = 0.0301$$

So, expected future spot rate at Date is 3.01%. The expected bond price at Date 1 is:

$$P_1 = \frac{\$4+\$100}{(1+0.0301)} = \$100.96$$

Endnotes

1. U.S. Department of the Treasury, Monthly Statement of Public Debt, Table IV Holdings of Treasury Securities in Stripped Form, Dec 31, 2019. www.treasurydirect.gov.
2. This equality is derived in the Appendix.
3. Friedman, Milton. *The Counter-revolution in Monetary Theory: First Wincott Memorial Lecture, Delivered at the Senate House, University of London, 16 September, 1970*; Institute of Economic Affairs. Occasional Paper No. 33. London: Institute of Economic Affairs, 1970.
4. Corporate debt includes all nonconvertible debt, medium term notes (MTNs), and Yankee bonds, but excludes CDs and federal agency debt.
5. Includes Asset-backed. Mortgage backed includes mortgage-backed bonds issued by government-sponsored enterprises (i.e., GNMA, FNMA, and FHLMC) as well as private -sector mortgage-backed securities.
6. Treasury includes all interest-bearing marketable coupon-bearing public debt.

CHAPTER 8

Stock Valuation and Market Efficiency

Learning Objectives

By the end of this chapter you will be able to:

1. Describe the primary features of stock and the stock market.
2. Compute the value of a preferred share.
3. Compute the value of common stock using the Dividend Discount Model.
4. Understand stock repurchases and compute the value of a stock using the Total Payout Method.
5. Compute the value of a stock using the P/E Valuation Model.
6. Explain the Efficient Markets Hypothesis.

In the earlier chapters, we learned that assets are valued by computing the present value of their future cash flows. We applied this method to the valuation of bonds. In each case, we identified the cash flows, estimated a discount rate, and computed a present value. In this chapter, we continue our study of investment valuation by learning to value stock. We find that though it becomes a little more complicated, the same concepts used to evaluate bonds applies to valuing stock. We begin with a brief summary about stock and the stock markets and then study a number of models for valuation.

8.1 Features of Stocks and Stock Markets

What is Stock?

Stocks (shares) are securities issued by incorporated companies. Stock represents equity or ownership in a company, and therefore a stockholder (shareholder) is a part owner of the company. Stockholders are entitled to control the corporation and to share in the company's profits. Control is exercised through the stockholder's right to vote. Common shareholders get voting rights, so that majority shareholders get control over the company. Shareholders attend an annual general meeting, where they receive annual financial statements, vote on special resolutions, and elect members to the board of directors.

stocks (shares)

A security that represents ownership in an incorporated company.

Tip

The board of directors is a body that represents the interests of the stockholders. The board oversees management's activities in order to ensure that the company's executives are running the company in the way that the shareholders desire.

A **public company's** shares are traded on a stock exchange, such as the New York Stock Exchange. A **private company's** shares are held by a relatively small number of individuals. Private company shares are not actively traded and are not listed on an exchange.

public company

A company that sells shares of stock to the public and whose shares are traded on a public exchange.

private company

A company where the ownership and shares are held by a limited number of stockholders and whose shares are not available to the public.

Tip

Cargill is the largest privately held company in the United States in terms of revenue. It would rank in the top 10 on the Fortune 500 list.

Common Shares

Common stock is the principal way that corporations raise equity or capital. **Common shares** typically give the owner one vote for each share. However, some shares have multiple votes, others have fractional votes, and still others are restricted in different ways. These "noncommon" shares are typically designated class B, class C, class D, and so on, which distinguishes them from common or class A shares.

As owners of the company, stockholders are entitled to what is left after all other obligations have been met. This makes them the **residual claimants** of the firm. In the case of liquidation of the firm, they receive the **liquidation value**. When there are profits, the board of directors may choose to distribute them to the stockholders. Profits can be distributed in two basic ways: dividends and **stock repurchases**.

common shares

Stock represents ownership in a corporation. A stockholder owns a percentage interest in a firm consistent with the percentage of outstanding stock held. Stockholders are residual claimants in the sense that they get whatever is leftover after all of the company's liabilities are paid off. Common shareholders exercise their control of the corporation by voting for directors who sit on the board, typically one vote per share. Common shareholders receive a dividend at the discretion of the board.

residual claimants

Having a claim on all assets and income after all liabilities have been met.

liquidation value

The value a firm will bring if the assets are sold, after subtracting all liabilities owned.

stock repurchases

The repurchase of stock by a firm from its existing stockholders. It is a method to distribute cash without paying dividends.

Tip

In an open market share repurchase, the firm instructs its broker to buy back shares on the open market. This gives the shareholders the option of selling some of their shares without reducing their proportionate ownership and thereby earning some income.

Dividends are usually paid every quarter on a regular schedule. Stock repurchases only take place when the directors determine excess cash has accumulated that should be distributed.

A sample common share certificate is shown in Figure 8.1. Notice how there is no par value and no indication of a dividend like we see on the preferred share in Figure 8.2. Common shareholders are not entitled to any fixed payment in the event of the dissolution of the company and the dividend is paid at the discretion of the board of directors. Buying a share is truly a leap of faith insofar as nothing is contractually promised.

FIGURE 8.1 **Common Stock Certificate Example**

1. Company Stock certificate number: an identifying number that uniquely describes this issue of stock; sometimes referred to as a CUSIP number. 2. Number of shares. 3. Company Name.

Scott Rothstein / Shutterstock.com

Tip

Stock certificates are rarely issued now. Instead, share ownership is documented as a book entry on record with your broker. Note the date on the stock certificate is shown. It is from 1906. It is hard to find actual stock certificates now since they are kept electronically. Since we couldn't locate a current one we used one from the far past.

As with any asset, we value common stock as the present value of all future cash flows. The cash flows a stockholder may earn from stock are dividends, stock repurchases, sales price, or all three. In the next few sections, we develop an understanding of the dividend valuation model. This model is used when dividend information is available and reliable. We then present the price earnings model that can be used when future cash flow data is limited. We also present a valuation model that incorporates stock repurchases since this has become a very frequent occurrence.

Preferred Shares

dividends

Periodic distributions of cash made by a firm to its stockholders, usually paid quarterly.

cumulative dividends

When a board of directors elects to suspend preferred divided payments; all skipped preferred dividends must be paid before a firm can pay any common stock dividends.

Preferred stock is a hybrid instrument because it has characteristics of both common stock and bonds. Like bonds, preferred stock pays a fixed amount each period. Like common stock, preferred stock does not usually mature and the periodic payments are in the form of **dividends** rather than interest. Unlike common stock shareholders, preferred stock shareholders typically do not have voting rights. Bond interest payments are paid before preferred dividends, but preferred dividends are paid before common stock dividends. Most preferred stock has **cumulative dividends**. This means that when the board of directors elects to suspend preferred dividend payments, all skipped preferred dividends must be paid before the firm can pay any common stock dividends. Second, in the event that a company is liquidated, preferred shareholders are entitled to their par value before common shareholders receive anything.

An example of a preferred share is shown in Figure 8.2. Note that the par value of the share is $100, which is indicated at the bottom of the certificate. If you look closely you can read that the dividend is 5% of the par value ($5) annually and that the dividends are non-cumulative.

FIGURE 8.2 Preferred Stock Certificate Example

1. Stock certificate number. 2. Number of shares this certificate represents. 3. Name of issuing company. 4. Par value of shares. This is the value of the shares if the company calls back the shares.

Shutterstock.com

Stock Markets

The **primary market** is the market for newly issued shares. When a company does an **initial public offering (IPO)**, where it first becomes a public company and issues stock, or a **seasoned offering**, where a firm that already has publicly traded stocks sells more shares, the trades occur in the primary market. Any trading done on these stocks after their initial issuance occurs in the **secondary market**.

primary market

The market where securities are traded for the first time and where initial offerings to the public are made.

initial public offering (IPO)

Where a firm first offers shares to the public and the firm becomes a public company.

seasoned offering

An issue of stock that was offered in the past and has been traded since.

secondary market

The market for trading securities after they have been issued.

Tip

Examples of secondary markets are the NYSE and NASDAQ.

Stock Price Reporting

Stock prices are listed in the financial press daily. Table 8.1 is typical of the information reported.

TABLE 8.1 Typical Stock Listing

High	Low	Stock	Sym	High[1]	Low[2]	Close[3]	Chg[4]	Vol 100s[5]
38.02	24.75	Suncor Enr	SU	34.48	33.88	34.02	+0.12	16032
15.03	8.32	Sunopta	SOY	10.66	10.39	10.39	−0.11	77
0.10	0.015	Systech Re	SYS	0.025	0.02	0.02	−0.005	811
2.99	1.22	Systm Xcel	SXC	1.48	1.40	1.47	+0.07	76

Trading Stocks

Positions: Long and Short

In a **long position** for a stock, bond, commodity, or currency, the investor owns the security. This is the most common approach to investing in securities. In a long position, the investor first purchases the security and then sells the security. You take a long position when you expect an increase in the asset price. Long positions are profitable if you buy at a low price and sell at a high price. (Buy low, sell high.)

long position

An investment where ownership is taken before the security is sold. This is the usual form investments take.

Tip

A good example of a long position is the investment in your house. With home ownership, the purchase precedes the sale. You hope that the price of the house will rise and so you will sell it at a higher price than the price that you paid.

short position

The investor initially borrows the security. It is then sold. Later the security is bought back to repay the loan.

A **short position** is the reverse of the normal buy–sell sequence. In a short position, the investor first sells the asset, and then buys it back later, hopefully at a lower price. A short position is initiated in the anticipation of a decrease in the asset price. Like a long position, a short position is profitable only if you buy low and sell high. You might wonder how you can sell something if you don't already own it. The answer is that you first borrow the security. Your stock broker will lend you shares in most publicly listed stocks for a small fee. When you complete the short position by buying the shares back you return them to the lender.

Explain It: Short Selling

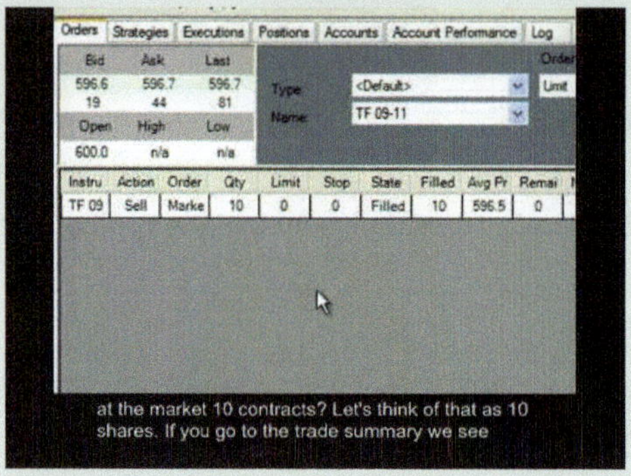

View in the online reader

Orders: Market and Limit

market order

An order to buy or sell that is to be executed as soon as it is received by the broker.

A **market order** is an order to buy or sell that is to be executed as soon as possible at the best price obtainable.

Explain It: Market Orders and the Long Position

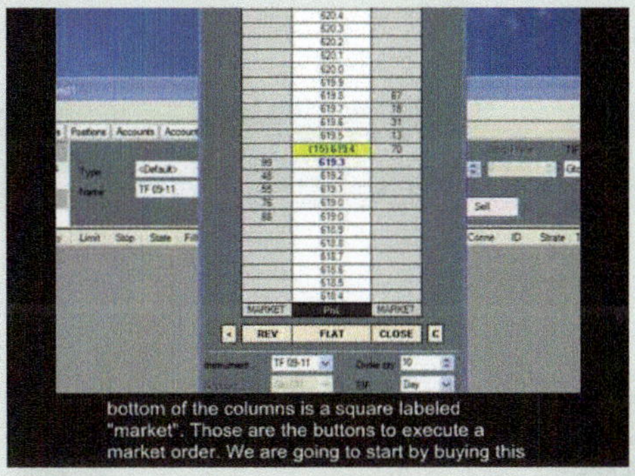

View in the online reader

A **limit order** is a conditional order to buy or sell. The investor specifies a price in the order, and the order is filled if the asset price is equal to the specified price or better. In particular, a limit order to buy is executed at the specified price or a lower price. A limit order to sell is executed at the specified price or higher.

limit order

A conditional order to buy or sell a security where it is only filled if the sell price is above a given level or the buy price is below a given level.

Explain It: Limit Orders

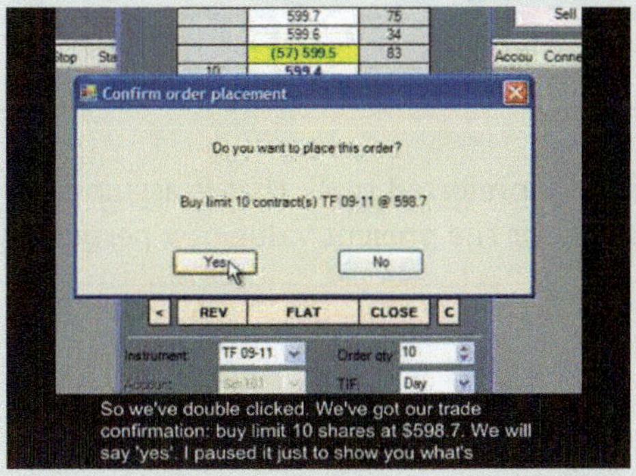

View in the online reader

Margin

margin

The amount of money the investor must provide to purchase a security. The balance is supplied by the broker. The minimum margin is 50%.

Buying on margin means borrowing money to make an investment in stocks (or any security). The lender is your broker. The term **margin** refers to the amount of money provided by the investor. The loan from the broker makes up the total. Brokers are usually restricted to lending no more than half of the total value of the investment. Thus, investors must provide a margin of at least 50% of the initial cost of a long position.

Explain It: Trading on Margin

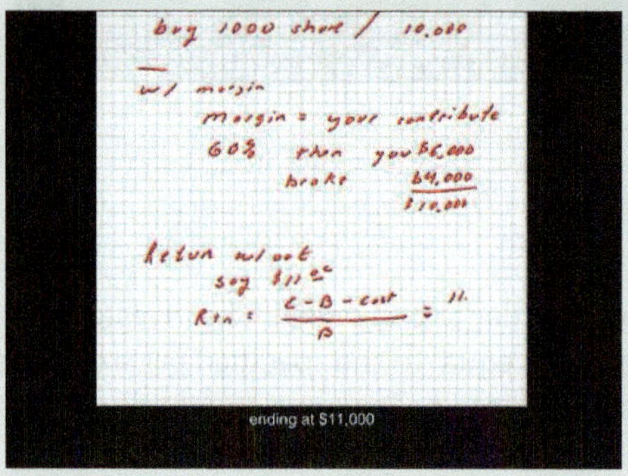

View in the online reader

8.2 Valuation of Preferred Stock

In this chapter, we focus on simple preferred stock that is assumed to pay dividends in perpetuity (forever). We can use the formula for the present value of a perpetuity. Equation 8.1 computes the value of preferred stock.

EQUATION 8.1

$$P_{\text{Preferred}} = \frac{D}{k}$$

where

$$P_{Preferred} = \text{the price of the preferred share}$$
$$D = \text{the periodic dividend}$$
$$k = \text{the required return of preferred shareholders}$$

Tip

Note that we denote the interest rate as *k* instead of *i*. The *k* notation is meant to capture the idea that this is the return required on this particular type of security. Sometimes, we will use *kp* to denote that this is the required return on preferred stock.

Example 8.1 Valuation of Preferred Stock

If investors require a 12.5% return, and the stock pays an annual end-of-year dividend of $1.50, what is the market price per share?

SOLUTION

Algebraic Solution

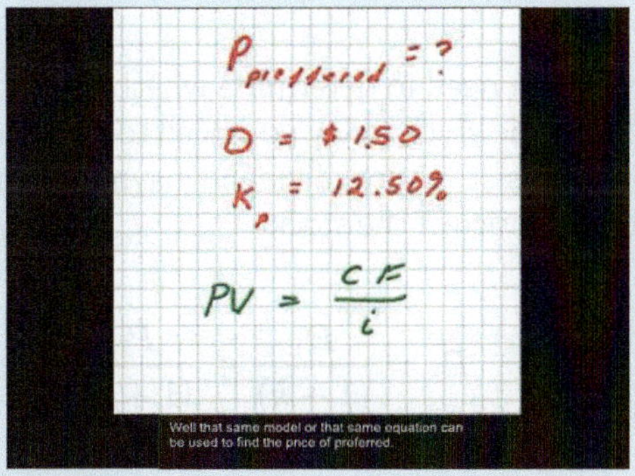

View in the online reader

Use Equation 8.1 to find the market price per share.

$$P_{\text{Preferred}} = \frac{D}{k}$$

$$P_{Preferred} = \$1.50/0.125 = \$12.00$$

What would make the price of a preferred share change? The answer is anything that makes the dividend or the required return (*k*) change.

Tip

Since the dividend is contractually fixed, it doesn't fluctuate unless the company's ability to pay dividends is threatened.

Like bonds, the price of a preferred share varies inversely with the rate of return required by preferred shareholders, *k*. That rate, in turn, varies with long-term interest rates and the perceived risk of the dividend payments being suspended.

8.3 The Valuation of Common Stock Using the Dividend Discount Model

The One-Period Valuation Model

Suppose you have some extra money to invest for 1 year. After a year, you will need to sell your investment to pay tuition. After listening to *Bloomberg*, you decide that you want to buy Intel Corp. stock. You call your broker and find that Intel is currently selling for $50.00 per share and pays $0.16 per year in dividends. The analyst on *Bloomberg* predicts that the stock will be selling for $60 in 1 year. Should you buy this stock?

To answer this question, you need to determine whether the current price accurately reflects the analyst's forecast. To value the stock today you need to find the present value of the expected cash flows. The cash flows consist of one dividend payment plus the sales price 1 year from now. Equation 8.2 computes the price of the stock.

EQUATION 8.2

$$P_0 = \frac{D_1}{(1+k)} + \frac{P_1}{(1+k)}$$

where

$$\begin{aligned} P_0 &= \text{the current price of the stock} \\ D_1 &= \text{the dividend paid at the end of year 1} \\ k &= \text{the required return of stockholders} \\ P_1 &= \text{the price at the end of year 1} \end{aligned}$$

Explain It: The One-Period Valuation Model

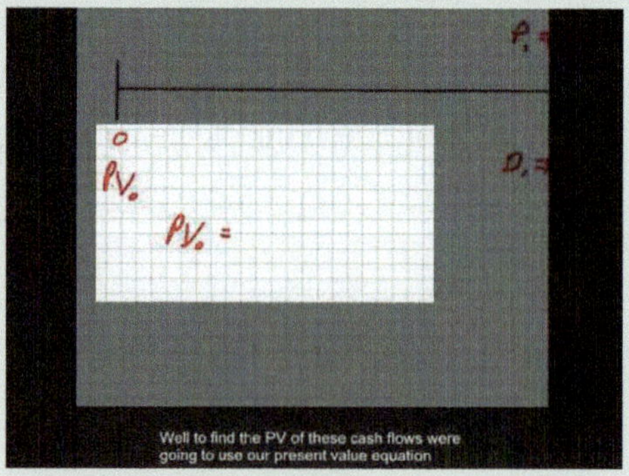

View in the online reader

Example 8.2 Valuation of Common Stock after Holding for One Period

Digital Downloads

Example 8.2_One_Period_Valuation_Model.xls
https://catalog.flatworldknowledge.com/a/34711/Example_8_2_One_Period_Valuation_Model-7e16.xls

Find the price of the Intel stock given the figures reported on the previously $(D_1 = 0.16 \text{ and } P_1 = \$60)$. You will need to know the required return of stockholders to find the present value of the cash flows. Assume that you would be satisfied to earn 12% on the stock.

SOLUTION

Spreadsheet Solution

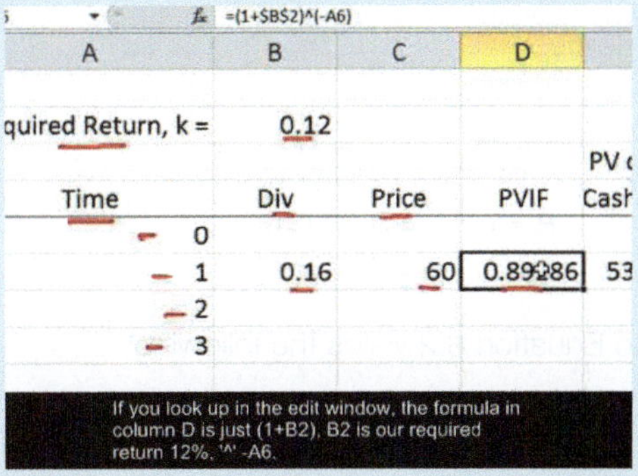

View in the online reader

Algebraic Solution

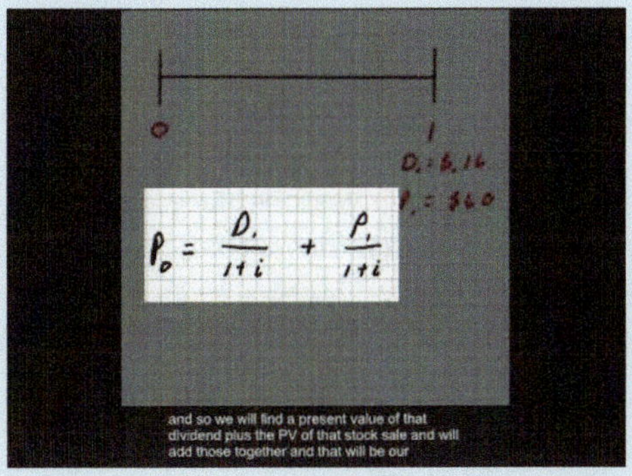

View in the online reader

Calculator Solution

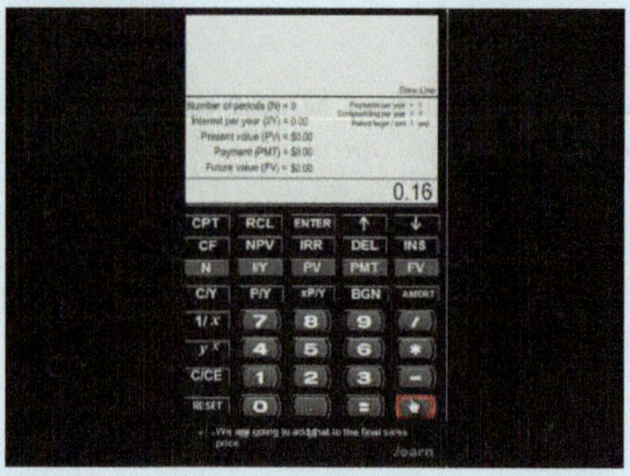

View in the online reader

Begin by preparing a timeline.

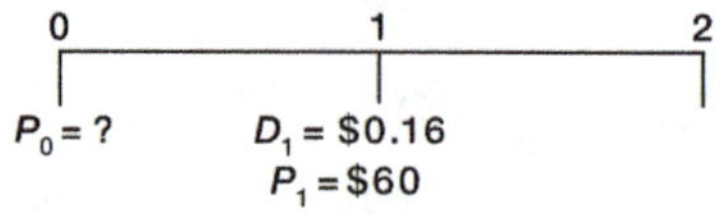

Putting the numbers into Equation 8.2 yields the following:

$$P_0 = \frac{D_1}{(1+k)} + \frac{P_1}{(1+k)}$$
$$P_0 = \frac{\$0.16}{(1+0.12)} + \frac{\$60}{(1+0.12)}$$
$$P_0 = \$0.14 + \$53.57 = \$53.71$$

Based on your analysis, you find that the stock is worth \$53.71. Since the stock is currently available for \$50.00 per share, you would choose to buy it. But you may wonder why the stock is selling for less than \$53.71. It could be that other investors place a different risk on the future cash flows or they are more pessimistic about future cash flows than you.

Tip

Whenever you buy stock, you are buying from someone who thinks it is overpriced. Only time will tell whether you or the seller is correct.

The Generalized Dividend Valuation Model

generalized dividend valuation model

A model used to compute the value of stock that assumes its price is the present value of all future cash flows.

The concept used in the last example to value a share of stock can be extended to allow for any number of periods. This valuation method is called the **generalized dividend valuation model**. However, the concept remains the same. The value of stock is the present value of all future cash flows. The only cash flows that an investor will receive are dividends and a final sale price when the stock is ultimately sold. The generalized formula for stock can be written as in Equation 8.3.

EQUATION 8.3

$$P_0 = \frac{D_1}{(1+k)} + \frac{D_2}{(1+k)^2} + \ldots + \frac{D_m}{(1+k)^n} + \frac{P_n}{(1+k)^n}$$

Tip

We are assuming for the current discussion that there are no stock repurchases.

If you were to attempt to use Equation 8.3 to find the value of a share of stock, first you must estimate the value the stock will have at some point in the future before you can estimate its value today. In other words, you must find P_n in order to find P_0 . P_n will be the present value of all future dividends plus a future sales price. That future sales price will also be the present value of all future dividends plus an even more distant sales price. This process continues so that the current price of the stock is found as the present value of a stream of dividends plus the present value of a very, very distant future stock price. Remember that the present value of a sum to be received far in the future is actually going to be *very* small and can be ignored.

Tip

For example, the present value of a share of stock that sells for \$50 75 years from now at a 12% discount rate is just one cent $[\$50/(1.12^{75}) = \$0.01]$.

This means that the current value of a share of stock can be found as simply the present value of the future dividend stream. The generalized dividend model is rewritten in Equation 8.4 without the final sales price.

EQUATION 8.4

$$P_0 = \sum_{t=1}^{\infty} \frac{D_t}{(1+k)^t}$$

Why do firms that pay no dividends have valuable stock that increases in price over time? *Buyers of the stock expect that the firm will pay dividends someday.* Most of the time, a firm starts paying dividends as soon as it has completed the rapid growth phase of its life cycle. The stock price increases as the time approaches for the dividend stream to begin.

Explain It: The Importance of Dividends

View in the online reader

Figure 8.3 shows how the stock price increases over time as the constant dividend phase of its life approaches, even though nothing has changed except the time until dividend payments start. In Figure 8.3, the company starts paying a perpetual annual dividend of $4.80 at date 5. The shareholders of the company require a 12% rate of return.

FIGURE 8.3

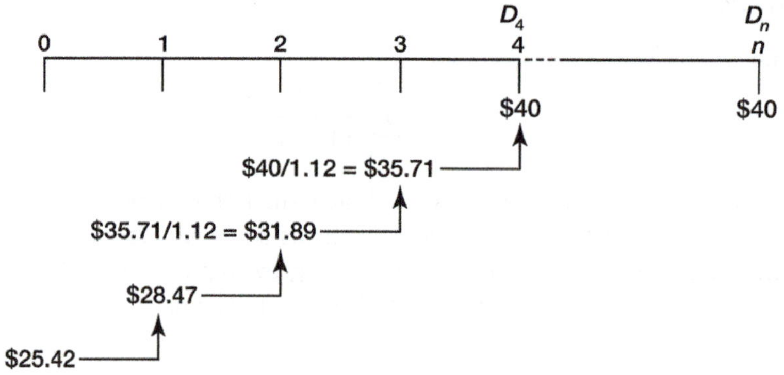

Explain It: The Increase in Price of a Nondividend Paying Stock

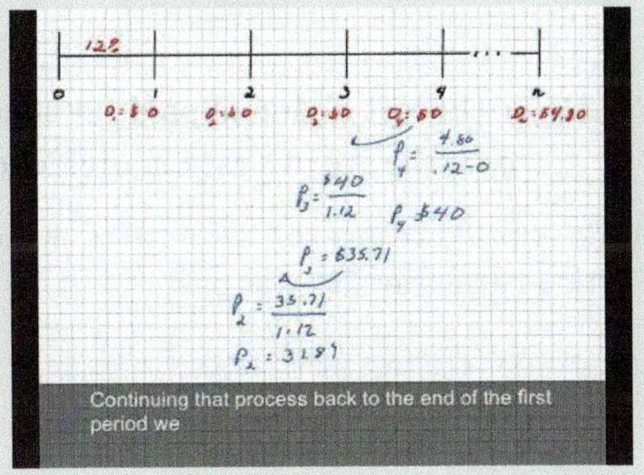

View in the online reader

The generalized dividend valuation model requires that we compute the present value of an infinite stream of dividends, a process that could be difficult, to say the least. Therefore, simplified models have been developed to make the calculations easier. One such model is the **constant growth model** that assumes constant dividend growth.

constant growth model

A model for computing the value of stock that assumes dividends grow at a constant rate forever and that the price is the present value of these dividends.

Tip

The generalized dividend model is only presented to make the theory behind the constant growth model make sense.

The Constant Growth Model

Many firms strive to increase their dividends at a constant rate each year. In this section, we assume that dividends grow at a constant periodic rate, forever. A typical sequence of dividends for a company is shown in the timeline in Figure 8.4.

Tip

We know that the dividends will not really increase at a constant rate forever, but given the uncertainty in estimating dividends this can often be a reasonable simplifying assumption.

FIGURE 8.4 Timeline of Constant Growth Dividends

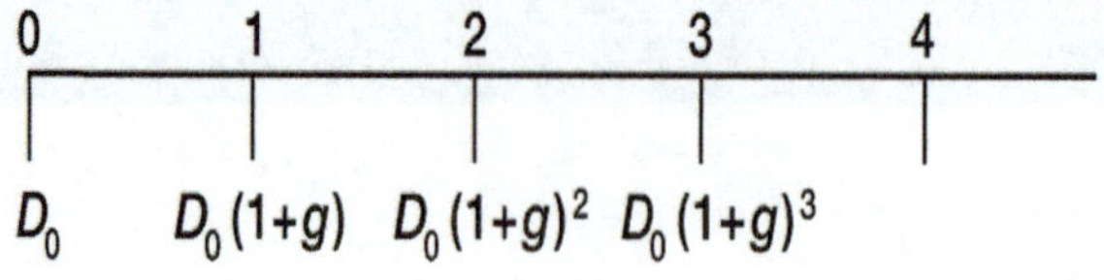

where

$$D_0 = \text{the last dividend paid (at time zero)}$$
$$g = \text{the growth rate in dividends}$$

We refer to D_0 as the last dividend paid because the assumed timing of this model is that we are standing at the beginning of period 1 just after D_0 was paid.

Tip

Think of this as New Year's Eve. The dividend (D_0) was paid at 11:59 pm on December 31 and now we are standing at 00:01 am on January 1.

The next dividend occurs one period later and is *g*% bigger than D_0. We can rewrite Equation 8.4 to reflect this constant growth in dividends.

EQUATION 8.5

$$P_0 = \frac{D_0 \times (1+g)}{(1+k)} + \frac{D_0 \times (1+g)^2}{(1+k)^2} + \ldots + \frac{D_0 \times (1+g)^\infty}{(1+k)^\infty}$$

The rate used to discount the dividends, *k*, is the required return of stockholders.

We can simplify Equation 8.5 to yield the constant growth model. Note, in particular, the inverse relationship between the stock price and the required return, *k*.

EQUATION 8.6

$$P_0 = \frac{D_0 \times (1+g)}{k-g} = \frac{D_1}{k-g}$$

Tip

The most common error students make applying the constant growth model is to use the wrong dividend in the numerator. D_0 is the dividend just paid. It is assumed that the investor will not receive this dividend. It is only a benchmark to use for estimating the next dividend (D_1) that the investor will receive. If the problem gives you D_1, do not multiply by $(1+g)$. If the problem gives you D_0, be sure that you compute D_1.

This model is useful for finding the value of stock under two chief assumptions: 1) the growth is constant forever; and 2) $k > g$.

1) The growth rate is constant forever.

Actually, as long as they are expected to grow at a constant rate for an extended period of time the model should yield reasonable results. This is because errors about distant cash flows become small when discounted to the present.

2) k>g

Myron Gordon, in his development of the model, demonstrates that this is a reasonable assumption. In theory, if the growth rate were larger than the rate demanded by holders of the firm's equity, in the long run, the firm would grow impossibly large.

The difficult part of valuing the stock will be estimating the long-term average growth rate to use in the model. One way to do this is to look at the past change in dividends and use this rate as an estimate of the future change. For example, review the dividends paid by Risky Ventures over the past 5 years in Table 8.2.

TABLE 8.2 Example Dividend Stream

Dividends Paid per Year	
Year	**Dividend**
20X1	$0.66
20X2	$0.70
20X3	$0.80
20X4	$0.88
20X5	$1.00

The average growth rate in dividends is computed by using the equation for solving for an interest rate (in the context of the future value of a lump sum). We have replaced the term *i* with *g* to make it clear we are computing a growth rate.

EQUATION 8.7

$$g = \left(\frac{FV_n}{PV_0}\right)^{\frac{1}{n}} - 1$$

PV will be the earliest occurring dividend, and *FV* will be the most recently occurring dividend. *n* will be the number of intervals during which the dividends can grow. For example, there is one interval between 20X1 and 20X2, a second between 20X2 and 20X3, and so on, for a total of four intervals. To find the growth in dividends, substitute the dividends into the growth equation as follows.

Tip

The most common error is counting the years instead of the intervals. Note that there are four intervals between 20X1 and 20X5, not 5.

$$g = \left(\frac{\$1.00}{\$0.66}\right)^{\frac{1}{4}} - 1$$

$$g = 1.1095 - 1 = 0.1905 \text{ or } 10.95\%$$

We can now use Equation 8.6 to find the current market price of our stock. The following Explain It video shows how to find the growth rate using your financial calculator.

Explain It: Computing Growth Rates Using the Calculator

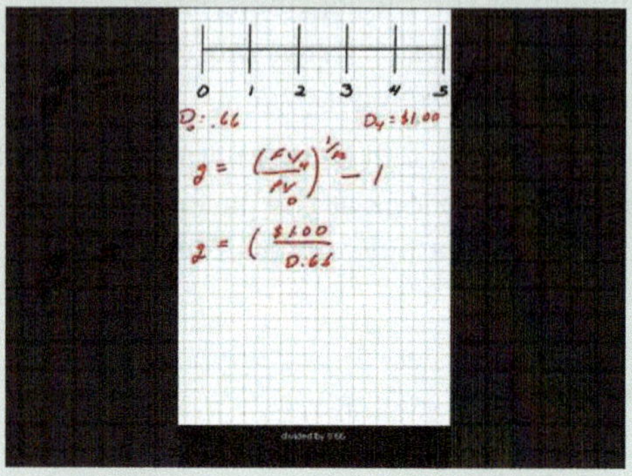

View in the online reader

Example 8.3 Valuation of Common Stock with Constant Growth Model

Digital Downloads

Example 8.3_Growth_Model.xls
https://catalog.flatworldknowledge.com/a/34711/Example_8_3_Growth_Model-616e.xls

Find the current market price of stock assuming dividends grow at a constant rate of 10.95%, $D_0 = \$1.00$, and the required return is 13%.

SOLUTION

Spreadsheet Solution

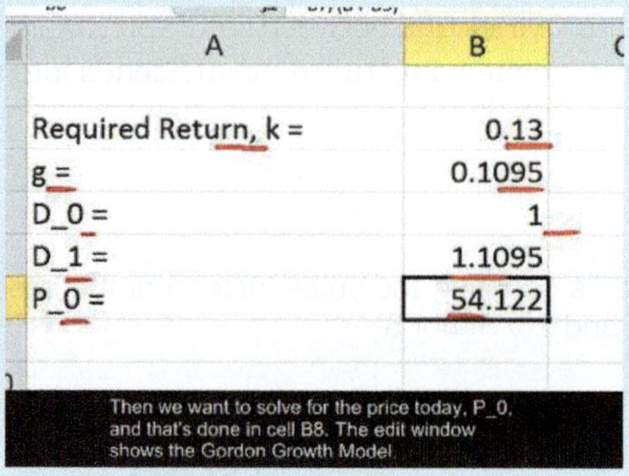

View in the online reader

Putting the numbers into Equation 8.6 yields the following:

$$P_0 = \frac{D_0 \times (1+g)}{k-g}$$

$$P_0 = \frac{\$1 \times (1+0.1095)}{0.13-0.1095}$$

$$P_0 = \$54.12$$

The stock should sell for $54.12 if the assumption regarding the constant growth rate and required return are correct.

Stock Market Volatility

An interesting application of the dividend growth model is in explaining stock market volatility. On any given day, individual stock prices can experience dramatic swings. To understand why this happens, take a look at the basic constant growth model:

$$P_0 = \frac{D_1}{k-g}$$

The price today is based on estimates formed by traders in the stock. They must estimate the next dividend as well as the required return and the expected future growth rate. Any change to the market's assessment of these values will change the value of the stock. For example, if the perceived risk of the firm increases, the required return will rise. This will lower the price. An increase in the growth rate will likewise increase the stock price. Since news is constantly being produced and analyzed about companies and their futures, it is not surprising that stock prices are constantly changing.

Explain It: Explaining Stock Market Volatility

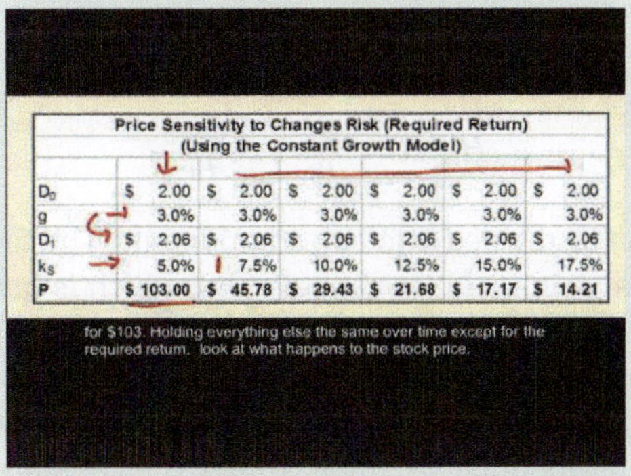

Price Sensitivity to Changes Risk (Required Return)
(Using the Constant Growth Model)

D_0	$ 2.00	$ 2.00	$ 2.00	$ 2.00	$ 2.00	$ 2.00
g	3.0%	3.0%	3.0%	3.0%	3.0%	3.0%
D_1	$ 2.06	$ 2.06	$ 2.06	$ 2.06	$ 2.06	$ 2.06
k_s	5.0%	7.5%	10.0%	12.5%	15.0%	17.5%
P	$ 103.00	$ 45.78	$ 29.43	$ 21.68	$ 17.17	$ 14.21

View in the online reader

Computing the Required Return on Stock

If a company pays dividends that grow at a constant rate, then we can use the stock market price to infer the discount rate used by the market to price the stock. In other words, we can solve for stockholders' required rate of return. We do this by rearranging the constant growth model to solve for $\boldsymbol{k}$.

$$P_0 = \frac{D_1}{k-g}$$
$$P_0(k-g) = D_1$$
$$(k-g) = \frac{D_1}{P_0}$$

EQUATION 8.8

$$k = \frac{D_1}{P_0} + g$$

Here we see that the required return on equity is equal to the dividend yield, (D_1/P_0) plus the dividend growth rate, *g*. The dividend yield is the dividend expressed as a percentage of the firm's current stock price.

To better understand Equation 8.8, let's think about buying a stock, holding it for 1 year and then selling it after receiving the annual dividend. The cash flows are shown in Figure 8.5.

FIGURE 8.5 Timeline of Stock Cash Flows

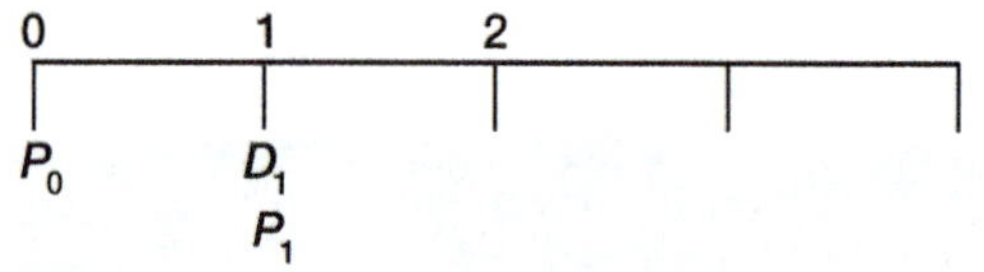

Let's denote the 1-year holding period return as HPR. The holding period return is equal to the profit (or loss) due to price appreciation (depreciation) plus the dividend expressed as a proportion of the investment (the purchase price).

$$HPR = \frac{P_1 - P_0 + D_1}{P_0}$$
$$HPR = \frac{D_1}{P_0} + \frac{P_1 - P_0}{P_0}$$

The holding period return can be divided into two components. The first part is the dividend yield. The second part is the capital gain yield (or capital gain), which is just the proportionate change in the price of the stock. Let's compare this two-part return to Equation 8.8, which solves for the required return, *k*. If stock holders expect to earn the rate *k*, then you would expect the holding period return each year to equal *k*. In both equations, the first term is the dividend yield. Thus, for HPR to equal *k*, the second terms must be equal. Under the constant growth model, the capital gain yield is equal to *g*. In other words, with constant dividend growth of *g*%, the stock price will increase at *g*% as well.

Tip

When we equate the 1-year holding period return, HPR, to the required return in Equation 8.8, we are assuming that the stock is priced fairly. When a stock is priced fairly the actual return matches the required return. When a stock is underpriced, then the actual return will exceed the required return.

A stock can provide a return to the investor by paying a dividend, increasing in value (due to growth, *g*), or by some combination of the two. **High yield stocks** pay out a large portion of their net earnings as dividends. Alternatively, **zero or low yield stocks** retain all or most of their earnings and reinvest them in the company.

high yield stocks

Stocks that pay out a relatively high percentage of their income in the form of dividends.

zero or low yield stocks

Stocks that pay out a low percentage of their income as dividends, instead investing in growth.

Tip

Notice the terminology used in the above paragraph. A high-yield stock is not one that offers unusually high returns. It is one where a large *portion* of the return is paid as a dividend.

Nonconstant Growth Model

The constant dividend growth model is useful for finding the value of firms that have reached maturity and have exhausted most of their high-growth opportunities. It may be fair to assume that these firms will maintain a constant growth rate into the foreseeable future. Alternatively, some firms may be experiencing an unusual dividend stream either because of an aggressive expansion program or a difficult business environment. It is inappropriate to use the constant dividend model to value these firms. A nonconstant growth or variable growth model may be used when the first few dividends are not constant and not anticipated to continue. For example, in 1996, Apple Computer posted a $740 million first-quarter loss. It suspended dividends and received a great deal of negative publicity. Analysts began projecting that Apple would either become a niche player, fail altogether, or merge with another firm. At this time, analysts had to project future cash flows for Apple in order to make buy or sell stock recommendations. It would have been inappropriate to use the historic average growth in dividends to value this firm since it was undergoing drastic changes in its business structure. A superior approach would have been to project when dividends would resume and at what level. Let us examine how this might be done.

For companies where dividends grow at a nonconstant rate, we value the shares using a three-step method:

1. Determine the dividend expected at the end of each year during the nonconstant growth period. For example, Apple may be projected to have zero dividends for 2 years, then to establish a $1.00 dividend.
2. Estimate the constant growth rate and use it to price the dividend stream that begins after the nonconstant growth period.
3. Find the present value of the nonconstant dividends and add the sum to the present value of the price found in step 2.

An example should help make these steps clear.

Example 8.4 Stock Valuation, Nonconstant Growth

Assume that Apple Computer pays no dividends for the next 2 years. At the end of the third year, it pays a $1.00 dividend and then establishes a dividend growth rate of 5% per year from then on. Draw a timeline and compute the current price of Apple stock assuming a 15% discount rate.

SOLUTION

Spreadsheet Solution

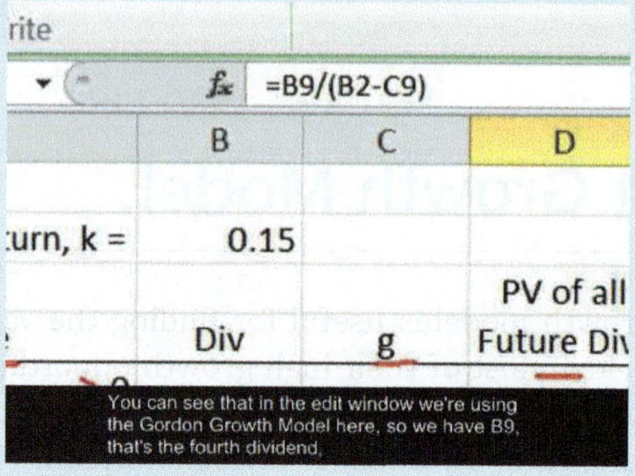

View in the online reader

Algebraic Solution

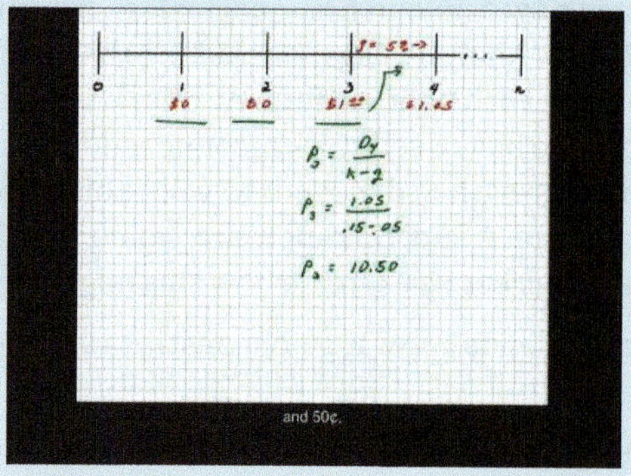

View in the online reader

Calculator Solution

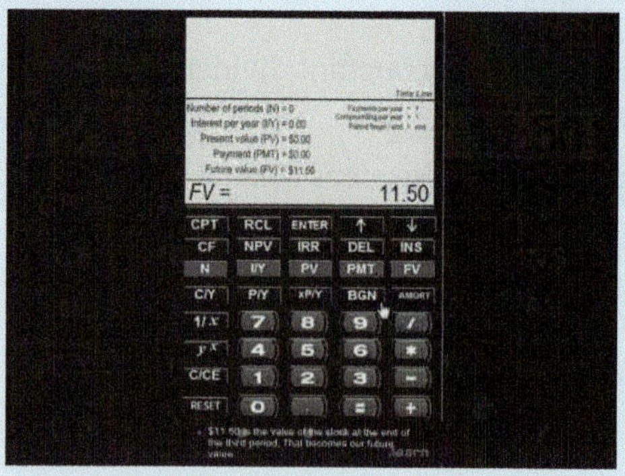

View in the online reader

Begin by drawing a timeline.

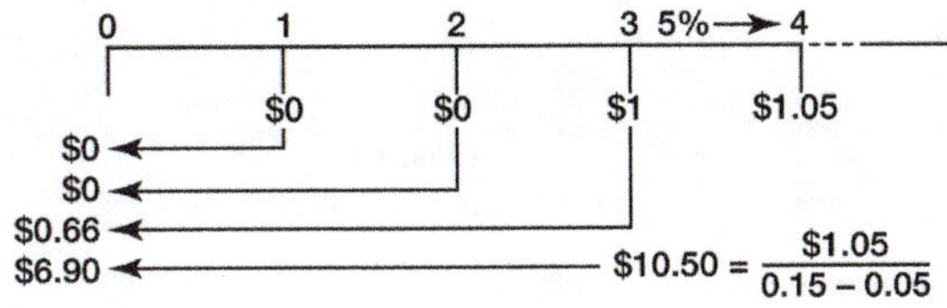

Steps 1 and 2: The relevant dividends are $0 paid for 2 years then $1 followed by 5% growth.

Step 3: The present value of the first two dividends is $0. The present value of the next dividend of $1 is $\$0.66(\$1/1.15^3 = \$0.66)$. The present value of the stream of dividends having a constant 5% growth rate following the $1 dividend is found using the constant growth model. Application of this model will provide a stock price at the end of the third period, not at the end of the fourth. The constant growth model discounts the dividend stream back *one* period. The price as of time 3 must be discounted back three *more* periods and added to the present value of the other dividends to find the current price.

$$P_3 = \frac{\$1.05}{0.15 - 0.05}$$

$$P_3 = \frac{\$1.05}{0.10} = \$10.50$$

$$P_0 = \$0 + \$0 + \$0.66 + \$10.50/\left(1.15^3\right)$$

$$P_0 = \$0 + \$0 + \$0.66 + \$6.90 = \$7.56$$

Another variation of nonconstant growth is the situation where a company experiences very fast dividend growth—a situation called supernormal growth. With supernormal growth, we assume a short period of high dividend growth followed by a perpetuity of slower, constant growth. To find the value of a supergrowth firm, we first determine each dividend in the supernormal growth phase. Next, we find the value of the stock at the time the constant growth phase is projected to begin. Finally, we sum the present value of the nonconstant dividends and the present value of the future price. This is demonstrated in "Example 8.5 Stock Valuation, Supernormal Growth".

Example 8.5 Stock Valuation, Supernormal Growth

Digital Downloads

Example 8.5_Supernormal_Growth_Model.xls
https://catalog.flatworldknowledge.com/a/34711/Example_8_5_Supernormal_Growth_Model-a1c7.xls

The last dividend paid was $2.00 per share. The stock is expected to grow at 20% for the next 3 years, then at a constant 10% thereafter. If the required return is 15%, what should the stock sell for today?

SOLUTION

Spreadsheet Solution

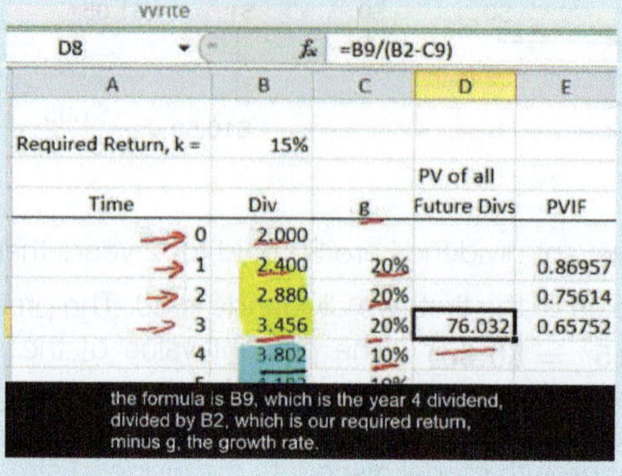

View in the online reader

Algebraic Solution

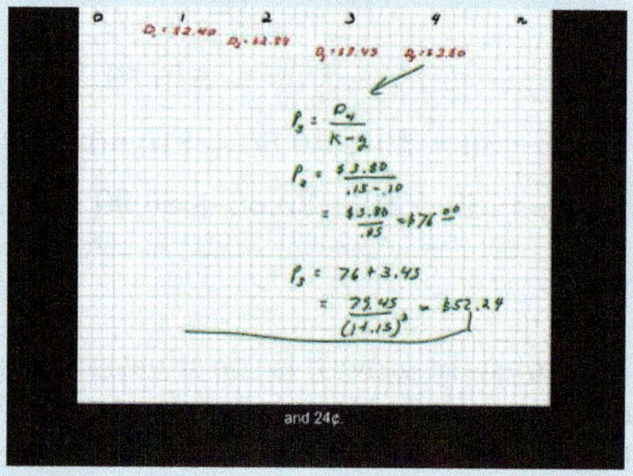

View in the online reader

Calculator Solution

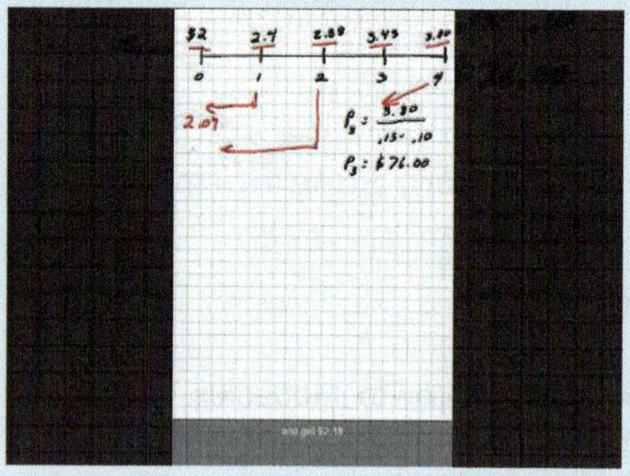

View in the online reader

TIP: *This is a good example of how the timeline can be a critical tool. You need it to visualize how many periods to discount the stock's cash flows.*

Begin by drawing a timeline.

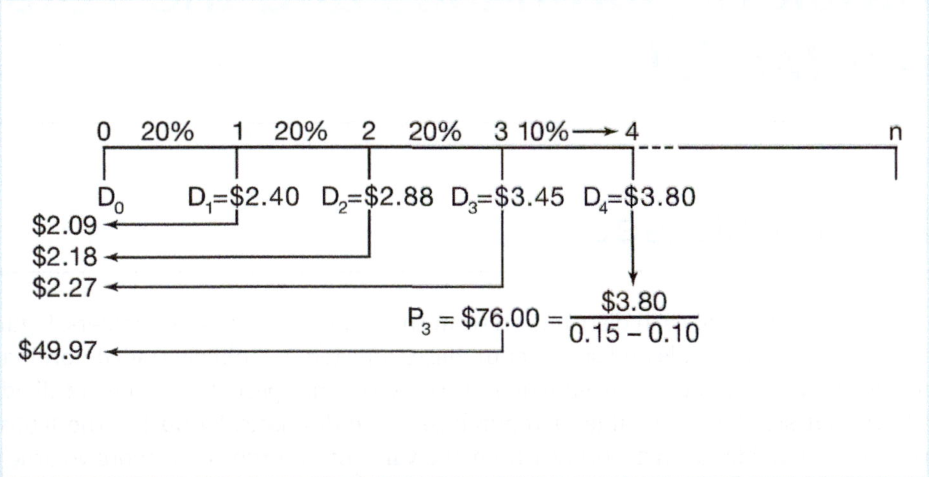

Step 1: Compute the dividends and put them on the timeline. The last dividend paid was $2.00. The next one will be 20% larger, which is computed by multiplying $\$2.00 \times 1.20$ and is $2.40. Each subsequent dividend is computed by multiplying by the appropriate growth rate.

Step 2: Compute the price of the stock when the constant growth phase of the company's life cycle begins. In this example, the 10% constant growth rate begins at the end of the third period. We compute P_3 using the constant growth model and the dividend that will be paid one period later (D_4).

Step 3: Find the present value of all of the dividends, except D_0. We do not include D_0 in the pricing process because it is assumed to have already been paid to the current owner of the stock. The present value of the dividends is computed as follows:

> **TIP:** *D_3 and P_3 could be added together to save time, as both are divided by the same factor. They are kept separate in this example only to show how the calculation is made.*

$$P_0 = \frac{\$2.40}{1.15} + \frac{\$2.88}{1.15^2} + \frac{\$3.45}{1.15^3} + \frac{\$76.00}{1.15^3}$$

$$P_0 = \$2.09 + \$2.18 + \$2.27 + \$49.97 = \mathbf{\$56.51}$$

The stock should sell for $56.51 today.

8.4 Stock Repurchases and the Total Payout Model

Stock Repurchases

A stock repurchase is a form of cash distribution from the company to its shareholders. Figure 8.6 shows the total value of dividends and stock repurchases affected by publicly traded nonfinancial corporations in the United States between 1991 and 2019. Over that period, the value of dividends increased slowly but steadily. The value of repurchases rose dramatically during the 1990s and exceeded the value of dividends in 2000. Over time, the value of repurchases is more volatile than the value of dividends and it seems to vary with the business cycle with lows following the tech slump of 2000–2001 and the financial crises in 2008.

FIGURE 8.6 The Value of Dividends and Repurchases

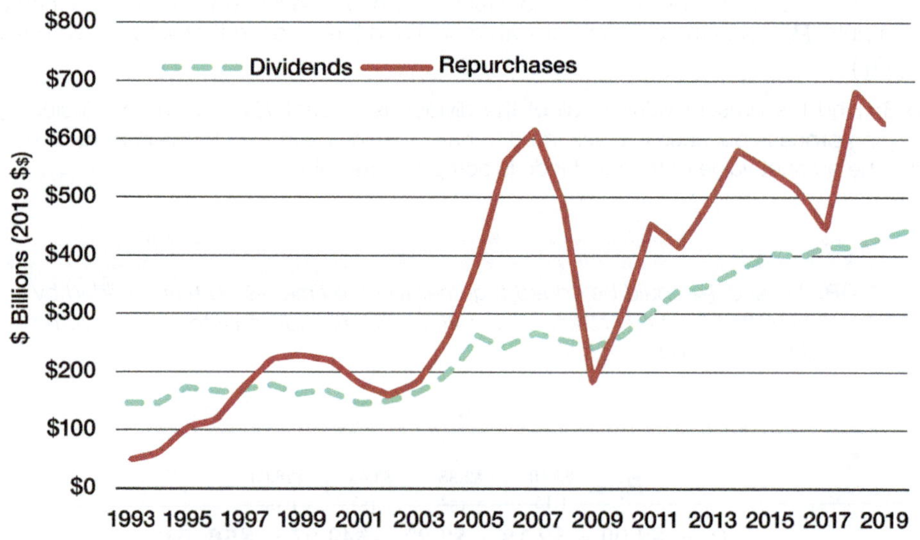

Source: Data obtained from Standard & Poor's Compustat.

There are three kinds of repurchase methods: (1) **open market**; (2) **fixed-price tender offer**; and (3) **Dutch auction**. The open market repurchase method is by far the most common. A detailed discussion of the three types is provided in the chapter on distributions. Here we present a brief overview.

In an open market repurchase, the firm instructs its broker to buy shares on the open market at prevailing market prices. The shares are then cancelled and the number of shares outstanding is reduced. As the Explain It! video shows, if the shares are repurchased at the same price as prevails before the repurchase, then the stock price does not change as a result of the repurchase. The repurchase impacts shareholder wealth by changing the form of the shareholders' wealth from shares to cash. In that sense, it is a distribution of cash.

Explain It: An Introduction to Stock Repurchases

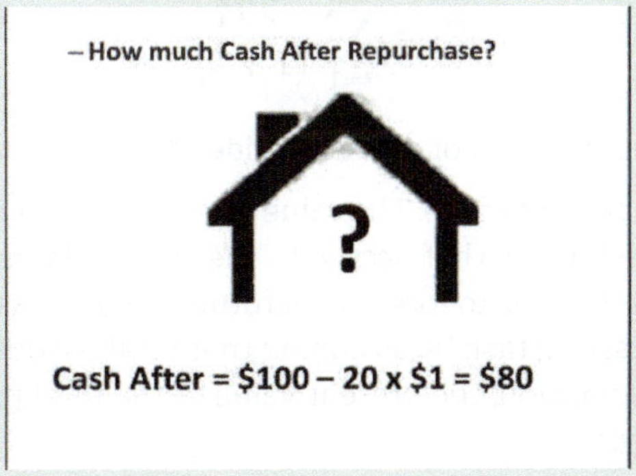

View in the online reader

An attractive feature of repurchases is that they are voluntary. None of the shareholders have to sell. Some may choose not to sell and their proportionate ownership of the company rises. With repurchases, shareholders get to choose when they receive the distribution. This option is not available with dividends. The option to defer is valuable because the tax liability associated with the income can also be deferred.

Explain It

A repurchase is taxed as a capital gain. The gain is the difference between the sale price and the original purchase price. This tax is assessed at the time of the sale of the shares.

As Figure 8.6 shows, cash flows to shareholders include both dividends and repurchases. The dividend discount model, presented earlier, ignores repurchases. In the next section we add repurchases to the dividend discount model. The amended model is called the total payout model.

open market

A company instructs its broker to buy shares on the open market at prevailing market prices. The shares are then cancelled and are no longer outstanding.

fixed-price tender offer

The company makes an offer to buy a fixed quantity of shares at a fixed price. A fixed-price offer is analogous to a tender offer in a merger or acquisition, but the offer originates from the firm itself. As a result, fixed-price offers are also called self-tender offers. Shareholders have to formally offer their shares for sale to the company. If more shares are offered than were targeted, then the company buys a pro-rata share of everyone's offer.

Dutch auction

A company announces a target repurchase quantity and invites shareholders to offer their shares for sale. The company provides a range of prices within which it will accept offers. Shareholders select a price in the range and offer a quantity. The company ranks the offers by price and accepts the offers up to the point where it achieves its target quantity. All accepted offers receive a price equal to that asked by the last accepted offer. All offers with higher prices are declined.

The Total Payout Method

In this section we explain the total payout model (TPM), which provides an estimate of the stock price by discounting both dividends and share repurchases.

The TPM values a company's total equity, denoted *E*. To calculate the share price, the total equity is divided by the number of shares outstanding:

EQUATION 8.9

$$P_0 = \frac{E_0}{N}$$

where *P* = the stock price, and *N* = the number of shares outstanding.

In the TPM, the value of the firm's (total) equity is simply equal to the present value of all payouts to all shareholders when discounted at the shareholders' required return, *k:*

EQUATION 8.10

$$E_0 = \sum_{t=1}^{\infty} \frac{TP_t}{(1+k)^t}$$

where *TP* (total payouts) is the sum of all cash dividends plus the value of shares repurchased.

This model makes good intuitive sense. The value of owning a company's shares is simply equal to the present value of all cash flows that accrue to the shareholders. The challenge with implementing Equation 8.10 is that we have to forecast all future payouts. As with the dividend discount model, we simplify this forecasting task by assuming that total payouts grow at a constant rate, *g*, in perpetuity. Under that assumption, the present value of the total payouts is similar to the dividend discount model stock price.

Tip

The most common error students make is to use the wrong payouts in the numerator. TP_0 are the total payouts just paid. It is assumed that the investor will not receive those payouts. It is only a benchmark to use for estimating the next payouts (TP_1) that the investor will receive. If the problem gives you TP_1 , do not multiply by $(1+g)$. If the problem gives you TP_0 , be sure that you compute TP_1 .

EQUATION 8.11

$$E_0 = \frac{TP_0 \times (1+g)}{k-g} = \frac{TP_1}{k-g}$$

This looks very similar to the dividend discount model, with two differences: (1) we model total payouts, not just cash dividends per share; and (2) the present value is the value of total equity, E_0 , not the value of an individual share.

Example 8.6 Total Payout Model with Constant Growth

Last year the Neversag Underwear Company had earnings of $330M and paid $47.4M in dividends and repurchased $17M worth of shares. Assume that all payouts occur annually and last year's payouts were made yesterday. Next year's payouts (due in 1 year) are expected to be 7% bigger than last year's and are expected to grow at that same rate in perpetuity. Stockholders require a return of 9% and there are 78 million shares outstanding. What is the fair price for Neversag's shares today?

SOLUTION

Algebraic Solution

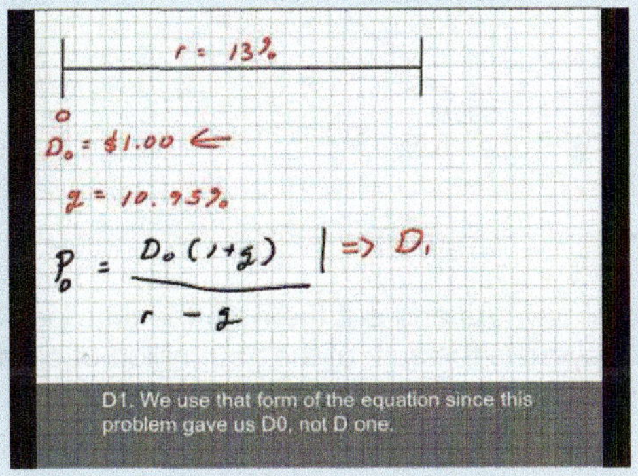

View in the online reader

First we solve for the value of Neversag's equity using Equation 8.11.

$$E_0 = \frac{TP_0 \times (1+g)}{k-g}$$

$$E_0 = \frac{(\$47.4+\$17)\times(1+0.07)}{0.09-0.07}$$

$$E_0 = \$3,445.40 \text{ million}$$

The fair stock price is:

$$P_0 = \frac{E_0}{N}$$

$$P0 = \$3,445.40/78 = \$44.17$$

If total payouts do not grow at a constant rate, then a nonconstant growth model can be used instead of the constant growth model.

Example 8.7 Total Payout Model with Nonconstant Growth

Because of the weak economy, Libby's Confections Inc. has suspended stock repurchases for the current year. Libby's makes its payouts annually at the end of each year. Today is the first day of a new year. Libby's has announced that it will pay total dividends of $50M at the end of the current year. Next year it will also pay out $50M in dividends and it will resume stock repurchases. It plans to spend $40 million repurchasing shares. In the years following, it plans to grow payouts every year (in perpetuity) at 2% per annum. Stockholders require a return of 9% and there are 100 million shares outstanding. What is the fair price for Libby's shares today?

Begin by drawing a timeline.

TIP: *This is a good example of how the timeline can be a critical tool. You need it to visualize how many periods to discount the stock's payouts.*

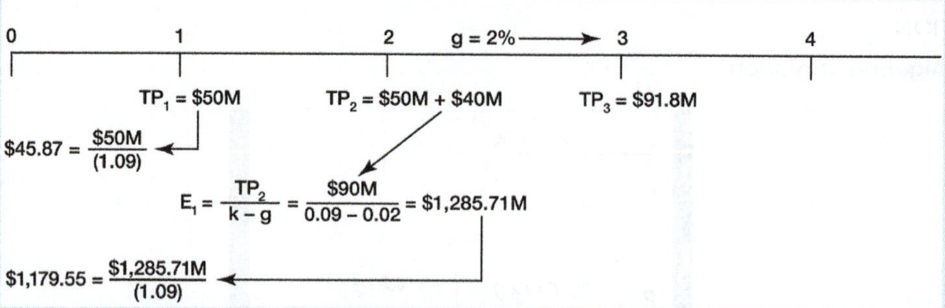

Step 1: Compute the total payouts and put them on the timeline. The next payout is $50 million of dividends. The year 2 payout is the sum of the $50 million of dividends and $40 million of share repurchases. Each subsequent payout is 2% larger.

Step 2: Compute the value of the equity 1 year before the first payout in the constant growth perpetuity. In this example, the 2% constant growth rate begins at year 2. We compute E_1 using the constant growth model and the total payout that will be paid one period later TP_2 .

$$E_1 = \frac{TP_2}{k - g} = \frac{\$90M}{0.09 - 0.02} = \$1,285.71$$

Step 3: Find the preset value of all of the payouts.

$$E_0 = \frac{\$50}{1.09} + \frac{\$1,285,71}{1.09}$$

$$E_0 = \$45.87 + \$1,179.55 = \$1,225.43$$

Step 4: Find the stock price.

$$P_0 = \frac{E_0}{N} = \frac{\$1,225.43}{100} = \$12.25$$

The stock should sell for $12.25 today.

8.5 Price Earnings Valuation Method

An alternative to the valuation models discussed above may be needed when dividend and repurchase data is not available. Among the more popular is the price/earnings multiple. The price/earnings (P/E) ratio is a widely watched measure of how much the market is willing to pay for $1 of earnings from a firm. It is computed as the current market price for a share of stock divided by the earnings per share of the firm.

The P/E ratio can be used to estimate the value of a firm's stock. Start with the definition of the ratio:

EQUATION 8.12

$$P/E = \frac{P_0}{EPS}$$

where P/E is the P/E ratio, EPS is the projected earnings per share, and P_0 is the stock price. Multiply both sides by EPS and rearrange to yield:

EQUATION 8.13

$$\frac{P}{E} \times EPS = \frac{P_0}{EPS} \times EPS$$

$$P_0 = \frac{P}{E} \times EPS$$

This formula produces an estimate of the (fair) stock price P_0, which is equal to the product of the P/E ratio and earnings per share. If we use the company's own current P/E ratio, then this equality is trivial. It is simply an identity. When we use the P/E pricing formula to price a stock, we don't use the company's current P/E ratio. We treat the P/E ratio as if it is a known value like a physical constant (e.g., speed of light, force of gravity, etc.). Let's call this the P/E constant. If a company has a P/E constant of 12, then we estimate its fair price as $P_0 = 12 \times EPS$.

The challenge to implementing this model is finding the correct P/E constant for each company. The most common approach is to use the average P/E for the industry (or for a group of close competitors).

The correct earnings per share to use is the earnings expected over the next period. The reasoning behind using projected earnings rather than last period's earnings is that buyers of the stock will not get last period's earnings. Those go to the current owner. The buyer will get next period's earnings so the price must reflect that value.

The average P/E can be adjusted up or down to compensate for risk, opportunities, or other factors unique to the firm. The P/E ratio approach is especially useful for valuing privately held firms and firms that do not pay dividends.

Example 8.8 Stock Valuation, P/E Approach

Consider Applebee's, the pub restaurant chain. Applebee's earnings-per-share (EPS) is $1.13. The average industry P/E ratio for restaurants is 23. Let's assume that this value is the long-run average P/E for Applebee's. What is the fair price for Applebee's?

SOLUTION

Spreadsheet Solution

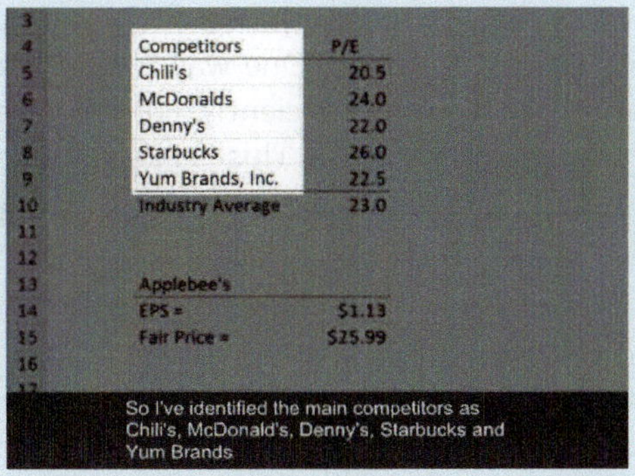

View in the online reader

Algebraic Solution

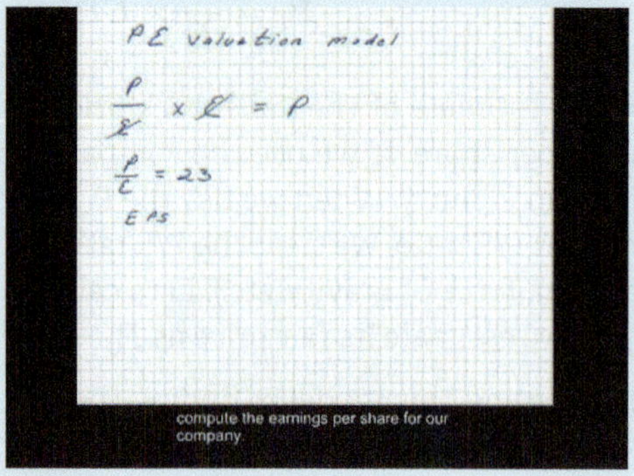

View in the online reader

Using Equation 8.13 and the data given, we find:

$$\text{Price} = \frac{P}{E} \times EPS$$

$$\text{Price} = 23 \times \$1.13$$

$$\text{Price} = \$25.99$$

8.6 The Efficient Markets Hypothesis

efficient markets hypothesis (EMH)

The hypothesis that markets price securities fairly at all times and that new information is rapidly reflected in the price.

Webster defines *efficient* as acting or functioning competently, with minimum waste or extra motion. The term retains this meaning in the context of the **efficient markets hypothesis (EMH)**. An efficient market must function competently, without waste or extra movement. What do we mean by functioning competently, however? One way to address this question is by looking at examples of markets that do *not* function efficiently. For example, it is easy to find highly rated wines selling for far less than mediocre wines. This is likely due to reputational value or efficient marketing, but still represents an apparent market failure in pricing. We might say that in this case the market is functioning inefficiently.

An efficient market adjusts prices rapidly and accurately. By contrast, an *inefficient* market adjusts prices slowly and not every unit of a particular type is priced the same. For example, before grocery stores used electronic inventory tracking systems that enabled instantaneous price changes on all like grocery items, each item had a to have a price sticker attached manually. Time constraints sometimes restricted price changes to only adjusting prices on new inventory as it was tagged manually by clerks. College students on tight budgets regularly searched items on the backs of shelves to see if any items had old tags with lower prices still attached.

Now that we have explored a few examples of inefficient markets, let us define what an *efficient* market is. In efficient markets, all prices accurately and rapidly adjust to reflect the true intrinsic value of securities. Note several features about this definition. First, we say that prices are set accurately. This precludes situations like poor-quality wines costing more than great wines. Second, the definition includes a time component. Prices must adjust quickly to changes in the environment. This precludes situations such as those we used to find in grocery stores.

Consider what it means to investors if the financial markets are really efficient. If every stock is correctly priced then it makes absolutely no difference which stock you buy because every stock is fairly priced. It is a waste of time and energy to research the stock market because no amount of study will identify one security that will perform better than another.

Does this mean you will be as well off buying Walmart stock as Kmart stock? The surprising answer is yes. If the financial markets are efficient, the price of Kmart will have adjusted down to reflect the risk inherent in the company's future and the price of Walmart will have adjusted up to reflect its expected future cash flows. "Bad" stocks will be cheap. "Good" stocks will be expensive. Both will be priced fairly for what the investor gets.

What Makes the Markets Efficient?

Suppose you go into McDonald's this afternoon for lunch. As you enter, you note that the restaurant is busy and that there are four registers open. What are the chances that you will be able to walk directly up to the counter and place your order? Virtually none. The reason is that everyone there has the same goal, to get waited on as quickly as possible. Customers, acting rationally in their own best interest, will seek out the shortest line. When you review your options, usually you will find that it does not make much difference which line you choose. They will all appear to provide about the same wait.

Does this mean that it really makes no difference which line you choose? Actually, they will not all move at the same speed. The guy in line two may be ordering lunch for a whole construction crew. Until you observe this order being placed, line two may have appeared to be a good option. Once this new information becomes available, you may choose to move to another line. The point is that when you initially picked a line, they all appeared to be equal given the information available to you at the time. Only the arrival of new information changes this.

Now suppose that line three unexpectedly shortens because two people in a row only order soft drinks. Now line three is a good deal. Anyone who gets in that line will have a shorter wait than if they get in any of the other lines. Who will get to take advantage of this good deal? The shorter wait will go to the customer who is alert to the opportunity and who moves most quickly to take advantage of it. The guy texting at the end of line four never stands a chance. Line three rapidly adjusted and the opportunity disappeared before he even knew a good deal existed.

Sorbis / Shutterstock.com

Let's review what makes the lines at McDonald's efficient.

1. Everyone has the same goal.
2. There are a large number of customers competing for good deals.
3. Some of the customers are alert to changes and new information.
4. Some of the customers react quickly to changes and new information.

The security markets share these same characteristics. Everyone who participates in the financial markets has the *same goal*, to earn the greatest return possible for a given level of risk.

Additionally, there are a *large number of investors* in the market. Currently, there are over 8,000 separate mutual funds, each with a well-informed manager searching for good deals for his clients. In addition, there are millions of individual investors who actively participate in the security markets, again each looking for good deals.

Tip

Larger investment funds have industry specialists who devote all of their time to studying one particular industry, such as steel, oil, or automobiles. They are constantly alert to any news reports that bear on the firms in their industry. These specialists have access to news as soon as it is released through industry contacts and costly news sources. Some even have access to industry insiders who will help them analyze information as it is released.

Finally, many participants in the security markets are willing and able to *quickly react to new information*. Electronic networks and modern communications allow for near instantaneous execution of stock trades.

The efficient market hypothesis (EMH) is based on the combined effect of (1) many competitive investors, (2) all with the same goal of locating securities that provide the highest risk-adjusted return, and (3) all willing and able to take advantage of new, changing conditions.

We can look to the security market line for another explanation for why we think the markets may be efficient. Review Figure 8.7. Security A is providing a higher risk-adjusted return (R') than other securities. Alert investors will identify this security and attempt to buy it. As demand pressure mounts for security A, its price will rise. Since the market price of the security will not affect its cash flows or dividends, a rising price will mean that the return will fall. Its return will continue to fall until the security is back on the line (at R).

FIGURE 8.7 The Price of Security A will rise until its return falls to *R*

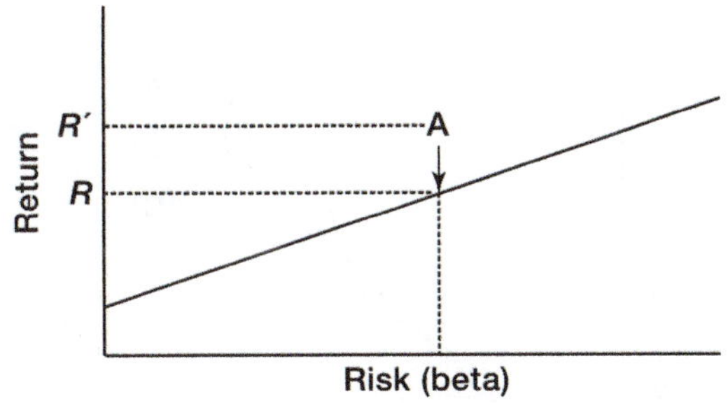

How many investors does it take to cause the price of security A to adjust to its proper level? Only one, if that investor has sufficient wealth to buy the security until its price adjusts. With thousands of well-informed investors, all looking for any firm whose return deviates from the security market line, any deviation is expected to disappear very quickly.

Explain It: Why are Security Prices Efficient?

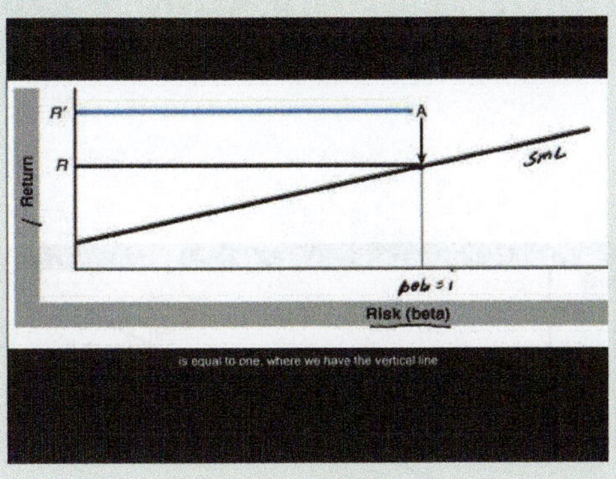

View in the online reader

Stock Follows a Random Walk in Efficient Markets

If the financial markets are indeed efficient, then past trends in stock prices should have no bearing on future price changes. For example, just because a stock's price has had a series of price increases, as shown in Figure 8.8, we cannot assume that tomorrow's price will be at A (assume that today is day 5). This is because everyone in the market has access to past stock prices. Suppose that if the stock price increases 5 days in a row there will be an increase on the 6th day as well. Investors would bid the price up on the 5th day instead of waiting for the 6th (the dotted line in Figure 8.8). As a result, the increase on the 6th day would disappear. In an efficient market, investors could not predict on day 5 whether the stock price on day 6 would be A, B, or C. If they could, an investment opportunity would exist that would provide superior returns.

FIGURE 8.8 Historical Trends Do Not Predict Future Prices

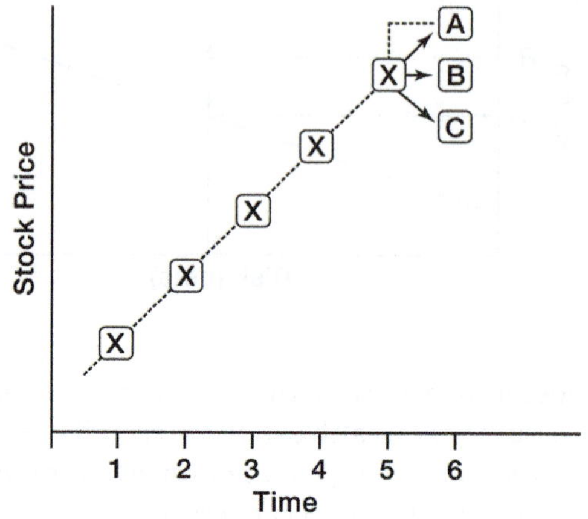

The implication of Figure 8.8 is that the best prediction of tomorrow's price is today's price. For this reason the efficient market hypothesis is sometimes referred to as the *random walk hypothesis*.

Explain It: Why Today's Stock Price is the Best Predictor of Tomorrow's Stock Price

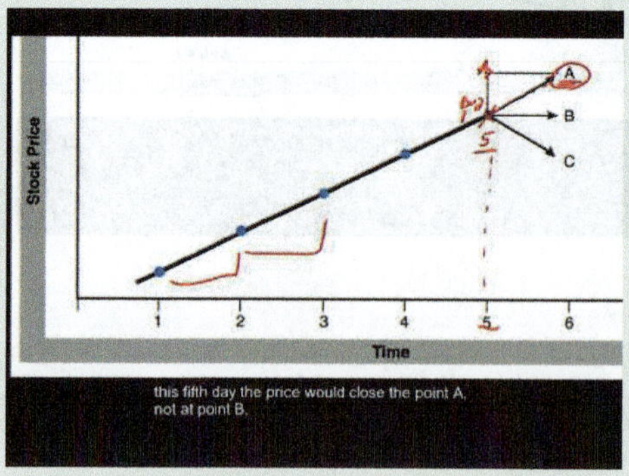

View in the online reader

Market Efficiency—The Evidence

A number of studies have identified evidence that is inconsistent with the efficient markets hypothesis. These studies identify what are called **anomalies**. Past anomalies include the **size effect**, the January effect, the **momentum effect**, and the **weekend effect**. The anomalies are persistent abnormal returns accruing to particular investment strategies. For example, a number of authors observed that portfolios of small company stocks outperform portfolios of large company stocks even after controlling for risk. This suggested that prices were not efficient and that investors were not processing information rationally. However, recent studies show that the size effect has disappeared. This pattern is true for all of the anomalies listed above. In each case, an anomaly was detected by academics in the 1970s or 1980s, the results were published in academic journals, and the effect was observed to disappear in the 1990s and 2000s.

The irony is that this is fully consistent with the efficient markets hypothesis (EMH). The EMH predicts that if a profitable opportunity is identified, then it will be exploited until it disappears. This is precisely what has happened. The most prominent evidence in support of the EMH is that mutual fund managers consistently underperform passive benchmarks. Because of management costs, this underperformance is expected in a market where prices are fair on average.

anomalies

In the financial context, events that occur on occasion that appear to violate the tenants of market efficiency.

size effect

This effect found that smaller firms tend to have higher risk adjusted returns than large firms.

momentum effect

The momentum effect was that when stocks went either up or down significantly, they tended to go too far and then corrected over the next several trading periods.

weekend effect

Stock prices tend to fall from closing Friday to closing on Monday.

What Market Efficiency Means to Financial Decision Making

If the financial markets are even reasonably efficient, most of the time most securities will be correctly priced. What does this mean to the investor and to the financial manager?

Do Not Try to Outsmart the Market

If markets are efficient, security prices are based on all available information. This means that to outsmart the market you not only have to know more than anyone else; you need to know more than *everyone* else. Only when you truly believe this to be true, can you justify short-term trading aimed at beating the market.

> **Tip**
>
> The time you are most likely to know more than everyone else is when you have inside knowledge about a firm. Of course, trading on this information is illegal.

Do Not Waste Money or Time Looking for Good Deals

Many investors spend great amounts of time and energy searching for good deals in the market. The current evidence on market efficiency suggests that the best investment strategy is a passive strategy—that is, you purchase a well-diversified portfolio of securities that has the amount of systematic risk that you can tolerate and you hold.

Endnotes

1. Daily high.
2. Daily low.
3. Price at close of last trading day.
4. Change in price from open to close.
5. Number of shares traded.

CHAPTER 9

Capital Budgeting: Introduction and Techniques

Learning Objectives

By the end of this chapter you will be able to:

1. Explain the purpose of capital budgeting.
2. List the steps in the capital budgeting process.
3. Analyze projects using the payback period method.
4. Analyze projects using the net present value and profitability index methods.
5. Analyze projects using the internal rate of return and modified internal rate of return methods.

Simply put, investment decisions have a greater impact on a business's future than any other decisions it makes. Businesses that invest profitably make money and provide a fair return for their owners. Those that do not are unlikely to survive in competition. This chapter investigates methods for evaluating long-term investment decisions. We use many of the tools that we have already discussed. For example, we must adjust an investment's cash flows to take into account the time value of money. Additionally, we must adjust for the risk of those cash flows.

9.1 Why Do Capital Budgeting?

The term *capital* refers to long-term securities and investments. The term retains the same meaning in this chapter. **Capital budgeting** is the process of deciding which long-term investments or projects a firm will acquire. The term *budgeting* is appropriate because most firms have more ways to spend money than they have available funds. They must allocate these limited funds in such a way as to provide the most long-term profits. Keep in mind that the goal of the financial manager is to increase shareholder wealth. This chapter provides techniques for selecting projects that accomplish this goal.

capital budgeting
The method for allocating the firm's long-term capital to long-term assets.

Most firms are constantly seeking new investment ideas and opportunities. For our purposes, we assume management has investment ideas to evaluate. Do not lose sight of the fact that the collection of these ideas spells the success or failure of the firm.

9.2 Steps in the Capital Budgeting Process

The capital budgeting process is so critical to the survival of a firm that it is worth discussing the full scope of the capital budgeting process, rather than simply presenting how the evaluation tools are computed. These ideas may be as simple as replacing two low-output copiers with one high-speed unit. Alternatively, an investment may change the entire face of a firm once a possible project has been identified. A firm's management must evaluate whether firm value will be increased if the project is accepted. We can identify five steps a firm should follow:

1. **Identification of opportunities.** Initially, the firm must have some method in place by which new opportunities are identified and brought to management's attention. Management is often removed from the factory floor or direct customer contact. Employees on the front lines must have both the incentive and the means to communicate ideas to those who have the authority to implement them.
2. **Evaluation of opportunities.** Once the firm identifies an opportunity, it must be evaluated. This requires that all costs and benefits be tabulated. These data are then subjected to analysis. Here, we focus on how to analyze data once they have been prepared. Later, we learn how to organize the cash flows from an investment opportunity.
3. **Selection.** Often, firms have more good projects than they can accept in any given year. This may be because of limited funds or because of human or physical constraints the firm faces. In this chapter, we look at how a firm might rank projects to facilitate selecting among them.
4. **Implementation.** Once a project has been selected, it must be implemented. Machines will be purchased, people hired, or investments made. Management must be vigilant at this stage to ensure the costs reflect what was initially proposed and evaluated. For example, Twentieth-Century Fox decided to produce the movie *Titanic* in 1995. They projected costs to be about $100 million and decided the project would be profitable. Unfortunately, by 1997, cost overruns brought the total cost to more than $200 million, making it the most expensive movie ever made to that point. Total movie revenues would have to exceed $350 million for the project to be profitable. Although this did happen (by 2006, total gross was about $1.8 billion, making it the highest-grossing film of all time), the risk of the project was much greater than originally anticipated.
5. **Post audit.** Once the project has been completed, management must compare the costs and revenues with the original projections. This is a critical step that is often overlooked. Holding employees responsible for errors in their projections gives them an incentive to make more accurate future cost and revenue projections. Employees who know they must later explain deviations from projections will study the results of their last estimates to improve their future performance.

Taken together, these steps can dramatically improve a firm's ability to select wealth-increasing projects, bring them to fruition, and learn from each experience.

9.3 Overview of Techniques for Analyzing Projects

The financial analyst first estimates the cash inflows and outflows an investment will generate. Then, these cash flows are evaluated to determine whether the project should be accepted. In the next few sections we investigate methods for evaluating the cash flows.

Explain It: Summary of Capital Budgeting Techniques

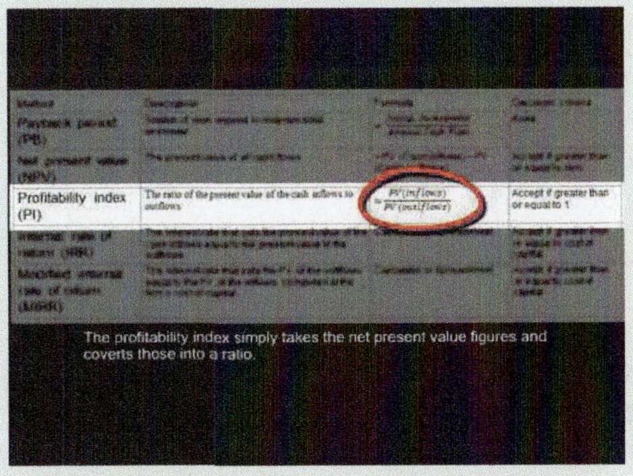

View in the online reader

There are a number of techniques used by businesses to evaluate potential projects. Some have many problems but continue to be used because they are simple. We discuss all of the common techniques. Summarized, they include:

TABLE 9.1

Method	Description	Equation	Decision Criteria
Payback Period (PB)	Number of years required to recapture initial investment	$= \frac{initial\ investment}{annual\ cash\ flow}$	None
Net Present Value (NPV)	The present value (PV) of all cash flows	$= PV\ (cash\ inflows) - PV\ (cash\ outflows)$	Accept if greater than or equal to zero
Profitability Index (PI)	The ratio of the present value of the cash inflows to outflows	$= \frac{PV\ (inflows)}{PV\ (outflows)}$	Accept if equal to or greater than 1
Internal Rate of Return (IRR)	The interest rate that sets the present value of the cash inflows equal to the present value of the outflows	Calculator or Spreadsheet	Accept if greater than or equal to cost of capital
Modified Internal Rate of Return (MIRR)	The interest rate that sets the present value of the outflows equal to the future values of the inflows, computed at the firm's cost of capital	Calculator or Spreadsheet	Accept if greater than or equal to cost of capital

Payback Period

The financial analyst first estimates the cash inflows and outflows an investment will generate. Then, these cash flows are evaluated to determine whether the project should be accepted. In the next few sections we investigate all of the methods listed in Table 9.1 that are used for evaluating cash flows. In this section we discuss the payback method.

payback period (PB)

The number of years it takes to recover an initial investment.

The **payback period (PB)** method is mechanically the easiest to compute, but theoretically the worst evaluation method available. The payback period is simply the number of years it takes to recover the initial investment. The timing and riskiness of the cash flows are ignored. Despite this method's drawbacks, it continues to be used because it is easy to understand and explain to others. This method is also used to supplement more sophisticated techniques.

Tip

Another reason PB is frequently used is that some projects are too small to justify the complexity of the other methods.

Computation

The calculation of the payback period is very easy if the annual cash flows are annuities. The payback period is found by dividing the initial investment by the annual annuity cash flow.

> **Tip**
>
> Remember that annuities are equal payments received at equal intervals.

EQUATION 9.1

$$Payback = \frac{initial\ investment}{annual\ cash\ flow}$$

In "Example 9.1 Using Payback Period to Evaluate an Annuity", we use the payback period method to evaluate an annuity. In "Example 9.2 Payback Period: Unequal Cash Flows", we address how to compute a payback where there are unequal annual cash flows. In the latter case we build a table to show the declining balance and then compute a percentage of the year for the final year. This is then converted into months.

Example 9.1 Using Payback Period to Evaluate an Annuity

In 2015, *Consumer Reports* listed Chateau Ste. Michelle Merlot as a best buy in its taste test. If Chateau Ste. Michelle wanted to expand production to take advantage of the increased sales this report could generate, it would have to expand its facilities. Assume expansion of its winery would cost $1 million. If this can generate after-tax cash inflows of $235,000 for 8 years, what is the payback period?

SOLUTION

Algebraic Solution

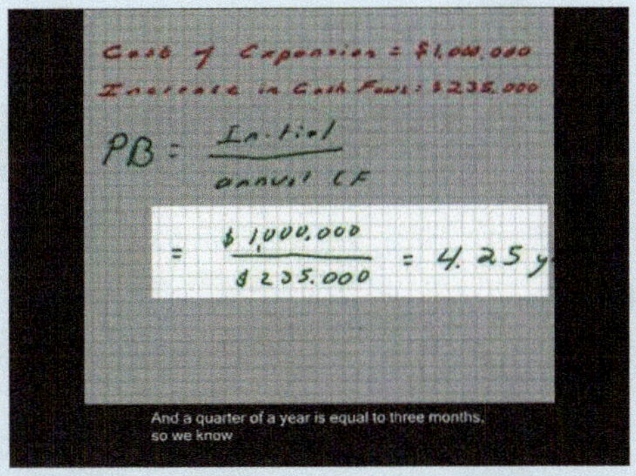

View in the online reader

Because the annual cash inflows are equal, simply divide them into the initial investment.

$$Payback = \frac{initial\ investment}{annual\ cash\ flow}$$

$$Payback = \frac{\$1,000,000}{\$235,000} = 4.25 = 4\ years\ 3\ months$$

The calculation is somewhat more complicated if the cash inflows are not equal. An accumulation table can be constructed to compute payback. We demonstrate this by evaluating an investment with unequal cash flows in "Example 9.2 Payback Period: Unequal Cash Flows".

Example 9.2 Payback Period: Unequal Cash Flows

Suppose, after reviewing its cash flow estimates, Chateau Ste. Michelle decides the publicity provided by the *Consumer Reports* article will dwindle over time. As a result, cash inflows would decline 10% the first year and 15% per year thereafter, as shown in the following table. What is the payback period?

Year	Initial Investment	Cash Inflow	Accumulated Inflow	Balance
0	–$1,000,000.00	0	0	–$1,000,000.00
1		$235,000.00	$235,000.00	–765,000.00
2		211,500.00	446,500.00	–553,500.00
3		179,775.00	626,275.00	–373,725.00
4		152,808.75	779,083.75	–220,916.25
5		129,887.44	908,971.19	–91,028.81
6		110,404.32	1,019,375.51	+19,375.51

SOLUTION

Spreadsheet Solution

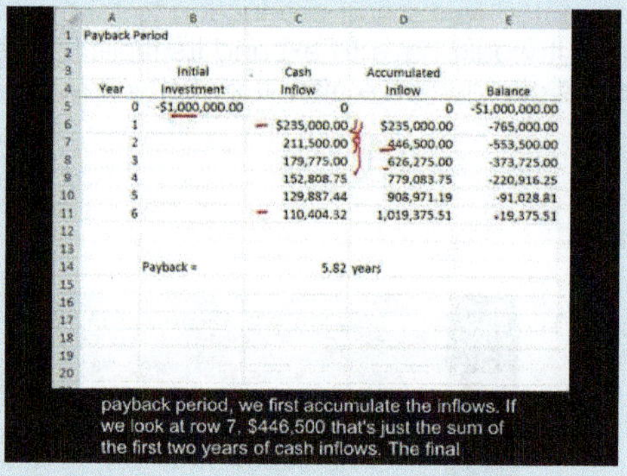

View in the online reader

Algebraic Solution

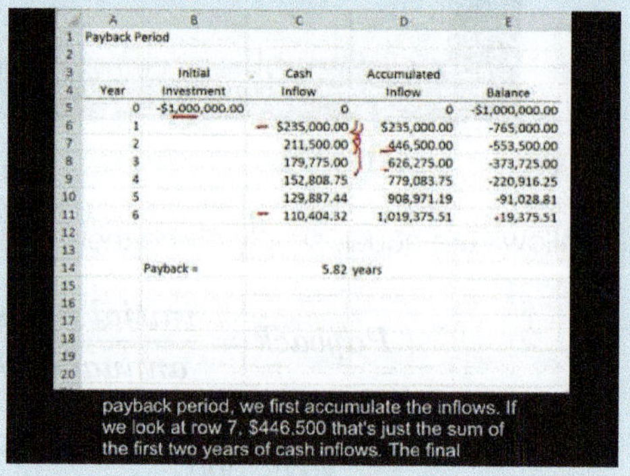

View in the online reader

Set up a table, as subsequently presented. The initial investment and cash inflow are given. The next column is the sum of the cash inflows. The last column is computed by subtracting the accumulated inflow column from the initial investment.

The final year can be estimated by dividing the remaining balance by the cash inflow and multiplying the product by 12 $(\$91,028.81/\$110,404.32 = 0.824 \times 12 = 9.89 \text{ months})$.

It would take about 5 years and 10 months to recover the initial investment if the cash flow estimates are correct $(5 \text{ years} + 9.89 \text{ months})$.

Advantages to the Payback Method

The principal advantage of the payback period method is its simplicity. It also provides information about how long funds will be tied up in a project. The shorter the payback period, the greater the project's liquidity.

Disadvantages to the Payback Method

There are many problems with the payback method:

- *No clearly defined accept/reject criteria:* Is a 4-year payback period acceptable?
- *No risk adjustment:* Risky cash flows are treated the same as low-risk cash flows. The required payback period could be lengthened for low-risk projects, but the exact adjustment is still arbitrary.
- *Ignores cash flows beyond the payback period:* Any cash inflows that occur after the payback period are excluded from analysis.
- *Ignores time value of money:* The order of the cash flows is not considered, so large, early cash flows are valued as much as small, early cash flows.

Explain It: Disadvantages to Payback Approach to Capital Budgeting

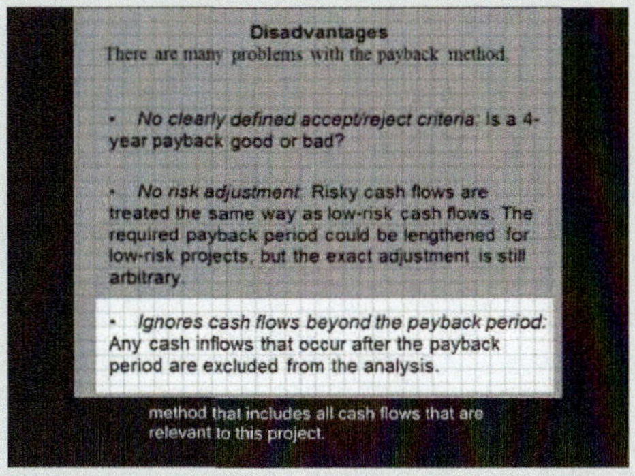

View in the online reader

discounted payback method

The amount of time it takes for a project to recoup the investment and the cost of capital.

The **discounted payback method** computes the PV of each cash flow then finds the payback based on these discounted values. Although this method takes into account time value of money (TVM) principles, it still suffers from the other problems listed for the payback period method.

9.4 Net Present Value and Profitability Index

Net Present Value

net present value (NPV)

The sum or net of all cash flows from a project. It is often described as the net of the present value of the cash inflows minus the present value of the cash outflows.

The **net present value (NPV)** method is the most popular and theoretically sound evaluation tool available to analysts. Its interpretation requires a fundamental understanding of the time value of money. Surveys of large national corporations find that more than 70% now apply the NPV to project evaluation, although most companies continue to use other methods as well.

To properly evaluate investment projects, we need a method that does not suffer from the payback method problems. One reason to learn the payback period method is to demonstrate a poor method of analysis so that you can appreciate a theoretically sophisticated method like that of the NPV. Going forward, pay attention to how the NPV approach differs from the payback method.

Theory

Most investments have some funds being spent today in the hope that greater amounts are received in the future. Because the cash inflows and the cash outflows occur at different times, they cannot be compared directly. Instead, they must be translated into a common time period. It is usually easiest to convert all of the cash flows into current dollars because at least some expenditure is probably made at time 0. After the conversion into present values, the cash inflows are compared with the cash outflows. If inflows exceed outflows, the project is acceptable. The difference between the cash outflows and the cash inflows is the NPV.

Tip

Do not simply add together cash flows that occur at different points in time. This will never be correct. You must always adjust for the time value of money before combining cash flows.

Computation

The formula for calculating the NPV can be written several ways. Equation 9.2 summarizes the concept as simply the net of the inflows against the outflows:

EQUATION 9.2

$$NPV = PV\ (cash\ inflows) - PV\ (cash\ outflows)$$

We rewrite Equation 9.2 to include the calculation of the present values in Equation 9.3.

EQUATION 9.3

$$NPV = \sum_{t=1}^{n} \frac{CF_t}{(1+i)^t} - \textit{initial investment}$$

The first term on the right-hand side of the equation computes the present value of the cash inflows, where *i* is the discount rate. This discount rate is equal to the firm's cost of capital when evaluating projects similar in risk to others in the firm's portfolio. The initial investment is assumed paid at time 0, so no discounting is required. If the initial investment is actually paid over a period of time, the present value of the initial investment must be found. Each year's cash outflows must be discounted back to the present before subtracting from the present value of the inflows.

Interpretation

You can interpret a positive NPV as meaning the current value of the income exceeds the current value of the expenditure, so the project should be accepted. A negative NPV means the project costs more than it will bring in, so it should be rejected. The decision criteria for the NPV can then be summarized as follows: accept the project if the NPV is greater than or equal to 0; reject the project if the NPV is negative.

Example 9.3 Net Present Value Calculation: Single Period Investment

Digital Downloads

Example 9.3_NPV.xls
https://catalog.flatworldknowledge.com/a/34711/Example_9_3_NPV-5fc9.xls

The owner of a gas station in Nevada is considering buying a slot machine to put in his small convenience store. The slot machine costs $6,000 and is expected to bring in about $10 per day after expenses. The machine is expected to last 3 years before a newer model will be needed to attract gamblers. If the average cost of funds to the gas station is 15%, should the slot machine be installed?

SOLUTION

Spreadsheet Solution

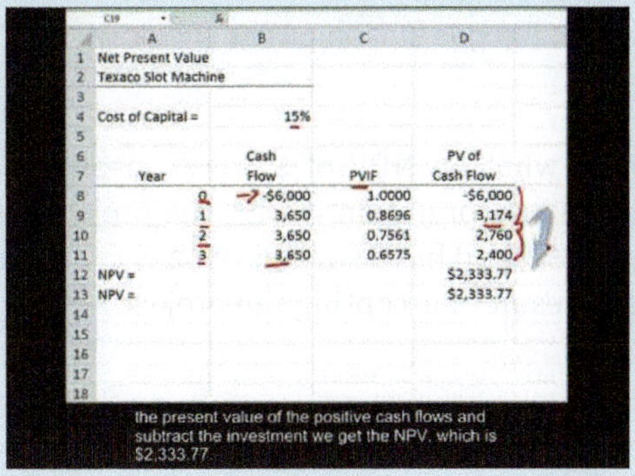

View in the online reader

Algebraic Solution

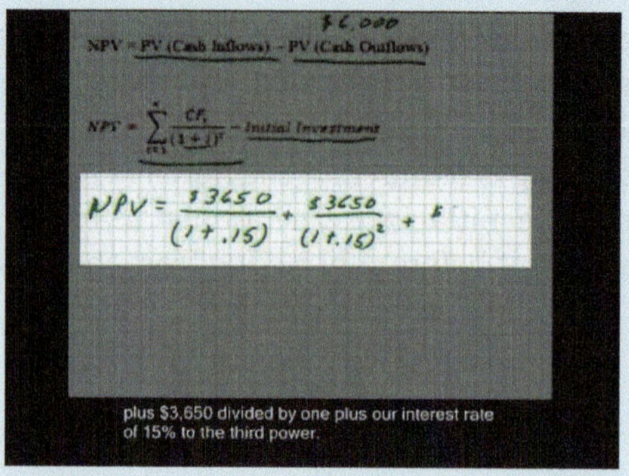

View in the online reader

Calculator Solution

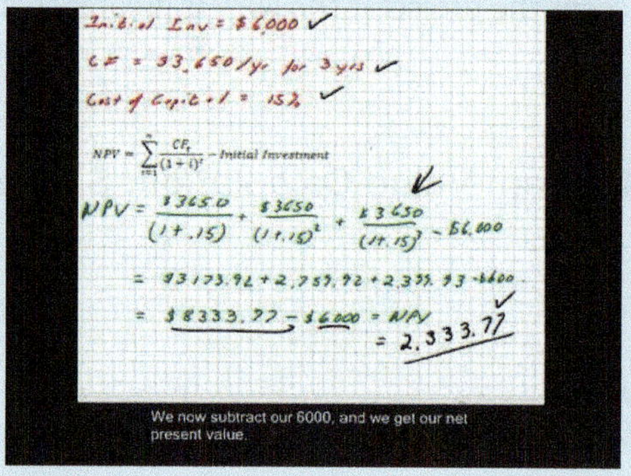

View in the online reader

Putting the numbers into Equation 9.3 yields the following:

$$NPV = \sum_{t=1}^{n} \frac{CF_t}{(1+i)^t} - \textbf{Initial investment}$$

$$NPV = \frac{\$3{,}650}{(1.15)^1} + \frac{\$3{,}650}{(1.15)^2} + \frac{\$3{,}650}{(1.15)^3} - \$6{,}000 = \$2{,}333.77$$

Because the NPV is positive, the gas station owner should install the slot machine.

How would you explain what an NPV of $2,333.77 means to someone who has not taken a finance course? One accurate interpretation is that the project has repaid the initial investment, returned the cost of capital (15%), and has a surplus of $2,333.77. In other words, the value of the firm will increase by $2,333.77 as a result of accepting the project.

Explain It: The Intuition Behind NPV

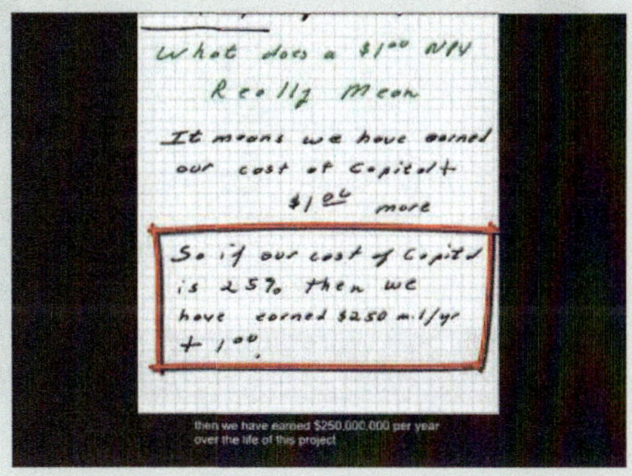

View in the online reader

Net Present Value of Multiperiod Investments

Not all investments are made in one lump sum. Sometimes the initiation of the project takes several years. We need to compute the NPV of all the periods and then subtract the present value of the outflows from the present value of the inflows to determine whether to invest in the opportunity.

Example 9.4 Net Present Value Calculation: Multiperiod Investment

Digital Downloads

Example 9.4_NPV_TransAlaska.xls
https://catalog.flatworldknowledge.com/a/34710/Example_9_4_NPV_TransAlaska-ac46.xls

The Trans-Alaska Pipeline took 4 years to complete, at a total cost of $8 billion. Suppose $1 billion was spent the first year, $1 billion the second year, $2 billion the third year, and $4 billion the last year. (Assume all investments are made at the beginning of the year.) If the revenues are expected to be $2 billion per year for 20 years and the discount rate is 15%, should the pipeline have been built? (Assume all cash inflows occur at the end of the year and begin at the end of year 4. So, the first cash inflow arrives at year 5.)

SOLUTION

Spreadsheet Solution

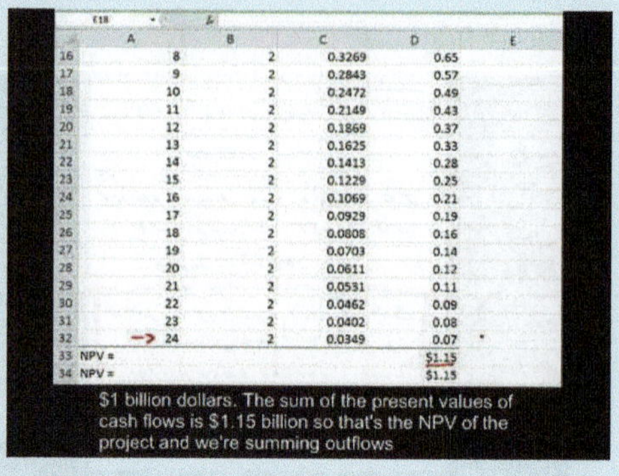

View in the online reader

Algebraic Solution

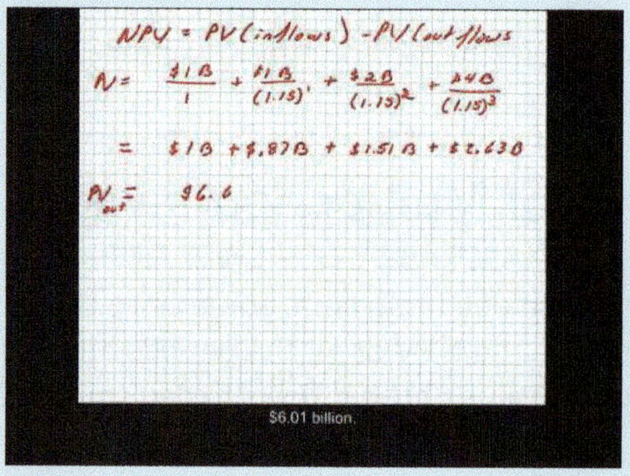

View in the online reader

Calculator Solution

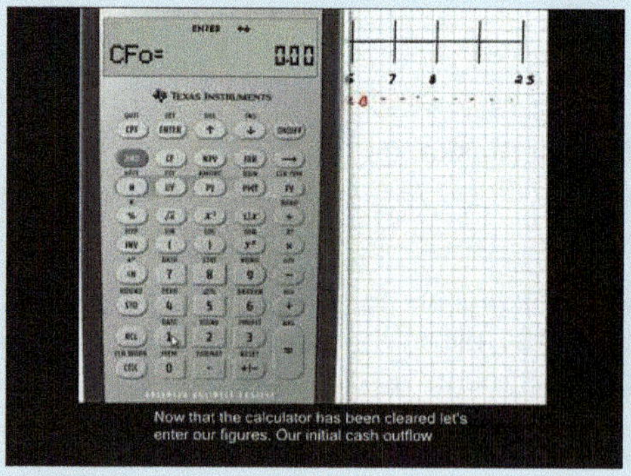

View in the online reader

We first compute the present value of the cash outflows, and then we compute the present value of the cash inflows. Finally, we compute the NPV by subtracting the present value of the outflows from the present value of the inflows.

Step 1:

$$PV(outflows) = \frac{\$1\text{ billion}}{1} + \frac{\$1\text{ billion}}{(1.15)^1} + \frac{\$2\text{ billion}}{(1.15)^2} + \frac{\$4\text{ billion}}{(1.15)^3}$$

$$PV(outflows) = \$1\text{ billion} + \$0.87\text{ billion} + \$1.51\text{ billion} + \$2.63\text{ billion}$$

$$PV(outflows) = \$6.01\text{ billion}$$

Step 2:

$$PV(inflows) = \$2\text{ billion} \times \left(\frac{\left(1 - \frac{1}{(1.15)^{20}}\right)}{0.15}\right)\frac{1}{(1.15)^4}$$

$$PV(inflows) = \$2\text{ billion} \times (6.2593) \times (0.5718) = \$7.16\text{ billion}$$

Step 3:

$$NPV = PV(inflows) - PV(outflows)$$

$$NPV = \$7.16\text{ billion} - \$6.01\text{ billion} = \$1.15\text{ billion}$$

Because the NPV is greater than zero, the pipeline should have been built.

Advantages

The new present value method solves the problems listed with the payback period approach.

- *Uses time value of money concept*: The cash flows are discounted back to the present, so all cash flows are compared at the same point in time.
- *Clear decision criterion*: Accept the project if the NPV is zero or greater. Reject if less than zero.
- *Discount rate adjusts for risk*: By increasing or decreasing the discount rate, the firm can adjust for the riskiness of the cash flows.

Tip

The discount rate used to evaluate capital budgeting projects is the firm's cost of capital, which is the average cost of its debt and equity. The cost of capital reflects the risk of the firm and the firm's average required rate of return on its investments.

Disadvantages

The primary disadvantage to the NPV method is that it may be difficult for someone without a background in financial theory to understand. This lack of understanding regarding the NPV perpetuates the popularity of the other, simpler methods we will study.

NPV Profile

NPV profile

A graph of the net present value of a project at a variety of different discount rates. It shows the sensitivity of the project to the firm's cost of capital.

An **NPV profile** graphs the NPV at a variety of discount rates. The NPV profile demonstrates how sensitive the NPV is to changes in the discount rate. It is very difficult to accurately and confidently estimate the cost of capital for a firm. At best, we can determine an approximate value. Before we recommend a firm accept or reject a project, we should determine whether a small error in our cost of capital estimate is important. We can do this by preparing an NPV profile. Once the profile is prepared, we can note whether small changes in the cost of capital will result in major changes to the NPV. This is an application of sensitivity analysis.

Tip

We are evaluating how sensitive the NPV is to the cost of capital. We can also compute the sensitivity to sales, fixed costs, or any other variable input. This is called sensitivity analysis.

Let us prepare an NPV profile for a simple series of cash flows.

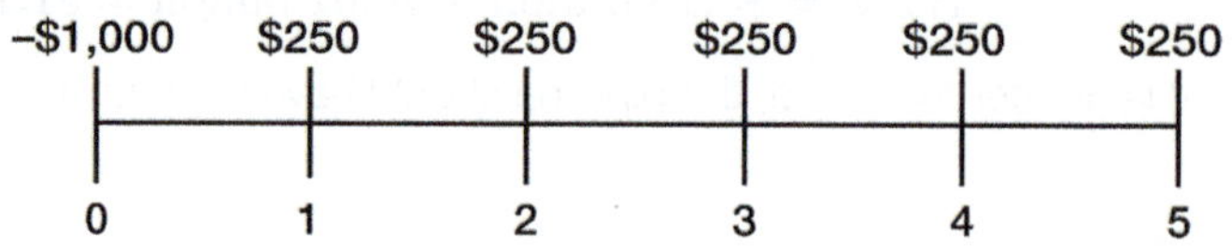

To compute the NPV profile, select a number of different discount rates and compute the NPV for each. You may use any discount rates you choose. Continue using increasingly larger discount rates until the NPV turns negative. We have computed the NPVs for five interest rates using the simple cash flows.

Tip

It is usually easiest to begin at 0% because then the NPV is found simply by summing the cash flows.

Discount Rate	NPV
0.0%	$250.00
5.0	82.37
7.5	11.47
10.0	–52.30
12.0	–98.81

These numbers are graphed in Figure 9.1. We can read the point at which the graph crosses the horizontal axis. This occurs at about 8%. This is the point at which the $NPV = 0$. To the left of this point, the NPV is positive and the project is acceptable. To the right of this point, the NPV is negative and the project should be rejected. If you are confident the cost of capital (the average cost of funds to the firm) is less than the crossover point, accept the project.

FIGURE 9.1 NPV Profile

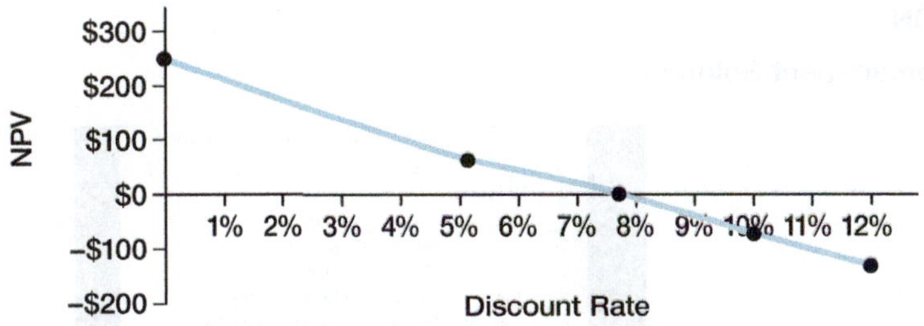

Explain It: Understanding NPV Profiles

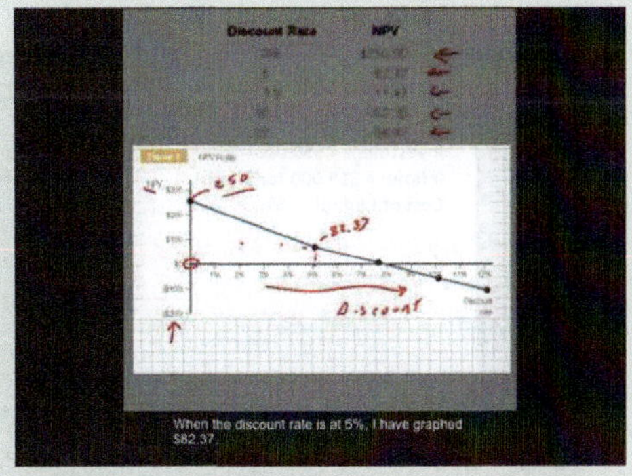

View in the online reader

Example 9.5 Preparing an NPV Profile

Digital Downloads

Example 9.5_PreparingNPVProfile.xls
https://catalog.flatworldknowledge.com/a/34711/ Example_9_5_PreparingNPVProfile-6947.xls

You are contemplating an investment in a Putt-Putt miniature golf course. If you invest $50,000 today, you expect to receive annual cash flows of $15,000 for the next 5 years. You are not certain of your cost of capital but expect it to be around 15%. Prepare the NPV profile and discuss whether the investment should be made.

SOLUTION

Spreadsheet Solution

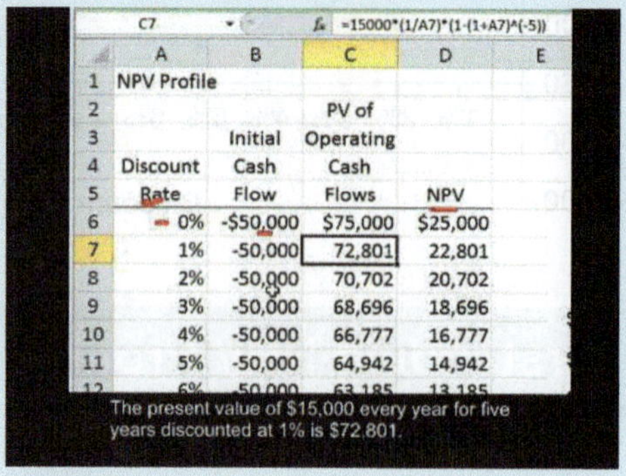

View in the online reader

Algebraic Solution

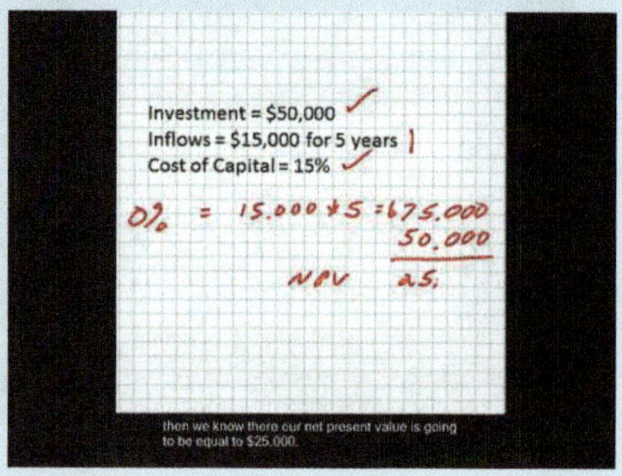

View in the online reader

Calculator Solution

View in the online reader

We need to compute the NPV at a variety of different discount rates. We begin with the discount rate equal to zero and compute the NPV using increasingly larger discount rates until the NPV is negative. The formula for computing the NPV is:

$$NPV = \$15,000 \times \frac{\left[1 - \frac{1}{(1+i)^5}\right]}{i} - \$50,000$$

We compute the NPV at different discount rates until the NPV is negative. The results are reported in the following table.

Discount Rate	NPV
0%	$25,000
5	14,935
10	6,862
15	282
20	–5,141

We now graph the results to obtain our NPV profile:

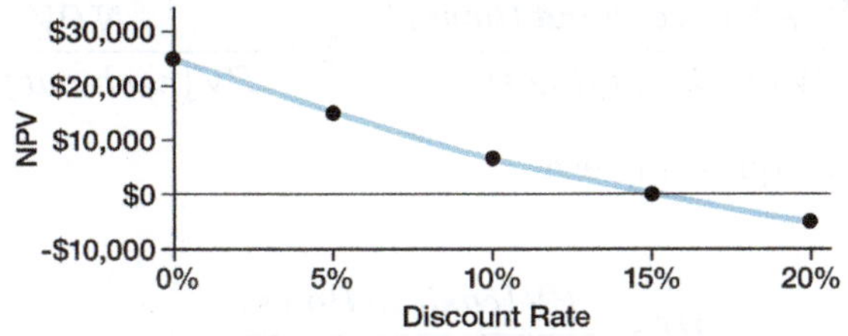

From the NPV profile, we see that we would accept the project as long as the cost of capital was less than about 15.25% because the NPV is positive in that range. Alternatively, we would reject the project if the cost of capital was greater than about 15.25%. In this example, as long as you are sure the cost of capital is 15% or less, you would make the investment.

Explain It: NPV Profile

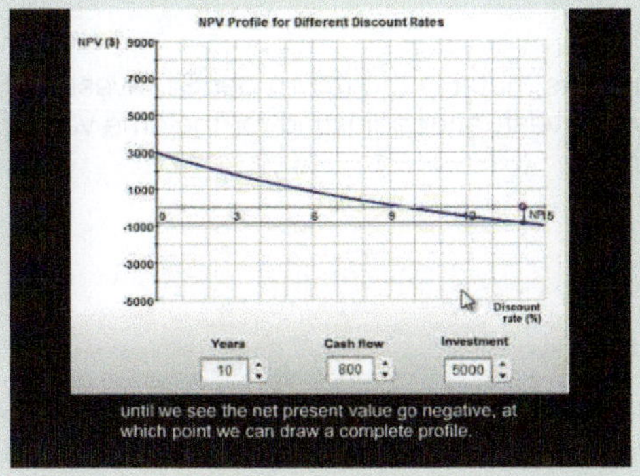

View in the online reader

Profitability Index (Cost–Benefit Ratio)

profitability index (PI)

The ratio of the PV of the cash inflows to the PV of the cash outflows. It provides a measure of the bang for the buck provided by investing in the project.

The **profitability index (PI)** uses the same inputs as the NPV, but by converting the results to a ratio, it provides additional information. Equation 9.4 computes the PI:

Tip

Recall that $NPV = PV(cash\ inflows) - (cash\ outflows)$.

We can use this definition to express the profitability index as:

$$PI = \frac{NPV + PV(cash\ outflows)}{PV(cash\ outflows)} = 1 + \frac{NPV}{PV(cash\ outflows)}$$

These versions are sometimes quicker to use.

EQUATION 9.4

$$PI = \frac{PV(cash\ inflows)}{PV(cash\ outflows)}$$

or

$$PI = \frac{PV(cash\ inflows)}{initial\ investment}$$

The numerator is the present value of the benefits of taking the project, and the denominator is the present value of the cost. A simple interpretation is that the PI is the bang for the buck provided by the project. When the NPV is zero, the PV (cash inflows) will equal the PV (cash outflows) and the PI will be 1. Thus, our decision criterion is to accept the project if the PI is greater than or equal to 1.

Tip

Another interpretation of the PI is that it is the return per $1 invested. So, a PI of 1.1 means that you get back $1.1 per $1 you invest, after adjusting for the time value of money.

Computation

To compute the PI, simply find the present value of the cash inflows and divide by the PV of the cash outflows. If you are also computing an NPV, these values were already computed. "Example 9.6 Profitability Index" uses the figures provided by "Example 9.3 Net Present Value Calculation: Single Period Investment" to illustrate the process.

Tip

The NPV and PI will *always* give the same accept/reject decision because all of the inputs to both models are *exactly* the same.

Example 9.6 Profitability Index

Digital Downloads

Example 9.6_Profitability_Index.xls
https://catalog.flatworldknowledge.com/a/34711/Example_9_6_Profitability_Index-7e4b.xls

Suppose a $6,000 investment will yield three cash inflows of $3,650 each. With a discount rate of 15%, what is the PI?

SOLUTION

Spreadsheet Solution

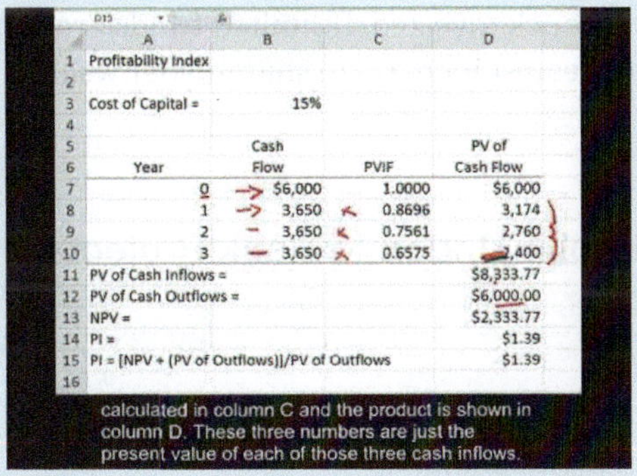

View in the online reader

Algebraic Solution

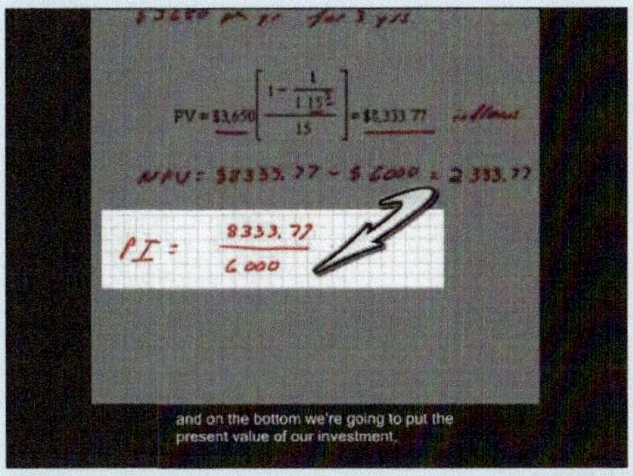

View in the online reader

The PV of the cash outflows is $6,000 because the entire investment is made today. The PV of the cash inflows is computed as:

$$PV = \$3,650 \left[\frac{1 - \frac{1}{1.15^3}}{0.15} \right] = \$8,333.77$$

Put these figures into Equation 9.4:

$$PI = \frac{PV(\text{cash inflows})}{PV(\text{cash outflows})}$$

$$PI = \frac{\$8,333.68}{6,000}$$

$$PI = 1.39$$

The profitability index is 1.39. Because it is greater than 1, we would accept the project. Notice that this is the same decision reached in "Example 9.3 Net Present Value Calculation: Single Period Investment". In fact, the PI and NPV will always provide the same answer to the accept/reject question.

Capital Rationing

As mentioned earlier, few firms have either the capital or human resources to pursue every good opportunity. In the end, firms must rank projects to conserve their capital. This is called *capital rationing*. One approach to capital rationing is to use the PI to rank projects since it provides a measure of the bang for the buck invested. If limited funds are available, we will want to invest in those that will provide the greatest increase in shareholder wealth. Using PI to rank projects can be a good first step.

Example 9.7 Profitability Index to Rank Projects

Digital Downloads

Example 9.7_Capital_Rationing.xls
https://catalog.flatworldknowledge.com/a/34711/Example_9_7_Capital_Rationing-cefc.xls

Suppose you have collected the following data on four possible projects. Rank the projects using the PI. If your capital budget is $1,000, which project(s) would you select?

Project	Net Investment	PV (cash inflows)	NPV
A	$500	$550	$50
B	100	90	−10
C	1,000	1,052	52
D	20	25	5

SOLUTION

Spreadsheet Solution

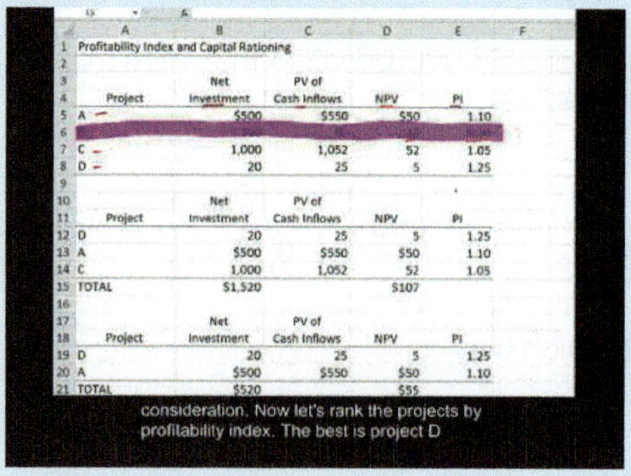

View in the online reader

Algebraic Solution

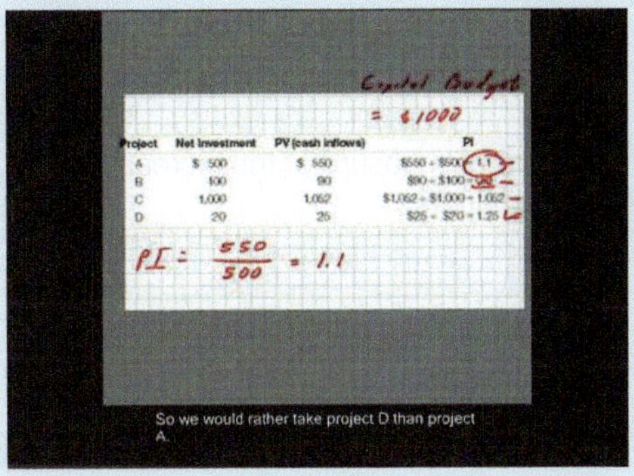

View in the online reader

Begin by computing the profitability index for each project:

Project	Net Investment	PV (cash inflows)	PI
A	$500	$550	$\$550/\$500 = 1.1$
B	100	90	$\$90/\$100 = 0.9$
C	1,000	1,052	$\$1,052/\$1,000 = 1.052$
D	20	25	$\$25/\$20 = 1.25$

Now, review the PI ratios to see which projects are acceptable. Because Project B has a PI less than 1, it is immediately rejected. Next, rank the projects in order from highest PI to lowest. Project D has the highest PI, A is second, and C is third. This analysis suggests we should accept Projects A and D, for a total capital budget of $520. The combined NPV of these two projects is $55, which is greater than the NPV of Project C by itself.

In "Example 9.7 Profitability Index to Rank Projects", NPV was maximized by selecting projects in the order they were ranked by the PI. However, ranking by PI only works if the projects use all of the budgeted capital. If the projects use less than the budget, then the top-ranked PI projects might not be the best. Remember, since the goal here is to achieve the greatest increase in shareholder wealth, we always want to choose the projects that combine to the highest total NPV. Sometimes, the top-ranked PI projects don't do that. For example, suppose you have collected data on three possible projects and want to rank them. As in Example 9.7, we would begin by computing the PI.

Project	Net Investment	NPV	PI
A	$9	$1.75	1.194
B	10	2.00	1.200
C	10	1.80	1.180

Now, if we rank the projects in order from highest PI to lowest, Project B has the highest PI, A is second, and C is third. If your capital budget is $20 we should accept Projects A and B, for a total capital budget of $19 and a total NPV of $3.75. However, if we select projects B and C our total capital budget is $20 and total NPV is increased to $3.80. The message here is that PI only provides a starting point for selecting projects under capital rationing. Once ranked by PI, the analyst must use trial and error to be sure that those projects selected actually maximize NPV.

PI can be used interchangeably with NPV to make an investment decision, since positive NPV projects have a PI that is greater than one. The disadvantage of PI is that it can rank projects incorrectly when capital is rationed. Under capital rationing, projects should be selected by NPV maximization. Ultimately, the goal of the financial manager is to maximize shareholder wealth. The PI may be used as a supplement to the NPV, but not as a replacement.

Tip

Remember that the NPV provides a measure of the increase in firm value resulting from a project. A PI does not provide this information.

9.5 Internal Rate of Return and MIRR

internal rate of return (IRR)

The discount rate that sets the present value of the cash inflows equal to the present value of the cash outflows. It is the discount rate that sets net present value to zero.

The **internal rate of return (IRR)** is the discount rate that sets the present value of the cash inflows equal to the present value of the cash outflows. Alternatively, **IRR can be defined as the discount rate that sets the NPV equal to zero**. If the IRR is greater than the cost of capital, the project is accepted. If the IRR is less than the cost of capital, the project is rejected.

The IRR is more difficult to calculate than the NPV and usually requires the use of a financial calculator or computer. However, it is far easier to interpret. For this reason, it is used almost as often as the NPV.

Theory

Suppose your roommate offers you an opportunity to invest in his mail-order computer parts business. If you invest $100 today, you will receive $110 in 1 year. What is the return on this investment? You probably answered 10%, without needing paper and pencil. The return on this investment is independent of what else is happening to external market returns, so we call it an internal return.

Would you accept your roommate's offer? That depends on what you require as a rate of return. If your cost of capital is 12%, you would reject the proposal.

Let us continue with this example by demonstrating how we would compute the NPV. The figures are initially put into Equation 9.3:

$$NPV = \frac{\$110}{1+i} - \$100$$

If we know the discount rate (i), we can compute the NPV. The IRR approaches the problem from a slightly different angle. Rather than inputting a discount rate and computing the NPV, we ask what the discount rate should be to make the NPV exactly equal to zero. For example:

$$\begin{aligned} NPV = 0 \quad &= \frac{\$110}{1+i} - \$100 \\ \$100 &= \frac{\$110}{1+i} \\ 1+i &= \frac{\$110}{\$100} = 1.10 \\ &= 0.10 = 10\% \end{aligned}$$

The 10% interest rate is the value of the discount rate that sets the present value of the cash inflows equal to the present value of the cash outflows. If the 10% return is acceptable, the project should be undertaken. In this example, because capital cost is 12%, we reject the project. Thus, the decision criterion for the IRR can be summarized as: **Accept the project if the IRR is greater than or equal to the cost of capital.**

Explain It: The Intuition Behind the Internal Rate of Return

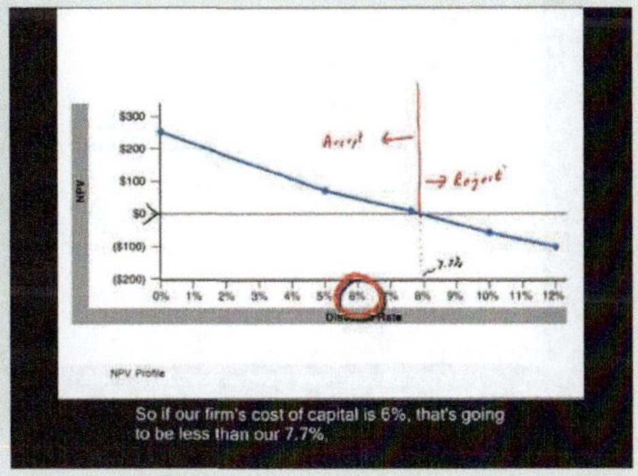

View in the online reader

Review Figure 9.1. We can read the IRR directly off the NPV profile. The IRR is the discount rate at which the $NPV = 0$. This is the point at which the profile crosses the horizontal axis.

Computation

In the preceding example, we see that the calculation of the IRR is fairly straightforward when there is a single cash inflow. It becomes much more complicated when there are multiple cash flows. If there are only a few cash flows, it is possible to find a close approximation using trial and error. However, in practice, the IRR is computed using spreadsheets and financial calculators.

Example 9.8 Computing IRR

Digital Downloads

Example 9.8_IRR.xls
https://catalog.flatworldknowledge.com/a/34711/Example_9_8_IRR-bb24.xls

If the initial investment is $500 and the cash inflows are $200 for 3 years, compute the IRR.

SOLUTION

Spreadsheet Solution

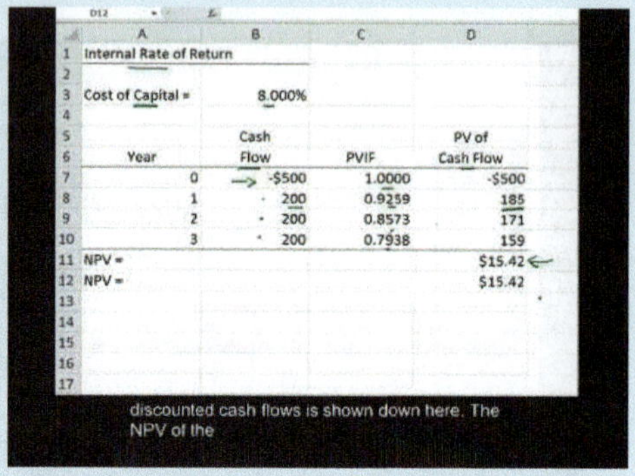

View in the online reader

Algebraic Solution

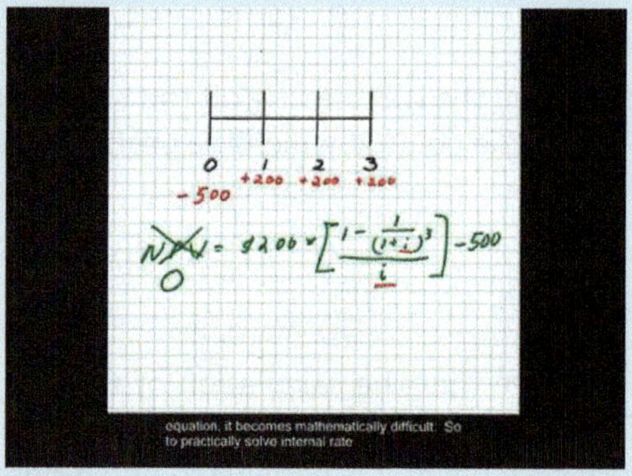

View in the online reader

Using a financial calculator input:

$$N = 3$$
$$PMT = \$200$$
$$PV = -\$500$$
$$CPTI = 9.7\%$$

Advantages

The primary advantage of the IRR method of investment analysis is that it is easy to interpret and explain. Investors normally speak in terms of annual returns when evaluating investment options. For this reason, many firms that use the NPV also compute the IRR. Note that the NPV and IRR will always provide the same accept/reject decision.

Disadvantages

There are several serious problems with the IRR that must be understood. They do not necessarily invalidate the model, but rather must be considered before its application.

1. *Reinvestment Rate Assumption:* The IRR assumes the cash flows are reinvested at the internal rate of return when they are received. The reinvestment rate assumption is most serious when using the IRR to rank projects. Look at Figure 9.2, which graphs the NPV profiles of Projects A and B. Project A has the highest NPV for all discount rates less than 12%. Project B is superior for all discount rates greater than 12%. The project's rank depends on the discount rate. **Because the IRR method does not evaluate the project at a particular discount rate, it cannot be used for ranking mutually exclusive projects.**

FIGURE 9.2 IRR Ranking

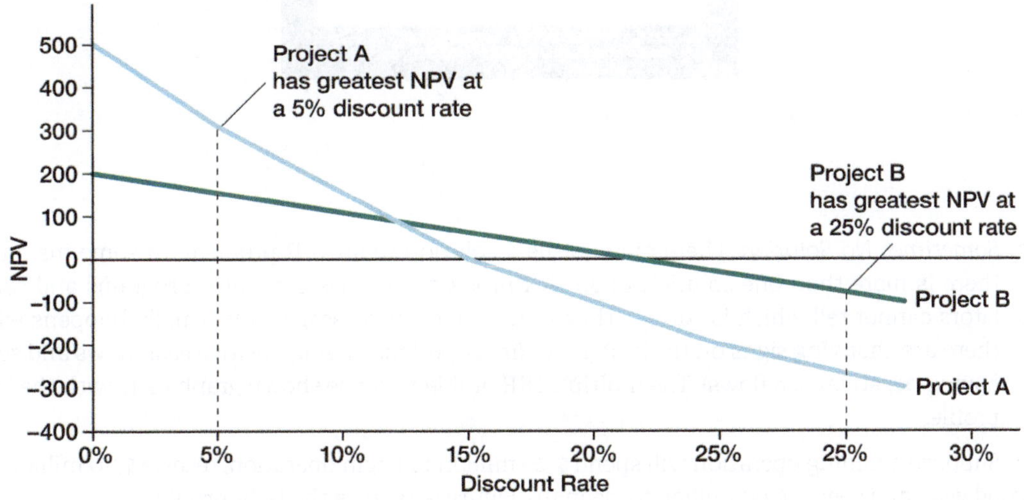

Explain It: IRR May Rank Projects Incorrectly because of the Reinvestment Rate

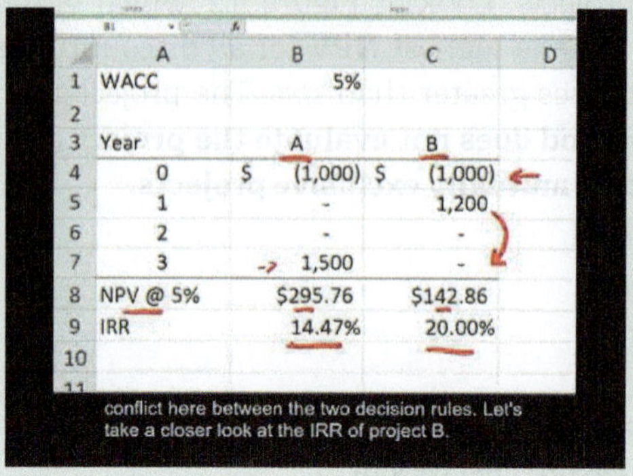

View in the online reader

2. *Sometimes No Solution:* There may not be a solution to an IRR problem. In some instances, there is more than one solution to an IRR problem. Because computer programs and calculators cannot tell which is correct, they return an error message. This usually happens when there are changing signs on the cash flows (most periods having positive cash flows and some having negative cash flows). The multiple IRR problem can be shown graphically with the NPV profile.

Suppose a mining operation will spend $120 million to begin operation, receive $310 million the second year, and spend $200 million to clean up. Figure 9.3 shows the NPV profile.

FIGURE 9.3 NPV Profile with Multiple IRRs

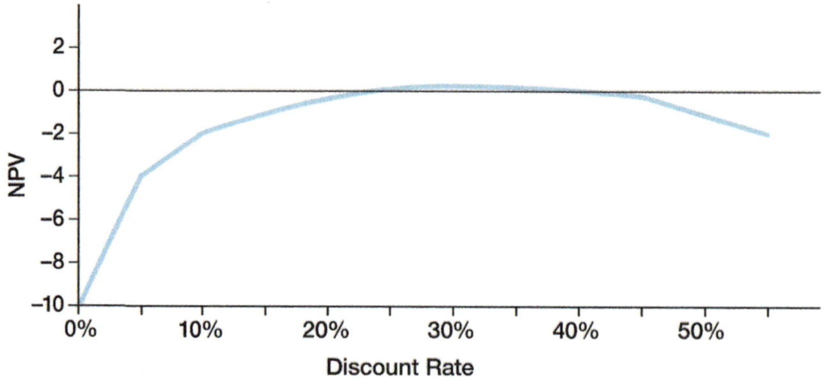

The NPV is initially negative, becomes positive, and then becomes negative again. Because it crosses the zero NPV line twice, there are two IRRs. Because cash flows often alternate signs, this can be a serious problem.

Explain It: Problems with IRR Caused by Alternating Cash Flows

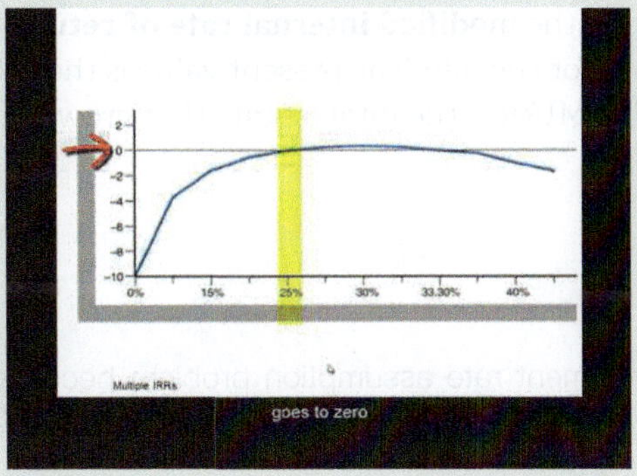

View in the online reader

3. *Accurate Calculation Often Requires a Financial Calculator:* You probably will not want to attempt many IRR calculations without the help of a financial calculator or spreadsheet program.
4. *IRR Ignores Differences in Scale:* Suppose you had the choice of buying the Kinston Indians (a small-town baseball team in North Carolina) or the Atlanta Braves. You can buy the Indians for $10,000. The Atlanta Braves cost $10 million, but contractual provisions limit you to owning only one baseball team of any kind. If both have an IRR of 25%, which would you take if you could afford either? The IRR does not give you any help because it converts the cash flows to percentages and ignores differences in the size or scale of projects considered.

NPV versus IRR

Which method should you use to evaluate a project? It depends on who your audience is, whether you're ranking projects or simply determining which are acceptable, and whether the project has alternating signs on the cash flows.

If you are a small business owner doing calculations for your own business, you do not have to worry about the sophistication of your audience. However, most of the time, you will be presenting your analysis to other investors. How successful would you be in convincing your art major roommate to invest in your new mail-order pizza business if you spoke only of net present values, cost of capital, risk-adjusted discount rates, and the like? Once you were convinced your numbers were correct by using the NPV, a simplified presentation using the IRR and payback may be more successful.

The choice of analysis methodology also depends on whether you are selecting among many good projects or simply determining the acceptability of a single project. Remember that the IRR cannot be used to rank projects, but always gives the same accept/reject decision as the NPV.

Modified Internal Rate of Return (MIRR)

modified internal rate of return (MIRR)

The discount rate that sets the terminal value of the cash inflows equal to the present value of the cash outflows, where the PV and terminal values are computed using the firm's cost of capital.

Because of the problems with the internal rate of return, analysts have developed an alternative evaluation technique similar to the IRR but without the reinvestment rate problem. The cash outflows are discounted back to the present at the cost of capital, and the cash inflows are compounded at the cost of capital to the project's end. The future value of the cash inflows is called the terminal value. To solve for the **modified internal rate of return (MIRR)**, we set up a simple future value problem and solve for the rate. The present value is the PV of the outflows. The future value is the terminal value. The MIRR is the interest rate that grows the present value to equal the future value.

Tip

The MIRR solves the reinvestment rate assumption problem because all cash flows are compounded at the cost of capital. It also solves the problem of changing cash flow signs resulting in multiple IRRs.

The calculation of the MIRR, although it takes several steps, is not difficult.

1. Find the present value of all cash outflows at the firm's cost of capital.

Tip

Often, the only cash outflow is the initial investment. If any subsequent cash outflows are required, such as a future modification, compute the present value of these outflows as well.

2. Find the future value of all cash inflows at the firm's cost of capital. All positive cash flows are compounded to the point at which the last cash inflow is received.
3. Compute the rate that compounds the present value of the outflows so that they equal the future value of the inflows. This rate is the MIRR.

Example 9.9 Modified Internal Rate of Return

Digital Downloads

Example 9.9_MIRR.xls
https://catalog.flatworldknowledge.com/a/34711/Example_9_9_MIRR-b455.xls

Compute the MIRR for the following cash flow stream. Assume a cost of capital of 10%. The initial investment is $500. The cash inflows are $300 per year for 2 years, followed by a $200 expenditure and then one more $300 inflow.

SOLUTION

Spreadsheet Solution

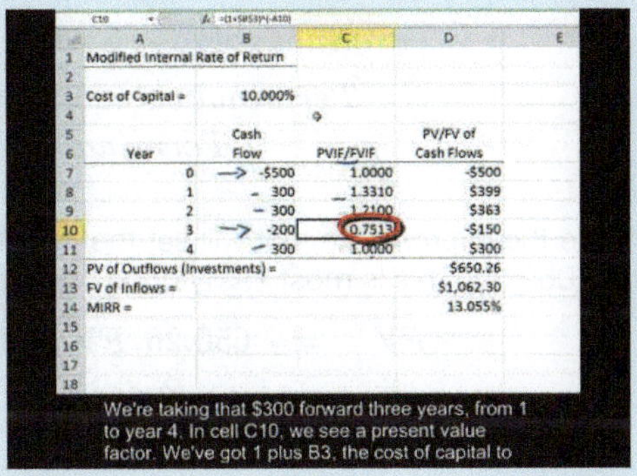

View in the online reader

Algebraic Solution

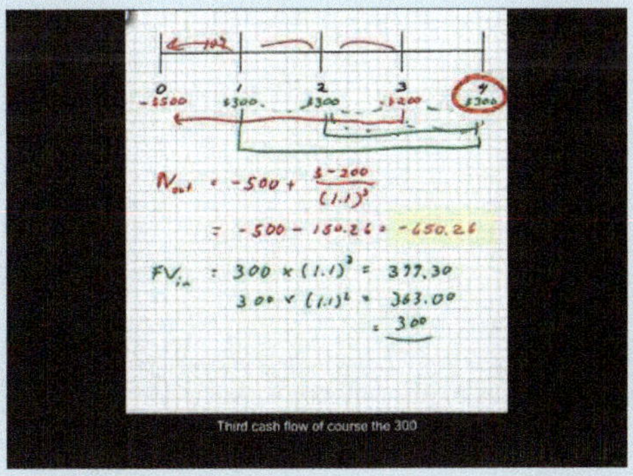

View in the online reader

Prepare a timeline to better visualize the process:

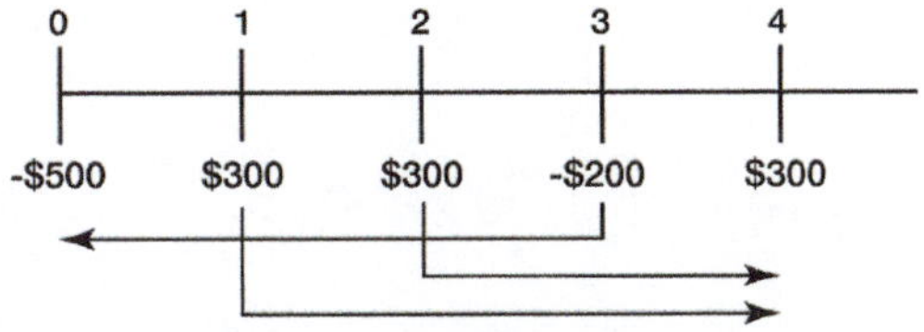

1. The investment is:

$$-\$500 - \$200\left(\frac{1}{1.1^3}\right) = -\$650.26$$

2. There are three positive cash inflows that must be compounded to the end of the fourth period. The first \$300 cash flow is compounded for three periods. The second \$300 cash flow is compounded for two periods, and the last \$300 earns no interest. The sum of the future value of the cash flows is the terminal value:

$$\textit{Terminal value} = \$300\left(1.10^3\right) + \$300\left(1.10^2\right) + \$300$$
$$\textit{Terminal value} = \$399.30 + \$363.00 + \$300$$
$$\textit{Terminal value} = \$1,062.30$$

3. In this step, compute the interest rate that will set the investment of \$650.26 equal to the terminal value of \$1,062.30. This is most easily done using a financial calculator.

$$PV = -650.26, FV = \$1,062.30, N = 4, PMT = 0$$
$$\textit{Press CPT}. I = 13.05\%$$

CHAPTER 10

Capital Budgeting: Estimating Cash Flows

Learning Objectives

By the end of this chapter you will be able to:

1. Calculate free cash flow.
2. Calculate the cash flows for an expansion project (without depreciation).
3. Calculate the cash flows for a replacement project (without depreciation).
4. Understand some advanced topics in capital budgeting.
5. Understand how MACRS affects the cash flows of expansion projects.
6. Understand how MACRS affects the cash flows of replacement projects.

The Channel Tunnel (Chunnel) is a 31-mile-long undersea tunnel linking Great Britain and France. In 1985, the Channel Tunnel Group estimated that the cost of construction for the tunnel would be 2.6 billion pounds sterling. The project was plagued by cost overruns, and construction was halted several times while additional funds were raised. By the time the tunnel was completed in 1994, the total cost was 4.65 billion pounds sterling—an 80% cost overrun. The Chunnel was completed because of government backing. Private-sector companies do not have government support. Capital budgeting errors of the magnitude experienced by the Chunnel would cause most private-sector firms to fail.

As we saw in the Chunnel example, a capital budgeting decision is only as good as its cash flow projections. This chapter shows how project cash flows are calculated. We start by defining free cash flow and its three component parts. In Sections 2 and 3, we show how to calculate project cash flows for expansion and replacement projects. In Section 4, we discuss some subtleties associated with capital budgeting (e.g., comparing projects with unequal lives). The appendices show how to adjust expansion and replacement project cash flows for depreciation tax deductibility and tax on salvage.

Depreciation Tax Deductibility and the Organization of this Chapter

The IRS allows businesses to deduct some of the cost of large capital expenditures against income earned in the business in order to reduce taxes. In some cases, businesses can deduct the entire cost in the year of the expenditure, but in other cases businesses must depreciate the cost.

In recent years, Congress has raised the limit for capital expenditures that qualify for Section 179 treatment. Under Section 179, capital expenditures are expensed rather than depreciated over time. In 2017, the Section 179 limit was raised to just over $1 million. Assets costing more than $1 million are depreciated using the Modified Accelerated Cost Recovery System (MACRS).

This dual treatment informs the organization of this chapter. In Sections 2 and 3, we present the calculation of project cash flows (for expansion and replacement projects) assuming that there is no depreciation deductibility and no tax on the sale of used assets. These assumptions are appropriate for projects that qualify for Section 179 treatment. Since most projects involve expenditures less the $1 million we have moved the treatment of MACRS depreciation and the treatment of project cash flows with depreciation to an Appendix.

The Incremental Approach

Suppose you are considering whether to add a new production line to a factory. You would proceed with the project if the company was more valuable with the new production line than without it. The decision criteria (accept projects that increase the value of the company) implies that, to evaluate projects, the analyst has to conduct two valuations: with the new project and without it. The project is only accepted if the value with is greater than the value without. In this chapter we present an alternative, the incremental approach, which is also consistent with maximizing the value of the company. For each project, we will compute the incremental cash flows—the costs and revenues that change because of the new project. If those incremental cash flows have a positive NPV, then we know the value of the company is greater if it adopts the project and the change in the company's value is equal to the NPV of the incremental cash flows. The Explain It video provides a deeper explanation of the incremental approach.

Explain It: The Incremental Approach to Capital Budgeting

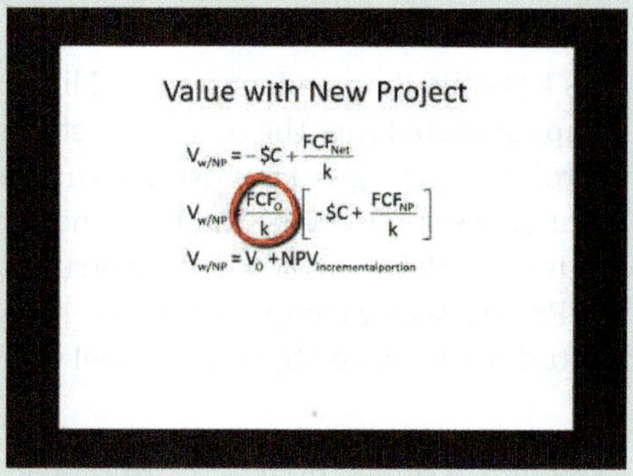

View in the online reader

10.1 Free Cash Flow

When we calculate free cash flow for a whole company, we interpret the value as being the amount of money that you would receive at the end of each year if you were the only owner of the company (assuming no debt). Project free cash flow is the amount of money you would receive from a new project if you were the sole owner of the business. The present value of the project's free cash flows is the incremental value of the project. We also call it the net present value of the project.

For companies that are partially debt financed, we interpret free cash flow as the total amount of money generated by the project that is available to be paid, in total, to the two sets of claimholders: bondholders and shareholders.

The free cash flow for a project is made up of three components as shown in Equation 10.1. In the next three sections, we explain each in turn.

EQUATION 10.1

$$FCF = OCF - \Delta NWC - CAPEX$$

where

$$OCF = \text{Operating Cash Flow}$$
$$\Delta NWC = \text{Investment in (or recovery of) net working capital}$$
$$\Delta CAPEX = \text{Expenditures on (or receipts from sale of) fixed assets}$$

Explain It: Free Cash Flow

View in the online reader

Operating Cash Flow

Operating cash flow (OCF) is the cash derived from the day-to-day operations of a business. It is sales revenue less out-of-pocket costs and taxes:

EQUATION 10.2

$$OCF = Sales - COGS - SG\&A - Taxes$$

where

$$COGS = \text{Cost of Goods Sold}$$
$$SG\&A = \text{Selling, General, and Administrative Expenses}$$

We do not subtract interest in the computation of OCF. Free cash flow is intended to represent the amount of money available to be paid to bondholders and shareholders, so we do not want to subtract one of the cash flows to bondholders (interest). Ignoring interest results in an overestimate of taxes, since interest is tax deductible. The work-around for this is that interest tax deductibility is incorporated into project valuation through the weighted average cost of capital when we use the after-tax cost of debt.[1]

We do not deduct depreciation because it is a noncash expense. It is not an amount of money that is actually paid to anyone. However, depreciation, like interest, is tax deductible. Next we'll explain how we manage depreciation tax deductibility in this chapter.

First, let's derive an expression for OCF and show where depreciation enters. We'll start by substituting an expression for taxes into our definition of OCF in Equation 10.2. Ignoring interest, taxes are computed as:

EQUATION 10.3

$$Taxes = T \times (Sales\text{–}COGS\text{–}SG\&A\text{–}Depr)$$

where

$$Depr = \text{Depreciation Expense}$$

Next, substitute Equation 10.3 into Equation 10.2 and simplify.

$$OCF = Sales - COGS - SG\&A - T \times Sales - COGS - SG\&A - Depr)$$
$$OCF = (Sales - COGS - SG\&A) \times (1 - T) + T \times Depr$$

EQUATION 10.4

$$OCF = EBITDA \times (1\text{–}T) + (T \times Depr)$$

where

$$EBITDA = Sales\text{–}COGS\text{–}SG\&A$$

Equation 10.4 shows that operating cash flows are the sum of two pieces, of which only the second involves depreciation. This additive separability allows us to calculate each piece separately and then add the two together. That is the approach we use in this chapter. In Sections 2 and 3, we analyze expansion and replacement projects ignoring depreciation and then, in the appendices, we adjust the cash flows to incorporate depreciation tax deductibility.

Investments in Net Working Capital

An increase in net working capital (NWC) is a use of cash, and a reduction in net working capital is a source of cash, so our focus is on the change in net working capital defined as:

EQUATION 10.5

$$\Delta NWC = NWC_{t+1}\text{–}NWC_t = \Delta CA\text{–}\Delta CL$$

where

$$\Delta NWC = \text{Change in net working capital}$$
$$\Delta CA = \text{Change in current assets}$$
$$\Delta CL = \text{Change in current liabilities}$$

Explain It

In the chapter on corporate valuation, we will use a slightly different definition of net working capital. We will exclude cash from current assets and short-term debt from current liabilities. The distinction won't affect this chapter.[2]

An increase in current assets constitutes an increase in net working capital (e.g., buying more inventory) and a decrease in current assets constitutes a decrease in net working capital. Similarly, an increase in current liabilities causes a decrease in net working capital (e.g., an increase in accounts payable).

An increase in NWC is a use of cash (e.g., buying more inventory) and a decrease in NWC (e.g., selling inventory) is a source of cash. Following Equation 10.1, an increase in NWC is subtracted from operating cash flows and reduces free cash flow. Conversely, a decrease in NWC (a negative increase) adds to operating cash flow and so increases free cash flow.

Example 10.2 Changes in Net Working Capital

As a result of a new machine, your production process has changed. This change requires you to keep $12,000 of additional widgets on hand. Accounts payable are expected to increase by $3,000 because you will rely on vendor financing as much as possible. What is the change in net working capital?

SOLUTION

The increase of $12,000 in widgets means that you have to increase inventory. Because inventory is a current asset, this increase affects net working capital. Similarly, accounts payable is a current liability. Using Equation 10.5, we get the following:

$$\Delta NWC = \Delta CA - \Delta CL$$
$$\Delta NWC = \$12,000 - \$3,000 = \$9,000$$

Current assets go up by $12,000. This increased need for assets is funded partly by an offsetting increase in current liabilities of $3,000. The increase in the net working capital is $9,000. This amount would be subtracted in the calculation of cash flows at the beginning of a project.

Finally, net working capital will typically rise and fall with sales, so there can be investments in (or returns of) working capital in any year of a project. In all of our examples, we will make the simplifying assumption that investments in working capital occur at the beginning of the project's life and are returned at the end of the project's life.

CAPEX

CAPEX is short for capital expenditures. CAPEX is the amount of money spent on purchases of long-term assets such as machinery and equipment. CAPEX is subtracted from operating cash flow and so reduces free cash flow. In most of the examples and homework for this chapter, we will assume that the investment in CAPEX occurs as soon as the project is initiated, which we will indicate as time 0. In the terminal year of a project, we assume that long-term assets are sold (the sale value is also called the **salvage value**). Salvage is negative CAPEX and so adds to free cash flow.

salvage value

The resale value of an asset at the end of a project. Also called scrap value.

Explain It

Our timing assumption is a simplification. Large projects can take a number of years before revenues are realized. Also, most (all) projects require ongoing capital investments throughout their operating lives.

Free Cash Flow from a Project

"Example 10.3 Free Cash Flow for Mike Mulligan's New Project" shows a typical capital budgeting example and computes free cash flow. Pay attention to the timing of cash flows, as most of the examples and homework problems follow this same pattern.

Example 10.3 Free Cash Flow for Mike Mulligan's New Project

Mike Mulligan wants to expand his heavy equipment business into excavation. He plans to buy a used excavator for $300,000. The excavator requires an inventory of spare parts worth $10,000. These investments will occur immediately. Mulligan will operate the excavation business for two years and expects EBITDA of $200,000 at the end of each year. He will close his business at the end of the second year, sell the equipment for $100,000 and liquidate the inventory of spare parts. Mulligan pays a tax rate of 25%. Using this information, compute the appropriate values for operating cash flow, investments in net working capital, CAPEX and free cash flow for each year of the project.

SOLUTION

	Year 0	Year 1	Year 2
OCF	$0	$150,000	$150,000
Less: Increase (decrease) in NWC	10,000		–10,000
Less: CAPEX	300,000		–100,000
=FCF	–310,000	150,000	260,000

Year 0

$$FCF_0 = \$0 - \$10,000 - \$300,000 = -\$310,000$$

Year 1

Operating cash flow from Equation 10.4 $(Depr = 0)$:

$$OCF = EBITDA \times (1-T) = \$200,000 \times (1-0.25) = \$150,000$$

Year 2

In the terminal year, the $10,000 investment in inventory from year 0 is liquidated (a decrease in net working capital) and the long-term assets are sold (salvage) for $100,000. Thus, the increase in NWC is negative (a decrease) and CAPEX is negative (salvage). Following Equation 10.1, free cash flow is:

$$FCF_2 = \$150,000 - (-\$10,000) - (-\$100,000) = \$260,000$$

10.2 Expansion Projects: Basic

We classify projects as either expansion or replacement projects. The reason we need to identify which type of project we are analyzing is that we treat them somewhat differently. A replacement project is a project in which an old asset is replaced by a new asset. In expansion projects, only the cost of the new asset must be considered; there are no old costs and revenues to complicate the analysis. We present expansion projects in this section and cover replacement projects in the next section.

In this section, we will calculate project free cash flow under the simplifying assumptions that depreciation is not tax deductible and that there are no taxes associated with the sale of an asset. These assumptions are appropriate for projects that qualify for Section 179 treatment. In the appendices of this chapter, we show how to adjust project cash flows to account for depreciation tax deductibility and the taxation on salvage. We have organized this chapter so that Section 5 and Section 6 show the additional cash flows that must be added to (or subtracted from) the cash flows developed here and in Section 3.

In almost all of our examples and problems, we assume the following pattern of cash flows:

1. Investments in net working capital and fixed assets (CAPEX) occur when the project is initiated (at time zero);
2. Operating cash flows occur at the end of each year during the life of the project commencing one year after the investments; and
3. Fixed assets are sold (and net working capital recovered) at the end of the final year of the project.

Initial Investment Cash Flows

Equation 10.6 shows how to calculate the initial cash flows for a project.

EQUATION 10.6

$$FCF_0 = 0 - CAPEX - Inc(Dec)\ in\ NWC$$

The zero on the right-hand side reflects the fact that, at the beginning of a project, there are no operating cash flows. The initial cash flow consists of the outflow associated with the initial purchases of fixed assets minus any increase in net working capital. Increases in NWC are subtracted because they are a use of cash and so lower free cash flow.

Tip

If working capital decreases at the outset of a project (which is rare), then the investment is negative (a decrease) and we subtract the negative number (add it) to the other initial cash flows.

The initial CAPEX is often the easiest and most accurate number to obtain. Include any taxes, tariffs, or other expenses that are part of the cost. Installation and shipping are also considered part of the initial cost of acquiring the asset and are included in the initial purchase price.

Example 10.4 Initial Cash Flows for an Expansion Project

A new Logan's restaurant costs $1 million to build and equip. Logan's restaurants typically have annual sales of $2 million. Assume that to open a new restaurant, owners must invest $100,000 in food and beverage inventory. What are the initial cash flows for opening a Logan's restaurant?

SOLUTION

CAPEX	$1,000,000
Increase in NWC	100,000
Initial cash flow	−1,100,000

Initial free cash flows are computed following Equation 10.6:

$$FCF_0 = \$0 - \$1,000,000 - \$100,000 = -\$1,100,000$$

Operating Cash Flows

In return for making an investment in plant, machinery, or equipment, the firm expects to receive a series of operating cash inflows. Only when the present value of these inflows exceeds the present value of the outflows will the project be accepted.

The formula for computing operating cash flows is given in Equation 10.4. As discussed earlier, in this section (and Section 3) we will assume that depreciation is not tax deductible. If we assume that depreciation is not tax deductible, then Equation 10.4 simplifies to:

EQUATION 10.7

$$OCF = EBITDA \times (1 - T) = EBITDA - (T \times EBITDA)$$

Note that taxes are computed as the tax rate times EBITDA.

Remember that only incremental changes are relevant to capital budgeting analysis. Incremental revenues are simply the new sales from the expansion project. Incremental costs can be a little more challenging to calculate. We review a number of issues related to incremental cash flows in Section 4.

Example 10.5 Computing Operating Cash Flows for an Expansion Project

Digital Downloads

Example 10.5 Expansion OCF Logans.xlsx
https://catalog.flatworldknowledge.com/a/34711/Example_10_5_Expansion_OCF_Logans-b74e.xlsx

Logan's Roadhouse Inc. owns a chain of restaurants that competes with Outback Steakhouse. If a new Logan's restaurant has revenues of $2 million and if the total expenses (cost of goods sold and SG&A expenses) are 60% of revenues, what will the annual cash inflows be over the expected 2-year life of the restaurant? Assume a 40% marginal tax rate.

SOLUTION

Logan's Roadhouse Inc.	Year 1	Year 2
Revenue	$2,000,000	$2,000,000
Operating Expenses	1,200,000	1,200,00
Gross Profit (EBITDA)	800,000	800,000
Taxes	320,000	320,000
OCF	480,000	480,000

Following Equation 10.7, annual cash inflows are:

$$OCF = \$800,000 - \$320,000 = \$480,000$$

Terminal Cash Flows

Terminal year cash flows are calculated using the same formula, Equation 10.1, as all other years:

$$FCF = OCF - \Delta NWC - CAPEX$$

We usually assume that the terminal year is a complete year with full operating cash flows. For most projects, the investment in NWC is negative, a decrease in NWC, so we would subtract a negative number (add). The intuition for this is that a decrease in net working capital is a source of cash and increases terminal year free cash flow. This can get a little confusing, so we will generally refer to the decrease in NWC (a positive value) and add it to operating cash flows.

Tip

It is not always the case that net working capital increases at the outset of a project and decreases at the end. Analysts must be prepared to deal with the reverse case. Remember: increases in NWC reduce free cash flow and decreases add to free cash flow.

In the terminal year, the used assets are sold (salvaged), not purchased, so CAPEX is a negative number. Following Equation 10.1, we would subtract the negative purchase. Like with NWC, this can become confusing and lead to mistakes, so we will instead add the salvage value of the used assets to terminal cash flows rather than subtract negative CAPEX.

These two amendments change the formula for free cash flow in the terminal year to:

EQUATION 10.8

$$FCF_T = OCF + \textit{Decrease in } NWC + \textit{Salvage}$$

Explain It

In this section, we assume that salvage is not taxable. This assumption is relaxed in Section 5 and Section 6.

Example 10.6 Terminal Cash Flow for an Expansion Project

Digital Downloads

Example 10.6 Expansion Terminal CF Logans.xlsx
https://catalog.flatworldknowledge.com/a/34711/Example_10_6_Expansion_Terminal_CF_Logans-0895.xlsx

A new Logan's restaurant costs $1 million to build and equip. Logan's restaurants typically have an operating cash flow of $480,000. Assume that, to open a new restaurant, owners must invest in $100,000 of food and beverage inventory. This inventory is sold at the end of the terminal year. Assume that the restaurant and its contents can be sold for $0.8M after two years. What is the terminal cash flow?

SOLUTION

The terminal cash flow is computed as follows:

Operating Cash Flows	$480,000
Decrease in NWC	100,000
Salvage	800,000
Terminal Cash Flow	1,380,000

Following Equation 10.8, terminal year cash flows are:

$$FCF = \$480,000 + \$100,000 + \$800,000 = \$1,380,000$$

Comprehensive Example of an Expansion Project

Example 10.7 Expansion Project NPV

Digital Downloads

Example 10.7 Expansion Boeing 797.xlsx
https://catalog.flatworldknowledge.com/a/34711/Example_10_7_Expansion_Boeing_797-21b1.xlsx

The Boeing 797-8 (the Skyliner) can carry 240 passengers at a cruising speed of Mach 0.95. The Skyliner is more comfortable for passengers because it has virus-proof sealed pods instead of seats. The airplane is more attractive to airlines because it uses 20% less fuel. Boeing has secured sales of 600 aircraft over the expected 3-year lifespan of the aircraft (200 aircraft per year starting in one year at $t = 1$). Each plane is priced at $160 million. The cost of building each plane is $140M (cost of goods sold and SG&A). Assume that sales (and costs) occur at the end of each year.

Boeing will build a factory to assemble the plane in Everett, Washington for $7 billion on land it already owns. Executives expect that they will be able to sell the factory and equipment for $5B in 3 years. Boeing expects to need additional inventory of parts equal to 5% of annual sales ($1.6B). Assume that the outlay for the factory and increased inventory occurs immediately (at time $t = 0$). Boeing's tax rate is 32%. Boeing's weighted average cost of capital is 11%.

Calculate the NPV of the project. Should Boeing go ahead with the Skyliner project?

SOLUTION

Spreadsheet Solution

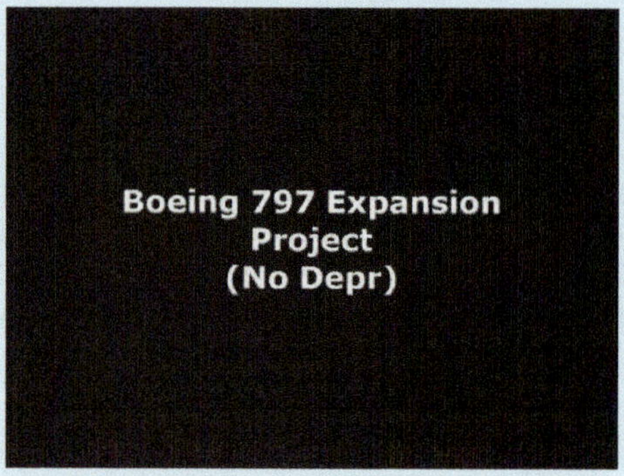

View in the online reader

($000,000s)	Year 0	Year 1	Year 2	Year 3
Revenue		$32,000	$32,000	$32,000
Operating Expenses		28,000	28,000	28,000

($000,000s)	Year 0	Year 1	Year 2	Year 3
Gross Profit (EBITDA)		4,000	4,000	4,000
Taxes		1,280	1,280	2,720
OCF		2,720	2,720	1,280
CAPEX/Salvage	7,000			5,000
Inc/Dec in NWC	1,600			1,600
Free Cash Flow	–8,600	2,720	2,720	9,320

Following Equation 10.6, initial free cash flows are:

$$FCF_0 = \$0 - \$7,000 - \$1,600 = -\$8,600$$

Following Equation 10.8, terminal year cash flows are:

$$FCF_3 = \$2,720 + \$1,600 + \$5,000 = \$9,320$$

The NPV of the project is:

$$NPV = -\$8,600 + \frac{\$2,720}{(1.11)} + \frac{\$2,720}{(1.11)^2} + \frac{\$9,320}{(1.11)^3} = \$2,873$$

Because the NPV is positive, Boeing should go ahead with the Skyliner project.

10.3 Replacement Projects: Basic

To evaluate a replacement decision, we compare two scenarios: (1) keeping the old equipment and (2) replacing it. Specifically, we calculate the free cash flows associated with the replacement scenario and subtract the cash flows that would have been received with the old equipment. The differences are the incremental cash flows associated with the replacement. To assess a replacement decision, we estimate the net present value of the incremental free cash flows. If the NPV is positive, then replacement is optimal. When evaluating replacement projects, we don't actually conduct two valuations: one with the new machine and one with the old machine. Instead, we try to calculate the incremental cash flows directly and compute their NPV.

The conceptually difficult part of calculating incremental cash flows for replacement projects is handling the incremental capital expenditures. As with our treatment of expansion projects, we will assume that the replacement is done immediately (new purchased and old sold) and that the new equipment will be sold at the end of the terminal year. (We will also assume that the old machine would have been sold at the end of terminal year if it had not been replaced.)

Explain It

As we did with expansion projects, we will assume that both projects (old and new) generate operating cash flow at the end of each year up until (and including) the terminal year. Also, we assume that the incremental investment in net working capital for the new (replacement) project occurs at time 0, the same time as the investment in fixed assets (CAPEX) for the new project.

Figure 10.1 shows a stylized timeline of the incremental capital expenditures (and receipts). The first row shows the CAPEX cash flows associated with keeping the old asset. The second row shows the CAPEX cash flows associated with replacing the asset. The bottom row shows the incremental CAPEX cash flows from replacement, that is, the cash flows associated with replacement minus the cash flows associated with keeping the old asset. At time 0 (the date of replacement), the incremental CAPEX cash flows are the proceeds from selling the old asset less the cost of buying the new asset. In the terminal year, we must calculate the salvage value of the new asset less the foregone salvage value of the old asset.

FIGURE 10.1 Incremental CAPEX Cash Flows for Replacement Decision

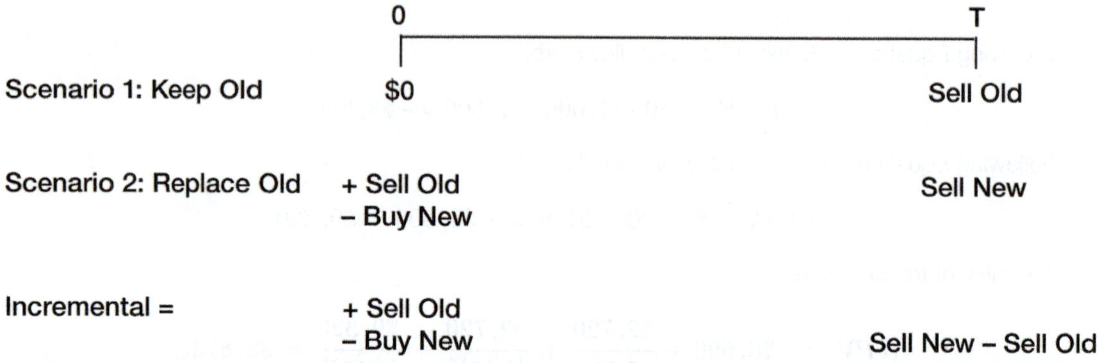

Explain It: Incremental Cash Flows for Replacement Projects

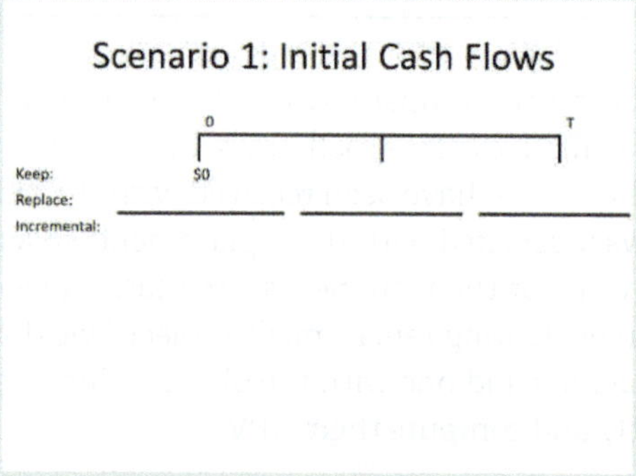

View in the online reader

As we did in Section 2, in this section we will assume that depreciation is not tax deductible and that there are no taxes associated with the sale of an asset. In Section 6 we show how to adjust the cash flows calculated here to account for depreciation tax deductibility and the taxation on salvage.

Initial Investment Cash Flows

The initial cash flows for a replacement project are the same as in Equation 10.6:

$$FCF_0 = 0 - CAPEX - Inc(Dec)\ in\ NWC$$

The difference with replacement projects is that the investment in CAPEX is the incremental CAPEX, which is the cost of the new assets less the proceeds from selling the old asset.

$$Incremental\ CAPEX = Price\ of\ new\ asset - Salvage\ value\ of\ old\ asset$$

If we substitute this expression for CAPEX into Equation 10.6, then we get an expression for initial cash flows for a replacement project:

EQUATION 10.9

$$FCF_0 = -Price_{new} + Salvage_{old} - Inc(Dec)\ in\ NWC$$

where

$$Price_{new} = \text{the price of the new asset on the replacement date}$$
$$Salvage_{old} = \text{the salvage value of the old asset on the replacement date}$$

Example 10.8 Initial Cash Flows for Replacement Project

Suppose Kmart is contemplating upgrading its computers, at a cost of $1.25 million, to allow for increased inventory control systems. Assume the old computer system, which originally cost $500,000, has been in service for 3 years. If the old system can be sold for $200,000 and net working capital decreases by $40,000, what is the initial cash flow?

SOLUTION

The initial cash flows:

Price of New Asset	$1,250,000
Salvage Value of Old Asset	200,000
Increase in NWC	–40,000
Initial Cash	–1,010,000

Using Equation 10.9, the initial cash flows:

$$FCF_0 = -\$1,250,000 + \$200,000 - (-\$40,000) = -\$1,010,000$$

Note that the increase in NWC is negative. The problem states that net working capital decreases by $40,000. We show the decrease as a negative increase. So the reduction in net working capital is added to initial cash flows—just as if the firm had received a check in the mail. By lowering the required net working capital, the firm frees up assets that can be used elsewhere. If the net working capital had increased, we would have subtracted, rather than added, it to the initial cash flow.

Operating Cash Flows

The incremental annual operating cash flows for a replacement project are the difference between the operating cash flows after replacement and the operating cash flows with the old asset. Because we are ignoring depreciation tax deductibility in this section, we can express old operating cash flows as (Equation 10.7):

$$OCF_0 = EBITDA_0 \times (1-T)$$

Similarly, new operating cash flows (after replacement) are given by:

$$OCF_N = EBITDA_N \times (1-T)$$

Incremental operating cash flow (ΔOCF) is the difference between cash flows after the replacement minus the cash flows that would have been generated by the original asset.

$$\Delta OCF = OCF_N - OCF_O$$
$$\Delta OCF = EBITDA_N \times (1-T) - EBITDA_O \times (1-T)$$
$$\Delta OCF = (EBITDA_N - EBITDA_O) \times (1-T)$$

EQUATION 10.10

$$\Delta OCF = \Delta EBITDA \times (1-T) = \Delta EBITA - (T \times \Delta EBITDA)$$

Table 10.1 shows this method for calculating incremental operating cash flows and separates EBITDA into its constituent parts.

TABLE 10.1 Calculation of Operating Cash Flows for Replacement Project

+	(New Sales Revenue–Old Sales Revenue)
–	(New Operating Expenses–Old Operating Expenses)
=	Gross Profit (EBITDA)
–	Incremental Taxes
=	Incremental Operating Cash Flow

Explain It

Operating expenses are cost of goods sold plus selling, general, and administrative (SG&A) expenses.

Example 10.9 Incremental OCF for Replacement Project

Digital Downloads

Example 10.9 Incremental OCF for Replacement Project.xlsx
https://catalog.flatworldknowledge.com/a/34711/ Example_10_9_Incremental_OCF_for_Replacement_Project-bcdf.xlsx

As the manager of a movie theater, you attended a local trade show and were impressed with a new-generation popcorn machine. Despite being smaller than your old model, it pops corn faster. You are analyzing the financial implications of replacing the old popper. The old popper generates revenues of $50,000 per year. It costs $10,000 to operate. The new popper pops faster so popcorn sales revenues will increase to $65,000, and costs will rise to $11,000. Assume a 40% tax rate and compute the incremental operating cash flows for the next 3 years.

SOLUTION

Incremental Operating Cash Flows	Year 1	Year 2	Year 3
(New Sales Revenue–Old Sales Revenue)	$15,000	$15,000	$15,000
(New Operating Expenses–Old Operating Expenses)	1,000	1,000	1,000
Gross Profit (EBITDA)	14,000	14,000	14,000
Less: Taxes	5,600	5,600	5,600
Operating Cash Flow (OCF)	8,400	8,400	8,400

Terminal Cash Flows

Terminal year cash flows for replacement projects are calculated using the same formula as for expansion projects (Equation 10.8) except that we add incremental salvage to the other cash flows. As shown in Figure 10.1, incremental salvage is the sale price of the new asset less the foregone sale price of the old asset. Equation 10.11 amends Equation 10.8 accordingly:

EQUATION 10.11

$$FCF_T = \Delta OCF + Decrease\ in\ NWC + Salvage_{new} - Salvage_{old}$$

where

$$Salvage_{new} = \text{the salvage value of the new asset at the end of the terminal year}$$
$$Salvage_{old} = \text{the salvage value of the old asset at the end of the terminal year}$$

We usually assume that the proceeds from selling the new asset exceed what we might have received from selling the old, so the incremental salvage is positive and adds to terminal year free cash flow.

Example 10.10 Terminal Cash Flow for a Replacement Project

As the manager of a movie theater, you are considering whether to replace your old popcorn popper. The new machine costs $25,000, has a 3-year operating life. It is expected that the new machine can be sold for $10,000 in 3 years. Two years ago, the old machine cost $15,000. Today, the old machine is worth $7,000, and in 3 years it will be worth $2,000. Calculate the terminal year cash flows if you were to buy the replacement machine. Assume that the incremental terminal year operating cash flows are $8,400 and assume there is no change in working capital.

SOLUTION

Incremental Operating Cash Flow	$8,400
Decrease in NWC	0
Salvage of New Asset	10,000
Salvage of Old Asset	2,000
Terminal Cash Flow	16,400

Following Equation 10.11, terminal year cash flows are:

$$FCF_T = \$8,400 + \$0 + \$10,000 - \$2,000 = \$16,400$$

Comprehensive Example of a Replacement Project

Example 10.11 Replacement Project NPV

Because of unexpectedly high demand, Pizzas-by-Mail finds it may need a larger oven. The old oven cost $20,000 when it was purchased and has been in use for 1 year. It can be sold today for $12,000. If the old oven were kept for another 3 years, then it could be sold for $1,000. The new oven, which makes perfect envelope-sized pizzas, costs $36,000. The new oven will be worth $4,000 in 3 years. The larger oven will require an additional inventory of $500 be held. Revenues will increase $20,000 (from $25,000 per year to $45,000 per year), and costs will increase by $3,000. Assume a 40% tax rate and 15% discount rate and compute the NPV. Should Pizza-by-Mail replace the oven?

SOLUTION

Digital Downloads

Example 10_11 Replacement Project NPV.xlsx
https://catalog.flatworldknowledge.com/a/34711/Example_10_11_Replacement_Project_NPV-057f.xlsx

Spreadsheet Solution

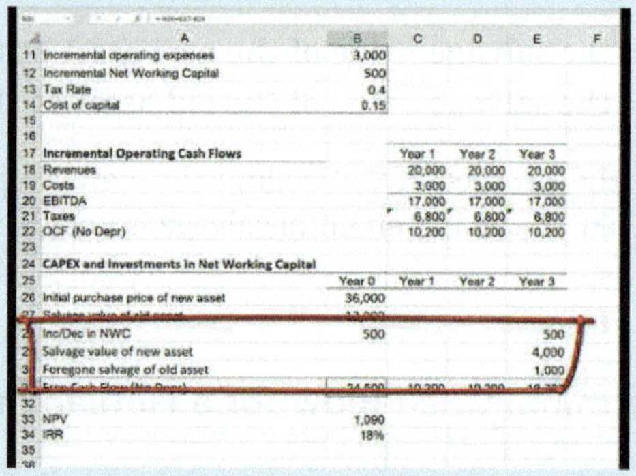

	A	B	C	D	E	F
11	Incremental operating expenses	3,000				
12	Incremental Net Working Capital	500				
13	Tax Rate	0.4				
14	Cost of capital	0.15				
15						
16						
17	**Incremental Operating Cash Flows**		Year 1	Year 2	Year 3	
18	Revenues		20,000	20,000	20,000	
19	Costs		3,000	3,000	3,000	
20	EBITDA		17,000	17,000	17,000	
21	Taxes		6,800	6,800	6,800	
22	OCF (No Depr)		10,200	10,200	10,200	
23						
24	**CAPEX and Investments in Net Working Capital**					
25		Year 0	Year 1	Year 2	Year 3	
26	Initial purchase price of new asset	36,000				
27	[illegible]	[illegible]				
28	Inc/Dec in NWC	500			500	
29	Salvage value of new asset				4,000	
30	Foregone salvage of old asset				1,000	
31	[illegible]	[illegible]	[illegible]	[illegible]	[illegible]	
32						
33	NPV	1,090				
34	IRR	18%				
35						

View in the online reader

Step 1: Initial Investment Cash Flows	
Price of New Asset	$36,000
Salvage Value of Old Asset	12,000
Increase in NWC	500
Initial Cash Flow	–24,500

Using Equation 10.9, the initial cash flows are:

$$FCF_0 = -36,000 + \$12,000 - \$500 = -\$24,500$$

Step 2: Operating Cash Flows	**Year 1**	**Year 2**	**Year 3**
Incremental Operating Cash Flows			
(New Sales–Old Sales)	$20,000	$20,000	$20,000
(New Expenses–Old Expenses)	3,000	3,000	3,000
Gross Profit (EBITDA)	17,000	17,000	17,000
Less: Taxes	6,800	6,800	6,800
Operating Cash Flow (OCF)	10,200	10,200	10,200

Step 3: Terminal Cash Flows	
Incremental Operating Cash Flow	$10,200
Decrease in NWC	500
Salvage of New Asset	4,000
Salvage of Old Asset	1,000
Terminal Cash Flow	13,700

Following Equation 10.11, terminal year cash flows are:

$$FCF = \$10,200 + \$500 + \$4,000 – \$1,000 = \$13,700$$

Step 4: NPV

$$NPV = -\$24,500 + \frac{10,200}{(1.15)} + \frac{10,200}{(1.15)^2} + \frac{13,700}{(1.15)^3}$$

$$NPV = \$1,090$$

Because the NPV is positive, the popcorn machine should be replaced.

10.4 Capital Budget Refinements

We continue our study of capital budgeting by reviewing some specific problems that often arise in the process. These include:

- Estimating cash flows
- Adjusting the analysis to compare projects with very different lives
- Using sensitivity analysis to test the stability of our analysis

Incremental Cash Flows

There are some rules you should always follow when estimating cash flows:

indirect costs

A cost to a business that is not directly related to making the product or service. For example, insurance is an indirect cost. It is a necessary expense, but it doesn't affect the per unit cost of production.

1. Include **indirect costs**.

Explain It: Indirect Costs

View in the online reader

sunk costs

Irreversible past costs.

2. Disregard **sunk costs**.

Explain It: Sunk Costs

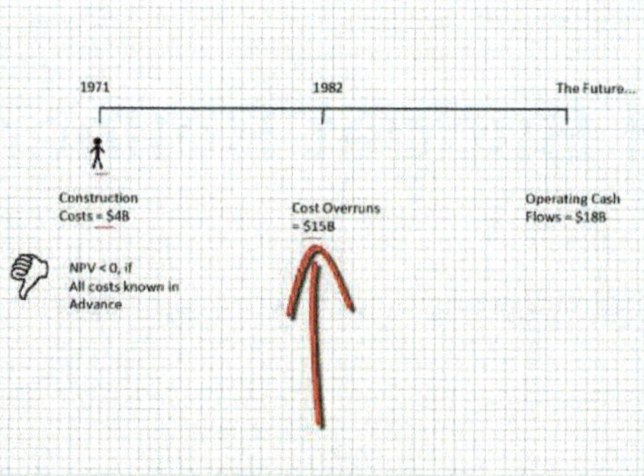

View in the online reader

opportunity costs

The full cost of a choice. It is the value of the best forsaken alternative.

3. Include **opportunity costs**.

Explain It: Opportunity Costs

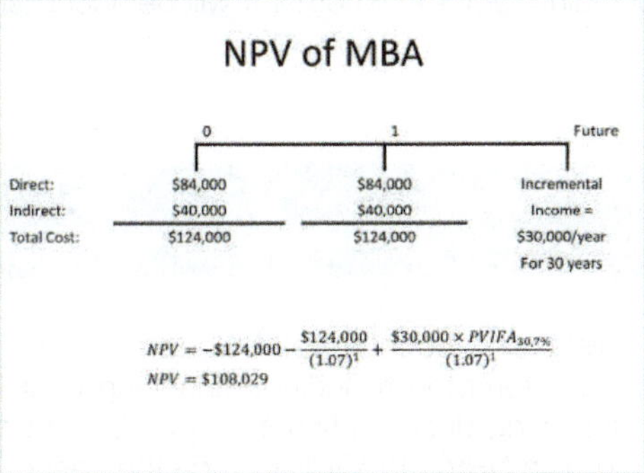

View in the online reader

4. Consider **externalities**.

externalities

A cost (or benefit) that accrues to a third person who is not a direct party to a transaction. A side effect.

Explain It: Externalities

View in the online reader

5. Adjust for taxes.

Explain It

As we develop the equations for computing cash flows, you will see that taxes add complexity to the calculations. It may be tempting to ignore the tax impact of a proposed project. However, the total of state, local, and federal taxes often exceeds 40% for corporations. The tax effect of a project can clearly be a deciding factor in whether it will be accepted.

6. Ignore financing costs.

Explain It

One of the most common mistakes students make when estimating cash flows is to include interest cost. You would be less tempted to include financing cost if a project were financed with retained earnings. The financing decision (whether to use debt or equity) is separate from the capital budgeting decision. The NPV and MIRR include the cost of funds by using a discount rate that reflects the required return. If we were to include interest expense in the cash flow estimate, we would be, in essence, double charging the project for financing.

Projects with Different Lives

Suppose you are evaluating two projects. One will be completed in 3 years, and the other will not be completed for 10 years. Is it still reasonable to choose the one with the greatest NPV? The longer-term project may have the largest NPV because it consumes company resources for a long time. It may be that a series of shorter-term projects would have a larger total NPV than one long-term project.

There are two methods for comparing projects with different lives. They both assume that, when the short-term project concludes, another similar project will be available. If this assumption is not realistic for your firm, these methods will not yield realistic results.

Replacement Chain Approach

replacement chain approach

An approach to comparing and choosing between two projects with unequal lives. Involves repeating each project until a common length is achieved and then comparing the net present values of the two streams of cash flows.

The **replacement chain approach** requires the analyst to string together as many short-term projects as necessary to equal the life of the long-term project. For example, if you are comparing a 5-year project with a 10-year project, the short project is doubled so that it will take the same amount of time as the long one. The net present values are then computed and compared in the usual way.

Example 10.12 Replacement Chain Approach

Digital Downloads

Example 10_12 Replacement Chain Approach.xlsx

https://catalog.flatworldknowledge.com/a/34711/
Example_10_12_Replacement_Chain_Approach-090f.xlsx

Disney built Epcot Center in Florida partly to display the world as it may be in the future. After it had been open for a number of years, an editorialist noted that one supposedly futuristic scene contained a rotary-dial telephone. Disney closed Epcot to remodel and update the displays. Disney's advisors presented two renovation alternatives: (1) a quick facelift or (2) a complete rebuild. The quick facelift would cost $10 million, would generate annual cash flows of $3.75 million per year on completion, and would last only 5 years until another facelift was needed. The complete rebuild would cost $17 million, would also generate annual cash flows of $3.75 million per year on completion, and would last 10 years until another renovation was needed. Which option should Disney choose? Assume a cost of capital of 12%.

SOLUTION

Algebraic Solution

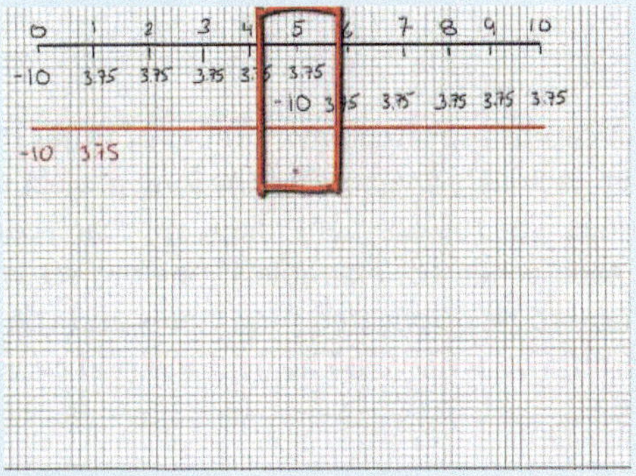

View in the online reader

Spreadsheet Solution

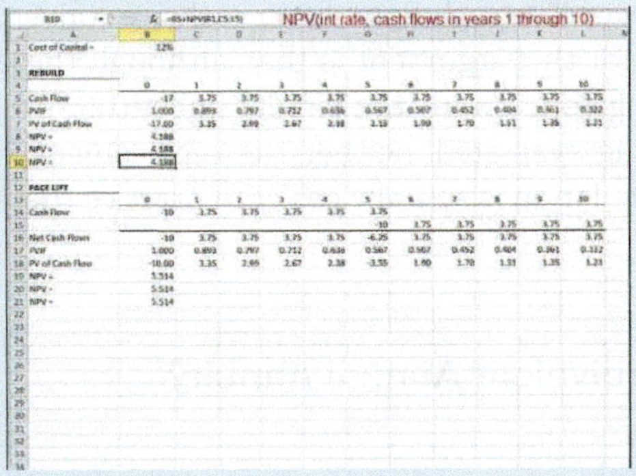

B10 | =B5+NPV(B1,C5:L5) | NPV(int rate, cash flows in years 1 through 10)

	A	B	C	D	E	F	G	H	I	J	K	L
1	Cost of Capital =	12%										
2												
3	**REBUILD**											
4		0	1	2	3	4	5	6	7	8	9	10
5	Cash Flow	-17	3.75	3.75	3.75	3.75	3.75	3.75	3.75	3.75	3.75	3.75
6	PVIF	1.000	0.893	0.797	0.712	0.636	0.567	0.507	0.452	0.404	0.361	0.322
7	PV of Cash Flow	-17.00	3.35	2.99	2.67	2.38	2.13	1.90	1.70	1.51	1.35	1.21
8	NPV =	4.188										
9	NPV =	4.188										
10	NPV =	4.188										
11												
12	**FACE LIFT**											
13		0	1	2	3	4	5	6	7	8	9	10
14	Cash Flow	-10	3.75	3.75	3.75	3.75	3.75					
15							-10	3.75	3.75	3.75	3.75	3.75
16	Net Cash Flows	-10	3.75	3.75	3.75	3.75	-6.25	3.75	3.75	3.75	3.75	3.75
17	PVIF	1.000	0.893	0.797	0.712	0.636	0.567	0.507	0.452	0.404	0.361	0.322
18	PV of Cash Flow	-10.00	3.35	2.99	2.67	2.38	-3.55	1.90	1.70	1.51	1.35	1.21
19	NPV =	5.514										
20	NPV =	5.514										
21	NPV =	5.514										

View in the online reader

Begin by computing the NPV for each option, ignoring the difference in lives:

$$NPV_{facelift} = \$3.750M \times PVIFA_{5,12\%} - \$10M$$

$$NPV_{\text{facelift}} = \$3.750\text{M} \times 3.604778 - \$10 = \$3.518\text{M}$$

$$NPV_{\text{rebuild}} = \$3.750\text{M} \times \text{PVIFA}_{10,12\%} - \$17\text{M}$$

$$NPV_{\text{rebuild}} = \$3.750\text{M} \times 5.650223 - \$17\text{M} = \$4.188\text{M}$$

Because the NPV of the rebuild is greater than that of the short-term facelift, we may be tempted to conclude that the long-term rebuild should be accepted. Let us continue the analysis, however, by assuming that, after 5 years, the facelift is repeated. The extended project is shown on the following timeline:

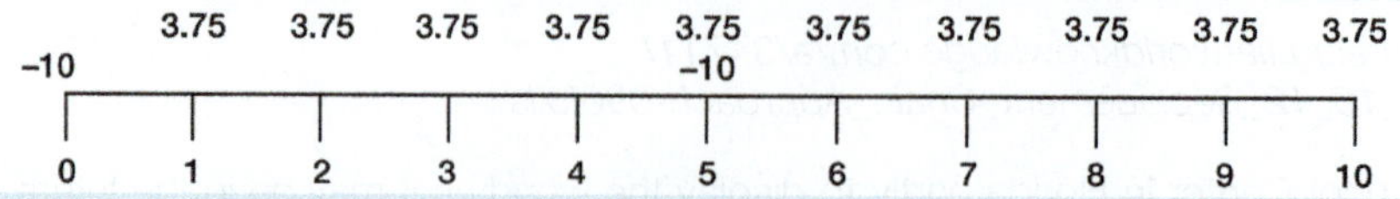

After 5 years, an additional \$10 million must be invested to continue the cash inflows. We now compute the NPV of this extended project:

$$NPV_{\text{facelift}} = \$3.750\text{M} \times \text{PVIFA}_{10,12\%} - \$10\text{M} \times 1/(1.12)^5 - \$10\text{M}$$

$$NPV_{\text{facelift}} = \$3.750\text{M} \times 5.650223 - \$10\text{M} \times 0.56743 - \$10\text{M} = \$5.514\text{M}$$

The NPV of the shorter-term facelift, if repeated twice, is greater than the NPV of the longer-term rebuild done once. In this example, because Disney is assured of being able to redo the facelift at the end of the first 5 years, it should choose the short option.

Data from www.lostepcot.com/land.html.

The short-term project can be repeated any number of times to equal the length of the longer-term project. If the short project lasts 6 years and the long project lasts 18 years, then the short one could be repeated three times. The replacement chain approach can become tedious if the projects are not even multiples of each other. For example, if one project is 4 years and another is 18 years, the short project would have to be duplicated nine times and the longer project duplicated twice before a common length would be achieved. The next method avoids this problem.

Equivalent Annual Annuity Method

equivalent annual annuity (EAA)

Essentially the net present value per year. It is an annual dollar amount (for each year of a project's life) that has a present value equal to the project's net present value.

The **equivalent annual annuity (EAA)** approach assumes both the short-term and long-term projects can be repeated forever. The cash flows from each are converted into annuities, which can be compared. The rationale for this argument is that, although these particular projects will not be repeated, a firm is a going concern in that similar substitute projects will be available. Again, if unusual projects are being evaluated, neither the replacement chain nor the EAA approach is appropriate. The EAA calculation is actually easier in practice than it sounds and is best explained with an example.

Example 10.13 Equivalent Annual Annuity

Digital Downloads

Example 10_13 Equivalent Annual Annuity.xls
https://catalog.flatworldknowledge.com/a/34711/Example_10_13_Equivalent_Annual_Annuity-e7be.xls

Disney is renovating Epcot Center and advisors have presented two renovation alternatives: (1) a quick facelift or (2) a complete rebuild. The quick facelift would cost \$10 million, would generate annual cash flows of \$3.75 million per year on completion, and would last only 5 years until another facelift was needed. The complete rebuild would cost \$17 million, would also generate annual cash flows of \$3.75 million per year on completion, and would last 10 years until another renovation was needed. Which option should Disney choose? Assume a cost of capital of 12%. Compute the equal annual annuity (EAA) for each project.

SOLUTION

Algebraic Solution

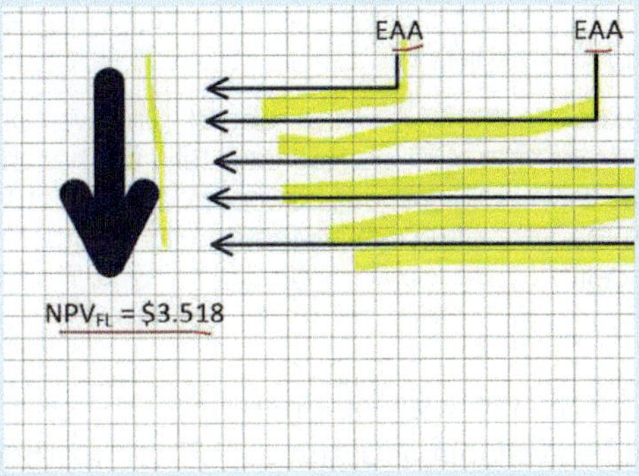

View in the online reader

Spreadsheet Solution

	A	B	C	D
1	Equivalent Annual Annuity			
2	Walt Disney and Epcot Center			
3				
4				
5		Face Lift	Rebuild	
6	NPV =	$3.518	$4.188	
7	Project Life =	5	10	
8	Cost of Capital =	12%	12%	
9	PVIF =	0.57	0.32	
10	PVIFA =	3.60	5.65	
11	EAA =	$0.976	$0.741	
12				
13				
14				

View in the online reader

Step 1: Compute the NPV for each project.

In "Example 10.11 Replacement Project NPV", we found $NPV_{rebuild}$ to be $4.188 million and $NPV_{facelift}$ to be $3.518M.

Step 2: Find the annuity payments that have the same present value as the NPV and the same number of periods as the project.

The rebuild has a life of 10 years and an NPV of $4.188M. We treat the NPV as if it is the present value of a 10-year annuity and solve for the annuity payments (recall that the cost of capital is 12%):

$$\$4.188\text{M} = PMT \times PVIFA_{10,12\%}$$
$$\$4.188\text{M} = PMT \times 5.650223$$
$$PMT = \$4.188\text{M}/5.650223 = \$0.7413\text{M}$$

The EAA for the rebuild is $0.7413M.

Review for a moment how this result is interpreted. An NPV of $4.188M is the same as having a 10-period annuity of $0.7413M, if the discount rate is 12%. We often convert annuities into present values. What we have done here is convert a present value back into an annuity.

Repeat this step for the facelift:

$$\$3.518M = PMT \times PVIFA_{5,12\%}$$
$$\$3.518\text{M} = PMT \times 3.60477$$
$$PMT = \$3.518\text{M}/3.60477 = \$0.9759\text{M}$$

The EAA for the facelift is \$0.9759M.

The EAA of the facelift exceeds the EAA of the rebuild. One way of thinking about EAA is to think of it as (roughly) the NPV per year. Our comparison tells us that the facelift generates more NPV per year than the rebuild. If we could repeat both projects perpetually, then the NPV of repeating the facelift is higher than the NPV of repeating the rebuild. In other words, firm value is maximized if Disney chooses the facelift.

Be aware of several problems with attempting to correct for unequal lives. First, similar replacement jobs may not be available, as assumed by both methods. Second, because of inflation, subsequent costs may be higher than initially projected. Third, all of the errors we have discussed with estimating cash flows are compounded when we assume the cash flows will repeat. Despite these problems, it is often better to correct for unequal lives than to ignore the issue entirely.

Sensitivity Analysis

Project ideas may originate from anywhere within a firm. Once identified, many different individuals may participate in the evaluation exercise. Marketing will estimate sales and pricing. Production will estimate the cost of producing the new product. Accounting may provide historic numbers to help with these estimates. Finally, the financial manager gets the opportunity to evaluate the numbers. The financial manager often knows that many of the estimates are merely educated guesses. This does not imply incompetence, only that it can be extremely difficult to make estimates about costs and revenues for a product or activity that has never been attempted.

sensitivity analysis

A series of analyses that reflect the effects of different assumptions.

In the early 1980s, IBM introduced a small, inexpensive home computer, called the PC Junior, to compete against the wildly popular Apple. The PC Junior was a resounding failure largely because of small keyboard keys, which prevented real typing. Likewise, for Christmas in 1996, the Tickle Me Elmo doll was the hottest toy on the market. Tyco underestimated demand, and there was a shortage. Parents fought each other in toy aisles and bid up to \$1,500 for a \$29 toy. How can the financial manager incorporate uncertainty into NPV estimates? One way is to produce a series of analyses that reflect the effects of different assumptions. This approach, called **sensitivity analysis**, tells the analyst how sensitive the results are to changes in the estimates. If a very small change in the sales projection makes a large difference in the NPV, then the estimates may require additional review.

The ability to play what-if games with the cash flow estimates is one reason capital budgeting should be done using spreadsheets. By changing any of the inputs, new NPVs can be easily computed. The following steps help produce the data needed to make difficult capital budgeting decisions:

1. Prepare a complete cash flow estimation schedule using a spreadsheet.
2. Compute the NPV of the cash flows.
3. Vary each of the uncertain estimates over its reasonable range and record the resulting NPV from each change in a table.
4. Graph the results of Step 3.
5. **Scenario analysis**. Prepare additional evaluations by changing more than one input. For example, evaluate the effect on NPV if sales are below projections and costs are above projections.

After many such iterations, the analyst will garner a clearer view of the project and will better understand the risk involved.

For example, look at Figure 10.2. A spreadsheet analysis of two projects was prepared. The level of sales was allowed to vary between 100 and 800. The NPV of each project was computed for each level of sales, and the results were graphed. Both projects have positive NPVs when sales are estimated at 450 units. However, Project 2 is much more sensitive to the sales estimate. A small error estimating sales has a much larger effect on its NPV than on Project 1's NPV. If sales turn out to be 350 units, Project 1 still has a positive NPV, but Project 2 will have a negative NPV.

scenario analysis

Scenario analysis is similar to sensitivity analysis. With scenario analysis, a group of assumptions are changed simultaneously to determine the impact on a project's profitability. The assumptions are connected by a theme. Typical scenarios include a boom case (everything goes right for the project) and a bust case (everything goes wrong for the project).

FIGURE 10.2 Sensitivity Analysis

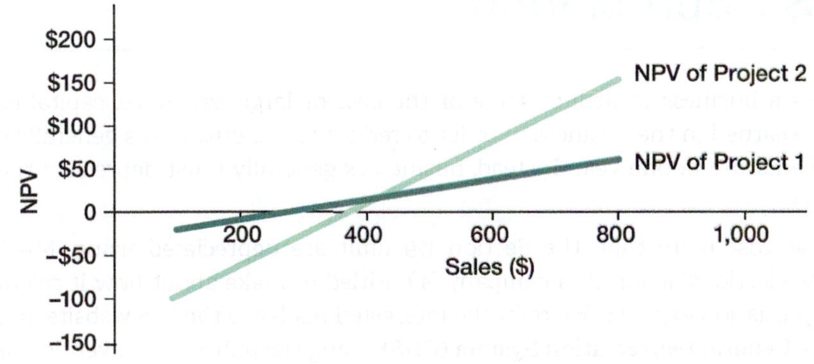

Sales is only one of many variables that can be evaluated when performing sensitivity analysis. You can also look at how cost estimates, sales growth rates, or interest rates affect the NPV of projects. Sensitivity analysis is an essential and critical part of the capital budgeting process.

10.5 Appendix 1: Expansion Projects Using MACRS

In this section we present a more complete analysis of expansion projects. In particular, we include depreciation tax deductibility and the taxation of salvage in the project cash flows. This analysis would apply to any project that does not qualify for Section 179 treatment, which includes projects requiring investments over one million dollars.

Incorporating the tax deductibility of depreciation and taxes on salvage does not require us to re-compute all of the project cash flows. Both the tax shields and the taxes on salvage add to (or subtract from) the cash flows computed in Section 3. Thus, we can calculate them separately, add them to the cash flows from Section 3, and then discount the result to compute the NPV of the project.

For example, consider the tax shields. As shown in Section 1, operating cash flows can be expressed as (Equation 10.4):

$$OCF = EBITDA \times (1-T) + (T \times Depr)$$

depreciation tax shield

The amount by which taxes are reduced due to depreciation tax deductibility. Equal to the product of the depreciation expense and the tax rate.

Modified Accelerated Cost Recovery System (MACRS)

The Modified Accelerated Cost Recovery System is the system used by the Internal Revenue Service to calculate depreciation expenses for income tax purposes.

The second term is the **depreciation tax shield**. The depreciation tax shield is equal to the product of the tax rate and the depreciation expense. It is the amount by which taxes are lowered as a result of depreciation tax deductibility. In Section 3, we assumed that depreciation was not tax deductible so we ignored the second term. In this section we show how to calculate depreciation expenses under the MACRS system so we can compute the tax shields in each year. Since the tax shields are added to the first term in Equation 10.4, we can add them to the operating cash flows computed in Section 3 to get an estimate of operating cash flows that incorporate depreciation tax deductibility.

This section is organized as follows. The first sub-section explains the depreciation system used by the IRS, the **Modified Accelerated Cost Recovery System (MACRS)**. The second section shows how to calculate the tax shields with MACRS depreciation. The third section explains taxation of the proceeds from salvage. The fourth section shows how to adjust terminal cash flows to incorporate tax on salvage and the fifth section presents a comprehensive example.

MACRS Depreciation

The IRS allows a business to deduct some of the cost of large assets (i.e. capital expenditures) against income earned in the business in order to reduce taxes. Businesses generally can't deduct the entire expenditure in one year. Instead, businesses generally must depreciate the cost of the assets over time.

General Depreciation System (GDS)

The General Depreciation System (GDS) is one of two depreciation systems under MACRS. The other is the Alternative Depreciation System (ADS). The two systems have different depreciation methods and recovery periods. You generally must use GDS unless you are specifically required by law to use ADS or you elect to use ADS.

Assets that cost more than the Section 179 limit are depreciated using MACRS. MACRS involves many "elections" (choices) a company is entitled to make about how it calculates its tax-deductible depreciation expense. We refer the interested reader to the IRS website. In this chapter, we assume the **General Depreciation System (GDS)**, using the half-year convention and the 200% declining balance method. This will give you a general sense for the MACRS system. Within the GDS system, assets are allocated to "property classes." Each property class has a different recovery period. The recovery period is the time over which the asset is depreciated to zero. Table 10.2 gives some examples of various property classes.

TABLE 10.2 MACRS Asset Classes

Type of Asset	Life
Manufacturing Tools	3-year
Cars, Light Trucks, Computers	5-year
Industrial Equipment, Office Furniture	7-year
Heavy-Duty Types of Equipment	10-year
Residential Rental Property	27.5-year
Nonresidential Real Property	39-year

Each asset class has a set of annual depreciation rates for each year of an asset's life (see the Explain It for an example of those rates).

Explain It

MACRS Percentage Table

GDS, 200% Declining Balance, Half-Year Convention

Recovery Period	3-Year	5-Year	7-Year	10-Year	15-Year
1	33.33%	20.00%	14.29%	10.00%	5.00%
2	44.45	32.00	24.49	18.00	9.50
3	14.81	19.20	17.49	14.40	8.55
4	7.41	11.52	12.49	11.52	7.70
5		11.52	8.93	9.22	6.93
6		5.76	8.92	7.37	6.23
7			8.93	6.55	5.90
8			4.46	6.55	5.90
9				6.56	5.91
10				6.55	5.90
11				3.28	5.91
12					5.90
13					5.91
14					5.90
15					5.91
16					2.95

Note that the recovery period is actually depreciated over $n+1$ years. This is because we employed the half-year placed-in-service convention. The first-year depreciation is for 6 months. That leaves 6 more months to be depreciated during the final year.

Depreciation Expense

The annual depreciation expense for an asset is simply the product of these rates and the **basis** of the asset. The basis is the original cost of the asset plus any other costs associated with installing the asset (which we denote C_0).

basis

The original cost of an asset.

Example 10.14 MACRS Depreciation

Digital Downloads

Example 10.14 MACRS Depreciation Expense.xlsx
https://catalog.flatworldknowledge.com/a/34711/Example_10_14_MACRS_Depreciation_Expense-a172.xlsx

Calculate the depreciation expense in the first and second years for $300,000 of office furniture in class 7. The depreciation rates (for 7-year property) in the first two years are 14.29% and 24.49%.

SOLUTION

The original cost of the asset is $C_0 = \$300,000$.

Year	Depreciation Rate	Depreciation Expense
1	0.1429	$\$300,000 \times 0.1429 = \$42,870$
2	0.2449	$\$300,000 \times 0.2449 = \$73,470$

Book Value

book value

The original cost of an asset minus its accumulated depreciation. Also known as the adjusted basis.

adjusted basis

The original cost of an asset minus its accumulated depreciation. Also known as the book value.

accumulated depreciation

The sum of all depreciation expenses claimed for an asset.

The **book value** (**adjusted basis**) of an asset is the undepreciated or leftover value of the asset. The book value at date t, B_t is equal to:

EQUATION 10.12

$$B_t = C_0 - ADepr_t$$

where

$$C_0 = \text{the original cost of the asset (basis)}$$
$$ADepr_t = \text{accumulated depreciation at date } t$$

Example 10.15 Book Value

Digital Downloads

Example 10.15 Book Value.xlsx
https://catalog.flatworldknowledge.com/a/34711/Example_10_15_Book_Value-8181.xlsx

Determine the book value after 2 years for $300,000 of office furniture in class 7. The depreciation rates (for 7-year property) in the first two years are 14.29% and 24.49%.

SOLUTION

First, we calculate the depreciation expenses in each year as we did in the previous example.

Year	Depreciation Rate	Depreciation Expense
1	0.1429	$\$300,000 \times 0.1429 = \$42,870$
2	0.2449	$\$300,00 \times 0.2449 = \$73,470$

The book value at the end of the second year is:

$$B_2 = C_0 - ADepr_2$$

Accumulated depreciation at the end of year 2 is the sum of the first two depreciations' expenses:

$$ADepr_2 = \$42,870 + \$73,470 = \$116,340$$

Thus, book value is:

$$B_2 = \$300,000 - \$116,340 = \$183,660$$

Tax Shields Under MACRS

Now that we know how to calculate depreciation expenses under the MACRS system, we can compute the **tax shields**. The next example shows how.

tax shields

The amount by which taxes are reduced due to a tax-deductible expense. Used for both interest and depreciation deductibility

Example 10.16 Tax Shields Under MACRS

Digital Downloads

Example 10.16 Tax Shields under MACRS Logans.xlsx
https://catalog.flatworldknowledge.com/a/34711/Example_10_16_Tax_Shields_under_MACRS_Logans-d94b.xlsx

A new Logan's restaurant costs $1 million to build and equip. Assume that the assets are classified as 15-year property with MACRS depreciation rates of 5% and 9.5% in the first two years. Assume a tax rate of 40% and a cost of capital of 11%. What are the tax shields in each of the two years of operations?

SOLUTION

Depreciation Schedule	Year 1	Year 2
Basis	$1,000,000	$1,000,000
MACRS Rates	0.05	0.0950
Depr	50,000	85,500
Tax Shield = (T × Depr)	20,000	34,200

Following Equation 10.4, the tax shields would be added to the FCF calculated without depreciation tax deductibility.

The final step, which we tackle in the next section, is to calculate the taxes associated with salvaging the assets in the terminal year.

Tax Impact of Salvage

When an asset is sold, the proceeds from the sale are a positive cash flow. The sale price of an asset is called the **salvage value** of the asset (denoted *S*). The proceeds from selling an asset are not taxable. The corporate tax system taxes income from the ongoing business of the company, not the proceeds from the sale of the company's assets.

salvage value

The resale value of an asset at the end of a project. Also called scrap value.

If an asset is sold for more than its purchase price, then the difference is a taxable capital gain. This situation is rare, and we do not consider it further.

When an asset is sold for less than its purchase price, there is a tax adjustment at the end of the year that depends on the relative sizes of the salvage value and the book value.

Recaptured Depreciation

recaptured depreciation

Depreciation recapture is assessed when the book value of an asset is smaller than the salvage value. The difference between these figures is added to taxable income, which raises taxes owing in the terminal year. Thus the excessive tax shields are "recaptured" by the tax authorities.

The situation in which the salvage value exceeds the book value is called **recaptured depreciation**. The salvage value exceeds the book value when the asset did not depreciate (economically) as much as the MACRS system allowed. As a result, the company has had too many depreciation tax shields, and it must pay extra tax to compensate. In a sense, the government is recapturing the excessive depreciation expenses it offered the business.

In a recaptured depreciation situation, the company adds the difference between the salvage value and the book value $(S-B)$ to its taxable income in the year in which the asset is sold. The additional taxes resulting from the sale are given by:

EQUATION 10.13

$$Tax\ on\ Sale = T \times (S-B)$$

This is a positive number (since $S > B$), and it is subtracted from the gross salvage value, so it reduces cash flows in the terminal year of the project.

Ordinary Loss

ordinary loss

An ordinary loss occurs when the book value of an asset is greater than the salvage value. The difference between these figures is deducted from taxable income. This reduces taxes owing in the terminal year.

Ordinary loss is the situation in which the salvage value is less than the book value of the asset. In this case, the asset has depreciated (economically) by more than the MACRS system allowed. The company has not had sufficient depreciation expenses, and it has paid too much tax. The company can deduct the difference from taxable income, which reduces taxes owing and so acts as a tax rebate. The amount of the tax rebate is:

$$Tax\ on\ sale = T \times (S-B)$$

This is a negative number (since $S < B$) and should be interpreted as a refund.

Tip

Notice that the tax on sale term is the same in both cases (recapture versus ordinary loss), so you don't need to memorize two formulas.

Net Salvage

net salvage

The salvage value of the asset minus the taxes paid on the sale of the asset.

We define **net salvage** as:

EQUATION 10.14

$$Net\ salvage = S - Tax\ on\ sale$$

In the case of recaptured depreciation, net salvage is equal to the proceeds received from selling the asset minus the taxes paid on the sale of the asset. In cases of an ordinary loss, net salvage will be greater than the proceeds from the sale of the asset. Net salvage is greater because we subtract the tax on sale from the salvage value, but the tax on sale number is negative under ordinary loss. Subtracting a negative number is the same as adding.

Tax on Salvage and Terminal Cash Flows

Now that we understand how the IRS taxes the proceeds from salvage, we have to incorporate those taxes into our calculation of terminal cash flows.

Recall that our calculation of free cash flows in Section 3 already includes salvage, *S*. So, to incorporate the tax impact of salvage separately, all we need to do is subtract the *tax on sale*. We do that in the next example.

Example 10.17 Tax on Sale

Digital Downloads

Example 10.17 Tax on Sale (and NPV for Logans).xlsx
https://catalog.flatworldknowledge.com/a/34711/Example_10_17_Tax_on_Sale_and_NPV_for_Logans_-d35a.xlsx

A new Logan's restaurant costs $1 million to build and equip. Assume that the assets are classified as 15-year property with MACRS depreciation rates of 5% and 9.5% in the first two years. Suppose the company plans to sell the restaurant to the manager after 2 years for $800,000. What is the tax on sale? Assume a tax rate of 40% and a cost of capital of 11%.

SOLUTION

After 2 years, accumulated depreciation is $135,500 (see the calculation in the spreadsheet).

The book value is:

$$B = C_0 - ADepr$$
$$B_2 = \$1,000,000 - \$135,500 = \$865,000$$

The tax on the sale is:

$$Tax\ on\ sale = (S - B) \times T$$
$$Tax\ on\ sale = (\$800,000 - \$865,000) \times 0.4 = -\$25,800$$

The negative sign indicates this is a negative tax—an inflow from the IRS. Logan's will receive a tax refund in the terminal year because the sale price was much smaller than the book value of the restaurant. This is known as an ordinary loss situation. This negative number is subtracted from terminal cash flows and so it increases free cash flow in the terminal year and thus increases the NPV of the project.

Now that we know the tax on sale we are in a position to compute the NPV of the Logan's Restaurant project. We start with the cash flows computed in Section 3, which ignored depreciation deductibility and tax on salvage. Those cash flows were computed in Examples 10.4–10.6 and are labelled "Free Cash Flow (No Depr.)" in the table below. Then we add the tax shields, subtract the tax on sale, and discount the resulting free cash flows.

TABLE 10.3 Free Cash Flow Logan's Restaurant ($000s)

	Year 0	Year 1	Year 3
FCF (No Depr.)	$-1,100,000	$480,000	$1,380,000
Tax Shields		20,000	34,200
Tax on Sale			–25,800
Free Cash Flow	–1,100,000	500,000	1,440,000

The terminal year cash flows are given by:

EQUATION 10.15

$$FCF_T = FCF(No\ Depr)_T + (T \times Depr) - Tax\ on\ Sale$$

For Logan's restaurant that is:

$$FCF_T + \$1,380,000 + \$34,200 - (-25,800) = \$1,440,000$$

The NPV of the project is the present value of the free cash flows discounted at the company's cost of capital (11%):

$$NPV = -\$1,100,000 + \frac{\$500,000}{(1.11)} + \frac{\$1,440,000}{(1.11)^2} = \$519,187$$

Comprehensive Example of an Expansion Project

Example 10.18 Expansion Project NPV

Digital Downloads

Example 10.18 Expansion Project NPV w Depr.xlsx
https://catalog.flatworldknowledge.com/a/34711/Example_10_18_Expansion_Project_NPV_w_Depr-3396.xlsx

The Boeing 797-8 (the Skyliner) can carry 240 passengers at a cruising speed of Mach 0.95. The Skyliner is more comfortable for passengers because it has sealed pods instead of seats. The airplane is more attractive to airlines because it uses 20% less fuel. Boeing has secured sales of 600 aircraft over the expected 3-year lifespan of the aircraft (200 aircraft per year starting in one year at $t = 1$). Each plane is priced at $160 million. The cost of building each plane is $140 million (Cost of Goods Sold and SG&A). Assume that sales (and costs) occur at the end of each year.

Boeing will build a factory to assemble the plane in Everett, Washington for $7 billion on land it already owns. Executives expect that they will be able to sell the factory and equipment for $5 billion in 3 years. Boeing expects to need additional inventory of parts equal to 5% of annual sales ($1.6B). Assume that the outlay for the factory and increased inventory occurs immediately (at time $t = 0$) and that the plant is categorized as 15-year property (with depreciation rates of 5%, 9.5% and 8,6% in the first three years). Boeing's tax rate is 32%. Boeing's weighted average cost of capital is 11%.

Calculate the NPV of the project. Should Boeing go ahead with the Skyliner project?

SOLUTION

Spreadsheet Solution

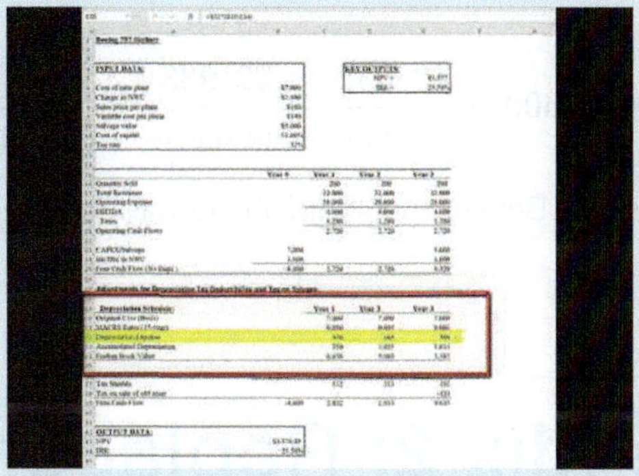

View in the online reader

In "Example 10.7 Expansion Project NPV", we compute the free cash flows under the assumption of no depreciation tax deductibility and no tax on salvage. To complete the calculation of NPV, we simply add the tax shields and subtract the tax on sale to the cash flows from Example 10.7 and then discount at the cost of capital.

Step 1: Cash Flows Ignoring Depreciation and Tax on Salvage

	Year 0	Year 1	Year 2	Year 3
FCF (No Depr)	−8,600	2,720	2,720	9,320

Step 2: Add Tax Sheilds

Depreciation Schedule	Year 1	Year 2	Year 3
Original Cost (Basis)	$ 7,000	$ 7,000	$ 7,000
MACRS Rates (15-year)	0.050	0.095	0.086
Depreciation Expense	350	665	599
Accumulated Depreciation	350	1,015	1,614
Ending Book Value	6,650	5,985	5,387
Tax Shields	112	213	192

Step 3: Subtract Tax on Sale

The tax on the sale is (in millions of dollars):

$$Tax\ on\ sale = (S - B) \times T$$

$$Tax\ on\ sale = (\$5,000 - \$5,387) \times 0.32 = -\$123.68$$

Step 4: Free Cash Flow

	Year 0	Year 1	Year 2	Year 3
FCF (No Depr)	−8,600	2,720	2,720	9.320
Tax Shields		112	213	192
Tax on Sale				124
Free Cash Flow	−8,600	2,832	2,933	9,635

Following Equation 10.15, the terminal year cash flows are:

$$FCF_T = \$9,320 + \$192 - (-\$124) = \$9,635$$

Step 5: Net Present Value (NPV)

The NPV of the project is:

$$NPV = -\$8,600 + \frac{\$2,832}{(1.11)} + \frac{\$2,933}{(1.11)^2} + \frac{\$9,635}{(1.11)^3} = \$3,377M$$

Because the NPV is positive, Boeing should go ahead with the Skyliner project.

10.6 Appendix 2: Replacement Projects Using MACRS

In Section 3 we showed how to calculate incremental cash flows for replacement projects under the simplifying assumptions that depreciation is not tax deductible and that there are no taxes associated with the sale of an asset. In this section, we show how to adjust the section 3 cash flows to incorporate the incremental depreciation tax shields and the tax on salvage. The first sub-section shows how to calculate incremental tax shields. The second subsection shows how to adjust initial and terminal cash flows to include tax on the sale of assets. The third subsection presents a comprehensive example.

Incremental Tax Shields for Replacement Projects

The incremental operating cash flows (ΔOCF) are the difference between cash flows after the replacement minus the cash flows that would have been generated by the original asset.

$$\Delta OCF = OCF_N - OCF_0$$

Substituting in Equation 10.4 for OCF yields:

$$\Delta OCF = EBITDA_N \times (1 - T) + T \times Depr_N - EBITDA_0 \times (1 - T) + T \times Depr_0$$

EQUATION 10.16

$$\Delta OCF = \Delta EBITDA \times (1 - T) + T \times \Delta Depr$$

where

$$\Delta EBITDA = EBITDA_N - EBITDA_0$$
$$\Delta Depr = Depr_N - Depr_0$$

In Section 3 we only calculated the first term in Equation 10.16—we ignored the second term. To include the impact of depreciation deductibility we will estimate the second term, the change in the tax shields, and add it to the incremental operating cash flows calculated in section 3.

Tip

Many students are confused by the calculation of incremental depreciation. It may seem reasonable that, because the old machine was sold, there should not be any depreciation on it. Stay focused on the idea that we are computing changes resulting from replacing the machine. One of the changes is in the depreciation amount. If the new machine had not been purchased, the old depreciation amount would have continued.

Example 10.19 Incremental Tax Shields

Digital Downloads

Example 10_19 Incremental Tax Shields.xlsx
https://catalog.flatworldknowledge.com/a/34711/Example_10_19_Incremental_Tax_Shields-b28c.xlsx

As the manager of a movie theater, you are considering whether to replace your popcorn popper. Two years ago, the old machine cost $15,000. The new machine costs $25,000 and will also depreciate over 3 years. Both machines are classified as 3-year property with MACRS rates of 33.33%, 44.45%, 14.81%, and 7.41%. Assume a 40% tax rate. What are incremental depreciation tax shields associated with replacing the old popping machine?

SOLUTION

The depreciation calculations require you to compute the depreciation on both the new and old machines and figure the difference. The old machine has already been depreciated for 2 years. (Year 1 in the table below is the end of the first year following replacement.)

Old Machine	**Year 1**	**Year 2**	**Year 3**
Basis (cost)	$15,000	$15,000	$15,000
MACRS Rate	0.1481	0.0741	0.0000
Depreciation Expense	2,222	1,112	0
New Machine			
Basis (cost)	25,000	25,000	25,000
MACRS Rate	0.3333	0.4445	0.1481
Depreciation Expense	8,333	11,113	3,703
ΔDepr	6,111	10,001	3,703
T × ΔDepr	2,444	4,000	1,481

Adjusting for Tax on Salvage

Initial Cash Flows

When we include tax on salvage in our analysis of a replacement project, the only change to initial cash flows is that salvage value is replaced by net salvage value. Equation 10.17 shows the revised formula:

EQUATION 10.17

$$FCF_0 = -Price_{new} + Net\ Salvaged_{old} - Inc(Dec)\ in\ NWC$$

where

$$Price_{new} = \text{the price of the new asset on the replacement date}$$
$$Net\ Salvage_{old} = \text{S}_{\text{old}} - \text{Tax on sale}_{\text{old}}$$
$$S_{old} = \text{Sale price of old asset on the replacement date}$$

In Equation 10.9 we incorporated all of these cash flows except the tax on sale term. To adjust the initial cash flows calculated in section 3 to include tax on salvage, we subtract the tax on sale associated with the disposal of the old asset.

Terminal Cash Flows

In Equation 10.11, we calculated terminal year cash flows as:

$$FCF_T = \Delta OCF + Decrease\ in\ NWC + S_{new} - S_{old}$$

where

$$S_{new} = \text{Salvage}_{\text{new}}$$
$$S_{old} = \text{Salvage}_{\text{old}}$$

To incorporate tax on salvage, all we need to do is replace gross salvage with net salvage:

$$F_T = \Delta OCF + Decrease\ in\ NWC + (S_{new} - Tax\ on\ Sale_{new}) - (S_{old} - Tax\ on\ Sale_{old})$$

Finally, rearrange:

$$FCF_T = \Delta OCF + Decrease\ in\ NWC + S_{new} - S_{old} - Tax\ on\ Sale_{new} + Tax\ on\ Sale_{old}$$

Notice that Equation 10.17 is identical to Equation 10.11 except for the last two terms. We will label the FCF from Equation 10.11 as "FCF (No Depr)" so we can express this more simply as:

$$FCF_T = FCF(No\ Depr) - Tax\ on\ Sale_{new} + Tax\ on\ Sale_{old}$$

Finally, following an earlier discussion, we must add the incremental tax shields:

$$FCF_T = FCF(No\ Depr) + T \times \Delta Depr - Tax\ on\ Sale_{new} + Tax\ on\ Sale_{old}$$

To adjust terminal year free cash flows so that it incorporates depreciation tax deductibility and the tax on sale, all we need to do is add the incremental tax shields, subtract the tax on sale for the new asset, and add the tax on sale for the old asset. We show an example in the next section.

Comprehensive Example of a Replacement Project

Example 10.20 Replacement Project NPV

Digital Downloads

Example 10_20 Replacement Project NPV w Depr.xlsx
https://catalog.flatworldknowledge.com/a/34711/Example_10_20_Replacement_Project_NPV_w_Depr-da95.xlsx

Because of unexpectedly high demand, Pizzas-by-Mail finds it may need a larger oven. The old oven cost $20,000 when it was purchased and has been in use for 1 year. It is classified as 3-year property and currently has a book value of $13,334. It can be sold today for $12,000. If the old oven were kept for another 3 years, then it could be sold for $1,000. The new oven, which makes perfect envelope-sized pizzas, costs $36,000. The new oven will be worth $4,000 in 3 years. Both ovens are classified as 3-year property with MACRS rates of 33.33%, 44.45%, 14.81%, and 7.41%. The larger oven will require an additional inventory of $500. Revenues will increase $20,000 (from $25,000 per year to $45,000 per year), and costs will increase by $3,000. Assume a 40% tax rate and 15% discount rate. Compute the NPV. Should Pizza-by-Mail replace the oven?

SOLUTION

Spreadsheet Solution

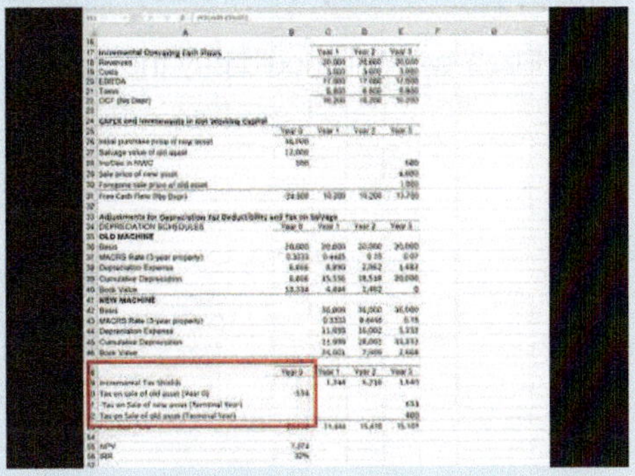

View in the online reader

The top of the following table shows the project cash flows without including depreciation or tax on salvage (from "Example 10.11 Replacement Project NPV"). The bottom of the table includes those cash flows. The final row is the sum of the free cash flow ignoring depreciation and the adjustment cash flows. For more detail, refer to the downloadable spreadsheet or watch the video solution.

	Year 0	Year 1	Year 2	Year 3
OCF (No Depr)		$10,200	$10,200	$10,200
CAPEX and Investments in Net Working Capital				
Price of New Asset	36,000			
Salvage Value of Old Asset	12,000			
Inc/Dec in NWC	500			500
Sale Price of New Asset				4,000

	Year 0	Year 1	Year 2	Year 3
Foregone Sale Price of Old Asset				1,000
FCF (No Depr)	–24,500	10,200	10,200	13,700
Adjustments for Depreciation Tax Deductibility and Tax on Salvage				
Incremental Tax Shields		1,244	5,216	1,540
Tax on Sale of Old Asset	–534			
Tax on Sale of New Asset				533
Tax on Sale of Old Asset				400
Free Cash Flow	–23,966	11,444	15,416	15,107

We adjust initial cash flows (Year 0) by subtracting the tax paid on the sale of the old asset (which is negative due to an ordinary loss):

$$FCF_0 = -\$24,500 - (-\$534) = -\$23,966$$

Following Equation 10.17, the free cash flow in the terminal year is:

$$FCF_T = \$13,700 + \$1,540 - \$533 + \$400 = \$15,107$$

The NPV of the project is:

$$NPV = -\$23,966 + \frac{\$11,444}{(1.15)} + \frac{\$15,416}{(1.15)^2} + \frac{\$15,107}{(1.15)^3} = \$7,574$$

Because the NPV is positive, Pizza-by-Mail should buy the new oven.

Endnotes

1. The incorporation of interest deductibility in the cost of capital is explained in Section 2 of Chapter 11, titled "After-Tax Cost of Debt."

2. For more information on the modified definition, see chapter 3, "Measuring Cash Flows" of Damodaran (2006). Damodaran, Aswath. 2006. *Damodaran on valuation: security analysis for investment and corporate finance.* Hoboken, N.J.: John Wiley & Sons.

CHAPTER 11

Cost of Capital

Learning Objectives

By the end of this chapter you will be able to:

1. Explain why firms need to compute the cost of capital.
2. Compute the cost of debt.
3. Compute the cost of preferred stock.
4. Compute the cost of equity.
5. Compute the weighted average cost of capital (WACC).
6. Select the correct WACC in multiple-division companies.

11.1 Why Compute the Cost of Capital

Earlier, we learned how to compute net present values (NPVs) and internal rates of return (IRR). To compute a net present value, you discount the future cash flows back to the present and subtract the present value of the cost of the project. The calculation of NPV requires that we have a **discount rate**. Up to now, we simply assumed that we knew the required return to the firm and used this rate. Similarly, the decision criterion for the internal rate of return required that the project's IRR exceed the firm's required rate of return to be acceptable. In this chapter, we learn how to compute the required return. We call this required return the **cost of capital**, which is the return required by investors.

discount rate

The rate of interest used to compute the present value of a cash flow.

cost of capital

The cost, expressed as a percentage rate, that a firm must pay investors for the use of debt and equity financing.

Timing is Important

Suppose you open a Sunglass Hut, having determined that it will yield a 12% return that can be financed with a 10% loan. Now, suppose a subsequent opportunity to open a custom shoe outlet becomes available with a 16% return, but because of the first loan, additional capital will cost 20%. As a result, you must reject the shoe outlet opportunity.

weighted average cost of capital (WACC)

The average cost of debt and equity financing where the average is computed as a weighted average using the long-term target weights of debt and equity in the balance sheet. Also referred to as the average cost of funds.

You imagine there must be a better way to evaluate investments. There is! Use a **weighted average cost of capital (WACC)** (also referred to as the average cost of funds), rather than the cost of the capital raised to finance a particular investment. Suppose, over the long run, you plan to raise money in equal parts debt and equity. What is your average cost of funds? In this example, the average is simply 10% plus 20% divided by 2, which equals 15%. If you had evaluated the Sunglass Hut using a 15% cost of funds, you would have rejected it. On the other hand, you would continue to find the custom shoe outlet attractive. This is demonstrated in Table 11.1 and discussed further in "Explain It: Choosing Investment Projects".

TABLE 11.1 Choosing Investment Projects

Business Opportunity	Expected Return	Cost of Borrowing	Cost of Equity	Average Cost of Money $(10\% + 20\%)/12$
Sunglass Hit	12%	10%		15%
Custom Shoe	16%		20%	15%

Explain It: Choosing Investment Projects

View in the online reader

Before you can compute an average cost of funds, you must first compute the cost of each type of capital. You then compute an average based on the proportion of each type of capital in your target capital structure. The cost of capital for a variety of companies is discussed in the Explain It video.

Explain It: Cost of Capital for Various Companies

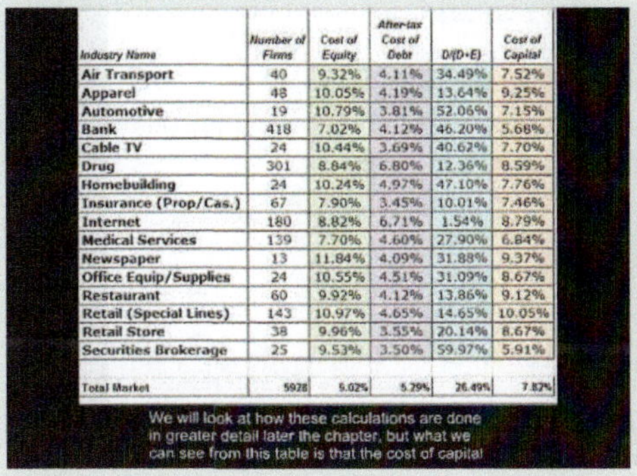

Industry Name	Number of Firms	Cost of Equity	After-tax Cost of Debt	D/(D+E)	Cost of Capital
Air Transport	40	9.32%	4.11%	34.49%	7.52%
Apparel	48	10.05%	4.19%	13.64%	9.25%
Automotive	19	10.79%	3.81%	52.06%	7.15%
Bank	418	7.02%	4.12%	46.20%	5.68%
Cable TV	24	10.44%	3.69%	40.62%	7.70%
Drug	301	8.84%	6.80%	12.36%	8.59%
Homebuilding	24	10.24%	4.97%	47.10%	7.76%
Insurance (Prop/Cas.)	67	7.90%	3.45%	10.01%	7.46%
Internet	180	8.82%	6.71%	1.54%	8.79%
Medical Services	139	7.70%	4.60%	27.90%	6.84%
Newspaper	13	11.84%	4.09%	31.88%	9.37%
Office Equip/Supplies	24	10.55%	4.51%	31.09%	8.67%
Restaurant	60	9.92%	4.12%	13.86%	9.12%
Retail (Special Lines)	143	10.97%	4.65%	14.65%	10.05%
Retail Store	38	9.96%	3.55%	20.14%	8.67%
Securities Brokerage	25	9.53%	3.50%	59.97%	5.91%
Total Market	5928	5.02%	5.29%	26.49%	7.87%

View in the online reader

Interpreting the Weighted Average Cost of Capital

A firm must earn at least the weighted average cost of capital or the value of the firm will fall. So, the WACC is the return a firm must earn on its investments; it is the rate you will use to evaluate long-term capital projects and it is the discount rate you will use in your NPV and IRR calculations. As the term implies, the WACC is computed by finding the average cost of funds to the firm. Despite how we compute the WACC, we must keep in mind that it is a measure used to evaluate investments. Thus, the rate must be adjusted and interpreted in light of how the funds will be used because the way the funds are invested affects the risk and the return expected by the investor. Most of the time, it is appropriate to assume that future company investments will look much like those in the past, and that the current cost of capital is appropriate. When firms evaluate projects that are very different from historical investments, they must adjust the discount rate to reflect risk appropriately.

Computing the Cost of Each Type of Security

Funds are raised from a number of sources. For example, a firm may borrow from a bank, issue bonds, or sell stock. Each of these sources of funds has a unique cost. In this chapter, we discuss how the cost of each type of financing is computed; then we put them all together to compute a weighted average cost. The calculation of weighted averages is discussed in the Explain It video.

Explain It: Simple Average versus Weighted Average

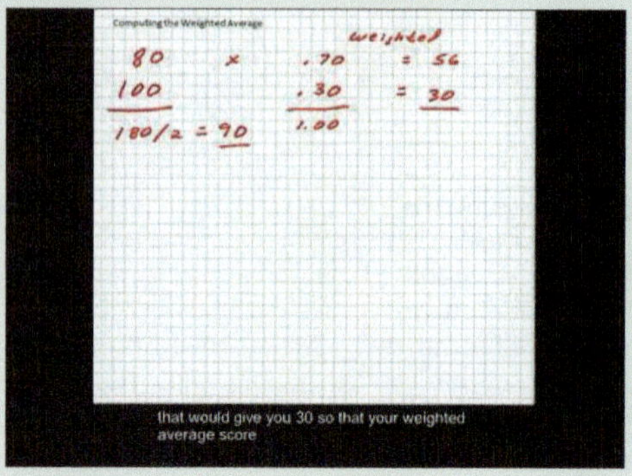

View in the online reader

One pleasant surprise is that you have already learned how to do the calculations required for this section.

11.2 After-Tax Cost of Debt

The cost of debt is the return that the firm's lenders demand on new borrowing. In other words, it is the interest rate on new borrowing, and we observe it from the interest rates quoted in the bond markets. If a company has existing bonds trading in the bond market, then the cost of debt is the yield to maturity of those bonds.

Tip

We do not use the coupon rate on existing bonds because that reflects the cost of debt when the bonds were issued; the coupon rate is usually set equal to the yield-to-maturity at the time of issue, so that the bond sells for its face value.

Recall that the equation for the price of a bond was given by the equation:

$$P_{\text{bond}} = \frac{C}{(1+k_d)^1} + \frac{C}{(1+k_d)^2} + \ldots + \frac{C}{(1+k_d)^n} + \frac{FV}{(1+k_d)^n}$$

where

$$\begin{aligned} P_{bond} &= \text{current market value of the bond} \\ C &= \text{coupon interest payment} \\ FV &= \text{face value of the bond} \\ n &= \text{number of periods until the bond matures} \\ k_d &= \text{required return on debt} \end{aligned}$$

Tip

We have added the subscript $_d$ to denote that this is the cost of debt. We also add subscripts to preferred and common equity to help to keep them separate.

We solved for k_d when computing the yield to maturity. Often, k_d is published in the firm's annual reports, or by bond services such as Moody's Bond Record. However it is obtained, k_d is not the true cost of debt to a company. Interest on debt is tax deductible. The tax deductibility of debt lowers the cost of debt financing because the government is paying a portion of the debt expense by reducing the taxes due from the company. The tax deductibility of interest reduces the cost of debt by $(1-T)$, where *T* is the firm's tax rate. For example, if the pretax cost of debt is 10% and the tax rate is 40%, the after-tax cost is 6% $(10\% \times (1-0.4)) = 6\%)$. When you learned how to compute the cash flows for capital budgeting, you did not deduct the interest expense on debt. By computing the cost of debt as $k_d(1-T)$, the interest expense and its tax deductibility are reflected in the cost of capital.

The cost of debt is stated in the following equation:

EQUATION 11.1

$$After\ tax\ cost\ of\ debt = k_d(1-T)$$

The cost of debt reflects the cost of borrowing at current market interest rates. That is, the cost of debt is the rate at which new debt could be issued. This means that the cost of debt rises and falls with market rates, regardless of whether any new debt is issued.

Example 11.1 Cost of Debt

Digital Downloads

Example 11.1_Cost_of_debt.xls
https://catalog.flatworldknowledge.com/a/34711/ Example_11_1_Cost_of_debt-2d83.xls

Suppose your company wants to issue bonds to finance research and development. The bonds have a face value of $1,000 and will net the firm $980 each. If the coupon rate is 10% and the bonds mature in 20 years, what is the cost of debt? Assume annual compounding and a 40% tax rate.

SOLUTION

Spreadsheet Solution

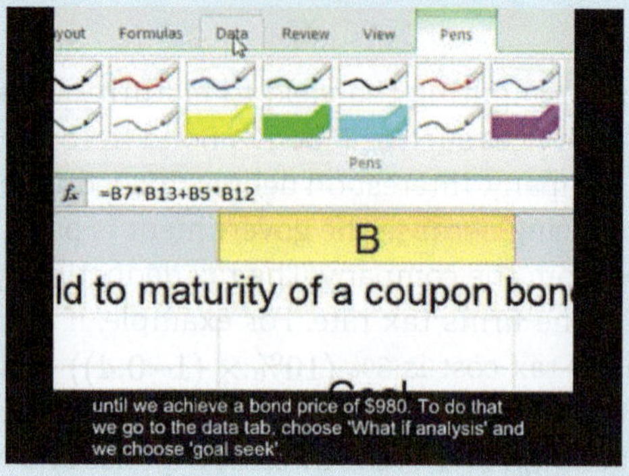

View in the online reader

Calculator Solution

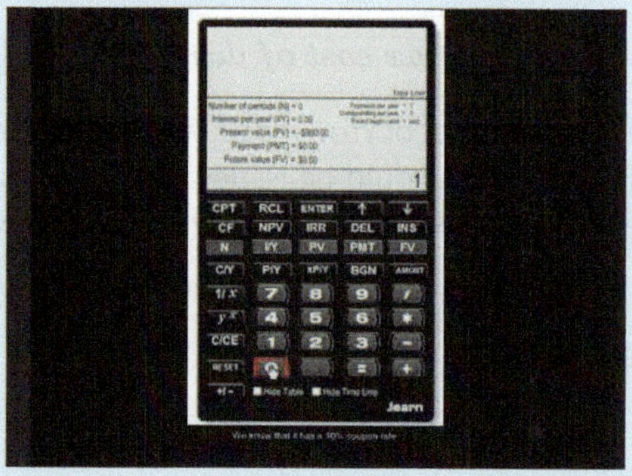

View in the online reader

If you use a financial calculator to solve for k_d then be sure to keep track of whether you are inputting cash inflows or outflows, and use the correct sign.

The pretax cost of debt is 10.24%. The after-tax cost of debt is found by multiplying by $(1 - T)$.

$$\begin{aligned} After\ tax\ cost\ of\ debt &= k_d(1-T) \\ &= 10.24\%(1-0.4) = 6.14\% \end{aligned}$$

11.3 Cost of Preferred Stock

About 5% of the average firm's capital is raised from issuing preferred stock. Do not be surprised if you find a firm that has no preferred stock outstanding; this is not unusual. Even though preferred stock has many of the characteristics of bonds, dividends are paid instead of interest. *Dividends are not tax deductible.* This makes the after-tax cost of preferred stock debt higher than the after-tax cost of similarly risky debt. This higher cost is one reason firms are reluctant to issue preferred stock. Given its close similarity to debt, most firms choose to sell bonds rather than issue preferred stock. The little preferred stock that has been issued in recent years has usually been part of merger packages, or has been convertible into the common stock of the company.

Earlier, we found that the price of preferred stock is:

$$P_{\text{preferred}} = \frac{D}{k_p}$$

which can be rearranged to solve for the cost of preferred stock,

EQUATION 11.2

$$k_p = \frac{D}{P_{preferred}}$$

where D is the annual dividend per paid share and $P_{preferred}$ is the price per share.

Example 11.2 Cost of Preferred Stock

Suppose Kmart tries to make the firm more competitive with Walmart by issuing additional shares of preferred stock to finance upgrading its inventory control and ordering systems. What is the cost of preferred stock if the stock pays a $1.00 dividend and sells at a price of $12?

To find the solution, use Equation 11.2:

SOLUTION

Algebraic Solution

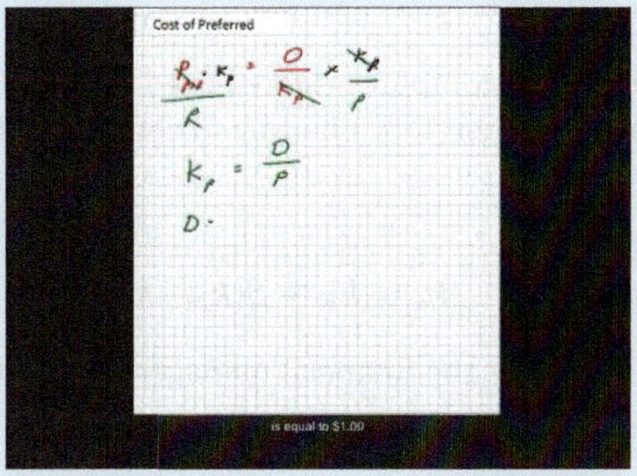

View in the online reader

$$k_p = \frac{\$1.00}{\$12.00} = 0.0833 = 8.33\%$$

The cost of preferred stock is 8.33%. Note that there is no tax adjustment for the cost of preferred stock.

11.4 Cost of Common Stock

The cost of equity is the return on investment required by investors in the stock of a company. Finding the cost of equity is far more difficult than finding the cost of either debt or preferred stock. Consider that the cash flows to bonds are very predictable. Similarly, we know what the promised dividend is for preferred stock. No such assurances are available for common stock. Since there is more uncertainty with the cost of equity, we use several different methods to compute its cost.

Before we dive into evaluating the cost of equity, let us consider an important point. Many students assume that equity has no real cost; after all, the firm does not have to pay dividends on equity capital. In fact, equity is the most expensive type of capital available. Recall the capital asset pricing model (CAPM). The CAPM computes the return that investors require to feel adequately compensated for the risk they incur from holding a firm's equity. If investors require a specific return, managers must earn that return or investors will sell the stock. When investors sell stock, its price falls, and falling stock prices often result in the replacement of managers. No executive can ignore shareholders, or fail to fairly compensate them. Equity has a cost that must be paid.

Clearly it is important to attach a cost to equity. The question is, what does equity cost? Let us review the three popular methods for computing the cost of equity.

Tip

If the cost of equity found by all of the methods is similar, we can be more confident that we have computed the correct cost. On the other hand, as frequently happens, the cost computed by the different methods may not be very similar at all. When this happens, we must reconcile costs. This reconciliation involves analyzing the inputs to each equation and attaching weights that represent your confidence in these inputs.

CAPM

We already noted that the CAPM computes the required return on equity. The required return is the same as the cost to the firm. Therefore, one way to determine the cost of equity is by using the CAPM equation:

EQUATION 11.3

$$k_e = k_F + \beta(k_M - k_F)$$

To compute the cost of equity, the financial manager must estimate the beta of the firm, the return on the market, and the risk-free rate of interest.

Tip

In 2002, Elroy Dimson, Mike Staunton and Paul Marsh published "Triumph of the Optimists: 101 years of Global Investment Returns." In that research, the team estimated the market risk premium ($k_m - k_f$) for 20 OECD countries using 101 years of data. Credit Suisse updates the Dimson, Marsh, and Staunton data annually, so you can easily obtain a market risk premium estimate based on over 120 years of data.

Example 11.3 Cost of Equity Using CAPM

The risk-free rate is 5.5%, and the expected return on the market portfolio is 12.5%. What is the cost of equity for a firm with a beta equal to 1.5?

SOLUTION

Algebraic Solution

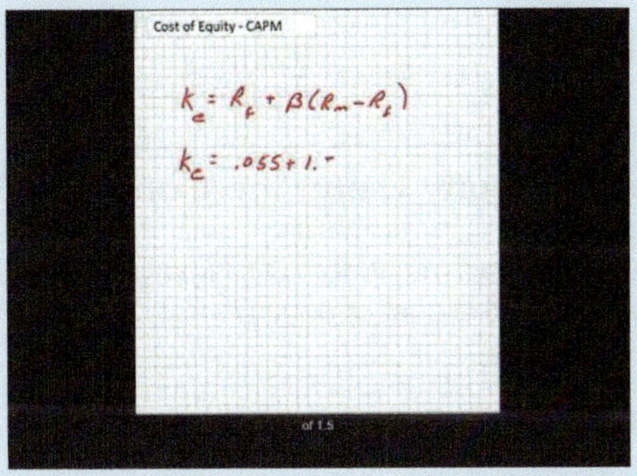

View in the online reader

Using the CAPM equation:

$$k_e = k_F + \beta(k_M - k_F)$$
$$k_e = 0.055 + 1.5(0.125 - 0.055) = 0.16 = 16\%$$

The cost of equity using CAPM is, theoretically, the most accurate method; however, there are many reasons you may not be confident in its result. The period that you use to estimate the beta can have a big impact on k_e. There are even disagreements about what value to use as the risk-free rate. With these concerns in mind, alternative approaches can be used.

Constant Growth Model

Previously, we rearranged the constant growth valuation model to show that the return was the sum of the dividend yield plus the capital gain. We use that equation here as one approach to estimating the cost of equity.

EQUATION 11.4

$$k_e = \frac{D_1}{p_0} + g$$

This equation computes the cost of equity given the current market price of the stock (P_0), an estimate of next period's dividend (D_1), and the constant growth rate the firm is expected to experience over the long run (g). Before, we noted the difficulty of determining these inputs accurately. This method only works well if the company conforms to the underlying assumptions of the constant growth dividend discount model. Those are: 1) the company pays dividends (most don't); 2) it doesn't repurchase stock; and 3) the dividends are expected to grow at reasonably constant rate for many years to come.

If a firm is paying dividends, then D_0 is known. Since D_1 is equal to $D_0(1+g)$ the difficult part of applying the constant growth model is estimating the growth rate.

Tip

Be sure to use D_1 in the numerator rather than D_0 . D_1 is the next dividend paid and may have to be computed by multiplying D_0 times $(1+g)$, where g is the expected growth rate in dividends.

Example 11.4 Cost of Equity Using the Constant Growth Model

The current stock price of HighTec, Inc, is \$25.00. Next year's dividend is projected to be \$3.00. If the growth rate is 7%, what is the cost of equity?

SOLUTION

Algebraic Solution

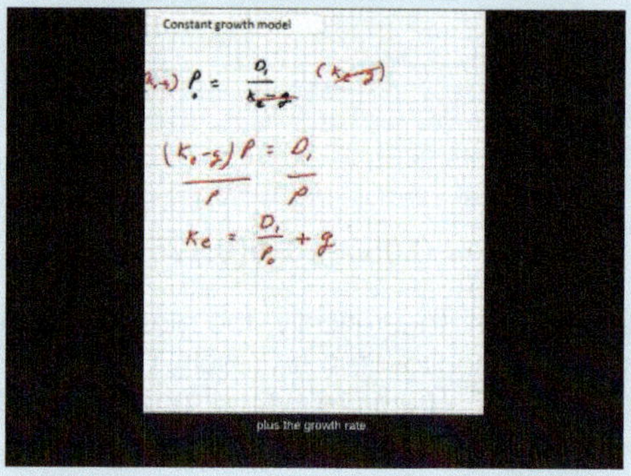

View in the online reader

Using Equation 11.4, we can find the cost of equity:

$$\begin{aligned} k_e &= \frac{D_1}{p_0} + g \\ &= \frac{\$3}{\$25} + 0.07 \\ &= 0.19 \text{ or } 19\% \end{aligned}$$

Bond Yield Plus Premium

risk premium

An additional return investors require due to the increased risk one investment has over another.

A third method used to compute the cost of equity involves adjusting the cost of debt by adding a **risk premium**. This method is based on the fact that bond yields can be computed with a reasonable degree of accuracy since all of the inputs are known. The bond yield captures certain elements of the risk of the firm. By adding a risk premium that captures the risk particular to equity, an alternative estimate of the cost of equity is achieved. This method is specified in Equation 11.5.

EQUATION 11.5

$$k_e = k_d + \theta$$

where θ , is the equity risk premium.

Most analysts project that the risk premium is usually between 3% and 5%; use 5% for more risky stocks and 3% for less risky ones. A better method for estimating is to use historical data to compute k_e and k_d at different points in the past. You should find that θ is relatively stable and the historical risk premium can be used to compute the current cost of equity.

Tip

One benefit of the bond yield plus premium approach is that it reminds us that the cost of equity is always larger than the cost of debt because equity has the residual claim on the firm's assets and so is riskier than debt.

Example 11.5 Cost of Equity Using the Bond Yield Plus Premium Approach

The pretax cost of debt (k_d) is 8%. If a 3% premium for the risk of equity over debt is appropriate, what is k_e ?

SOLUTION

Algebraic Solution

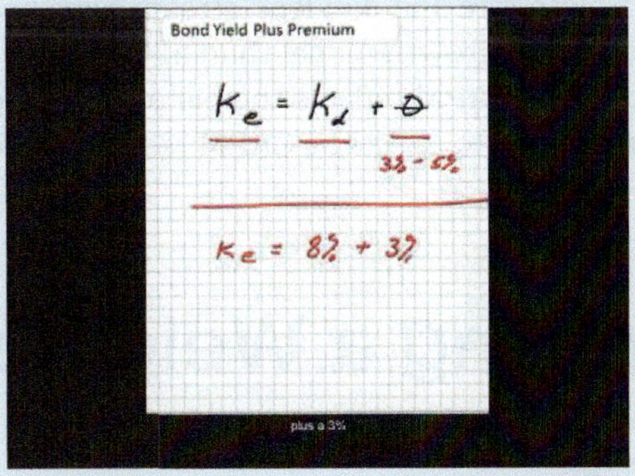

View in the online reader

Use Equation 11.5 to find the cost of equity:

TIP: *Remember to use the pretax cost of debt, not the after-tax cost, in Equation 11.4. This is because the cost of equity is not tax deductible.*

$$k_e = k_d + \theta$$
$$k_e = 8\% + 3\% = 11\%$$

Reconciling the Models

We have discussed three methods for accompanying the same task: computing the cost of equity. These methods are summarized below.

Method	Equation
CAPM	$k_e = k_F + \beta(k_M - k_F)$
Constant Growth Model	$k_e = \frac{D_1}{P_0} + g$
Bond Yield+Premium	$k_e = k_d + \theta$

Suppose you are interested in computing the cost of equity for a firm. Which method should you use? The answer is to use all of the methods for which you have the required data. As each method has inputs that are difficult or impossible to accurately estimate, the more methods we can use, the more confidence we will have in the final result.

Once you have computed k_e using each technique, you next need to reconcile the results. It is unlikely that each method will yield the same result. In fact, when real company data are applied, very different results are common. We need to determine one rate that best represents the true cost of equity capital. There is no clearly established approach to selecting this true cost. One obvious method would be to simply average the cost of equity as computed by each method. At times, this may be the best approach. However, it is possible that the analyst will be able to trust one method more highly than another because of a greater degree of confidence in the data input into the equation. For example, if the growth rate and dividend stream have been very stable, the analyst may have greater faith in the constant growth model than in the other models. Similarly, if the analyst knows that the beta used in the CAPM reflects the historical risk of the firm, but that the firm is now much less risky, she may wish to reject the CAPM results entirely.

11.5 Computing a Weighted Average Cost of Capital

In the past several sections, we computed the cost of debt, preferred stock, and equity. We now need to combine these cost estimates to find a single cost of capital for a firm. The first step is to determine the firm's target mix of debt, equity, and preferred stock. The target mix is the proportion of each type of financing resulting in the lowest average cost of funds. For now, assume that the target mix has already been established.

Computing Capital Structure Weights

The weights in the WACC formula are the proportion that each source of capital represents in the firm's capital structure. Let us denote the value of equity as E, the value of debt as D, and the value of preferred shares as P. The value of all of the company's securities is V.

EQUATION 11.6

$$V = D + P + E$$

V is the value of the whole company. The capital structure weights in the WACC formula are as follows:

$$\omega_d = D/V$$
$$\omega_p = P/V$$
$$\omega_e = E/V$$

The preferred method of computing the weighted average cost of capital is to use weights based on the firm's *target* capital structure. Only when target weights are unavailable should other methods be substituted. The reason for this preference is that the WACC is a rate to use in evaluating long-term projects. We need to develop it using the mix of securities that will comprise the firm's capital structure over this same period of time. In the long run, the firm can be expected to achieve its targets.

Tip

The target capital structure will be known to insiders of the company and may not look like the current structure of the firm at all. It is still appropriate to use these targets, since they are expected to be achieved in the long run.

It is often difficult for firm outsiders to determine a firm's target capital structure. The proportions of different types of capital may change frequently over time. Certainly, no firm raises all types of funds at one time. Instead, a firm will raise one type at a particular time, then when funds are needed, another type of security will be issued so that the target capital structure is approximately maintained. Firm management will know what this target mix is; however, outside analysts must guess. The usual method for outsiders to estimate the target capital structure is to look at the average capital mix over the past several years. Target weights should be based on the market values of the different securities. Although the market value approach is theoretically more accurate, book value weights may be used if security prices are not available.

Tip

Market security prices will not be available for privately held firms. In this case, you may have to use accounting values.

Note that the sum of the weights must equal 1 $(\omega_d + \omega_p + \omega_e = 1)$. A **weighted average** is found by multiplying each cost component by its weight.

weighted average

An average that is based on the proportion of each element in the total. A weighted average can be contrasted with a simple average that assumes each element is held in equal proportions.

Example 11.6 Computing Capital Structure Weights

Digital Downloads

Example11.6_Computing_Weights.xls
https://catalog.flatworldknowledge.com/a/34711/Example11_6_Computing_Weights-dab3.xls

Use the following data to determine which weights to use when computing the weighted average cost of capital.

Long-term debt	$500,000
Preferred Stock	$20,000
Common stock	$600,000

SOLUTION

Spreadsheet Solution

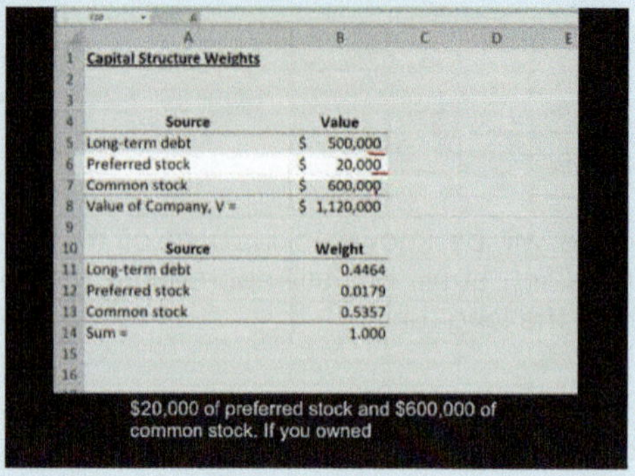

View in the online reader

First, sum the components of the firm's capital to compute the total value of the capital in the firm using Equation 11.6:

$$V = D + P + E$$
$$Value = \$500,000 + \$20,000 + \$600,000 = \$1,120,000$$

Next, divide each component by the value.

$$\omega_d = \$500,000/\$1,120,000 = 0.4464$$
$$\omega_p = \$20,000/\$1,120,000 = 0.0179$$
$$\omega_e = \$600,000/\$1,120,00 = 0.5357$$

Now, verify by seeing if they sum to 1.

$$0.4464 + 0.0179 + 0.5357 = 1$$

Putting It All Together: Computing the WACC

To find the WACC, multiply each component's cost by the proportion it occupies in the target mix. This method is specified by Equation 11.7.

EQUATION 11.7

$$WACC = \omega_d k_d (1 - T) + \omega_p k_p + \omega_e k_e$$

where

$$\omega_d, \omega_p, \omega_e = \text{proportion of debt, preferred and equity in the target capital structure}$$
$$k_d, k_p, k_e = \text{cost of debt, preferred stock, and equity}$$
$$T = \text{the firm's tax rate}$$

Explain It: The WACC Calculator

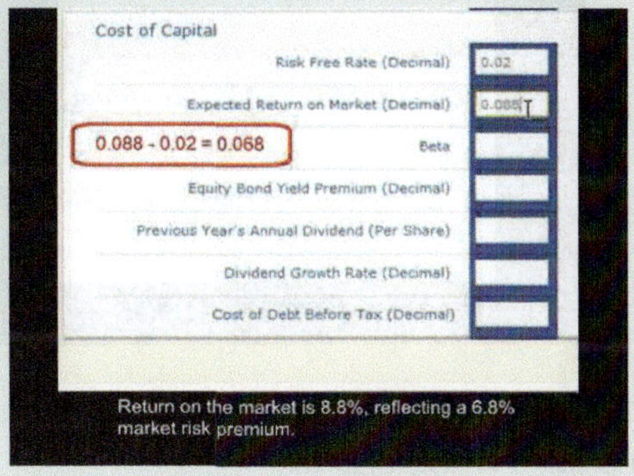

View in the online reader

In the next example, we put everything together to compute the WACC.

Example 11.7 Computing the WACC

Digital Downloads

Example11.7_WACC.xls

https://catalog.flatworldknowledge.com/a/34711/Example11_7_WACC-1459.xls

The pretax cost of debt is 10%. The cost of preferred stock is 11% and the cost of equity is 13%. The firm's capital structure is comprised of 40% debt, 10% preferred stock, and 50% equity. The tax rate is 40%. What is the firm's weighted average cost of capital after tax?

SOLUTION

Spreadsheet Solution

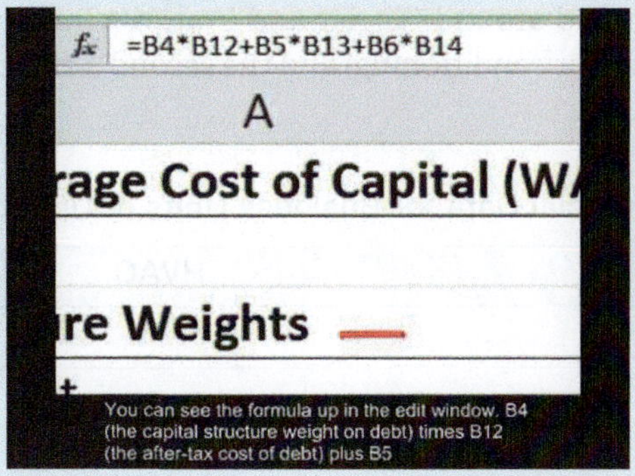

View in the online reader

Algebraic Solution

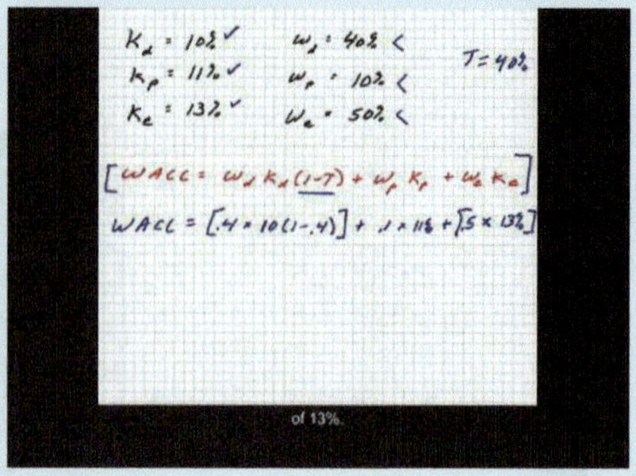

View in the online reader

Use Equation 11.7 to find the firm's WACC after tax:

$$WACC = \omega_d k_d(1-T) + \omega_p k_p + \omega_e k_e$$
$$WACC = (0.40 \times 0.10 \times (1-0.4)) + (0.10 \times 0.11) + (0.50 \times 0.13)$$
$$WACC = 0.10 \text{ or } 10\%$$

The WACC after tax is 10%.

11.6 Divisional Cost of Capital

divisional cost of capital

The cost of capital computed for a specific unit or division within a company that reflects that area's weighted average cost of funds.

Companies with multiple divisions should not use a single corporate WACC to evaluate projects. They should calculate a **divisional cost of capital** for each business unit. We show you why, using the example of United Technologies.

United Technologies is a conglomerate with business units that include Carrier (maker of residential heating and cooling systems), Otis (maker of elevators), Pratt & Whitney (maker of jet and rocket engines), and Sikorsky (maker of helicopters). To simplify, let's assume that United has two major business units centered around Carrier and Pratt & Whitney. We call the first HVAC (short for heating, ventilation, and air conditioning) and the second Aerospace. Additional data for the two divisions is given in Table 11.2.

TABLE 11.2 Selected Financial Data for Business Units of United Technologies

	HVAC	Aerospace
Cost of debt, k_d	5%	5%
Beta	0.5	1.5
Cost of equity, k_e	7%	13%
Tax Rate	35%	35%
$\omega_d = D/V$	0.533	0.205
$\omega_e = E/V$	0.467	0.795
WACC	5%	11%

Table 11.2 shows that the HVAC division has little business risk. This is not surprising, since demand for heating and cooling systems is relatively insensitive to the business cycle. The beta for the HVAC division is 0.5 and the required return of shareholder for that level of risk is 7%. The Aerospace division is much more cyclical; its beta is 1.5, and the required return on equity is 13%. The HVAC division is financed (almost) equally with debt and equity, and its divisional weighted average cost of capital is 5%. The Aerospace division is financed 20% by debt and its divisional weighted average cost of capital is 11%.

Let's assume that the two divisions are of equal size, so the corporate weighted average cost of capital is 8%. If United Technologies uses the corporate WACC to evaluate projects for the two divisions, then it could make two significant decision errors.

First, consider a new project in the HVAC division with a beta of 0.5 and an internal rate of return (IRR) of 7%. This project would be rejected, since the IRR is less than the corporate WACC of 8%. (Recall that if IRR < WACC, then NPV < 0.) However, it is a very profitable project when evaluated with the divisional WACC, since the IRR of 7% exceeds the divisional WACC of 5%. Using the corporate WACC causes United Technologies to forgo profitable, low-risk projects.

Second, consider a new project in the Aerospace division with a beta of 1.5 and an IRR of 10%. This project would be accepted, since the IRR is greater than the corporate WACC of 8%. However, it is an unprofitable project when evaluated with the divisional WACC, since the project IRR of 10% is less than the divisional WACC of 11%. The use of the corporate WACC causes United Technologies to accept unprofitable, high-risk projects.

To avoid these decision errors, multidivision companies need to develop separate estimates of the weighted average cost of capital for each division. The separate estimates must reflect the business risk of the division (beta) and the different financing mix of the division.

CHAPTER 12

Capital Structure

Learning Objectives

By the end of this chapter you will be able to:

1. Calculate measures of operating and financial leverage.
2. Understand the effect of leverage on EPS and ROE.
3. Calculate firm value and returns for levered companies when there are no corporate taxes.
4. Calculate firm value and returns for levered companies when there are corporate taxes.
5. Understand the impact of financial distress and agency costs on the capital structure choice.

In April 2013, Apple Inc. borrowed $17 billion. But Apple didn't need the money. At that time, it had over $120 billion in cash and short-term and long-term investments. This chapter explores some of the reasons why Apple added debt to its capital structure and the effect the debt had on its value.

The mix of debt and equity is the **capital structure** of the firm. In our study of portfolio theory, we found that buying stocks on margin increases risk and expected return. Corporate borrowing has similar effects: it increases the risks to shareholders and it increases the shareholders' expected return. Not surprisingly, anything that affects returns also affects value, since value is just the discounted present value of cash flows. Because the goal of financial managers is to maximize stockholder wealth (firm value), it is important for managers to understand how debt impacts firm value.

capital structure
The mix of long-term debt and equity used by the firm to finance its assets.

In this chapter, we start by looking at two measures of leverage: operating and financial. Financial leverage is another phrase for debt. In the second part, we examine the impact that borrowing has on the level and variability of corporate profits. The final sections of the chapter present two models of capital structure developed by Franco Modigliani and Merton Miller (M&M). We also present a refinement of the M&M models (the static trade-off theory) achieved by relaxing some of their assumptions.

12.1 Measures of Leverage

A lever is a machine that amplifies a force exerted at one end to produce a larger force at the other end. In Figure 12.1, a small downward force applied to the left end produces a larger upward force at the right end. The leverage effect is greater as the fulcrum moves right.

FIGURE 12.1 Leverage

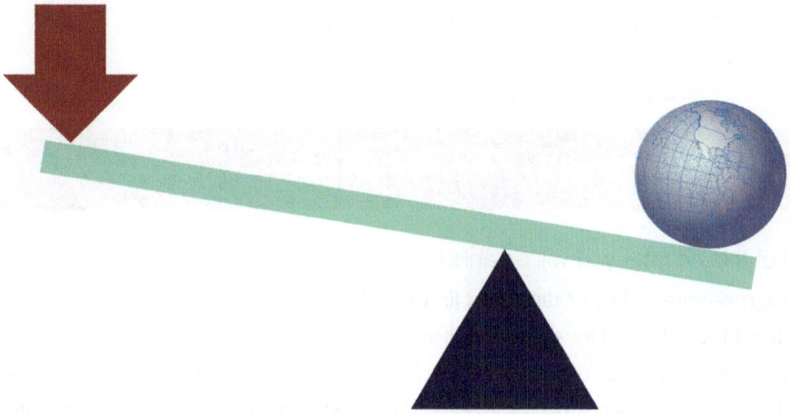

Operating Leverage

operating leverage

Fixed costs create operating leverage. Fixed costs accentuate the variability of operating profits relative to the variability of sales. Measured by the degree of operating leverage (DOL).

earnings before interest and taxes

Earnings before interest and taxes (EBIT) are deducted.

degree of operating leverage (DOL)

The percentage change in EBIT divided by the percentage change in sales.

In business, there are two types of leverage: operating and financial. **Operating leverage** is achieved through the use of fixed assets. The more fixed assets owned by a company, the further the fulcrum slides right. With a high degree of operating leverage, a small increase in sales (at the left end of the lever) produces a very big change in operating profit (measured by **earnings before interest and taxes**, or EBIT). The analogy of the lever does not apply perfectly because sales and profit move in the same direction. High operating leverage occurs in companies with a large amount of fixed assets because those companies typically have very low variable costs. Thus, one dollar of extra sales translates into almost one dollar of operating profit. We measure operating leverage by comparing the percentage change in sales to the percentage change in EBIT. Specifically, we define the **degree of operating leverage (DOL)** as

$$DOL = \frac{Percentage\ change\ in\ EBIT}{Percentage\ change\ in\ Sales} = \frac{\%\Delta EBIT}{\%\Delta Sales}$$

Example 12.1 Degree of Operating Leverage

Q9 Networks is a leading provider of outsourced data center infrastructure. As long as Q9 operates below capacity, it has high fixed costs and low variable costs. Use the selected financial data to calculate the DOL for 2015.

Selected Financial Information Q9 Networks ($000s)			
	2014	2015	% Change
Sales	$26,268	$37,829	44%
EBIT	448	913	104%
Operating Margin		2.14%	

SOLUTION

$$DOL = \frac{\%\Delta EBIT}{\%\Delta Sales} = \frac{104}{44} = 2.36$$

Explain It: Operating Leverage and the Operating Profit Margin

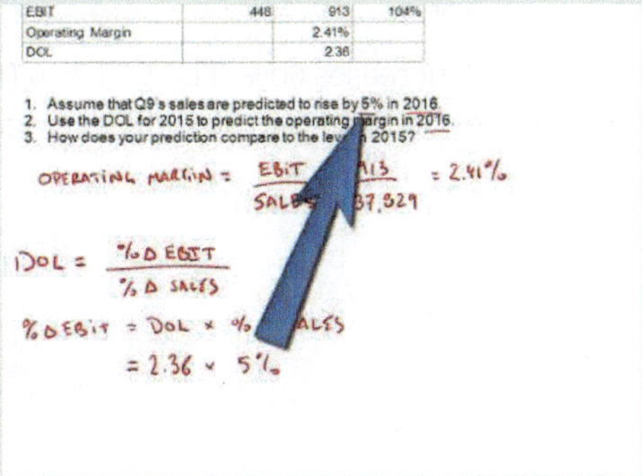

View in the online reader

Some firms, by virtue of the industry in which they operate, have high operating leverage. A steel mill, for example, must invest substantial sums in expensive plant and equipment. Similarly, automobile manufacturers, railroads, and the producers of computer chips must invest heavily before producing products. In these industries, the degree of operating leverage is high, so small changes in sales result in large changes in earnings before interest and taxes.

Financial Leverage

financial leverage

Debt creates financial leverage. Financial leverage increases the expected return on equity, but it also accentuates the variability of net income relative to the variability of operating profit. Measured by the degree of financial leverage (DFL).

earnings per share (EPS)

Net income (less preferred share dividends) divided by the number of common shares outstanding.

degree of financial leverage (DFL)

The percentage change in EPS divided by the percentage change in EBIT.

total leverage

A measure of leverage that combines operating and financial leverage.

degree of total leverage (DTL)

The percentage change in EPS divided by the percentage change in sales.

Financial leverage is achieved with debt. The more debt a company has, the further the fulcrum slides to the right (see Figure 12.1). With a high degree of financial leverage, a small increase in operating profit (at the left end of the lever) produces a very big change in shareholder profit (**earnings per share**, or EPS). The interest expense increases with the amount of debt and so the EPS becomes more sensitive to changes in operating profit (EBIT). We measure financial leverage by comparing the percentage change in the EPS to the percentage change in the EBIT. Specifically, we define the **degree of financial leverage (DFL)** as:

EQUATION 12.2

$$DFL = \frac{\text{Percentage change in } EPS}{\text{Percentage change in } EBIT} = \frac{\%\Delta EPS}{\%\Delta EBIT}$$

Suppose the EBIT increases by 10%. If the EPS increases by 20%, the DFL is 2 $(20\%/10\% = 2)$. The greater the change in the EPS given a change in the EBIT, the greater the financial leverage.

Total Leverage

Total leverage is a measure of leverage that combines operating and financial leverage. The formula for the **degree of total leverage (DTL)** is the product of the DFL and the DOL.

EQUATION 12.3

$$DTL = DOL \times DFL$$

$$DTL = \frac{\%\Delta EBIT}{\%\Delta \text{ Sales}} \times \frac{\%\Delta EPS}{\%\Delta EBIT} = \frac{\%\Delta EPS}{\%\Delta \text{ Sales}}$$

Suppose sales increase 10% and EPS increases 60%. The DTL is 6 $(60\%/10\%)$. The greater the change in the EPS given a change in sales, the greater the total leverage.

Tip

Notice that $\%\Delta EBIT$ cancels.

Besides pointing out there's more than one way to leverage a firm, the reason for presenting this discussion of leverage is to show one factor that will bear on the capital structure decision. Review Equation 12.3. Financial leverage and operating leverage are multiplied together, not summed. This means that an increase in either type of leverage has a large impact on the variability of the EPS.

If firms with high operating leverage (i.e., steel manufacturers) were to have high financial leverage as well, they might be too risky to be attractive to investors. For this reason, firms with high operating leverage often have low financial leverage, and vice versa. For example, the average debt ratio for all firms is 26%. The debt ratio for steel mills is 12.8% and for drug companies it's 7.8%.

Firms within an industry tend to have similar capital structures. One reason is that firms within an industry often have similar operating leverage. To keep risk within acceptable limits, they adjust their financial leverage. Thus, one determinant of capital structure is the level of operating leverage (fixed assets).

12.2 The Effects of Leverage

In this section we look at how financial leverage affects the level and variability of shareholder profits. In particular, we compare earnings-per-share (EPS) and return on equity (ROE) across two capital structures.

EPS and ROE as EBIT Changes

Suppose you're considering opening a chain of mail-order pizza restaurants. You have two ways to finance this investment. You could use all of your inheritance and have an all-equity firm, or you could finance it with 50% debt and 50% equity. What impact does this capital structure choice have on the earnings per share and return on equity? Table 12.1 reports the two alternatives in Panel A. Panel B of Table 12.1 reports the EPS and ROE for three possible sales forecasts assuming the firm is financed entirely with equity. Panel C reports the EPS and ROE for three possible sales forecasts assuming the firm is financed with 50% debt and 50% equity.

TABLE 12.1 Effects of Leverage on the EPS and ROE

Panel A	**All Equity**	**50% Debt**	
Assets	$1,000	$1,000	
Debt	$0	$500	
Equity	$1,000	$500	
Debt-Equity Ratio	0%	100%	
Shares Outstanding	100	50	
Share Price	$10	$10	
Panel B: All Equity Financing	**Weak Sales**	**Average Sales**	**Strong Sales**
EBIT	$25	$200	$400
–Interest	0	0	0
Net Income	$25	$200	$400
EPS	$0.25	$2.00	$4.00
ROE	3%	20%	40%
Panel C: 50% Debt Financing	**Weak Sales**	**Average Sales**	**Strong Sales**
EBIT	$25	$200	$400
–Interest	$50	$50	$50
Net Income	–$25	$150	$350
EPS	–$0.50	$3.00	$7.00
ROE	–5%	30%	70%

Digital Downloads

Table 12.1 Effects of Leverage on EPS and ROE.xls
https://catalog.flatworldknowledge.com/a/34711/

Table_12_1_Effects_of_Leverage_on_EPS_and_ROE-47a5.xls

Explain It: Effects of Leverage on EPS and ROE

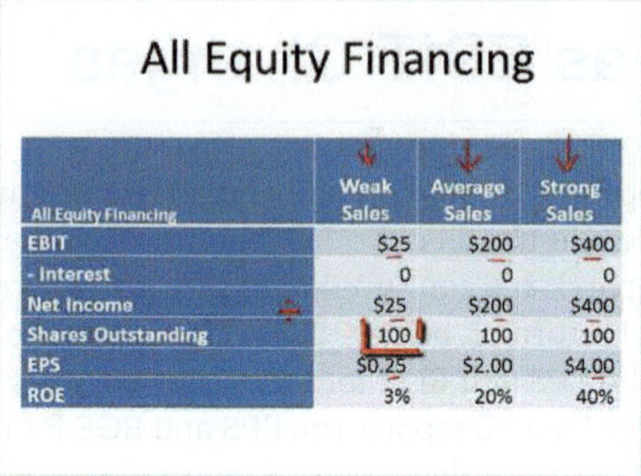

View in the online reader

We see in Panel B that even with weak sales, the all-equity firm earns a profit and reports an ROE of 2.5% $(\$25/\$1,000 = 2.5\%)$. In contrast, we see in Panel C that with weak sales the 50% debt-financed firm earns an ROE of -5% . The leveraged capital structure amplifies the poor performance in the weak state of nature. However, with strong sales, the debt-financed firm's ROE is 70% whereas the all-equity firm has an ROE of only 40%. The leverage also amplifies the good performance when the state of nature is strong.

EBIT—EBS Analysis

EBIT–EPS analysis is a visual method for evaluating the impact of capital structure choice on profitability (EPS). Figure 12.2 is a graphical representation of the analysis shown in Table 12.1. Figure 12.2 shows EBIT–EPS pairs in states of the economy (i.e., weak or strong) for each of the two capital structure choices. The dark green line is the all-equity choice, and the light green line is the 50%-debt (leveraged) choice.

FIGURE 12.2 EBIT—EPS Analysis

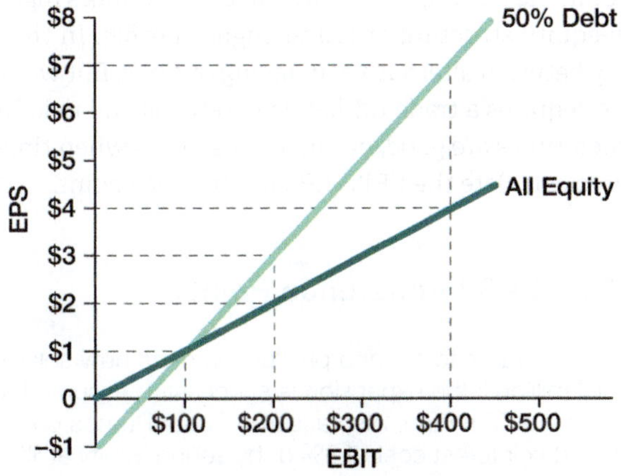

Explain It: EBIT—EPS Analysis

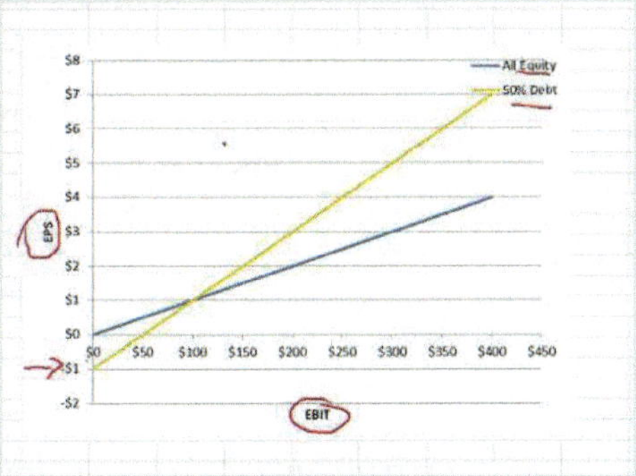

View in the online reader

The EBIT—EPS graph demonstrates both the advantage and disadvantage of using financial leverage.

- Leverage creates the risk of bankruptcy. With leverage and weak sales (i.e., below an EBIT of $50 where the light green line cuts the *x*-axis), you may not be able to pay your interest expense (so EPS is negative) and you could be forced out of business by creditors. This cannot happen if the firm is all-equity financed because there are no creditors to satisfy—notice that the all-equity line never enters the negative EPS range.
- Leverage increases shareholder profits (when times are good). With leverage and strong sales, the debt-financed capital structure produces an EPS of $7 but the all equity only generates $4. In effect, by using debt, the firm is able to earn money for shareholders by using someone else's money (lenders).
- Leverage increases risk. This is reflected by the steeper slope of the light green line. With leverage, there is a higher variance of profit (EPS or ROE), which explains why firms are considered to be more risky when they're leveraged.

The point where the two lines intersect in Figure 12.2 is called the EBIT–EPS indifference point. In this example the two capital structure choices produce the same EPS when EBIT is $100. At EBIT levels above this point, the leveraged capital structure produces higher profits for the owners. Below this point, the all-equity structure produces higher profits. In this way, EBIT–EPS analysis can be useful for selecting between alternative financing options. But we should not forget that the capital structure decision requires a trade-off between returns and risk. Increasing financial leverage improves returns when times are good, but increases losses when times are bad. The following example shows you how to calculate the EBIT–EPS indifference point.

Example 12.2 EBIT—EPS Indifference Point

Suppose Super Pumps Inc. wants to expand production of its new solar-powered bilge pumps. It projects the EBIT of $3 million if the expansion is successful. Assume the projected total funds needed for this expansion are $5 million. Also assume Super Pumps could finance the $5 million by selling bonds with a pretax interest cost of 8% or by selling equity at $20 per share. If there are a million shares outstanding and the firm's tax rate is 37%, calculate the EBIT–EPS indifference point. Given expected EBIT, which option should Super Pumps choose?

SOLUTION

Algebraic Solution

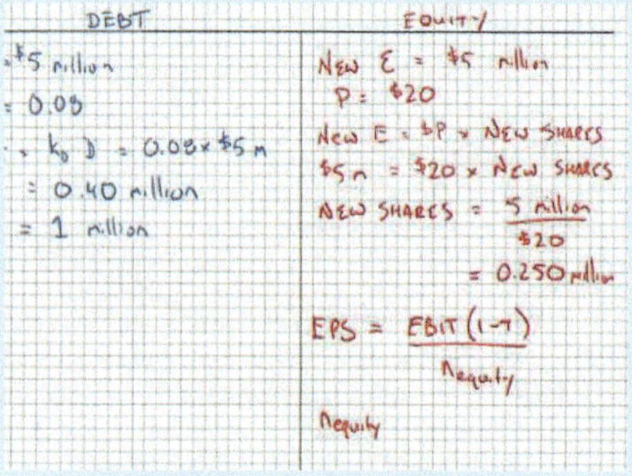

View in the online reader

EQUATION 12.4

$$EPS_{debt} = \frac{(EBIT\text{–}Interest) \times (1\text{–}T)}{n}$$

The EPS from financing with an equity option is computed the same way. The interest amount will be less and the number of shares may be more. The indifference point is found by setting $EPS_{debt} = EPS_{equity}$. This results in:

EQUATION 12.5

$$\frac{(EBIT\text{–}Interest_{debt}) \times (1-T)}{n_{debt}} = \frac{(EBIT - Interest_{equity}) \times (1-T)}{n_{equity}}$$

where

$$Interest_{debt} = \text{interest due under the debt option} = 0.08 \times \$5M = \$0.4M$$
$$Interest_{equity} = \text{interest due under the equity option} = \$0$$
$$n_{debt} = \text{number of shares under the debt option} = \$1M$$
$$n_{equity} = \text{number of shares under the equity option} = \$1.250M$$

By setting the terms equal to each other, we can compute the EBIT for which the two methods of financing give the same EPS.

For Super Pumps, with no interest under the equity option, we can simplify Equation 12.5 to yield:

$$EBIT = Interest_{debt} \times \left[\frac{n_{equity}}{n_{equity} - n_{debt}}\right]$$

The interest on the debt is $\$400,000[\$5,000,000(0.8) = \$400,000]$. If the equity option is used, 250,000 shares would have to be issued $(\$5,000,000/\$20 = 250,000)$. There are already 1 million shares outstanding. Inputting these into our expressions gives a breakdown EBIT of:

$$EBIT = \$400,000 \times \left[\frac{1,250,000}{250,000}\right] = \$2,000,000$$

Because the expected EBIT of \$3,000,000 is greater than the indifference point, Super Pumps should finance its expansion using debt rather than by selling stock. This results in the highest EPS. This solution is shown graphically in Figure 12.3.

FIGURE 12.3 EBIT—EPS Analysis of Super Pumps Inc.

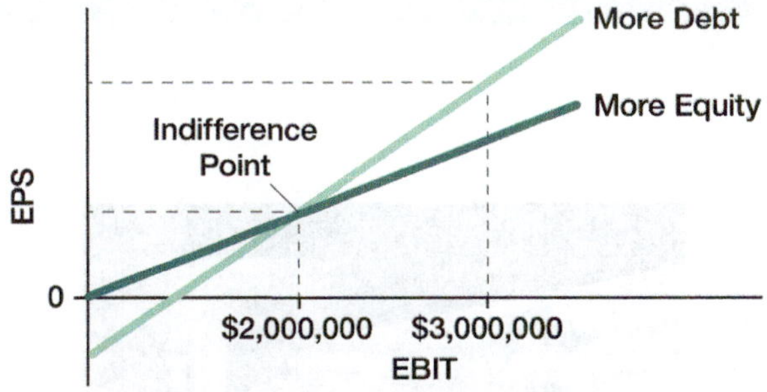

12.3 Capital Structure with No Taxes

In the remainder of this chapter, we build three models that explain how capital structure affects firm value. Each successive model highlights a different way in which debt affects corporate value. Each model builds on the previous one and so each model is more realistic than the last. Since this is your first exposure to capital structure theory, we end the presentation after the third model, but, in our conclusions, we list other determinants of capital structure that you will study in more advanced courses.

In the first model, we explore the impact of leverage on value assuming perfect capital markets. In particular, we assume no taxes, no costs of financial distress, no transactions costs, and no information asymmetries. The first model highlights the fact that leverage increases risk and the required return of shareholders, but it yields the surprising result that there is no **optimal capital structure**.

optimal capital structure

The capital structure that produces the highest firm value of all capital structures.

In the second model, we include the tax benefit of debt. (Remember that interest is tax deductible.) This model yields the result that the optimal capital structure is 100% debt. This conclusion simply follows from maximizing the tax benefit of debt. It is not realistic because we see no companies with 100% debt financing.

The first two models are based on the ideas of Merton Miller and Franco Modigliani, who both won the Nobel Prize in Economics for their work on capital structure. In our discussion, we refer to the models of Miller and Modigliani as M&M.

financial distress

The events leading up to and including bankruptcy, such as the violation of loan covenants.

principal–agent problems

The problems and costs that occur when an agent does not maximize the utility of the principal.

static trade-off theory

The theory that the optimal capital structure is determined by a trade-off of the value of tax shields against financial distress costs and the agency costs and benefits.

The third model includes transactions costs. First, we include the costs of **financial distress**, and second, we realize that transactions costs make contracting between corporate stakeholders imperfect. Specifically, we look at **principal–agent problems** and how they are ameliorated or exacerbated by debt. This third model is more realistic and yields an optimal capital structure that is less than 100% debt. This model is known as the **static trade-off theory**.

M&M Proposition 1: Debt and Value

M&M showed that the capital structure decision is irrelevant in a world without taxes and other costs. Their theory says that the value of the firm is not determined by how the assets are financed. Rather, the value of the firm is based on the earning power of its assets. Merton Miller explained his theory with an analogy of a pizza as shown in "Explain It: Intuition behind M&M Proposition". The value of the firm doesn't change with the number of claims on it, or, as in the case of the pizza, the number of slices.

Explain It: Intuition behind M&M Proposition

View in the online reader

The essence of the M&M proof is that investors can buy shares in an all-equity company and create their own leverage or buy shares in a levered company and undo the leverage. Because the company does nothing that investors can't do themselves, there is no reason to pay more for a levered (or unlevered) company.

no-arbitrage

This condition is the same as the law of one price. If two identical assets trade in two different markets, then they must trade for the same price. If not, then there are arbitrage trading opportunities.

In the next example, we look at the cash flows earned by an investor who borrows on his own account to buy shares in an all-equity company. This is a simple variation of M&M's very clever **no-arbitrage** argument, which was published in 1958.[1]

Example 12.3 Homemade Leverage

Assume that Mail-Order Pizzas chooses the all-equity capital structure (refer to Table 12.1). Leon Demargin, an investor, wants to buy shares in the company. He has $50 of his own money (his equity), but he wants to buy $100 worth of shares. Thus, he borrows $50. We assume that he can borrow at the same rate as the company or 10%. What are his annual cash flows from this investment strategy?

> **Tip:** *We choose $50 of borrowing so that Leon's portfolio is 50% debt financed. That way, his capital structure matches that of Mail-Order Pizzas in Panel C of Table 12.1.*

SOLUTION

Algebraic Solution

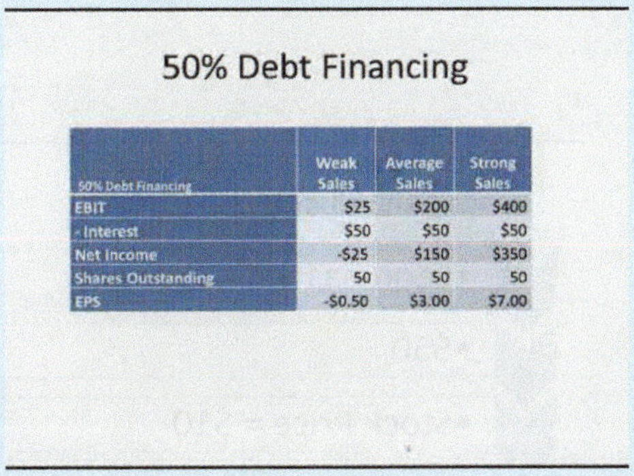
50% Debt Financing

50% Debt Financing	Weak Sales	Average Sales	Strong Sales
EBIT	$25	$200	$400
- Interest	$50	$50	$50
Net Income	-$25	$150	$350
Shares Outstanding	50	50	50
EPS	-$0.50	$3.00	$7.00

View in the online reader

Leon buys $100 worth of shares, which gets him 10 shares @ $10/share (the price of a share is shown in Table 12.1). The table calculates his net cash flows for each sales scenario. Assume that sales are weak. Leon will receive a dividend of $0.25 per share (assume all the EPS is paid out) or $2.50 in total. However, Leon must also pay interest on his loan at 10%. He borrowed $50, so his interest expense is $5.

> **Tip:** *Assume that the loan is a perpetuity, so Leon pays interest annually forever. That way, we don't have to worry about the principal repayment in this example.*

Leon's Investment Cash Flows			
All Equity Financing	**Weak Sales**	**Average Sales**	**Strong Sales**
EPS	$0.25	$2.00	$4.00
Leon's dividends	$2.50	$20.00	$40.00
–Interest	–$5.00	–$5.00	–$5.00
Net cash flows	–$2.50	$15.00	$35.00

Now let's consider what Leon would have earned if Mail Order Pizzas had adopted the 50% debt capital structure and Leon had invested his $50 in shares of the company. He would have purchased five shares (@ $10/share). Look at the EPS in Table 12.1, Panel C. If Leon had five shares, then his dividend cash flows would have been $2.50, $15.00, and $35.00 across the three scenarios. That is identical to what we calculated in "Example 12.3 Homemade Leverage". If the company does not borrow, then Leon can create the same investment cash flows (as a levered company would have generated) by borrowing on his own account. Leon does not regard the company as more valuable if it adopts the leveraged capital structure because he can do it himself.

The argument also works in the other direction. An investor can buy shares in a levered company and undo the leverage on her own account. The resulting portfolio cash flows are identical to what she would have earned if she had bought shares in the all-equity company. "Explain It: Unlever an Investment in 50% Debt-Financed Firm" walks through such an example.

Explain It: Unlever an Investment in 50% Debt-Financed Firm

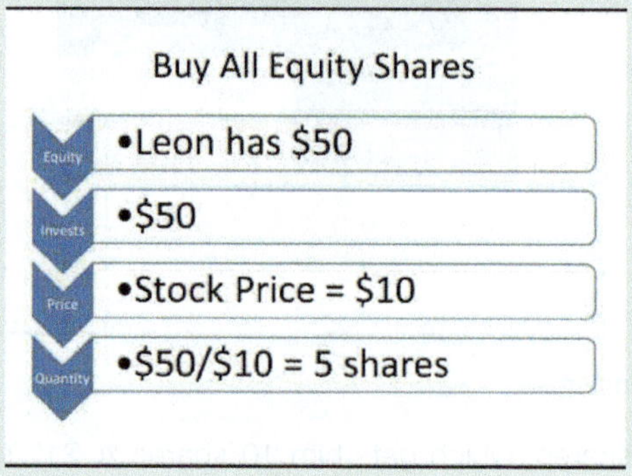

View in the online reader

Our examples show that investors don't care about capital structure and won't pay more for a levered company compared to an unlevered company. Now that we understand the argument, let's state the proposition formally. Consider two firms that are identical in every respect except capital structure. One company is all equity financed (unlevered) and the other company is partially debt financed (levered). M&M Proposition 1 states that the value of the two companies is equal.

EQUATION 12.6

$$V_U = V_L$$

where

$$\begin{aligned} V_U &= \textbf{value of the unlevered company} \\ V_L &= \textbf{value of the levered company} \end{aligned}$$

M&M Proposition 2: Debt and Required Returns

Another implication of Proposition 1 is that the weighted average cost of capital (WACC) is unaffected by leverage. We prove this (beginning with the following example), and then use the example to derive Proposition 2.

Example 12.4 Value of All-Equity Company

Assume that Mail-Order Pizzas generates perpetual annual operating income (EBIT) of $200. The company isn't growing so there are no investments in working capital or fixed assets. Assume that taxes are zero. Shareholders require a return of 20%. (Denote the required return of unlevered shareholders as k_U.) What is the market value of the company, V_U? (Assume that all cash flows occur at the end of the year and we are currently at the beginning of a year.)

SOLUTION

Algebraic Solution

Income Statement Mail Order Pizza Inc.	
EBIT	$200
- Interest	$0
EBT	$200
- Taxes	$0
Net Income	$200

NO TAXES

View in the online reader

The value of the company is just the present value of the cash flows when discounted at the investors' required return. There are no taxes, so the amount of cash available to be distributed to shareholders is just the EBIT. Because the cash flows are a perpetuity, the value of the company is just the present value of a perpetuity discounted at k_U.

EQUATION 12.7

$$V_U = \frac{EBIT}{k_U}$$

$$V_U = \frac{\$200}{0.2} = \$1,000$$

Let's assume that our perpetual Mail-Order Pizzas company (from "Example 12.4 Value of All-Equity Company") added some debt to its capital structure. Then, the value of the levered firm, V_L, is equal to:

EQUATION 12.8

$$V_L = \frac{EBIT}{k_W}$$

where k_w is the WACC. A derivation of Equation 12.8 is given in "Explain It: Proof that V=EBIT/WACC".

Explain It: Proof that V=EBIT/WACC

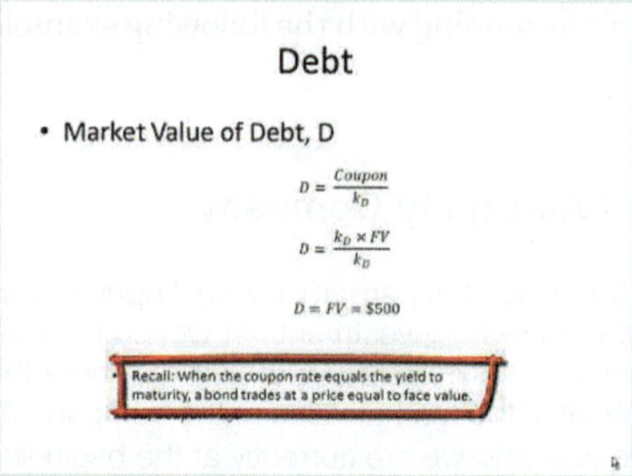

View in the online reader

The intuition is simple. The annual cash flows generated by Mail Order Pizzas for all claimholders (stockholders and bondholders) is the EBIT. So, Equation 12.8 is just the present value of the claimholders' cash flows discounted at their (average) required return.

M&M Proposition 1 tells us that $V_U = V_L$. If we equate Equation 12.7 and Equation 12.8, then it follows that $k_U = k_W$. In other words, the WACC is constant for all levels of debt at the rate of k_U .

EQUATION 12.9

$$k_U = k_W = \frac{E}{V}k_E + \frac{D}{V}k_D$$

If we solve Equation 12.9 for k_E , then we obtain M&M Proposition 2. (The algebra is shown in the accompanying "Explain It: M&M Proposition 2 (No Taxes)" below.)

EQUATION 12.10

$$k_E = k_U + (k_U - k_D)\,\frac{D}{E}$$

Explain It: M&M Proposition 2 (No Taxes)

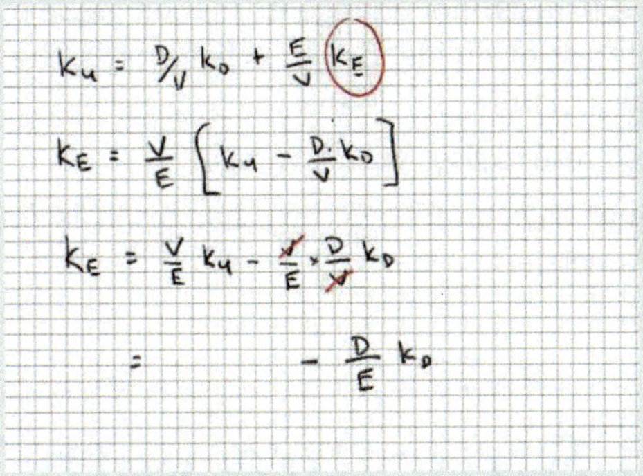

View in the online reader

Equation 12.10 shows that the required return on the shares of a levered company, k_E , increases in direct proportion to the debt/equity ratio. The return on equity is an increasing function of leverage because leverage makes equity riskier and shareholders compensate by requiring a higher return. The rate of increase is equal to the spread between k_U and k_D .

Proposition 2 is described in "Explain It: Modigliani & Miller Proposition 2 (No Taxes)". It also shows and graphs the WACC. Notice that the WACC is constant regardless of the level of debt. As leverage increases, the rising cost of equity offsets the lower cost of debt and causes the WACC to remain constant.

Explain It: Modigliani & Miller Proposition 2 (No Taxes)

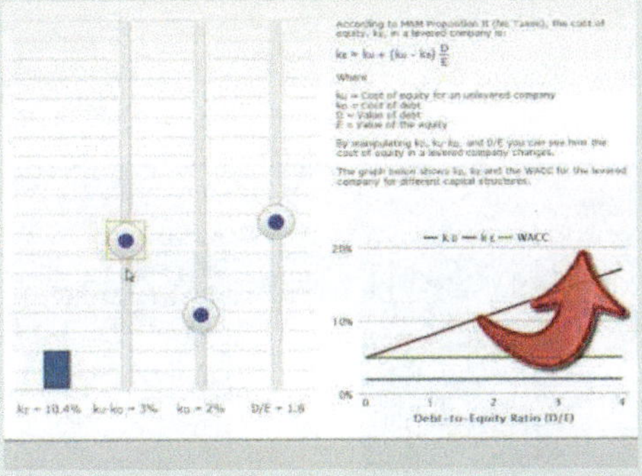

View in the online reader

Conclusions

M&M drew the following conclusions from Propositions 1 and 2:

- Firm value is determined by the left-hand of the balance sheet, the firm's assets, and the cash flow generated by them. A firm cannot change its market value by splitting its cash flows into different streams (i.e., interest or dividends). In other words, the market value of any firm is independent of its capital structure.
- The shareholder's required return rises with leverage.
- The WACC does not change as capital structure changes. It is determined by the riskiness of the company's business (assets).

12.4 Capital Structure with Taxes

We begin this section by describing the tax benefit of debt, which is called the interest tax shield. We then augment the M&M model to include interest tax deductibility. This produces a new relationship between the value of levered and unlevered firms and it changes the relationship between leverage and the required return of shareholders.

Interest Tax Shield

operating cash flow

Revenues less costs (including fixed costs) and taxes. Also equal to net income plus interest and depreciation.

Interest creates a tax shield in the same way as depreciation. Since interest is tax deductible, taxes are lower for companies that are debt financed. Look at Table 12.2 below, which shows taxes, net income, and **operating cash flow** for Mail-Order Pizzas for an EBIT of $200. The two columns in the table correspond to the two capital structures: all equity and 50% debt.

Explain It: The Interest Tax Shield

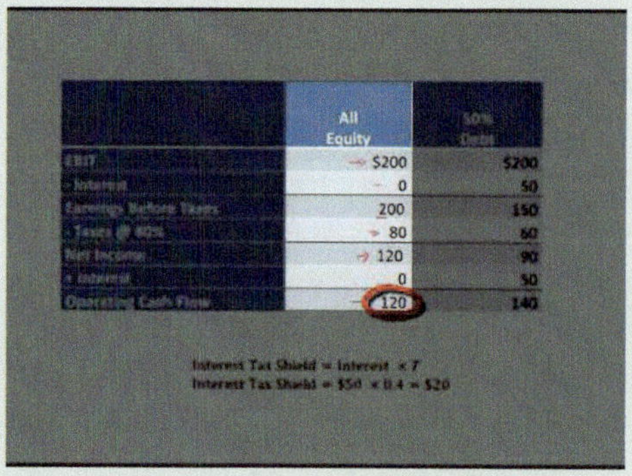

View in the online reader

TABLE 12.2
The Interest Tax Shield and Operating Cash Flows

	All Equity	50% Debt
EBIT	$200	$200
–Interest	$0	–$50
EBT	200	150
–Taxes @ 40%	80	60
Net Income	120	90
+Interest	0	50
=OCF	120	140

Tip

Operating cash flows are given by

$$OCF = EBIT - Taxes$$

But, we can also express them as

$$OCF = Net\ income + Interest$$

where

$$Net\ income = EBIT - Interest - Taxes$$

Tip

The amount of cash available for distribution to stock and bondholders is called free cash flow. Free cash flow is equal to operating cash flow when there are no investments in working capital or fixed assets, which is the case in all of our examples.

Operating cash flow is the amount of cash available to be distributed to stock and bondholders. The operating cash flow for Mail-Order Pizzas when it is all equity financed is $120, compared to $140 if it is 50% debt financed. Operating cash flows are higher with the debt financing because taxes are $20 lower. The difference is called the interest tax shield. The interest tax shield is equal to the product of the interest expense and the corporate tax rate. In this example, the interest tax shield is $\$20 = 0.4 \times \$50$.[2]

M&M Proposition 1: Debt and Value with Taxes

In Table 12.2, we saw that the operating cash flows generated with the 50% debt financing are larger than with all equity financing and the difference is equal to the interest tax shield.

We know that the value of a company is equal to the present value of its cash flows. Modigliani and Miller Proposition 1 (with taxes) shows that the value of the levered company is greater than the value of the unlevered company and the difference is equal to the present value of the tax shields.

M&M Proposition 1 (with taxes) states that the value of the levered company is equal to:

EQUATION 12.11

$$V_L = V_U + PV_{\text{Tax shields}} = V_U + (T \times D)$$

Explain It: M&M Proposition 1 (with Taxes)

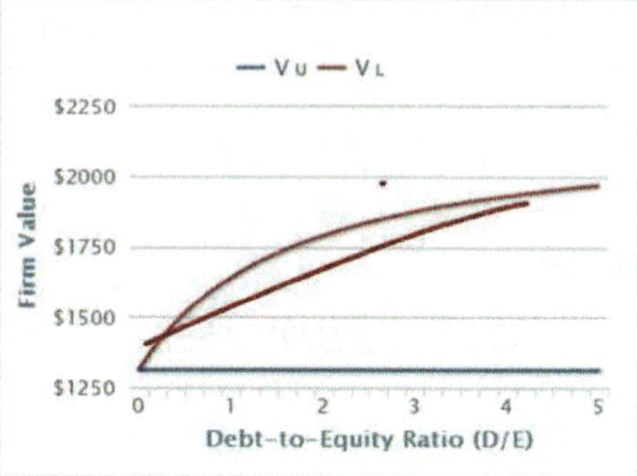

View in the online reader

The interest tax shield is just the interest expense (the bond coupon, $k_D D$) multiplied by the corporate tax rate, *T*. If the tax shields are a perpetuity (as we have been assuming in all of our examples), then the present value of the tax shields is just the annual tax shield divided by the appropriate interest rate. But what is the appropriate rate? The appropriate rate is k_D. The interest tax shields have the same risk as the bond coupons. Bondholders discount the coupons at k_D, so the tax shields should be discounted at k_D. The present value of the interest tax shield perpetuity is:

EQUATION 12.12

$$PV_{\text{Tax shields}} = \frac{k_D D \times T}{k_D} = D \times T$$

Tip

The present value of a perpetuity with annual cash flow of $PMT is $PV = \$PMT/i$.

A derivation of Proposition 1 is provided in "Explain It: Proof of M&M Proposition 1 (with Taxes)".

Explain It: Proof of M&M Proposition 1 (with Taxes)

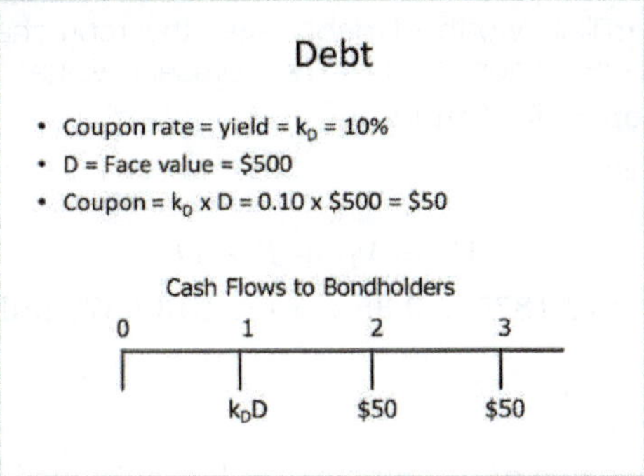

View in the online reader

The following example employs Proposition 1 to analyze the impact of a change in capital structure on the stock price.

Example 12.5 M&M Proposition 1 with Taxes

Initech Inc. is an all-equity firm that generates EBIT of $3 million per year in perpetuity. The required return of shareholders, k_U , is 16%, and its marginal tax rate, T, is 35%. Assume that all cash flows are paid annually at the end of the year and we are currently at the beginning of a year.

First, calculate the market value of Initech. Second, if Initech issues $4 million of perpetual debt with a coupon rate (and yield) of 9%, what is the market value of the firm? Assume that the debt is used to repurchase stock. The shares are cancelled after being repurchased. What is the market value of the firm's equity after the repurchase?

SOLUTION

Algebraic Solution

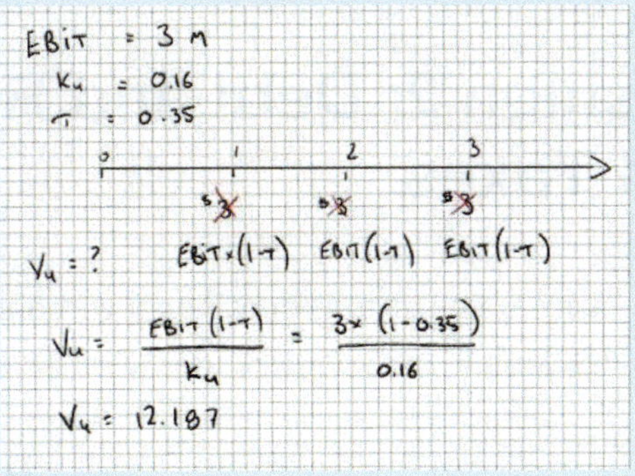

View in the online reader

Market Value before Share Repurchase

The market value of the all-equity firm is the present value of the operating cash flows when discounted at their required return, k_U :

$$V_U = \frac{EBIT \times (1-T)}{k_U} = \frac{\$3 \times (1-0.35)}{0.16} = \$12.1875 \text{ million}$$

Market Value after Share Repurchase

The company executes a share repurchase and buys $4 million worth of shares. The repurchase is financed by issuing $4 million worth of debt. After the repurchase, the value of the firm is given by Proposition 1 (Equation 12.11). The present value (PV) of the tax shield is $T \times D = 0.35 \times \$4 \text{ million} = \$1.4 \text{ million}$.

The market value of Initech is:

$$V_L = V_U + T \times D$$
$$V_L = \$12.1875 + 0.35 \times \$4 = \$13.5875 \text{ million}$$

With corporate taxes, the value of a company can be envisioned as a pie with three slices, as shown in Figure 12.4.

FIGURE 12.4 M&M with Taxes

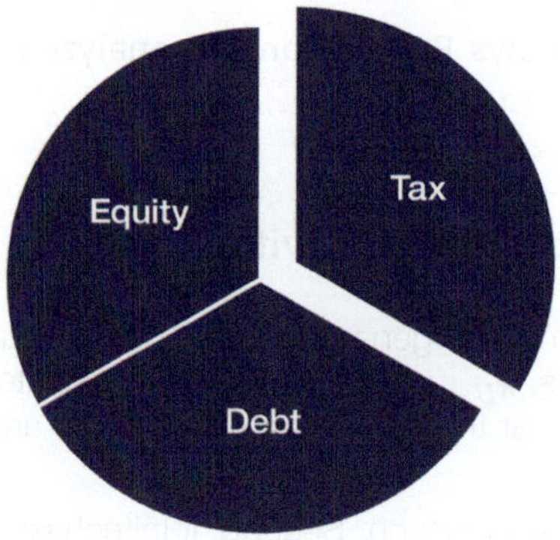

The stockholders control one slice and the bondholders control another. The sum of the two slices is the value of the levered firm. The third slice is the government's slice, which it takes as corporate income taxes. The main insight of Modigliani and Miller (with taxes) is that capital structure can affect firm value by reducing the size of the government's slice.

M&M Proposition 2: Debt and Required Returns with Taxes

M&M Proposition 2 with taxes is similar to Proposition 2 without taxes. The cost of equity is an increasing function of leverage.

EQUATION 12.13

$$k_E = k_U + (k_U - k_D)(1-T)\frac{D}{E}$$

Proposition 2 shows that the required return of shareholders of a levered company, k_E, increases in direct proportion to the debt/equity ratio, expressed in market values. The rate of increase is equal to $(k_U - k_D) \times (1-T)$. As leverage increases, the required return of bondholders is constant and the required return of shareholders rises. However, the return of shareholders rises more slowly than in the case with no corporate taxes and so the WACC declines as leverage increases. Notice how the WACC line declines slowly as the debt-to-equity ratio rises in the following video.

Tip

Recall that the WACC is constant as leverage increases with no corporate taxes.

Explain It: The M&M Proposition 2 (with Taxes)

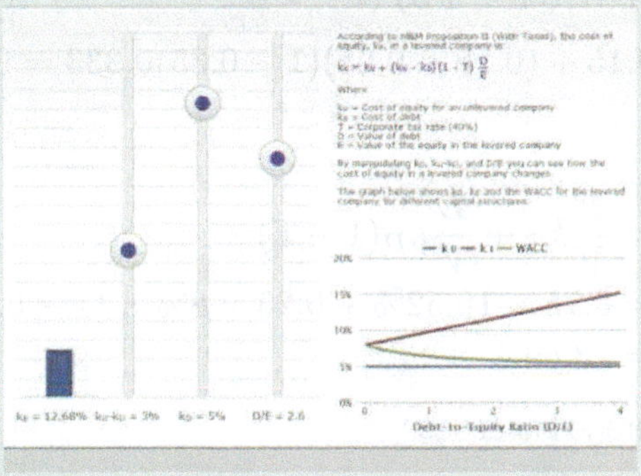

View in the online reader

The following example employs Proposition 2 to show how the required return on equity changes with increases in leverage.

Example 12.6 M&M Proposition 2 with Taxes

Vapid Motor Corp. has no debt, but can borrow at 8%. The firm's WACC is 15% and the tax rate is 35%. What is Vapid's cost of equity? If the firm converts to 25% debt $(D/V = 25\%)$ what will its cost of equity be, and what happens to the WACC?

SOLUTION

Algebraic Solution

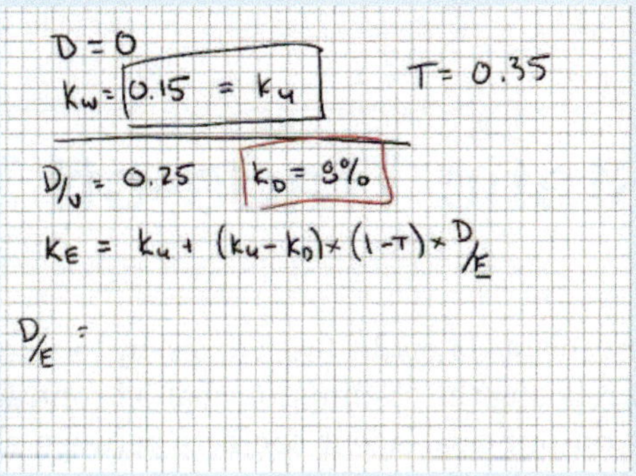

View in the online reader

If the firm is all equity financed, then the cost of equity is the WACC.

$$k_u = k_w = 15\%$$

If the firm converts to 25% debt $(D/V = 0.25)$, then its debt-to-equity ratio will be $D/E = 0.25/0.75 = 1/3$. We can use Equation 12.13 to solve the required return of the shareholders:

Tip: $D/E = (D/V)/(1 - D/V)$

$$k_E = k_U + (k_U - k_D)(1 - T)\frac{D}{E}$$
$$k_E = 0.15 + (0.15 - 0.08)(1 - 0.35)0.333 = 0.1652$$

WACC

$$k_W = \frac{E}{V}k_E + \frac{D}{V}k_D(1 - T)$$
$$k_W = 0.75 \times 16.52\% + 0.25 \times 8\% \times (1 - 0.35)$$
$$k_W = 13.69\%$$

The WACC declines as leverage increases.

Conclusions

With or without taxes, M&M showed how leverage increases the risk of equity and the required return of shareholders. With no taxes, M&M showed that capital structure is irrelevant—there is no one capital structure that maximizes the value of the company. With the addition of taxes, M&M showed that the optimal capital structure is 100% debt. But this implication isn't realistic. The average ratio of debt to value is around 27%.[3]

M&M made a number of assumptions to arrive at their conclusions. If we don't like the conclusions, then we have to relax the assumptions. To derive a theory that predicts an optimal capital structure of less than 100% debt, we relax the assumption of no transactions costs. In particular, in the next section, we assume that financial distress is costly and that contracts between corporate stakeholders are not perfect.

12.5 The Static Trade-off Theory

In this section, we augment the M&M model (with taxes) by relaxing the assumption that financial distress is costless and by relaxing the assumption that all contracts are perfect. In particular, we look at the effect of debt on principal–agent conflicts between shareholders and managers and between shareholders and bondholders.

Financial Distress Costs

When a company cannot make interest or principal payments to its creditors, it declares bankruptcy. Federal bankruptcy laws govern how companies reorganize or liquidate. A bankrupt company can use Chapter 11 of the Federal Bankruptcy Code to reorganize its business and try to become profitable again. Management continues to run the business but is closely supervised by lenders and the bankruptcy court. Alternatively, a bankrupt company can cease operations and go out of business. The assets are liquidated by a trustee, and the proceeds are used to pay off debt.

Tip

Creditors can also petition for bankruptcy. This is called "liquidation" under Chapter 7 of the Federal Bankruptcy Code.

In bankruptcy, secured creditors (e.g., banks or secured bondholders) are paid first. Unsecured creditors (e.g., banks, suppliers, and **debenture** holders) have the next claim. Shareholders have a residual claim and usually receive nothing.

debenture
Unsecured bonds.

There are direct and indirect costs to bankruptcy. The formal cost of filing with the bankruptcy court, paying attorneys, and so forth are the direct bankruptcy costs. These are small compared with the indirect costs. Indirect bankruptcy costs arise because a firm facing financial distress must work to recover its economic health. In addition to the managerial time and effort that will be expended dealing with creditors and attorneys, there may be a loss of customers and key employees. Customers often avoid purchasing from financially distressed firms, and good employees often tend to seek new employment when a firm's probability of bankruptcy increases.

Explain It

Customers tend to avoid buying durable goods from financially weak firms. Chrysler and General Motors filed for bankruptcy in 2009. In addition to problems caused by the continuing recession, sales suffered because customers did not want to buy a car from a company that might not survive to perform warranty work and supply parts. In the late 1990s, Apple Computer faced the same problem. Even die-hard Apple fans were reluctant to buy Apple computers out of concern the firm might not survive to service the units.

A firm does not have to declare bankruptcy to incur bankruptcy costs. As the debt-equity ratio increases, so does the probability of bankruptcy. Because some of these costs are incurred prior to bankruptcy, it is more accurate to label them **financial distress costs** (because they are incurred when a company is in distress but not yet bankrupt). We can model financial distress costs as a rising function of the debt-to-equity ratio, as shown in Figure 12.5.

financial distress costs
The direct and indirect costs of bankruptcy that are incurred prior to and in bankruptcy.

FIGURE 12.5 Financial Distress Costs

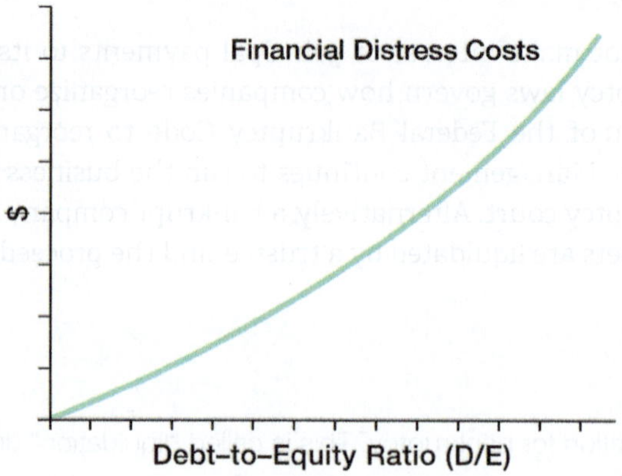

The static trade-off theory of capital structure incorporates financial distress costs into the Modigliani and Miller model with taxes. Under the static trade-off theory, the value of the levered firm is equal to the sum of the value of the unlevered firm and the value of tax shields (as per Equation 12.11) less the present value of financial distress costs.

EQUATION 12.14

$$V_L = V_U + PV_{\text{Tax shields}} - PV(\text{Financial distress costs})$$

In Figure 12.6, we graph the value of the firm for our three models: (1) M&M with no taxes, (2) M&M with taxes, and (3) the static trade-off theory with financial distress costs. With no taxes, there is no optimal capital structure. Firm value is invariant to capital structure. With taxes, the optimal capital structure is 100% debt. Under the static trade-off theory, there is an optimal D/E ratio that produces a maximum firm value. That is the optimal capital structure. Higher levels of debt produce increases in financial distress costs that are greater than the marginal increase in tax shields.

FIGURE 12.6 Firm Value and Capital Structure with Financial Distress Costs

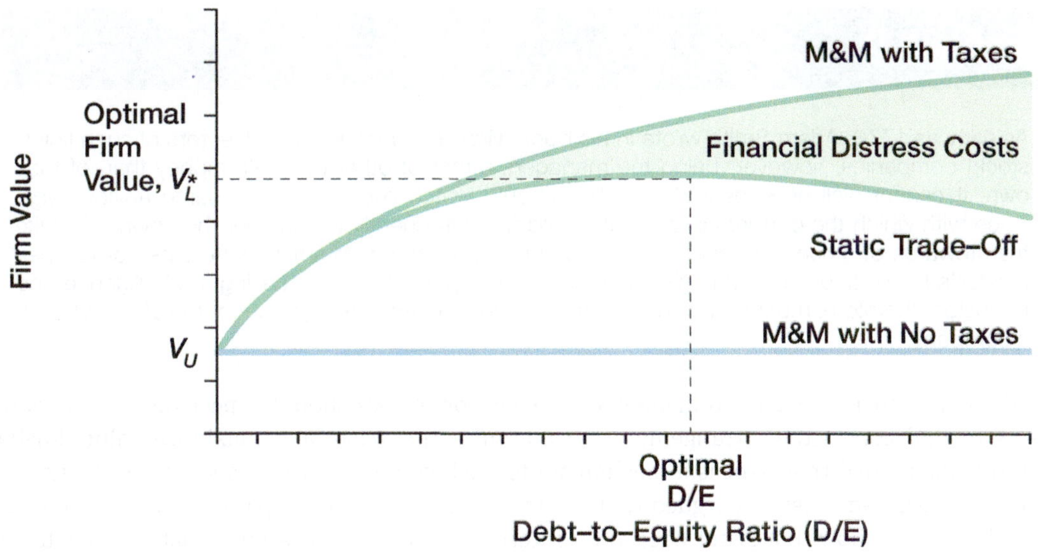

Agency Costs

Berle and Means (1933) observed that there is a separation of ownership and control in modern corporations.[4] Stockholders have no operational control over the companies they own. Stockholders are entitled to vote for members of the board of directors who hire the CEO and/or president and review major decisions. The president hires senior managers, and the senior executive team controls the company and makes operational decisions.

The separation of ownership and control creates the potential for a misalignment of objectives. Managers may not act in the best interest of stockholders. This is known as the principal–agent problem. A principal–agent problem occurs when the agent does not act in the best interest of the principal. Principal–agent problems are costly: First, there are contracting costs associated with efforts to make sure that agents act in the best interest of the principal, and second, there is the waste associated with bad decisions made by managers pursuing their own self-interests. The following Explain Its tell two stories of wasteful managers and remind us that principal agent problems aren't new since old economists like Adam Smith wrote about them in 1776.

Explain It

A good example of agency costs is the story of Armand Hammer, who was CEO of Occidental Petroleum from 1957 until his death at age 92 in 1990. Under a golden coffin agreement, Hammer's estate continued to receive his salary of $2.3 million for 8 years after his death. Hammer purchased a Leonardo Da Vinci manuscript titled The Codex Hammer using $5.6 million of Occidontal's money. Hammer used $95 million of Occidental's money to collect impressionist paintings. To house his collection, he used approximately $250 million of Occidental's money to build the Armand Hammer Museum of Art and Cultural Center, which is alongside Occidental's corporate headquarters in Los Angeles. In 1986, Hammer had Occidental acquire a 5% share (costing about $15 million) in Church & Dwight, who were manufacturers of Arm & Hammer brand baking soda. The acquisition was motivated by the similarity between the product and his name.

Explain It

As early as 1776, Adam Smith wrote in his book, *Wealth of Nations*: the directors of such [joint-stock] companies, however, being the managers rather of other people's money than of their own, it cannot well be expected that they should watch over it with the same anxious vigilance with which the partners in a private copartnery frequently watch over their own. . . . Like the stewards of a rich man, they are apt to consider attention to small matters as not for their master's honor and very easily give themselves a dispensation from having it. Negligence and profusion, therefore, must always prevail, more or less, in the management of the affairs of such a company.[5]

Because principal–agent problems reduce share prices, we should expect rational economic agents to find contractual arrangements to minimize the waste and maximize value. Michael Jensen (1986) argued that debt is a mechanism for reducing the waste associated with the principal–agent problem.[6] Jensen argued that waste can only arise in companies that have free cash flow. That is, cash flow that is not needed for internal investment. He argued that one way to stop the waste is to remove the cash from management's discretion by paying it out as interest on debt. Thus, increased leverage can increase firm value if it reduces agency costs.

covenants

Covenants are conditions that the issuer must meet. Covenants include such things as maximum debt-to-equity ratios, minimum working capital levels, restrictions on dividend policy and capital expenditures, reporting requirements, and any other conditions the lender feels will increase the probability of timely repayment. If the borrower fails to keep any of the covenants, then the lender has the right to declare the borrower in default and to demand immediate repayment.

The owner–manager relationship is not the only principal–agent relationship in the corporation. Jensen and Meckling (1976) argue that agency costs arise between owners and lenders.[7] Consider a company where the entrepreneur invests $10,000 of equity and lenders contribute $100 million of debt. With that financial structure, the entrepreneur has an incentive to accept projects that are long shots, especially if the company is in financial distress. Long shots are projects with a low probability of a very high payoff. If the long shot pays off, then the entrepreneur captures most of the gains; if it turns out badly, the lenders bear the costs (because they own the bankrupt company). To protect themselves, lenders include **covenants** in their loans in order to limit the ability of managers to select long-shot projects. Additionally, bondholders demand higher interest rates as leverage increases.

We can incorporate agency costs into the static tradeoff theory and expand Equation 12.14 as follows:

EQUATION 12.15

$$V_L = V_U + PV_{\text{Tax shields}} - PV(\text{Financial distress costs}) - PV(\text{Agency costs}) + PV(\text{Agency benefits})$$

where PV(Agency costs) is the present value of costs due to agency conflicts between shareholders and bondholders, and PV(Agency benefits) is the present value of the reduction in costs associated with conflicts between shareholders and managers.

Figure 12.7 depicts Equation 12.15 graphically. Figure 12.7 is similar to Figure 12.6 except that we have added agency costs (the shaded yellow area). When agency costs are added to financial distress costs, the set of leveraged firm values (the purple line) shifts down compared to the set available when we only considered financial distress costs (the green line). As a result, the optimal capital structure is lower. In this figure, we have assumed that agency costs outweigh agency benefits. The balance of costs and benefits varies from company to company, and so will the optimal capital structure.

FIGURE 12.7 Firm Value and Capital Structure with Agency Costs

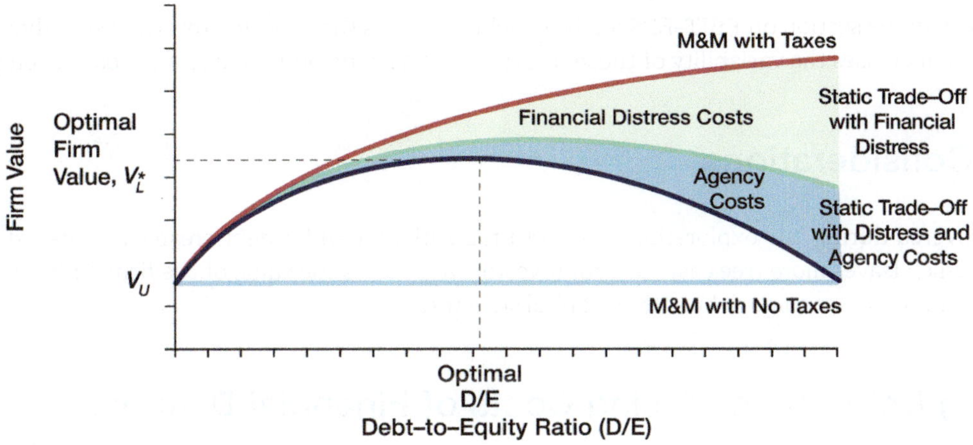

Conclusions about Optimal Capital Structure

Table 12.3 shows that there are big differences in capital structures across industries.[8] These differences reflect the fact that the optimal capital structure varies by industry, and even by firm within industries.

TABLE 12.3 Debt Ratios (Debt-to-Value) by Industry

Industry	Debt Ratio
Aerospace/defense	19%
Automotive	52%
Bank	46%
Drug	12%
Electronics	16%
Paper/forest products	42%
Petroleum	16%
Power	50%
Railroads	21%
Semiconductor	6%
Telecom	46%
Average	27%

Do financial managers really have target capital structures as theory suggests they should? In a survey of Fortune 500 firms, 81% of financial managers admitted to either a flexible or strict capital structure target.[9]

What can we tell financial managers about selecting their target capital structure? Despite the many years of research and effort put into identifying the optimal capital structure, there is no simple answer to the question. In fact, there is much we don't yet understand about capital structure. Let's review what we *do* know.

Risk and Return

As we saw in the section on EBIT–EPS analysis, debt increases the expected return to shareholders but it also increases the variability of those returns. Debt also introduces the risk of bankruptcy.

Tax Considerations

As discovered during our exploration of M&M Propositions 1 and 2, debt creates an interest tax shield, which leaves more free cash flow for investors and raises the value of the firm. This implies that firms should use some debt in their capital structure.

Rising Debt Means Rising Costs of Financial Distress

As debt increases, so do financial distress costs. The optimal debt level balances this cost against the tax benefit of using debt.

Debt Affects Principal–Agent Conflicts

As debt increases, managers have less free cash flow that they can waste, but shareholders are increasingly likely to accept long-shot projects. Debt has agency benefits and costs. Each company's exposure to these costs is different, and so the balance of benefits and costs is different.

Differences in Risk among Firms

Different firms are subject to different levels of risk. Firms with variable sales and/or high operating leverage have a higher probability of financial distress and are likely to maintain low debt ratios to keep total risk reasonable.

Other Considerations

Also pertinent to the capital structure decision:

- Some firms value the flexibility provided by low debt more than other firms do.
- Some owners and managers are more concerned about risk than others.
- Some owners want to retain control of their companies and so prefer debt over equity (since new equity will dilute their ownership).
- Finally, not all companies need the interest tax shield and so use less debt. Graham and Tucker (2006) study a sample of 44 companies that use tax shelters to reduce their corporate taxes.[10] Those companies have debt ratios that are about 8% lower than comparable companies.

Endnotes

1. Miller, Merton H., and Franco Modgiliani, "The Cost of Capital, Corporation Finance and the Theory of Investment," *American Economic Review 48*, no. 3 (1958): 261–97.
2. The tax rate is 40%.
3. Damodaran, Aswath. From Damodaran online. http://pages.stern.nyu.edu/~adamodar/. Debt ratio uses market value of debt. Data from annual reports, Value Line, Capital IQ, and Bloomberg.
4. Berle, Adolph A., and Gardiner C. Means, *The Modern Corporation and Private Property* (New York: Macmillan, 1933).
5. Adam Smith, *The Wealth of Nations (1776)*, Part II, "Of the Expense of Justice."
6. Jensen, Michael C., "Agency Costs of Free Cash Flow, Corporate Finance and Takeovers," *American Economic Review 76*, no. 2 (1986): 323–29.
7. Jensen, Michael C., and William H. Meckling, "Theory of the Firm: Managerial Behavior, Agency Costs, and Ownership Structure," *Journal of Financial Economics 3*, no. 4 (1976): 305–60.
8. Damodaran, Aswath, "Debt Ratio Uses Market Value of Debt," http://pages.stern.nyu.edu/~adamodar/. Data from annual reports, Value Line, Capital IQ, and Bloomberg.
9. Graham, John R., and Campbell R. Harvey, "The Theory and Practice of Corporate Finance: Evidence from the Field," *Recent Developments in Corporate Finance 1* (2005): 122–78; *International Library of Critical Writings in Financial Economics* (Cheltenham, UK: Elgar, 2005).
10. Graham, John R., and Alan L. Tucker, "Tax Shelters and Corporate Debt Policy," *Journal of Financial Economics 81* (2006): 563–94.

CHAPTER 13

Dividends, Repurchases, and Splits

Learning Objectives

By the end of the chapter you will be able to:

1. List the types of distributions; understand the aggregate value of payouts and the way distributions are taxed.
2. Understand the mechanics of dividends and how dividends impact stock prices and shareholder wealth.
3. Understand the mechanics of stock repurchases and how repurchases affect stock prices and shareholder wealth.
4. Understand the mechanics of stock splits and how they impact stock prices.

Distributions are payments of cash to shareholders. Distributions come in two forms: dividends and stock repurchases.

In a perfect world, the question of when companies should distribute cash is simple. Companies should retain cash when there are positive net present value (NPV) projects. The retained cash is used to finance the projects. Shareholders then earn an (internal) rate of return that is higher than their required return. Companies should distribute cash when the internal rate of return (IRR) on the available projects is less than the shareholders' required return (negative NPV projects). In this case, shareholders can earn higher returns by investing in other companies that have better projects.

In an imperfect world with taxes, **asymmetric information**, and agency problems, the issues of how much a company should distribute and how the market reacts to distributions are more complicated.

asymmetric information

Information that is not shared equally across individuals. Some know more than others.

This chapter explains the institutional mechanics of dividends and repurchases. It shows the impact that distributions have on the stock price under the assumption of perfect markets and it briefly explores the impact of taxes, asymmetric information, and agency problems (i.e., imperfect markets).

13.1 Distributions

In this section, we explain the different types of dividends and repurchases, show the history of how much of each type has been paid, look at how many firms make payouts and how much they tend to pay, and discuss the taxation of dividends and repurchases.

Distributions Defined

share repurchase

Same as a stock repurchase. When a company buys back its own shares so that the shares are no longer outstanding.

A distribution is a payment to shareholders. There are two primary forms of distributions: dividends and **share repurchases**.

There are three types of dividends, which are listed in Table 13.1, along with an example of a press release announcing each type of distribution.

TABLE 13.1 Types of Dividends

Regular cash dividend	For the 50th year in a row, an increase in the quarterly dividend rates was announced on April 26, 2012, at the annual meeting of Johnson & Johnson shareholders. The 7% increase is reflected in the $0.61 per share quarterly dividend payment, up from the previous quarter's payment of $0.57 per share. Johnson & Johnson pays its next quarterly dividend on June 12, 2012, to shareholders of record as of May 29, 2012.[1]
Extra (special) dividend	Citing significant growth in revenues and net income due to increased truck production, financial services revenues, and "aftermarket" sales in 2011, PACCAR's Board of Directors declared not only a quarterly cash dividend of $0.18 per share but also a special cash dividend of $0.70 per share. The special dividend is payable on January 5, 2012, to shareholders of record on December 19, 2011. The next quarterly dividend is payable on March 15, 2012, to shareholders of record on February 17, 2012. Mark Pigott, PACCAR's chairman and chief executive officer, said that these successes are directly reflected in PACCAR's increase in operating cash flow in the amount of $1.15 billion for the first three quarters of 2011.[2]
Stock dividend	Shareholders of common stock and Class B common stock of Tootsie Roll Industries will receive an extra 3% stock dividend on April 7, 2011. This dividend was declared by the Tootsie Roll's Board of Directors on February 22, 2011. Fractional shares will receive a cash payment based on the closing price on the NYSE on the date of record, March 8, 2011.[3]

The most common distribution is regular cash dividends. Cash dividends are typically paid quarterly. A stock dividend is not cash; it is additional shares in the company. We explore stock dividends in the final section of this chapter.

There are three types of share repurchases listed in Table 13.2. In a share repurchase, the company buys back some of its shares and so the number of shares outstanding is reduced. Open-market repurchases are the most common, so they are our main focus.

TABLE 13.2 Types of Share Repurchase

Open-market share repurchase	**Chase Manhattan** On March 13, 2012, Jamie Dimon, Chairman and CEO of JP Morgan Chase, announced Chase's $15 billion equity repurchase program. The number of shares repurchased will depend on a number of factors: (1) market conditions, (2) operating cash flows, (3) the company's capital structure, and (4) the availability of new investment opportunities. The repurchase program will be accomplished in the open market (with no price targets) or it may be privately negotiated (including purchases under Rule 10b5-1 programs). The program may be terminated at any time. The company will buy back at least as many shares as are issued for employee stock purchase and employ stock option programs. The company will buy back more shares if its operating cash flow exceeds investment needs and if the repurchase opportunities provide value to the existing shareholders.[4]
Fixed-price share repurchase	**TechTarget** On November 9, 2010, the Board of Directors of TechTarget, Inc. (NASDAQ: TTGT) announced a tender offer to repurchase up to 10 million common shares at a price of $6.00 per share. The number of shares targeted for repurchase is 23.5% of the 42.6 million shares outstanding. TechTarget's common shares closed at a price of $5.13 per share on November 5, 2010. This offer expires on December 9, 2010, at 5:00 p.m. EST unless TechTarget extends the deadline. If more than 10 million shares are tendered, then TechTarget will repurchase the tendered shares on a pro rata basis. Cash payments (net in cash minus any taxes and no interest) to shareholders will be made after the expiration of the tender period.[5]
Dutch auction share repurchase	**Expedia** On December 8, 2006, Expedia, Inc. (Nasdaq: EXPE) announced it will repurchase up to 30 million shares of its common stock using a modified Dutch auction. Between December 11, 2006, and January 10, 2007, shareholders are invited to submit offers to sell. Offers must indicate the number of shares and a price within the company's specified range of $18.50 to no greater than $22. The repurchase is targeting to buy back approximately 9.8% of common shares outstanding. Based on the number of shares tendered and prices specified by tendering stockholders, the company will determine the lowest price per share that will enable it to purchase 30 million shares, or a lesser number as are properly tendered. Expedia will not purchase shares below a stockholder's stipulated price, but may, in some cases, purchase shares at prices above it. Expedia, Inc.'s directors and officers and Liberty Media Corporation have advised the company that they do not intend to tender any shares.[6]

A History of Dividends and Repurchases

Figure 13.1 shows the total value of dividends and stock repurchases affected by publicly traded nonfinancial corporations in the United States between 1993 and 2019. The value of dividends has increased slowly but steadily. The value of repurchases rose dramatically during the 1990s to exceed the value of dividends by the late 1990s. The value of repurchases is more volatile than the value of dividends, and it seems to vary with the business cycle with lows following recessions. Look in particular at the large drop in the value of repurchases following the financial crises in 2008.

FIGURE 13.1 The Value of Dividends and Repurchases

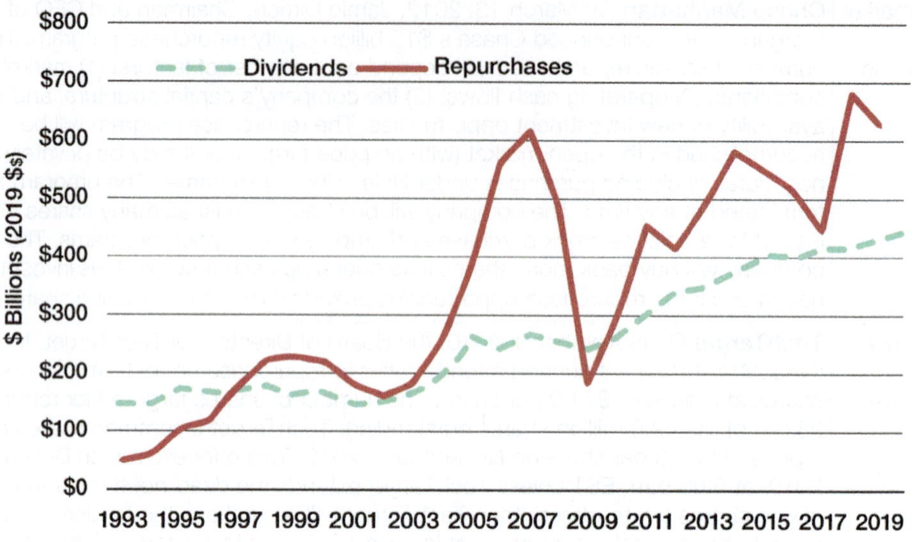

Who Pays and How Much?

distribution yields

The value of cash distributed during the year divided by the market value of the company's equity.

Figure 13.2 presents a histogram of **distribution yields** across public nonfinancial corporations in 2013.

FIGURE 13.2 Distribution Yield

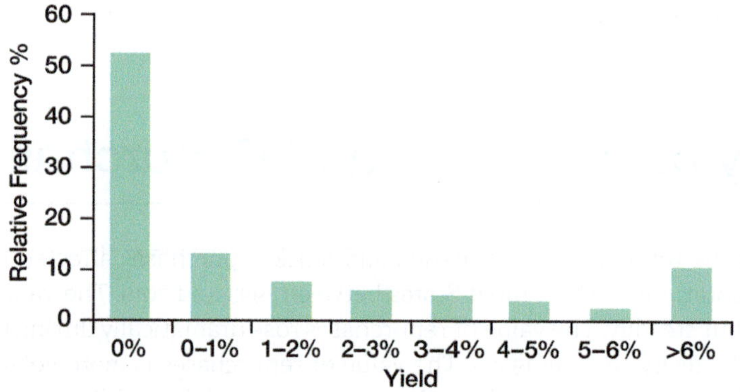

Most companies (52%) have a yield of 0%. That is, most companies distribute nothing to their shareholders. These companies include smaller, younger companies that are reinvesting in their growth. It also includes companies enduring difficult business circumstances who cannot afford to make distributions. Of the companies that do make distributions, the median yield is 2.6%.

Figure 13.2 suggests that dividends are not common. Research shows that a small number of companies pay most of the dividends and generate most of the earnings.[7] For example, one study found that, in the year 2000, 25 firms accounted for over half of profits earned and dividends paid. Figure 13.3 presents some of the results from that study. (Read "Explain It" for a description of the results shown in Figure 13.3.)

FIGURE 13.3 Dividend Yield (Payout Rate)

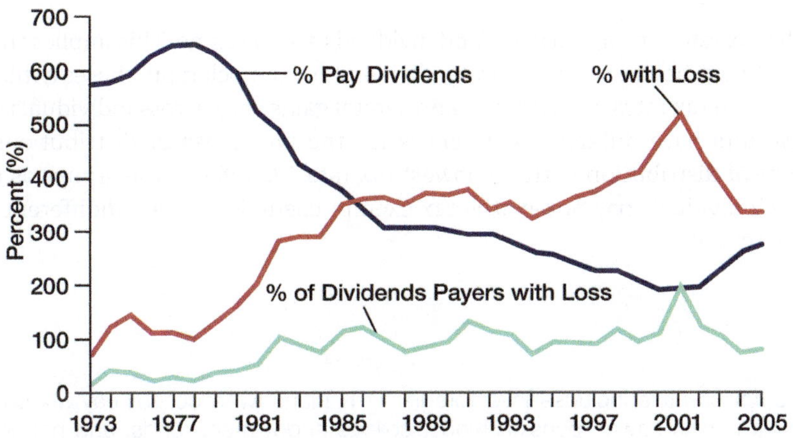

Data from DeAngelo, H., L. DeAngelo, and D. J. Skinner, "Corporate Payout Policy," *Foundations and Trends in Finance 3*, nos. 2–3 (2008): 95–287.

Explain It

The blue line shows the proportion of industrial firms that pay dividends. The proportion fell to about 20% in 2001 but recently it has risen toward 25%. In other words, only about one-quarter of all (industrial) companies pay dividends. The red line shows the proportion of all companies that reported a loss in the given year. The green line shows the proportion of the dividend-paying companies that reported a loss. The proportion of dividend payers with a loss is much smaller than the proportion of companies with a loss in the overall population. The takeaway from this graph is that few companies pay dividends and the companies that do pay dividends tend to be the most profitable.

Taxes on Dividends and Capital Gains

When dividends are declared, stockholders must pay tax on the dividend in the year the dividend is paid. When companies repurchase shares, the shareholders who sell realize a capital gain (or loss) at the time of the sale. The size of the gain depends on the average cost (basis) of the shares sold. The tax rates for 2020 on dividends and capital gains are shown in Table 13.3.[8] Notice that the rates are identical for capital gains or dividends and are greater for those in the earning more than $441,450 (in 2020).

TABLE 13.3 Marginal Federal Tax Rates (2020)

Tax Rates by Types of Income			
Taxable Income	Ordinary Income	Qualified Dividends	Capital Gains
=$40,000	12%	15%	15%
>$441,450	35%	20%	20%

qualified dividends

Dividends paid by a U.S. corporation when the stock is held for more than 60 days prior to an ex-dividend date.

capital gains

Earnings that are due to an increase in the price of security held for more than 1 year.

Tax Clienteles and Distribution Policy

clienteles

A group of investors who have similar preferences for a firm that follows a particular distribution policy. The preference usually derives from the tax rate paid by the group, but it can also stem from other sources such as "prudent man" guidelines, which encourage institutions to hold dividend paying stocks.

Notice that the tax rates on capital gains and dividends are the same. This implies that investors in each tax bracket have no tax reason to prefer dividends over stock repurchases (which are taxed as capital gains). When tax rates on dividends and capital gains vary across individuals, then different groups of investors have different preferences for the two types of distributions. Each group prefers the type of distribution with the lowest tax rate. We refer to the groups as **clienteles**. For example, some individuals pay no tax (the tax-exempt clientele) and are indifferent between dividends and repurchases.

Tip

The tax exempt clientele includes investors in 401K plans (who do not pay tax on investment income until it is withdrawn), pension funds, college endowment funds, and nonprofit foundations.

In 2003, the Jobs and Growth Tax Relief Reconciliation Act (JGRRA) reduced the maximum federal tax rate on dividends from 35% to 15%, and on capital gains from 20% to 15%. This change increased the size of the clientele that preferred dividends. The increased demand for dividend-paying companies would be expected to change dividend policies and stock prices. A company that switched from repurchases to dividends might enjoy an increase in its stock price as the top-income (high tax rate) clientele bid for its shares.

Consistent with this argument, Figure 13.3 shows an increase the proportion of firms paying dividends after 2003. One study estimates a large increase in the percentage of firms that pay dividends and an increase in the level of regular (and special) dividends following JGRRA.[9] Another study reports that about one-third of the firms that initiated dividends in 2003 simultaneously scaled back their level of stock repurchases, which is consistent with the argument that the tax rate changes caused companies to switch from repurchases to dividends.[10]

This argument is the essence of the tax-clientele hypothesis regarding distribution policy. The argument asserts that companies adjust their distribution policy to suit the preferences of underserviced clienteles. Under this hypothesis, the cross section of distribution policies is determined by tax rates. A change in tax rates will cause a change in prices and policies. However, once a new equilibrium is achieved, a company's incentive to change its distribution policy disappears.

13.2 Dividends

This section is all about cash dividends. First, we describe the mechanics of how dividends are paid. Second, we look at a simple model of how dividends should impact stock prices and investor wealth. The simple model assumes perfect markets. In the third subsection, we list some other factors that should affect the stock price reaction to dividends when the assumption of perfect markets is relaxed. Fourth, we look at the empirical evidence of how prices actually react to dividends. Finally, we present some models of how firms actually set their dividends.

Dividend Mechanics and Timing

The first step in the process of paying dividends is for the Board of Directors to vote to do so. As the payment of a dividend is considered a material piece of information for investors, the Board's decision to pay a dividend must be broadly disseminated to the company's investors. This is typically done through newswire releases, as shown in the following Explain It.

Explain It

On April 10, 2018 (for the 128th consecutive year), Procter & Gamble (NYSE: PG) announced its quarterly dividend payment. For the 62nd consecutive year, the company increased its dividend, which demonstrates its commitment to returning cash to shareholders. This quarter, the dividend is 4% more than its previous quarterly dividend payment of $0.6896 per share. Shareholders of record on April 20, 2018, will receive $0.7172 payment per share of common stock on or after May 15, 2018. The Company expects total dividend payments for the year to be $7.5 billion.[11]

FIGURE 13.4 Timing for P&G Dividend

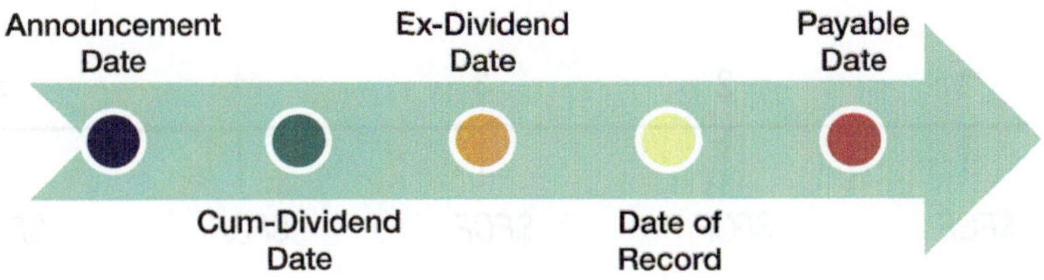

announcement date

The date that the dividend is announced.

cum-dividend date

Two business days before the day of record. The last day on which an investor can buy the stock and receive the forthcoming dividend.

ex-dividend date

One business day prior to the day of record. This is the first day on which the buyer will not be entitled to receive the forthcoming dividend.

date of record

The day on which the list of dividend recipients is created. Registered owners on the date of record receive the dividend.

payable date

The date when the dividend is distributed to holders of record.

1. **Announcement Date:** April 10, 2018. The date that the dividend is announced.
2. **Cum-Dividend Date:** Wednesday, April 18, 2018. Two business days before the date of record. This is the last date on which a buyer can buy the stock and receive the announced dividend. Because of the 2-business-day settlement delay, a buyer is not an owner of record until 2 business days after the trade date. If you were to buy P&G on Wednesday, April 18, 2018, then you would be a registered owner on Friday, April 20, and you would receive the announced dividend.
3. **Ex-Dividend Date:** Thursday, April 19, 2018. The ex-dividend date is 1 business day before the date of record. This is the first date when the buyer of the stock will not be entitled to the dividend. The timing of the ex-dividend day is determined by the 2-day settlement delay mandated by the Securities and Exchange Commission. The 2-day settlement delay is known colloquially as "T+2." Because of the settlement delay, it takes 2 business days from the time you purchase stock until you are recorded as the rightful owner of the stock. Until the 2 days haves passed, the seller of the stock is still registered as the owner. This means that if you buy the stock 1 business day before the date of record you will not become a registered owner until the day after the date of record.
4. **Date of Record:** Friday, April 20, 2018. The day on which the list of dividend recipients is created. Registered owners on the date of record receive the dividend.
5. **Payable Date:** May 15, 2018. This is the date when the dividend is distributed to holders of record.

The Impact of Dividends on the Stock Price

Modigliani and Miller (henceforth M&M) argue that dividend policy is irrelevant.[12] In a perfect world, dividends have no impact on investor wealth. Investors can create "homemade dividends" by selling off a small part of the stock they own, or undo dividends by reinvesting the dividend cash. To make the irrelevance argument, M&M assume perfect markets. That is—no taxes, no asymmetric information, and no transaction costs (no agency problems).

Consider an all-equity financed company with some cash (denoted \$C), and a factory that generates a perpetual, level annual amount of free cash flow (denoted \$FCF). The timeline of cash flows is shown in Figure 13.5.

FIGURE 13.5 Timeline of Cash Flows

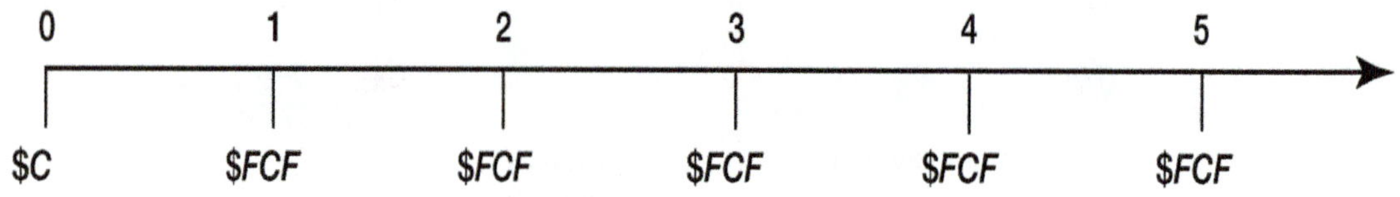

The value of the company (*V*) and its equity (E) is the sum of the cash and the present value of the stream of free cash flow.

Tip

We assume that the first cash flow occurs at the end of the current year. Because the free cash flow stream is a perpetuity, the present value is $\$FCF/k$.

If we assume that all free cash flow is paid out as dividends, then this is just a dividend discount valuation:

EQUATION 13.1

$$V_{cum} = E_{cum} = \$C + \frac{\$FCF}{k}$$

where k is the required return of shareholders.

The company has N shares outstanding, so the current stock price, P_{cum} , is:

EQUATION 13.2

$$P_{cum} = \frac{E}{N} = \frac{\$C}{N} + \frac{1}{N} \times \frac{\$FCF}{k}$$

The company is considering paying out all of the cash as a divided, so the per share dividend (denoted D) is simply:

EQUATION 13.3

$$D = \frac{\$C}{N}$$

After the dividend is paid, the value of the firm's equity is:

> **Tip**
>
> We use the $_{ex}$ subscript to indicate the ex-dividend period. The ex-dividend period starts 1 business day before the day of record.

EQUATION 13.4

$$E_{ex} = \frac{\$FCF}{k}$$

and the price is:

EQUATION 13.5

$$P_{ex} = \frac{E_{ex}}{N} = \frac{1}{N} \times \frac{\$FCF}{k}$$

If you compare Equation 13.2 with Equation 13.5, the difference is $\$C/N$, which is just the per-share dividend. Thus, the price falls by the amount of the dividend.

Explain It: Stock Prices Around the Ex-Dividend Date

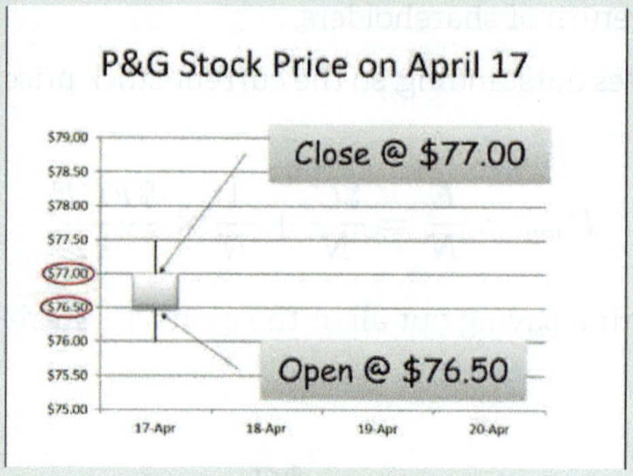

View in the online reader

Explain It: Short Selling Around the Ex-Dividend Date

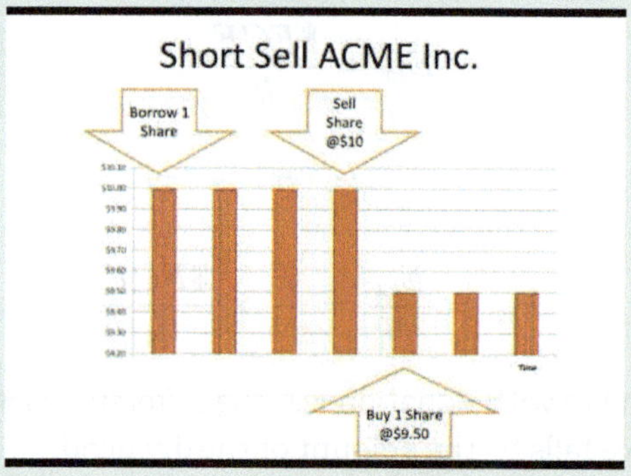

View in the online reader

Example 13.1 Price Impact of a Dividend

Chalk Dust Disposal Inc. has $10 cash and operates an incinerator that generates free cash flow of $5 per year in perpetuity (starting in 1 year). Chalk Dust is all-equity financed, its shareholders require a return of 10%, and it has 100 shares outstanding. The company is considering paying a dividend of $0.1 per share. What is the stock price before the dividend and what is the price after the dividend?

SOLUTION

Algebraic Solution

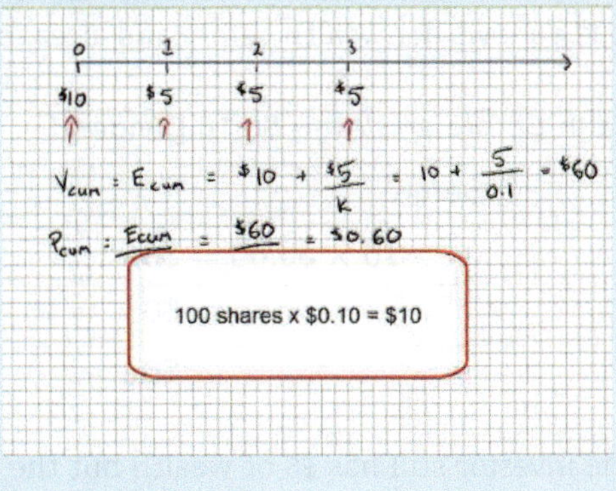

View in the online reader

Following Equation 13.1, the value at time 0 is:

$$V_{cum} = E_{cum} = \$10 + \frac{\$5}{0.1} = \$60$$

Following Equation 13.2, the stock price before the dividend is:

$$P_{cum} = \$60/100 = \$0.60$$

Using Equation 13.4, the value of the company (and its equity) after the dividend is computed is:

$$V_{ex} = E_{ex} = \frac{\$5}{0.1} = \$50$$

Using Equation 13.5, the stock price after the dividend is determined is:

$$P_{ex} = \$50/100 = \$0.50$$

The price fell by the amount of the dividend or $0.10.

Wealth Effects

Let's consider the wealth impact of the dividend. Consider an investor with 10 shares before the dividend (worth $6). Table 13.4 shows her wealth before and after the dividend.

TABLE 13.4 Investor Wealth Before and After $0.10 Dividend

	Before	After
Shares	$10 \times \$0.60 = \$6$	$10 \times \$0.50 = \$5$
Cash	$0	$10 \times \$0.10 = \$1$
Total	$6	$6

After the dividend, the investor still has $6 of wealth but the wealth is now divided between cash and shares. If she did not want $1 of cash, then she could buy two more shares with her $1 of cash. In other words, she could undo the dividend.

Alternatively, if the company had not issued the dividend, but she had wanted $1 of cash, then she could have sold 1.67 shares. After the sale, she would have had 8.33 shares worth $5, and $1 of cash. In other words, she could have made a homemade dividend.

Since there are no wealth impacts from dividends, and since investors can undo a dividend or create a homemade dividend, dividends are said to be irrelevant.

Other Factors Affecting Dividends

The example in the last section assumed perfect markets, which means (1) no taxes, (2) no information asymmetries, and (3) no agency problems. If one relaxes these assumptions, then arguments can be made that dividends are relevant.

Taxes

If there are taxes on dividends, then the ex-dividend day price reaction to a dividend will not be exactly equal to the size of the dividend, as shown in "Example 13.1 Price Impact of a Dividend". If dividend tax rates are higher than capital gain tax rates (for the clientele who holds the company's shares), then the price will fall by less than the amount of the dividend on the ex-dividend day.[13]

Information Asymmetries and Signaling

A survey of corporate financial managers about their dividend policy found that managers try to maintain a stable level of dividends, are reluctant to cut dividends, and only increase dividends when **sustainable earnings** increase.[14] Sustainable earnings are a good predictor of future earnings, so these findings imply that managers increase dividends when they expect higher future earnings. A number of academics have hypothesized that managers use dividends to intentionally signal higher future earnings to the market.[15] This is known as the **signaling hypothesis**, and is described in "Explain It". If this hypothesis is correct, then dividend increases should cause an increase in the stock price and should be followed by an increase in future earnings. We review some empirical evidence in the next section.

sustainable earnings

Earnings after the removal of nonrecurring items or expenses. Sustainable earnings are a good predictor of future average earnings.

signaling hypothesis

Signalling is a market solution to the problem of asymmetric information. In corporate finance, the biggest asymmetric information problem is that companies have better knowledge of their future cash flows than investors. Signalling is an action undertaken by high cash flow companies to separate themselves from low cash flow companies. A number of corporate actions are considered signals, such as dividends, stock repurchases and new issues of debt. A signal is believable if low cash-flow companies would never find it optimal to use the signal to trick investors. The implication of the hypothesis is that the market should raise the valuation of the company following the signal as it revises its estimate of future cash flows.

Explain It

In his famous article titled "Job Market Signaling," Michael Spence argued that when employee quality is hard to measure, then education can act as a believable indicator (signal) of an individual's quality. The fact that quality is hard to measure means that the information about quality is asymmetric—the employee has it and the employer doesn't. To overcome the asymmetry, the two players need a way to communicate the information in a believable way. Spence argues that an employee can "signal" her quality through the extent of her education. The signal is believable if the high-quality individual finds the signal cheaper to send, because then there is usually some level of signal that the low-quality type will find too costly to send.[16]

Agency Problems

As we discussed in Chapter 1, managers are supposed to act as the shareholders' agents. When monitoring is imperfect (contracting is costly) and a company generates lots of free cash flow, then self-interested managers may be tempted to use the cash to their own advantage. For one example of waste, look at the "Explain It". A high dividend lessens the amount of cash at a manager's discretion and so reduces the scope for waste. If this hypothesis is correct, then a dividend increase should cause an increase in the stock price as it implies that the company's cash flows will not be wasted. The positive reaction should be greater for firms with bigger agency problems (i.e., firms with more free cash flow), since they experience a larger loss in value due to waste.[17]

Explain It

On July 21, 2002, WorldCom (since renamed MCI) filed for Chapter 11 bankruptcy protection. With a peak market capitalization of $186 billion (in April 1999), it was the largest bankruptcy in U.S. history to date. In the year 2000, the telecommunications industry entered a downturn and WorldCom suffered a serious setback when it was forced to abandon its proposed merger with Sprint. By that time, WorldCom's stock price was declining. Beginning in mid-1999 and continuing through May 2002, Worldcom (under the direction of CEO Bernard Ebbers) used fraudulent accounting methods to mask its declining earnings to prop up the price of WorldCom's stock. Ebbers had a personal stake in the fraud as he had substantial holdings of WorldCom common stock, some of it purchased on margin. The price declines triggered margin calls. During 2001, Ebbers persuaded WorldCom's board of directors to provide him corporate loans and guarantees in excess of $400 million to cover his margin calls. The board agreed—ostensibly to support the stock price. The price continued to fall, the strategy failed, and Ebbers was ousted as CEO in April 2002.[18]

Empirical Evidence about the Price Reaction to Dividends

dividend initiation

The first instance where a firm pays out cash dividends.

dividend omission

A temporary suspension of dividends.

dividend suspension

The cancellation of dividend payments.

dividend increase

An increase in the level of per-share dividends.

dividend decrease

A decrease in the level of per-share dividends.

Changes in dividend policy (**dividend initiation**, **dividend omission**, **dividend suspension**, **dividend increase**, and **dividend decrease**) convey information to the market and so precipitate price changes. Studies have shown that dividend increases result in a stock price increase and dividend decreases result in a price decrease.[19] The academic literature has not reached consensus on what causes this association, but we briefly summarize some of the empirical findings.

Dividend Decreases are Uncommon and Usually Bad News

Dividend increases are 10 times more likely than dividend decreases.[20] Dividend decreases result in an average stock price decline of about 3% on the 3 days surrounding the announcement of a dividend cut.[21] But not all decreases are bad. The market's negative reaction is focused mainly on dividend reductions by firms that have experienced recent declines in earnings.[22]

Dividend Increases are Good News

Stock prices rise (on average) after dividend increases. Blau et al. (2011) find significant positive abnormal returns on the day of (and following) the announcement of dividend increases.[23] From this evidence we know that dividend increases convey positive information to the market, but there is disagreement about the nature of that good news. Some argue that dividend changes signal managers' private information about future earnings. One study found a positive relation between abnormal returns around dividend initiations (and omissions) and subsequent changes in earnings.[24] A later study that included increases and decreases of regular dividends did not find a relationship with future earnings.[25] A more recent study finds that dividend changes signal the persistence of past earnings changes.[26] They argue that a dividend increase signals that past earnings increases will not be reversed in the future.

Dividend Policy

How do companies set their dividend? Obviously, the dividend decision is related to the amount of cash on hand, the amount of free cash flow generated by operations, and the company's capital investment plans. In previous sections, we argued that the dividend decision is also affected by:

1. Taxes
2. Asymmetric information (signaling)
3. Agency problems

Academic finance doesn't have a formula that weighs each of these factors to provide financial managers with a simple way of setting their dividend. In this section, we review two simple dividend policy models. Neither incorporates all of the issues discussed above, but each provides some insight into the dividend decision.

Stable Dividends

The **stable dividend policy** is a policy of keeping dividends steady. Dividends are set as a function of expected, future sustainable earnings. With a stable dividend policy, dividends only increase if earnings rise to a "sustainably" higher level.

"Example 13.3 Residual Dividend Policy" shows earnings per share and dividends for Precision Bearings (PB). PB's dividends are a good example of a stable dividend policy. Even though there were large fluctuations in PB's earnings per share, the dividend maintains a slow and steady increase.

stable dividend policy

It is a policy of keeping dividends steady. Dividends are set as a function of expected future sustainable earnings. With a stable dividend policy, dividends only increase if earnings rise to a sustainably higher level.

FIGURE 13.6 Quarterly Dividends and Earnings per Share for Precision Bearings, 2010–2021

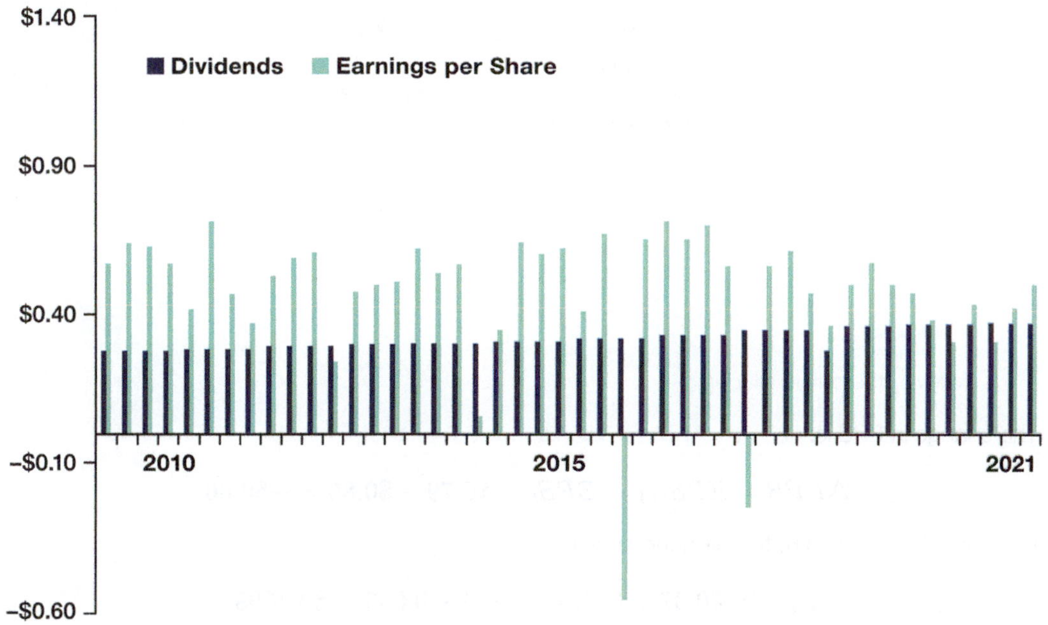

Target Payout Policy

The target **payout policy** is one example of a stable dividend policy. Surveys show that managers try to maintain a stable level of dividends, are reluctant to cut dividends, and only increase dividends when sustainable earnings increase and seem to have a target payout rate. The **target payout model** incorporates all of these characteristics into one formula:[27]

EQUATION 13.6

$$D_{t+1} = D_t + \Delta EPS \times \text{ Target payout } \times \lambda$$

where

$$\begin{aligned} D_t\ (D_{t+1}) &= \text{dividend in the current period } t \text{ (the next period, } t+1) \\ EPS_t &= \text{earnings per share in period } t \\ \Delta EPS &= EPS_{t+1} - EPS_t = \text{the change in EPS} \\ \text{Target payout} &= \text{target payout ratio} \\ \lambda &= \text{adjustment factor} \end{aligned}$$

payout policy

A company's financial plans for future distributions. The payout policy encompasses decisions about the mix of distribution types, dividends or repurchases, as well as the levels and rates of change of those distributions.

target payout model

A model of dividends developed by John Lintner (1956). Dividends are both smoothed and based on a target payout ratio.

The model provides a formula for setting the next period's dividend. It is equal to the current period's dividend plus an additional factor. The additional factor is the product of three terms: the change in EPS, the payout rate, and an adjustment factor. When the adjustment factor is small, then dividends do not rise even when earnings rise.

Example 13.2 Target Payout Rate

Jerry Stamp, the CFO of Precision Bearings, is trying to set the dividend for the coming quarter. Last quarter, the dividend was $0.37 per share and EPS was $0.85 per share. PB uses a target payout ratio model with a payout ratio of 60% and an adjustment factor of 0.005. Jerry expects EPS to be $0.79 in the coming quarter. What should the dividend be?

SOLUTION

Algebraic Solution

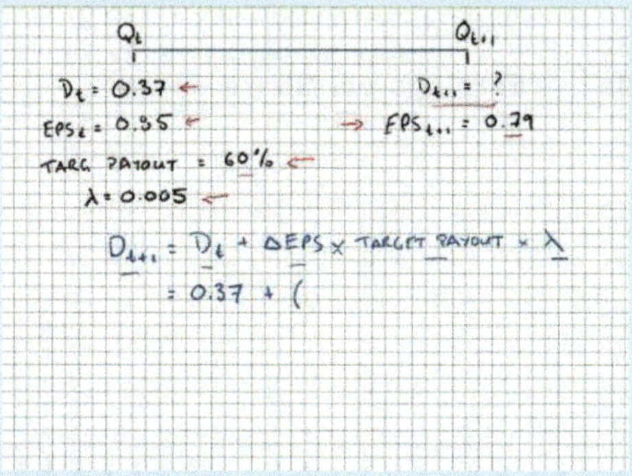

View in the online reader

The change in EPS is:

$$\Delta EPS = EPS_{t+1} - EPS_t = \$0.79 - \$0.85 = -\$0.06$$

Following Equation 13.6, the dividend should be:

$$D_{t+1} = \$0.37 + (-0.06) \times 0.6 \times 0.005 = \$0.3698$$

Residual Dividend Policy

residual dividend policy

It recognizes that internal equity is a cheap source of project financing and sets dividends as a leftover.

The **residual dividend policy** recognizes that internal equity is a cheap source of project financing and sets dividends as a leftover. First, the company calculates the amount of retained earnings it needs to finance new projects. Second, it subtracts the needed earnings from net income and then pays the remainder as a dividend. The residual dividend policy does not typically lead to a stable dividend. The residual dividend policy can be expressed using the following formula:

EQUATION 13.7

$$D_t = \frac{\text{Net income}_t - \omega_E \times \$\text{Investments}_t}{\text{Shares outstanding}}$$

where

$$D_t = \text{dividend per share}$$
$$\$Investments_t = \text{investments in fixed and net working capital during period } t$$
$$\omega_E = \text{target capital structure weight for equity}$$

Investments are the amount of money that the company plans to spend on fixed assets and net working capital for new projects. The target capital structure weight is the proportion of the company's long-term capital that is financed by equity. The product of those two variables (the second term in the numerator of Equation 13.7) is the equity required to fund the new projects. The amount available for distribution as dividends is net income less the equity required.

Example 13.3 Residual Dividend Policy

Jerry Stamp, the CFO of Precision Bearings, is trying to set the dividend for the coming quarter. PB has a residual payout policy with a target capital structure weight for equity of 70%. Jerry expects net income to be $158 million. Jerry is waiting for the COO's report on the new projects and the capital required for each. In anticipation of that report, Jerry wants to calculate dividends under three scenarios for three levels of investment: (1) $75M, (2) $125M, and (3) $200M. PB has 250 million shares outstanding. What will the dividend (per share) be under each of the investment scenarios?

SOLUTION

Algebraic Solution

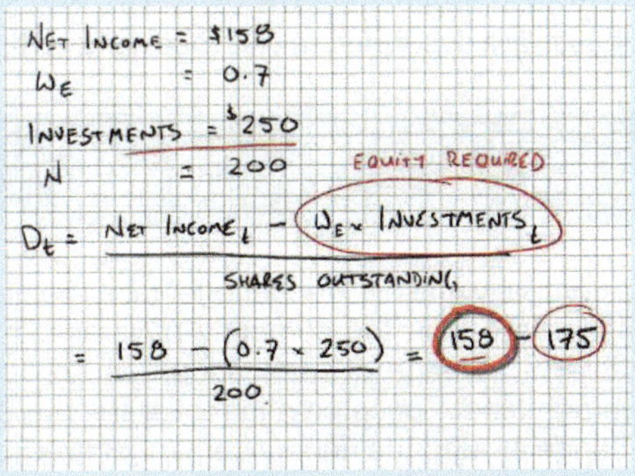

View in the online reader

	Scenario 1	Scenario 2	Scenario 3
Net Income ($millions)	$158	$158	$158
Equity Weight	0.7	0.7	0.7
Investments ($millions)	75	125	250
Equity Required	52.5	87.5	175
Total Dividends ($millions)	105.5	70.5	–17
Shares Outstanding (millions)	200	200	200
Dividend per Share	0.5275	0.3525	–0.085

Look at the third scenario in "Example 13.3 Residual Dividend Policy". Of course, the dividend cannot be negative. In that scenario, project investments are $250 million and the equity required to fund those investments is $175M. The remaining $75M would be obtained by borrowing. However, PB only expects to generate $158M of net income. Thus, internal equity is not sufficient to finance all of the projects. In this situation, the company would cancel the dividend and would have to raise $17M of new equity; that is, if it wanted to adhere strictly to its target capital structure weights. Under the residual dividend policy, dividends will vary with the size of new projects and with net income.

13.3 Stock Repurchases

This section presents an introduction to stock repurchases. First, we describe the mechanics of how stock is repurchased. Second, we look at a simple model of how repurchases should impact stock prices and investor wealth. The simple model assumes perfect markets. In the third sub-section, we list some other factors that should affect the stock price reaction to repurchases when the assumption of perfect markets is relaxed. Fourth, we present some reasons why repurchases are chosen as a means of distribution instead of dividends.

Repurchase Mechanics and Timing

There are three types of repurchases: (1) fixed price, (2) Dutch auction, and (3) open market. Open-market repurchases are far more popular than the other two and so they are our focus. Fixed-price and Dutch auction repurchases are described in the following Explain Its.

Explain It

In a fixed-price offer, the company makes a tender offer (at a premium) for its own shares. If more shares are offered than wanted, then the company buys an equal proportion of each shareholder's tendered shares. The average quantity sought in fixed-price offers is 20% of shares outstanding, and the average tender price premium over the pre-announcement price is almost 21%. The stock price change around the announcement of fixed-price offers averages 12.3%.

Explain It

A Dutch auction is a type of auction in which the auctioneer begins with a high asking price, which is lowered until a bidder is willing to accept the auctioneer's price. In a Dutch auction repurchase, the company announces a range of acceptable prices and invites shareholders to submit sale offers at a price within the range. The company ranks the sale offers by price from lowest to highest. The company accepts all of the lowest-priced offers up to the quantity it targeted. All accepted offers receive the price of the marginal offer. The average proportion of shares sought in Dutch auctions repurchases is 17%, and the range of prices varies between 3% and 16% (average of 13%) above the pre-announcement price. Dutch auctions are cheaper for companies than fixed-price offers because the premium paid is smaller, but the market reaction to Dutch auction announcements is only about 75% of the reaction to fixed-price offer announcements.

In an open-market repurchase, the firm instructs its broker to buy shares on the open market at prevailing market prices. The shares are then cancelled and the number of shares outstanding is reduced. The average proportion targeted for repurchase is 7% of shares outstanding.[28] It can take up to 2 or 3 years for the repurchase to be completed.[29] There is no legal requirement for the company to buy all of the shares that it targets to repurchase.

Repurchases are another means of distributing cash to shareholders. Consider the following example: a company has five shareholders each owning 20 shares. The company announces that it will repurchase 10 shares. The shares outstanding will fall from 100 to 90. If each shareholder sells two shares, then each receives some cash and their proportionate ownership in the company does not change. After the repurchase, each shareholder owns 18 shares, but that continues to represent 20% of the (90) outstanding shares.

An attractive feature of repurchases is that they are voluntary. None of the shareholders have to sell. Some may choose not to sell and their proportionate ownership of the company rises. With open-market repurchases, shareholders get to choose when they receive the distribution. This option is not available with dividends. The option to defer is valuable because, along with deferring the realization of the distribution, the tax liability associated with the distribution can be deferred.

Explain It

Some firms use repurchases to offset dilution due to employee and executive stock options. Repurchases don't offset those options; the options still represent a transfer of wealth from shareholders to employees (executives). The repurchase can restore the number of shares outstanding to its original number. Even with this motive, the repurchase still represents a distribution of cash to shareholders.

Price Reaction to Stock Repurchases

In this section, we explore what happens to the stock price following an open-market repurchase. Let's continue working with the firm described earlier (whose cash flows are shown in Figure 13.5). The value of the company was given in Equation 13.1 and the share price prior to any form of distribution is given in Equation 13.2. We use the subscripts "B" and "A" to refer to the period before and after the repurchase.

We denote the price paid for repurchased shares as P_R and the number of shares repurchased as N_R. The cost of the repurchase is the product of the shares repurchased and the price, or $P_R N_R$.

Tip

If the company uses all of its cash to repurchase shares, then $P_R N_R = \$C$.

To understand how the repurchase affects the stock price, we start by considering how the repurchase affects the total value of all of the equity (denoted E). For example, consider a company with equity worth $100 that repurchases $10 worth of shares. All else held constant, the equity is worth $90 after the repurchase. The intuition is shown in Figure 13.7.

FIGURE 13.7 Value of Equity Before and After a Repurchase
Before: E_B. Repurchase: $P_R \times N_R$. After: $E_A = E_B - P_R \times N_R$.

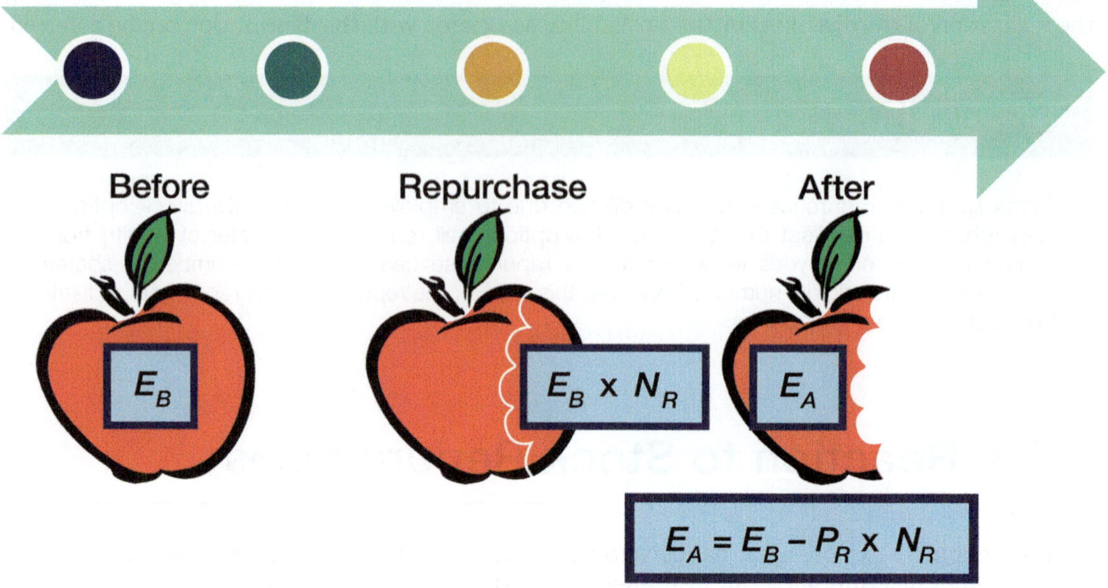

Equation 13.8 shows that, after the repurchase, the value of the firm's equity (denoted E_A) is equal to the value of the equity before the repurchase minus the cost of the repurchase.

> **Tip**
>
> We are assuming that the company is all equity financed, that the repurchase is paid for with cash, and that there are no changes in the company's operations or the market's information about the company. The first two assumptions ensure that there is no change in value due to a change in leverage.

EQUATION 13.8

$$E_A = E_B - P_R N_R$$

We can use this equality to derive an expression for the stock price after the repurchase. Equation 13.9 shows that, before the repurchase, the value of the equity is just equal to the stock price multiplied by the number of shares outstanding.

EQUATION 13.9

$$E_B = P_B N_B$$

The number of shares outstanding after the repurchase is equal to $N_A = N_B(1 - f)$ where f is the fraction of shares repurchased. For example, if a company initially has 100 shares outstanding $(N_B = 100)$ and repurchases 10 shares $(N_R = 10)$ then the fraction repurchased is 10% $(f = 10/100 = 0.10)$ and there are 90 shares outstanding afterward $(N_A = 100(1 - 0.1) = 90)$. Thus, we can express the value of the equity after the repurchase as:

EQUATION 13.10

$$E_A = P_A N_B(1 - f)$$

If we insert Equation 13.9 and Equation 13.9 into Equation 13.8 (view "Explain It: Solving for the Price After Repurchase" to see the algebra), then we get the following expression for the price after the repurchase.

EQUATION 13.11

$$P_A = P_B \frac{1}{1-f} - P_R \frac{f}{1-f}$$

Explain It: Solving for the Price After Repurchase

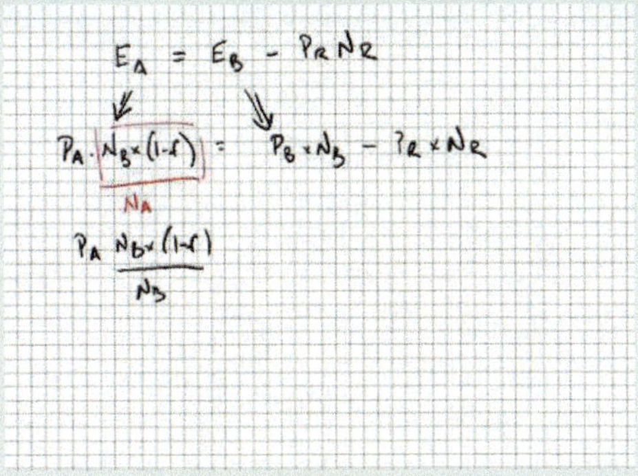

View in the online reader

Equation 13.11 says that the stock price after the repurchase is a weighted average of the price before the repurchase and the repurchase price. Consider an open-market repurchase where shares are repurchased at the pre-repurchase price, so $P_R = P_B$. If we substitute this equality into Equation 13.11, then we get the result that $P_A = P_B$. In other words, the post-repurchase price is equal to the pre-repurchase price when shares are repurchased at the pre-repurchase price. "Explain It: The Impact of a Repurchase on the Stock Price" gives you an opportunity to explore the relationship between the price after, the price before, and the repurchase price.

Explain It: The Impact of a Repurchase on the Stock Price

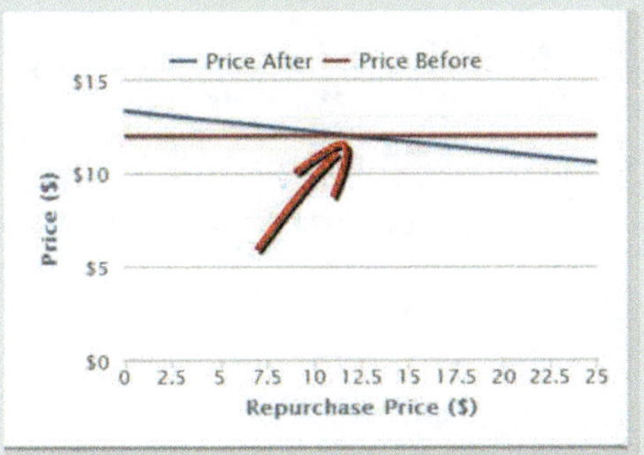

View in the online reader

If a company can repurchase its shares at a price below its pre-repurchase price (below fair market value, $P_R < P_B$), then the price after the repurchase will rise: $P_A > P_B$. View "Explain It: Analyzing a Repurchase at a Discount" to see the algebra. In this case, there is a wealth transfer from shareholders who sell their shares (at a price below fair value) to shareholders who hold. Many companies motivate their share repurchases (in their press releases) by arguing that the company's shares are occasionally undervalued and that the repurchase is motivated to take advantage of those opportunities.

Explain It: Analyzing a Repurchase at a Discount

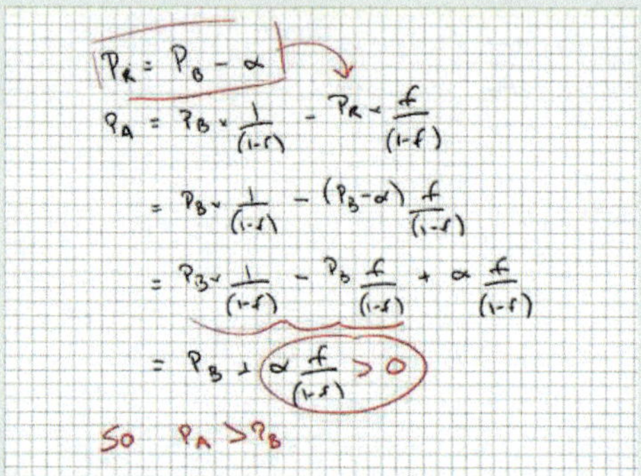

View in the online reader

Example 13.4 Price Impact of an Open-Market Stock Repurchase

Chalk Dust Disposal Inc. has $10 cash and operates an incinerator that generates free cash flow of $5 per year in perpetuity (starting in 1 year). Chalk Dust is all-equity financed, its shareholders require a return of 10%, and it has 100 shares outstanding. The company has announced a $10 repurchase (it will use all of its cash) and will buy shares at the price prevailing prior to the repurchase announcement. What is the stock price before the repurchase, what proportion of shares are repurchased, and what is the price after the repurchase?

SOLUTION

Algebraic Solution

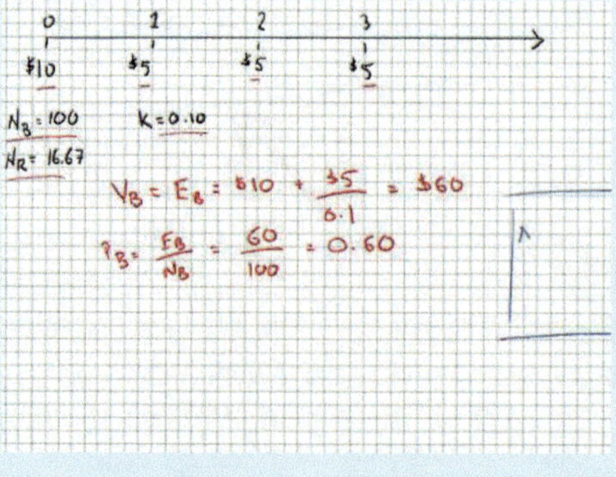

View in the online reader

Following Equation 13.1, the value of the equity at time 0 is:

$$V_B = E_B = \$10 + \frac{\$5}{0.1} = \$60$$

The stock price before the repurchase is:

$$P_B = \$60/100 = \$0.60$$

The number of share repurchased is:

$$f = N_R/N_B = 16.67/100 = 16.67\%$$

Using Equation 13.11, the price after the repurchase is:

$$P_A = \$0.60\frac{1}{1-0.1667} - \$0.60\frac{0.1667}{1-0.1667}$$
$$P_A = \$0.60$$

The price remains at \$0.60 after the repurchase.

Wealth Effects

Let's consider the wealth impact of the repurchase. Consider an investor with 10 shares before the repurchase (worth \$6). We assume that the investor sells 16.67% of her holdings (1.667 shares), which gives her \$1 of cash $(1.67 \times \$0.60)$ and \$5 worth of shares $(8.33 \times \$0.60)$. Her wealth is unchanged by the repurchase but its form has changed: from all shares to a mix of shares and cash.

If she did not want \$1 of cash, then she could refrain from selling any of her shares. In other words, she could undo the repurchase. If she did not sell any shares, then her proportionate ownership of the company would rise from 10% to 12%, but her wealth would remain at \$6.

Alternatively, if the company had not repurchased shares, but the investor had wanted \$1 of cash, then she could have sold 1.667 shares. After the sale, she would have had 8.333 shares worth \$5 and \$1 of cash. In other words, she could have made a homemade repurchase.

Like dividends, repurchases are irrelevant in perfect markets. They do not change the wealth of the investors.

EPS

Repurchases reduce the number of shares outstanding. All else held constant, the reduction increases earnings per share. Some market participants think that repurchases increase share prices because of this increase in EPS. As we saw earlier, this perception is incorrect. Repurchases reduce shares outstanding, but they reduce the cash (or cash flows) of the business in an equal and offsetting way.

Taxes, Asymmetric Information, and Agency Problems

The example in the last section assumed perfect markets, which means: (1) no taxes, (2) no information asymmetries, and (3) no agency problems. If one relaxes these assumptions, then arguments can be made that repurchases are relevant.

A debt-financed repurchase will substantially change leverage. If corporate taxes are not zero, then a repurchase can increase the stock price by increasing the company's interest tax shields. Of course, value will only increase if the company starts with a debt-to-equity ratio below its optimum (recall Figure 12.7).

Tip

Chapter 12 contains a number of examples showing how a debt-financed repurchase increases the stock price.

Like dividend increases, repurchases have also been proposed as signals of future earnings. The idea is that managers use repurchases to signal that future earnings will be higher and so increase the stock price.[30]

Repurchases are also a means of removing free cash flow from wasteful managers. Thus repurchases, like dividends, can be used to reduce agency costs and so increase firm value as a result.

Studies have documented an average price increase of 2.57% in the 3 days following the announcement of an open-market repurchase.[31]

Tip

The 7-day announcement returns around fixed-price and Dutch auction repurchases are 12.3% and 8.3%, respectively.[32]

In perfect markets, there should be no price increase. (If the repurchase price is fair.) The observed price increase is due to one of the reasons listed earlier, but different firms repurchase for different reasons, so one motive does not explain all observed behavior.

Stock Repurchase Policy

flexibility hypothesis

The hypothesis that repurchases are used to distribute a temporary excess of cash (but dividends are used to distribute a permanent increase in cash). Repurchases are more flexible because they do not increase investor expectations as do dividends.

How and when do companies choose to repurchase shares? The **flexibility hypothesis** provides one explanation, and the presence of employee stock options provides another.

Flexibility

As we saw earlier, dividend increases create an expectation among investors that future earnings are permanently higher (or past earnings increases will not be reversed). One advantage of repurchases relative to dividends is that they do not raise expectations and implicitly commit the firm to future payouts. This gives companies more flexibility to use repurchases selectively.

Some evidence suggests that repurchases are used flexibly—they complement dividends as a means of paying out a short-term excess of cash. Looking at the historical pattern of distributions (Figure 13.1) dividends are fairly smooth, repurchases are more volatile, and appear to be positively correlated with the business cycle. (That is, they are higher at the top of a cycle and lower in recession.) This historical evidence is consistent with the view that dividends are paid out of sustainable cash flows while repurchases are paid out of a temporary excess of cash flows. Consistent with this view, note that the value of shares repurchased hit an all time high in 2018. This was a result of the 2017 Tax Cuts and Jobs Act (TCJA), which lowered tax rates on repatriated earnings from foreign subsidiaries. Many firms decided to distribute the excess cash because they decided that their shareholders could earn higher returns than they could by reinvesting. In 2018, total payouts exceeded $1 trillion for the first time.

Stock Options

As we saw earlier, dividends cause stock prices to fall (on the ex-dividend day), but repurchases leave the price unchanged. Anything that reduces the stock price will reduce the value of stock options. Thus, executives and directors with stock options prefer repurchases to dividends. Not surprisingly, the popularity of repurchases coincides with the advent of stock options as a method of executive compensation. Consistent with this argument, researchers found a positive relationship between repurchases and management stock options.[33]

13.4 Stock Dividends and Splits

A stock dividend is a distribution of additional shares to the owners of the company. A 1% stock dividend means that a shareholder will receive one additional share for every 100 shares she owns. If the stock dividend exceeds 25%, it is referred to as a stock **split**.

Stock splits are expressed in the form of a **split ratio**. The split ratio (denoted *S*) is defined as:

EQUATION 13.12

$$S = \frac{Shares\ outstanding\ after\ split}{Shares\ outstanding\ before\ split}$$

Table 13.5 presents some examples of different split ratios.

TABLE 13.5 Split Ratios and Shares Outstanding

Split	Shares Outstanding Before	Shares Outstanding After	Split Ratio	New Shares Issued
4-for-3	100	133	1.33	33
3-for-2	100	150	1.50	50
2-for-1	100	200	2	100
3-for-1	100	300	3	200

split

An increase in the number of shares outstanding. If a company with 1 million shares executes a two-for-one split, the company would have 2 million shares. Each investor's share holdings rise by the same proportion and so percentage holdings are unaffected by a split. Since shares outstanding rise, the share price falls.

split ratio

The ratio of shares outstanding after the split to shares outstanding before the split.

The Price Impact of a Stock Split

Since stock dividends and splits affect neither the underlying cash flows of a business nor the systematic risk of those cash flows (and thus the required return of shareholders), the value of the business should not change. A two-for-one split will simply leave a company with double the number of shares selling at half their pre-split price. More generally, the price after a split is equal to:

EQUATION 13.13

$$P_A = \frac{P_B}{S}$$

Example 13.5 Price Impact of a Stock Split

Shoe Carnival, Inc. (NASDAQ: SCVL) is a leading footwear and accessories retailer. The company announced a three-for-two stock split of common shares. Stockholders will receive a stock dividend of one common share for every two shares of stock owned as of the close of business on Friday, April 13, 2012. The stock dividend payment date is April 27, 2012. The NASDAQ stock market will report the split-adjusted price and shares outstanding commencing Monday, April 30, 2012. According to CEO Mark Lemond, the stock split is motivated by the recent stock price performance. The company wants to make its shares more accessible, increase the number of shareholders, and so improve the liquidity of the market for its shares.

Read the press release for Shoe Carnival's stock split. There were 13.6 million shares outstanding prior to the split announcement. The closing price on the last cum-dividend day was $29.50 (April 10, 2012). How many shares are outstanding after the split, and what will the opening price be on the morning of the ex-dividend day (April 11, 2012)? (Assume no change in information between the Tuesday close and the Wednesday open.)

SOLUTION

Algebraic Solution

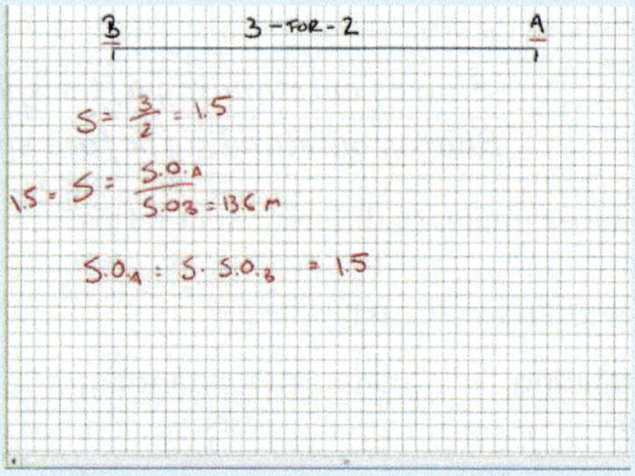

View in the online reader

Following Equation 13.12, the split ratio is:

$$S = 3/2 = 1.5$$

The number of shares outstanding after the split is:

$$\textit{Shares outstanding after the split} = S \times \textit{shares outstanding before the split}$$

$$\textit{Shares outstanding after the split} = 1.5 \times 13.6\ \textit{million} = 20.4\ \textit{million}$$

Following Equation 13.13, the stock price after the split is:

$$P_A = P_B/S = \$29.50/1.5 = \$19.67$$

Based on "Shoe Carnival Announces Three-for-Two Stock Split," Shoe Carnival, Inc. news release, March 23, 2012.

Motive for Stock Splits

One benefit of splits is that the stock price moves to a lower trading range. This is important to small retailer investors. Consider an investor who wants to invest $2,000, but wants to buy shares in amounts of at least one **board lot** (100 shares). This means that she would prefer to buy a $20 rather than a $40 stock. If the retail investor can only buy 50 shares, then she will be trading an **odd-lot** (less than board lot), which means that because of exchange trading rules, her order may be subject to extra price volatility. As a consequence, stock dividends and splits are expected to increase the interest of retail investors and so broaden demand for the company's stock. A broader pool of retail investors ought to increase the liquidity of the stock. The following Explain It presents Warren Buffett's attitude about this motive for stock splits.

board lot

A quantity of shares, typically 100.

odd-lot

A quantity of shares that is less than one board lot.

Explain It

"We often are asked why Berkshire does not split its stock. The assumption behind this question usually appears to be that a split would be a pro-shareholder action. We disagree. Let me tell you why. One of our goals is to have Berkshire Hathaway stock sell at a price rationally related to its intrinsic business value. The key to a rational stock price is rational shareholders, both current and prospective. If the holders of a company's stock and/or the prospective buyers attracted to it are prone to make irrational or emotion-based decisions, some pretty silly stock prices are going to appear periodically. Such aberrations may help us in buying and selling the stocks of other companies. But we think it is in both your interest and ours to minimize their occurrence in the market for Berkshire. To obtain only high-quality shareholders is no cinch. Mrs. Astor could select her 400, but anyone can buy any stock. Entering members of a shareholder "club" cannot be screened for intellectual capacity, emotional stability, moral sensitivity, or acceptable dress.

I believe well over 90%—probably over 95%—of our shares are held by those who were shareholders of Berkshire or Blue Chip five years ago. Among companies with at least several thousand public shareholders and more than $1 billion of market value, we are almost certainly the leader in the degree to which our shareholders think and act like owners. Upgrading a shareholder group that possesses these characteristics is not easy. Were we to split the stock or take other actions focusing on stock price rather than business value, we would attract an entering class of buyers inferior to the exiting class of sellers. At $1,300, there are very few investors who can't afford a Berkshire share. Would a potential one-share purchaser be better off if we split 100 for 1 so he could buy 100 shares? Those who think so and who would buy the stock because of the split or in anticipation of one would definitely downgrade the quality of our present shareholder group. People who buy for nonvalue reasons are likely to sell for nonvalue reasons. Their presence in the picture will accentuate erratic price swings unrelated to underlying business developments. We try to avoid policies that attract buyers with a short-term focus on our stock price and try to allow policies that attract informed long-term investors focusing on business values. One of the ironies of the stock market is the emphasis on activity. Brokers, using terms such as "marketability" and "liquidity," sing the praises of companies with high share turnover (those who cannot fill your pocket will confidently fill your ear). But investors should understand that what is good for the croupier is not good for the customer. A hyperactive stock market is the pickpocket of enterprise."

Warren Buffett wrote the comments, quoted above, in March 1984 for his 1983 Shareholder Letter to Berkshire Hathaway shareholders (www.berkshirehathaway.com). In January 2010, Berkshire shareholders approved a 50-for-1 split of its class B shares. The split was conducted to facilitate a share-based acquisition of Burlington Northern Santa Fe Corp. The class B shares were trading for about $3,500 prior to the split. The class A shares have never been split and traded for $347,815 at the time of writing.[34]

Reverse Split

reverse split

A decrease in the number of shares outstanding. If a company with 1 million shares executes a 1-for-10 split, the company would have 100,000 shares. Each investor's share holdings fall by the same proportion and so percentage holdings are unaffected by a reverse split. Since shares outstanding fall, the share price rises.

A **reverse split** occurs when a company reduces the number of shares held by each shareholder by the same proportion. For example, a 1-for-10 reverse split means that the 1,000 shares of a company will be replaced by 100 shares. The price should increase by a factor of 10. Companies will undertake reverse splits when they think that the optimal trading range for the stock is substantially higher than the current price. Two reasons why companies prefer higher stock prices are:

1. Some stock exchanges will de-list a stock if it trades below a price of $1 for too long.
2. Some brokerages will not lend to investors (for margin purchases) if the stock trades below a threshold price (i.e., $3).

Endnotes

1. Based on "Johnson & Johnson Announces Dividend Increase of 7.0%," news release from Johnson & Johnson, April 16, 2012.
2. Based on "PACCAR Announces Extra Cash Dividend and Regular Quarterly Dividend," news release from PACCAR Inc., December 6, 2011.
3. Based on "Tootsie Roll Declares 3% Stock Dividend," Bloomberg.com, April 7, 2011.
4. Based on "JPMorgan Chase to Increase Quarterly Common Stock Dividend to $0.30 Per Share," JP Morgan Chase & Co. news release, March 13, 2012.
5. Based on "TechTarget, Inc. Announces Commencement of Tender Offer to Repurchase up to 10,000,000 Shares of its Common Stock at Price of $6.00 Per Share," TechTarget, Inc. news release, November 9, 2010.
6. Based on "Expedia, Inc. to Repurchase up to 30 Million of Its Common Shares in Tender Offer," Expedia, Inc. news release, December 8, 2006.
7. DeAngelo, H., L. DeAngelo, and D. J. Skinner, "Are Dividends Disappearing?: Dividend Concentration and the Consolidation of Earnings," *Journal of Financial Economics 72*, no. 3 (2004): 425–56.
8. The rates in Table 13.3 are the U.S. federal tax rates in 2014.
9. Chetty, R., and E. Saez, "Dividend Taxes and Corporate Behavior: Evidence from the 2003 Dividend Tax Cut," *Quarterly Journal of Economics 120* (2005): 791–833.
10. Brown, J. R., N. Liang, and S. Weisbenner, "Executive Financial Incentives and Payout Policy: Firm Responses to the 2003 Dividend Tax Cut," *Journal of Finance 62* (2007): 1935–65.
11. Based on "P&G Declares a 7% Dividend Increase," Procter & Gamble news release, April 10, 2018.
12. Miller, M. H., and F. Modigliani, "Dividend Policy, Growth, and the Valuation of Shares," *Journal of Business 34* (1961): 411–33.
13. Elton, E. J., and M. J. Gruber, "Marginal Stockholder Tax Rates and the Clientele Effect," *Review of Economics and Statistics 52*, no. 1 (1970): 68–74.
14. Lintner, J., "Distribution of Incomes of Corporations among Dividends, Retained Earnings, and Taxes," *American Economic Review 46* (1956): 97–113.
15. Miller, M., and K. Rock, "Dividend Policy under Asymmetric Information," *Journal of Finance 40* (1985): 1031–51.
16. Spence, M., "Job Market Signaling," *Quarterly Journal of Economics 87*, no. 3 (1973): 355–74.
17. Jensen, M. C., "Agency Costs of Free Cash Flow, Corporate Finance, and Takeover," *American Economic Review 76* (1986): 323–29.
18. Wikipedia.com
19. The first major study is Charest, G., "Dividend Information, Stock Returns and Market Efficiency," *Journal of Financial Economics 6* (1978): 297–330.
20. Koch, A. S., and A. X. Sun, "Dividend Changes and the Persistence of Past Earnings Changes," *Journal of Finance 59* (2004): 2093–116.
21. Lie, E., "Operating Performance following Dividend Decreases and Omissions," *Journal of Corporate Finance 12* (2005): 27–53.
22. Asem, E., "Prior Earnings, Dividend-Reducing Announcement Returns and Future Earnings Performance," Working Paper, University of Lethbridge, 2012.
23. Blau, Benjamin M., Kathleen P. Fuller, and Robert A. Van Ness, "Short Selling Around Dividend Announcements and Ex-Dividend Days," *Journal of Corporate Finance 17*, no. 3 (2011): 628–39.
24. Healy, P. M., and K. G. Palepu, "Earnings Information Conveyed by Dividend Initiations and Omissions," *Journal of Financial Economics 21* (1988): 149–75.
25. Benartzi, S., R. Michaely, and R. Thaler, "Do Changes in Dividends Signal the Future or the Past?" *Journal of Finance 52* (1997): 1007–34.
26. Koch, A. S., and A. X. Sun, "Dividend Changes and the Persistence of Past Earnings Changes," *Journal of Finance 59* (2004): 2093–116.
27. Lintner, J., "Distribution of Incomes of Corporations among Dividends, Retained Earnings, and Taxes," *American Economic Review 46* (1956): 97–113.
28. Simkovic, M., "The Effect of Enhanced Disclosure on Open Market Stock Repurchases," Working Paper. Harvard Law School, 2007.
29. Stephens, C. P., and M. S. Weisbach, "Actual Share Reacquisitions in Open-Market Repurchase Programs," *Journal of Finance 53* (1998): 313–33.
30. Comment, R., and G. Jarrell, "The Relative Signaling Power of Dutch Auction and Fixed-Price Self-Tender Offers and Open-Market Share Repurchases," *Journal of Finance 46*, no. 4 (1991): 1243–71.
31. Grullon and Michaely (2002).
32. Comment and Jarrell (1991).
33. Fenn, G. W., and N. Liang, "Corporate Payout Policy and Managerial Stock Incentives," *Journal of Financial Economics 60*, no. 1 (2001): 45–72.
34. The material is copyrighted and used with permission of the author: Warren Buffett, © March 1984, www.berkshirehathaway.com.

CHAPTER 14

Financial Planning and Forecasting

Learning Objectives

By the end of this chapter you will be able to:

1. Forecast sales.
2. Budget cash receipts and disbursements.
3. Forecast financial statements and calculate additional funds needed.
4. Calculate additional funds needed and maximum growth rates using formulas.

No firm plans for failure, but a failure to plan can lead to just that. In this chapter, we investigate how firms plan for success. Financial managers spend a substantial amount of their time in the process of strategic and financial planning.

Strategic planning is the process of determining the company's goals, and how to allocate resources to achieve those goals. **Financial planning** is the process of forecasting the financial implications of the strategic plan in order to identify how much money is needed to fulfill the plan. Money may not be available unless it is arranged in advance of the need. The timing of new issues of debt and equity is sensitive to market conditions. For example, few firms could raise money during the financial crisis in 2008. Financial planning allows the financial manager to anticipate shortages of money before they occur and time new issues advantageously for the firm.

strategic planning

The process of determining the company's goals, the direction the company will take, and how to allocate resources to achieve those goals.

financial planning

The process of forecasting the financial implications of a strategic plan in order to identify how much money is needed to fulfill the plan. Short-term financial planning focuses on week-by-week cash receipts and disbursements to identify short-term cash imbalances. Long-term financial planning involves forecasting financial statements to identify shortages (or excesses) of capital.

Planning is a multistep process. It usually begins with the strategic plan, which identifies what assets are to be acquired in the future and what new revenues are projected. This leads to the preparation of long-term financial plans. Long-term financial plans allow the manager to prepare short-term financial plans, called *cash budgets*. Together, these plans help managers direct the company's future, rather than just react to it.

Financial planning uses the same process to project cash flows as capital budgeting. The difference is that financial planning focuses on the *whole company* and not on a *single project*.

discounted cash flow (DCF) valuation

A company valuation technique. Analogous to a project net present value calculation. A company's free cash flows are discounted at the weighted average cost of capital. The present value is the value of a whole company (debt plus equity).

Financial planning is not just a tool for internal use. Analysts in investment banking and portfolio management use the tools of financial planning to estimate the fair value of a firm's equity to make investment decisions. This method is called **discounted cash flow (DCF) valuation**.

Tip

Accountants use the term *pro forma* to refer to financial statements that incorporate hypothetical assumptions about the future, for example, to extrapolate fiscal-year statements from a few quarters. They use the expression "financial statements forecasting" to refer to the process that we describe in this chapter. In deference to our accounting colleagues, we do not use the term *pro forma*, but do not be surprised to hear finance people use the expression in this context.

The first step in all financial plans is a **sales forecast**. Sales forecasting could be the subject of an entire book, so our treatment is a brief introduction. In the second section, we examine short-term financial planning, which is called **cash budgeting**. The third section presents **long-term financial planning**. We explain the **percent-of-sales method** of forecasting financial statements (also known as **pro forma financial statements**). The final section presents a shortcut method of calculating **additional funds needed (AFN)** and explores the relationship between sales growth and AFN.

sales forecast

The prediction of the firm's sales over a given period, based on external and/or internal data, and used as the key input to the financial planning process.

cash budgeting

Short-term financial planning. The process of forecasting cash receipts and disbursements to identify cash imbalances.

long-term financial planning

The process of forecasting financial statements to identify shortages (or excesses) of capital.

percent-of-sales method

A method of forecasting financial statements based on the assumption that many accounts will remain at a fixed percentage of sales. For example, assume that cost of goods sold is 80% of sales. If sales are forecast to rise, then cost of goods sold would be forecast as 80% of the new level of sales.

pro forma financial statements

Refers to financial statements that incorporate hypothetical assumptions about the future. For example, to extrapolate fiscal year statements from the first half of the year. Often used (mistakenly) as a synonym for forecasted financial statements.

additional funds needed (AFN)

Additional external funds required by a company to finance assets or bridge a temporary cash shortage. Can be debt or equity. Identified using a financial planning tool (e.g., cash budget, financial statements forecast, or formula).

14.1 Sales Forecasting

A sales forecast can be qualitative or quantitative. Qualitative forecasts include market surveys, surveys of the sales force, or executive opinion. Quantitative methods include time-series models based on historic data and associative forecasts. An associative forecast is a forecast based on explanatory variables. That is, the forecast is based on a functional relationship (association) between sales of the product and publicly observable values (i.e., GDP growth). In this section, we focus on associative forecasts. They are useful to managers forecasting sales of new products (where no historical sales data is available) and by outsiders such as equity analysts. Sales forecasting could be the subject of an entire book. It is more art than science and requires an integration of many facets of economics and business. In this section, we provide a few examples as an introduction to the general idea of associative forecasts.

The Sales Model

To forecast sales we start by building a sales model for the business. The sales model is the functional connection between sales and the explanatory variables. This approach is based on the idea that the right-hand side variables are easier to forecast than the left-hand side variables. The simplest sales model is the product of price and quantity.

EQUATION 14.1

$$Sales_t = P_t \times Q_t$$

where

$$Sales_t = \text{revenue in period } t$$
$$P_t = \text{price of the product in period } t$$
$$Q_t = \text{sold in period } t$$

To forecast sales we need to forecast price and quantity. For multiproduct companies this is difficult, as few firms provide price and quantity data for all of their product lines. In those situations, we model sales revenue. Next, we present a simple sales model for a multiproduct company. Then, we present a comprehensive example of an associative forecast for a single-product company. Finally, we present a specialized model for retailers.

Market Share Forecasting

For a multiproduct company, the simplest sales model is based on industry sales and market share. We can express sales revenue in any year:

EQUATION 14.2

$$Sales_t = ISales_t \times ms_t$$

where

$$ISales_t = \text{industry sales in period } t$$
$$ms_t = \text{market share of the firm in period } t$$

To forecast with this model, we need an industry sales forecast from a third party like a market research company. The market share forecast has to come from the analyst based on a qualitative analysis of product features, marketing, product innovation, and the competitive environment. A company with good products in a reasonably contestable market would be expected to increase its market share over time.

Example 14.1 Forecast of Orange's Smartphone Sales

North American smartphone sales were $200 billion last year. Orange's smartphone market share was 47% last year and is expected to remain constant next year. A market research company expects a 3% increase in sales next year. What is Orange's forecasted sales revenue for next year?

SOLUTION

Forecast sales using Equation 14.2:

$$Sales_{t+1} = ISales_{t+1} \times ms_{t+1}$$
$$Sales_{t+1} = (\$200 \times 1.03) \times 0.47 = \$96.82 \text{ billion}$$

Comprehensive Example of an Associative Forecast

Let's forecast sales for a luxury home builder. Last year, the company completed 2,611 houses at an average price of $576,000, for total revenues of just over $1.5 billion. Nationally, there were 609,000 houses constructed (AKA housing starts), so the company's market share was 0.429%. The revenue model for this company is simple: price times quantity as in Equation 14.1. But, we can express quantity as the product of national housing starts and the company's market share. We do this because national housing starts is easier to forecast. So, the sales model is:

EQUATION 14.3

$$Sales_t = P_t \times (ms_t \times IQ_t)$$

where

$$Sales_t = \text{sales revenue in period}_t$$
$$Sales_t = \text{the average sale price of a house in period}_t$$
$$ms_t = \text{the company's market share in period}_t$$
$$IQ_t = \text{industry quantity (national housing starts) in period}_t$$

Model Drivers

In this model we think of national housing starts as the main **driver** for the company's sales.

> **Tip**
>
> Price and market share are also drivers, but, in this example, we assume that they don't change so they are not an important part of the story (thesis).

driver

An underlying economic factor that determines the future path of a variable. For example, the price of gasoline is one driver for car sales.

A driver is an explanatory variable in the model. It is an economic factor that determines (or is related to) sales of the product. Here are a few examples.

- Sales of beer are determined by weather.
- Mountain bike sales are determined by geography and the number of young men living in the area.
- Nursing home demand is determined by the number of retirees in the area.

Forecasting the Drivers

Given the sales model, to forecast sales we need to forecast the drivers: average price, the company's market share, and national housing starts. Barring a dramatic change in the company's product mix, the best forecast of next year's price is last year's price (plus inflation). Forecasting market share is a qualitative process that draws on an analysis of the quality of the company's products and the dynamics in the industry. In this example, let's assume that market share remains constant. Finally, we need a forecast of housing starts. These can be obtained from public sources (i.e., the National Association of Home Builders) or can be forecast with a regression model. The second approach is the more challenging, and so we discuss it next.

Associative Regression Forecast

Some variables are difficult to forecast directly, but they depend on (or are associated with) other variables (drivers) that are easier to forecast. For example, housing starts depend on interest rates and income. Consumers buy more new homes when rates are low and disposable income is high. We can estimate the (historical) relationship between these variables using a regression and then use the regression equation to forecast housing starts.

The regression equation is as follows:

EQUATION 14.4

$$House\ Starts_t = \beta_0 + \beta_1 i_t + \beta_2 Inc_t$$

where

$$House\ Starts_t = \text{number of housing starts in year } t \text{ (000s)}$$
$$i_t = \text{the 5-year mortgage rate in year } t$$
$$Inc_t = \text{average disposable income in year } t$$

Using historic data we estimate the regression and obtain the following results:

TABLE 14.1 Housing Starts Regression Results

Coefficient	Estimate
β_0	521
β_1	–8.73
β_2	0.004

We can use the regression to forecast housing starts for next year. First, we need forecasts for the interest rate and disposable income. Those can be obtained from private- or public-sector sources.

Tip

Because of this associative regression model, the driver for sales is not housing starts, but, instead, it is interest rates and disposable income because they are the drivers for housing starts. When selecting drivers, it is best to use variables for which forecasts are easily available.

Say that the 5-year mortgage rate is forecast to be 2% and average disposable income is $41,000. Then, using Equation 14.4, the forecast number of housing starts is:

$$HouseStarts_t = 521 + -8.73 \times 2 + 0.004 \times 41,000$$
$$HouseStarts_t = 667.524 \text{ (in thousands)}$$

Now we have all of the pieces to forecast sales for the home builder. The average price of a home is forecast to be 2% greater than last year due to inflation, so $587,520. Market share is forecast to remain constant at 0.429% and national housing starts are forecast to be 667,524. Thus, using Equation 14.4, sales are forecast to be:

$$Sales_t = \$587,520 \times (0.00429 \times 667,524)$$
$$Sales_t = \$1,682.47 \text{ million}$$

This example is somewhat unique. A home builder is a single-product company and so simpler to model. Sales models vary by business and industry and it is impossible to list them all. Our goal here is to recommend a process of modeling sales as a function of underlying drivers. To forecast sales, one must forecast the underlying drivers. The advantage of this approach is that it focuses the manager's (or analyst's) attention on the economic determinants of sales. As we said above, the sales model varies by industry. One very common model is the retail sales model, which we present in the next section.

Sales Forecast for Retailers

Let's forecast sales for the retailer Build-A-Bear Workshop, Inc. (BAB). BAB operates a chain of over 344 stores in North America and the United Kingdom at which customers make their own stuffed animals.

Since BAB has a multitude of products, we cannot model price and quantity separately as proposed in Equation 14.1. Instead, we model and forecast total sales revenue. With retailers, the two drivers are (1) the number of stores and (2) sales per square foot. Sales revenues are modeled as:

EQUATION 14.5

$$Sales_t = Stores_t \times Area_t \times \$Sales\ per\ square\ foot_t$$

where

$$\#Stores_t = \text{the number of stores owned by the company in year } t$$
$$Area_t = \text{average area of a store in year } t$$
$$\$\ Sales\ per\ square\ foot_t = \text{the average annual revenue per square root in year } t$$

For example, in 2010, the average area for a BAB store was 3,161 square feet. Sales per square foot were $356. Thus, total retail sales for BAB were:

$$Sales_{2010} = 344 \times 3.161 \times \$356 = \$387 \text{ million}$$

To forecast sales, we need to know two things: (1) how many new stores BAB intends to open each year and (2) how sales per square foot will change.

To estimate the number of new stores, one typically starts with management's forecast. If no management forecast is available (i.e., for a new business), then the analyst must look at demand for the product and also at the experience of similar retailers.

The growth in sales per square foot is called **same-stores sales growth (SSSG)**. SSSG is likely to rise with inflation. Beyond inflation, one must look at the competitive landscape of the industry. A high level of competition usually leads to slow price growth. Finally, one can look at SSSG in competing businesses. For example, since BAB is in the toy business, one could look at SSSG for Toys-R-Us.

same-stores sales growth (SSSG)
The rate of growth of sales in existing stores (not including sales growth due to the addition of new stores). Also equal to the growth of sales per square foot.

14.2 Cash Budgeting

Explain It

Sadler Development Company is a property developer. The company buys land, builds, and leases commercial and retail space. A manager at Sadler claims to have spent 80% of his time developing cash budgets for the firm during its peak construction periods. Weekly cash outflows were fairly constant due to payrolls and purchases. However, bank loan disbursements were made only when specific phases of the construction were completed. Often, Sadler found that disbursements exceeded revenues. By constructing detailed cash budgets, management was able to delay certain disbursements and to adjust construction schedules to ensure that paychecks didn't bounce. Although the employees weren't told, the firm occasionally worked them overtime to complete a phase of a project so that a loan disbursement could be requested and the employees paid on time.

The cash budget is a detailed statement of cash inflows and outflows that summarizes the cash position of the firm. Cash budgets are prepared for various intervals: weeks, months, or quarters. Although many firms are not as cash strapped as Sadler (the company profiled in the above "Explain It"), every firm can benefit from knowing its cash position. If the cash budget shows a firm will be short of cash at some point in the future, it will have time to make arrangements for a loan, an equity infusion, or deferred disbursements. If the cash budget shows the firm will have a cash surplus, those funds can be invested in income-producing securities or otherwise put to work. In its simplest form, the cash budget contains the elements in Figure 14.1.

FIGURE 14.1 Elements of a Cash Budget

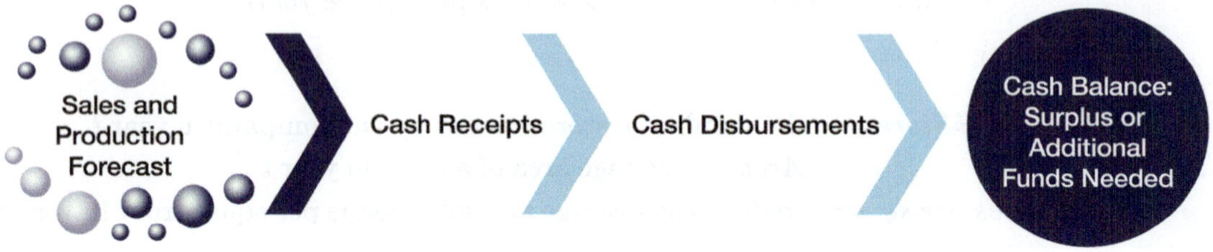

The cash budget starts with a sales and production forecast. The forecast identifies sales revenues, operational costs, financing outlays, taxes, and any fixed asset requirements. Once the assumptions are made, specific forecasts of cash receipts and outlays are made to identify net cash flows in each period. Finally, the net cash flows are used to identify whether additional funds are needed or whether the company will have a surplus of cash.

This section presents a simple approach to preparing a cash budget. In our examples, we make specific assumptions about how credit sales are collected and when accounts payable is paid. Keep in mind that the assumptions can be modified to fit the needs of any firm.

Cash Receipts

Not all sales generate immediate cash receipts. Usually, a portion of sales is for cash and the rest is for credit. Table 14.2 shows sales and cash receipts for Mammoth Mart Groceries (Panel A) and Yingling Breweries Inc. (Panel B). Mammoth does not extend credit to customers—all of its sales are for cash. In each month t, Mammoth's cash receipts are equal to total sales in the same month.

EQUATION 14.6

$$Cash\ receipts_t = Sales_t$$

On the other hand, half of Yingling's sales are for cash and the other half are on credit. Yingling collects its credit sales one month after the sale. Cash receipts for Yingling in month t are equal to one-half of sales in the same month (cash sales) plus one-half of sales in the previous month $(t-1)$.

EQUATION 14.7

$$Cash\ receipts_t = 0.5 \times Sales_t + 0.5 \times Sales_{t-1}$$

TABLE 14.2 Patterns of Cash Receipts

	Nov.	Dec.	Jan.
Panel A. Sales Collections for Mammoth Mart Groceries			
Sales	$9,500	$10,000	$11,000
Cash Sales	9,500	10,000	11,000
Collections from Last Month	0	0	0
Cash Receipts	9,500	10,000	11,000
Panel B. Sales and Collections for Yingling Breweries Inc.			
Sales	$9,500	$10,000	$11,000
Cash Sales	4,250	5,000	5,500
Collections from Last Month		4,250	5,000
Cash Receipts		9,250	10,500

Cash Disbursements

Determining whether an item is a cash disbursement is simple. If it reduces the bank account, it's a cash disbursement. Cash disbursements include:

1. **Payments for inputs and supplies.**
2. **Operating expenses.** Wages, rent, taxes, selling, general, and administrative expenses.
3. **Capital expenditures.** Purchases of fixed assets.
4. **Financing expenses.** Interest, dividends, stock repurchases, and repayment of principal.

Tip

Spreadsheets are an ideal tool for building cash budgets.

Payments to Suppliers

Supply purchases are made prior to the sale of a finished product. It is common for suppliers to extend credit and buyers usually pay the invoice in the month after the purchase. We model payments to suppliers in two steps: (1) the purchase and (2) the payment of the accounts payable.

Tip

Modeling payments in two steps may seem pedantic, but it increases transparency and reduces errors.

Purchases are a function of sales. If purchases are equal to 25% of sales and occur 1 month before the sale, then we can express purchases in month *t* as:

EQUATION 14.8

$$Purchases_t = 0.25 \times Sales_{t+1}$$

Payments to suppliers are modeled as a function of purchases. If purchases are made on credit and paid 1 month after the purchase, then we can express payments to suppliers as:

EQUATION 14.9

$$Payments_t = Purchases_{t-1}$$

Net Cash Flows

EQUATION 14.10

$$Net\ cash\ flow_t = Cash\ receipts_t - Cash\ disbursements_t$$

Example 14.2 Net Cash Flows for the Furthur Bus Company

Digital Downloads

Example 14.2 Net Cash Flows for the Furthur Bus Company.xlsx
https://catalog.flatworldknowledge.com/a/34711/
Example_14_2_Net_Cash_Flows_for_the_Furthur_Bus_Company-7aee.xlsx

Sales for Furthur Bus Company are shown in the table below.

	November	December	January	February	March
Sales	$9,500	$10,000	$11,000	$12,100	$13,310

All sales are for credit, with 80% collected the following month and 20% collected during the second month. Purchases of raw materials equals 60% of sales. Purchases are made in the month of the sale, but suppliers are paid in the month following the purchase. Wages are $1,000 per month, rent is $1,500, taxes are $500, and a $1,000 loan payment is due in February. Monthly interest expense is $200. What are the net cash flows in January, February, and March?

SOLUTION

Spreadsheet Solution

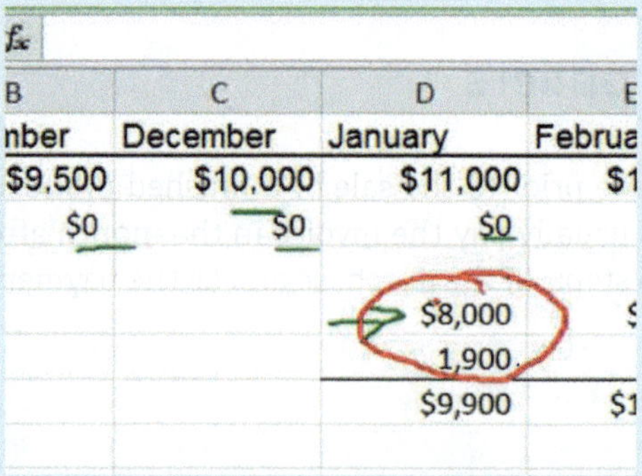

B	C	D	E
nber	December	January	Februa
$9,500	$10,000	$11,000	$1
$0	$0	$0	
		$8,000	$
		1,900	
		$9,900	$1

View in the online reader

	November	December	January	February	March
Sales	$9,500	$10,000	$11,000	$12,100	$13,310
Collections					
1 Month Ago			8,000	8,800	9,680
2 Months Ago			1,900	2,000	2,200
Total Cash Receipts			9,900	10,800	11,880
Purchases		$6,000	$6,600	$7,260	$7,986
Payments to Suppliers			6,000	6,600	7,260
Wages			1,000	1,000	1,000
Rent			1,500	1,500	1,500
Taxes			500	500	500
Interest			200	200	200
Principal Payment			—	1,000	—
Total Disbursements			9,200	10,800	10,460
Net Cash Flow			700	0	1,420

Cash Balance: Surplus or Additional Funds Needed

Table 14.3 shows the net cash flows and the cash balance for the Furthur Bus Company.

TABLE 14.3 Cash Balance for the Furthur Bus Company

	January	February	March
Beginning Cash Balance	$3,000	$3,700	$3,700
Plus: Net Cash Flows	700	0	1,420
Ending Cash Balance	3,700	3,700	5,120
Less: Minimum Cash Balance	3,000	3,000	3,000
Surplus (AFN)	700	700	2,120

The cash balance is just the amount of cash in the cash account. The beginning cash balance is the balance forwarded from the previous period. Let's assume that the beginning cash balance for the Furthur Bus Company in January is $3,000.

The ending cash balance is the beginning balance plus the net cash flows during the month.

14.3 Financial Statements Forecasting

We begin our discussion by demonstrating the preparation of very simple forecasted statements. We then add more realism (and accuracy) to the model in the second section. Throughout this section we employ the percent-of-sales (POS) method. With the POS method, most of the accounts are related to sales and we use a sales forecast to generate forecasted statements.

Simple Forecast

The Income Statement and Balance Sheet for Mug o' Pizza (the only pizza in a mug) are presented in Table 14.4.

TABLE 14.4 Financial Statements for Mug o' Pizza

Mug o' Pizza	
Income Statement	
Sales	$2,000
Cost of Goods Sold	1,600
Net Income	400

Mug o' Pizza			
Balance Sheet			
Assets	$3,000	Debt	$500
		Equity	2,000
Total	3,000	Total	3,000

With the POS method, (almost) every accounting item is related to sales with a ratio. Once we have a sales forecast, we can use the ratios to forecast the rest of the statements. Table 14.5 provides some important ratios, which were obtained from the statements in Table 14.4.

TABLE 14.5 Key Ratios for Mug o' Pizza

Ratio	Value
Cost-to-Sales	0.8
Assets per $1 Sales	1.50

Mug o' Pizza's CEO expects sales to grow by 50% next year as more and more people discover the benefits of eating pizza in a mug. In Table 14.6, we repeat the historical financial statements (in the columns labeled Historic) and show the forecasted statements using the ratios from Table 14.5.

Cost of goods sold are a good example of an account that maintains a fixed proportion to sales. As such, we can forecast future values of costs by using the ratio in Table 14.5 and the following formula:

EQUATION 14.11

$$\textit{Cost of goods sold}_{t+1} = \textit{Sales}_{t+1} \times \textit{Cost to sales ratio}$$

The value for cost of goods sold in the forecasted statements is $2,400, which is just 80% of the forecasted level of sales.

Digital Downloads

Table 14.6 Forecasted Financial Statements for Mug O Pizza.xlsx
https://catalog.flatworldknowledge.com/a/34711/Table_14_6_Forecasted_Financial_Statements_for_Mug_O_Pizza-8c77.xlsx

TABLE 14.6 Forecasted Financial Statements for Mug o' Pizza

Income Statement		
	Historic	**Forecast**
Sales	$2,000	$3,000
Cost of Goods Sold	1,600	2,400
Net Income	$400	$600

Balance Sheet					
	Historic	**Forecast**		**Historic**	**Forecast**
Assets	$3,000	$4,500	Debt	$500	$500
			Equity	2,500	3,100
Total	$3,000	$4,500	Total	$3,000	$3,600

Notice that Forecasted Assets are 1.5 times forecasted sales in the Income Statement.

Many accounts, particularly capital accounts on the right-hand side, do not maintain a proportionate relationship to sales. For example, in Table 14.6, equity does not rise with sales. It increases from $2,500 to $3,100 because of retained earnings (net income).

Notice that the balance sheet does not balance. The firm faces a capital shortfall of $900. We call this shortfall the AFN. If the funds cannot be raised, then the firm cannot afford to increase assets and so it will not be able to increase sales as planned. If the AFN are obtained by borrowing, then debt will rise to $1,400 and the balance sheet will balance. Alternatively, the firm could obtain the AFN by issuing equity.

When we add the AFN to one of the accounts, then we refer to that account as the **plug account** or **plug variable.**

plug account

The account used to make the balance sheet balance when forecasting financial statements. Also known as a plug variable.

plug variable

The account used to make the balance sheet balance when forecasting financial statements. Also referred to as a plug account.

The choice of plug accounts is up to management. Debt and equity values are chosen to reflect the firm's target capital structure.

Forecasted financial statements are an important planning tool. They give financial managers the ability to forecast capital needs before they arise.

Forecasting Accounts Not Tied to Sales

From the example in the last section, it seems there are two categories of accounts: (1) those that are tied to sales and (2) plug accounts. There is a third category: accounts that are not directly tied to sales. In the last section, we identified retained earnings as one such account. Other examples include taxes, dividends, and goodwill. Taxes are a percentage of taxable income. Dividends are a percentage of net income. Goodwill is assumed to be constant, since it is created by acquisitions and we usually do not model growth through acquisitions.

Tip

We do not model growth through acquisitions because we would need to know the net present value of the acquisition and that is only known by the acquiring firm after much analysis.

capital expenditures (CAPEX)

Purchases of fixed assets such as property, plant, and equipment. Also referred to as capital expenditures.

In this section, we are going to show you how to handle four other accounts that are not tied to sales: (1) interest expense, (2) depreciation, (3) **capital expenditures (CAPEX)**, and (4) net fixed assets (net property plant and equipment).

Interest Expense

The interest expense is not tied to sales. Rather, it is tied to debt. When we studied time value of money, we calculated the future value as follows:

EQUATION 14.12

$$FV_1 = PV_{t-1} \times (1 + i) = PV_{t-1} + (PV_{t-1} \times i)$$

The term $(PV_{t-1} \times i)$ is the interest earned (paid) over the period t. It is the product of the amount owed at the beginning of the period and the interest rate. To forecast interest, we use the same equation. We obtain the amount owed from the previous year's balance sheet. We calculate the interest expense by taking the product of the interest rate and the book value of debt from the end of the last period. For example, if Dutch Ovens has long-term debts of $200 at the end of the most recent year and if its interest rate is 6%, then its interest expense in the coming year is $12.

Tip

This method underestimates the interest expense if new debt is added during the period (year). The workaround is to forecast quarterly. Alternatively, some analysts add a small premium to their interest rate.

Depreciation

The depreciation expense is not driven directly by sales. Rather, it is related to fixed assets. So, it makes sense to model depreciation as a function of fixed assets. The simplest approach is to use a declining balance depreciation system.

The declining balance system deducts a fixed percentage of an asset's value each year. Thus, the annual depreciation expense is:

EQUATION 14.13

$$Depreciation_t = dr \times Book\ value_{t-1}$$

Explain It

Example of Declining Balance Depreciation: Mike Mulligan purchased a new steam shovel for $100,000. The shovel is depreciated at a rate of 15%. What is the book value at the end of the second year?

Starting Book Value	Depreciation Rate	Annual Depreciation Expense	Accumulated Depreciation	Ending Book Value
$100,000	15%	$15,000	$15,000	$85,000
$85,000	15%	$12,750	$27,750	$72,250

The depreciation expense in the first year is:

$$\textit{Depreciation}_1 = \mathbf{0.15 \times \$100,000 = \$15,000}$$

The accumulated depreciation at the end of year 2 is:

$$\textit{Accumulated depreciation}_2 = \mathbf{\$15,000 + \$12,750 = \$27,750}$$

The book value at the end of year 2 is:

$$\textit{Book value}_2 = \textit{Original cost} - \textit{Accumulated depreciation}_2$$
$$\textit{Book value}_2 = \mathbf{\$100,000 - \$27,750 = \$72,250}$$

where

$$\textit{Book value}_t = \textit{Purchase price of asset} - \textit{Accumulated depreciation}$$
$$\textit{Accumulated depreciation}_t = \textbf{sum of depreciation expenses to the end of period } t$$
$$dr = \textbf{the depreciation rate}$$

If the book value of assets is $100,000 at the end of last year, and the depreciation rate is 15%, then this year's depreciation expense is $15,000.

Equation 14.13 implicitly assumes that no new assets are purchased during the year. New asset purchases are called *capital expenditures* or *CAPEX*. We can extend Equation 14.13 to incorporate CAPEX as follows:

EQUATION 14.14

$$\textit{Depreciation}_t = dr \times [\textit{Book value}_{t-1} + CAPEX_t]$$

Tip

This equation assumes that new assets (CAPEX) are depreciated for the full year. In the terminology of the IRS, the placed-in-service date is assumed to be January 1.

When we forecast financial statements, we treat all of the fixed assets as one, so the book value is equal to net fixed assets (net property, plant, and equipment) from the balance sheet.

Assume that Dutch Oven had net fixed assets of $100 at the end of last year. The firm's average depreciation rate is 10% and it plans to purchase assets (CAPEX) worth $20 to support the growing level of sales. Using Equation 14.14, the depreciation expense for this year is forecast to be:

$$\textit{Depreciation} = \mathbf{0.1 \times (\$100 + \$20) = \$12}$$

Net Fixed Assets

Explain It

View in the online reader

Recall that when an asset is depreciated, regardless of method, the value of net fixed assets (book value) at the end of any year *t* is given by:

EQUATION 14.15

$$Net_t = Net_{t-1} - Depreciation_t$$

where Net_t refers to net fixed assets at the end of year *t* (net property plant and equipment or book value). For example, consider a company with net fixed assets (at the end of last year) of $100 that are depreciated at 25%. The current year's depreciation expense is $25. The value of net fixed assets at the end of the year is $100 - 25 = 75$.

When companies add fixed assets during the year (CAPEX), Equation 14.15 becomes:

EQUATION 14.16

$$Net_t = Net_{t-1} - Depreciation_t + CAPEX_t$$

CAPEX

maintenance CAPEX

Assets that are purchased to replace worn-out equipment.

growth CAPEX

The assets that must be purchased in order to grow sales.

CAPEX can be divided into two parts: **maintenance CAPEX** and **growth CAPEX**. Maintenance CAPEX are the assets that are purchased to replace worn-out equipment. Growth CAPEX are the assets that must be purchased in order to grow sales. In our examples and problems, we do not distinguish between maintenance and growth CAPEX. We provide the total amount of CAPEX. However, as you become more experienced with financial forecasting, you should forecast each separately.

Example 14.3 Forecasting Depreciation, CAPEX, and Net Fixed Assets for Dutch Oven

Use the information in the following table to forecast depreciation and net fixed assets for Dutch Oven.

Selected Financial Values for Dutch Oven	
Depreciation Rate, *dr*	20%
$\text{Net Fixed Assets}_t$	$100
CAPEX_{t+1}	$30

SOLUTION

Digital Downloads

Example 14.3 Forecasting Depr CAPEX and Net Fixed for Dutch Ovens.xlsx
https://catalog.flatworldknowledge.com/a/34711/Example_14_3_Forecasting_Depr_CAPEX_and_Net_Fixed_for_Dutch_Ovens-2e98.xlsx

Depreciation

From Equation 14.14:

$$Depreciation_{t+1} = dr \times [Net_t + CAPEX_{t+1}] = 0.2 \times [\$100 + \$30] = \$26$$

Net Fixed Assets

From Equation 14.16:

$$Net_{t+1} = Net_t - Depreciation_{t+1} + CAPEX_{t+1} = \$100 - \$26 + \$30 = \$104$$

Income Statement Forecast

With the forecasted values of interest and depreciation, we now have everything that we need to forecast the income statement.

Example 14.4 Forecasted Income Statement for Dutch Oven

Digital Downloads

Example 14.4 Forecasted Income Statement for Dutch Oven.xlsx
https://catalog.flatworldknowledge.com/a/34711/Example_14_4_Forecasted_Income_Statement_for_Dutch_Oven-8a46.xlsx

Forecast the income statement for Dutch Oven using the following assumptions. Assume that sales are forecast to rise by 20% (to $600). Assume that the cost of debt is 6%, the depreciation rate is 12.5%, CAPEX is $40, and the tax rate is 50%.

SOLUTION

Cost of goods sold and SG&A expenses are forecast as a fixed percentage of sales. Cost of goods sold was historically 80% of sales, as indicated in the column labeled "Ratio to Sales." SG&A expenses were 4% of sales. We forecast these values by assuming that their ratio to sales remains constant. For example, if sales are forecast to be $600 in the next period, then cost of goods sold is forecast to be $0.8 \times \$600 = \$480$.

	Historic	Ratio to Sales	Forecast
Sales	$500		$600
Cost of Goods Sold	400	80%	480
Selling, General, and Admin. Expenses	20	4%	24
Depreciation	25		26
EBIT	55		70
Interest	15		12
Pre-Tax Income	40		58
Taxes (@50%)	20		29
Net Income	$20		$29

statutory rate

A statutory tax rate is the legally imposed corporate income tax rate.

apparent tax rate

The apparent rate is just the amount of taxes claimed on the income statement divided by pretax income.

Taxes can be calculated using the **statutory rate** or the **apparent tax rate**. The apparent rate has the advantage that it reflects any tax credits or special rates enjoyed by the company.

Explain It

If Dutch Ovens had historically paid out 40% of earnings, then dividends would be forecast as $0.4 \times \$29.50 = \$11.8$ and retained earnings as $17.70.

Dividends and retained earnings are forecast by assuming that the firm's historical payout ratio remains constant. When we forecast the balance sheet for Dutch Oven, we assume that the company pays out nothing.

Balance Sheet Forecast

Current Assets and Liabilities

Current assets and current liabilities are forecast as a percentage of sales. In other words, the turnover and payable ratios are assumed to remain constant. It is up to the analyst to decide whether cash and short-term debt are modeled as a percentage of sales. Alternatively, the amounts can remain constant or can be used as plug accounts. In this example, we model cash as a percentage of sales (the historic ratio is 20%) and we can ignore short-term debt because Dutch Oven doesn't have any. Table 14.7 shows the historic financial statements and the forecasted values for those accounts.

Digital Downloads

Table 14.7 Partial Balance Sheet Forecast for Dutch Oven.xlsx
https://catalog.flatworldknowledge.com/a/34711/ Table_14_7_Partial_Balance_Sheet_Forecast_for_Dutch_Oven-0a8f.xlsx

TABLE 14.7 Partial Balance Sheet Forecast for Dutch Oven

	Historic	Forecast
Cash	$100	$120
Accounts Receivable	150	180
Inventories	200	240
Total Current Assets	$450	$540
Fixed Assets, Net	$100	
Total Assets	$550	
Accounts Payable	$100	$120
Total Current Liabilities	100	120
Long-Term Debt	200	
Common Stock	100	
Retained Earnings	150	179
Stockholders' Equity	250	
Total Liabilities and Equity	$550	

The forecasted values for accounts receivable, inventories and accounts payable are calculated using the historic ratios to sales: 30%, 40%, and 20%, respectively.

Long-Term Assets

Earlier, we explained the method for forecasting net fixed assets. Other common long-term assets are items such as goodwill, patents, and other intangibles. None of those accounts are proportionate to sales and so all should be forecast at a constant level equal to their historic value.

Debt and Equity—The Plug Variables

Debt (both short-term and long-term) and equity are not forecast as a percentage of sales. They are both determined as a matter of financial policy. As we learned previously, the choice between debt and equity is a function of the firm's target capital structure. If the firm has less debt than its target level, then it will raise capital by borrowing. If it has too much debt, then it will raise capital by selling new shares.

Of course, equity rises automatically by the amount of retained earnings. You will notice that retained earnings in the partial balance sheet rises from $150 to the new level of $179. The difference is just the amount of retained earnings from the forecasted income statement.

In this scenario, the AFN is $45. If we assume that debt is the plug variable, then it takes the value of $245 and the forecasted balance sheet is as shown in Table 14.8.

Digital Downloads

Table 14.8 Above Forecasted Balance Sheet for Dutch Oven_Debt_Plug.xlsx
https://catalog.flatworldknowledge.com/a/34711/
Table_14_8_Above_Forecasted_Balance_Sheet_for_Dutch_Oven_Debt_Plug-d834.xlsx

TABLE 14.8 Forecasted Balance Sheet for Dutch Oven

	Historic	Forecast
Cash	$100	$120
Accounts Receivable	150	180
Inventories	200	240
Total Current Assets	450	540
Fixed Assets, Net	100	104
Total Assets	550	540
Accounts Payable	100	120
Total Current Liabilities	$100	$120
Long-Term Debt	200	245
Common Stock	100	100
Retained Earnings	150	179
Stockholders' Equity	250	279
Total Liabilities and Equity	$550	$644

The implication is that the firm must borrow an additional $45 in order to finance the increase in sales from $500 to $600 this year. Forecasted financial statements are used by financial managers to identify capital needs before they arise. This gives them time to arrange the financing in the cheapest manner possible. The spreadsheet shows the forecasted balance sheet if the plug account had been equity.

Digital Downloads

Table 14.8 Below Forecasted Balance Sheet for Dutch Oven_equity_plug.xlsx
https://catalog.flatworldknowledge.com/a/34711/
Table_14_8_Below_Forecasted_Balance_Sheet_for_Dutch_Oven_equity_plug-bc4d.xlsx

Comprehensive Example

Example 14.5 Forecasting Financial Statements

Digital Downloads

Example 14_5 Forecasting Financial Statements.xlsx

https://catalog.flatworldknowledge.com/a/34711/ Example_14_5_Forecasting_Financial_Statements-9249.xlsx

Forecast the financial statements for Pennybags Corp. Assume that sales grow by 5%, the cost of debt is 7%, the depreciation rate is 22%, and Pennybags invests $153,025 in CAPEX.

SOLUTION

The solution is provided in the spreadsheet and is explained in the spreadsheet video.

Spreadsheet Solution

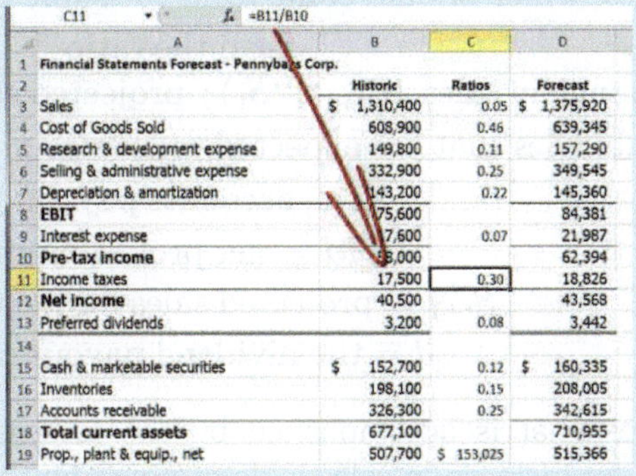

C11 =B11/B10

	A	B	C	D
1	Financial Statements Forecast - Pennybags Corp.			
2		Historic	Ratios	Forecast
3	Sales	$ 1,310,400	0.05	$ 1,375,920
4	Cost of Goods Sold	608,900	0.46	639,345
5	Research & development expense	149,800	0.11	157,290
6	Selling & administrative expense	332,900	0.25	349,545
7	Depreciation & amortization	143,200	0.22	145,360
8	EBIT	75,600		84,381
9	Interest expense	17,600	0.07	21,987
10	Pre-tax income	58,000		62,394
11	Income taxes	17,500	0.30	18,826
12	Net income	40,500		43,568
13	Preferred dividends	3,200	0.08	3,442
14				
15	Cash & marketable securities	$ 152,700	0.12	$ 160,335
16	Inventories	198,100	0.15	208,005
17	Accounts receivable	326,300	0.25	342,615
18	Total current assets	677,100		710,955
19	Prop., plant & equip., net	507,700	$ 153,025	515,366

View in the online reader

14.4 Additional Funds Needed and Growth

In the previous section, we used forecasted financial statements to find how much assets must increase if sales increase as projected. This increase in assets must be financed somehow. Part of the financing comes from retained earnings and some comes from a spontaneous increase in liabilities. Specifically, current liabilities, such as accounts payable, often increase with sales.

If the increase in assets is greater than retained earnings and the spontaneous increase in liabilities, then additional funds are required. This is the plug figure that balances total assets to liabilities and owners' equity.

The firm may choose to raise AFN from an increase in notes payable, long-term debt, or equity. For example, a smaller dividend could be paid. Another option available to management is to curtail growth, so it doesn't need additional funds. Remember, the purpose of financial planning is to give management options. By projecting a cash shortage, management can choose the option that best fits the firm's strategic plan.

Additional Funds Needed

Computing the AFN from forecasted financial statements provides analysts the opportunity to pick which specific accounts will vary with sales. The equation approach is simpler and may be more appropriate if only a rough estimate of cash requirements is needed. The equation for estimating the AFN is:

EQUATION 14.17

$$AFN = \frac{A^*}{S_t}\Delta S - \frac{L^*}{S_t}\Delta S - [PM \times S_{t+1} \times (1 - d)]$$

where

$$AFN = \text{additional funds needed}$$
$$A^* = \text{assets that are expected to change proportionally with sales}$$
$$S_t = \text{prior year sales, which should come from the same period as the asset balances used to form the ratio}$$
$$\Delta S = \text{the change in sales } (S_{t+1} - S_t)\text{; projected sales minus last period's sales}$$
$$L^* = \text{liabilities that are expected to change proportionately with sales (i.e., accounts payable)}$$
$$PM = \text{net profit margin}$$
$$S_{t+1} = \text{projected sales for next period}$$
$$d = \text{the dividend payout ratio}$$

Equation 14.17 summarizes what is accomplished by the forecasted financial statements. The increase in assets due to an increase in sales is determined by the first term to the right of the equals sign. Spontaneous sources of financing, which include increases in liabilities and retained earnings, are then subtracted from this figure.

The AFN equation works well for the simple Mug o' Pizza in Table 14.6 as shown in Equation 14.18.

EQUATION 14.18

$$AFN = \frac{\$3,000}{2,000}\$1,000 - \frac{\$0}{2,000}\$1,000 - [0.20 \times 3,000 \times (1 - 0)] = \$900$$

We get the same AFN using Equation 14.18 as we found using the forecasted financial statements (in Section 3.1). The two methods yield the same result when all accounts (other than plug accounts, taxes, and payouts) are modeled as a percentage of sales. In other words, the equation is derived from the assumption that all accounts are a percentage of sales. When interest, depreciation, and CAPEX are not modeled as a percentage of sales (as in Section 3.2), then the growth rate of assets is not the same as sales and the profit margin changes gradually over time. Then, the forecasted statements and Equation 14.17 produce different estimates of AFN.

One advantage of Equation 14.17 is that it can easily be used in a spreadsheet to map the AFN at different projected sales or payout ratios. Because sales are only a forecast, a graph of the AFN at various sales levels will help management determine the likelihood that additional funds will be required. Figure 14.2 is a graph of the AFN for various sales projections.

Digital Downloads

AFN_and_Sales_for_Dutch_Oven.xlsx
https://catalog.flatworldknowledge.com/a/34711/AFN_and_Sales_for_Dutch_Oven-7dde.xlsx

Explain It: AFN with Different Sales Growth Projections

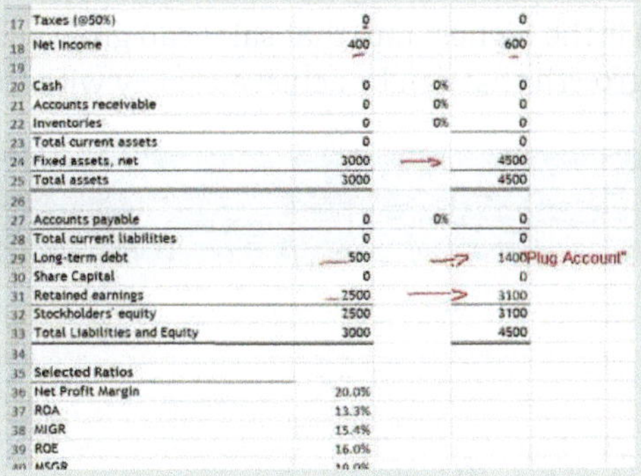

17	Taxes (@50%)	0		0
18	Net Income	400		600
19				
20	Cash	0	0%	0
21	Accounts receivable	0	0%	0
22	Inventories	0	0%	0
23	Total current assets	0		0
24	Fixed assets, net	3000		4500
25	Total assets	3000		4500
26				
27	Accounts payable	0	0%	0
28	Total current liabilities	0		0
29	Long-term debt	500		1400Plug Account"
30	Share Capital	0		0
31	Retained earnings	2500		3100
32	Stockholders' equity	2500		3100
33	Total Liabilities and Equity	3000		4500
34				
35	Selected Ratios			
36	Net Profit Margin	20.0%		
37	ROA	13.3%		
38	MIGR	15.4%		
39	ROE	16.0%		
40	MSGR	10.0%		

View in the online reader

FIGURE 14.2 AFN with Different Sales Growth Projections

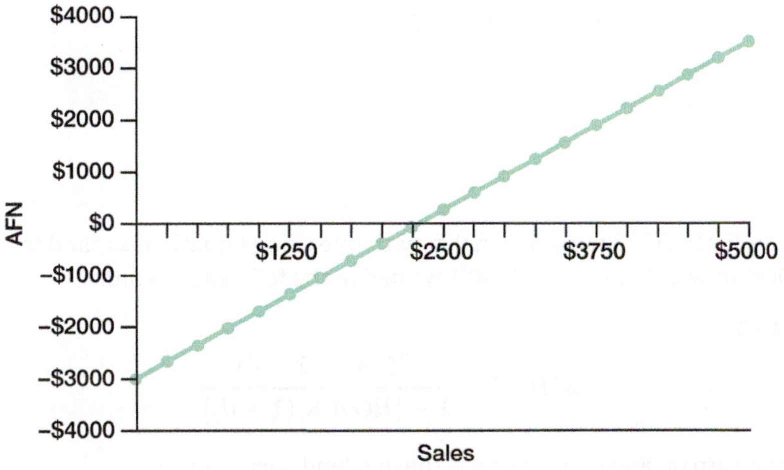

In Figure 14.2, if sales are below about $2,307, no additional funds are required. As sales increase above $2,307, more funds must be raised. Figure 14.2 points out an important issue in finance: Firms can grow too fast. Success can lead to failure unless capital needs are provided for. The good news is that growth firms are usually able to raise additional capital from a number of sources as long as they start the process before they find themselves in financial distress.

We learned two approaches to determining the AFN: (1) using forecasted financial statements and (2) using Equation 14.17. Two advantages of forecasting the statements explicitly are (1) it allows for changes in the relationship between sales and the asset and liability accounts and (2) it allows us to model lumpy capital expenditures, operating leverage, and economies of scale. In contrast, the equation approach holds all relationships with sales constant.

Projecting the Maximum Internal Growth Rate

maximum internal growth rate (MIGR)

The highest rate that sales can grow without a firm needing additional funds.

The AFN and growth are clearly closely related topics. In Figure 14.2 the line crosses the *x*-axis at about $2,307. This means that as long as the firm doesn't increase sales more than $307, no external funds are required. This increase represents a 15.4% maximum internal growth rate. The **maximum internal growth rate (MIGR)** is the highest rate that sales can grow without the firm needing additional funds. It is the rate of growth that can be achieved solely with internal financing.

Explain It: MIGR

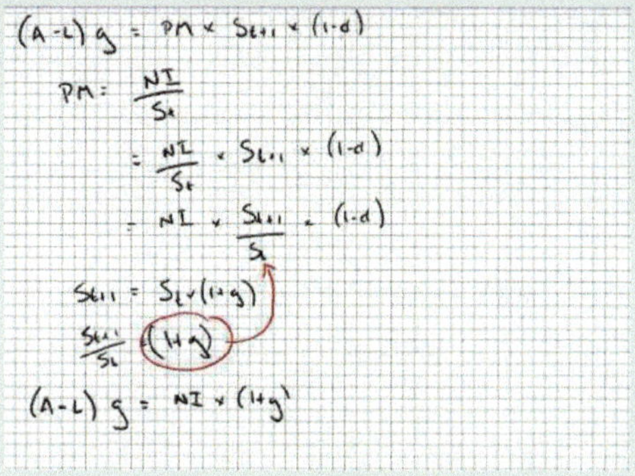

View in the online reader

We can solve for the maximum internal growth rate using Equation 14.17 and setting $AFN = 0$. With some algebra (see "Explain It: MIGR"), we derive the following formula:

EQUATION 14.19

$$MIGR = \frac{ROA \times (1 - d)}{1 - [ROA \times (1 - d)]}$$

ROA is the return on assets, and the *d* is the dividend payout ratio.

Example 14.6 Maximum Internal Growth Rate

Digital Downloads

Example 14_6 Maximum Internal Growth Rate.xlsx
https://catalog.flatworldknowledge.com/a/34711/Example_14_6_Maximum_Internal_Growth_Rate-faf0.xlsx

The ROA for Mug o' Pizza is 13.3% more info and Mug o' Pizza pays no dividends. What is the maximum rate of growth that Mug o' Pizza can maintain using internally generated funds only?

SOLUTION

Spreadsheet Solution

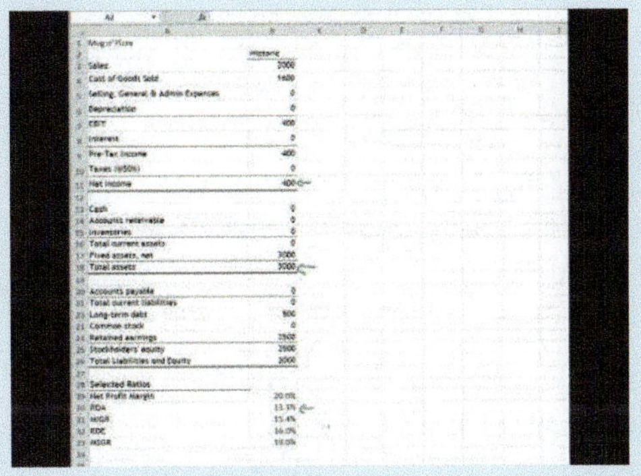

View in the online reader

Using Equation 14.19 and plugging in the figures yields:

$$g = \frac{0.133 \times (1 - 0)}{1 - [0.133 \times (1 - 0)]} = \frac{0.133}{0.867} = 0.154 \text{ or } 15.4\%$$

Mug o' Pizza can grow 15.4% per year indefinitely without resorting to outside capital.

Projecting the Maximum Sustainable Growth Rate

The internal growth rate is the growth rate a firm can maintain without any outside financing. An alternative is the **maximum sustainable growth rate (MSGR)**. The MSGR is the highest growth that a firm can sustain using only internal equity (retained earnings) and borrowing just enough to maintain a constant debt-to-equity ratio.

maximum sustainable growth rate (MSGR)

The highest growth that a firm can sustain using only internal equity (retained earnings) and borrowing just enough to maintain a constant debt-to-equity ratio.

As firms grow they generate retained earnings. If debt is fixed, then the debt-to-equity ratio will slowly fall over time. As we learned in Chapter 12, there is an optimal debt-to-equity ratio that maximizes firm value. If companies grow and want to maintain their optimal debt-to-equity ratio, then they will borrow each year to offset the increase in equity. The funds so provided allow an increase in assets and therefore support an increase in sales. The MSGR is that sales growth rate.

Explain It: MSGR

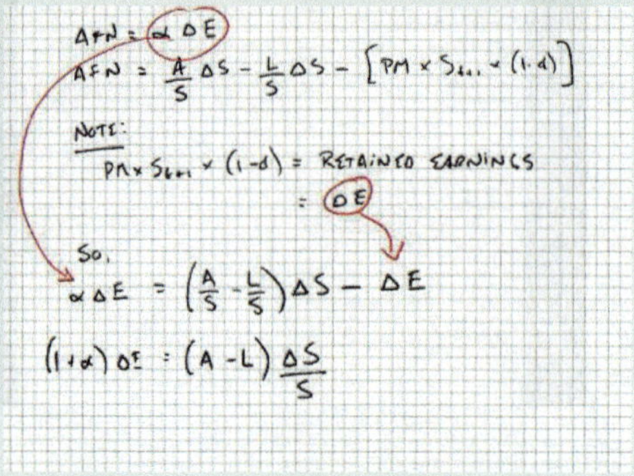

View in the online reader

We can solve for the MSGR using Equation 14.17. We set the AFN equal to the amount of debt that must be raised to offset the increase in retained earnings and so maintain the company at its optimal debt-to-equity ratio. With some algebra (see "Explain It: MSGR"), we derive the following formula:

EQUATION 14.20

$$MSGR = \frac{ROE \times (1 - d)}{1 - [ROE \times (1 - d)]}$$

ROE is the firm's return on equity, computed as net income divided by equity.

The maximum sustainable growth rate is the rate of growth a firm can maintain while keeping its financial leverage constant and not issuing additional equity.

Example 14.7 Maximum Sustainable Growth Rate

Digital Downloads

Example 14_7 Maximum Sustainable Growth Rate.xlsx
https://catalog.flatworldknowledge.com/a/34711/Example_14_7_Maximum_Sustainable_Growth_Rate-9f72.xlsx

The ROE for Mug o' Pizza is 16% and Mug o' Pizza doesn't pay dividends. What is the firm's MSGR?

SOLUTION

Spreadsheet Solution

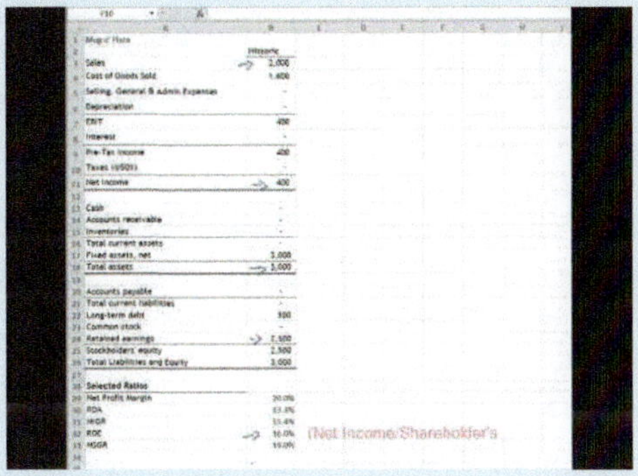

View in the online reader

Using Equation 14.20 and plugging in the figures yields:

$$MSGR = \frac{0.16 \times (1 - 0)}{1 - [0.16 \times (1 - 0)]} = \frac{0.16}{0.84} = 0.19 \text{ or } 19\%$$

Mug o' Pizza can grow at 19% indefinitely without issuing additional equity. Earlier, we found that Mug o' Pizza's MIGR was 15.4%. Because debt is increasing, the MSGR is greater than the MIGR.

How to Influence Growth Rates

In Chapter 2, we developed the DuPont method, which shows the ROE to be the product of profit margin, total asset turnover, and leverage (the equity multiplier). If we review Equation 14.20, we see that anything that increases the ROE will increase the maximum sustainable growth rate. Putting Equation 14.20 together with the DuPont ratio shows that the following factors affect a firm's ability to sustain its growth without issuing additional equity:

1. **Profit margin:** The greater the profit on sales, the more cash is available to finance growth.
2. **Total asset turnover:** The more rapidly assets turn over, the more sales are generated by each dollar of assets. This decreases the amount of assets needed as sales increase.
3. **Financial leverage:** The greater the percentage of debt in the firm's optimal capital structure, the less equity is required to support growth.
4. **Dividend payout ratio:** The greater the net income kept by the firm to finance growth, the greater the maximum sustainable growth rate.

Every firm should know its sustainable growth rate. If growth exceeds this rate, management can expect cash flow problems to develop. It also helps to illustrate the effect management can have on the growth of the firm. Increasing profitability, turnover, and leverage increases the rate at which a firm can grow.

Keep in mind that Equation 14.19 and Equation 14.20 are approximations. They assume that the asset and liability accounts change proportionately with sales.

CHAPTER 15
The Management of Working Capital

Learning Objectives

By the end of this chapter you will be able to:

1. Calculate the operating period and cash conversion cycle.
2. Understand how to manage inventory.
3. Understand how to manage Accounts Receivable.
4. Understand how to manage cash.
5. Recognize short-term financing alternatives.

In this chapter, we focus on short-term assets and liabilities. The major short-term (current) assets include cash, accounts receivable, and inventory. Current assets make up 15–50% of most firms' assets. Managing these effectively can produce major savings. Consider Walmart's inventory control system. In the highly competitive discount retailing industry, any cost savings are extremely important. Walmart has made a science of inventory control, and many industry analysts point to this as the single most important reason for the firm's success.

We study each of the major types of current assets. Our goal is to determine what managers can do to optimize the return on each type of asset. In addition, we review the primary short-term sources of funds. The major short-term liability is accounts payable. Most firms both give credit and take advantage of credit offered by their vendors. We extend our discussion of credit policy to how it affects a firm's liability management.

15.1 The Operating Period and Cash Conversion Cycle

A firm's working capital management policies will be largely determined by its operating period and cash conversion cycle. The **operating period** is the amount of time it takes to buy inventory, sell it, and collect on the sale. The length of the operating period can vary widely across firms and industries. Within the operating period is the **cash conversion cycle**. This is the amount of time between when we pay for our inputs and when we receive payment for selling our products. Contrast the cash management requirements of a car dealer against those of a grocery store. The car dealer will buy a car for inventory that may not sell for 6 months, while the grocery store sells its milk and lettuce in a few days. These two companies have very different operating periods and cash conversion cycles. The problem each firm faces is that the timing of the cash inflows is not synchronized with the cash outflows. We can better understand the issue by looking at each more closely.

operating period

The inventory period plus the collection period. The amount of time required to acquire, sell, and receive payment on a company's merchandise.

cash conversion cycle

The time between when we pay for our products and when we receive payment for selling them.

The Operating Period

Suppose you decide to start a small business that sells custom fingernail polish. You order the paints, bottles, and labels from a vendor that requires payment of $200 in 45 days. You make up the polish and set up your website to take orders. When orders are received, you mail the polish. On average, it takes 90 days to sell each batch. All sales are by credit card and you receive payment 3 days after the sale. We summarize this in Table 15.1.

TABLE 15.1 Operating Period

Stage	Day in the Cycle	Cash Flow	
Order Raw Materials (or Inventory)	0	$0	Inventory Period
Pay for Raw Materials (or inventory)	45	–200	
Sell Product	90	0	Collection Period
Collect on Sales	93	500	

inventory period

The length of time it takes to acquire, process, and sell the inventory.

collection period

The length of time from the sale of the product until payment is received.

Within the operating period, we can identify two separate periods: the inventory period and the collection period. The **inventory period** is the time it takes to acquire and sell the inventory. This may include building a product or just holding an item for sale on a shelf. The **collection period** is the time from the sale of the product until funds are actually received from the buyer. In our example, the inventory period is 90 days and the collection period is 3 days. The operating period is defined in Equation 15.1.

EQUATION 15.1

$$\textit{Operating period} = \textit{Inventory period} + \textit{Collection period}$$
$$\textit{Operating period} = 90 \textit{ days} + 3 \textit{ days} = 93 \textit{ days}$$

The operating period is 93 days because that is the number of days between when the process is initiated and when it is completed. This would be much shorter for a grocery store and much longer for most car dealers, home builders, and jewelry stores.

The Cash Conversion Cycle

accounts payable period

The amount of time the vendor gives a company to pay for its purchases of inventory.

Although the operating period in our example is 93 days, the cash conversion cycle is much shorter. This is because we do not pay for the raw materials at the time of purchase. We need to adjust the operating period to determine exactly how long our funds will be in use. The adjustment is to subtract the time the vendor gives us to pay. We call this time the **accounts payable period**. The cash conversion cycle is summarized by Equation 15.2 and shown graphically in Figure 15.1.

FIGURE 15.1

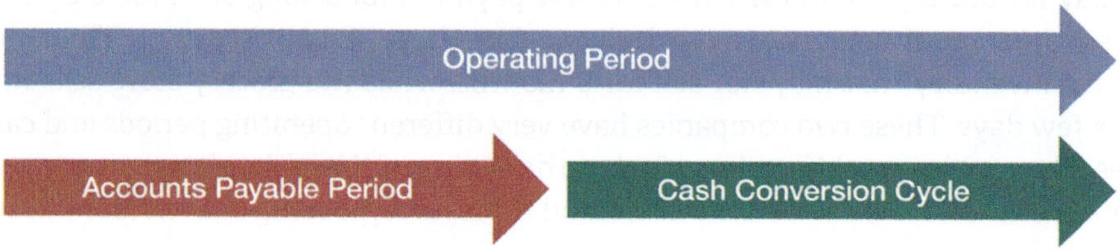

EQUATION 15.2

$$\textit{Cash conversion cycle} = \textit{Operating period} - \textit{Accounts payable period}$$
$$\textit{Cash conversion cycle} = 93\ \textit{days} - 45\ \textit{days} = 48\ \textit{days}$$

Explain It: Cash Conversion Cycle

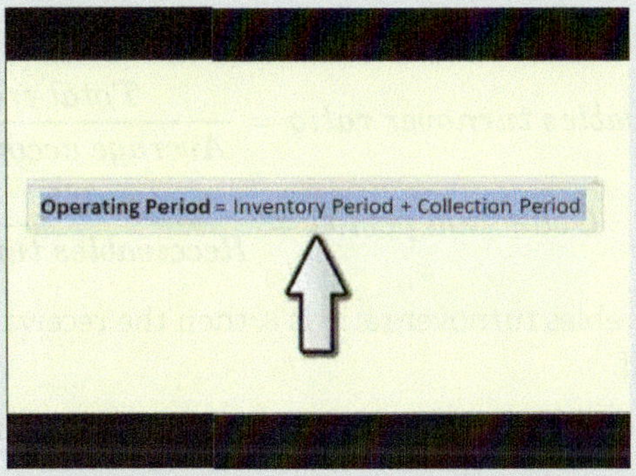

View in the online reader

How to Calculate the Cash Conversion Cycle

The cash conversion cycle was easy to compute in the simple example used in the previous section. In practice, it gets a little more complicated. We need to compute averages based on financial sheet data that can be used in Equation 15.1 and Equation 15.2.

Step 1: Compute the Operating Period

To compute the operating period, we need to compute both the average inventory period and the average collection period.

a. **Average inventory period:** We begin with the inventory turnover ratio and then divide this into 365 to find the average inventory period.

average inventory period

The average length of time it takes to acquire and sell inventory.

EQUATION 15.3

$$\textit{Inventory turnover} = \frac{\textit{Cost of goods sold}}{\textit{Average inventory}}$$
$$\textit{Average inventory period} = \frac{365}{\textit{Inventory turnover}}$$

For example, if the inventory turns over 12 times per year, then the average time to sell the inventory is 30.4 days $(365/12 = 30.4)$ or about 1 month.

Tip

Notice how we used the average level of inventory over the year. We use the average level of the asset for all three ratios that are used in computing the cash conversion cycle. You may also see these ratios computed with the year-end level of the asset. Either approach is correct. You just need to be consistent.

b. **Average collection period:** We begin with the receivables turnover ratio and then divide this into 365 to find the average collection period.

EQUATION 15.4

$$Receivables\ turnover\ ratio = \frac{Total\ credit\ sales}{Average\ accounts\ receivable}$$

$$Collection\ period = \frac{365}{Receivables\ turnover}$$

For example, if the receivables turnover ratio is 8, then the receivables period would be 45.6 or about a month and a half.

c. **Operating period:** We now have the pieces to compute the operating period.

Step 2: Calculating the Cash Conversion Cycle

Because the cash conversion cycle is just the operating period minus the payables period, the only missing piece is the payables period. We calculate the payables turnover ratio and then divide this into 365 days.

EQUATION 15.5

$$Payables\ turnover = \frac{Cost\ of\ goods\ sold}{Average\ payables}$$

$$Accounts\ payables\ period = \frac{365}{Payables\ turnover}$$

For example, if the payables turnover ratio is 10, the receivables period would be 35.6 days. Putting this all together, we compute the cash conversion cycle using Equation 15.2.

$$Cash\ conversion\ cycle = Operating\ period - Accounts\ payable\ period$$
$$Cash\ conversion\ cycle = 76\ days - 36.5\ days = 39.5\ days$$

The interpretation of the cash conversion cycle is that there are 36.5 days between when we pay for our merchandise and when we receive payment for its sale. This is the length of time we need to provide for internal short-term financing. As a firm grows, its need for inventory typically grows as well. The longer the cash conversion cycle, the more cash a firm will require.

Tip

Suppose you had a very short operating period, say 14 days. If your average payables period was 30 days, then you could finance your inventory completely by using vendor credit. Walmart has largely been able to accomplish this especially between 2018–2020 when its cash cycle was 2 days or less. Operationally, this means that it could buy merchandise and sell it in about the same time it took to pay its suppliers. Financially this means that supplier credit largely financed its inventory and little long-term capital was needed to finance short-term assets.

Example 15.1 Calculating the Cash Conversion Cycle

At the beginning of year 1, inventory is $1,000, accounts payable are $200, and accounts receivable are $900. At the beginning of year 2, inventory is $1,200, accounts payable are $250, and accounts receivable are $930. If the cost of goods sold is $5,000 and total credit sales is $8,000, what is the cash conversion cycle?

SOLUTION

Video Solution

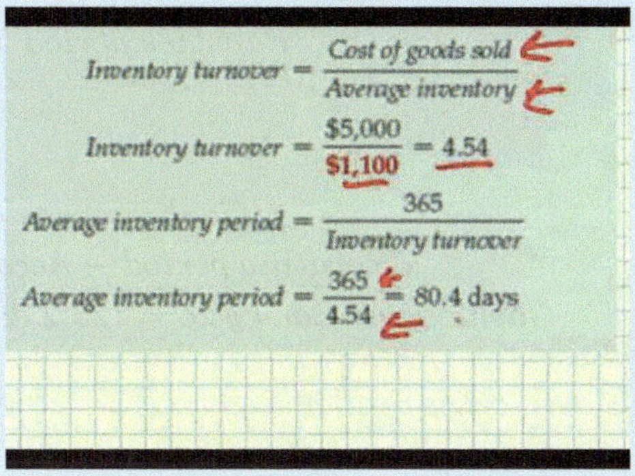

View in the online reader

Step 1.

Compute the inventory period:

$$Inventory\ turnover = \frac{Cost\ of\ goods\ sold}{Average\ inventory}$$

$$Inventory\ turnover = \frac{\$5,000}{\$1,100} = 4.54$$

Calculate the average collection period:

$$Receivables\ turnover\ ratio = \frac{Total\ credit\ sales}{Average\ accounts\ receivable}$$

$$Receivables\ turnover\ ratio = \frac{\$8,000}{\$915} = 8.74$$

$$Collection\ period = \frac{365}{Receivables\ turnover}$$

$$Collection\ period = \frac{365}{8.74} = 41.8\ days$$

Calculate the operating period:

$$Operating\ period = Inventory\ period + Collection\ period$$

$$Operating\ period = 80.4 + 41.8 = 122.2\ days$$

Step 2. Subtract the payable period from the operating period.

Compute the payables turnover and the payables period:

$$\textit{Payables turnover} = \frac{\textit{Cost of goods sold}}{\textit{Average payables}}$$

$$\textit{Payables turnover} = \frac{\$5,000}{\$225} = 22.2$$

$$\textit{Payables period} = \frac{365}{\textit{Payables turnover}}$$

$$\textit{Payables period} = \frac{365}{22.2} = 16.4\ \textit{days}$$

Compute the cash conversion cycle:

$$\textit{Cash conversion cycle} = \textit{Operating period} - \textit{Accounts payable period}$$

$$\textit{Cash conversion cycle} = 122.2\ \textit{days} - 16.4\ \textit{days} = 105.8\ \textit{days}$$

Using the Cash Conversion Cycle in Working Capital Management

Now that we have examined the details of computing the cash conversion cycle, we see how this focuses our efforts to manage our working capital. Table 15.2 lists the variables that impact the cash conversion cycle and how each affects its length.

TABLE 15.2 Changing the Cash Conversion Cycle

Variable	Impact on Cash Conversion Cycle
Accounts Receivable ↑	Increases cash conversion cycle
Accounts Payable ↑	Decreases cash conversion cycle
Inventory ↑	Increases cash conversion cycle
Cost of Goods Sold ↑	Increases cash conversion cycle

15.2 How to Manage Inventory

We can see from Table 15.2 that efforts to lower average inventory will result in reducing the average cash conversion cycle and lead to reduced cash requirements.

Inventory represents a major asset for many firms. Typical manufacturing firms have at least 15% of their assets tied up in inventory, and retailers can have 25% or more of their total assets in inventory. With so much of the firm's net worth at stake, managers must make every effort to manage it wisely. We should recognize that the financial manager may not have primary control over the level of inventory. Marketing, purchasing, and production also impact the inventory decision. Marketing and production typically compete for greater inventory, whereas finance attempts to point out its cost.

Reasons to Hold Inventories

For a manufacturing firm, there are three types of inventory: raw materials, work in process, and finished goods. Retailers typically hold only goods ready for resale. The type of inventory influences why it is held and how much is required. Retailers can seldom sell a product they don't have in inventory, although mail-order houses, Web retailers, and some distributors are successful in this area. Shoppers love a selection and stores that fail to offer it may not be able to compete. On the other hand, inventory is expensive to hold. In manufacturing, where inventory doesn't necessarily influence sales, tight inventory control can be especially valuable.

The Costs of Holding Inventory

The combined costs of holding inventory are called **carrying costs**. As inventory levels increase, so do each of the following costs:

- Opportunity cost of funds tied up in inventory
- Storage cost
- Insurance cost
- Cost of obsolescence, damage, and theft

carrying costs
The variable costs per unit of holding an item in inventory for a specified time period.

At the other end of the spectrum are costs that fall as inventory increases. **Shortage costs** are associated with the consequences of running out of inventory. An entire assembly line can be shut down for lack of a certain type of bolt. Shortage costs can be enormous, and many firms maintain large inventories to ensure that a stockout never occurs.

shortage costs
The cost associated with running out of inventory.

Firms must also be aware of reorder costs. These are costs related to the processing, restocking, and paying for each new order. We generally assume that each new order has a fixed cost, although some variation exists because of differences in order size. Clearly, reorder costs fall when larger inventory levels are maintained. For an example of this, consider Figure 15.2.

FIGURE 15.2 Relationship of Average Inventory, Order Size, and Order Frequency

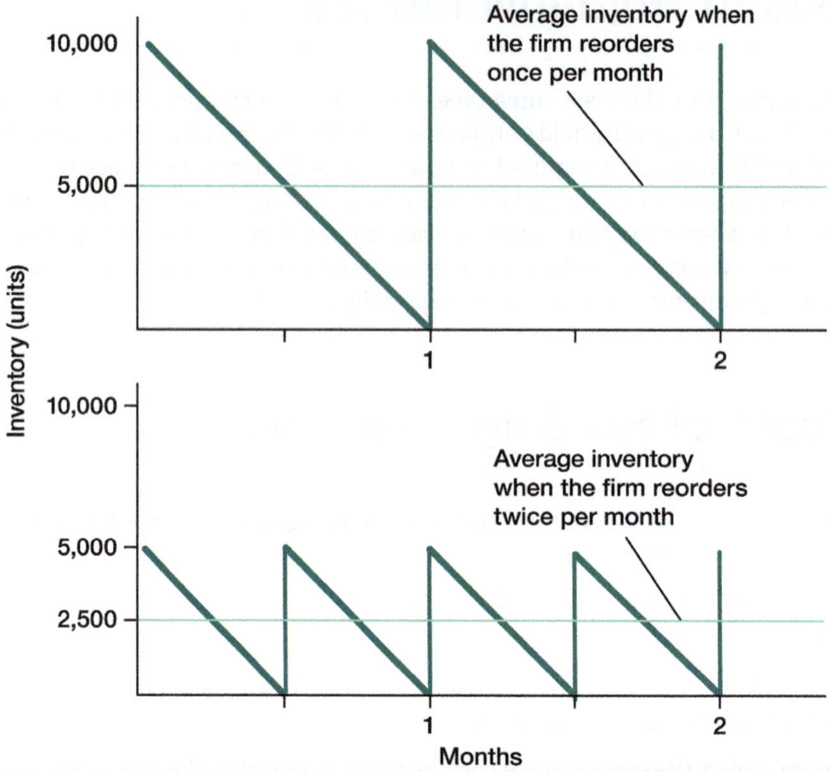

Explain It: Average Inventory Size

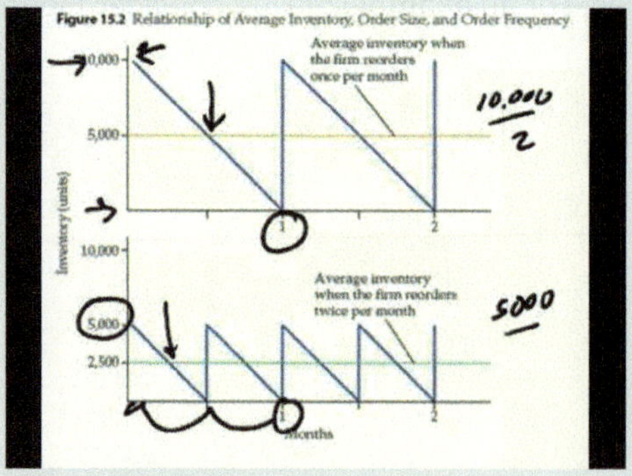

View in the online reader

If a firm sells 10,000 units a month and reorders new inventory once each month, then each order will be for 10,000 units. Because the inventory begins at 10,000 and falls to 0, the average inventory during the month is 5,000. The second panel in Figure 15.2 shows what happens when the firm reorders twice per month. The firm still sells 10,000 units, but now 5,000 units are ordered at a time and the average inventory falls to 2,500. With four orders per month, the average inventory level falls to 1,250.

The average inventory is computed with a simple equation.

Tip

For this discussion, we assume constant sales volume throughout the month.

EQUATION 15.6

$$Average\ inventory = \frac{Q}{2}$$

With more orders, the average order size and inventory level continue to fall. The costs of holding inventory fall, but reorder costs increase. The question then becomes, how many orders per month is optimal?

Optimal Inventory Level

Office Outlet is a discount office supply store that stocks and sells, among many other items, copy paper. One store estimates it sells about $250,000 of a particular type of paper per year, with a cost of $3.29 per ream. If the store ordered only once per year, it would order $\mathbf{\$250,000/\$3.29 = \$75,988}$ reams. Because the paper sells continuously throughout the year, the average number of reams on hand would be $\mathbf{75,988/2 = 37,994}$. All of the carrying costs listed earlier apply to holding this inventory of paper. If the local Office Outlet orders the paper twice per year, the order amount drops to 37,994 and the average inventory drops to $\mathbf{37,994/2 = 18,997}$. If the number of orders per year increases, carrying costs decline but the reorder costs increase.

Figure 15.3 graphs the costs of holding inventory. As the size of the average inventory order increases, reorder costs fall but carrying costs increase. The goal of inventory management is to find the order size that minimizes the total costs of holding inventory, or the optimal inventory level. This occurs on the graph at Q^*. Note that Q^* is independent of the total annual inventory purchases during the year because that is dictated by sales. What we are concerned with here is determining the amount of inventory that should be kept on hand at any particular moment.

FIGURE 15.3 Cost of Holding Inventory

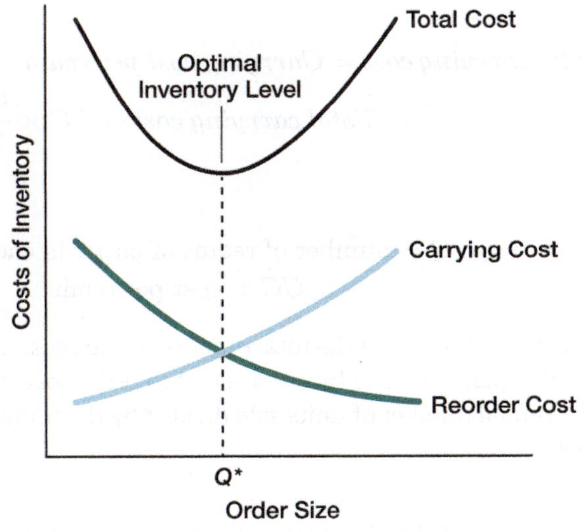

Explain It: Cost of Holding Inventory

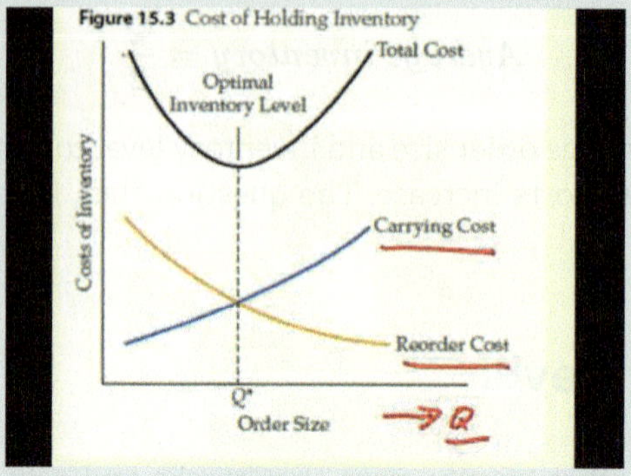

View in the online reader

Computing the Economic Order Quantity

economic order quantity (EOQ) model

An inventory management technique for determining an item's optimal order quantity, which is the one that minimizes the total of its order and carrying costs.

The **economic order quantity (EOQ) model** is the best-known and simplest approach for computing the optimal inventory level, Q^*. Notice in Figure 15.3 that the minimum total cost occurs where carrying costs are equal to order costs. You can derive the economic order quantity (EOQ) model by setting carrying costs equal to order costs and solving for Q^*.

We first need to derive an equation to compute the carrying cost. This cost includes the opportunity cost of the funds tied up in inventory, the costs of shelf space and storage, insurance, and so forth. Suppose these costs are estimated to be $0.50 per ream of paper. The annual total carrying cost is:

EQUATION 15.7

$$\textit{Total carrying cost} = \textit{Carrying cost per ream} \times \textit{Average inventory}$$

$$\textit{Total carrying cost} = CC \times \frac{Q}{2}$$

where

$$Q = \text{number of reams of paper in each order}$$
$$CC = \text{cost per ream}$$

Next, we need an equation to compute the total order cost. This cost involves the clerical and handling expense required to place and pay for an order. Each order costs the same, and the number of orders per year is the annual number of units sold divided by the number of reams purchased each time an order is placed:

EQUATION 15.8

$$\textit{Total order cost} = \textit{Order cost} \times \textit{Orders per year}$$

$$\textit{Total order cost} = OC \times \frac{S}{Q}$$

where

$$OC = \text{order cost}$$
$$S/Q = \text{order per year (sales/quantity)}$$

Explain It: Solving for Optimal Order Quantity

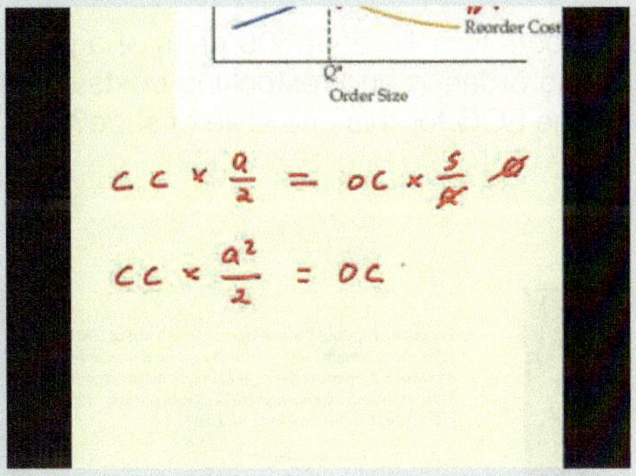

View in the online reader

Notice that as Q increases in Equation 15.7, the total carrying cost also increases. However, in Equation 15.8, Q is in the denominator, so as it increases, total order cost falls. Next, let's set Equation 15.7 equal to Equation 15.8 and solve for Q^*:

EQUATION 15.9

$$CC \times \frac{Q^*}{2} = OC \times \frac{S}{Q^*}$$
$$CC \times \frac{(Q^*)^2}{2} = OC \times S$$
$$(Q^*)^2 = \frac{(2 \times OC \times S)}{CC}$$
$$Q^* = \sqrt{\frac{(2 \times OC \times S)}{CC}}$$

Continuing our example, if the carrying cost per ream of paper is \$0.50, the order cost per order is \$20.00, and the number of reams sold per year is 75,988, then Q^* the optimal number of reams of paper to purchase with each order is found using Equation 15.9:

$$Q^* = \sqrt{\frac{2 \times OC \times S}{CC}}$$
$$Q^* = \sqrt{\frac{2 \times \$20 \times 75,987}{0.50}}$$
$$Q^* = 2,465.55 = 2,466$$

Tip

Notice that we rounded our result up to the nearest whole number because only whole reams of paper can be ordered.

Office Outlet should order 2,466 reams of paper each time it orders. If we order 2,466 reams with each order, we'll make $75,988/2,466 = 30.81$ orders per year, or about one every couple of weeks. We can determine from Equation 15.9 that, as order cost increases, the number of units purchased with each order increases and the number of orders per year falls. Conversely, when carrying costs increase, the number of units purchased with each order falls, so the number of orders per year increases.

Example 15.2 Economic Order Quantity

Suppose Lady Foot Locker expects to sell about 500 pairs of a particular style of running shoe this year from one store. Assume ordering and restocking costs are $20 per order and carrying cost is $2.75 per pair. What is the EOQ for this one style of shoe?

SOLUTION

Algebraic Solution

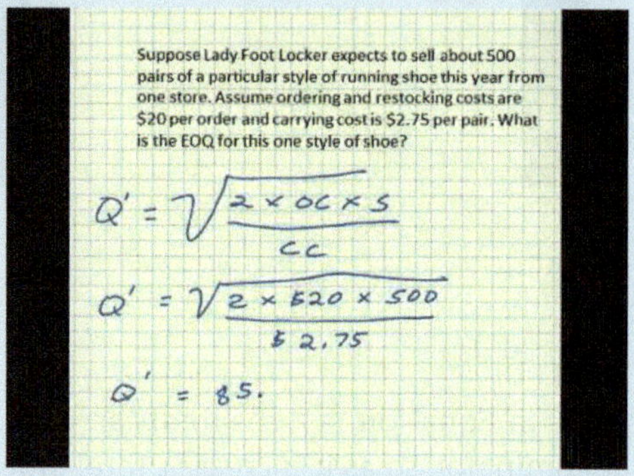

View in the online reader

The CC is $2.75, the sales are 500, and the OC is $20. Use Equation 15.9 to compute the EOQ:

$$Q' = \sqrt{\frac{2 \times OC \times S}{CC}}$$

$$Q' = \sqrt{\frac{2 \times \$20 \times \$500}{\$2.75}}$$

$$Q' = 85.28 = 86 \text{ pairs}$$

Lady Foot Locker should order 86 pairs of shoes each time it places an order. The store will place $500/86 = 6$ orders per year, or one order every 2 months.

Adding a Safety Stock

The EOQ assumes that the firm lets the inventory run down to zero before new inventory is purchased. In reality, firms prefer to order prior to this point to avoid stockouts and the resulting production delays or loss of customers.

safety stock

The amount of inventory a firm holds to protect against the cost incurred in running out of inventory.

A **safety stock** is a minimum level of inventory a firm keeps on hand. Ideally, the inventory never falls below this level except in emergencies, such as when the supplier has problems or demand unexpectedly surges. Holding a safety stock doesn't change the fundamentals of the EOQ. The first order is simply increased to include the extra number of units to be held as safety stock. Subsequent orders represent the EOQ.

Firms also must consider the delay between order placement and delivery. The timing of the order should be such that delivery is made as inventory hits zero or reaches the safety stock.

Figure 15.4 illustrates when an order will be placed, allowing for delivery delay and a safety stock. When the inventory falls to point A, an order is placed. This allows time for delivery. The inventory arrives when the inventory level has fallen to point B. The new inventory returns the stock to point C. Management experience is required to determine the time difference between points A and B, and how large a safety stock is required.

FIGURE 15.4 Reorder Point with Safety Stock

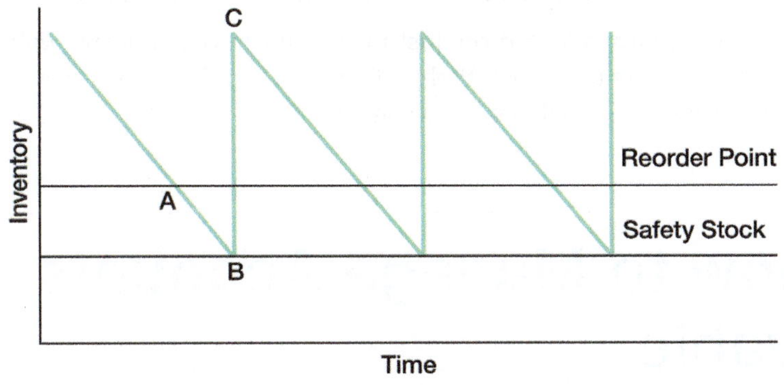

Explain It: Reorder Point with Safety Stock

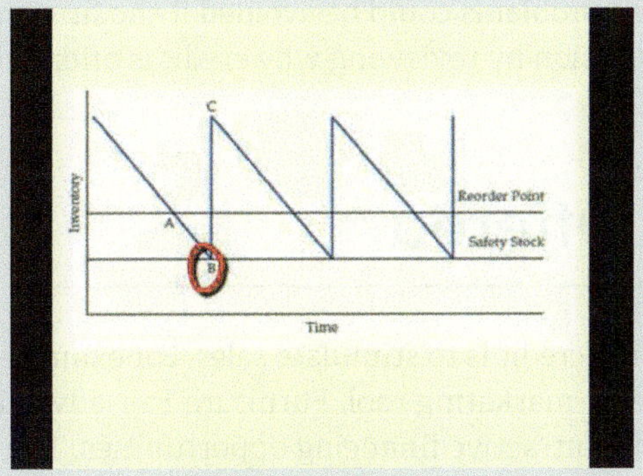

View in the online reader

Other Inventory Methods

Some firms choose a much simpler approach to inventory control. The method is sometimes called the basket method. In essence, inventory is separated into three bins (baskets) when it arrives. The first is the normal operating inventory. When this bin is empty, new inventory is ordered and the firm operates out of the second bin. The third bin is the safety stock. This approach may be appropriate for low-valued inventory items or when inventory represents a very small part of the firm's assets. For example, a law firm may use the basket approach to control office supplies.

An alternative to holding inventory is the just-in-time inventory method. The idea behind just-in-time inventory is that parts and supplies are delivered just as the firm needs them, often mere hours ahead of time.

The downside of just-in-time inventory is that it increases the likelihood of a stockout. If the supplier isn't reliable, any savings the method provides will be lost when the plant is shut down by a parts shortage. However, technology has made the just-in-time inventory method and its derivatives easier to manage. By tying the buyer's computer system to its own system, the supplier is able to track parts usage and production requirements so that parts can be delivered as needed.

Many major retailers have adopted the just-in-time inventory concept. Walmart, for example, requires many of its suppliers to restock shelves from the supplier's inventory so that the store is not required to inventory beyond what's on its shelves.

15.3 How to Manage Accounts Receivable

accounts receivable turnover ratio

Accounts receivable turnover=Sales / Average accounts receivable.

In this section, we investigate the management of accounts receivable. In Chapter 2, we learned a number of ratios managers can use to track accounts receivable, such as the **accounts receivable turnover ratio** and average collection period. Although these ratios deserve management attention, there is much more to managing accounts receivable than simply attempting to collect what's due as fast as possible. For example, firm managers must decide how aggressively collection efforts should be pursued, who should receive credit, and what discounts the firm will give to customers who pay promptly. All of these problems could be avoided if the firm simply refused to offer credit. Therefore, let's begin our discussion by reviewing why credit is offered.

Why Credit is Offered

The primary reason for offering credit is to stimulate sales. For example, the furniture industry has learned to use credit as a major marketing tool. Furniture Fair advertises with "buy now with no payments for a year" and other attractive financing opportunities. The only reason the store offers these terms is because they induce customers to buy furniture.

trade credit

Credit offered by suppliers and used by firms that sell products or services.

Alternatively, in many industries, **trade credit** is so frequently offered that any firm failing to give credit would probably not survive. For example, lumber stores usually allow contractors to buy on credit. The real decision in cases such as these is not whether to offer credit, but rather what terms to offer.

Developing a Credit Policy

credit policy

The determination of credit selection, credit standards, and credit terms.

Once a firm has decided to offer credit, either because the competitive nature of the industry demands it or because the firm expects increased sales, it must then decide on the credit terms. A firm's **credit policy** stipulates how it will handle each phase of the credit decision. This includes what goods will be sold on credit, who will receive credit, what the credit terms will be, and how the firm will collect on delinquent accounts.

There are three elements to the typical credit sale: the credit period, the discount amount, and the discount period.

Credit Period

The credit period is the length of time the customer has before payment is due. Although the credit period varies among industries, it's usually between 30 and 120 days. Longer credit periods often are offered as a means of inducing customers to buy the firm's products. Not all customers are given the same terms. Higher-value customers, such as those with an established credit history, and those whose business is most desired, may be given longer periods to pay.

Another factor to consider when establishing the credit period is the buyer's inventory period and collection period. As discussed earlier, the inventory period is the length of time it takes the buyer to acquire, process, and sell the inventory. The **collection period** is the length of time it takes to collect on the sale. The credit period serves to finance a portion of the buyer's operating period. The longer the buyer's operating period, the longer the credit period the buyer will require. Trade credit, as this is often called, is often an important part of a firm's source of funds.

collection period

The typical length of time it takes to collect on sales.

If the credit period is longer than the buyer's operating period, the supplier is financing a portion of the buyer's operations beyond what is related to inventory. For this reason, we typically avoid credit periods that exceed the customer's operating period.

Other issues the firm should consider before establishing the credit period include:

- Whether the product is perishable or has continuing collateral value
- Consumer demand for the product
- The credit risk of the buyer
- The competition in the market

The Effective Annual Rate for Taking a Cash Discount

Cash discounts are widely used as a method to speed up the collection of accounts receivable. The usual terms offer a 1 or 2% discount if the customer pays the outstanding balance within some short period, such as 10 days. Credit terms are quoted using a shorthand notation where the discount and discount period are listed first, and the credit period is listed last. For example, 2/10, net 30, means that a 2% discount is available if the customer pays the bill within 10 days; otherwise, the bill is due in full in 30 days. In this case, by forgoing the 2% discount, the customer obtains a $\mathbf{30 - 10 = 20}$ day loan for 2% of the amount due. Although this may initially seem like a low interest rate, remember that the 2% is for only 20 days. An important question both the supplier and the customer may ask is, "What is the annualized cost of this credit?"

To compute the effective annual rate for a cash discount, we first need to determine how many discount periods there are in a year. There are $\mathbf{365/20 = 18.25}$ discount periods in 1 year. If the amount of the discount is 2%, then the customer is paying $2 to borrow $98 for 20 days. The holding period cost of the loan is $\mathbf{\$2/\$98 = 0.02041}$. We annualize this by compounding this rate for 1 year and using the equation for effective interest rate (EIR).

Tip

While not obvious, the holding period rate given by (discount/1-discount), or \$2/\$98 as in this example, is the same as i/m in the effective interest rate equation. For example, $\$2/\$98 = 0.02041$ is the holding return *i* for 20 days. There are $365/20 = 18.25$ such periods in a year, so the annual nominal rate is $0.02041 \times 18.25 = 0.372449$. Thus $i/m = 0.372449/18.25 = 0.02041$, the same as we get simply by dividing $\$2/\$98$.

Explain It: The Cost of Trade Discounts

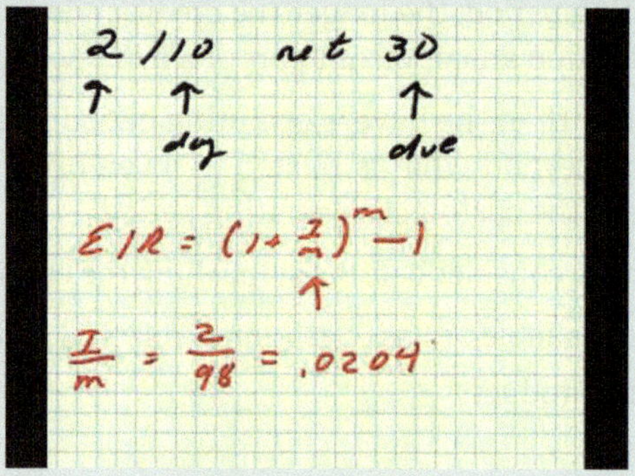

View in the online reader

$$EIR = (1.02041)^{18.25} - 1 = 44.59\%$$

From both the buyer's and seller's viewpoints, this is very high-cost financing. The seller is paying a high rate of interest to speed collections, and the buyer is paying a very high rate of interest to borrow short-term money. It's important that buyers keep the correct perspective when dealing with trade credit. The price after the discount is taken isn't really a discounted price. It's the price the typical customer will pay who visits the seller's place of business and purchases the goods across the counter. The undiscounted price reflects a markup over the real price that includes the cost of financing the purchase for the credit period. It is not free credit, as some business managers are inclined to think. In fact, it's very expensive credit that usually should be financed with some other source of short-term money. Trade credit is free only for the length of the discount period; for example, the 10 days in the 2/10, net 30, terms.

Example 15.3 Cost of Trade Credit

You have received an invoice from your major supplier of pink widgets used in your production process. The invoice says 1/15, net 30. Compute the effective interest rate and the annual percentage rate if you don't pay the invoice within 15 days. If you can borrow short-term money from your bank at 8%, should you pay within the 15-day grace period?

SOLUTION

Algebraic Solution

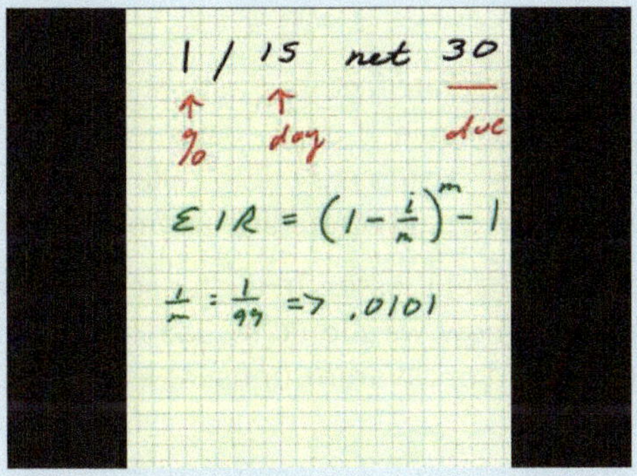

View in the online reader

Calculator Solution

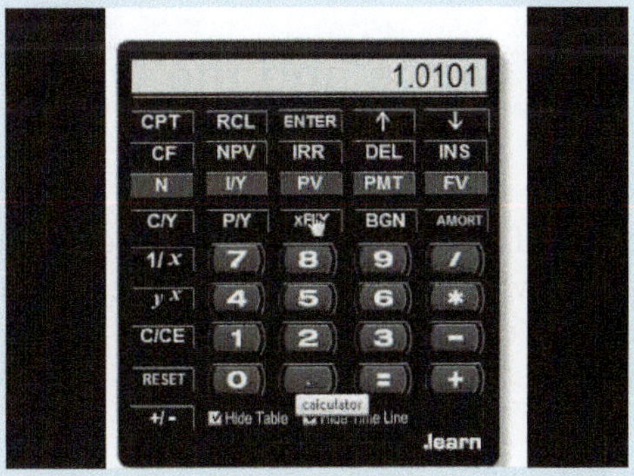

View in the online reader

EIR:

First, compute the number of periods in a year: $m = 365/15 = 24.33$

Next, compute the percentage holding cost per period: $i = 1/99 = 0.0101$

Finally, input the values into the equation for EIR:

$$EIR = (1 + i)^m - 1$$

where

$$EIR = \text{effective } annual\ interest\ rate$$
$$m = 365/\text{difference between the net period and the grace period}$$
$$i = amount\ of\ discount/(100 - amount\ of\ the\ discount)$$

$$EIR = (1 + 0.0101)^{24.33} - 1 = 27.70\%$$

APR:

$$APR = Periodic\ rate \times Number\ of\ periods$$
$$0.0101 \times 24.33 = 0.246 = 24.6\%$$

If you can borrow money at 8%, pay within the 15-day grace period.

Despite the high cost to buyers, trade credit remains a very popular means of financing. With this in mind, suppliers must establish an optimal credit policy. Theoretically, the optimal credit policy is one in which the increased profit from sales is exactly equal to the increase in the cost of carrying and administering accounts receivable. Let us identify these costs more precisely.

Cost of Credit

The cost of credit includes three separate factors. First, there's the cost of holding increased current assets in the form of accounts receivable. If most customers pay within the discount period, there are no offsetting revenues. If most customers fail to take advantage of the discount, or if no discount is offered, the increased prices paid by credit customers can turn out to be a revenue source.

A second cost of credit is bad debt losses. In a later section, we discuss the factors that determine who is to receive credit. For now, we should realize that if credit is extended, there's a chance it won't be repaid. Default rates of 1 or 2% aren't unusual, even for firms with careful screening procedures.

The third cost of offering credit is the cost of administering the accounts receivable. Staff must be employed to analyze credit, send out bills, and collect on past due accounts. This entire department can be eliminated if no credit is offered.

Total Cost of Credit Curve and the Optimal Amount of Credit

We now can combine the cost of receivables with their revenues to generate a total cost curve, as shown in Figure 15.5. The downward-sloping line represents revenues earned by extending credit and increasing sales. The more credit is offered, the more sales will be generated and the more income the firm will receive.

FIGURE 15.5 Net Cost of Extending Credit

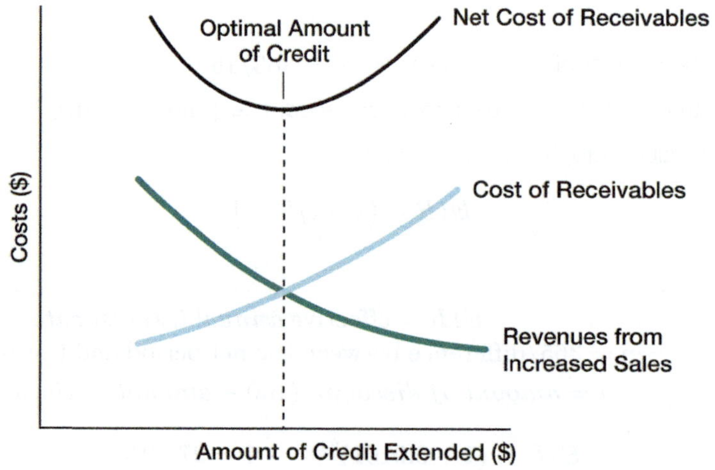

Explain It: The Net Cost of Extending Credit

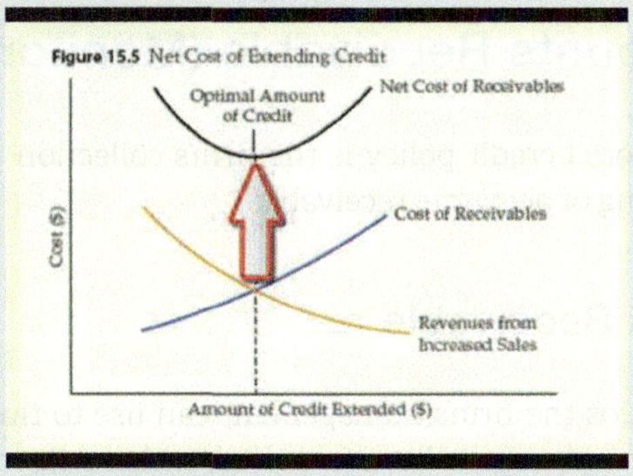

View in the online reader

The upward-sloping line represents the combined cost of offering credit. Increased trade credit requires more administration and more bad debt losses.

The net cost of receivables curve in Figure 15.5 combines the income from advancing credit with the cost of offering credit. The optimal credit policy is one in which the net cost of receivables curve is lowest. The general shape of this curve should look very familiar to you by now, but it's difficult to quantify the costs and revenues. Most firms must experiment with their credit policy to find the terms that minimize costs. A typical approach is to begin with a credit policy that's standard for the industry. The firm can then make small adjustments and carefully observe the resulting effects.

The Five Cs of Credit Analysis

Once the firm has made the decision to extend credit, it must decide to whom credit will be extended and how much credit will be allowed. Some firms use complex computer programs to analyze credit applications. Many others rely on less sophisticated methods. Because firm managers often don't know nearly as much about the finances of customers as they might like, they must find alternative methods for judging creditworthiness. The classic approach is to use the five Cs of credit:

- **Character:** The willingness of the borrower to pay obligations owed.
- **Capacity:** The ability of the borrower to pay. If the capacity to pay isn't present, the best intentions of the borrower are of little use.
- **Capital:** The financial reserves of the firm. The more capital the firm has at its disposal, the more likely is repayment.
- **Conditions:** The general economic and business climate. Favorable conditions increase the probability of repayment.
- **Collateral:** The value of the assets that could be seized if the customer doesn't pay on the debt. If all else fails, the customer may be forced to liquidate to pay debts. The lender's priority of payment in the event of liquidation and the value of the assets affect the likelihood of repayment.

A variety of sources of information are available to the firm that's considering offering a customer credit. The best information may be from the firm's own prior experience with the customer. When this is unavailable, the manager may obtain information from credit rating companies, such as Dun & Bradstreet and Experian. Dun & Bradstreet provides financial statement information, and Experian provides payment history.

Collection of Accounts Receivable (Monitoring)

An important part of the overall credit policy is the firm's collection policy. The collection policy begins with careful monitoring of accounts receivable.

Monitoring Accounts Receivable

There are several activity ratios the firm's management can use to track accounts receivable. The most important of these is the average collection period, which tells managers how long the average credit remains outstanding. With experience, managers learn to factor out seasonal variation in the average collection period and use it to help evaluate how well the credit policy is functioning. If the average collection period begins to stretch out, it may be that many customers are taking a little longer to pay or a few are taking much longer. Either alternative requires additional investigation.

aging schedule

A schedule used to evaluate credit and/or collection policies that shows the proportion of the accounts receivable balance that has been outstanding for a specified period of time.

Another tool managers use to evaluate the firm's accounts receivable is an **aging schedule**. An aging schedule is simply a list of the amounts due, organized by due dates. Most modern accounting packages used by even the smallest firms have built-in accounts receivable aging schedules. An example is presented in Table 15.3.

TABLE 15.3 Accounts Receivable Aging Schedule

Age of Account	Amount	Number of Accounts
0–10 days	$1,000,000	60
11–30 days	75,000	40
31–45 days	10,000	5
46–60 days	3,000	2
Over 60 days	1,500	1

Explain It: Accounts Receivable Aging Schedule

Table 15.3 Accounts Receivable Aging Schedule

Age of Account	Amount	Number of Accounts
0–10 days	$100,000	60
11–30 days	75,000	40
31–45 days	10,000	5
46–60 days	3,000	2
Over 60 days	1,500	1

View in the online reader

Any interval may be used for reporting purposes. The first one usually extends from zero to the end of the discount period, and the second period goes from the end of the discount period to the end of the credit period. In the example cited earlier, with credit terms of 2/10, net 30, an aging schedule similar to the one in Table 15.3 would be useful to track how many customers are taking advantage of the discount and how many are truly delinquent.

Collection Effort

Most computerized accounting packages also provide specialized reports that list the details of delinquent accounts so that the firm can follow up with additional collection efforts. An important part of the overall credit policy is collection procedures. Firms usually are concerned with treading a middle ground between losing customers by being too aggressive with collections versus having bad debt losses because they're too lax. The firm should follow a sequence of steps that are progressively more insistent.

Management must closely monitor the activities of both the sales force and the collection department. Clearly, they operate with different primary motives. The sales personnel are most concerned with moving the product. If their compensation is based on their sales volume, they will tend to sell to customers who may be known credit risks. On the other hand, the collection department may antagonize normally good customers by being overly threatening. It's the responsibility of management to balance these two opposing approaches to maximize profits and, as always, to maximize shareholder wealth.

15.4 How to Manage Cash

In one sense, holding cash is a waste of resources. Cash balances in themselves do not generate any income, and there's typically little or no interest paid on corporate checking account balances. Still, virtually all firms keep significant amounts of cash on hand. In this section, we investigate ways to minimize cash and to compute the optimal level of cash a firm should hold.

Float

Float occurs because of delays in the banking system. It's the time difference between when a check is written and when the funds are removed from the account. Most students have learned the basics of float management with their own funds. The result of float is that there's a difference between your actual bank balance and what your books reflect. Whether the bank shows a greater or smaller balance than your books depends on whether disbursement or collection float dominates.

Disbursement Float

disbursement float

The lapse between the time when a firm deducts a payment from its checking account ledger (disburses it) and the time when funds are actually withdrawn from its account.

Disbursement float occurs when there's a delay between when the firm issues a check and when the funds are removed from the checking account balance at the bank. For example, if your parents mail a check to the university to pay your tuition, the check may be in the mail 2 or 3 days, and it may be several more days before the university's bank presents the check to your parents' bank for payment. It's only then that the funds are removed from the checking account.

Disbursement float works to increase the balance in your account relative to your book balance. A corporation can issue checks and not put the funds into the bank for several days if the financial managers can predict disbursement float accurately.

Collection Float

collection float

The delay between the time when a customer deducts a payment from their checking account ledger and the time when the payee or vendor actually receives the funds in a spendable form.

hold

A tag placed on a deposit that prevents the funds from being used until the underlying deposit has been collected by the bank.

Collection float occurs when there's a delay between when you receive payment and when the bank gives you credit. Suppose you deposit a check into your account at the bank. The bank must process that check, but will not receive the funds for several days. Therefore, it may put a hold on your account while the check clears. Clearing a check is the process of sending it through the banking system and having funds transferred back. A **hold** is an annotation put on a checking account preventing funds that haven't been cleared from being spent. The available balance is the amount of funds on deposit that can be spent. Large corporate checks may have holds put on them because the bank doesn't want to disburse large sums it hasn't received yet. Smaller personal checks may have holds placed by the bank if the bank is uncertain whether the check is good.

Net Float

Disbursement float increases the available balance, and collection float decreases the available balance. A firm should be more concerned with the available balance than with the book balance because this is what can be used to pay bills. We calculate the net float as the difference between the firm's available balance and the firm's book balance. This calculation is shown in Equation 15.10.

Tip

Note that book balance is what you show in the checkbook and it acts like all funds are moved instantly.

EQUATION 15.10

$$\textit{Net float} = \textit{Available balance} - \textit{Book balance}$$

Electronic Funds Transfer

Electronic funds transfer or **EFT** is a broad term that generally refers to the transfer of funds around the world electronically, as opposed to by paper document. According to the Department of Treasury, it costs the government a little over a dollar to process a check while the same transaction can be done electronically for 10 cents. In addition to the savings in processing cost, float is reduced to virtually zero. It is little wonder that the government, banks, and businesses are rapidly moving toward a paperless and floatless world. Research from the Federal Reserve shows that the use of electronic payment systems rose from 16% to 73% of all transactions from 2000 to 2018.

electronic funds transfer (EFT)

A method of moving funds from one bank to another by wire.

FIGURE 15.6 Use of Checks and Electronic Payment Systems in the U.S.

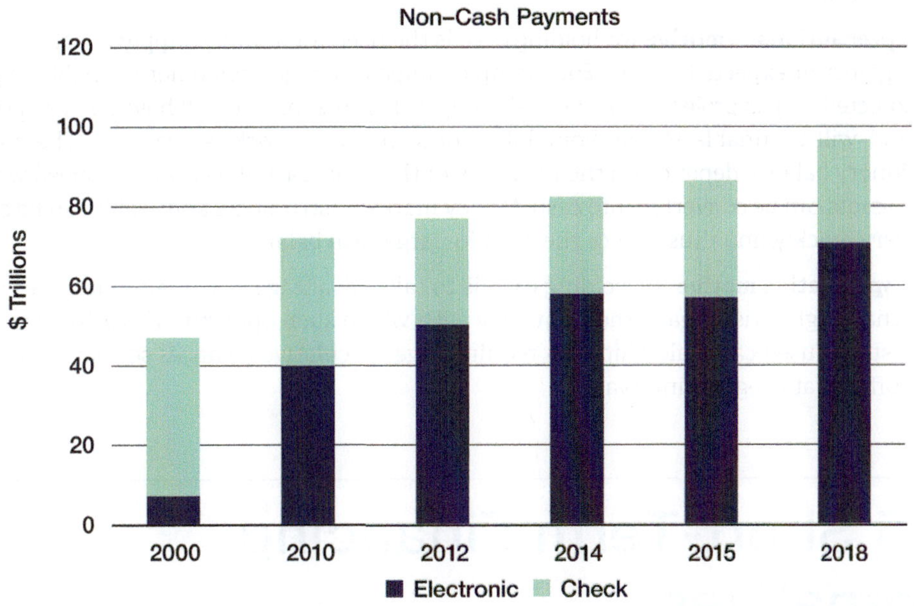

As the use of debit cards, direct payroll deposits, direct payments of bills, and other digital forms of payment increase, float management will become a less significant issue and EFT management will take precedence. Even small businesses are now able to accept debit cards in the field via cell phone data connections. In a few years, the written check may be all but replaced with digital alternatives that lower cost and eliminate float concerns.

Computing the Optimal Cash Balance

Our discussion so far has centered on methods for reducing the amount of cash required by reducing the cash conversion cycle. Another related question is, "How much cash should a firm hold?" In 1995, Kirk Kerkorian made an attempt to buy Chrysler Motor Company because it had over $7 billion in cash. He argued that, with that kind of cash surplus, "someone is going to come after them. Why not me?" Kerkorian felt that the excess cash should be returned to shareholders rather than being held as idle funds by the firm. His takeover attempt failed, but Chrysler was shocked into increasing its dividends.

Reasons to Hold Cash

Traditionally, there are three reasons why firms should hold cash. The most obvious is to satisfy transactional needs. Beyond this reason, we can identify two others: the precautionary motive and the speculative motive.

transactional motive

The need to hold cash to pay debts that arise as a regular consequence of doing business.

The **transactional motive** for holding cash is the need to pay debts that arise as a regular consequence of doing business. These include disbursements to pay wages, trade debts, taxes, and so forth. Cash inflows occur as goods and services are sold, and these inflows should be sufficient to cover the outflows. In a perfect world, cash deposits made each day would cover that day's cash disbursements, and any extra could be invested or returned to shareholders. The problem is that cash inflows and cash outflows aren't perfectly synchronized. As a result, some level of cash is needed as a buffer.

precautionary motive

The need for a safety supply of cash to act as a financial reserve against unexpected events.

The **precautionary motive** for holding cash is the need for a safety supply to act as a financial reserve against unexpected events. For example, suppose a major customer is unable to pay their bill as expected and as projected on the cash budget. This means you will have less cash than forecasted and will be unable to pay your bills unless a safety stock is available. The size of the precautionary balance depends on the reliability of the firm's cash flows and the speed with which its other assets can be converted into cash. Money market instruments and T-bills can be converted to cash very quickly, and thus reduce the need for large cash balances.

speculative motive

A reason for holding cash that is to take advantage of bargain purchase or opportunities that might arise.

The **speculative motive** for holding cash is to take advantage of bargain purchases or opportunities that might arise. Again, the frequency with which such opportunities arise varies by firm and industry. A used car dealership may require large speculative balances so that it can buy cars that are offered at irregular intervals.

15.5 Short-Term Financing Alternatives

So far, this chapter has focused on short-term asset management. When a firm requires more short-term assets than it can accumulate through careful management, it may use alternative sources. There are many sources of short-term funds. The two alternatives discussed here are short-term bank loans and trade credit.

Bank Loans

Many businesses use banks to supply short-term funds needed for the firm's operations. Banks tend to specialize in customizing short-term loans. In fact, these short-term business loans are the bread and butter for most banks. The advantage to the bank is that it can charge fees every time a new loan is made. The advantage to the firm is that the bank can be much more flexible in its terms and conditions than is possible with publicly issued debt.

Short-term interest rates tend to be lower than long-term rates. This means firms may prefer to obtain short-term loans instead of long term because they may be less costly. Of course, there's additional risk from using short-term money in that the cost of borrowing can rise if interest rates increase.

Self-Liquidating Loans

Short-term bank loans are often self-liquidating, meaning the loan is made to finance an asset that will pay off the loans. For example, a bank may make a loan to finance accounts receivable. When the receivables are paid, the proceeds are given to the bank to retire the debt.

Receivable financing usually requires the firm to pledge its accounts receivable to the bank as collateral for the loan. The bank will typically lend the firm no more than 80% of the book value of receivables. Additionally, accounts that are past due are often excluded from financing. If the firm defaults on its loan, the bank can notify those who owe the firm money that all payments are to be made to the bank.

Inventory financing is also a very common type of short-term financing. The firm borrows a portion of the value of its inventory and pays off the loan from the proceeds generated by selling the inventory. For example, an auto dealer may borrow money to pay for its inventory of cars. Each time a car is sold, the car dealer must pay an agreed-upon amount to the bank.

Banks often require that the firm completely pay off its short-term loans every year. This is to keep the short-term money from being used to finance long-term assets.

Lines of Credit

Firms often reach an agreement with banks regarding how much credit the bank will extend. The total amount that can be borrowed is the firm's line of credit. Usually, once the line of credit has been established, little effort is required by the firm to obtain a disbursement of funds. For example, a firm may have a line of credit of $100,000. If the current total of loans outstanding is $50,000, a request for a $25,000 loan secured by accounts receivable can often be obtained almost immediately and without a bank visit.

CHAPTER 16
International Finance

Learning Objectives

By the end of this chapter you will be able to:

1. Explain the basics of exchange rates.
2. Understand how purchasing power parity establishes exchange rates.
3. Understand how interest rate parity relates to interest rates and exchange rates.
4. Discuss international finance risk.
5. Explain how to make foreign investments.

In this chapter, we investigate financial aspects of international business. This investigation includes:

- What exchange rates mean and how to read and interpret them
- How currency exchange rates are established and what they accomplish
- How exchange rate risk affects international trade
- Other areas of international risk that firms incur
- How the international markets can be used to raise capital

16.1 Basics of Exchange Rates

Few people will deny the value of international trade to both firms and consumers. The question is, "How can firms do business in countries where goods and services are priced in foreign currencies?" The answer lies in exchange rates that allow the firm to convert its domestic currency into foreign currency, and back. The **exchange rate** is the price of one country's money quoted in terms of another country's money. For example, if you're planning a trip to England and have located a hotel in London that will cost 50 pounds, you may well wonder what this will cost in U.S. dollars. The exchange rate is used to make this conversion.

exchange rate

The factor used to convert the value of one currency into another currency.

Role of Exchange Rates

Exchange rates tell us how to convert one currency into another. If you're quoted the price of a product in terms of a foreign currency, you must determine what that product will cost in your own currency to know whether the price is acceptable. Exchange rates are important because they affect the relative price of domestic and foreign products. For example, suppose you're an importer of Porsche 911s. You learn that the new model will sell for 80,000 euros in Germany. How much will this car cost in U.S. dollars? If the exchange rate is $1.25 to the euro $(1.25 \text{ U.S.\$/€})$ the car will cost $100,000. If the exchange rate changes to $1.35 to the euro, the price of the Porsche becomes $108,000 in U.S. dollars. Conversely, if the exchange rate falls, the car becomes cheaper in U.S. dollars. These changes could significantly affect your ability to sell the cars.

Tip

There are a number of conventions used to report exchange rates. At one time, the term "U.S. dollar equivalent" was the standard because that was the way they were reported in the *Wall Street Journal*. Now that rates are reported online by different reporting agencies, there are various ways to express currency relationships.

From this simple example, we can make two deductions. First, exchange rates have a powerful effect on exports and imports because they affect the price of imports for buyers. If the domestic price increases because of a change in the exchange rate, demand is likely to fall. Alternatively, if the exchange rate makes foreign goods less expensive, demand will increase and imports are likely to rise.

Tip

For example, in the early 1970s, the exchange rate between Japan and the United States made Japanese cars cheap. Demand increased dramatically, nearly bankrupting Chrysler Corporation. In the early 1990s, exchange rates made Japanese cars more expensive and demand fell, resulting in record profits for domestic auto manufacturers.

exchange rate risk

The risk that changes in the exchange rate between when a transaction begins and when it is completed will cause a negative return.

The second conclusion we can draw from our Porsche example is that exchange rates introduce a new kind of risk to international trade—**exchange rate risk**, or the risk of loss due to exchange rates moving over time. For example, suppose a U.S. exporter agrees to sell goods abroad in exchange for a sum to be paid in a foreign currency when the goods are delivered in 2 months. If the value of the foreign currency falls relative to the dollar, the exporter may take a loss on the sale. We discuss methods to reduce >exchange rate risk later in this chapter.

Reading Exchange Rate Quotes

direct rate

The amount of U.S. dollars required to purchase 1 unit of a foreign currency.

indirect rate

The amount of U.S. dollars 1 unit of a foreign currency will purchase.

Exchange rate quotes are published in the financial press. Table 16.1 lists rates for several major currencies. Until you get used to the format of this list, it can be quite confusing. The first column lists the U.S. dollar equivalent of one unit of a foreign currency. This is called the **direct rate**. The second column lists the amount of foreign currency one U.S. dollar will buy. This is called the **indirect rate**.

Explain It: Table 16.1 Reading Exchange Rates

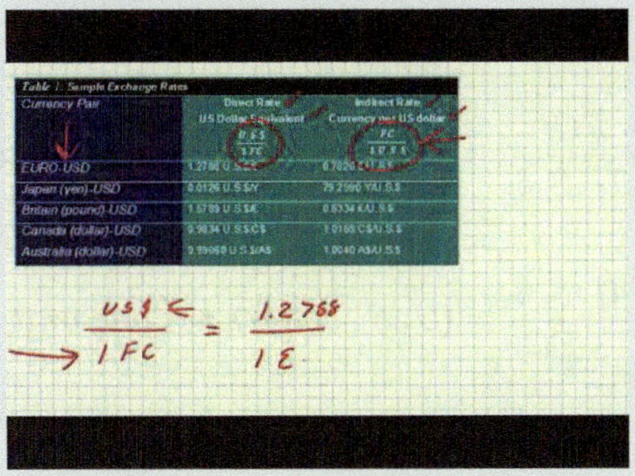

View in the online reader

TABLE 16.1 Sample Exchange Rates

Currency Pair	Direct Rate U.S. Dollar Equivalent U.S.$/1FC	Indirect Rate Currency per U.S. Dollar FC / 1U.S.$
Euro–USD	1.2788 U.S.$/€	0.7820 € / U.S.$
Japan (yen)–USD	0.0126 U.S.$ / ¥	79.2990 ¥ / U.S.$
Britain (pound)–USD	1.5789 U.S.$ / £/£	0.6334 £ / U.S.$
Canada (dollar)–USD	0.9834 U.S.$ / C$	1.0169 C$ / U.S.$
Australia (dollar)–USD	0.99060 U.S.$ / A$	1.0095 A$ / U.S.$

Tip

It is common to report currency pairs as is show in Table 16.1 and on the Yahoo and Bloomberg websites. There, EUR–USD 1.2788 is interpreted as one euro is exchanged for U.S.$1.2788.

base rate

In exchange rate quotes, the currency with 1 unit in the rate.

counter rate

In exchange rate quotes, the counter rate is the number of units of a currency required to exchange for 1 unit of the base rate.

spot exchange rate

The rate of exchange between two currencies on any given day. Also commonly referred to as "spot rate."

A good way to think about how exchange rates are reported is as fractions. The denominator represents one unit of a currency (also called the **base rate**) and the numerator is the other currency (the **counter rate**). The direct rate uses the foreign currency as the base, while the indirect rate uses the local rate as the base. Another term for the indirect rate is the **spot exchange rate** or spot rate (S_0). The spot rate tells you how many units of a foreign currency you can exchange for one unit of your currency. These relationships are shown by Equation 16.1 and Equation 16.2. Note that the indirect rate is simply the inverse of the direct rate.

EQUATION 16.1

$$Indirect\ rate = S_0 = \frac{FC}{1\,U.S.\$} = (foreign\ currency\ per\ one\ unit\ of\ local\ currency)$$

EQUATION 16.2

$$Direct\ rate = 1/S_0 = \frac{U.S.\$}{1\,FC} = (U.S.\ dollars\ per\ one\ unit\ of\ foreign\ currency)$$

Using Exchange Rates to Convert Prices

Table 16.2 shows how to use exchange rates to convert prices.

TABLE 16.2 Using the Currency Trading Column to Convert Currency

To convert a price in a foreign currency into U.S. dollars	Multiply by direct rate (U.S. dollar equivalent)	$P\$ = (1/S_0) \times PFC$
To convert a price in U.S. dollars into a foreign currency	Multiply by indirect rate (currency per U.S. dollar)	$PFC = S_0 \times P\$$

Example 16.1 Using Exchange Rates

Suppose you're planning a trip to England and have located a hotel on the Internet that lists the price of the rooms as 50 pounds per night. Using the rates listed in Table 16.1, how much will these rooms cost you in U.S. dollars?

SOLUTION

To convert from British pounds to U.S. dollars, we need to multiply 50 pounds by the direct rate, which is listed in the table as $\mathbf{1.5789\ U.S.\$/£}$.

$$P_{\$}(1/S_0) \times P_{FC}$$

$$P_{\$} = 1.5789\frac{U.S.\$}{£} \times £50$$

Notice that there are pound symbols in the numerator and denominator. They cancel, which leaves the results in U.S. dollars.

$$P_{\$} = \mathbf{1.5789\ U.S.\$ \times 50 = U.S.\$78.94}$$

Your hotel room will cost $78.94 per night based on the exchange rates now in effect. If those rates change by the time you're required to pay for the room, the cost in dollars may be more or less, depending on how the rates move.

Computing Cross Rates

We can tell from Table 16.1 what rate to use to convert to or from U.S. dollars, but there are times when we want to convert between two non-U.S. currencies. We can use Table 16.1 to compute **cross rates**. A cross rate is computed using the exchange rates between the U.S. dollar and two other currencies to find the exchange rate between those currencies. Say we want to know the direct cross rate for British pounds to yen $(£/1¥)$. We can use the fraction notation introduced in the last section to help keep us organized. If we want to end up with pounds in the numerator and yen in the denominator, then we want to multiply the indirect pound to U.S. rate times the direct yen to U.S. rate. The U.S. dollars cancel and we are left with our cross rate.

cross rates

A conversion of two non–U.S. dollar denominated currencies where one is expressed in terms of the other.

$$\frac{£}{1\,U.S.} = 0.6334$$

$$\frac{U.S.\$}{1¥} = 0.0126$$

$$\frac{£}{1\,U.S.\$} \times \frac{U.S.\$}{1¥} = \frac{£}{1¥} = 0.6334 \times 0.0126 = 0.00798\ £/1¥$$

Example 16.2 Computing a Cross Rate

You are traveling from England to France and find that you have 1,000 pounds in your wallet that you want to convert into euros. Given the exchange rates in Table 16.1 compute the cross rate between the euro and the pound $(€/1£)$.

SOLUTION

Algebraic Solution

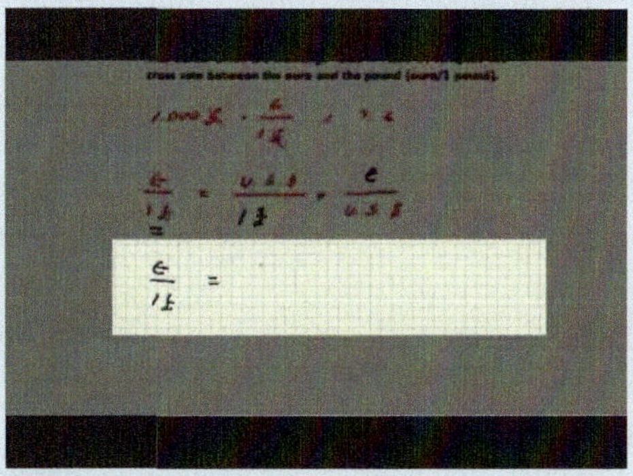

View in the online reader

We want to end up with the fraction $€/1£$.

Multiply the direct exchange rate for pounds times the indirect for the euro. The U.S. dollar cancels and we end up with our cross rate.

$$\frac{U.S.\$}{1£} \times \frac{€}{1\,U.S.\$} = \frac{€}{1£}$$

$$1.5789 \times 0.7820 = 1.2347$$

Tip

The best way to keep the exchange rate relationship straight in your mind is learn a few stable rates so that you can interpret the reporting accurately. For example, for decades, 1 U.S. dollar has been worth about 0.6 pounds.

Foreign Exchange Markets

There's no central place you can go to watch foreign exchange rates being determined; they aren't traded on organized exchanges, such as the New York Stock Exchange. Instead, the foreign exchange market is organized much like the over-the-counter stock market, where hundreds of dealers conduct business over telephones and computers. The volume of these transactions worldwide exceeds $1 trillion per day. Because of the rapid flow of information among these traders, the market is very competitive and functions much like a centralized market.

If you're planning to exchange dollars for an upcoming trip to England, you'll buy foreign currency from dealers such as American Express or a bank. Because retail exchange rates allow for a profit to the dealer, you'll receive less foreign currency than indicated by the exchange rates quoted on the Internet.

There are two ways to exchange funds in the currency markets. The most common is called a spot transaction, which involves the exchange of bank deposits immediately. Spot exchange rates apply to exchanges of funds that occur at the present time, rather than at some point in the future.

forward transactions

A financial arrangement in which prices or exchange rates are agreed upon in the present for an exchange that will occur in the future.

forward exchange rates

The rate of exchange between two currencies at some specified future date.

appreciation

An increase in value; when a currency increases in value relative to another currency.

depreciation

The systematic charging of a portion of the costs of fixed assets against annual revenues over time.

Forward transactions involve the exchange of funds at some specified point in the future, and **forward exchange rates** are the exchange rates put into forward exchange contracts. Forward transactions are used by businesses that want to reduce exchange rate risk. By entering into a forward contract, they protect themselves from undesirable shifts in exchange rates by locking into a specified rate. Of course, by using a forward transaction, the firm loses the possibility of benefiting from favorable exchange rate movements. In effect, the exchange rate risk has been transferred from the firm to a speculator in the exchange rate market who buys the forward contract. Exchange rate speculators are often employed by large money center banks that trade extensively in the foreign markets. They project future exchange rates for contracts to be settled 30, 90, and 180 days in the future.

The financial press often reports on the strength of the dollar. On a daily basis, analysts watch how the rate of exchange between the dollar and other foreign currencies changes. If the value of the dollar strengthens (**appreciation**) on average, $1 will buy more foreign currency. Alternatively, if the dollar buys less foreign currency, then it has weakened (**depreciation**).

Now that we know how exchange rates are quoted and who uses them, the next step is to investigate what factors cause exchange rates to be set at a particular level and what factors cause them to change.

16.2 How Exchange Rates are Established

For a firm's managers to assess properly the risk of doing business in the international marketplace, they must understand how exchange rates are established and what factors could cause them to change over time. Unfortunately, there's no single factor at work, nor a simple explanation. Instead, many issues affect exchange rates, including the supply and demand for each country's currency, the relative prices of goods, and the returns that can be earned on international investments in securities.

Supply and Demand for Currency Affect Exchange Rates

Suppose a U.S. firm sells goods in Japan through one of its subsidiaries. The subsidiary receives yen that must be converted back into U.S. dollars. This increases the demand for dollars and the supply of yen in the exchange markets. Similarly, when Toyota sells cars in the United States, it must convert U.S. dollars back into yen to transfer the profits back to the parent company. This increases the demand for yen and the supply of dollars on the international exchange markets.

As long as the flow of currencies between countries is equal, the exchange rate can remain constant. However, when the demand for one currency increases and the supply of another increases, the exchange rate adjusts so that the market for the currencies reaches equilibrium. For example, if Japan consistently sells more goods in the United States than the United States sells in Japan, Japanese firms may have trouble converting their U.S. dollars into yen. The excess dollars offered for sale in the currency markets cause the value of the dollar to fall compared with the value of the yen.

Governments become very concerned with their exchange rates because they directly affect the domestic economy. When exports decrease because of an appreciating currency, domestic firms will have slower growth and reduced profits, and they'll employ fewer workers. The country's central bank may attempt to affect the exchange rate by buying or selling currencies. However, because of the size of the markets, a central bank cannot control the level of exchange rates in the long run.

In addition to the supply and demand for currencies, other factors affect the level of exchange rates. Foremost among these is the relative price of goods in different countries. We discuss this in the next section.

Relative Prices Affect Exchange Rates: The Law of One Price

To understand how the relative prices of goods and services between countries affect exchange rates, recall the law of one price introduced in Chapter 1. The law of one price says that two identical products produced in two different countries should cost the same to traders in any other country. For example, oil produced in Kuwait and oil produced in Saudi Arabia should cost the same to traders in the United States. The reasoning is that, if the law of one price did not hold, buyers would shun the product that is more expensive and buy only the cheaper one. This increased demand for the cheaper product would increase its price, while the lack of demand for the more expensive product would lower its price. These price changes would continue until the prices of the two goods became equal.

Before we continue to investigate the role of exchange rates in the law of one price, we must first acknowledge its limitations. Oil is a homogeneous commodity (one barrel of oil is much like another barrel) and cheaply transported, so traders can take advantage of price differences that may emerge. Some products are not so easily substituted or transported. For example, if you learn that haircuts cost less in France than in England, there's little you can do to earn a profit with this opportunity. Because haircuts aren't transportable, the forces of supply and demand won't cause prices to adjust. In addition, it is often difficult to determine whether goods from different countries are truly the same.

Tip

For example, many connoisseurs believe California and Washington wines are now equivalent to the best French wines. Others disagree. Such comparisons are matters of opinion and aren't addressed by the law of one price.

Purchasing Power Parity

Absolute Purchasing Power Parity

purchasing power parity (PPP)

The idea that due to arbitrage, prices for similar goods will be the same around the world.

absolute purchasing power parity

The idea that exchange rates are determined by the differences in the prices of goods at a particular point in time.

Remember that our reason for discussing the law of one price was to explain exchange rates and how they change over time. The idea behind **purchasing power parity (PPP)** is that exchange rates must adjust over time to maintain the law of one price. **Absolute purchasing power parity** says that exchange rates are determined by the differences in the prices of goods at a particular point in time. In the examples presented above, we assumed exchange rates did just that. If a slice of pizza cost $2 in Atlanta, Georgia, and the exchange rate between dollars and British pounds $(S_0 = (FC)/(1\,U.S.\$))$ is 0.5422 pounds to the dollar, then the pizza should cost 1.08 pounds in England $(\mathbf{0.5422 \times \$2 = 1.08\ pounds})$. The PPP theory says that the exchange rate between dollars and pounds will adjust to ensure that the price of the pizza is indeed the same in both countries, after adjustment using the exchange rate.

We can state the formula for PPP more formally as an equation. If $P_\$$ is the price of pizza in dollars and $P_£$ is the price of pizza in pounds, then PPP expressed algebraically is:

EQUATION 16.3

$$P_£ = S_0 \times P_\$$$

Explain It: Purchasing Power Parity

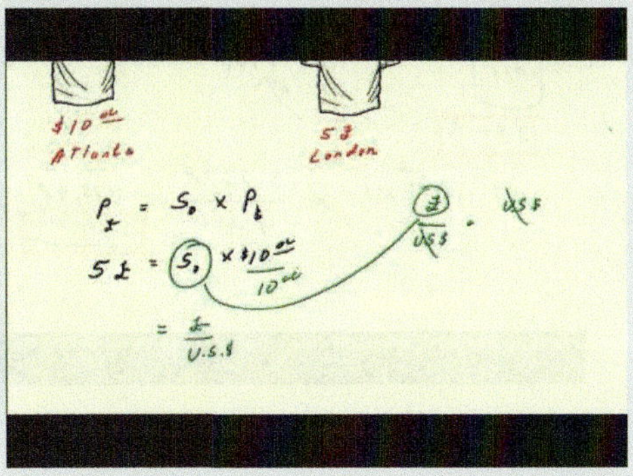

View in the online reader

PPP says that the price of a good in the United States is equal to the price of that same good in another country when multiplied by the exchange rate. If this condition didn't hold, two things would occur. First, the price of the goods would change because merchants would buy the cheap good and avoid the expensive one. Thus, the forces of supply and demand would cause the prices to adjust.

Second, the exchange rate would adjust due to arbitrage. To **arbitrage**, you buy and sell equal amounts of a good so that you have zero net investment while earning a return on the transaction. **Purchasing power arbitrage** is the act of trading to profit from a violation of the law of one price. The guiding rule of arbitrage is to buy low and sell high. Consider the following example.

arbitrage

A trading strategy that involves the simultaneous purchase and sale of an identical security in two different markets at two different prices. Perfect arbitrage involves no investment and no risk.

purchasing power arbitrage

The act of trading to profit from a violation of the law of one price.

Explain It

Suppose the price of oil in Saudi Arabia was below the price of oil in Alaska, even after adjusting for exchange rates. Oil companies would be converting U.S. dollars into riyals to buy Saudi oil. This would increase the international supply of U.S. dollars and the demand for riyals. As a result, the value of the riyal would increase compared with the value of the U.S. dollar, which would be reflected in a change in the U.S. dollar/riyal exchange rate. Because it would take more dollars to buy a riyal, the U.S. dollar cost of Saudi oil would increase. The combined effect of the price changes and the exchange rate adjustments would bring PPP into line.

Example 16.3: Purchasing Power Arbitrage

Assume the following:

1. Price of oil per barrel in Saudi Arabia = 350ريال (the symbol for the Saudi riyal).
2. Price of oil per barrel in Alaska =$100.
3. Indirect exchange rate =S_0=3,759ريال /U.S.$.

SOLUTION

Algebraic Solution

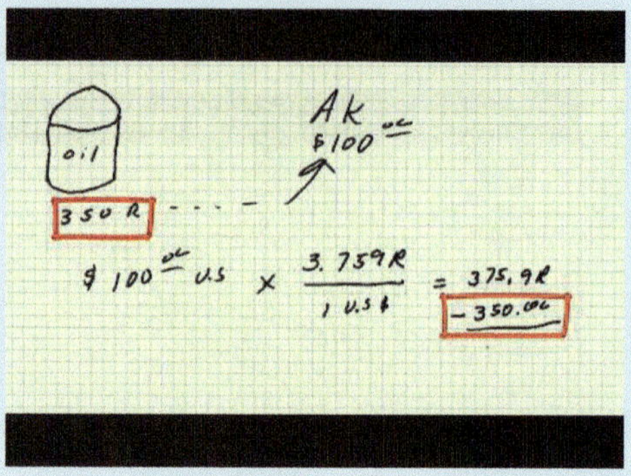

View in the online reader

What are the trades and profits to a Saudi arbitrageur? Assume free shipping.

An arbitrage trader will execute the following trades:

1. Buy a barrel of oil in Saudi Arabia for 350 ریال.
2. Sell the barrel of oil in Alaska for $100.
3. Sell the $100 of U.S. currency in the foreign exchange market and buy riyals at the indirect exchange rate and receive:

   $P\$ \times S_0 = P$ریال

   $\$100 \times 3.75$ریال/U.S.$=375.9ریال

The trader has profited by 25.9 ریال.

If this transaction is repeated, then supply of U.S. dollars will increase and demand for Saudi riyals will rise. The exchange rate will adjust until there is no more profit from arbitrage. This occurs when the indirect exchange rate is 350 ریال/U.S.$. This is the PPP exchange rate.

The key points from this discussion are:

- PPP occurs when the price of a good in one country equals its price in another country, after adjustment for exchange rates.
- The PPP theory depends on traders taking advantage of deviations from PPP through arbitrage (buying the cheap good and selling the expensive one). This trading causes both the prices of the goods and the exchange rate to adjust.
- PPP won't hold if the goods aren't transportable or close substitutes.
- Strict PPP requires a good that has zero transportation costs and is perfectly substitutable. Some goods that are technically transportable are legally restricted from moving across borders due to tariffs, taxes, and other political restraints. Examples include items you typically see in the duty-free shops at the airport.

Few goods meet all of these conditions. Transportation costs are seldom zero, and few goods are identical to their counterparts around the world. As a result, PPP is seldom found to hold exactly. In fact, large deviations often occur.

One example of a near-perfect good for PPP is the McDonald's Big Mac. *The Economist* magazine publishes the Big Mac Index that tracks the cost of the Big Mac around the world. A sample of prices reported in U.S. dollars is presented in Table 16.3. We can see clearly that prices vary. However, when reviewing the complete list, we see that most are within $1 of the U.S. price. This continues to confirm the point that PPP only holds approximately.

TABLE 16.3 The Big Mac Index

Country	Cost of Big Mac at July 2020 Exchange Rate in $US
Australia	4.58
Brazil	3.91
Britain	4.28
Canada	5.08
China	3.10
Germany	4.79
Japan	3.64
Mexico	2.23
Russia	1.91
United Kingdom	4.02
United States	5.71

Data from "Daily Chart: The Big Mac Index," *The Economist* Online, July1, 2020.

Changes in Purchasing Power Parity

We have been discussing absolute PPP, which posits that exchange rates are determined by the differences in the prices of goods at a particular point in time. Although absolute PPP may not hold very often, it does provide a basis for understanding how long-term changes in price levels between countries can affect exchange rates. Consider what happens to the relative prices of goods if one country experiences a higher level of inflation than another. For example, suppose PPP holds between the United States and Mexico today, and the exchange rate is 8 pesos to $1 $(S_0 = 8)$. Now, suppose the inflation rate is 20% per year in Mexico and 0% per year in the United States. If the exchange rate doesn't adjust to reflect the changing prices in each country, PPP will soon be violated. In this example, because the prices of goods in Mexico are appreciating 20% per year faster than in the United States, the exchange rate must adjust 20% per year as well. Initially, it must appreciate 20%, to 9.6, due to inflation differences. Now it takes 9.6 pesos (rather than 8 pesos) to buy $1. This is an example of **relative purchasing power parity**—changes in inflation rates cause exchange rates to adjust. The following example demonstrates how this adjustment maintains PPP.

relative purchasing power parity

Changes in inflation rates cause exchange rates to adjust.

Example 16.4 Maintaining Purchase Power Parity

Suppose a merchant in the United States has been importing wool shirts from England for the past several years. The price of the shirts to the importer is 10 pounds per shirt. The exchange rate is $S_0 = 0.5£/U.S.\$$. If inflation is 10% in England and 0% in the United States, how must the exchange rate adjust for the price to the importer to remain unchanged?

SOLUTION

Algebraic Solution

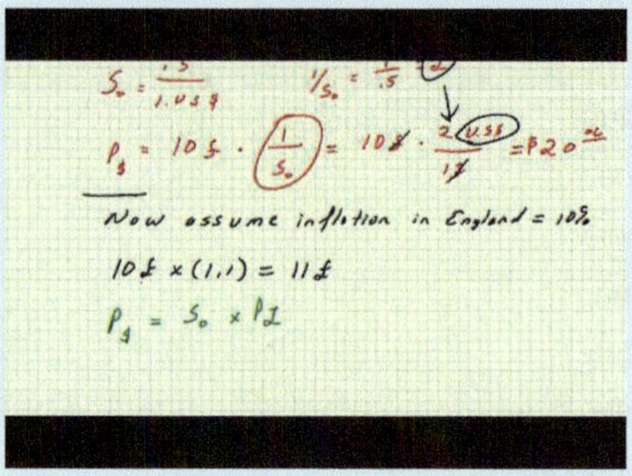

View in the online reader

We must first compute the original price of the wool shirts in dollars.

$$P_{\$} = P_{£} \times 1/S_0$$
$$1/S_0 = 1/(0.5£/U.S.\$) = 2\ U.S.\$/£$$
$$P_{\$} = 10£ \times 2\ U.S.\$/£ = \$20$$

The importer sells the shirts for $20 to American consumers. Now, if inflation in England causes the price of the shirts to increase 10% to 11 pounds, the exchange rate must adjust so that the dollar price remains constant at $20 because U.S. consumers haven't experienced inflation and won't be willing to pay a higher price.

$$P_S = P_{£} \times 1/S_0$$
$$\$20 = £11 \times 1/S_0$$
$$S_0 = £11/\$20 = 0.55£/\text{U.S.}\$$$

The cost of buying one U.S. dollar rises by 10%, from £0.50 to £0.55.

In "Example 16.4 Maintaining Purchase Power Parity", the exchange rate adjusts so that the price in U.S. dollars is constant. But what would happen if the United States were also experiencing inflation? If the U.S. inflation rate were equal to the inflation rate in England, the exchange rate wouldn't need to adjust. However, if there were a difference, the exchange rate would have to compensate. For example, if the inflation rate is 10% in England and 6% in the United States, the U.S. dollar equivalent must adjust up 4% $(10\%-6\% = 4\%)$. In Example 16.4, the new exchange rate would be 0.52.

We can formalize this relationship with Equation 16.4:

EQUATION 16.4

$$E[S_t] = S_0 \times [1 + Inf_f - Inf_{U.S.}]^t$$

where

$$E[S_t] = \text{expected currency per U.S. dollar exchange rate at time } t$$
$$S_0 = \text{spot rate or indirect rate}$$
$$Inf_f = \text{foreign rate of inflation}$$
$$Inf_{U.S.} = \text{U.S. rate of inflation}$$

Example 16.5 Relative Purchasing Power Parity

If the inflation rate in the United States is expected to average 3% in the future, and the inflation rate in England is expected to average 5%, what spot rate is expected to be in effect in 3 years? Assume the S_0 is now 0.62.

SOLUTION

Algebraic Solution

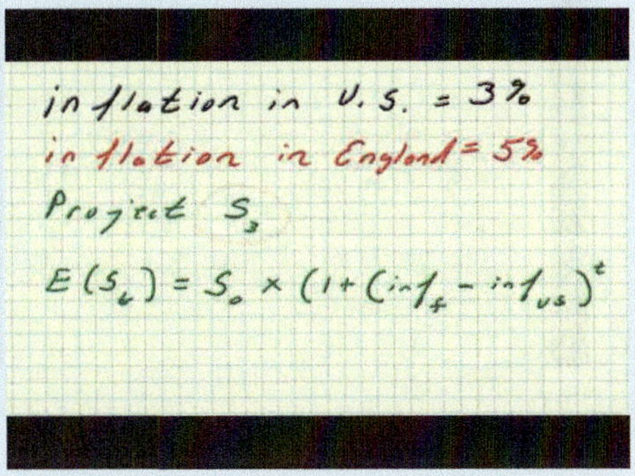

View in the online reader

Using Equation 16.4, we obtain:

$$E[S_t] = S_0 \times [1 + (\text{Inf}_f - \text{Inf}_{U.S.})]^t$$
$$E[S_3] = 0.6200 \times [1 + (0.05 - 0.03)]^3$$
$$E[S_3] = 0.6200 \times 1.0612 = 0.6579$$

Because of the greater inflation in England than in the United States, the number of pounds you can buy with $1 is expected to increase from 0.6200 to 0.6579 after 3 years.

In "Example 16.5 Relative Purchasing Power Parity", the exchange rate expected to be in effect in 3 years is 0.6579. This demonstrates how forward exchange rates are established. Traders must anticipate the relative inflation rates between two countries and set a forward rate that compensates for the difference. The forward rate represents a best guess as to what the spot rate will be in the future.

We have already noted that absolute PPP does not hold very well for most goods because of transportation costs and other restrictions to trade. We might now ask how changes in relative PPP reflect differences in inflation rates. Studies show that, in the short run, relative PPP doesn't explain changes in exchange rates well. However, over the long run, relative PPP does do a good job of explaining exchange rate changes. The reason for this is that, in the short run, other factors affect the prices of goods, such as changes in demand, droughts, and production problems. These influences tend to cancel in the long run, where the relationship between inflation and exchange rates dominates the short-run effects.

Tip

Absolute PPP describes the relationship between the prices of goods at a particular point in time. Relative PPP focuses on the changes over time in the relative prices of goods between countries. Absolute PPP does not hold well when examined; however, relative PPP does a good job of explaining exchange rate movements over the long run.

Explain It: Relative versus Absolute PPP

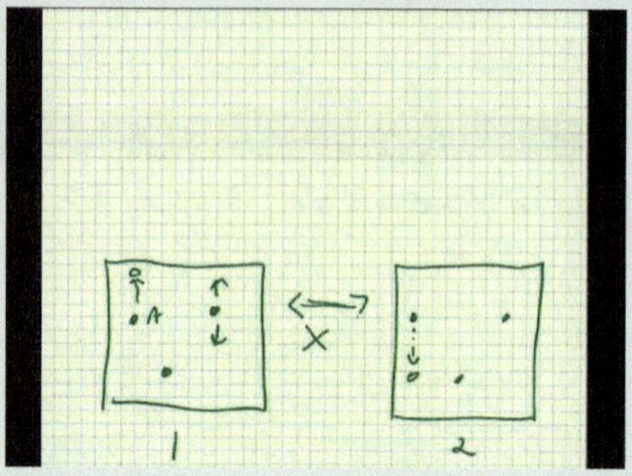

View in the online reader

16.3 Interest Rate Parity

Another factor that influences exchange rates is the return earned on investments in different countries. Exchange rates must adjust so that there is no reason for funds to flow from one country just to take advantage of better returns in another.

interest rate parity (IRP)

A theory that interest rates around the world will adjust so that investors earn the same return, regardless of where they invest.

In the previous section, we explained the PPP theory by arguing that if PPP did not hold, traders could buy the goods in the cheaper country and sell them where they're more expensive. However, we also noted that various barriers to trade prevented PPP from being true much of the time. What if a good that was essentially costless to transport was exactly equivalent around the world and had an easily obtainable price quote? We might expect this particular good to adhere to PPP very accurately. In fact, there is such a good: money. Money can be transferred from one country to another electronically, has universal value, and has an easy-to-determine price: the interest rate. Interest rates behave so much more consistently than the prices of goods that a special term has been applied to international interest rate relationships: **interest rate parity (IRP)**. Understanding IRP requires that we first understand interest rate arbitrage.

Interest Rate Arbitrage

If you can invest $1 in a risk-free dollar-denominated investment while simultaneously borrowing $1 at the rate paid on British pounds, you have zero net investment. If you can earn a return on this transaction, you have an arbitrage opportunity. Interest rate arbitrage maintains the IRP relationship.

Table 16.4 lists interest rates available on risk-free deposits in different countries in 2015.

TABLE 16.4 Central Bank Interest Rates

Country	Percent per Year
Japan	(0.10)
United States	0.25
United Kingdom	0.10
Canada	0.25
Reserve Bank—Australia	0.10
China	4.20
Hungary	0.90
Brazil	2.00
Egypt	8.75

Data from https://en.wikipedia.org/wiki/List_of_countries_by_central_bank_interest_rates

Assume for this example that interest rates are 1.0% in Canada and 9.25% in Egypt. You might think it wise to borrow from Canada at 1.0% and invest in Egypt at 9.25%. Let's examine this transaction in greater detail.

To invest in Egyptian pounds, you must:

Step 1: Convert your dollars to pounds using the spot exchange rate.

Step 2: Buy the Egyptian risk-free investment.

Step 3: Convert the pounds back to dollars when the investment matures. To make this a risk-free transaction, you would lock in a future exchange rate by buying a forward exchange contract.

FIGURE 16.1 Currency Timeline

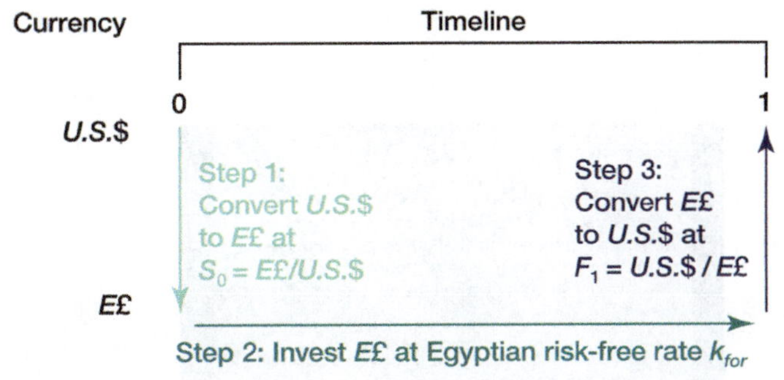

Let's find out how much we could earn if we borrowed $10,000 in Canada at 1%, converted the $10,000 into Egyptian pounds, invested at 9.25%, and finally converted the pounds back into dollars 1 year later. Assume Egyptian pounds per U.S. dollar (S_0) is 6.

Step 1: You must convert the $10,000 into pounds by multiplying by the S_0 :

$$\textit{Egyptian pounds} = \$10,000 \times 6 = 60,000\ E\pounds$$

Step 2: You now invest these pounds at 9.25%, so you'll have 65,550 E£ at the end of 1 year.

Step 3: Now, you must convert your pounds back into dollars. To be sure you don't suffer if exchange rates move, you lock in an exchange rate at the time of the initial investment by buying a contract, called a *forward contract*, that lets you convert Egyptian pounds back into dollars when your investment matures. Suppose this forward contract sets the $1/F_1$ to be 0.1542. (Multiplying by the $1/F_1$ will convert your pounds into dollars.) Then

$$\textit{Dollars from investment} = \textit{Pounds at end of year} \times 1/F_1$$
$$\textit{Dollars from investment} = 65,550E£ \times 0.1542 = \$10,107.81$$

To determine your net income from the investment, you must compute how much the loan of the $10,000 cost you. You borrowed $10,000 at 1% for 1 year, so you'll have to pay back $10,000 times $(1 + 0.01)$:

$$\textit{Amount due on loan of } \$10,000 = \textit{Loan amount} \times (1 + \textit{Interest rate})$$
$$\textit{Amount due on loan of } \$10,000 = \$10,000 \times (1.01) = \$10,100$$

The net income is $\$10,107.81 - \$10,100 = \$7.81$. You're investing none of your own equity in this transaction, and it's completely riskless because you're investing in risk-free securities and have locked in a contract to convert the pounds to dollars when the investment matures; thus, you have a positive arbitrage opportunity. As long as the opportunity continues to exist, you, as well as other arbiters, will continue to borrow more dollars and invest in more Egyptian pound-denominated investments. Predictably, as the demand for dollars increases, the cost of dollars will rise. This means the interest cost on borrowed dollars will rise. Similarly, as investments flow into Egypt, the return on the investments will fall. Finally, as the demand for forward contracts rises, the rate will increase. The main point of this discussion is that eventually, all of these forces will cause the arbitrage opportunity to disappear because exchange rates and interest rates will adjust.

We can summarize the IRP relationship by noting that, when no arbitrage opportunity exists, the return earned on an investment in dollars must equal the return earned when dollars are converted to a foreign currency, invested, and then converted back to dollars. This is shown by the following equation:

Explain It: Interpreting Interest Rate Parity Equations

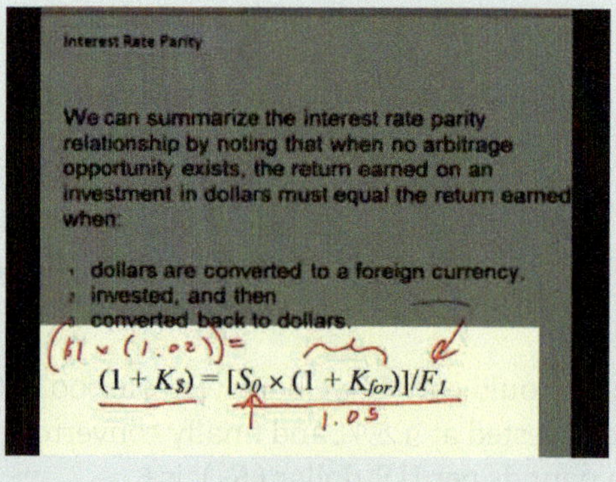

View in the online reader

EQUATION 16.5

$$(1 + K_{\$}) = [S_0 \times (1 + K_{for})]/F_1$$

where

$$K_{\$} = \text{the risk-free rate of return on an investment denominated in dollars}$$
$$K_{for} = \text{the risk-free rate denominated in a foreign currency}$$
$$F_1 = \text{the forward exchange rate available at the time of the investment quoted as currency per U.S. dollar}$$

The term on the left side of the equal sign is what will result from investing $1 domestically. The term on the right is what will result from a foreign investment after converting to and from the foreign currency. By rearranging Equation 16.5, we arrive at the equation that represents the IRP relationship:

EQUATION 16.6

$$F_1/S_0 = (1 + K_{for})/(1 + K_{\$})$$

Let's use Equation 16.6 to estimate what forward exchange rate was likely to be quoted to investors:

$$F_1/S_0 = (1 + K_{for})/(1 + K_{\$})$$
$$F_1/6 = (1.0925)/(1.01)$$
$$F_1 = 6.4901 \text{ or } \frac{6.4901\ E£}{1\text{U.S.}\$}$$
$$\text{currency per U.S. dollar or}$$
$$1/6.4901 = 0.1541$$

If the forward rate had been 0.1541 in our example, rather than 0.1542, we wouldn't have earned any arbitrage profits from our foreign investment. Speculators can take advantage of arbitrage opportunities so quickly and, at no cost, few arbitrage opportunities last long. The result is that tests of IRP show that it holds very well around the world. In other words, it's rare that similar risk investments in one country earn more than in another country, after converting money to and from the foreign currency using spot and forward exchange rates.

Example 16.6 Interest Rate Parity

If the risk-free rate in the United States is 0.25%, the risk-free rate in England is 0.5%, and the currency per U.S. dollar spot rate is 0.6, what should the 1-year forward rate be?

SOLUTION

Algebraic Solution

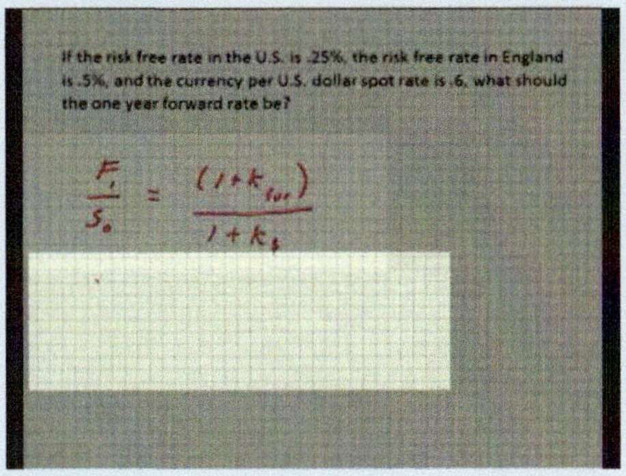

View in the online reader

Use Equation 16.6.

$$F_1/S_0 = (1 + K_{for})/(1 + K_\$)$$
$$F_1/0.6 = (1 + 0.005)/(1 + 0.0025)$$
$$F_1 = 0.6015$$

The point of this section is that arbitrageurs, working to make profits for themselves with riskless transactions, also help exchange rates adjust to their correct levels rapidly and accurately.

16.4 International Finance Risk

Engaging in international business involves risk not normally faced when engaging in business domestically. For example, we discussed exchange rate risk earlier and demonstrated that a business may suffer losses due to unexpected changes in exchange rates. Firms investing in foreign countries are also subject to political risk—the risk that changing politics may adversely affect the business' interests. We examine these sources of risk in this section.

Controlling Exchange Rate Risk

hedge

Buying and selling securities where a change in the price of one offsets a change in the price of the other. Hedges are used to reduce risk from market fluctuations.

In the previous section, we used futures contracts (contracts that lock in forward rates) to lock in an exchange rate when setting up a risk-free arbitrage for interest rates. These futures contracts can also be used to reduce the exchange rate risk associated with normal international business transactions by allowing the firm to **hedge** against exchange rate fluctuations. The concept behind a hedge is straightforward. If a drop in the exchange rate will cost a firm money, a futures contract is sold so that the same drop will cause the value of the hedge to increase by exactly the amount of the loss. The gain on the futures contract cancels the loss suffered from the change in exchange rates on the business transaction being hedged. If exchange rates move so that the original business transaction would have enjoyed a gain due to exchange rates, a loss will occur on the futures contract. Either way, the firm ends up earning the same as if exchange rates hadn't moved. The exchange rate risk is transferred to a speculator, who essentially insures the firm against exchange rate losses.

Explain It: Hedging with Forward Contracts

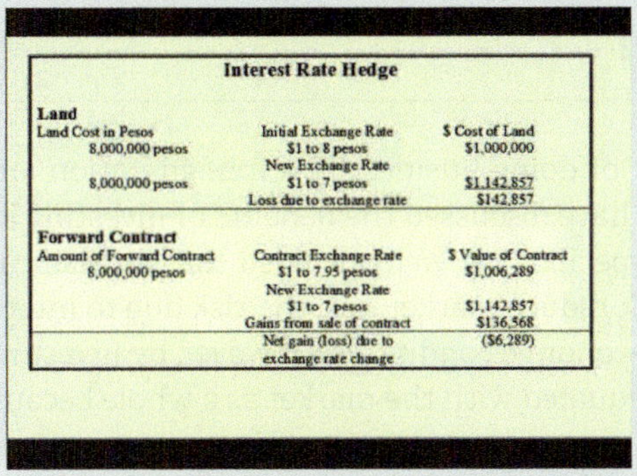

Interest Rate Hedge

Land		
Land Cost in Pesos	Initial Exchange Rate	$ Cost of Land
8,000,000 pesos	$1 to 8 pesos	$1,000,000
	New Exchange Rate	
8,000,000 pesos	$1 to 7 pesos	$1,142,857
	Loss due to exchange rate	$142,857
Forward Contract		
Amount of Forward Contract	Contract Exchange Rate	$ Value of Contract
8,000,000 pesos	$1 to 7.95 pesos	$1,006,289
	New Exchange Rate	
	$1 to 7 pesos	$1,142,857
	Gains from sale of contract	$136,568
	Net gain (loss) due to exchange rate change	($6,289)

View in the online reader

An alternative method of avoiding exchange rate risk is to insist that contracts be denominated in U.S. dollars. The U.S. dollar is as close to a worldwide currency as there is. Its stability and the size of the U.S. economy allow it to be used in trade around the world. This means that businesses in many countries are willing to accept dollars in exchange for goods because these dollars can be used to satisfy other obligations of the foreign firm. Although establishing contracts in dollars is not always possible, it is clearly one avenue that international firms should investigate.

Political Risk

Although it's possible to create hedges to reduce exchange rate risk, it's much more difficult to deal with political risk. Suppose your firm has built a facility in a small South American country to process coffee before shipping it to plants in the United States for final packaging. If the government of that country is overthrown, the new government may not choose to recognize any ownership claims established under the old regime. In fact, the new government may see taking your firm's plant (a process called **nationalization** or expropriation) as an opportunity to enrich itself. For example, China nationalized all business assets owned by foreign firms in 1949, as did Cuba in 1959. Today, events in Bolivar, Ecuador, and Russia are causing losses to foreign firms.

nationalization

The process where a country takes ownership of businesses, both foreign and domestic.

Other less drastic circumstances can arise from political problems. The local government in a foreign country may impose import or export duties, or tariffs, that may make the operation of a firm from another country unprofitable. Labor laws may change, causing the cost of labor to rise, erasing the advantage initially provided by the foreign location. One of the more common risks is that the local government will impose additional unexpected taxes on businesses from other countries. The foreign government may choose to tax the income, the property, or the value added by the manufacturer. Firms doing business in foreign countries must recognize that the government has little interest in the outside firm's health and often makes every effort to extract as much benefit as possible from businesses headquartered in other countries. In addition to high taxes, governments may require foreign firms to hire local labor, which may prevent the firm from using its own specialized personnel. Finally, the foreign government may pass laws limiting the ability of the outside firm to convert currency; such a rule prevents outside firms from taking profits or income out of the country.

Foreign investments may offer returns and opportunities for growth and diversification far greater than can be achieved domestically. Evaluating these opportunities involves the same principle used to evaluate any investment maximizing the value of the firm by accepting positive net present value projects.

Diversification

Offsetting the increased risk of doing business in a foreign nation are the benefits realized from increased diversification. We have discussed the benefits of investing in a variety of different firms and projects to reduce firm-specific risk. We concluded that diversification could almost eliminate firm-specific risk, but couldn't reduce market risk, the risk due to interest rate changes, raw material shortages, and changing economic conditions. However, by investing in foreign countries, firms may reduce the risk usually equated with the market as a whole because different economies don't necessarily move together. For example, in 1993–1995 Japan was experiencing a recession while the U.S. economy was very strong. Alternatively, in 1989–1991, the United States suffered a mild recession while Japan's economy was strong. Firms doing business in both countries would have had smaller fluctuations in income than firms with operations limited to one country. The recession that began in 2008 was unique in its global impact. Few countries escaped the downturn.

The economies of many developing countries are less closely related to that of the United States. This makes them attractive to domestic companies seeking to stabilize their cash flows. We have learned it's possible to reduce the risk of a portfolio by adding a high-risk investment if it's negatively correlated with other investments. Similarly, the risk of a firm can be reduced by adding investments in high-risk countries if their economies have a low correlation with the business cycles of the firm's other investments. In fact, the desire to insulate the firm's income from fluctuations is often one of the driving motivations behind foreign investment and expansion.

16.5 Foreign Investments

Evaluating foreign investment opportunities involves the same principle used to evaluate any investment—maximizing the value of the firm by accepting positive net present value projects.

Evaluating Foreign Investments

The process of evaluating foreign investments is conceptually the same as evaluating any investment; however, analysts should be aware of additional complicating factors. First, estimating the cash flows is more difficult than on similar domestic projects. This is because the international firm may not be as aware of indirect expenses and operating conditions as it is when operating in more familiar territory. Given the problems firms have in estimating domestic cash flows accurately, estimating them in foreign countries can add a whole new level of error.

The usual method for adjusting a project's cash flows for increased risk is to increase the discount rate used when computing the net present value of the cash flows. The analyst usually determines the amount of the increase from experience with similar projects or from examining the risk of other firms performing similar activities. However, the financial analyst may have little experience to draw on for evaluating a foreign investment and there may be no other firms to use for comparison. As a result, the evaluation may not have a great deal of value. As firms grow more familiar with a particular part of the world, it becomes easier to properly evaluate and quantify risk.

How Foreign Investments are Financed

Although both domestic and international firms have access to foreign markets, more international firms take advantage of the opportunities foreign markets offer for raising capital. Of course, international firms may finance their international investments with the usual sources of capital, such as retained earnings, bank loans, or domestically marketed bonds and stock. The international financial markets offer attractive alternatives to these sources. One such source is the **Eurodollar** market. Eurodollars are dollar-denominated deposits held in foreign banks. Firms may often borrow short-term funds in the Eurodollar market at attractive interest rates. Eurodollar loans are usually unsecured and have maturities from 30 days to 1 year. The interest rate on the loans tends to be based on the **London Interbank Offered Rate (LIBOR)**. LIBOR is similar to the prime rate quoted by large banks in the United States, but is set by large international banks for loans among themselves. The lowest-risk borrower pays 0.75% to 1% above the LIBOR rate.

Firms may also issue Eurobonds to attract long-term funds. **Eurobonds** may be in dollars or in the currency of another country with a strong economy, such as Germany. The primary advantage of Eurobonds is that they're not subject to U.S. Securities and Exchange Commission (SEC) registration and disclosure rules, which can substantially delay the issue and increase the costs.

Foreign countries also have stock exchanges in which equity capital can be raised and shares of foreign firms can be traded.

Eurodollar

Deposits of currency not native to the country in which the bank is located; negotiable, usually pay interest at maturity, and are typically denominated in units of $1 million.

London Interbank Offered Rate (LIBOR)

The London Interbank Offered Rate is a daily reference rate set by the British Banker's Association. It is an average of the rates at which banks borrow unsecured funds from one another in the London interbank market.

Eurobonds

A bond issued by an international borrower and sold to investors in countries with currencies other than the currency in which the bond is denominated.

CHAPTER 17

Corporate Valuation

Learning Objectives

By the end of this chapter you will be able to:

1. Perform advanced financial statement forecasting.
2. Calculate free cash flow.
3. Understand how to calculate the discounted cash flow value of a company.
4. Calculate free cash flow to equity.

Accurate valuation is critical to investing and to investment banking. Investors want to buy good companies at cheap prices. To identify cheap companies, equity investors compare the market price to the fair price. A cheap company is one where the market price is less than the fair price. Calculating a fair price is a critical activity for investors.

Two important parts of the investment banking business are (1) new issues of equity and (2) mergers and acquisitions. A big part of both activities is valuation. The biggest decision in a new issue is the price at which the shares will be offered. The biggest decision in an acquisition is the price that will be offered for the target company's shares. Calculating a fair price is a central activity for investment bankers.

In the chapter on stocks, we presented a number of models for estimating the fair price of a share. In this chapter we present the most detailed and complete method in the finance toolbox: the discounted cash flow (DCF) method. On the downside, the DCF method is more involved and time-consuming. On the upside, it creates the best understanding of the business, it provides the most accurate estimate of the price, and it offers the greatest insight into the nature of the investment. The last point is important—every equity investment hinges on a small number of business variables (i.e., the success of a new product). These are the variables that determine the success or failure of the investment. A good investor understands the drivers of success and failure, and the DCF method provides the best insight into those drivers.

Discounted cash flow valuation is very similar to capital budgeting. Like capital budgeting, we forecast the free cash flows generated by the company. Then, we discount the free cash flows at the weighted average cost of capital (WACC) to arrive at the value of the company. However, unlike capital budgeting, we want to know the value of a company, not a project.

This chapter has four sections. In the first section, we augment your financial statement forecasting techniques by showing you how to forecast capital expenditures (CAPEX) and depreciation. Then we show you how to calculate free cash flow. In the third section, we discount the free cash flows at the WACC to find the value of the company. The fourth section shows how to calculate the free cash flow to equity and the discounted cash flow value of equity.

17.1 Advanced Financial Statements Forecasting

In Chapter 14, we showed you how to forecast financial statements. In order to keep the presentation simple, we provided the depreciation rate and the amount of capital expenditures (CAPEX). In this section, we show you how to calculate and forecast the depreciation rate and CAPEX.

Net Fixed Assets

Recall from Chapter 14 that we can express this year's net fixed assets as:

EQUATION 17.1

$$Net_1 = Net_{t-1} - Depreciation_1 + CAPEX_t$$

where Net_t refers to net fixed assets at the end of year *t* (net property, plant, and equipment).

CAPEX

Purchases of fixed assets such as property, plant, and equipment. Also referred to as CAPEX.

Net fixed assets is the aggregate book value of all of the company's assets. **CAPEX** is the purchase price of only new assets. In other words, CAPEX represents the additions to fixed assets. We call Equation 17.1 the capital asset identity; we use it repeatedly in this section.

Depreciation

declining balance depreciation system

A depreciation system where a percentage of the undepreciated assets are depreciated each year.

The depreciation expense is related to fixed assets, so it makes sense to model depreciation as a function of fixed assets. The simplest approach is to use a **declining balance depreciation system**.

The declining balance system deducts a fixed percentage of an asset's value each year. In Chapter 14, we showed that the annual depreciation expense is:

EQUATION 17.2

$$Depreciation_t = dr \times [Net_{t-1} + CAPEX_t]$$

where

$$Net_t = \text{net fixed assets=net property, plant, and equipment}$$
$$dr = \text{the depreciation rate}$$
$$CAPEX_t = \text{additions to fixed assets in period } t$$

Example 17.1 Calculating Depreciation

Calculate the depreciation expense for Dutch Oven given the following:

$$Net_{t-1} = \$100$$
$$dr = 10\%$$
$$CAPEX_t = \$20$$

SOLUTION

Using Equation 17.2, the depreciation expense is forecasted as:

$$\text{Depreciation} = 0.1 \times (\$100 + \$20)$$
$$\text{Depreciation} = \$12$$

Estimating the Average Depreciation Rate

In order to calculate the depreciation rate, it is necessary to find an expression for it using the historical income statement and balance sheet. First, rearrange Equation 17.1 as follows:

EQUATION 17.3

$$Net_{t-1} + CAPEX_t = Net_t + Depreciation_t$$

Then, substitute the right-hand side of Equation 17.3 into the square brackets of Equation 17.2 and simplify:

EQUATION 17.4

$$dr = \frac{Depreciation_t}{Net_t + Depreciation_t}$$

The (average) depreciation rate is equal to the depreciation expense divided by the sum of ending net fixed assets and depreciation. In the denominator, adding depreciation back to year-end net fixed assets gives us the amount that was to be depreciated: net fixed assets from last year plus CAPEX from this year. The advantage of Equation 17.4 is that it can be calculated from values in the income statement and balance sheet.

Example 17.2 Calculating the Depreciation Rate

Digital Downloads

Example 17.2 Calculating the Depreciation Rate.xlsx
https://catalog.flatworldknowledge.com/a/34711/Example_17_2_Calculating_the_Depreciation_Rate-b0a0.xlsx

Calculate the average depreciation rate for American Railcar Industries using the following historic financial information:

Selected Financial Information (in millions), American Railcar Industries		
	Year 4	**Year 5**
Sales	355.1	608.2
Depreciation	6.2	6.8
Net Fixed Assets	77.0	93.0

SOLUTION

Using Equation 17.4, the depreciation rate in each year is:

$$dr_4 = 6.2/(77 + 6.2) = 0.075$$
$$dr_5 = 6.8/(93 + 6.8) = 0.068$$

The average rate is 0.0716 or 7.16%.

CAPEX

CAPEX can be divided into two parts: (1) maintenance CAPEX and (2) growth CAPEX. Maintenance CAPEX is the expenditure on assets to replace worn-out equipment. A company that is not growing must still invest in maintenance CAPEX to maintain its stock of fixed assets. Growth CAPEX is the expenditure on assets that are needed to make more products and grow sales. Maintenance CAPEX is tied to the existing stock of fixed assets, while growth CAPEX is tied to sales growth. Total CAPEX is the sum of maintenance and growth CAPEX.

Total CAPEX

We can use the capital asset identity (Equation 17.1) to calculate total CAPEX from the income statement and balance sheet as follows:

EQUATION 17.5

$$CAPEX_t = Net_t - Net_{t-1} + Depreciation_t$$

Example 17.3 Calculating CAPEX

Using the following information, calculate CAPEX for American Railcar in Year 5.

Selected Financial Information (in millions), American Railcar Industries		
	Year 4	**Year 5**
Sales	355.1	608.2
Depreciation	6.2	6.8
Net Fixed Assets	77.0	93.0

SOLUTION

Using Equation 17.2, CAPEX is:

$$CAPEX_5 = 93.0 - 77.0 + 6.8$$
$$CAPEX_5 = 22.841$$

Maintenance CAPEX

We can use Equation 17.1 and Equation 17.2 to solve for maintenance CAPEX (denoted mCAPEX). It is the amount of CAPEX necessary to make net fixed assets at the end of a year equal to the value at the end of the previous year (i.e., $Net_t = Net_{t-1}$).

EQUATION 17.6

$$mCAPEX_t = \frac{dr}{1 - dr} Net_{t-1}$$

Growth CAPEX

Growth CAPEX (denoted gCAPEX) is tied to new sales. We express growth CAPEX as a proportion of new sales. The ratio of growth CAPEX to new sales is denoted *gx*:

EQUATION 17.7

$$gx = \frac{gCAPEX}{\Delta Sales_t}$$

For example, if it requires $20 of growth CAPEX to grow sales by $100, then $gx = \$20/\$100$ or 0.2. This value means that the company needs to invest 20 cents in growth CAPEX to support each new dollar of sales. The amount of growth CAPEX is forecasted simply by multiplying new sales by this ratio.

Tip

Growth CAPEX can never be negative. If sales are forecast to decline, then growth CAPEX should be set equal to zero.

The *gx* ratio is calculated from historical financial statements. The process is somewhat involved, as the depreciation rate, total CAPEX, and maintenance CAPEX all need to be estimated first and then growth CAPEX is calculated as a residual. This is shown in the next example.

Tip

Make note of the order in which these values are calculated because it will help you when you do problems. First, calculate the depreciation rate; second, total CAPEX; third, maintenance CAPEX; and last, growth CAPEX.

Before we turn to the example, you should know two characteristics of growth CAPEX and the ratio:

1. In periods of declining sales, growth CAPEX is zero by definition. Growth CAPEX cannot be negative.
2. Growth CAPEX is lumpy. Companies don't add capacity in small amounts. A company that builds a new factory may have a *gx* ratio greater than 1 in the year of construction. This value should not be used to forecast the financial statements, as it will cause free cash flow to be negative. Instead, the analyst must average the *gx* ratio across earlier years.

Example 17.4 Calculating Maintenance CAPEX and the *gx* Ratio

Digital Downloads

Example 17.4 Calculating Maintenance CAPEX and the gx Ratio.xlsx
https://catalog.flatworldknowledge.com/a/34711/Example_17_4_Calculating_Maintenance_CAPEX_and_the_gx_Ratio-fd0c.xlsx

Use the information in the table to calculate the *gx* ratio for Year 5.

Selected Financial Information (in millions), American Railcar Industries		
	Year 4	**Year 5**
Sales	358.9	610.4
Depreciation	6.2	6.8
Net Fixed Assets	77.0	93.0
CAPEX		22.8
Depreciation Rate	0.075	0.068

SOLUTION

Spreadsheet Solution

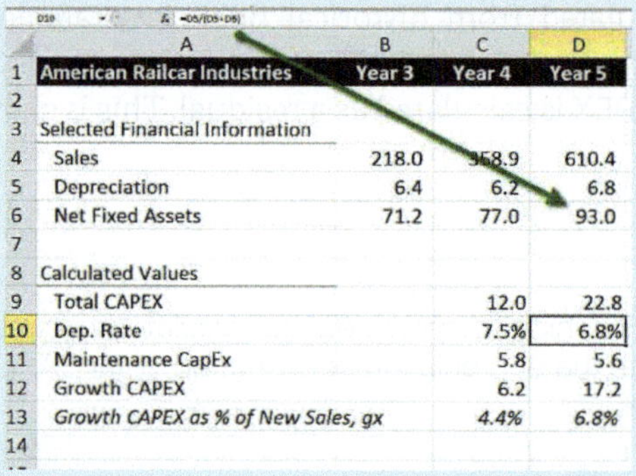

	A	B	C	D
1	American Railcar Industries	Year 3	Year 4	Year 5
2				
3	Selected Financial Information			
4	Sales	218.0	358.9	610.4
5	Depreciation	6.4	6.2	6.8
6	Net Fixed Assets	71.2	77.0	93.0
7				
8	Calculated Values			
9	Total CAPEX		12.0	22.8
10	Dep. Rate		7.5%	6.8%
11	Maintenance CapEx		5.8	5.6
12	Growth CAPEX		6.2	17.2
13	*Growth CAPEX as % of New Sales, gx*		*4.4%*	*6.8%*
14				

View in the online reader

Since we already have the depreciation rate and total CAPEX, the next step is to calculate maintenance CAPEX. From there, we can solve for growth CAPEX and the ratio.

Maintenance CAPEX

From Equation 17.6:

$$mCAPEX = [0.068/(1-0.068)] \times \$77 = \$5.633$$

Growth CAPEX

$$gCAPEX = CAPEX - mCAPEX$$
$$gCAPEX = 22.841 - 5.633 = 17.208$$

The Growth CAPEX ratio, *gx*, is:

$$gx = gCAPEX/\Delta Sales$$
$$gx = 17.208/(610.4 - 358.9) = 0.0684 \text{ or } 6.84\%$$

Example 17.5 Forecasting Depreciation, CAPEX, and net Fixed Assets

Digital Downloads

Example 17.5 Forecasting Depreciation CAPEX.xlsx
https://catalog.flatworldknowledge.com/a/34711/Example_17_5_Forecasting_Depreciation_CAPEX-4cdd.xlsx

American Railcar is forecasting sales of $646.1 million in Year 6. Use this information and your answers to "Example 17.4 Calculating Maintenance CAPEX and the gx Ratio" to forecast maintenance CAPEX, growth CAPEX, total CAPEX, net fixed assets, and depreciation for Year 6. Use the Year 5 values for the depreciation rate and the ratio of growth CAPEX to the change in sales.

SOLUTION

Spreadsheet Solution

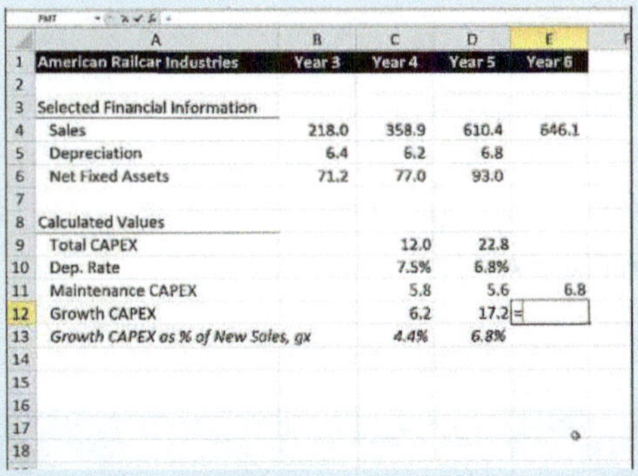

	A	B	C	D	E
1	American Railcar Industries	Year 3	Year 4	Year 5	Year 6
2					
3	Selected Financial Information				
4	Sales	218.0	358.9	610.4	646.1
5	Depreciation	6.4	6.2	6.8	
6	Net Fixed Assets	71.2	77.0	93.0	
7					
8	Calculated Values				
9	Total CAPEX		12.0	22.8	
10	Dep. Rate		7.5%	6.8%	
11	Maintenance CAPEX		5.8	5.6	6.8
12	Growth CAPEX		6.2	17.2	=
13	*Growth CAPEX as % of New Sales, gx*		4.4%	6.8%	
14					
15					
16					
17					
18					

View in the online reader

1. Maintenance CAPEX: From Equation 17.6

$$mCAPEX_6 = dr/(1-dr) \times Net_5 = [0.068/(1-0.068)] \times \$93 = \$6.807$$

2. Growth CAPEX

$$\begin{aligned} gCAPEX &= \Delta Sales_6 \times (gCAPEX/\Delta Sales) \\ &= (646.1 - 610.4) \times 0.0684 \\ &= \$2.432 \end{aligned}$$

3. Total CAPEX

$$\begin{aligned} CAPEX &= gCAPEX + mCAPEX \\ CAPEX &= 2.432 + 6.807 = 9.239 \end{aligned}$$

4. Depreciation: From Equation 17.6

$$Depreciation_6 = dr \times [Net_5 + CAPEX_6] = 0.068 \times [\$93 + \$9,239] = \$6.95$$

5. Net Fixed Assets: From Equation 17.1

$$Net_6 = Net_5 - Depreciation_6 + CAPEX_6 = \$93 - \$6.95 + \$9.239 = \$95.295$$

17.2 Free Cash Flow

Defining Free Cash Flow

Free cash flow is the amount of money that you would receive at the end of each year if you were the only owner of a company that had no debt. Since free cash flow is the amount of money you get to keep in a single year, the present value of all free cash flows is equal to the value of your company today. That is how much you would accept from a buyer if you sold your company today. It is what we call the discounted cash flow value.

If your company has debt, then free cash flow is the amount of money that you would receive if you were the sole owner and lender (of the debt). With debt, the present value of the free cash flows is equal to the value of equity and debt in the company.

Free cash flow is made up of three components as shown in Table 17.1.

We explain each in turn.

TABLE 17.1 Free Cash Flow

+	Operating Cash Flow
−	Investments in Net Working Capital
−	Investments in Fixed Assets
=	Free Cash Flow

Explain It: Free Cash Flow

View in the online reader

Operating Cash Flow

Operating cash flow (OCF) is the cash derived from the day-to-day operations of a business. It is sales revenue less out-of-pocket costs and taxes (see Equation 17.8).

EQUATION 17.8

$$OCF = Sales - COGS - SG\&A - Taxes$$

where

$$COGS = \text{Cost of Goods Sold}$$
$$SG\&A = \text{Selling, General, and Administrative}$$

We do not include depreciation because it is a noncash expense. Accountants include depreciation in the income statement because it provides an estimate of average fixed costs. In the calculation of free cash flow, we are interested in how much cash the company generates, *not* an estimate of profit.

Tip

Of course, depreciation is deducted in the calculation of taxes.

We do not subtract interest because it is a cash flow to bondholders. Free cash flow is the amount available to be paid to bondholders and shareholders, so we do not want to subtract interest when calculating it.

In the calculation of operating cash flows, taxes are given by:

EQUATION 17.9

$$Taxes = T \times (Sales - COGS - SG\&A - Depreciation)$$

or

$$Taxes = T \times EBIT$$

where *T* is the corporate tax rate.

Tip

EBIT is earnings before interest and taxes. It is defined as $EBIT = Sales - COGS - SG\&A - Depreciation$.

This definition of taxes omits the **interest tax shield**. Thus, it overestimates taxes compared to taxes on the income statement.

interest tax shield

Equal to the product of the interest expense and the corporate tax rate. It is the amount by which taxes are reduced due to interest tax deductibility.

Tip

On the income statement, taxes are calculated as the product of the tax rate, *T*, and pretax income. Pretax income is EBIT less interest. Thus, the OCF estimate of taxes is too high by an amount equal to $T \times \$Interest$. This is called the interest tax shield. It is the amount by which taxes are reduced due to interest deductibility.

The interest tax shield is incorporated into the valuation through the weighted average cost of capital when we use the after-tax cost of debt. This approach to treating the interest tax shield is explained in the following video.

Explain It: Taxes in the Calculation of Operating Cash Flow

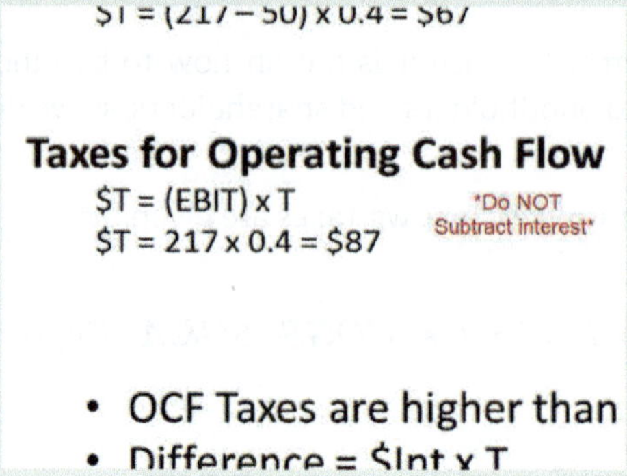

View in the online reader

Using the definition of EBIT, we can also re-express Equation 17.8:

EQUATION 17.10

$$OCF = EBIT \times (1 - T) + Depreciation$$

Explain It: Operating Cash Flow

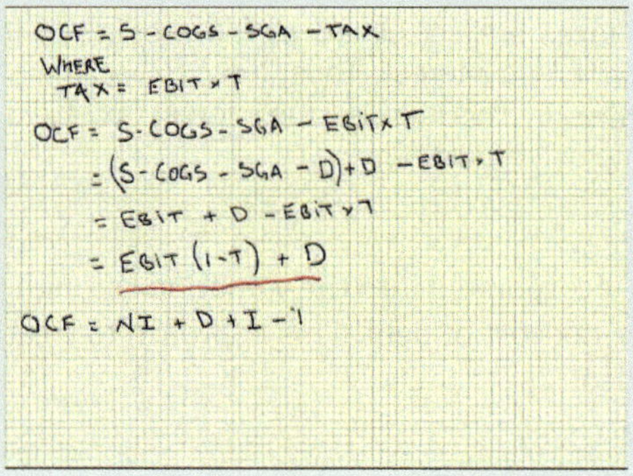

View in the online reader

Example 17.6 Operating Cash Flow at Vandalay Industries

Digital Downloads

Example 17.6 Operating Cash Flow at Vandalay.xlsx
https://catalog.flatworldknowledge.com/a/34711/_Example_17_6_Operating_Cash_Flow_at_Vandalay-4bad.xlsx

Calculate operating cash flow for Vandalay Industries.

Vandalay Industries Income Statement Year 1 (in millions)	
Sales	$730
Cost of Goods Sold	571
SG&A	52
Depreciation	30
EBIT	77
Interest	3
Pretax Income	74
Taxes @ 47.3%	35
Net Income	39

SOLUTION

Spreadsheet Solution

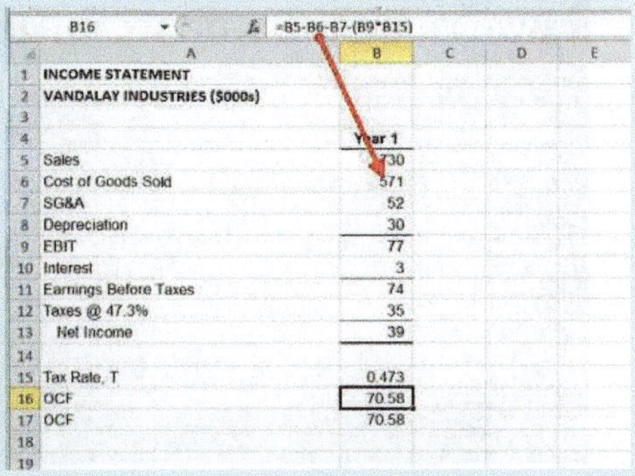

B16 =B5-B6-B7-(B9*B15)

	A	B	C	D	E
1	INCOME STATEMENT				
2	VANDALAY INDUSTRIES ($000s)				
3					
4		Year 1			
5	Sales	730			
6	Cost of Goods Sold	571			
7	SG&A	52			
8	Depreciation	30			
9	EBIT	77			
10	Interest	3			
11	Earnings Before Taxes	74			
12	Taxes @ 47.3%	35			
13	Net Income	39			
14					
15	Tax Rate, T	0.473			
16	OCF	70.58			
17	OCF	70.58			
18					
19					

View in the online reader

Taxes for the calculation of operating cash flows are:

$$Taxes = EBIT \times T$$
$$Taxes = \$77 \times 0.473 = \$36.419$$

This is a little higher than the amount shown in the income statement because this estimate does not include the interest tax shield.

$$Operating\ Cash\ Flow = Sales - COGS - SG\&A - Taxes$$
$$Operating\ Cash\ Flow = 770 - 571 - 52 - 36.419$$
$$Operating\ Cash\ Flow = 70.581$$

Investments in Net Working Capital

net working capital (NWC)

Current assets minus current liabilities.

An increase in **net working capital (NWC)** is a use of cash, and a reduction in net working capital is a source of cash. We subtract an increase in net working capital from operating cash flow. (A decrease is shown as a negative increase and so adds to operating cash flows.)

When calculating free cash flow, NWC is defined as:

EQUATION 17.11

$$NWC = (Short\ term\ assets - Cash) - (Current\ liabilities - Short\ term\ debts)$$

This is different from the accounting definition of NWC. We don't include cash on the asset side of NWC because if the increase in current assets is financed by running down the cash balance, then the firm has consumed cash and free cash flow should be negative. We don't include bank borrowing or short-term debt on the liability side of NWC because free cash flow is designed to indicate if more funds must be borrowed or invested to finance the business.

The investment in net working capital is the change in NWC. For example, if inventory or accounts receivable increase, then that is an investment in net working capital (and a use of free cash flow).

Explain It: Investments in NWC

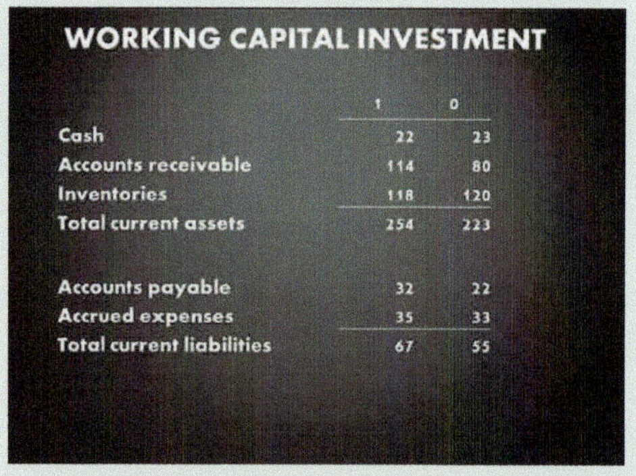

View in the online reader

Example 17.7 Investments in Net Working Capital at Vandalay Industries

Digital Downloads

Example 17.7 Investments in Net Working Capital at Vandalay.xlsx
https://catalog.flatworldknowledge.com/a/34711/ Example_17_7_Investments_in_Net_Working_Capital_at_Vandalay-089a.xlsx

Calculate the investment in net working capital for Vandalay Industries for Year 1.

Selected Financial Information (in millions) Vandalay Industries		
	Year 1	**Year 0**
Cash	$22	$23
Accounts Receivable	114	80
Inventories	118	120
Total Current Assets	254	223
Accounts Payable	32	22
Accrued Expenses	35	33
Total Current Liabilities	67	55

SOLUTION

Spreadsheet Solution

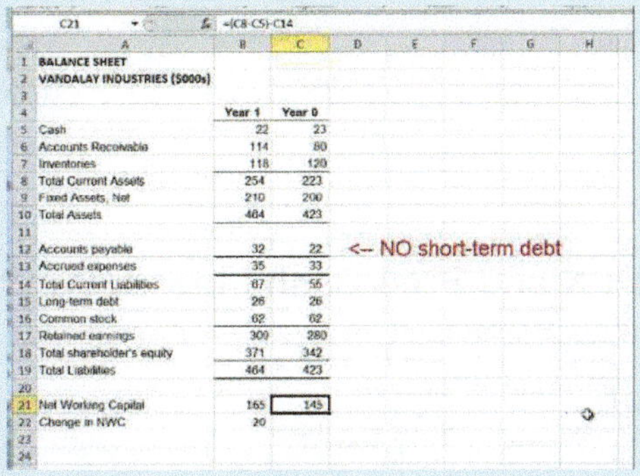

C21 =(C8-C5)-C14

	A	B	C
1	**BALANCE SHEET**		
2	**VANDALAY INDUSTRIES ($000s)**		
3			
4		**Year 1**	**Year 0**
5	Cash	22	23
6	Accounts Receivable	114	80
7	Inventories	118	120
8	Total Current Assets	254	223
9	Fixed Assets, Net	210	200
10	Total Assets	464	423
11			
12	Accounts payable	32	22
13	Accrued expenses	35	33
14	Total Current Liabilities	67	55
15	Long-term debt	26	26
16	Common stock	62	62
17	Retained earnings	309	280
18	Total shareholder's equity	371	342
19	Total Liabilities	464	423
20			
21	Net Working Capital	165	145
22	Change in NWC	20	

<-- NO short-term debt

View in the online reader

The investment in net working capital is the change in the level of net working capital.

$$\Delta NWC = NWC_1 - NWC_0$$
$$NWC_1 = (254 - 22) - (67) = 165$$
$$NWC_0 = (223 - 23) - (55) = 145$$
$$\Delta NWC = 165 - 145 = 20$$

On the asset side, accounts receivable increase and inventory decreases. On the liability side, both accounts payable and accrued expenses rise. The increase in liabilities partially offsets the increase in assets.

CAPEX and Free Cash Flow

CAPEX is short for capital expenditures. CAPEX is the amount of money spent on purchases of long-term assets such as machinery and equipment. The calculation of CAPEX was covered in Section 1.3.

Explain It: CAPEX

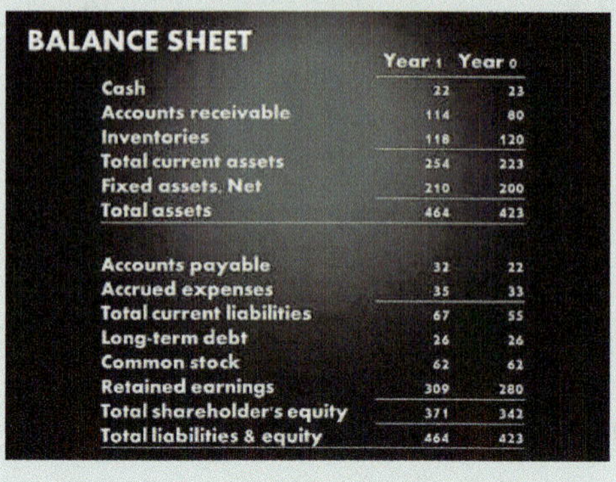

BALANCE SHEET

	Year 1	Year 0
Cash	22	23
Accounts receivable	114	80
Inventories	118	120
Total current assets	254	223
Fixed assets, Net	210	200
Total assets	464	423
Accounts payable	32	22
Accrued expenses	35	33
Total current liabilities	67	55
Long-term debt	26	26
Common stock	62	62
Retained earnings	309	280
Total shareholder's equity	371	342
Total liabilities & equity	464	423

View in the online reader

Example 17.8 CAPEX and Free Cash Flow at Vandalay Industries

Digital Downloads

Example 17.8 CAPEX and FCF at Vandalay.xlsx
https://catalog.flatworldknowledge.com/a/34711/Example_17_8_CAPEX_and_FCF_at_Vandalay-2857.xlsx

Calculate the investment in fixed assets (CAPEX) and free cash flow for Vandalay for Year 1.

Selected Financial Information (in millions), Vandalay Industries		
	Year 1	**Year 0**
Sales	$730	$668
Cost of Goods Sold	571	531
SG&A	52	54
Depreciation	30	24
Tax Rate	47.3%	47.3%
Cash	22	23
Total Current Assets	254	223
Fixed Assets, Net	210	200
Total Current Liabilities	67	55

SOLUTION

Spreadsheet Solution

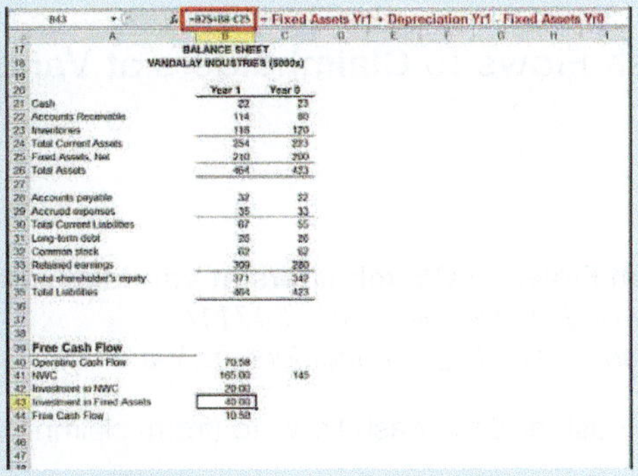

BALANCE SHEET
VANDALAY INDUSTRIES ($000s)

	Year 1	Year 0
Cash	22	23
Accounts Receivable	114	80
Inventories	118	170
Total Current Assets	254	273
Fixed Assets, Net	210	200
Total Assets	464	473
Accounts payable	32	22
Accrued expenses	35	33
Total Current Liabilities	67	55
Long-term debt	26	26
Common stock	62	62
Retained earnings	309	280
Total shareholder's equity	371	342
Total Liabilities	464	473

Free Cash Flow		
Operating Cash Flow	70.58	
NWC	165.00	145
Investment in NWC	20.00	
Investment in Fixed Assets	40.00	
Free Cash Flow	10.58	

View in the online reader

Investment in Fixed Assets (CAPEX)

$$CAPEX_1 = Net_t - Net_{t-1} + Depreciation$$
$$CAPEX_1 = 210 - 200 + 30 = 40$$

Free Cash Flow	
Operating Cash Flow	$70.581
–Investment in Net Working Capital	–20
–Investment in Fixed Assets	–40
=Free Cash Flow	10.581

The Free Cash Flow Identity

Free cash flow can go three places: into the cash account, to shareholders, or to lenders. Lenders receive interest and principal payments. Shareholders receive dividends or share repurchases.

This can be expressed formally as the free cash flow identity:

EQUATION 17.12

$$FCF = \Delta Cash + Cash\ flow\ to\ (from)\ Claimholders - \$Interest \times T$$

where

$$\Delta Cash = Cash_t - Cash_{t-1} (Change\ in\ the\ cash\ balance)$$
$$\$Int \times T = The\ interest\ tax\ shield$$

This equality is derived from the cash flow statement. For accounting aficionados, the spreadsheet video in the solution to "Example 17.9 Cash Flows to Claimholders at Vandalay Industries" shows the derivation. The interest tax shield appears on the right-hand side because our definition of taxes in operating cash flows omits it. If we use taxes from the income statement in the calculation of operating cash flow, then the interest tax shield term would not appear on the right-hand side of Equation 17.12.

Claimholders are just shareholders and the firm's lenders. Note the implied signs of the cash flows on the right-hand side. Payments to claimholders are shown with a positive sign. Cash flows received from claimholders (new debt or equity) carry a negative sign. New debt just means additional borrowing. New equity represents a new issue of shares.

Example 17.9 Cash Flows to Claimholders at Vandalay Industries

Digital Downloads

Example 17.9 Cash Flows to Claimholders at Vandalay.xlsx
https://catalog.flatworldknowledge.com/a/34711/ Example_17_9_Cash_Flows_to_Claimholders_at_Vandalay-1995.xlsx

Calculate the change in cash and the cash flows to (from) claimholders for Vandalay in Year 1.

Selected Financial Information (in millions) Vandalay Industries		
	Year 1	**Year 0**
Cash	$22	$23
Interest	3	3
Long-Term Debt	26	26
Dividends	10	10
Common Shares	62	62

SOLUTION

Spreadsheet Solution

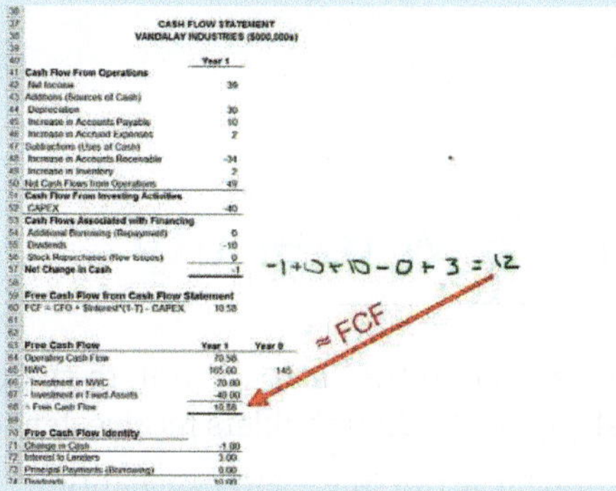

View in the online reader

The cash account drops by 1, so the change in cash is −1.Lenders received interest of $3. Long-term debt is unchanged in Year 1, so there is no additional borrowing (or repayment).

Tip: *If long-term debt was lower in Year 1, then that would indicate a principal repayment. Repayment is a cash flow to claimholders, and so would have a positive sign. Conversely, an increase in debt represents new borrowing, and the increase would have a negative sign.*

Shareholders received $10 of dividends. Common shares are unchanged, so there were no share repurchases or new issues.

Tip: *An increase in common shares from Year 0 to Year 1 would indicate a new issue of shares. A new issue is a cash flow from claimholders, and so would have a negative sign. Conversely, a reduction in common shares indicates a share repurchase. A repurchase is a flow to claimholders and would have a positive sign.*

We summarize these flows (in millions) as follows:

	Change in Cash=	−1
Flow to Lenders	Interest=	3
	Principal Repayment (Borrowing)=	0
Cash Flow to Shareholders	Dividends=	10
	Repurchased Shares (New Issues)=	0
Total		12

If we subtract the tax shield from this number ($1.419M), then we get the free cash flow value, which was calculated in "Example 17.8 CAPEX and Free Cash Flow at Vandalay Industries" ($10.581M).

17.3 Discounted Free Cash Flow Valuation

Overview of the DCF Method

How much is a business worth? The answer is "the amount the highest bidder is willing to pay for it." The successful bidder gets to keep all of the free cash flows generated by the firm each year. The most a bidder will pay for a business is the present value of the free cash flows. Thus, the value of a business is the present value of the free cash flows.

Here is another way to think about the value of a firm. To receive all of the cash flows from a company, an investor must own all of the securities issued by that company. So the value of a firm is the sum of the values of its issued securities. This is illustrated in Figure 17.1.

FIGURE 17.1 The Total Value of a Firm

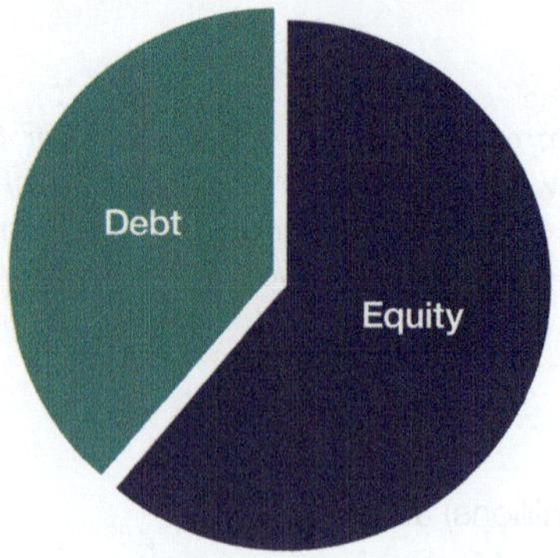

These two ways of thinking about value are equivalent. The market value of the securities is equal to the present value of the cash flows accruing to those securities. Thus, to value a firm we can value each security separately and add them up. Alternatively, we can find the present value of total free cash flow, since free cash flow is equal to the amount that is paid to all claimholders. The latter is the approach used by the discounted free cash flow method.

The DCF valuation method is similar to finding the net present value of a project. However, instead of valuing a project, we value the entire company.

The Cost of Capital

The DCF method, like the NPV method in capital budgeting, discounts the free cash flow generated by the assets. Because free cash flows are paid out to a combination of debt and equity holders, the discount rate applied to these cash flows should reflect the financing mix. We use the weighted average cost of capital (WACC) as the discount rate, since it is a weighted average of the required returns of the various claimholders.

The calculation of the WACC is covered in Chapter 11, so we do not review it here. An important assumption underlying the use of the WACC is that the financing proportions (i.e., the debt-to-value ratio) are assumed to remain constant over the company's life.

Another important point to remember is that we use the after-tax cost of debt in the calculation of WACC. This captures the interest tax shield, so we can safely omit it from the calculation of operating cash flows. This was explained earlier in "Explain It: Taxes in the Calculation of Operating Cash Flow".

Forecast Timeline

forecast period

The early part of a forecast with two-stages of growth.

terminal growth period

The final stage of a forecast. Usually continues in perpetuity and features constant growth.

The cash flows from a company normally extend well into the future. To make the analysis easy to understand, the future is typically broken into two sequential parts (see Figure 17.2): (1) a short-term period called the **forecast period**, and (2) a long-term period extending into perpetuity called the **terminal growth period**. In the forecast period, we allow that sales growth can vary. In the terminal period, sales (and free cash flow) are assumed to grow in perpetuity at a constant rate.

FIGURE 17.2 Timeline for Free Cash Flow Valuation

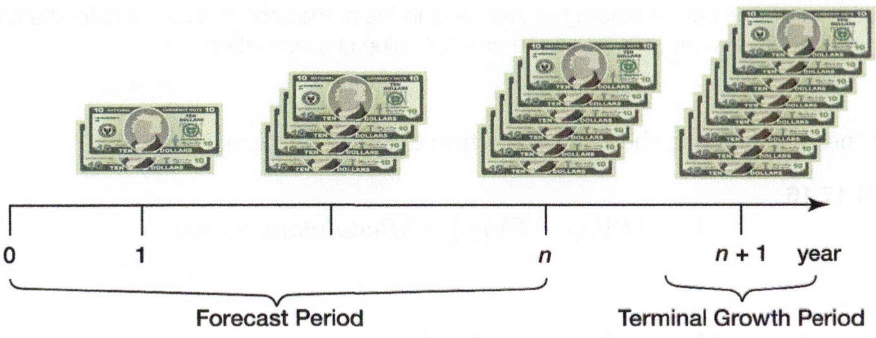

DCF Valuation

The value of the firm, V, is equal to the sum of the present value of the cash flows and the **redundant assets** when discounted at the WACC:

redundant assets
Assets not used for a company's operations. For example, unused land owned by the company.

EQUATION 17.13

$$V = PV\ of\ Free\ Cash\ Flows + \$Redundant\ Assets$$

Assets of a company can be divided into those that are expected to provide an ongoing stream of payments, the **operating assets**, and those that are not, the redundant assets. An example of a redundant asset is a tract of land that a company holds as a speculative investment and does not intend to use in its manufacturing operations. Another common redundant asset is cash and marketable securities. For example, at the time of writing, Apple Inc. had $205 billion of cash and marketable securities. A valuation based on free cash flows alone would significantly undervalue Apple.

operating assets
The assets used for a company's operations. The non-redundant assets.

The present value of free cash flows is equal to the sum of the present value of the cash flows from the forecast period and the terminal period. The present value of the cash flows from the forecast period is given by:

EQUATION 17.14

$$PV_{FP} = \sum_{t=1}^{n} \frac{FCF_t}{(1 + k_{WACC})^t}$$

where n is the length of the forecast period.

The present value of the cash flows in the terminal period is called the **terminal value**. The terminal value is found using the constant growth model, since it is assumed that those cash flows grow at a constant rate in perpetuity:

terminal value
The present value of cash flows generated in the terminal growth period.

EQUATION 17.15

$$PV_{TP} = \frac{1}{(1 + k_{WACC})^n} \cdot \frac{FCF_n(1 + g)}{k_{WACC} - g}$$

Tip

The second term on the right-hand side of the equation is the terminal value.

$$Terminal\ Value = [FCF_n(1 + g)]/(k_{WACC} - g)$$

> Be careful with the timing assumptions built in to the constant growth model. The formula gives the present value one period before the cash flow in the numerator. In this example, the cash flow in the numerator is at date $n+1$, so the present value is as of date *n*.

Using these expressions, the value of the firm can be re-expressed as:

EQUATION 17.16

$$V = (PV_{FP} + PV_{TP}) + \$Redundant\ Assets$$

Estimating the Share Price

Figure 17.1 shows that the value of the firm is equal to the value of the debt and equity securities:

EQUATION 17.17

$$V = E + D$$

where *E* is the value of equity and *D* is the value of debt.

The value of equity is given by:

EQUATION 17.18

$$E = V - D$$

D is the market value of debt. In practice, the market value is difficult to obtain. Instead, we use the book value, which is easy to obtain from the balance sheet. This is not an egregious error. Bonds are typically sold at a price equal to the face value and are worth their face value when they mature. Thus, face value (or book value) is not a bad approximation for market value.

To get an estimate of the stock price, *P*, we simply divide the aggregate value of equity, *E*, by the number of shares outstanding.

EQUATION 17.19

$$P = \frac{E}{N}$$

where *N* is the number of shares outstanding.[1]

DCF: An Example

Next we present a DCF valuation of the Grand Trunk Railway. This presentation has four steps. First, we forecast the financial statements. Second, we calculate free cash flow. Third, we calculate the WACC. Fourth, we find the present value of the forecasted free cash flow and estimate a share price.

Forecasting the Financial Statements

Before we present the forecast of the financial statements for Grand Trunk Railway, we present the forecast for CAPEX, depreciation, and net fixed assets. This will simplify the subsequent presentation.

Forecast of CAPEX, Depreciation, and Net Fixed Assets

Selected historical and forecasted values for the Grand Trunk Railway are shown in Table 17.2. The forecast is based on the following assumptions:

1. We assume that the forecast period is 1 year, so we only have to forecast the financial statements for Year 1.
2. We assume that sales will grow by 10% in Year 1.
3. We use the Year 0 ratios for the forecast.

Since these calculations were covered in Section 1 of this chapter, we do not review the details here.

Tip

There is a sequence for doing these calculations: (1) Calculate historical values and ratios. (2) Forecast maintenance CAPEX. (3) Forecast growth CAPEX. (4) Calculate total CAPEX. (5) Forecast Depreciation. (6) Forecast Net Fixed Assets.

TABLE 17.2 Fixed Asset Forecast for Grand Trunk Railway

	Historic		Forecast
	Year –1	**Year 0**	**Year 1**
Sales	$5,652	$6,110	$6,721
Depreciation	463	499	506
Net PP&E	16.723	16,898	17,131
Depreciation Rate, *dr*		0.0287	
Total CAPEX		674.0	739.4
Maintenance CAPEX, mCAPEX		493.8	499.0
Groth CAPEX, gCAPEX		180.2	240.4
Change in Sales		458.0	611
gCAPEX/Change in Sales		0.3934	

Digital Downloads

Grand_Trunk_Railway_F-S.xlsx
https://catalog.flatworldknowledge.com/a/34711/Grand_Trunk_Railway_F_S-5d73.xlsx

Table 17.2 Detailed Calculations

Historical (Year 0):

1. Depreciation Rate (Equation 17.12)

$$dr = Depr_t/(Depr_t + Net_t) = 499/(499 + 16,898) = 0.0287$$

2. Total CAPEX (Equation 17.5)

$$CAPEX_t = Net_t - Net_{t\text{-}1} + Depr_t = 16,898 - 16,723 + 499 = 674$$

3. Maintenance CAPEX (mCAPEX) (Equation 17.6)

$$mCAPEX_t = Net_{t\text{-}1} \times [dr/(1 - dr)] = 17,723 \times [0.0287/(1 - 0.0287)] = \$493.8$$

4. Growth CAPEX (gCAPEX)

$$gCAPEX = CAPEX – mCAPEX = 674 – 493.8 = 180.2$$

5. Growth CAPEX/ΔSales (gx) (Equation 17.7)

$$gx = gCAPEX / \Delta Sales = 180.2/458 = 0.3934$$

Forecast (Year 1):

1. Maintenance CAPEX (mCAPEX) (Equation 17.6)

$$mCAPEX_t = Net_{t\text{-}1} \times [dr/(1 – dr)] = 16,898 \times [0.0287/(1 – 0.0287)] = \$499$$

2. Growth CAPEX (gCAPEX)

$$gCAPEX_t = gx \times \Delta Sales_t = 0.3934 \times (6,721 – 6,110) = 240.4$$

3. Total CAPEX

$$CAPEX = mCAPEX + gCAPEX = 499 + 240.4 = 739.4$$

4. Depreciation (Equation 17.2)

$$Depr_t = dr \times [Net_{t\text{-}1} + CAPEX_t] = 0.0287 \times [16,898 + 739.4] = 506$$

5. Net PP&E (Equation 17.1)

$$Net_t = Net_{t\text{-}1} – Depr + CAPEX_t = 16,898 – 506 + 739.4 = 17,131$$

Explain It: Fixed Asset Forecast for Grand Trunk

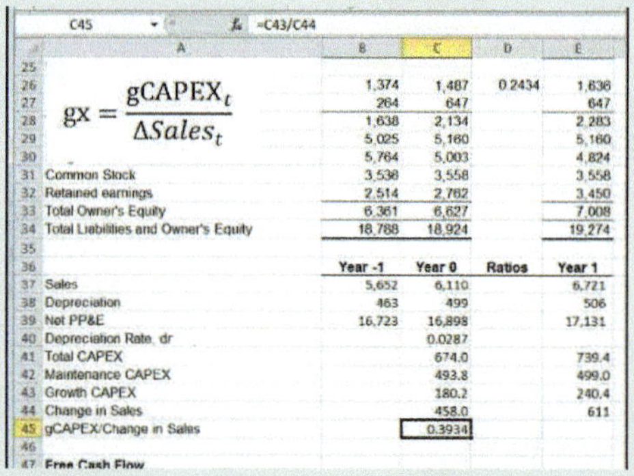
C45 =C43/C44

$$gx = \frac{gCAPEX_t}{\Delta Sales_t}$$

	A	B	C	D	E
25					
26		1,374	1,487	0.2434	1,636
27		264	647		647
28		1,638	2,134		2,283
29		5,025	5,160		5,160
30		5,764	5,003		4,824
31	Common Stock	3,538	3,558		3,558
32	Retained earnings	2,514	2,762		3,450
33	Total Owner's Equity	6,361	6,627		7,008
34	Total Liabilities and Owner's Equity	18,788	18,924		19,274
35					
36		Year -1	Year 0	Ratios	Year 1
37	Sales	5,652	6,110		6,721
38	Depreciation	463	499		506
39	Net PP&E	16,723	16,898		17,131
40	Depreciation Rate, dr		0.0287		
41	Total CAPEX		674.0		739.4
42	Maintenance CAPEX		493.8		499.0
43	Growth CAPEX		180.2		240.4
44	Change in Sales		458.0		611
45	gCAPEX/Change in Sales		0.3934		
46					
47	Free Cash Flow				

View in the online reader

Complete Financial Statement Forecast

TABLE 17.3 Forecast for Grand Trunk Railway

	Year –1	Year 0	Ratios	Year 1
Revenue	$5,652	$6,110		$6,721
COGS	3,823	4,495	0.7357	4,945
Depr	463	499	0.0287	506
EBIT	1,366	1,116		1,271
Interest Expense	247	277	0.0460	260
Pre-Tax Income	1,119	839		1,011
Income Taxes	392	268	0.3194	323
Net Income	727	571		688
ASSETS	**Year –1**	**Year 0**	**Ratios**	**Year 1**
Cash	$53	$25	0.0041	$28
Accounts Receivable	645	722	0.1182	794
Inventory	466	416	0.0681	458
Total Current Assets	1,164	1,163		1,280
Net PP&E	16,723	16,898		17,131
Other Assets	901	863		863
Total Assets	$18,788	$18,924		$19,274
LIABILITIES & OWNERS' EQUITY	**Year –1**	**Year 0**	**Ratios**	**Year 1**
Accounts Payable	$1,374	$1,487	0.2434	$1.636
Short-Term Debt	264	647		647
Total Current Liabilities	$1,638	$2,134		$2,283
Deferred Taxes	5,025	5,160		5,160
Long-Term Debt	5,764	5,003		4,824
Common Shares	3,536	3,558		3,558
Retained Earnings	2,514	2,762		3,450
Total Owners' Equity	$6,361	$6,627		$7,008
Total Liabilities & Owners' Equity	$18,788	$18,294		$19,274

Digital Downloads

Section 17.4 Grand Trunk Railway.xlsx
https://catalog.flatworldknowledge.com/a/34711/Section_17_4_Grand_Trunk_Railway-754d.xlsx

Table 17.3 Detailed Calculations

Historical (Year 0)

1. Tax Rate

$$Tax\ Rate = Income\ Taxes/Income\ before\ Taxes = 268/839 = 0.3194$$

2. Interest Rate

$$Interest\ Rate = Int_t/(Debt_{t\text{-}1}) = 277/(264 + 5,764) = 0.0460$$

Forecast (Year 1):

1. Sales

$$Sales_1 = Sales_0 \times (1.10) = 6,721$$

2. Interest

$$Interest_t = Interest\ Rate \times Debt_0 = 0.0460 \times (647 + 5,003) = 260$$

Explain It: F/S Forecast Grand Trunk Railway

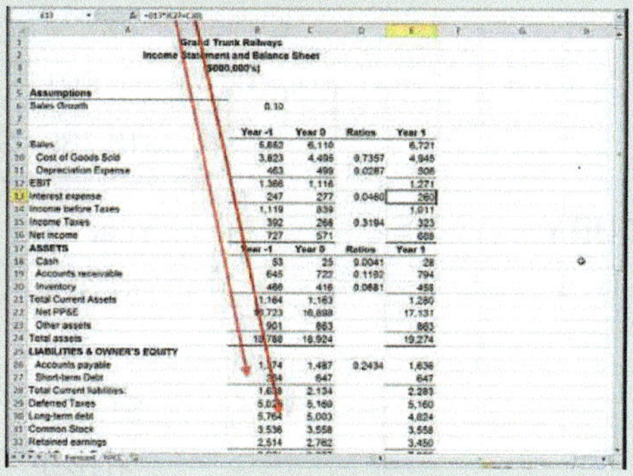

View in the online reader

Forecasting Free Cash Flow

In this example, the forecast period is Year 1. The terminal period commences after Year 1 and continues in perpetuity. See Figure 17.3 for a graphic depiction of the timeline. During the terminal period, we assume that free cash flow grows at a constant rate equal to the growth rate of nominal GDP (2%).

FIGURE 17.3 Timeline for Cash Flow Forecast

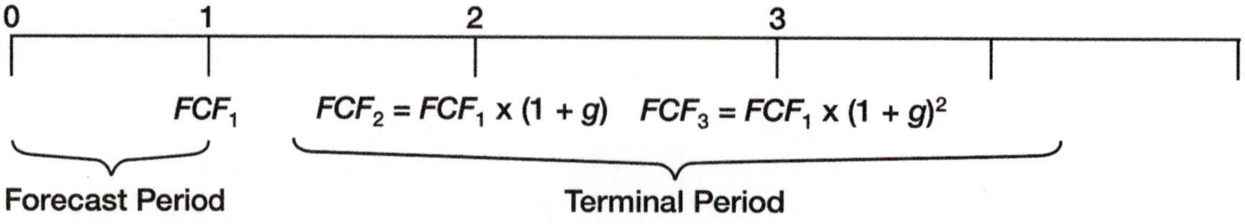

In the next subsections, we calculate free cash flows for Year 1.

Operating Cash Flow for Year 1

The operating cash flows are computed using Equation 17.10, as follows:

$$OCF = EBIT \times (1 - T) + Depreciation$$
$$OCF = 1,271 \times (1 - 0.3194) + 506 = \$1,370.6$$

Investment in Net Working Capital for Year 1

Table 17.4 shows selected financial values for Grand Trunk and net working capital in Years 0 and 1.

TABLE 17.4 Net Working Capital

	Year 0	Year 1
Cash	25	28
Total Current Assets	1,163	1,280
Short-Term Debt	647	647
Total Current Liabilities	2,134	2,283
Net Working Capital	–349	–384

Digital Downloads

Grand_Trunk_Railway_F-S.xlsx
https://catalog.flatworldknowledge.com/a/34711/Grand_Trunk_Railway_F_S-6975.xlsx

Note that net working capital is negative. This is caused by the fact that railways do not have much inventory because of the perishable nature of transportation services. The investment in net working capital is the change in net working capital from Year 0 to Year 1. The net working capital is computed using Equation 17.11.

$$Investment\ NWC = NWC_1 - NWC_0$$
$$= -384 - (-349) = -35$$

Investments in Fixed Assets (CAPEX) for Year 1

In Table 17.2, we forecasted CAPEX to be 739.4.

TABLE 17.5 Free Cash Flow for Year 1

	Year 1
Operating Cash Flow	1,370.6
–Investment in Net Working Capital	–(–34.9)
–CAPEX	–739.4
=Free Cash Flow	666.2

Digital Downloads

Grand_Trunk_Railway_F-S.xlsx
https://catalog.flatworldknowledge.com/a/34711/Grand_Trunk_Railway_F_S-4826.xlsx

Given the long-term growth rate 2%, the timeline for free cash flows is shown in Figure 17.4.

FIGURE 17.4 Timeline for Cash Flow Forecast

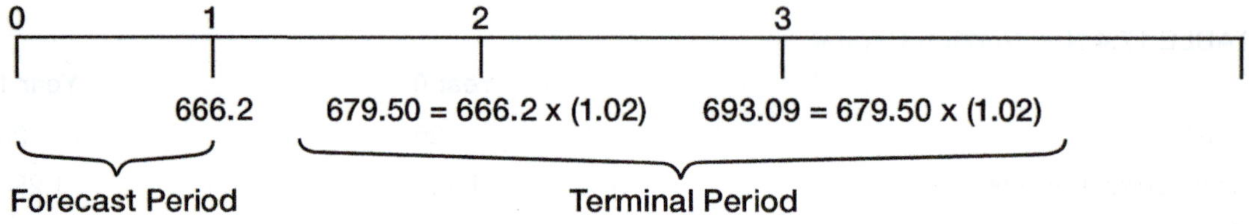

Weighted Average Cost of Capital

Next, we estimate a WACC to discount these free cash flows. Chapter 11 explains the calculation of WACC in detail. Readers should review that chapter if they have any questions. The calculation of WACC is presented in Table 17.6. We use the book value of debt from the Year 0 balance sheet instead of the market value because the corporate bonds are not actively traded, and we assume that the resulting capital structure weights are the company's long-run optimal weights.

TABLE 17.6 WACC for Grand Trunk Railway

Shares Outstanding at Year 0 (millions)	200	Risk-Free rate	3.0%
Share Price	$40	Expected Return on Market	9.5%
Value of Equity, *E*	8,000	Beta	0.95
Book Value of Debt, *D*	5,650	Expected Return on Equity	9.2%
Value of Firm, *V*	13,650	Pretax Cost of Debt	4.6%
Capital Structure Weight for Equity, W_E	0.586	Tax Rate	31.9%
Capital Structure Weight for Debt, W_D	0.414	After-Tax Cost of Debt	3.1%
		WACC	6.67%

Digital Downloads

Table 17.6 WACC for Grand Trunk Railway.xlsx
https://catalog.flatworldknowledge.com/a/34711/Table_17_6_WACC_for_Grand_Trunk_Railway-aa6c.xlsx

Table 17.6 Detailed Calculations

1. Value of Equity, E

   $$E = Price \times Shares\ Outstanding = \$40 \times 200\ million = 8,000\ million$$

2. Book Value of Debt, D

   $$Debt = Short\ Debt + Long\ Debt = 647 + 5,003 = 5,650$$

3. Value of Firm, F

   $$V = E + D = 8,000 + 5,650 = 13,650$$

4. Capital Structure Weight for Equity, w_E

   $$w_E = E/V = 8,000/13,650 = 0.586$$

5. Capital Structure Weight for Debt, w_D

   $$w_D = D/V = 5,650/13,650 = 0.414$$

6. Cost of Equity (from CAPM)

   $$E(k_E) = k_F + B \times [E(k_M) - k_F] = 0.03 + 0.95 \times [0.095 - 0.03] = 0.092$$

7. WACC

   $$WACC = wE \times kE + wD \times kD \times (1 - T)$$
   $$WACC = 0.586 \times 0.092 + 0.414 \times 0.031 = 0.0667 \text{ or } 6.67\%$$

Valuation

There are four steps remaining to estimate a share price for Grand Trunk: (1) calculate the terminal value, (2) discount the free cash flow to Year 0, (3) calculate the value of the equity, and (4) calculate the share price.

Terminal Value

The terminal value is the present value of the free cash flows during the terminal period as of the beginning of the terminal period (Year 1). The terminal period commences at Year 1 and continues in perpetuity. The first cash flow in the terminal period is at Year 2. Because of the assumption of constant growth in perpetuity, we can discount the cash flows using the constant growth dividend model in Equation 17.14:

$$\text{Terminal Value} = \frac{666.2 \times (1.02)}{0.0667 - 0.02} = \$14,544,838 \text{ million}$$

The constant growth model produces a present value one period prior to the first cash flow in the series. Thus, we will have to discount the terminal value by one period to get it to Year 0. Following Equation 17.15, the present value of the Year 1 free cash flow plus the terminal value is the value of the firm.[2]

$$V = (PV_{FP} + PV_{TP}) + \text{Redundant Assets}$$
$$V = \frac{\$666.2}{(1.0667)} + \frac{\$14,544,838}{(1.0667)}$$
$$= \$14,259,645 \text{ million}$$

Following Equation 17.17 the value of the equity is equal to the value of the firm less the value of the debt:

$$\begin{aligned} E = V - D &= 14,259,645 - 5,650 \\ &= 8,609,65 \end{aligned}$$

Our estimate of the fair share price is the total value of equity divided by the number of shares outstanding (200 million), or $43.05. The market price of the shares at Year 0 is $40 per share, so we conclude that the shares of Grand Trunk Railway are slightly undervalued.

17.4 Discounted Cash Flow to Equity

The analyst's goal when using the DCF valuation method is usually to estimate the value of equity (and the fair value of the stock price). You might wonder why we don't estimate the value of equity directly instead of valuing the business first. This section presents the direct approach: the discounted cash flow to equity (DCFE) model. The idea behind the model is simple: discount the cash flows to stockholders at their required return. The cash flow to stockholders is called the free cash flow to equity (FCFE). FCFE is just the part of free cash flow that is available to be paid to stock holders. With the DCFE model, we simply discount the FCFE at the required return of shareholders.

EQUATION 17.20

$$E = \sum_{t=1}^{T} \frac{FCFE_t}{(1 + k_E)^t}$$

where

$$\begin{aligned} E &= \text{the value of equity} \\ FCFE &= \text{Free cash flow to equity} \\ k_E &= \text{the required return of stockholders} \end{aligned}$$

How does the DCFE model compare to the total payout model from Chapter 8? If a company distributes all of the cash flow that it has available via dividends and stock buybacks, then the FCFE model will yield the same estimate of the stock price as the total payout model. However, if a company pays out less than it can, then the total payout model will underestimate the fair value and the FCFE model is more accurate.

This section has four sub-parts. In the first part, we derive a preliminary definition of FCFE from the DCF model under the assumption of no growth. This will help build intuition for the meaning of FCFE. In the second part, we develop a more general definition of FCFE. Finally, we present an example of using the general definition of FCFE and the DCFE model to value the shares of a company given its historic financial statements.

FCFE Definition #1: A No Growth Company

In this section, we derive a basic definition of FCFE and basic version of the DCFE model by valuing the equity in a company that does not grow. We'll relax the no-growth assumption in the next section. Our starting point is the DCF value of the firm. With no growth, the value of the firm is just the present value of the free cash flow perpetuity discounted at the WACC. (We assume that the company is perpetual to make the math simpler.):

$$V = \frac{FCF}{kw}$$

Multiply both sides by the weighted average cost of capital, k_W :

$$V \times kw = FCF$$

Substituting the definition of WACC on the left hand side yields:

$$V\frac{D}{V}k_D(1-T) + V\frac{E}{V}k_E = FCF$$

A little simplification yields the following expression for the value of equity:

$$E = \frac{FCF - D \cdot k_D \cdot (1-T)}{k_E}$$

or

$$E = \frac{FCFE}{k_E}$$

where

EQUATION 17.21

$$FCFE = FCF - D \cdot k_D \cdot (1{-}T)$$

Equation 17.21 is free cash flow to equity (FCFE) for a zero growth firm. It is equal to total free cash flow less the after-tax interest on the debt. The difference is the free cash flow available to be paid to owners.

The main reason for showing this basic definition of FCFE is to make students comfortable with the second term on the right-hand side of Equation 17.21: $D \cdot k_D \cdot (1{-}T)$ is the after-tax interest expense. That is the net cost of interest after taking account of the tax deductibility of interest. The reason it appears in this expression is two-fold. First, FCF is the cash available for all claimholders, not to stockholders alone. So, it shouldn't be surprising that we derive FCFE by subtracting interest from FCF. But you might wonder why the interest expense $D \cdot k_D$ is multiplied by one minus the corporate tax rate $(1{-}T)$. This occurs because of a trick we used in computing the DCF value of the firm. With DCF valuation, when we calculate operating cash flow (OCF), we ignore interest tax deductibility. This means that the estimate of taxes in OCF is too high. We compensate by discounting FCF with a weighted average cost of capital that is based on the after-tax cost of debt—$k_D \cdot (1{-}T)$. The tax deductibility of interest is included in the WACC and not in operating cash flows directly. When valuing equity directly, we incorporate the interest tax shield into the calculation of FCFE because we start with the same definition of OCF as used in DCF valuation and we don't discount that with WACC. Rather, we discount the FCFE with the required return of stockholders.

In summary, the second term in Equation 17.21 is adjusting FCF so it reflects what is available to be paid to stockholders (by subtracting interest) and adjusts the tax calculation in OCF to incorporate interest tax deductibility (which was intentionally not included in that calculation).

Example 17.10 A Basic FCFE Model with No Growth

Borus Entertainment Inc. will generate $100 million of free cash flow at the end of the year. Analysts expect the company to last forever and do not expect the free cash flow to ever change. Borus has debt worth $900.9009 million with an annual coupon (and yield) of 4%. Stockholders require a return of 5.667%. The company has a debt-to-value ratio of 40% and management plans to maintain that ratio. The corporate tax rate is 35%. What is the DCF value of the equity and the DCFE estimate?

SOLUTION

The DCF Approach:

The WACC for Borus is:

$$k_W = (D/V)k_D(1{-}T) + (E/V)k_E = 0.4 \times 0.04 \times (1{-}0.35) + 0.6 \times 0.05667 = 0.04444$$

The DCF value of Borus is:

$$V = FCF/k_W = 100/0.044 = \$2,252.252$$

The value of the equity is: $E = V - D = \$2,252.252 - 900.9009 = 1,351.351$

The FCFE Approach:

$$E = FCFE/k_E = [FCF - Dk_D(1-T)]/k_E$$
$$E = [\$100 - \$900.9009 \times (1 - 0.35) \times 0.04]/0.05667$$
$$E = \$1,351.351$$

FCFE Definition #2

For a company whose cash flows grow, the discounted cash flow value of equity is still given by Equation 17.20, but the definition of FCFE becomes a little more complicated. In particular, we have to allow for the likelihood that the company will repay some debt (or borrow more). Debt repayments reduce the cash available to be paid to shareholders, but new borrowing increases FCFE, all else remaining equal. With changes in debt, the definition of FCFE is:

EQUATION 17.22

$$FCFE = FCF{-}D \cdot k_D \cdot (1{-}T) + \Delta D$$

where

$$\Delta D = \textit{Net new debt} = \textit{New borrowing} - \textit{Debt repayment}$$

We will prove that Equation 17.22 is correct by example. We will show that the DCF value of the equity ($E = V{-}D$) is the same as the DCFE value using Equation 17.22.

Example 17.11 The DCFE Model with FCFE Definition #2

Illicit Pharmaceuticals Inc. is expected to generate free cash flow of $300 million at the end of the year. Analysts expect Illicit's cash flows to grow in perpetuity at the rate of 2.5%. Illicit has debt worth $1.619 billion. The annual coupon rate is 8% and the yield on the bonds is also 8%. Illicit's debt-to-value ratio is 40% and management plan to maintain that ratio in perpetuity. Illicit's stockholders require a return of 13%. There are 250 million shares outstanding. The tax rate is 34%. What is the DCF estimate of the value of the equity and what is the DCFE estimate?

SOLUTION

The DCF Approach:

The WACC for Illicit is:

$$k_W = (D/V)k_D(1{-}T) + (E/V)k_E = 0.4 \times 0.08 \times (1{-}0.34) + 0.6 \times 0.13 = 0.099$$

The DCF value of Illicit is (using the constant growth model):

$$V_0 = \frac{FCF_1}{k_W - g} = \frac{300}{0.099 - 0.025} = \$4,047M$$

The DCF value of the equity is (at $t = 0$).

$$E = V - D = 4,047 - 1,619 = \$2,428$$

The FCFE Approach:

To use the DCFE method we need to know net new debt in the first year. Since the company's cash flows are growing, so is its value. Since its capital structure policy is to maintain debt at 40% of value, the debt will grow each year as the company's value grows. We can solve for the amount of debt at Year 1 by taking 40% of the value of the company at Year 1.

$$D_1 = 0.4 \times V_1 = 0.4 \times FCF_2/(kw - g)$$
$$= 0.4 \times (\$300 \times (1.025))/(0.099 - 0.025) = 0.4 \times \$4,149 = \$1,659$$

This represents an increase of \$40 million compared to the debt outstanding at year 0. In other words, net new debt (ΔD) is \$40 million.

Now we can calculate the free cash flow to equity in year 1 and the DCFE.

$$FCFE_1 = FCF_1 - Dk_D(1-T) + \Delta D = \$308 - 0.08 \times (1-0.34) \times 1,619 + 40 = \$254.99$$

Using the direct approach, the value of the equity is:

$$E_0 = FCFE_1/(k_E - g) = \$254.99/(0.13 - 0.025) = \$2,428$$

Tip

Notice that we assumed a capital structure policy of maintaining a fixed debt-to-value ratio and that we used this policy to calculate the amount of debt. This capital structure policy assumption is implicit in the WACC/DCF valuation method, because we use fixed capital structure weights to discount the cash flows.

Different finance textbooks provide expressions for FCFE that differ from Equation 17.22. We'll explain some of the variants next.

First, let's express the definition of free cash flow in Table 17.1 as an equation:

$$FCF = OCF - Investments\ in\ NWC - Investments\ in\ fixed\ assets$$

Next, let's substitute in the expression for OCF from Equation 17.11.

$$FCF = EBIT \times (1-T) + Depr - Investments\ in\ NWC - Investments\ in\ fixed\ assets$$

Next, we recognize that the Investment in net working capital is the change in NWC (ΔNWC) and the investment in fixed assets is denoted CAPEX. Inserting these variable names yields the following expression for FCF:

$$FCF = EBIT \times (1-T) + Depr - \Delta NWC - CAPEX$$

Substitute the right-had side of the above expression for FCF in Equation 17.22:

EQUATION 17.23

$$FCFE = EBIT \times (1-T) + Depreciation - \Delta NWC - CAPEX - \$Interest(1-T) + \Delta D$$

where

$\$Interest \cdot (1{-}T) = D \cdot k_D \cdot (1{-}T)$

In other words, the interest expense on the income statement can be expressed as the product of the cost of debt times the amount of debt ($\$Int = k_D D$). We can re-arrange this as follows:

$$FCFE = [EBIT - \$Int] \times (1 - T) + Depr - \Delta NWC - CAPEX + \Delta D$$

The first term is simply net income (NI), so:

EQUATION 17.24

$$FCFE = NI + Depr - \Delta NWC - CAPEX + \Delta D$$

Many textbooks (for example, in the CFA curriculum) assume that the amount of CAPEX is equal to depreciation (i.e., $CAPEX = Depr$), so Equation 17.24 simplifies further to:

$$FCFE = NI - \Delta NWC + \Delta D$$

The assumption that CAPEX equals the depreciation expense is a simplifying assumption. Let's explore its meaning. Companies that don't grow still have CAPEX: they replace equipment as it wears out. This is called Maintenance CAPEX. Maintenance Capex is usually defined as the amount of CAPEX that will maintain net fixed assets constant over time. The amount that achieves this, following Equation 17.1, is $CAPEX = Depreciation$. Thus, when analysts assume that CAPEX equals depreciation, they are assuming that the company invests in only maintenance CAPEX and not growth CAPEX. This is really only appropriate for non-growing companies.

FCFE and the DCFE Model: An Example

Now that we have an expression for FCFE (Equation 17.24), we will show an example of how it is used to estimate the fair value of the stock. We will put ourselves in the position of an analyst who has two years of financial statements data and who wants to use that to estimate the fair value of the stock price. We'll present two examples: the first calculates FCFE from the historic financial statements, and the second inserts that estimate into the DCFE model to calculate the fair value of the shares.

Example 17.12 Calculating FCFE

What is free cash flow to equity in Year 2 for Eatmore Food Inc.?

Digital Downloads

Example 17.12 Calculating FCFE.xlsx
https://catalog.flatworldknowledge.com/a/34711/Example_17_12_Calculating_FCFE-7d2c.xlsx

Financial Statements Eatmore Food, Inc.		
	Year 1	**Year 2**
Revenue	$27,801	$29,210
Cost of Goods Sold		22,152
SG&A		5,245
Depreciation		621
EBIT		1,192
Interest		277
Earnings Before Taxes		915
Income Taxes		288
Net Income		$627
ASSETS		
Current Assets	**Year 1**	**Year 2**
Cash	$920	$1,467
Accounts Receivable	656	649
Inventories	2,125	2,269
Total Current Assets	3,701	4,385
Net Fixed Assets	9,372	9,637
Goodwill	688	678
Total Assets	$13,761	$14,700
LIABILITIES AND OWNERS' EQUITY		
Current Liabilities		
Short-Term Debt	$627	$715
Accounts Payable	2,535	2,936
Total Current Liabilities	3,162	3,651
Long-Term Debt	4,194	4,208
Other Liabilities	519	560
Total Liabilities	7,875	8,419
Common Stock	1,192	1,192
Retained Earnings	4,694	5,089
Total Owners' Equity	5,886	6,281
Liabilities & Owners' Equity	$13,761	$14,700

SOLUTION

These values are rounded to units for efficient exposition. For detailed calculations, open the accompanying spreadsheet.

Step 1: ΔNWC

$$\Delta NWC = NWC_2 - NWC_1 = -18 - 246 = -264$$

Step 2: CAPEX

Investments in fixed assets (from Equation 17.5):

$$CAPEX_2 = Net_2 - Net_1 + Depr_2 = 9,637 - 9,372 + 621 = 886$$

Step 3: ΔD

Net new debt is total debt (short- and long-term) in Year 2 less total debt in Year 1:

$$\Delta D = Debt_2 - Debt_1 = (4,208 + 715) - (4,194 + 627) = \$102$$

Step 4: FCFE (from Equation 17.23)

$$FCFE = NI + Depr. - \Delta NWC - CAPEX + \Delta D$$
$$FCFE = \$627 + 621 - (-246) - 886 + 102 = \$728$$

Tip

You may have noted that our definition of FCFE excludes changes in long-term liabilities that aren't debt (e.g., other liabilities). This omission is intentional. Our presumption is that if the analyst were to forecast the financial statements in order to compute FCFE, she would hold those accounts constant in dollar terms. Thus, omitting them in the computation of past FCFE provides the best estimate of future FCFE.

Example 17.13 DCFE for Eatmore Foods Inc.

What is the DCFE estimate of the fair price for shares of Eatmore Food Inc.?

Assume that Eatmore Food Inc. has 274.1 million shares outstanding currently (end of Year 2) and that its shareholders require a return of 9.6%. Analysts expect Eatmore's cash flows to grow at 2% in perpetuity. Cash flows are generated at the end of each year. Today is the first day of Year 3.

SOLUTION

The fair value of the equity today is the present value of FCFE:

$$E_2 = FCFE_2(1 + g)/(k_E - g)$$
$$E_2 = \$728 \times (1.02)/(0.096 - 0.02) = \$9.770.53$$

The stock price is:

$$P = \$9,770.53/241.1 = \$35.65$$

In "Example 17.13 DCFE for Eatmore Foods Inc." we assumed constant growth. This was for ease of exposition. Any pattern of growth can be used: two stage growth or three stage growth. It depends on the age of the company and the position of its products in their product life cycle. An example of two stage growth (e.g. Supernormal growth) is provided in Chapter 8 in the treatment of the dividend discount model.

Endnotes

1. We are assuming that the company has no preferred shares and only one class of common shares.
2. We are assuming there are no redundant assets.

CHAPTER 18

Futures and Options

Learning Objectives

By the end of this chapter you will be able to:

1. Understand the basics of forward contracts.
2. Understand futures contracts, how futures are traded, and the payoffs to futures contracts.
3. Describe how futures are used to hedge price risk.
4. Understand option contracts and how options are traded.
5. Understand the payoffs and profits to options contracts.
6. Understand intrinsic value and time value.

Futures and options are **derivative contracts**. The term "derivative" is used because the price of a future or option is *derived* from the price (level) of an underlying asset (variable). "Explain It: Derivative Markets and Products" presents an overview of the derivatives, markets, and some of the assets (variables) underlying Chicago Mercantile Exchange futures and options contracts.

derivative contract

A financial contract whose value depends on, or is "derived" from, an underlying asset or security.

Explain It: Derivative Markets and Products

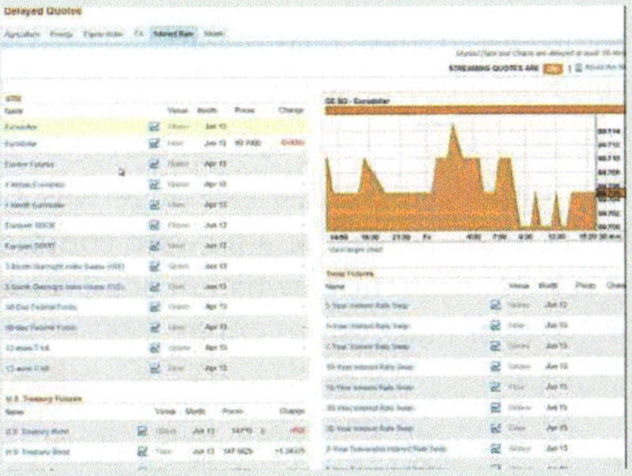

View in the online reader

In this chapter, we introduce derivatives as tools that companies use to reduce price risk. An action that reduces price risk is called a *hedge*. We focus here on hedging with derivatives. An action that increases price risk is called *speculating*. Speculators accept price risk in the hope of making a profit. The derivatives markets are a place where hedgers pass their price risk off to speculators.

Tip

This is a generalization. Not every derivatives trade features a hedger on one side and a speculator on the other. It is possible to have two hedgers on either side of a trade or two speculators.

"Explain It: Hedging Price Risk with Derivatives" provides a simple example of a business using a derivative (a futures contract) to hedge a price risk. Watch the video with the goal of understanding the price risk experienced by a company and the way that a derivative contract can offset it.

Explain It: Hedging Price Risk with Derivatives

View in the online reader

forward contracts

A forward contract is a modification of a spot contract where the price, quantity and quality of the good to be exchanged are agreed on at initiation, but the exchange of the goods for money occurs at a later date.

Chicago Board of Trade (CBOT)

The Chicago Board of Trade (CBOT) is a derivatives market. It is part of the CME Group. The CBOT trades a variety of futures and options contracts. The CBOT is one of the world's oldest derivatives markets, established in 1848. In 2007, the CBOT and CME (Chicago Mercantile Exchange) merged to form the CME group.

Commodities have been traded for money since at least the fifth century b.c. in ancient Greece. **Forward contracts** are known to have been used in rice markets in 17th-century Japan and may have been used even earlier.

In North America, the first organized futures exchange was the **Chicago Board of Trade (CBOT)** created in 1848. In 1851, there are records of a forward contract for corn. The forward contract provided a guarantee of price and quantity, which made it easier for eastern merchants to arrange financing for bulk purchases of Midwestern grains.

Tip

The word "contract" is important. A forward is not a security like a stock or a bond. It has no intrinsic value. If you found a forward contract lying on the sidewalk, you couldn't sell it to anyone.

In 1865, the CBOT formalized grain trading by developing standardized agreements called **futures contracts**. Futures contracts were standardized (by the exchange) in terms of quantity, quality, delivery month, and terms. The only thing left to negotiate was price. The contracts could be traded at the CBOT during designated trading hours. The exchange publicized the bids and offers as well as negotiated prices of the trades. Unlike forward contracts, an active secondary market for standardized futures contracts grew quickly.

futures contracts

A futures contract is an institutionalized version of a forward contract. Futures differ from forwards in that they are standardized, traded on exchanges, feature a clearinghouse, and involve margin and daily resettlement.

In the first section of this chapter, we describe first the forward contract (since it is the simpler precursor), and then focus on futures, which are much more common. In the second half of the chapter we explain the basics of options contracts.

18.1 Forward Contracts

The Elements of a Forward Contract

A **spot contract** is an agreement between a buyer and a seller to exchange a commodity (security or currency) immediately. In a spot market exchange, the terms of the exchange are agreed upon and the goods and money are exchanged immediately.

spot contract

An agreement between a buyer and seller to exchange goods for money immediately.

Tip

Actually, in a spot contract the exchange of money and goods occurs on the spot date, which is normally two business days after the trade date. The spot date is also called a *settlement date*. The consummation of the agreement is called *settlement*. The two-day lag between trade and settlement is known as the *settlement delay*.

The agreed-upon price in a spot contract is called the **spot price**.

spot price

The price agreed to in a spot contract.

maturity date

For a bond, the date on which the principal is required to be repaid. For futures and options contracts, the day that trading terminates—also known as the expiration date.

buyer

The counterparty in a spot, forward, futures, or options contract who agrees to pay a price and take delivery of the (underlying) asset. See also long position, owner, or holder.

seller

The counterparty in a spot, forward, futures, or options contract who agrees to receive the price and deliver the (underlying) asset. See also Short Position.

forward price

The price in a forward contract which the buyer agrees to pay when she takes delivery of the underlying asset (and the seller agrees to accept).

A forward contract differs from a spot contract in regard to the timing of the physical exchange of goods for money. With a forward contract, the terms of the exchange are agreed upon now, but the exchange of goods for money occurs at a specified date in the future—the **maturity date**. Like a spot contract, a forward is a contract between two parties: the **buyer** and the **seller**. The buyer agrees to buy the asset on the maturity date and the seller agrees to deliver the asset on that date. The price, or **forward price**, and quantity are agreed to when the contract is struck. The asset and payment are exchanged on the maturity date. The rights and obligations of the buyer and seller are summarized in Table 18.1.

TABLE 18.1 Rights and Obligations of Buyers and Sellers in a Forward Contract

Buyer (Long Position)	Seller (Short Position)
Pays price and Has OBLIGATION to BUY	Receives price and Has OBLIGATION to SELL
an underlying asset on the maturity date.	

A common example of a forward contract is when you place a pizza delivery order. The terms of the deal (price, quantity and contract specifics—e.g., anchovies) are negotiated when you make the telephone (or online) order. Money and goods are exchanged at maturity, when the pizza is delivered. You are the long side of the pizza forward contract, since you agree to take delivery of the pizza and pay. The pizza company is the short side of the contract since it agrees to deliver the pizza and receive the money.

Tip

One example of the spot market for pizza is Little Caesars, which advertises its "Hot and Ready" pizzas that are ready for immediate purchase and pick-up.

Forward contracts are negotiated privately. The contract terms are customized to satisfy the needs of the counterparties. There is no central exchange for forward contracts—contracts are negotiated through an international network of large banks and brokers who communicate electronically and by telephone. There is no secondary market for forward contracts. The only way to complete a forward contract is to follow through with the purchase/sale.

Forward Contract Example: Foreign Currency

currency contract

A contract to exchange one currency for another at an agreed rate of exchange. Can be spot or forward.

The most common type of forward contract is a **currency contract**. Consider the problem potentially faced by a large multinational, such as the Ford Motor Company. It generates sizable Canadian-dollar profits from its sale of cars and trucks in Canada and it needs to convert those to its home currency, U.S. dollars. Assume that Ford anticipates having CDN$10,000,000 of profit from sales at the end of the next quarter, in 3 months' time. Ford has two choices: It can wait until the end of the quarter and exchange the Canadian dollars for U.S. dollars at the then-prevailing spot exchange rate, or it can lock in the exchange rate now with a forward contract.

If it chooses to enter a forward agreement, then it will approach a bank, the typical counterparty in a currency forward contract, to sell the Canadian dollars and buy U.S. dollars. For example, Ford might contract to give the bank CDN$10,000,000 in exchange for USD$8,500,000 in 3 months' time. The forward exchange rate is 0.85 $USD/$CDN.

Hedging and Speculating

Ford will enter the forward contract rather than wait and use the spot market because it fears that the spot rate will be lower than 0.85 $USD/$CDN at the end of the quarter. This strategy is called a hedge transaction. A hedge is a transaction that reduces the risk (harm) associated with an adverse price movement in a commodity (security or currency). The alternative to hedging is **speculation**. A speculative transaction accepts the risk of adverse price changes in exchange for the opportunity to profit. Speculators trade an asset in the hope of profiting from anticipated price changes.

speculation

Speculation involves the acceptance of risk in exchange for the opportunity to profit. Speculators trade an asset in the hope of profiting from anticipated price changes.

18.2 Futures Contracts

The Elements of a Futures Contract

A futures contract is similar to a forward contract. Two important differences are that futures contracts are traded on an exchange and the terms of the contract are not privately negotiated. The terms of the futures contract (quantity, type of asset, and maturity date) are set by the exchange and cannot be changed by the counterparties. The only element negotiated by the counterparties is the price.

For example, the **Chicago Mercantile Exchange's (CME)** SRW wheat contract calls for the delivery of 5,000 bushels of soft red winter wheat. The short side of the contract (seller) has an option as to which type of wheat to deliver. The price is quoted in cents and quarter-cents per bushel with a **minimum tick size** of a quarter-cent per bushel (see the "Explain It" box for a description of the pricing convention).

Chicago Mercantile Exchange (CME)

A futures and options exchange in Chicago. The CME group owns the CME, the Chicago Board of Trade, and the New York Mercantile Exchange (NYMEX). The CME has both floor trading using open outcry and an electronic trading platform called CME Globex.

minimum tick size

The minimum boundary for the change of a futures or options price. Set by the exchange.

Explain It

The exchange uses a four-digit price quote, for example, 7350. The first three digits are cents per bushel; the fourth digit is 1/8 cent/bushel. Thus,

$$7350 = \$7.35/\text{bushel}$$
$$7352 = \$7.3525$$
$$7354 = \$7.3550$$
$$7356 = \$7.3575$$

Notice that last digit only takes the values 0, 2, 4, and 6. This is because the minimum price change for this contract is 1/4 of a cent.

There are five fixed maturity dates through the year: July, September, December, March, and May. The last trading day for each contract is the business day prior to the 15th calendar day of the month. The last delivery day (for the short side) is the 7th business day following the last trading day of the delivery month. Delivery is completed when the seller gets the wheat to an approved warehouse in the Chicago Switching District. Figure 18.1 presents a screen shot from the CME website showing prices for wheat futures.

FIGURE 18.1 Wheat Futures Price Quote

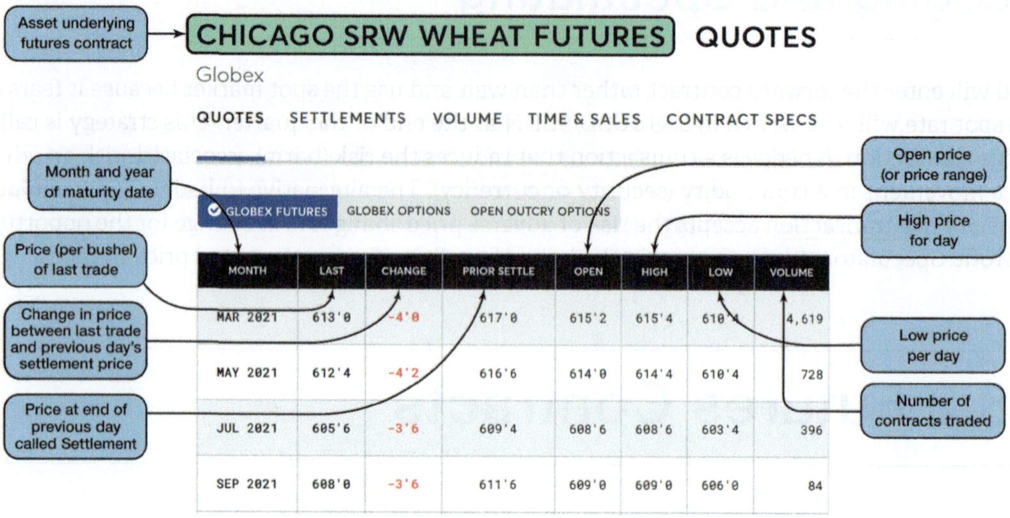

MONTH	LAST	CHANGE	PRIOR SETTLE	OPEN	HIGH	LOW	VOLUME
MAR 2021	613'0	-4'0	617'0	615'2	615'4	610'4	4,619
MAY 2021	612'4	-4'2	616'6	614'0	614'4	610'4	728
JUL 2021	605'6	-3'6	609'4	608'6	608'6	603'4	396
SEP 2021	608'0	-3'6	611'6	609'0	609'0	606'0	84

Futures Trading

open outcry

An auction method used to trade stocks, futures or options. The dominant trading method at the CBOT and CME until the mid-1990s. The CME group ended open outcry trading in 2015.

Most derivative contracts are traded on computer trading platforms, but some exchanges, like the CME, still operate a trading floor. At the time of writing, less than 3% of the CME's volume occurs on the floor and the remaining volume is traded on computer trading systems. The trading system used on the floor is called **open outcry**. It is fascinating to watch and is shown in a film called *Trading Places.*

Tip

Trading Places is a comedy that involves futures trading. It is worth watching.

Initiating a Futures Trade: Margin/ Performance Bond

Assume that you think wheat prices are going to rise and you want to speculate on that expectation. You place an order with your broker to buy one wheat contract at the market. Each contract is for 5,000 bushels, or 5,000bu. Let's say the order goes through on May 3 and one September contract is purchased at a price of **705'4**/bu (or $7.055/bu). You are now obliged to buy 5,000bu of wheat in mid-September for a total cost of $\$7.055 \times 5,000 = \$35,275$.

You do not have to have that much money when you place the order. Your broker will require you to create an account and to deposit in that account a performance bond (aka initial margin) equal to between 5% and 10% of the value of the position. For the wheat contract, the performance bond (initial margin) is $3,240. In turn, your broker maintains an account with the exchange's clearinghouse.

The Clearinghouse

An important feature of exchange-traded futures contracts is the **clearinghouse**. After a trade is consummated on the exchange floor (or electronically), both counterparties deal only with the clearinghouse. The clearinghouse interposes itself in each trade—a process called **novation**. The clearinghouse becomes the counterparty to each trader, as shown in Figure 18.2. The left-hand panel shows the trade, and the right-hand panel shows each trader's relationship with the clearinghouse after the trade.

clearinghouse

A clearinghouse works hand-in-hand with futures and options exchanges. The clearinghouse guarantees performance by inserting itself into every completed contract. It is the buyer for every seller and the seller for every buyer. The clearinghouse is also the central bank equivalent in the daily resettlement process. It debits the accounts of losers and credits the accounts of winners.

novation

The substitution of a new contract in place of an old one.

FIGURE 18.2 The Role of the Clearinghouse in Futures Markets

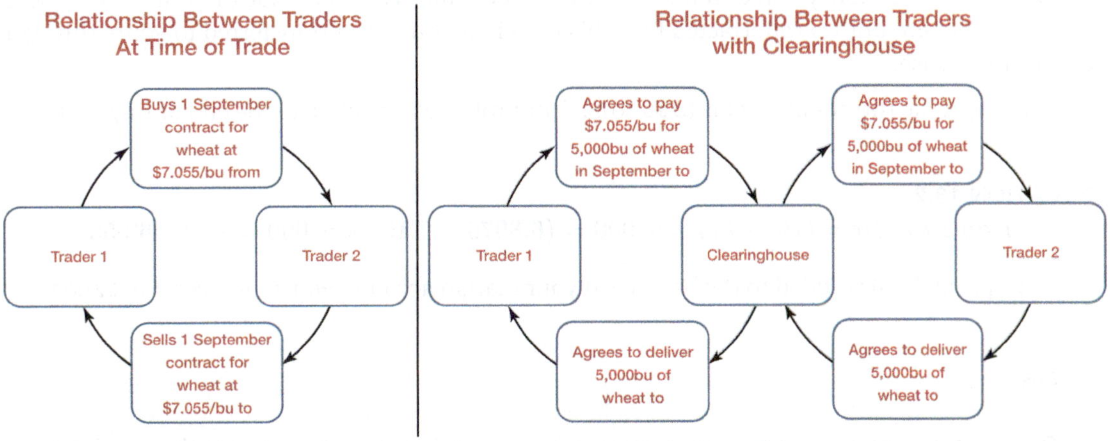

The clearinghouse serves as a guarantor, ensuring that the obligations of all traders are met and that no trader is hurt by a counterparty that reneges on an obligation. Since each trade starts with one buyer and one seller, there are as many buyers as there are sellers and the clearinghouse has no net exposure.

Let's assume that the wheat futures trade discussed above is the first trade for each trader. Each trader posts a performance bond with his or her broker. Each day after the trade, the clearinghouse tracks the details of each trade and calculates daily profits and losses. The clearinghouse credits the accounts of those who profit and debits the accounts of losers. Again, since futures trading is zero sum, the clearinghouse has no net exposure. In turn, the brokers credit and debit their clients' accounts. This process is called **marking-to-market** (or daily resettlement) and is described in the next section.

marking-to-market

The calculation and attribution of daily trading profits. At the end of each trading day, the clearinghouse will transfer money from the accounts of losers to the accounts of winners.

Daily Marking-to-Market

Each day, the clearinghouse credits gains and debits losses to each trader's account. This process is called marking-to-market.

settlement price

In derivative markets, the settlement price is the price used for daily marking-to-market. It is calculated as a volume-weighted average price over a short period at the end of the day. The calculation varies across exchanges and instruments.

Think about our wheat example. At the end of the first day of trading, assume that the **settlement price** for the wheat futures contract is $7.10. You have a long position, so you profit from the increase. Your gain is the difference between the settlement price and your purchase price ($7.055) multiplied by the number of bushels. The gain is calculated as if you have closed the position and sold the wheat at the settlement price. In a long position, the forward price when the contract is initiated is your purchase price.

EQUATION 18.1

$$\textit{Day 1 Profit} = (P_1 - P_0) \times 5,000 = (7.10 - 7.055) \times 5,000 = \$225$$

This gain is added to the balance in your margin account (the performance bond), so the account rises to $3,465.

Where did the money come from? Futures are zero sum. The short side of your contract lost $225, and that amount was subtracted from his margin account and transferred to yours through the clearinghouse.

On Day 2, the futures price falls to $6.8075. Your profit (loss) relative to the end of Day 1 is given by:

EQUATION 18.2

$$\textit{Day 2 Profit} = (P_2 - P_1) \times 5,000 = (6.8075 - 7.10) \times 5,000 = -\$1,462.50$$

This profit (loss) is added to the balance in your margin account, which reduces it to $2,002.50.

Tip

P_0 is the futures price when the long position is initiated. It is like the purchase price in a simple buy/sell transaction. The cumulative profit for a short position is the opposite: $(P_0 - P_2) \times 5,000$. For a short position, P_0 is the sale price.

Your cumulative profit is the sum of the two daily profits:

EQUATION 18.3

$$\textit{Cumulative Profit Day 2} = (P_2 - P_0) \times 5,000 = (6.8075 - 7.055) \times 5,000 = -\$1,237.50$$

Explain It: The Clearinghouse and Marking to Market

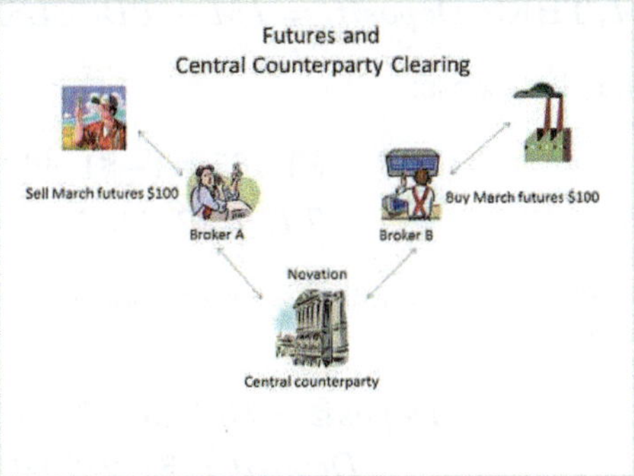

View in the online reader

Maintenance Margin

In the last example your account balance falls through a critical threshold called the **maintenance margin** level. The maintenance margin level for your wheat futures contracts is $2,400.

maintenance margin

Minimum maintenance margin levels are set by the exchange and vary across contracts and over time.

Tip

The exchange publishes the maintenance margin levels for all contracts.

When your account balance falls below the maintenance margin level, you are given a **margin call**. You have a choice of whether or not to respond to the margin call. If you respond, then you must deposit more money to the margin account. The amount deposited must bring the balance back to the initial margin level. In this case, you must deposit $1,237.50 in the margin account. The method for calculating the deposit is explained in the following Explain It box.

margin call

A message from a securities broker to a client requiring that the client either liquidate a security or add cash to the trading account. Occurs when the value in the account falls below the maintenance margin level.

Explain It

Margin Account Balance, *B*, on Day *t* is:

$$B_t = B_{t-1} + \boldsymbol{Daily\ Profit_t} + \boldsymbol{Deposit_t}$$

The Deposit on any day *t* depends on whether the daily profit, on its own, pushed the account balance below the maintenance margin (MM) level. If the balance falls through MM, then the deposit is the amount necessary to bring the account back to the initial margin (IM) level.

First calculate the temporary balance (TB) without any deposit:

$$TB_t = Balance_{t-1} + Daily\ Profit_t$$

If the temporary balance is above the maintenance margin level, then there is no deposit. If the temporary balance is (equal to or) below the maintenance margin level, then the deposit is:

$$Deposit_t = IM - TB_t$$

The following IF statement determines the size of the deposit:

$$\text{IF } TB_t <= MM, \text{THEN } Deposit_t = IM - TB_t \text{ ELSE } Deposit_t = 0$$

In this example, the temporary balance is:

$$TB = \$3,465 + (-\$1,462.50)$$
$$TB = \$2,002.50$$

The maintenance margin level is $2,400, which is larger than the temporary balance, so the trader must deposit into the account.

$$Deposit = \$3,240 - \$2,002.50$$
$$Deposit = \$1,237.50$$

If the margin call is not heeded, then the broker will close out the position. The margin call, in conjunction with the initial margin requirement and daily marking-to-market, protects brokers from losses in the event a client reneges on a futures position after an adverse price change.

Explain It: Marking to Market Explore It

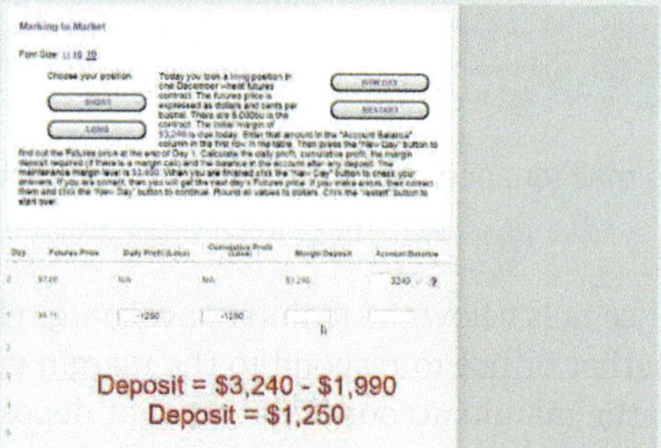

View in the online reader

Completing a Futures Trade

The most obvious way to complete a futures trade is to make or take delivery of the underlying asset.

Tip

With physical delivery, the buyer will pay the seller the futures price prevailing at maturity and once goods and payments are exchanged, then the clearinghouse will release the margin accounts of both parties. Thus, both parties realize their gains or losses through their margin accounts.

However, the clearinghouse provides a second way to complete a futures trade: through an **offset (reversing) trade**. It may surprise you to learn that fewer than 1% of all contracts are completed with physical delivery.

offset (reversing) trade
The elimination of a long or short position by executing a trade in the opposite direction.

Consider our wheat example. In May, you took a long position in one wheat contract for September delivery. The futures price when you initiated the long position was $7.055/bu. Let's say that the futures price of wheat for September delivery rises to $7.25/bu by August 25 and you want to close out the position and take your gains. Your cumulative profit on the long position is $925. The balance in your margin account will be the sum of your margin contributions and this profit.

How do you get out of the contract in the middle of its life? The answer is with an offset trade. Since you are long one September contract, you do the opposite: you sell one September contract. Afterward, the clearinghouse ignores you and you have no delivery obligations. Your position is closed and you get to keep the accumulated gain in the account. This is equivalent to selling a share after you have gone long.

To understand why the clearinghouse ignores you, think about its obligations vis-à-vis each trader, as shown in Table 18.2. In your first trade you went long wheat futures and agreed to take delivery in September. Let's call the short side of that contract Trader 2. Trader 2 agreed to deliver wheat in September. These obligations are shown in the middle column. In August you entered a new contract on the short side; you agreed to deliver wheat in September. Let's assume that you traded with a new counterparty, Trader 3.

TABLE 18.2 Obligations of Futures Traders to Clearinghouse

	Obligation to Clearinghouse	Clearinghouse's Action
Trader 1	1. Take delivery of 5,000bu of wheat in September. 2. Deliver 5,000bu of wheat in September.	Nothing
Trader 2	Deliver 5,000bu of wheat in September.	Pair Trader 2 with Trader 3
Trader 3	Take delivery of 5,000bu of wheat in September.	

You have an obligation to deliver wheat to the clearinghouse under your short position, but you have an obligation to take delivery of wheat from the clearinghouse under your long position. That is a lot of work for nothing. Thus, the clearinghouse waives your obligations. As shown in the right-hand column, it takes no action with you; you are irrelevant. Trader 2 still has an open obligation to deliver wheat to the clearinghouse and Trader 3 still has an open obligation to take delivery of wheat. The clearinghouse will simply give Trader 2's wheat to Trader 3. The clearinghouse has no net exposure at the end of the matching process.

The offset trade and the role of the clearinghouse in making it possible are explained in the following video.

The Clearinghouse and the Offset Trade

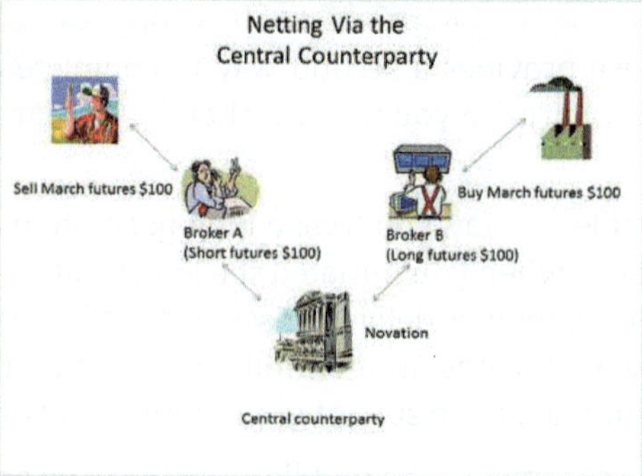

View in the online reader

The Differences Between Forward and Futures Contracts

1. Forward contracts are customized. Futures contracts are standardized.
2. Forward contracts are traded in a dealer (over-the-counter) market. Futures contracts are traded in an auction market.
3. Forward contracts can only be completed by making or taking delivery. Futures contracts can also be completed through an offset (reversing) trade.
4. Forward contracts are settled on the maturity date. Futures contracts have daily marking-to-market.

18.3 Hedging with Futures Contracts

To explain how companies hedge with futures, we first need to explain two concepts: basis and convergence.

Basis

Basis is the spot price minus the futures price for the same asset.

EQUATION 18.4

$$Basis = Spot\ Price - Futures\ Price$$

The spot price varies by location, and so does the basis. For example, the price of No. 2 Soft Red Wheat is probably not the same in Toledo as it is in Chicago.

Tip

The prices will vary because of different supply-and-demand conditions in each location and because transportation costs eliminate the profits from trying to arbitrage any difference in prices.

The basis also varies across different futures contract maturity dates. For simplicity, think of one location and one futures contract. For commodities like wheat that are costly to store, the basis is negative.[1] That is, the futures price is bigger than the spot price.

Convergence

Figure 18.3 graphs the spot and futures prices for a wheat futures contract over time. The basis is the difference between the two lines. Notice that the basis declines as the maturity date nears. This is a property of futures called convergence. The futures price gets closer and closer to the spot price as the maturity date approaches. The reason for this is simple: If a trader buys a futures contract on the maturity date and does not offset, then she will take delivery of the underlying asset almost immediately. In respect of the delivery time, the futures contract (on its maturity date) is equivalent to a spot contract. By the law of one price, the futures price must equal the spot price (the basis is zero) on the maturity date.

FIGURE 18.3 Convergence

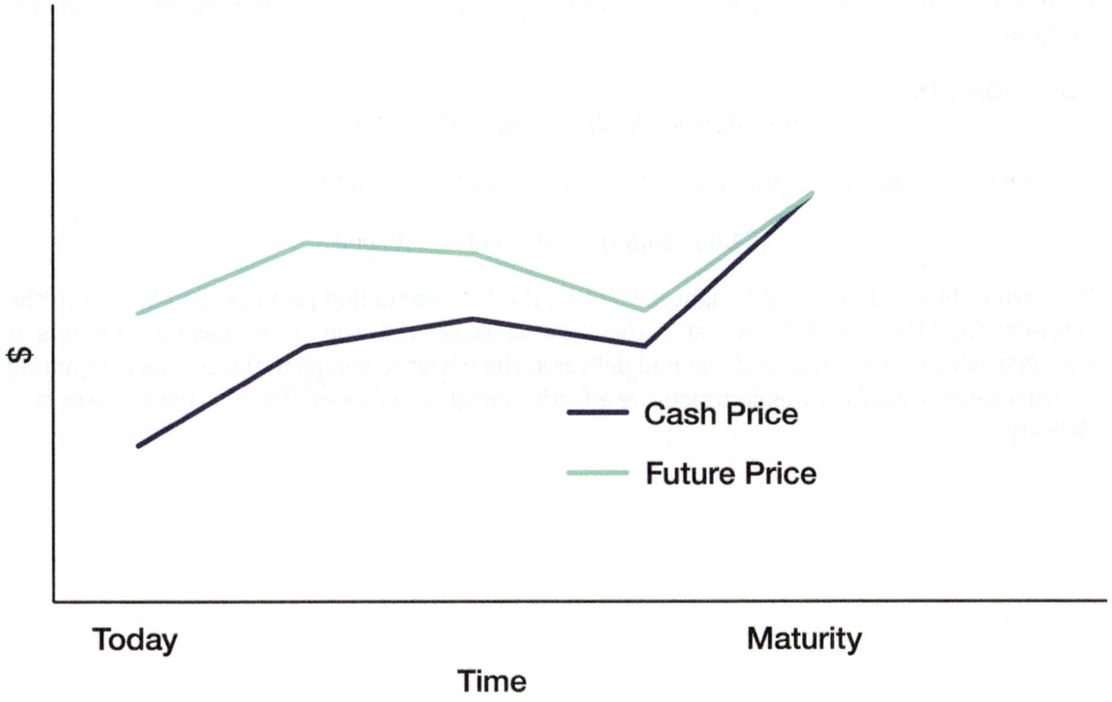

A Short Hedge

A short hedge is a short position taken by a hedger. Think of a wheat farmer who plants her crops in May. She plants enough seed to harvest 100,000 bushels. Assume that the December contract is trading at 400'0/bu ($4.00/bu). If the farmer likes the $4 price and is worried that the price of wheat might fall by harvest (in late October), then she could sell 20 December wheat futures contracts in May for $4/bu.

> **Tip**
>
> Each contact is for 5,000bu, so 20 contracts will involve 100,000bu.

Assume that late October arrives and the growing season was excellent—plenty of rain and hot weather. The farmer harvests her 100,000bu, but the spot price of wheat has dropped to $3.50/bu because of the excess supply. The farmer could simply wait for the middle of December and then transport her wheat to Chicago to fulfill the delivery requirements of her 20 short contracts. She would then, obviously, receive $4/bu for her wheat despite the drop in the spot price. She has locked-in the price and "hedged" the price risk with the futures contract.

However, the transportation costs associated with this completion method are very high, especially if her farm is any distance from Chicago. If that is the case, then she might prefer to sell her wheat to her local grain elevator operator. She would receive the spot price of $3.50/bu for total proceeds of $\mathbf{100,000}\boldsymbol{bu} \times \mathbf{\$3.50}$.

Of course, she still has the short futures position. To get out of those contracts she would execute an offset trade. She would buy 20 December contracts. Let's assume that convergence is complete and the futures price equals the spot price. The equation to determine the cumulative profit is:

EQUATION 18.5

$$\boldsymbol{Cumulative\ Profit} = (\boldsymbol{P_0} - \boldsymbol{P_1}) \times \mathbf{100,000}$$

The futures settlement price is $3.50/bu, so the cumulative profit is:

$$(\mathbf{\$4.00}\text{–}\ \mathbf{\$3.50}) \times \mathbf{100,000} = \mathbf{\$50,000}$$

The farmer has sold high and bought low. When the futures trading profit is combined with the revenues from the sale of the wheat to the elevator, we see that the farmer has total receipts of $400,000, which is the same as if she had delivered the wheat to complete the contracts (ignoring transportation costs). Futures contracts are effective hedging tools even if you do not make or take delivery.

18.4 Option Contracts

Options are contracts between two counterparties. There are two kinds of options: **calls** and **puts**. Calls give the **owner** the right to buy, and puts give the owner the right to sell.

> **Tip**
>
> Here is a good way to remember the difference between calls and puts. Call options let the owner *call* the underlying asset to them (from the call seller). Put owners can *put* the underlying asset onto the put seller.

The buyer of a call option pays a premium (price) and has a choice to buy an underlying asset before a specified date (**expiration date**) at a fixed price (**strike price or exercise price**). The seller of a call option receives the premium and must be ready to sell the asset (if the owner chooses to buy) before a specified date at the strike price.

The owner of a put option pays a premium and has the right to sell an underlying asset at a strike price before expiration. The **writer** of a put option receives the premium and must stand ready to buy the underlying asset (if the owner chooses to sell) at the strike price.

There are four things that you should notice about options:

1. They are contracts, like futures, and not securities.
2. There are two cash flows: the premium and the strike price.
3. Buyers, not sellers, have the option.
4. Buyers pay (the premium) for the option and the sellers receive the premium.

Table 18.3 summarizes the rights and responsibilities of buyers and sellers of call and put options.

TABLE 18.3 Rights and Obligations of Buyers and Sellers in Option Contracts

	a. Buyer (aka long position, holder, owner)	b. Seller (aka short position, writer)
CALL	Pays a premium and has the right to BUY	Receives a premium and has obligation to SELL
an underlying asset at the specified strike price before the expiration date.		
PUT	Pays a premium and has the right to SELL	Receives a premium and has obligation to BUY
an underlying asset at the specified strike price before the expiration date.		

The premium of the option contract is the price that is negotiated between the buyer and seller. All other elements of the contract—strike price, expiration, quantity, and quality of the underlying asset—are fixed by the exchange.

If the owner of an option decides to buy (sell), then they are **exercising** their option.

Call owners make money when the price of the underlying asset rises above the strike price, then they can buy the asset cheap (by exercising their option) and sell it for a higher price in the spot market. Call sellers want the price of the underlying asset to stay steady or fall so that the option owner lets the contract expire. Then the option seller gets to keep the premium. The highest profit that an option seller can earn is the premium. There is no further upside for them.

calls

The type of option that gives the owner of the option the right to buy the underlying asset (before the expiration at the strike price) to the seller of the option.

puts

The type of option that gives the owner of the option the right to sell the underlying asset (before the expiration at the strike price) to the seller of the option.

owner

The counterparty in an options contract who agrees to pay a price and take delivery of the (underlying) asset. See also buyer, long position, or holder.

expiration date

The date an option expires (matures). The option cannot be exercised after the expiration date.

strike price or exercise price

The price at which a call (put) owner can buy (sell) the underlying asset if they choose to exercise the option.

writer

The counterparty in an options contract who agrees to receive the price and accepts the obligation to sell (for a call) or buy (for a put) if the owner exercises. See also seller, or short position.

exercising

When an option owner chooses to buy (Call) or sell (Put) the underlying asset.

Explain It: The Call Option

View in the online reader

Put owners profit when the price of the underlying asset falls below the strike price. Then, the put owners can buy the asset cheap in the spot market and sell it for a higher price (by exercising their option). Like all option writers, put option writers want the owner to walk away without exercising so that they keep the premium.

Explain It: The Put Option

View in the online reader

offset trade

The elimination of a long or short position by executing a trade in the opposite direction.

The preceding two paragraphs convey the essential nature of the "bets" represented by options. We suggested that option contracts are completed through exercise. As with futures, options can also be completed through an **offset trade**. Offsetting is almost always better than exercising the contract. We prove this point with an example in a little while.

There are two varieties of options: **American** and **European**. The labels have nothing to do with where they are traded. American options can be exercised at any time prior to expiration. European options can only be exercised at expiration. At first, European options seem to contradict their very nature: they restrict the flexibility of the option. But if you recall what we asserted in the previous paragraph, it is (almost) never optimal to complete an option by exercising it, so the restriction on exercise is not that significant.

American option

A type of option that can be exercised at any time up to and including the expiration date.

European option

A type of option that can be exercised only on the expiration date.

Stock Options

There are many underlying assets for options contracts, some of which were listed in an earlier Explain It video (reproduced here again for your viewing convenience).

Explain It: Derivative Markets and Products

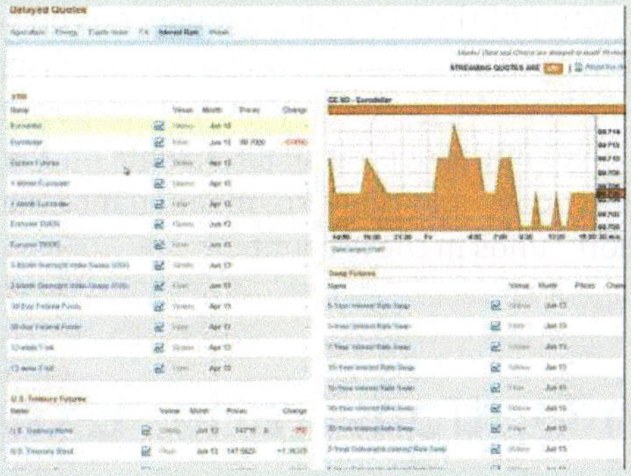

View in the online reader

Throughout this chapter we focus on one type of option: stock options. With a stock option, the underlying asset is 100 shares of a particular stock but, in most of our examples, we act like there is only one share to keep the numbers simple.

For example, consider the stock options on Big Heartless Corp. (BHC), a multinational conglomerate, which are traded on the NASDAQ OMX PHLX trading system (the PHLX used to be the Philadelphia Stock Exchange). The ticker for the option contract is BHO, and the ticker for the stock is BIG (listed on NASDAQ). The contract calls for the delivery of 100 of BHC's common shares. The option contract has a fixed schedule of dates on which the contracts expire throughout the year (September, October, December, January, and March). The contracts always expire on the third Friday of the month. There are a variety of strike prices.

Stock Option Price Quote

A typical stock option quote is shown in Table 18.4. The table shows that the shares of BHC closed at $42.50. Below the stock price information is information on prices and volumes for various call options with different strike prices and expiry dates. The October contract with a strike price of $40 last traded at a price (premium) of $9.00. If you had wanted to buy the option, you would have paid $\$9.00 \times 100 = \$900$ (stock option price quotes are expressed per share even though the contract is for 100 shares). This would have entitled you to buy 100 shares of BHC for $40 (per share).

TABLE 18.4 Call Option Price Quotes for Big Heartless Corp.

Company=BHC					Stock Price=$42.50
Date=Today					
Expiry	Strike	Last Sale	Change	Vol	Open Int.
Oct. 20XX	$40	9.00	−1.50	585	4,785
Oct. 20XX	$45	6.90	−1.50	585	6,858
Nov. 20XX	$40	10.30	−1.50	72	529
Nov. 20XX	$45	8.20	−1.40	301	1,021

Initiating an Options Trade

To initiate an options trade, a trader must deposit an initial amount (cash or securities) into an account with a broker. The amount of the initial deposit depends on whether the contract is a put or a call, whether the trader is long or short, and the type of underlying asset. For long positions in both puts and calls on stock options, the trader only needs to deposit the option premium in their account. Each exchange publishes initial deposit requirements on their websites. As with futures, the account is marked-to-market daily and there are maintenance margin levels that, if breached, require the trader to invest more funds in the account.

Completing an Option Trade: Exercise or Offset

Consider buying the October call option with the $40 strike price shown in Table 18.4. The stock price is $42.50 and you pay $9.00 for the option. Let's assume that you initiated the position in July and that by September the price of BHC has climbed to $50 (the premium has risen to $14.30). Now you think that it is time to get out of the option and take your profits. You have two choices in completing this option position:

1. You can exercise your option (assuming that it is an American option) and buy the underlying BHC stock for $40 a share for a total cost of $4,000. Once you have received the shares you can sell them in the stock market. Your profit is equal to the proceeds of the sale minus the cost of exercise and minus the option premium that you paid to buy the options when you initiated the position.
2. You can execute an offset trade. An offset trade is a trade in the opposite direction (long or short) in the same option with the same strike price and expiry. Offset trades in the options market work in the same manner as they do in the futures market, so we won't repeat that explanation here. We refer curious readers back to Section 2. Since you were initially long the BHC Oct 40 call option, the offset is to write (sell) a BHO Oct 40 call option. Since you are writing (selling), you will receive the call premium that prevails when you place your order. You have no further obligations, so your profit is the difference between the call premium that you received when you executed the offset trade and the premium that you paid when you initiated the position.

We will revisit the difference between offset and exercise in the final section of this chapter.

18.5 Option Payoffs and Profits

A good way to understand options is to draw profit diagrams. A profit diagram shows the profit from holding an option position at expiration for hypothetical values of the stock price. It is a "what if" exercise: What if you held the option to maturity, and what if the stock price was at various levels? Of course, you don't have to hold to maturity—you can close a position at any time with an offset trade.

Long Call

Consider an example where you purchase a BHO Oct 50 call option for a premium of $3.50. Let's fast forward to expiration on the third Friday of October. Let's say that the stock price on that Friday is $60.

> **Tip**
>
> If you hold the option at maturity, it is automatically exercised for you if the stock price is larger than the strike price. If it is a call option, then you have to deposit funds in your account to cover the strike price. Brokers will lend part of the strike price. In other words, you can buy on margin.

If you sell the shares after exercise, then what is your profit from the option? We calculate profit in two steps. First, we calculate the payoff of the option. Second, we subtract the premium (you pay the premium in a long position).

Payoff is the amount earned from buying the share for $X by exercising the option and selling the share at the market price of $$S_t$ (on date *t*). The payoff can be represented with the following function:

EQUATION 18.6

$$Payoff_t = MAX(0, S_t - X)$$

> **Tip**
>
> In Excel the *MAX*(...) function selects the highest value in the list.

In this example, if you exercise the option, then you buy the share for $50 and sell it at the market price for $60. The payoff is $10.

The payoff cannot be negative because the **holder** will not exercise the call option when the stock price is below the strike price. If there is time until the expiration date, then the holder will wait. If it is the expiration day, then the holder will abandon the option.

> **holder**
>
> The counterparty in an options contract who agrees to pay a price and take delivery of the (underlying) asset. See also buyer, long position, or owner.

The profit is the payoff less the premium:

EQUATION 18.7

$$Profit = Payoff - Premium$$
$$Profit = \$10 - \$3.50 = \$6.50$$

Remember, this is on a per-share basis. Your profit for the whole contract is $650.

Table 18.5 presents payoffs and profits for a variety of hypothetical closing prices on the expiration date. One interesting example is if the stock price is $50 at expiration. In this case, it is not worth exercising your option. The payoff is zero and the profit is -$3.50 per share. Indeed, for all prices under $50, that is the profit.

TABLE 18.5 Call Option Payoffs and Profits

Stock Price	Payoff	Profit
$0	$0	–$3.50
40	0	–3.50
50	0	–3.50
60	10	6.50
70	20	16.50
80	30	26.50

Figure 18.4 presents a graph of the values in Table 18.5. The graph shows both the payoff and profit from the call option.

FIGURE 18.4 Profit (Payoff) Diagram for One Long Call Option

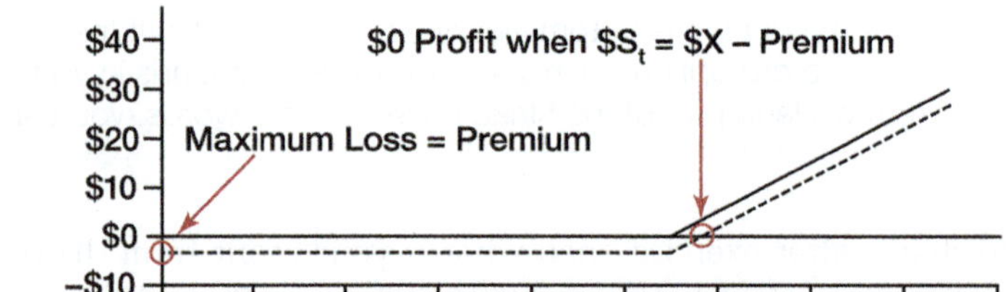

	$0	$10	$20	$30	$40	$50	$60	$70	$80
— Payoff	$0	$0	$0	$0	$0	$0	$10	$20	$30
--- Profit	–$3.5	–$3.5	–$3.5	–$3.5	–$3.5	–$3.5	$6.50	$16.5	$26.5

Stock Price

Tip

Payoff and profit diagrams are sometimes referred to as "hockey stick" pictures. Notice that the graph is drawn as if there is only one share underlying the contract.

Digital Downloads

ExplainIt Profit Diagram for a Long Call.xlsx
https://catalog.flatworldknowledge.com/a/34711/ExplainIt_Profit_Diagram_for_a_Long_Call-8dbb.xlsx

Explain It: Profit Diagram for a Long Call

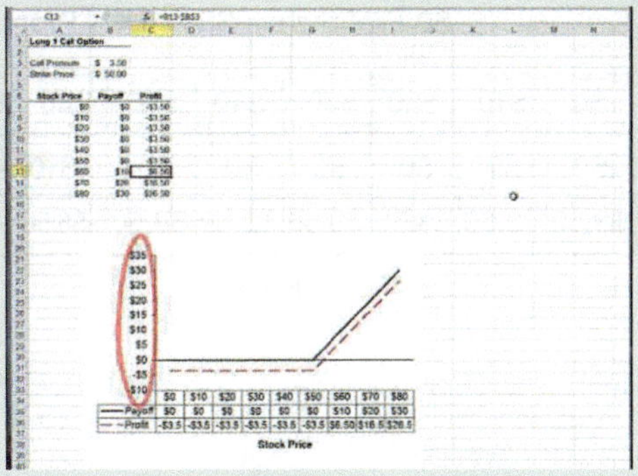

View in the online reader

Short Call

To understand the payoff and profit to an option writer, it is best to think of what the owner of the option will do in each situation and then consider the impact on the writer. Let's say that you wrote the call in the previous example—the BHO Oct 50 call option for a premium of $3.50. If the option holder does not exercise, then you get to keep the $3.50. As we saw above, this happens for all stock prices at or below $50. At prices above $50, the writer starts to get in trouble. Consider a price of $60. The option holder will exercise and the writer is obliged to sell shares to the holder for $50—the option's strike price. This represents a loss to the writer of $10. The writer's payoff is the opposite of the holder's payoff. The writer gets to keep the premium, which partially offsets the negative payoff.

Example 18.1 Profit to a Call Writer

You wrote the BHO Oct 50 call option for a premium of $3.50. The expiration day is today and the stock is trading for $60. What is your profit?

SOLUTION

The payoff for the writer is equal to –1 times the payoff to the holder.

$$Payoff = -MAX(0, S_T - X)$$
$$Payoff = -MAX(0, \$60 - \$50) = -\$10$$

The premium is added to the payoff because the option writer receives the premium.

$$Profit = Payoff + Premium$$
$$Profit = -\$10 + \$3.50 = -\$6.50$$

Figure 18.5 presents a graph of the payoffs and profits to a call writer.

FIGURE 18.5 Profit (Payoff) Diagram for One Short Call Option

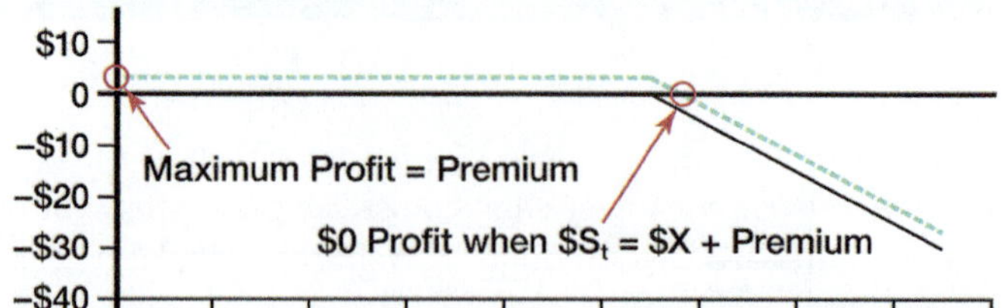

	$0	$10	$20	$30	$40	$50	$60	$70	$80
— Payoff	$0	$0	$0	$0	$0	$0	–$10	–$20	–$30
--- Profit	$3.50	$3.50	$3.50	$3.50	$3.50	$3.50	–$6.50	–$16.5	–$26.5

Stock Price

Digital Downloads

Short_Call_Profit_Diagram.xlsx
https://catalog.flatworldknowledge.com/a/34711/Short_Call_Profit_Diagram-7da1.xlsx

Explain It: Profit Diagram Short 1 Call

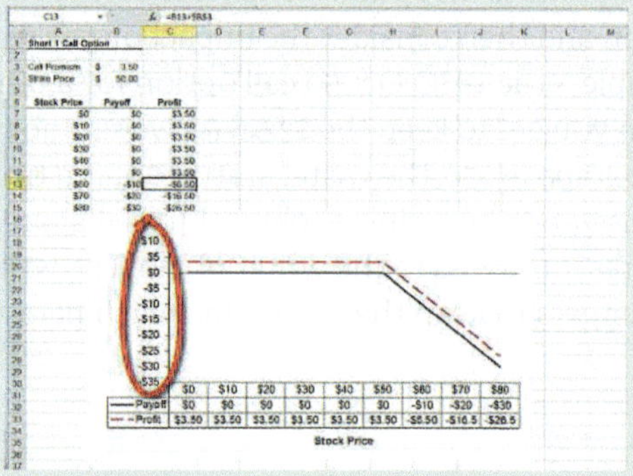

View in the online reader

Long Put

Now consider owning a put option on BHC shares. Assume that you bought the BHO Oct 50 put option for a premium of $3.00. The put option gives you the right to sell 100 shares of BHC common shares for a price of $50 per share at any time before the option expires in October. The right to sell the shares at a fixed price becomes more valuable as the price of the underlying shares drops. Ideally, the company goes bankrupt. In that case, you can acquire 100 shares for nothing and then exercise your put. When you exercise the put, you sell the shares to the put writer at the strike price. Your payoff is the strike price, since the purchase price is zero. In general, we can express the payoff as:

EQUATION 18.8

$$Payoff_t = MAX(0, X - S_t)$$

The payoff to a put owner is the greater of zero or the difference between the strike price and the stock price. The minimum payoff is zero because you cannot be forced to exercise the option if it is disadvantageous to you. That is, you cannot be forced to sell at the strike price if the market price is higher. If the market price is lower than the strike price, then your payoff is equal to the amount of money you would earn if you bought the shares today at a price of $\$S_t$ and sold them for \$X by exercising the put.

The profit is the payoff minus the premium, since the owner of an option pays the premium.

EQUATION 18.9

$$Profit = Payoff - Premium$$

Figure 18.6 presents a graph of the payoffs and profits to a put owner.

FIGURE 18.6 Profit (Payoff) Diagram for One Long Put Option

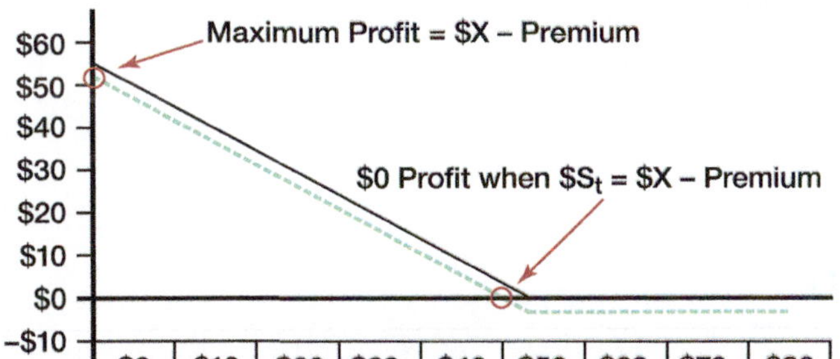

	$0	$10	$20	$30	$40	$50	$60	$70	$80
— Payoff	$50	$40	$30	$20	$10	$0	$0	$0	$0
--- Profit	$47.0	$37.0	$27.0	$17.0	$7.00	–$3.0	–$3.0	–$3.0	–$3.0

Stock Price

Digital Downloads

Long_Put_Profit_Diagram.xlsx
https://catalog.flatworldknowledge.com/a/34711/Long_Put_Profit_Diagram-95fa.xlsx

Explain It: Profit Diagram for a Long Put

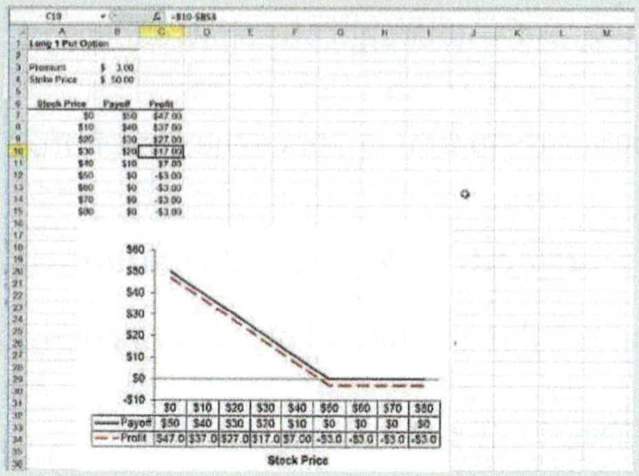

View in the online reader

Short Put

Now consider writing the BHO Oct 50 put option for a premium of \$3.00. The put option obliges you to buy 100 shares of BHC common shares for a price of \$50 per share if the owner exercises. You receive the premium of \$3.00.

The writer of the option wants the holder to walk away—to not exercise their option. In that case, the writer keeps the premium, which is his profit. The put owner will walk away if the share price is above the strike price at expiration. Consider a situation where the owner does not walk away. Consider a final share price of \$40. The put owner, as we demonstrated in the last example, exercises at this price. She sells the shares for \$50 to the put writer. The put writer is therefore buying shares that are overpriced by \$10, since they only trade for \$40 on the stock market. The put writer's payoff is the opposite of the put owner's: -\$10. The put writer receives the premium, which partially offsets this negative payoff.

Example 18.2 Profit to a Put Writer

You wrote the BHO Oct 50 put option for a premium of \$3.00. The expiration day is today and the stock is trading for \$40. What is your profit?

SOLUTION

The payoff for the writer is equal to –1 times the payoff to the holder.

$$Payoff = -MAX(0, X - S_T)$$
$$Payoff = -MAX(0, \$50 - \$40) = -\$10$$

The premium is added to the payoff because the option writer receives the premium.

$$Profit = Payoff + Premium$$
$$Profit = -\$10 + \$3 = -\$7$$

Digital Downloads

Explain It Short Put Profit Diagram.xlsx
https://catalog.flatworldknowledge.com/a/34710/Explain_It_Short_Put_Profit_Diagram-dd97.xlsx

Spreadsheet Solution

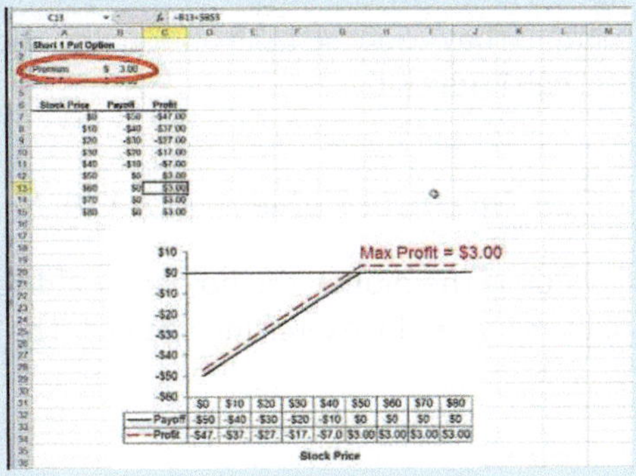

View in the online reader

FIGURE 18.7 Profit (Payoff) Diagram for One Short Put Option

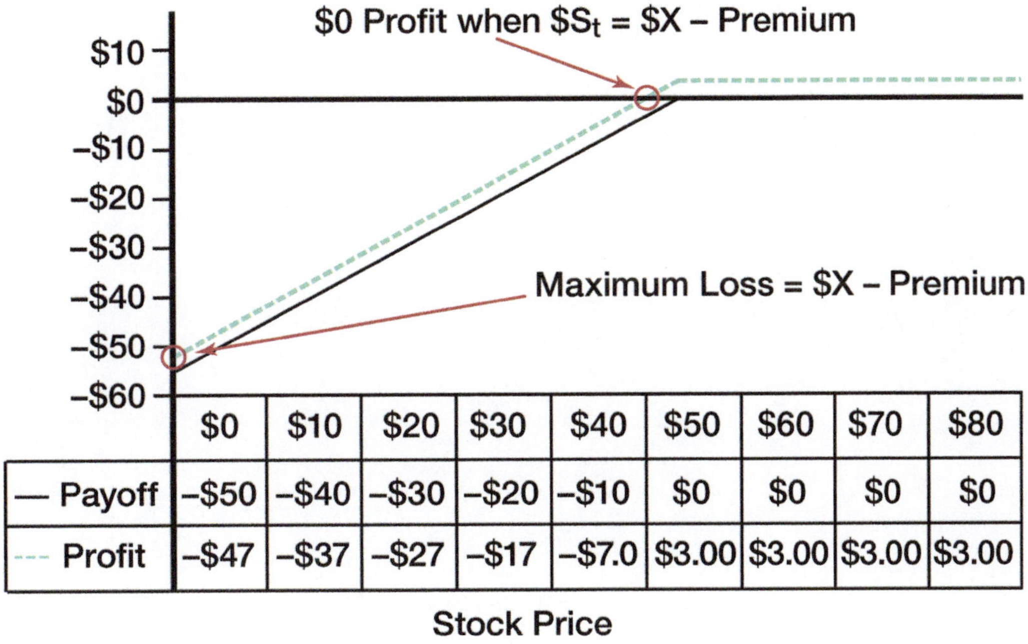

18.6 Option Pricing

Intrinsic Value

intrinsic value

The value of an option (to the owner) if it were exercised immediately at the current stock price.

The **intrinsic value** of an option is simply the payoff to the option holder. For a call, it is the money the holder would receive today if they exercised the option and then sold the shares at the market price. The intrinsic value of a call is given by:

EQUATION 18.10

$$Call\ Intrinsic\ Value = MAX(0, S_t - X)$$

For a put, the intrinsic value is the money the holder would receive if they bought the shares at the market price and sold the shares by exercising the put. The intrinsic value of a put is given by:

EQUATION 18.11

$$Put\ Intrinsic\ Value_t = MAX(0, X - S_t)$$

The intrinsic value cannot be negative, since the option holder can choose not to exercise and, in a sense, walk away from the option.

Moneyness

An option with positive intrinsic value is said to be **in-the-money**. An option with an intrinsic value of 0 is said to be **out-of-the-money**. When the share price equals the strike price, then the option is said to be **at-the-money**. Table 18.6 relates the share price, the exercise price, and intrinsic value to **moneyness**.

in-the-money

An option is said to be "in-the-money" when it has positive intrinsic value.

out-of-the-money

An option is said to be "out-of-the-money" when it has zero intrinsic value (and the asset's market price is not equal to the stroke price).

at-the-money

A situation with options where the asset's market price equals the strike price.

moneyness

The relative position of the current price of the underlying asset (e.g., a stock) with respect to the strike price. If the owner would make money if the option were to expire today, then it is in the money. If the owner would not exercise, then the option is out of the money. If the current price and strike price are equal, then the option is at the money.

TABLE 18.6 Moneyness for Puts and Calls

	$S_t > X$	$S_t < X$
CALL	In-the-money	Out-of-the-money
	Intrinsic value>0	Intrinsic value=0
PUT	Out-of-the-money	In-the-money
	Intrinsic value=0	Intrinsic value>0

Intrinsic Value and Price

An option premium is almost never less than the intrinsic value. If it is, then there can be an arbitrage opportunity—that is, an easy profit opportunity. As traders exploit the opportunity, the option price changes until the price is above the intrinsic value.

For example, consider the BHO Oct 50 call option. Assume that it is an American option, the price of the stock is currently $55, and the premium is $1. The intrinsic value of the option is $5, which is greater than the premium of $1. Could you structure a sequence of trades to take advantage of this situation? Yes. Buy the option for $1, exercise it, and buy the shares for $50, then sell the shares on the stock market for $55. Your profit is $4. Traders would flock to such an opportunity and the premium would quickly be bid over $5. At that level, there is no easy profit opportunity.

Time Value

Option premiums are usually higher than the intrinsic value. The difference is called the **time value or time premium** of the option:

time value or time premium

The difference between an option's price and its intrinsic value.

EQUATION 18.12

$$\textit{Time value} = \textit{Option premium} - \textit{Intrinsic value}$$

The time value reflects the likelihood that the stock price will rise (for calls) or fall (for puts) between now and the expiration date.

The main factors that affect the time value are time and volatility.

With more time comes the increased likelihood of a change in the stock price. In the short run, the odds of something happening to a company are small. Over a longer time period, the odds rise. Time values rise as the time to expiration rises and fall as the time to expiration nears. On the expiry date of the option the time value is zero.

The second factor that affects the time value is volatility. The higher the volatility of the price of the underlying asset, the higher will be the time value, all other things being equal. More volatile assets are more likely to jump up (or down).

Completing a Call Option and Time Value

Assume that, last July, you bought an October call option on shares of BHC with the $40 strike price. At the time, the stock price was $42.50 and you paid $9.00 for the option. (This is a continuation of the example we used earlier when we started our discussion on completing an option position.) Today it is mid-September, the price of BHC stock has climbed to $50 and the option now trades for $14.30. You think that BHC's stock price has peaked and now is the time to get out of your option position. As we discussed earlier, you have two completion choices: exercise (assuming it is an American option) or offset.

If you exercise your option, then you buy 100 shares of BHC for $40 (the option's strike price) at a total cost of $4,000. At the same time, you would sell the shares on the stock market for $5,000 yielding a payoff of $1,000. Since you had to invest $900 to pay the option premium, this represents a profit of $\mathbf{\$1,000 - \$900 = \$100}$.

Alternatively, you would execute an offset trade by writing (selling) a BHO Oct 40 call option. Given today's option premium of $14.30 you would receive a total of $1,430. Your net profit is the difference between the premium received ($1,430) and paid ($900) = $530.

We can see from this example that offset yielded a higher profit than exercise. This is usually the case, although there are a number of fairly technical exceptions.

The reason that offset is superior is that exercise burns the time value of the option. With exercise, all you capture is the intrinsic value of the option. Note that the intrinsic value of the option, today, is $MAX(0, S-X)$ or $10 per share. But the option premium today is $14.30, so the time value is the difference or $4.30 ($430 for the full contract). Notice that the difference in profits between offset and exercise is $430—the amount of the time value of option.

When you execute an offset trade you receive the full premium, which includes both the intrinsic value and the time value. When you exercise, you only receive the intrinsic value. For this reason, it almost always better to complete an options position with an offset trade rather than by exercising the option. The obvious exception to this rule is the expiry date of the option. On that day, exercise yields the same profit as offset, since the time value of the option is zero on the expiry day.

Endnote

1. You will learn the reason for positive or negative basis in an elective course on futures and options.

Index